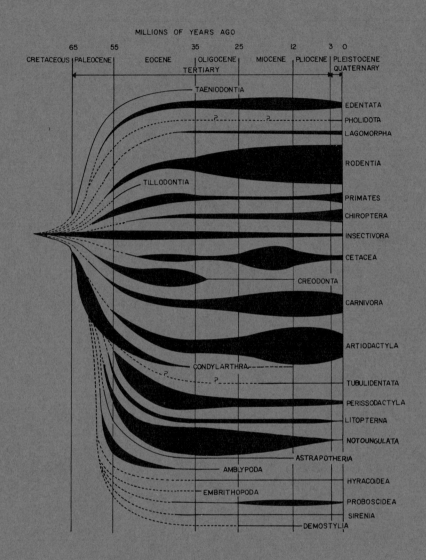

MILLIONS OF YEARS AGO

Radiation of the placental mammals. Records for 25 extinct and extant orders
are shown. Width of lines is in proportion to the abundance of each order;
dashed lines mean that no fossil record exists for the indicated interval; question
marks imply doubt as to the systematic position of specimens referred to the
order in question. [Redrawn from Kurtén, 1969, after Romer; revised by
B. Patterson.]

Evolution, Mammals, and Southern Continents

Evolution, Mammals, and Southern Continents

EDITED BY
ALLEN KEAST,
FRANK C. ERK,
BENTLEY GLASS

STATE UNIVERSITY OF NEW YORK PRESS, ALBANY, 1972

Published by State University of New York Press
99 Washington Avenue, Albany, New York 12210

© *1968, 1969, 1971, 1972 Stony Brook Foundation, Inc.*
All rights reserved

Printed in the United States of America
Designed by Anne Souza

Library of Congress Cataloging in Publication Data

Evolution, mammals, and southern continents.
Revision of papers originally prepared for the XVI
International Congress of Zoology.

Bibliography: p.
1. Mammals, Fossil—Addresses,
essays, lectures. 2. Mammals—Southern Hemisphere
—Addresses, essays, lectures. 3. Evolution—
Addresses, essays, lectures. 4. Zoogeography—
Addresses, essays, lectures. I. Keast, Allen, ed.
II. Erk, Frank C., 1924-   ed. III. Glass, Hiram
Bentley, 1906-   ed. IV. International Congress
of Zoology, 16th, Washington, D. C., 1963.
QE881.E85   599′.03′ 8   75-152519
ISBN 0-87395-086-0
ISBN 0-87395-186-7 (microfiche)

Contents

VIII

The Editors

Allen Keast (who is also a contributing author) is Professor of Biology, Queen's University, Kingston, Ontario, and a member of the Advisory Board of *The Quarterly Review of Biology*.

Frank C. Erk is Professor of Biological Sciences, State University of New York at Stony Brook, and Coeditor of *The Quarterly Review of Biology*.

Bentley Glass is Distinguished Professor of Biological Sciences, State University of New York at Stony Brook, and Coeditor of *The Quarterly Review of Biology*.

The Contributors

H. B. S. Cooke is Carnegie Professor of Geology, Dalhousie University, Halifax, Nova Scotia.

R. C. Bigalke is Professor of Nature Conservation, Faculty of Forestry, University of Stellenbosch, Stellenbosch, South Africa.

Bryan Patterson is Professor of Vertebrate Paleontology, Museum of Comparative Zoology, Harvard University, Cambridge, Massachusetts.

Rosendo Pascual is Professor of Vertebrate Paleontology, Department of Natural Sciences and Museo de La Plata, Universidad Nacional de La Plata, Argentina.

Philip Hershkovitz is Research Curator of Mammals, Field Museum of Natural History, Chicago, Illinois.

Preface

For the XVI International Congress of Zoology, held in Washington D. C. during the Summer of 1963, Professor Allen Keast organized a symposium on the evolution of mammals on the southern continents of Africa, Australia, and South America. The papers prepared for that symposium were such an outstanding contribution to this subject that it was decided by the Editors to devote almost a year's issues of *The Quarterly Review of Biology* to their publication. For this series, each author revised and brought up-to-date his own articles, which made it possible to include recent work in each area.

The response to that series of articles (*The Quarterly Review of Biology*, September 1968 through June 1969) was the most enthusiastic in the history of the journal. Clearly there was a need felt by workers and students in the areas of evolution, biogeography, and mammalogy for this knowledge to be brought together and made more generally available. Since that series appeared, new work and discoveries in geology and paleontology have focussed attention on and generated excitement about the earlier speculations on continental drift. The implications for the evolution of life on the southern continents are many.

In the light of the need to incorporate this new work, it was agreed by the Editors of *The Quarterly Review of Biology* and the authors of the articles to once again revise and expand this series, this time to make them available in book form. This volume thus presents the latest knowledge about the evolution of mammals on southern continents and adjoining areas. The individual chapters were contributed by outstanding authorities on the fossil and contemporary mammals of these areas. In addition, Professor Keast has prepared a new chapter assessing present views on the occurrence and importance of continental drift, especially as it affects our understanding of the distribution of mammals and other organisms on the southern continents.

For the purposes of this volume we have included charts showing the history in geologic time of the major groups of mammals and their progenitors; also included are an author index, an index to scientific and vernacular names, and a subject index. It is our hope that these new materials will variously serve the needs of professional biologists and students who would pursue their interest in the origin, evolution, and current status of mammal faunas, particularly those of the southern continents.

In the original publication of the articles and in the preparation of the manuscript for this volume the lion's share of the work has fallen to the Managing Editor of *The Quarterly Review of Biology*, Mrs. Rosemary G. Smolker. She has done a superb job at every stage, and without her tireless labors and her endless patience with the Editors and the authors, this volume would not have been possible.

THE EDITORS

I Introduction: The Southern Continents as Backgrounds for Mammalian Evolution

by Allen Keast

INTRODUCTION

The three southern continents, supplied with basically different mammalian raw material at the end of Cretaceous, and then more or less isolated throughout the Tertiary, provide an unusual opportunity for a comparative study of the dynamics of mammalian evolution. The fossil record shows that at the time of its isolation, South America had a fauna restricted to a few marsupials, edentates, and primitive ungulates. Australia, with the oldest fossils extending only from the Upper Oligocene, presumably had only marsupials and monotremes. Africa probably obtained a faunistic nucleus from the "world continent" fauna in the Cretaceous, but the nature of this nucleus is unknown since the fossil record begins only at the end of the Eocene (Patterson, 1965; Patterson and Pascual, 1968).

The three continents are alike in that they have been distributional dead ends; entry to each continent was possible, at least after the early Tertiary, from the north. Australia actually may have obtained its original marsupial stocks from the south, as will be discussed in the next chapter, but it was undoubtedly isolated throughout most or all of the Tertiary. Entry of placental mammals into Australia (bats and rodents) occurred relatively late, probably in the Miocene (or Oligocene) for bats and the early Pliocene for rodents.

Faunistic movements with respect to the southern continents have been one way, except in the case of Africa, which contributed forms to Eurasia in the Late Oligocene, Late Miocene, and Late Pliocene (Cooke, 1968; Chapter III). With the exception of megalonychid sloths, South America apparently contributed forms to North America only after the completion of the Panamanian land-bridge in the Late Pliocene. Australia apparently has not provided any new colonizing families or higher categories of mammals to other areas.

There is now no doubt that South America, Africa, and Australia have been isolated from each other throughout the Tertiary. Their oldest mammalian fossil faunas (Paleocene in the case of South America, Upper Eocene for Africa, Upper Oligocene for Australia) are dominated by distinctive autochthonous orders.

Africa and South America apparently have occupied the same general positions relative to the Equator throughout the Tertiary even if, as the latest paleomagnetic data suggest, Australia initially occupied a more southern position. Certainly, as suggested by oxygen isotope and other data, the three must have gone through comparable climatic phases. The periodic north-south climatic sweeps of the later Tertiary and Pleistocene must have entailed comparable south-north movements of the vegetation belts. The same kinds of environments and range of available vegetation types must have been available on the three southern continents during the Tertiary, even if not at exactly the same times. It is also noteworthy that, in contrast with the northern continents, Pleistocene glaciation was never widespread in the southern continents, being restricted to the highest mountains and the southern tip of South America. Severe cold was not, therefore, a major factor in the extermination of life. Proximity to the Equator insured the continuance of tropical or, in the case of Australia, subtropical zones. A broad latitudinal spread, and periods of mountain building, maintained a continuous diversity of habitats. Again, since each continent is built around a large Precambrian shield (or shields), there has been a considerable measure of geological stability. Tectonic shifts have been restricted to the margins.

ZOOGEOGRAPHICAL DIFFERENCES AMONG THE CONTINENTS

The three southern continents differ in their relative sizes (Fig. 1), latitudinal positions, degree and history of isolation, and in many basic physiographic features. Africa has a land area of 11,700,000 square miles, South America, 7,000,000, and Australia, 2,950,000. Australia is thus only one-quarter the size of Africa, South America being intermediate. The equator passes through the middle of Africa, through the north of South America, and lies well to the north of Australia. Only one-twentieth of Africa lies south of the Tropic of Capricorn (23.5° S), whereas one-quarter of South America and two-thirds of Australia do so. Since Australia is broader than long, it does not extend nearly as far south as South America, which approaches Antarctica at its southern limits. The equal distribution of Africa on either side of the Equator probably accounts, in part, for the persistence of its exceptionally rich "Pleistocene" large mammal fauna. North-south climatic movements would merely contract or expand the tropical belt, not compress it into the far south as in the case of North America.

Physiographically the three southern continents differ greatly today. South America alone has a major north-south mountain range, the Andean Cordillera. The average height along this chain is 7,000 feet, but

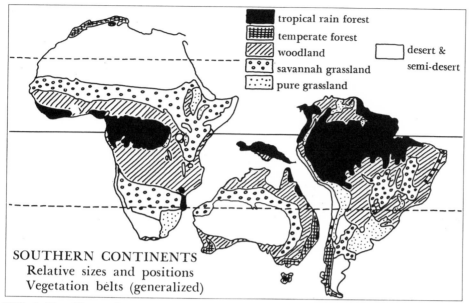

FIG. 1. The Three Southern Continents to Show Relative Sizes, Latitudinal Positions, and Distribution of Major Vegetation Formations

New Guinea, which lies on the Australian continental shelf, was part of the continent for part of the Tertiary and was repeatedly and broadly connected during the Pleistocene. Hence, its fauna must be added to that of Australia in any zoogeographic comparisons.

Data for African vegetation regions from Keay (1959); for Australian vegetation regions from Wood (1950) and Williams (1960); and for South American vegetation regions from Linton (1951).

higher peaks exceed 20,000 feet. This range of mountain heights produces a very marked series of altitudinal life zones. These zones have parallels in North America and the Himalayas, but not in Africa or Australia. South America also has an extensive highland belt in the east and northeast, the Guianan and Brazilian highlands composed of ancient igneous and metamorphosed rocks. Notwithstanding the prominence of its mountains, plains and river basins cover two-thirds of South America.

Australia and Africa are continents of low to moderate relief, with long degradational histories. The major mountain system of Australia, the Great Divide (so called because it divides the watershed of eastern Australia into eastward-flowing and westward-flowing components), extends from north to south, paralleling the eastern coastline. It was partly elevated in the Miocene. While there was further elevation in the Pliocene, it did not experience the very strong late Pliocene and Pleistocene upthrusts that brought the Andes to their present height. The Great Divide is only 3,000 to 5,000 feet high for much of its length, and has never been more than a couple of thousand feet higher. The highest peak today, Mount Kosciusko on the New South Wales-Victoria border, is only 7,300 feet in height.

Africa has mainly a rolling plateau surface. Volcanic peaks in central and eastern Africa reach considerable heights (Kilimanjaro, 19,300 feet; Kenya, 17,000 feet), but are both too scattered and too recent to have served as centers of evolution. Isolated highland areas such as those of east Africa, the Cameroons in west Africa, and the Abyssinian Highlands however, do support relicts or outliers of forest faunas. These are more pronounced in birds and insects than in mammals.

The three continents differ markedly today in the relative areas covered by rain forest, woodland, and desert (Fig. 1). Rain forest covers possibly 20 per cent of South America and 6 to 7 per cent of Africa. In Australia this formation is limited to a few pockets, mainly in the northeast. The largest of these would not be much more than 1,000 square miles. They can be thought of as outliers from New Guinea to the north, where tropical rain forest is well developed. Woodland and grassland areas are extensive on all three continents. Deserts are strikingly developed in Africa and Australia but are limited in extent and peripheral in western South America. Whereas in Australia the desert is continuous through the central areas of the continent, in Africa the deserts are broken up into three segments, the Kalahari in the southwest, Sahara in the north, and Somali arid in the northeast. Each has a series of distinctive mammalian faunal elements.

LITERATURE CITED

COOKE, H. B. S. 1968. The fossil mammal fauna of Africa. *Quart. Rev. Biol.,* 43: 234-264.

KEAY, R. W. J. 1959. *Vegetation Map of Africa South of the Tropic of Cancer, with Explanatory Notes.* L'Association pour l'Étude Taxonomique de la Flore d'Afrique Tropicale, with the assistance of UNESCO. Oxford University Press, London.

LINTON, D. L. 1951. Vegetation map of the world. In C. Lewis, J. D. Campbell, D. P. Bickmore and K. F. Cook (eds.), *The American Oxford Atlas,* p. viii. Oxford University Press, London.

PATTERSON, B. 1965. The fossil elephant shrews (Family Macroscelididae). *Bull. Museum Comp. Zool., Harvard,* 133: 297-335.

PATTERSON, B., and R. PASCUAL. 1968. The fossil mammal fauna of South America. *Quart. Rev. Biol.,* 43: 409-451.

WILLIAMS, R. J. 1960. Vegetation map of Australia. In G. W. Leeper (ed.), *The Australian Environment,* p. 67-84. Commonwealth Scientific and Industrial Research Organization and Melbourne University Press, Melbourne. [Third edition.]

WOOD, J. G. 1950. Vegetation map of Australia. In G. W. Leeper (ed.), *The Australian Environment,* p. 77-96. Commonwealth Scientific and Industrial Research Organization and Melbourne University Press, Melbourne. [Second edition.]

II Continental Drift and the Evolution of the Biota on Southern Continents

by Allen Keast

INTRODUCTION

Continental drift has become a question of increasing importance, and it is no longer possible to consider mammalian evolution on southern continents without a thorough review of our current understanding of this issue. It is fundamental, accordingly, to determine (1) if continental drift has occurred; (2) if so, whether the southern continents were in direct contact during the Triassic, at the time the first mammals appeared; (3) what the spatial relations of the continents were in the Cretaceous and early Tertiary, when mammals became increasingly diversified and are supposed to have reached South America and Australia; and (4) if the distribution of the world's major land masses has changed from the Early Tertiary to the present, in such a way that this factor has to be taken into account in explaining contemporary mammalian evolutionary and distributional patterns.

Three main lines of evidence are available for testing the continental drift hypothesis (reviewed in detail later) and for bringing together relevant data: (1) the basic geological data, old and new; (2) the terrestrial fossil records for each continent for the different periods, from the Triassic onward; and (3) analysis of their contemporary biotas. The fossil and contemporary biological evidence can be used to bring out whether, and to what extent, the floras and faunas exhibit special taxonomic relationships to each other which apparently can only be explained by former direct links. Should such relationships exist, it then becomes desirable to see if the biota exhibit different *levels* of relationship and whether, on this basis, an *order* of separation of the continents can be postulated. Archaic plant and animal groups are, of course, of particular relevance here.

Continental drift is now finding increasing acceptance by geologists, but much of the evidence advanced in its support remains tentative and confusing. A balanced appraisal of the whole concept is a prerequisite to the consideration of its significance in the evolution of mammals.

Various challenging problems in mammalian evolution and history are linked to the possibility of continental drift. None, however, is more intriguing than the origin of the Australian marsupials. South America and Australia, alone among the continents, have extensive faunas of marsupials, and advocates of continental drift have long used this as supporting evidence for their theory (e.g., Harrison, 1924). Subsequent mammalogists, however, have discounted this suggestion (e.g., Simpson, 1940a). More recently, Ride (1964) has again raised the possibility of Australia having received her mammals from the south, basing this idea on the paleomagnetic findings of Irving, Robertson, and Stott (1963), which suggest that since Mesozoic Australia has been moving slowly northward relative to the Antarctic, and achieved its present latitude only during the later Tertiary. The newer geological data on sea-floor spreading has initiated added support for the southern entry theory for Australian marsupials, and recent writers who advocate it include Hoffstetter (1970) and Cox (1970).

Serventy (1972) has recently suggested that some Australian bird groups may have entered the continent from the south.

THE MESOZOIC ORIGIN OF MAMMALS

Mammals first emerged in the Late Triassic, approximately 190-200 million years ago. Several families are recognizable by the beginning of the Jurassic, and by the start of the Cretaceous some nine families had differentiated (Cox, 1967). Until the end of the Cretaceous period, however, the mammals remained small and insignificant elements of the terrestrial fauna, most of them being in the size range of modern small rodents and shrews (Clemens, 1970). Marsupials and placental mammals became differentiated during the Cretaceous. The rise of mammals to the position of dominant terrestrial vertebrates commenced towards the end of that period, some 65,000,000 years ago, about the time of the final extinction of the dinosaurs. A rapid radiation took mammals into a whole series of new adaptive zones, including those of the larger terrestrial herbivores and carnivores that had previously been occupied by the dinosaurs.

The Permian predecessors of the mammals were the therapsids, or mammal-like reptiles, a group so successful that they numbered 170 genera by the end of that period (Robinson, 1971). At this time they greatly outnumbered their labyrinthodont and cotylosaur contemporaries. The therapsids remained important in the Early Triassic, various genera like *Lystrosaurus* and *Cygnognathus* (see later) being abundant and widespread. By the end of the Triassic, however, the therapsids were excelled by the diapsid or sauropsid reptiles, which by then had differentiated into some 83 genera, compared to the 17 of the declining therapsids (Robinson, 1971). The sauropsids fell into two groups, the archosaurs (first crocodiles, saurischian and ornithischian dinosaurs), and the lepidosaurs (rhynchocephalians and ancestral lizards).

Throughout the Jurassic and Cretaceous the dinosaurs were the dominant and largest land vertebrates. Hence it is to their fossils that we must look for possible evidences of continental spatial relationships. The reasons for the success of the diapsid reptiles in the later Mesozoic, the long suppression of the mammals, and then the tremendous success of mammals at the end of the Cretaceous, has been the subject of much speculation. The subject has recently been discussed by Cox (1967) and by Robinson (1971). One suggestion is that the mammals only evolved many of their more advantageous physiological and anatomical attributes (such as endothermy, an advanced reproductive system, enlarged brain) relatively late. Another suggestion is that the basic physiological characteristics of the diapsids and mammals were optimal for different kinds of environmental conditions. Robinson (1971) suggests that it was environmental changes in the late Cretaceous that finally swung the balance in favor of mammals. The changes, she suggests, may have been associated with shifts in the distribution of the world's land, since a series of smaller isolated continents, each surrounded by sea, would have had different climates from single supercontinents.

The Late Triassic therapsid-mammalian transition has been extensively documented. The presence of a dentary-squamosal articulation, forming part or all of the joint between the skull and lower jaw, has been regarded as the best criterion of having reached the mammalian grade (Kermack and Mussett, 1958). Subsequently, however, certain additional characters, notably dental criteria, have been introduced to make the definition more restrictive (Hopson and Crompton, 1969; Clemens, 1970). A feature of the Triassic reptilian-mammalian transition is that a series of reptilian lineages was acquiring mammalian characters at the same time. Simpson (1959) has listed four to nine of these. With the more restrictive definition of Hopson and Crompton (1969), this may be reduced to two or three (Clemens, 1970).

Upper Triassic mammals have been described from Europe, China, and Africa (Clemens, 1970). They are, as yet, unknown from South America, although cynodont reptiles, in which the dentary bone is in contact with the squamosal and is taking part in the lower jaw articulation, are known from the Chañares beds of South America (Romer, 1969). Two Upper Triassic morganucodontid mammals are known from South Africa: *Erythrotherium parringtoni* (Crompton, 1964) and *Megazostrodon ruderae* (Crompton and Jenkins, 1968).

The only Jurassic mammal known from the Southern Hemisphere is *Brancatherulum tendaguruense* from the late Jurassic Tendaguru beds of Tanzania (Dietrich, 1928). Simpson (1928) regards it as a primitive paurodontid pantothere (Cooke, 1968; Chapter III, this volume). See Simpson (1971) for a list of the latest literature on Mesozoic mammals in Africa. There is also an alleged mammalian footprint from Santa Cruz Province, Argentina (Casamiquela, 1961).

Riek (1970) records two lower Cretaceous fleas from Australia which he suggests are of a mammalian type.

Cretaceous mammals, while present in North America and Eurasia, are unknown from the southern continents, except for some unidentified fragments of marsupials and part of a jaw of a primitive condylarth (?) of presumed Late Cretaceous age (*Perutherium*) from South America (Patterson and Pascual, 1968; Chapter VI, this volume).

No Mesozoic mammals are known from Australia, but the contemporary Monotremata could represent the relics of a Mesozoic dispersal into Australia.

The first Tertiary fossil records of mammals in the southern continents are as follows: South America, Paleocene (Patterson and Pascual, Chapter VI); Africa, Upper Eocene (Cooke, Chapter III); Australia, Upper Oligocene (?) (Keast, Chapter V).

THE GEOLOGICAL EVIDENCE OF CONTINENTAL DRIFT IN THE SOUTHERN HEMISPHERE

The Historical Development of the Continental Drift Concept

Continental drift, as a comprehensive theory of the evolution of the earth's crust, can be ascribed to Alfred Wegener (1924). Contrary to common belief, earlier writers such as Francis Bacon in 1620, François Placet in 1668, and A. von Humboldt in 1801, cannot be regarded as anticipating the theory: von Humboldt did notice the parallelism and complementary geology of the opposing shores of the Atlantic but he saw this only as the two sides of a valley opened up by marine erosion (Carozzi, 1970). Most early writers were catastrophists and were preoccupied with The Deluge: they saw the oceans and separation of continents as the result of the flooding of preexistent land. Anthony Snider, in 1886, came closest to formulating a drift concept, in suggesting that the Atlantic was formed by an initial cracking of the earth's surface (the result of underground fires) and expansion as a result of the Deluge (Carozzi, 1970). Snider has been quoted as noting a matching of the Carboniferous fossil plants of Europe and North America (see Hurley, 1968), but a perusal of his book, "La Création et ses Mystères dévoilés," does not support this (J. M. Schopf, pers. commun.). Neumayr (1887), however, felt that the distribution patterns of Jurassic ammonites indicated a different relationship of sea and land at that time.

It is to the geologist Suess (1906) that we owe the concept of a former southern supercontinent, Gondwanaland. His supercontinent was, however, very different from that of du Toit (1937), for he saw continuity between Africa, India, and Australia being achieved by elevation of the Indian Ocean bed, not by continental displacement (J. M. Schopf, pers. commun.).

Serious scientific consideration of continental drift as a theory stems back no further than Alfred Wegener and F. B. Taylor, who independently conceived the idea about 1910 (Holmes, 1965; J. M. Schopf, pers. commun.). Wegener and later supporters, such as the South African geologist du Toit (1937) and the Tasmanian geologist Carey (1958), envisaged the clustering of the southern continents about Antarctica, either as part of a single world continent, Pangaea, or a southern super-continent, Gondwanaland. There were initially four major lines of geological and fossil evidence for this view: (1) The contours of the continents permitted a generalized fit—see recent computer-plotted fits (with good geologic control) for the continents fringing the South Atlantic by Bullard, Everett, and Smith (1965), and those of Sproll and Dietz (1969), and Dietz and Sproll (1970) for Antarctica (where good geologic control is difficult to achieve); and for additional recent reconstructions of Gondwanaland, see Smith and Hallam, 1970; Schopf, 1970a; and Tarling, 1971). (2) Certain important geological formations—e.g., those in west Africa and Brazil, New Zealand and Antarctica, Australia and Antarctica, and Andes and Antarctica—are of similar age or duplicate each other structurally (reviews in du Toit, 1937; Adie, 1963; Hurley et al, 1967; Hamilton, 1967; Cullen, 1967; Hurley and Rand, 1968; Martin, 1968; Halpern, 1968; Allard and Hurst, 1969; Schopf, 1970a; Bonatti, Ball, and Schubert, 1970; and Smith and Hallam, 1970). (3) Africa, South America, Australia, India, and Antarctica shared a widespread, exclusively Southern Hemisphere glaciation in the Permo-Carboniferous (for latest review see Hamilton and Krinsley, 1967). (4) In the Permian, these southern land masses shared a unique flora, dominated by the widespread genera *Glossopteris, Gangamopteris, Neoggeranthiopis* and *Paracalamites* (e.g., Just, 1952; Kummel, 1961; Melville, 1969). Schopf (1970b, p. 64) has noted, with respect to these fossil plants, that "most of the specimens in every assemblage are referable to the same small group of species, regardless of the continent from which the specimens were obtained." Notwithstanding this, certain northern plants were prominent in Argentina during the Permian (Archangelsky and Orrondo, 1969). (There are also similarities in the Permo-Carboniferous marine faunas of Australia and Argentina—see Amos and Sabattini, 1969.)

The vigorous arguments raised against the continental drift theory in Wegener's day, and in subsequent decades, are well known (e.g., there was no known mechanism by which continents could move). In the early 1960's, however, the theory underwent a striking resurgence with the discoveries of terrestrial paleomagnetism, which suggested that the continents of the world had, indeed, changed their positions relative to the magnetic pole in geologic time (Runcorn, 1962). Thus, paleomagnetic results from the Permian of Africa suggested that this continent occupied a different latitude at that time (Gough, Opdyke, and McElhinney, 1964) and supported the suggestion that it then lay adjacent to Antarctica. Australian results (Irving, Robertson, and Stott, 1963) suggested a series of changes in paleolatitudes for that continent which indicated a progressive drift northward across the Southern Ocean.

The plotting of Paleozoic paleomagnetic pole positions has now also served to indicate a former clustering of the southern continents and

India in the far south (see, e.g., Francheteau and Sclater, 1969; Creer, Embleton, and Valencio, 1970; Larson and La Fountain, 1970; Vilas and Valencio, 1970; McElhinney and Briden, 1971).

Continental drift, insofar as it affects the southern continents, should be thought of in terms of two distinct phases, an initial fragmentation of the Gondwana cluster—that is, the separation of India, Australia, New Zealand, South America, and Africa, from a position about Antarctica; and subsequently, a series of separations of the individual continents from each other—e.g., South America from Africa, Australia from Antarctica.

Various workers have advanced different dates for the break-up of Gondwanaland. Included in these are Fairbridge (1965) who placed its start as the end of the Cambrian, Creer (1964) as the end of the Permian and, later (as quoted in Fell, 1967b) as "about 150-200 million years ago," which would mean late Triassic to mid-Jurassic. Dietz and Holden (1970) suggest that the break-up began in the Triassic.

Later workers, using newer techniques, such as the paleomagnetism of the ocean floor, to date sea-floor spreading (see later), have emphasized that the break-up of Gondwanaland was progressive and have advanced dates for the various phases (detailed discussions in Heirtzler et al., 1968; Dietz and Holden, 1970). Fig. 1 shows a postulated series of stages in the break-up. Thus, while the split between the South American and African continents may have begun in the early Mesozoic, simultaneously with these continents breaking free from Antarctica, it was not finally completed until the Cretaceous (Heirtzler et al., 1968). Hurley (1968), reasoning partly from data on offshore sediments, gives the middle Triassic as the starting date for the rift that separated west Africa from North America, and the Cretaceous as the final date of separation of its southern parts from South America; the east coast of Africa, he reasons, opened up earlier, in the Permian. Australia, by contrast, did not break free from Antarctica until the Cretaceous (Dietz and Holden, 1970), and a date as late as the Eocene has been suggested by Le Pichon (1968).

Comparisons of the paleomagnetism of terrestrial rocks serve as indicators of relative displacement among continents through geologic time, but are subject to various interpretive uncertainties (see Graham, Helsley, and Hales, 1964; Darlington, 1965). Also, they provide no information on paleolongitudes, only on paleolatitudes. These shortcomings are partly resolved, for various parts of the world, by the newer findings stemming from the study of marine paleomagnetism and sea-floor spreading.

Plate Tectonics as a Mechanism for Continental Drift

Plate tectonics (Morgan, 1968; Dietz and Holden, 1970), which as a theory is still somewhat in a state of flux, envisages the earth's crust as being composed of a rigid outer shell or lithosphere, perhaps 100 kilometers thick, resting on an underlying and less rigid asthenosphere. The outer shell, presumably as a result of processes in the asthenosphere, is broken up into some six (Le Pichon, 1968) to ten (Dietz and Holden, 1969) major plates and subplates of varying shapes and size that are in a state of motion, relative to each other. The plates are margined (1) by trenches, where they converge and override each other and the lithosphere is resorbed in the underlying mantle; (2) by rifts, where they diverge and drift away from each other and volcanism produces new lithosphere in the gap; and (3) by transform faults or megashears, where they slide along past each other. The plates are rigid and more or less free of internal distortion (Heirtzler et al., 1968). Because the plates are interlocked to form the earth's carapace and the earth's circumference is assumed to be invariant, any shifting must be integrated in a systematic global pattern. The plates are segments of a spherical shell, and therefore the relative motion between any two plates can be described as a rotation about an axis through the center of the earth (Dietz and Holden, 1970). Plates may move in semi-unison, shear past each other (indicated by a fracture or megashear zone), or dip under each other. Deep-sea trenches characteristically are areas where plates are dipping, or being resorbed, into the mantle. These are called subduction zones.

Many individual plates contain both continental and oceanic segments of the earth's crust. The continental crust rises as a plateau within a plate because it consists of relatively lighter sialic (granite-like) rock. In terms of plate tectonics, continental drift involves the rifting of the continents and then the passive rafting of fragments of continental crust over the surface of the earth on the backs of the global conveyor-belt formed by a crustal plate that is being consumed at one place while growing by accretion at another. The realization, since 1964 (Vine, 1966), that linear magnetic anomalies on the sea floor might be ascribed to the accretionary lateral growth of the earth's crust along a rift by sea-floor spreading during fluctuations in the polarity of the earth's magnetic field has provided a remarkable new tool for studying the history of the evolving plates and of the large displacements among the continental fragments. The magnetic polarity changes can be dated, and they fix the time at which the oceanic rocks that produce the linear magnetic anomaly were formed. The velocity of relative movement between plates determined in this way ranges up to 10 centimeters per year (Heirtzler et al., 1968).

The actual mechanisms whereby plates move is uncertain. They could be thought of as being pushed, or pulled, or driven by gravitational forces, or carried by convection cells into the mantle; Dietz and Holden (1969) prefer a model based on pulling. They suggest that the plates may be colder and heavier at one boundary than elsewhere, and that it is here that they dive down into the earth's mantle.

Throughout the world the boundaries of the major plates are the loci of the main tectonic activity in the earth's lithosphere. Thus, most earthquakes are confined to narrow continuous belts that bound large stable areas (Isacks, Oliver, and Sykes, 1968). The major earthquake zones of

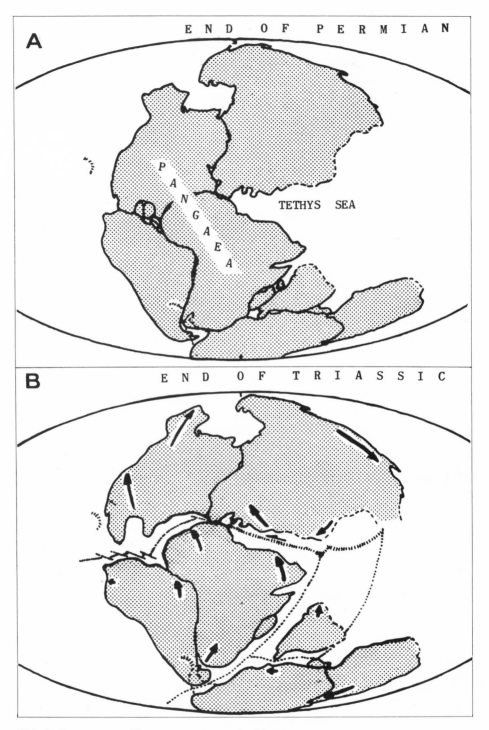

FIG. 1. CONTINENTAL MOVEMENTS DURING THE MESOZOIC

Reconstructions according to Dietz and Holden (1970) and based on the latest marine paleomagnetic and sea-floor spreading data and ideas. These authors assume the existence of a single supercontinent (Pangaea) in the Permian (A) and thus differ from some other authors who postulate both southern and northern continents. The southern and northern continents, Gondwana and Laurasia, separated by the Tethys Sea, appeared at the end of the Triassic (B), by which time South America, Africa, and

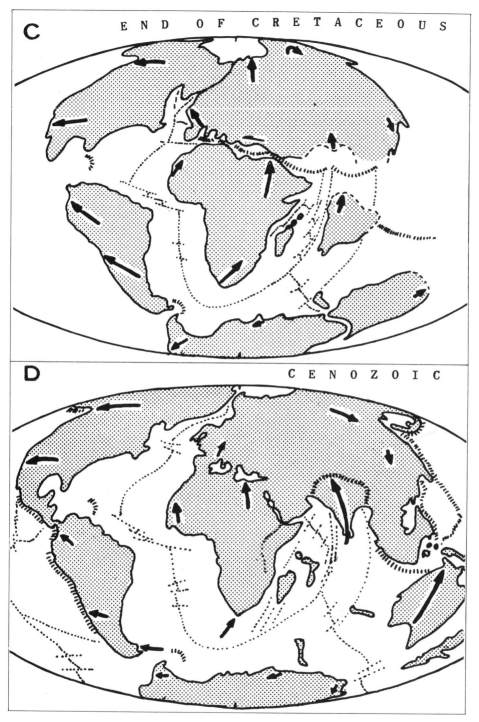

India had broken free from Antarctica. By the end of the Cretaceous (C), South America and Africa had drifted well apart, and the Indian plate was approaching Asia. According to this view, Australia did not separate from Antarctica until the end of the Cretaceous. The Cenozoic distribution of the continents is shown in D.

Rifts and oceanic ridges, from which sea-floor spreading is occurring, are shown by dotted lines, subduction zones by the banded lines. Arrows indicate directions of continuing movement patterns.

the earth are shown in Fig. 2, taken from Hurley (1968), and based partly
on data of the above authors. The latest maps of earthquake distribution
are contained in Barazangi and Dorman (1969). Physiographically, the
zones correspond with young mountain belts, oceanic ridges, island arcs,
and great faults. The Andes, for example, represent an area where oceanic
rocks of one plate are moving down beneath the continental rocks of
another plate (Fig. 2). The locus of the downward-moving plate of cold
lithosphere is marked by a zone of shallow earthquakes followed by zones
of medium and then deep earthquakes inland. This zone of earthquake
foci sloping into the depths of the mantle has been called a Benioff zone
and is taken to be the locus of a subduction zone in which a downward-
moving plate of the lithosphere is resorbed in the mantle.

The Himalayas represent another type of plate margin in which both
the overriding and underriding plates contain a thick crust of light continental rocks. The Indian plate is being subducted beneath the Asian
plate after having been rifted from Gondwanaland before its long Cenozoic migration northward from Antarctica. A zone of deep earthquakes is
absent here, presumably because the Indian plate contains relatively
light continental crustal rocks which resist being displaced into the deep
mantle because of their buoyancy.

Island arcs represent a third important variant among zones of convergence between lithosphere plates; here, both plates contain oceanic
crustal rocks, and the light granitic rocks that are typical of the continental crust are replaced by basaltic and andesitic volcanics extruded
above the subduction zone. Island arcs and ocean floor sediments and volcanic rocks are commonly accreted to the continental margin as a result
of the convergence between continental and oceanic crust at subduction
zones. The confused mass of basalts, greywackes, and schists that form the
Franciscan complex along the coast of California is an example of this
(W. Hamilton, pers. commun.; Dietz and Holden, 1969).

The current status of the plate tectonics theory in geology has recently
been summarized by Gilluly (1971), in a paper devoted to the magnetic
features that seem clearly related to plate motion and those that seem to
be independent of it. After stating that "So far as I know, no one has
suggested a model for the generation of plate motion that is acceptable
to anyone else," Gilluly goes on to say (page 2383):

> . . . nevertheless, the arguments from magnetic strips, from the distribution
> of blue schists and ophiolite belts, from sedimentary volumes, from the mu-
> tual relations of volcanic and plutonic belts, ocean ridges and deeps, and
> from the JOIDES drill cores, are cumulatively so compelling that the reality
> of plate tectonics seems about as well demonstrated as anything ever is in
> geology.

The latest workers in plate tectonics differ from the older ones in that
their postulated reconstructions involve large numbers of small plates
as well as large ones, rather than just the latter. See, for example, the

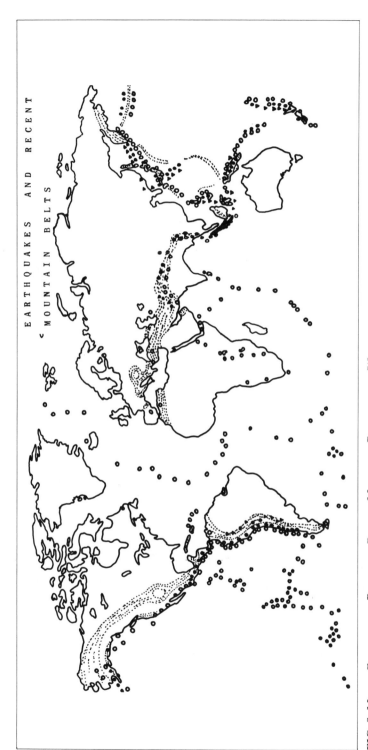

EARTHQUAKES AND RECENT MOUNTAIN BELTS

FIG. 2. MAJOR EARTHQUAKE BELTS AND RECENT MOUNTAIN BELTS OF THE WORLD

▼, deep earthquakes; ●, earthquakes at medium depths; ○, shallow earthquakes. Most of these are associated with plate margins. Upwelling (at the oceanic ridges) seems to coincide only with shallow tectonic movements. According to the new concepts of plate tectonics, the Rocky Mountains and the Andes result from oceanic plates subducting continental ones. The presence of a deep earthquake zone in the Andes signifies that the leading edge of the plate is here penetrating at a shallow angle. The Himalayas result from the subduction of the Asian plate by the Indian one at the end of its long movement northward from Antarctica. Here the contact is limited to the more superficial layers of the crust, and deep earthquakes are absent. Redrawn from Hurley (1968), and based on the kind of data reviewed in Isacks, Oliver, and Sykes (1968), and others.

work of Dewey (1971) and of Hamilton (1971), as presented at the Geological Society of America meetings in Washington in November, 1971.

Sea-Floor Spreading and Radiometric Dating Relative to Continental Drift

The theory of plate tectonics stems from recent findings with respect to the bathymetry, volcanicity, and earthquake activity of the sea floor, the analysis of deep-sea cores, and the anomalies in the earth's magnetic field over the oceans. As spreading occurs between plates moving outwards from the oceanic ridges, new oceanic floor is being created by the eruption and intrusion of basalt lavas in the zone of dilation between the plates (Vine, 1966; Burckle, et al., 1967; Riedel, 1967).

The rate of spreading outwards from the ridge axis can be determined from analysis of the magnetic anomalies measured above the ocean basins and by taking cores of the deep ocean sediments and determining the distance from the ridge axes to the nearest occurrence of sediments of progressively greater age. As the new volcanic rocks are poured out along the ridge axes, the magnetic particles within them become oriented to correspond with the local direction of the earth's field, and this magnetization is frozen into the lava as it cools. Periodically, due to reasons unknown, the earth's magnetic field reverses its polarity. Hence successive strips of volcanic rocks outwards from the ridge axis form a series of broad alternating bands or strips with normal and reversed magnetic polarity that disrupt the normal strength of the earth's field and create anomalies in it. These anomalies can be recorded, and their widths measured. Research ships towing magnetometers measure the strength of the earth's field while sailing series of transects outwards from the ridge axes. Zones of positive magnetization are those where the magnetization of the sea bottom lavas reinforce the earth's field, and zones of reversed magnetization are where they counteract it. The magnetic record is almost equally clearcut, whether the volcanic rocks are at the surface or are buried beneath an extensive cover of sediments, because the sediments are only weakly magnetized. A striking feature of the magnetic anomaly profiles is that they are symmetrical about the axis of the ridge. The exact mirror image (diagrams in Heirtzler, 1968), on either side of the ridge, supports the sea-floor-spreading hypothesis by demonstrating that the spreading rates on either side of the ridge are the same.

The sequences of polarity reversal recorded in the magnetization of oceanic rocks in themselves do not provide an absolute time scale. An absolute time scale has been worked out on the more accessible terrestrial volcanic rocks, however, by dating rocks with normal and reverse polarity, using radioactive decay systems such as potassium-argon, uranium-lead, and rubidium-strontium.

This scale has now been calibrated back to about four million years ago (Cox, Doell, and Dalrymple, 1968). The individual polarity epochs

range from some 0.7 to 1.75 million years. When marine magnetic
anomaly sequences are calibrated by extrapolating the scale back into
time, dates of up to 80 million years are obtained for some of the older
anomalies (Heirtzler et al., 1968).

Sediments are continuously being deposited on the ocean floor, and
probably at a constant rate. New volcanic rock along the crest of the
ridges will only be overlain by contemporary sediments. Those further
out from the axis will be overlain by sediments of increasing ages and
depths, with layers of successively younger sediments above. Rotary drill
cores from the sea floor provide a record of the sediments of different
geological layers preserved in them. Dating of the sediment is carried out
largely from the analysis of calcareous nanoplankton and planktonic
foraminifera. In this way it has been proven that the oldest sea floor
occurs near the continents. In the case of the South Atlantic, the ocean
basin that has been analyzed in greatest detail, the oldest sediments on
the floor are of Cretaceous age and are slightly less than 80 million years
old (Maxwell et al., 1970). These authors conclude that spreading has
continued in the South Atlantic at essentially a constant rate of two centimeters a year for the past 67 million years. By back calculating, they estimate that the separation of Africa and South America began about 130
million years ago. Calculations are based on the interpretation of magnetic anomalies and the dating by fossils in the sediments. The oldest
known sea-floor sediments in the world, it has been believed, occur in the
western north Pacific. A considerable portion of the abyssal floor there
was "already receiving pelagic sediment in late Jurassic time" (Fischer
et al., 1970, p. 1210). More recently, however, Fox, Heezen, and Johnson
(1970) have also described Jurassic sea floor from the tropical Atlantic,
and Dietz and Holden (1971) have directed attention to the possibility
that even older sea floor may occur in the Wharton Basin area of the
Indian Ocean.

A third line of data providing evidence of sea-floor-spreading rates is
provided by the magnetic record of the sediments contained in the cores
(Opdyke, 1968). Magnetization of sediments is weak compared to that of
the lavas. All sediments, however, contain some magnetic material which,
in the course of deposition, takes up an orientation controlled by the
local orientation of the earth's magnetic field. Hence the record here is
in successive shifts in the direction of magnetic polarization from top to
bottom through the core. The technique, which has been extensively
applied to Antarctic cores, shows polarity reversal sequences exactly corresponding to those revealed by the terrestrial volcanic rocks (Opdyke,
1968).

These combined techniques have now demonstrated sea-floor-spreading
rates for different parts of the world as follows: 4.5 cm per year for the
northeast Pacific and Pacific-Antarctic Oceans, 3.5 cm per year for the
southern Indian Ocean, 2 cm per year for the South Atlantic, and 1 cm
per year for the North Atlantic Reykjanes Ridge off Iceland (Heirtzler,

1968). More recently, Van Andel and Moore (1970) have given spreading rates of 1.6-2.0 cm per year for the northern South Atlantic. Since, as noted, the continents are carried along passively within the plates during sea-floor spreading, a basis is provided both for determining the age of the movements between continents and, when taken in conjunction with the distribution of such features as fault planes, for determining their direction of relative movement. It is obvious, of course, that the further one goes back into the Mesozoic the poorer the record and the less reliable the "reconstructions" are going to be. This is partly due to the diminishing amounts of old sea floor, partly to increasing difficulties in interpreting the evidence. The confusion could be compounded, in part, by a more active period of spreading in the mid-Mesozoic.

Continental Movements in the Southern Hemisphere: Recent Reconstructions

The newer thinking about continental movements in the Mesozoic and Cenozoic eras is summarized by the series reconstruction of Dietz and Holden (1970)—see Fig. 1A-1D. According to this view, the clustering of the southern continents about Antarctica was still complete at the end of the Permian (225 million years ago), although the extreme South Atlantic Ocean may have already opened up slightly. The creation of the North Atlantic rift in the Triassic separated North America from the bulge of Africa and the rifting of plate boundaries initiated the primitive Caribbean Sea. North America drifted northwest with respect to South America. The breakup of Gondwana in the south was a mid-Triassic phenomenon, resulting from the creation of the pan-Antarctic rift system. The rift split off a West Gondwana (Africa and South America) from an East Gondwana. The split of India from Antarctica was initiated. The Gondwana plates began to rotate, Africa and, initially, South America rotating sinistrally, as did India in lesser degree, and Antarctica. The disposition of the continents at the end of the Triassic Period is shown in Fig. 1B. The prominence of the Tethys Sea between Africa and Laurasia is a feature.

The general disposition of the land masses remained similar in the Jurassic Period, although South America and Africa moved northward from a fixed Antarctica. In the late Jurassic, or possibly in the early Cretaceous, an incipient South Atlantic rift was created within West Gondwana, as Africa and South America began to rift apart. India was now rapidly being rafted northward. Australia remained attached to Antarctica.

By the end of the Cretaceous (65 million years ago), according to the Dietz-Holden reconstruction (Fig. 1C), Africa and South America were widely separated, the South Atlantic being 3000 km wide. Their map shows South America and North America, which had hitherto apparently moved as one, being separated at this time. In another paper, however,

Dietz and Holden (1969, p. 37) refer to these continents being "rejoined" as a result of volcanism and the arching upward of the earth's mantle. As a result of their westward drift the Americas had, by the end of the Cretaceous, over-run or displaced a continuous north-south trench along their western margins. Africa drifted northward about 10°, rotating still further sinistrally so that the Tethys Sea became almost completely closed. Madagascar was split off. Australia now began to rift away from Antarctica. India by now had covered about two-thirds of its journey northward toward Eurasia.

The early Tertiary saw the splitting off of New Zealand from Australia and a rapid northward movement of Australia. Later, India collided with Eurasia, and the Australian plate, which included New Guinea, reached its present latitude and proximity to Indonesia.

There is now a considerable literature dealing with different phases of the above series of events. Most of the newer papers provide additional data for specific areas and, hence, update or reinterpret aspects of the Dietz-Holden reconstructions. It is obvious, moreover, that while there is a general consensus about the past histories of one or two areas, considerable disagreement and controversy surround the others.

Most writers seem to agree that the South Atlantic rift that initiated the separation of Africa and South America probably began in the Jurassic or Early Cretaceous (see, e.g., Valencio and Vilas, 1969; Creer, 1970; Larson and La Fountain, 1970; Maxwell et al., 1970). Funnell and Smith (1968) find that the marine deposits on the western margin of Africa began with the Upper Jurassic beds of Senegal, and that there is an abundance of Lower Cretaceous evaporite-type beds in the Senegal, the Congo, and Gabon. Smith and Hallam (1970) state that there are no major coastal sediments until the Cretaceous. The consensus is that the final separation of Africa and South America was probably a mid-Cretaceous event.

Dingle and Klinger (1971) record the discovery of Upper Jurassic margin sediments in the Knysna region of southeastern Africa and hence, by dating the invasion of the sea here, help pinpoint the time of separation of eastern Gondwana from western Gondwana. They point out that the Late Jurassic date for the first marine sediments is not in conflict with the mid-Triassic date advanced by Dietz and Holden (1970) for the separation but that it would appear to effectively disprove the later Cretaceous date advanced by Veevers, Jones, and Talent (1971).

Hamilton (1967) has discussed the plate tectonics of the Antarctic continent and has brought out that east Antarctica and west Antarctica are, geographically speaking, quite distinct units.

An important paper on the geological history and time of separation of South America and Antarctica has recently been published by Dalziel and Elliot (1971). These authors assess all the old and new data on the controversial Scotia Arc area that lies between the two continents, and confirm that it represents a displaced and fragmented section of a for-

merly continuous north-south Andean cordillera that extended from the
Andes to the Antarctic Peninsula. By dating the onset and history of
tectonic instability in the area, and incorporating South Atlantic sea-floor
spreading and other data, Dalziel and Elliot conclude that fragmentation
of the Scotia Arc region, and the eastward dispersal of the South Orkneys,
South Georgia, and related features occurred between the beginning of
the Tertiary and 20 to 25 million years ago. This relatively late separation of South America and Antarctica would have great implications from
the viewpoint of the direct transference of Southern Hemisphere floras
and faunas.

The date for the separation of Australia from Antarctica is given as
Late Eocene by Heirtzler et al. (1968), rather later than the separation of
New Zealand (Upper Cretaceous). Le Pichon (1968) suggests that New
Zealand left Antarctica in the Paleocene, moving northward very rapidly
at first. By the early Eocene its rate of movement had slowed considerably.
When Australia broke free from Antarctica in the late Eocene it developed a rate of movement twice that of New Zealand. The two masses
apparently were then moving in closely parallel paths and, for a time,
came into close contact, before separating more widely.

Creer (1964, 1970), after a study of Mesozoic pole positions suggests a
much earlier date for the separation of Australia from Antarctica, the
Early Triassic. The Eocene date is based on sea-floor spreading data (Le
Pichon, 1968; Le Pichon and Heirtzler, 1968; McElhinney and Wellman,
1969). Christoffel and Ross (1970) link a major change in the pattern
of ocean-floor spread in the Antarctic, which occurred about the time of
the Paleocene-Eocene boundary, with this event. Tarling (1971) suggests
that Australia and Antarctica were connected until the Paleocene. Jones
(1971) notes the occurrence of a marine transgression along the southern
margin of Australia in the Late Eocene. In contrast to this, Veevers,
Jones, and Talent (1971) suggest that Africa, Australia, and India, all
began to drift north in the mid-Cretaceous. This date, as noted, is actually
apparently too late for the separation of Africa (Dingle and Klinger, 1971).

Additional data on the presumed past spatial relationships of New
Zealand, Madagascar, and India, is considered later in the sections devoted
to those areas. India is treated in considerable detail because its past history
is the source of considerable conflict. This largely revolves around three
opposing concepts, namely that it (1) drifted northward more or less in
isolation, starting in the late Triassic or early Jurassic onward (the Deitz-
Holden concept); (2) remained close to Africa in the early stages (e.g.,
Schopf, 1970a; Smith and Hallam, 1970); and (3) was spatially associated
with Australia until the latest Jurassic, or earliest Cretaceous—see Veevers
et al. (1971), who reason on the basis of similar sedimentary deposits in
Western Australia and India. Up to this time, these authors believe,
southwest Australia and peninsular India had lain within the interior
of Gondwanaland (since their sedimentary deposits are dominantly non-
marine), and northwest Australia and Himalayan India (which have

marine deposits) had lain along its margin. Collision of the detached Indian and Australian blocks with Asia was "marked by regression, thrusting, orogeny, and subsequent molasse deposition" (Veevers, et al., 1971, p. 385). The northeast part of the Indian block, they believe, collided with Asia at the end of the Eocene, while Australia (which separated from Antarctica in the Eocene) collided with Asia in the Middle Miocene, "as suggested by thrusting and emplacement of block clay (argille scagliose) on Timor, broad folding of the floor of the Timor Sea, and deposition of Pliocene molasse in Timor" (Veevers et al., 1971, p. 385).

The evolution of the Indian Ocean, and the northward movements of Australia in the Cenozoic have also recently been reviewed by McElhinny (1970), and Jones (1971). Shor, Kirk, and Menard (1971) review some of the problems associated with the evolution of the Tasman Sea and the geological relationships of Australia and New Zealand.

The above brings out how little agreement there is, as yet, among geologists as to the spatial relationships of Australia to other land masses in the late Mesozoic and Early Tertiary. The problem is of basic importance in explaining both the occurrence of Jurassic and Cretaceous dinosaurs on both, and the origin of Australia's marsupials (see later).

Data Not Consistent with Continental Drift

Two recent geologists have produced strong arguments against the view that the continents of the world have drifted in geologic time. These are Beloussov (1967), and Meyerhoff (1970a,b). Beloussov's main argument is based on calculations of heat flow from the interior of the earth. Over continents, most of the heat flow is accounted for by radioactive substances in the lighter, superficial, granitic rocks. Hence, if oceans have formed as a result of the splitting and drifting apart of continents, heat-flow levels in the newly formed floors (since they contain no granite) must be low indeed. This is not the case, however. Heat-flow levels at the bottom of the oceans is just as high as on the continents. Radioactive material, hence, must be scattered through the mantle beneath the ocean floor, and the ocean bottoms must be ancient and permanent. Beloussov also argues against placing much significance on the matching and parallelism of continental coasts (e.g., on opposite sides of the Atlantic) as evidence of drift, suggesting that the same general "laws" seem to govern the formation of coastal outlines everywhere, and hence similar configurations might be expected.

The major objections of Meyerhoff (1970a,b) stem from his detailed analyses of the distribution of the world's evaporite belts (marine evaporites, coal, desert eolian sandstones, tillites) from the Proterozoic to Miocene. It was found that these have not changed in position in geologic time. Thus, (1) 95 per cent of all evaporite deposits (anhydrite, gypsum, halite, potash salts) crop out in or underlie the present dry wind belts—

i.e., belts which today receive less than 100 cm of annual rainfall; (2) the positions of the earth's desert belts have remained constant; (3) the earth's evaporite and coal zones, since the middle Proterozoic and Devonian times, respectively, have been symmetric with respect to the present rotational axis. Hence, the world's planetary wind and ocean-current circulation patterns cannot have changed, and this could only apply if the positions of the rotational pole, ocean basins, and continents have been consistent throughout. Meyerhoff also takes issue with various assumptions made by the "advocates of continental drift," including deductions based on the alleged changes in position of the paleopoles, because of the low level of consistency obtained in successive determinations.

In a still later paper Meyerhoff and Teichert (1971) argue that the existence of continental glaciations in the Proterozoic and Paleozoic, and the large coal fields of the Paleozoic, Carboniferous, and Permian, demonstrate that the world's land could not have been grouped into two supercontinents at these times. This is because glaciation and large-scale coal deposition require an adequate water supply and that this would not have been available in the middle of supercontinents. Bonatti, Ball, and Schubert (1970) also discuss evaporite distribution and continental drift.

It is too early to pass judgment on the views of Beloussov and Meyerhoff. Since their interpretations are so at variance with the bulk of contemporary geological thinking there is a real need for a dissection of their ideas. At the same time, Meyerhoff's warning against the rash acceptance of all the new concepts concerning drift is well taken. It is also impossible, as yet, to evaluate the random geophysical objections that are sometimes raised against drift—e.g., Jeffrys (1970, p. 1007) remarks: "Imperfection of elasticity in the Earth follows a law that forbids convection and continental drift."

In the last decade a few Southern Hemisphere geologists (mainly Australian) have come out against continental drift, at least in so far as it affects Australia, and have assembled a range of arguments that conflict with it. These include Teichert (1959, quoted in Glaessner, 1962), Audley-Charles (1966) and, in particular, Glaessner (1962). Glaessner has pointed out that the occurrence of marine strata ranging in age from early Paleozoic to late Tertiary along most of the west coast of Australia is clearly inconsistent with a supposition that this coast was formerly part of another land mass (but note the remarks of Veevers et al., 1971, concerning this). Glaessner argues that much of the Late Carboniferous and early Permian glaciation in Australia can be interpreted as mountain, not continental, glaciation and hence does not necessarily indicate a more southern geographic position for the continent. Glaessner's parting shot against continental drift is that the "assemblies of continents drawn by various adherents of this hypothesis (Wegener, du Toit, King, Carey) and even successive versions produced by individual authors, differ so widely that they are mutually exclusive" (p. 244). This argument is of doubtful relevance.

Fossil marine invertebrate studies, which have great potential for resolving many questions concerning drift, currently provide rather confused and inconclusive results. Arguing against drift are Stehli and Helsley (1963), and Fell (1967a,b), who have mapped the distribution of a range of invertebrate groups during the different geological periods. They base their interpretations on two considerations: (1) groups are almost invariably restricted to specific latitudinal belts, being tropical, temperate, or cold water forms; and (2), more important, that, in the past just as now, adjoining and adjacent landmasses had closely related faunas whereas distant ones had dissimilar faunas. Their conclusions were that faunas have been distributed along the same latitudinal belts from the Ordovician to the present (i.e., the latitudinal distribution of a typical "tropical" element has remained unchanged). India could not, accordingly, have drifted 60° of latitude northward in post-Jurassic times, as suggested by the paleomagnetic data. Again, since Ordovician times the affinities of the pericontinental shelf faunas of South America have been with North America, Africa with Eurasia, and Australia with Asia. These sets of faunas, in turn, have remained distinct from each other since the Ordovician. This, it is argued, could not have been the case had the southern continents been part of a common Gondwanaland mass at any time. The argument is thus essentially a biological parallel to that of Meyerhoff.

Alternatively, however, Hallam (1967, p. 201), following an analysis of the fossil mollusk faunas at different times during the Mesozoic, has come to the opposite conclusions: "The distribution of many Mesozoic faunas appears to demand the existence of land and/or shelf sea connections between continents where none exists today. The old concept of trans-oceanic land bridges being considered unsatisfactory, an interpretation based on Late Mesozoic and Early Tertiary continental drift is preferred, taking into account other geological and geophysical data. None of the paleozoogeographic data surveyed is obviously incompatible with drift, and much is difficult to explain without it."

Of equal significance to the above conflict of opinion is evidence that Australia has been at its present latitude since at least the early Mesozoic. Stratigraphers such as Teichert (1941), Audley-Charles (1966), and Veevers (1969) have either argued for this view or have produced evidence that Australia is closely linked stratigraphically with Timor, an island which, to judge from its very rich Triassic fauna of warm-water invertebrates (Kummel, 1961), has long enjoyed an equatorial, or near-equatorial, position. Moreover, an Upper Eocene anthracothere, a semiaquatic artiodactyl resembling a small hippopotamus, has been discovered on Timor (von Koenigswald, 1967). This fact would certainly seem to confirm this island's proximity to Asia at that time. A recent expedition to locate the fossil site from which this skull fragment was obtained and hence confirm this tantalizing zoogeographic find failed, however, its discoverer only remembering that he picked it up in a river (D. A. Hooijer, pers. commun.). Audley-Charles (1966) has stated that Timor and northern Australia share many Permian fossils and, on the basis of this and his own stratigraphic interpretations, has produced a series of maps showing Australia lying close to Asia throughout the Mesozoic. A direct land connection is suggested for the Upper Jurassic, with a wide separation commencing between the Lower and Upper Cretaceous as a result of widespread marine transgressions. (Audley-Charles's maps are reproduced in the chapter on Australian mammals, in order to illustrate the northern theory of marsupial colonization of this continent). Veevers (1969), in the course of interpreting the results of deep-bore drillings into offshore reefs to the northwest of Australia, lists a series of stratigraphic similarities between Australia, the Sahul Shelf, and Timor.

Irrespective of past geological relationships between Australia and Timor, there is, of course, no reason for necessarily believing that this island has always had its present spatial relationship with southeast Asia. The island, like northern New Guinea and some other Indonesian land masses, shows evidence of great physiographic distortion (W. Hamilton, pers. communun.); deep-water trenches, moreover, lie both to the southeast and northwest of Timor. Furthermore, a map in Menard (1964), reproduced in Hallam (1967), draws attention to the arc of deep trenches that extend from Indonesia, around the north of Australia, and then southeast toward New Zealand. Other evidence that the Australia-New Guinea continental plate drifted northward in later geologic times, then crashed into the pre-existing island arcs to the northwest, north, and northeast, stems from the contorted and confused geology of these areas today (see Shor, et al., 1971; Veevers, et al., 1971).

In a paper given at the 1971 meetings of the Geological Society of America (Washington, D.C., November), Hamilton (1971) reviewed the results of recent studies on plate tectonic evolution in Indonesia. An extremely involved and complicated history was indicated, involving virtually all the island systems from New Guinea to Java, Borneo, and the Philippines. The sum evidence was consistent with "continuous Late Cretaceous and Cenozoic westward motion of the Pacific plate, and northward motion of the Indian Ocean-Australia-New Guinea plate, into changing Indonesian and western Pacific subduction zones" (Hamilton, 1971, p. 589).

Confirmatory evidence from invertebrate fossils that Australia has moved progressively northward from the Mesozoic onward is lacking. J. M. Dickens (pers. commun.) states: "The evidence from the Permian faunas is in fact rather clear, although it can be interpreted in various ways. Briefly, the lowermost invertebrate Permian faunas are of the Gondwana type, i.e., closely related to those of India and South America, in particular. In Western Australia during the Lower Permian this fauna is replaced by Tethyean type faunas. This relationship persists through the Permian into the Triassic. In the lowermost Triassic it might be remembered that in any case the faunas are relatively very cosmopolitan.

In eastern Australia and New Zealand a series of faunas developed derived more or less directly from the early Gondwana type. This of course is rather over-simplified and an exact description would require many pages. In Western Australia, irrespective of other relationships, Tethyean relationships persist through into the Tertiary. From Permian into the Tertiary a fairly persistent temperate zone is recognizable in southern Australia with a warmer zone to the north. The evidence for this is to be found in a number of publications."

Evidence from invertebrate fossils is now awaited in order to see if the concept that Australia has only more recently arrived at its present latitude can be substantiated. Deep cores put down into Wreck Island, at the southern end of the Great Barrier Reef, indicate that this was a site of reef deposition even as far back as the Miocene (J. M. Dickins, pers. commun.). This *could* be consistent with the view that Australia only reached subtropical latitudes at this time. Oxygen isotope data on paleo-temperatures, given by Dorman (1966), provide some support for this possibility. Thus, data derived from the mollusks *Chlamys, Pecten,* and *Ostrea* from southern Victoria indicate a steep rise in mean sea temperatures from 15 to 20° C in the mid-Oligocene up to 23 to 25° C in the early Miocene. This rising temperature possibly indicates the time when Australia reached its present position. The sharp drop from mid-Miocene onward is in accord with a world-wide drop in temperatures at that time (Dorman, 1966).

An alternative explanation for the above evidence of higher water temperatures in southeastern and eastern Australia during the late Oligocene and Miocene is that some change in patterns of marine currents then brought warmer waters to these coasts.

THE MESOZOIC FOSSIL RECORD ON THE SOUTHERN CONTINENTS

Triassic

A symposium organized in 1952 to consider the biological evidence for direct Mesozoic connections between Africa and South America presented conflicting opinions (Mayr, 1952). These differences particularly applied to the fossil tetrapods, the immediate terrestrial predecessors of mammals. Thus, Colbert (1952) noted that the Triassic faunas of the world were comparatively homogeneous. South America and Africa had 75 per cent of reptile families in common; South America and North America, 63 per cent; South America and Europe, 75 per cent; and South America and Australia, 12 per cent. Colbert was noncommittal as to the necessity of continental drift to explain these relationships. Romer (1952), however, pointed out that to group broadly the Early Triassic and Late Triassic faunas, as Colbert had done, obscured trends. In actual fact the equivalent Middle Triassic Santa Maria Beds of Brazil and the Manda Beds of Tanzania had remarkably similar tetrapod faunas, the differences being no greater than might be expected in two parts of the same continent. Romer, accordingly, was inclined to argue for direct junction of Africa and South America during the mid-Triassic.

In later years, a number of workers (Bonaparte, 1967; Romer, 1967; Sill, 1969; Colbert, 1971) reviewed similarities and parallels in the fossil synapsid reptiles of Africa and South America. Bonaparte (1967) has noted, in particular, closely related species of the dicynodont *Kannemeyeria* in the two areas, and Romer (1967) has commented on the herbivorous traversodontid cynodonts of the Tanzanian Manda beds and those of the South American Chañares beds. Cox (1965) discussed the difficulties attending the exact dating and correlation of the Triassic faunal successions in the two continents.

The recent discovery in Antarctica of a Lower Triassic tetrapod fauna, characterized by the therapsid *Lystrosaurus* (Elliot, et al., 1970), is an exciting development, not only by reason of demonstrating that this continent supported tetrapods in the early Triassic but further that it must then have been joined to other land masses. *Lystrosaurus* is particularly prominent in the Early Triassic of South Africa and India, both "Gondwana" continents, but it is also known from Sinkiang, China (Tripathi and Satsangi, 1963; Cox, 1967). The discovery of *Lystrosaurus* in Antarctica is accepted by various workers (e.g., Simpson, 1970) as proving the reality of continental drift and the existence of a former Gondwana supercontinent. (*Lystrosaurus* has not yet been recorded from South America or Australia, but that it also occurred in at least the former continent is now presumed to be the case.)

In a recent extensive review Colbert (1971) has given a full list of the tetrapods occurring with *Lystrosaurus* in the new Lower Triassic Antarctic deposits, and has compared them in detail with Lower Triassic labyrinthodont and reptile faunas of Africa, South America, and India. Two distinct Lower Triassic faunas occur in South Africa, a lower *Lystrosaurus* assemblage, in which that genus makes up about 90 per cent of all the fossils, and an overlying *Cynognathus* fauna. The South African and Antarctic *Lystrosaurus* faunas almost exactly replicate each other, sharing such genera as *Thrinaxodon* (a therapsid cynodont), *Procolophon* (a small cotylosaur), the labyrinthodont *Lydekkerina*, and other forms. The Antarctic deposits are, however, rather richer in prolacertids (ancestral lizards). Colbert stresses that such a close resemblance would not be possible unless both assemblages inhabited a common land mass. The Indan "*Lystrosaurus* Zone" also bears close resemblances to the South African one, the genera *Lystrosaurus* and *Chasmatosaurus* being common to both. Colbert regards this resemblance as proof that India was also part of the same major land mass. The occurrence of *Lystrosaurus* in China, beyond the limits of Gondwanaland, requires explaining. Colbert believes that it represents a secondary extension of range by way of northwest Africa (the so-called "Spanish abutment"), where reconstructions (see Fig. 1) suggest that Gondwana and Laurasia were tenuously joined.

The African *Cynognathus* zone fauna does not occur in Antarctica (or, rather, has not yet been found there). It is, however, well developed in South America (where the genera *Cynognathus* and *Kannemeyeria* are also prominent). There is again a slightly different, but equivalent, fauna in India, and a comparable one, characterized by different genera, in China. The latter fact Colbert suggests also represents a secondary extension of range via northwest Africa.

These southern Lower Triassic faunas, Colbert states, represent a relatively uniform group. They differ strikingly, moreover, from contemporary ones in Europe and North America. These Laurasian assemblages are dominated by labyrinthodonts and the large thecodont *Chirotherium*. Therapsids, so important in the southern continents, are completely absent. These differences, Colbert argues, are persuasive evidence for the existence of separate southern and northern supercontinents in the Early Triassic.

Colbert's general conclusions about the proximity of the southern continents in the Early Triassic would seem to be reasonable. Difficulties, of course, remain. Dicynodonts, as a group, occurred far beyond the postulated limits of Gondwana, and their apparent marked success in one hemisphere and not in the other may reflect differences in environmental conditions at the various sites of deposition. In recent years, the known distribution of certain reptilian groups has been broadened; thus phytosaurs have been found in Madagascar and rhynchosaurs in Nova Scotia (Cox, 1967). Lastly, the Australian Triassic tetrapod picture is not as clear as we would like it to be. Australia and South America shared only 12 per cent of reptile families in the Triassic (Colbert, 1952). The Australian Triassic reptile fossil data are, however, limited and what there is requires reappraisal. The recent discovery of scattered labyrinthodont and thecodont reptilian remains in Lower Triassic deposits near Rolleston, central Queensland, offers potentially interesting material (Bartholomai and Howie, 1970). Included in the specimens since removed from this deposit are two or three species of lepidosaurian reptiles that these authors provisionally ally with the Paliguanidae, or short-skulled eosuchians, other members of which have been described from South Africa and Central Asia. Synapsid reptiles, however, are absent (Bartholomai and Howie, 1970). Middle to Upper Triassic dinosaur footprints are known from coal mines at Dinmore, near Brisbane (Bartholomai, 1966). Most of the Australian Triassic labyrinthodont amphibians have been placed in endemic genera. One genus (*Paratosaurus*), however, also occurs in Germany and Arizona, and one of its species has a skull similar to that of a genus of labyrinthodonts in the *Cynognathus* zone of South Africa (Cosgriff, 1967). Recently in a paper read before the Linnean Society of New South Wales, Howie (1971) described a new species of brachyopid labyrinthodont from the Lower Triassic Rewan formation of Queensland that is closely related to one from the Mangali beds of India.

The Triassic floras of South Africa, Australia, South America, and

India are, however, closely related (Menéndez, 1969). They, too, thus suggest ongoing spatial continuity or near continuity of these continents at that time.

Jurassic

Rich dinosaur fossil beds of the type necessary for the comparison of continental faunas, unfortunately, are lacking from the Jurassic until near the end of that period. These are characterized by a worldwide uniformity of type (Colbert, 1962). Thus, the Jurassic dinosaur *Bothriospondylus* is known from Europe, Australia, and Madagascar. The Jurassic flora of South America is also more cosmopolitan than the Triassic one (Ménendez, 1969). Few significant data are forthcoming from marine fossil invertebrates to complement the terrestrial data. Hallam (1967), however, has noted that although the Lower Jurassic marine mollusks are cosmopolitan, certain similarities between those on either side of the Atlantic persist into the Late Jurassic.

Cretaceous

The freshwater ostracods of the Upper Jurassic (?) to Lower Cretaceous deposits of the Congo, Angola, and Gabon on the one hand, and Brazil on the other, are remarkably similar. Eighteen species are shared (Krommelbein, 1965a,b). Martin (1968) argues for caution in accepting these data as proving continental junctions. He pointed out that not enough is yet known about Lower Cretaceous nonmarine ostracods from other parts of the world. Certainly, the findings applying to this group should be tested against freshwater mollusks and other invertebrates of that habitat. Reyment (1967, 1969) has studied fossil ammonites relative to the opening of the Atlantic. Hallam (1967) records that the Lower Cretaceous marine trigoniid mollusks of Africa and South America are remarkably similar. This would also suggest close contact between these continents then or in the recent past; or, at least, that the same marine currents washed their shores. Slightly more puzzling is the apparent occurrence of the boa *Madtsoia* in the Upper Cretaceous of Madagascar and the Paleocene-Eocene of Patagonia, based on Hoffstetter's identification of vertebrae (Del Corro, 1968).

The Cretaceous fossil plants of South America do not provide any real data concerning possible land connections. The Lower Cretaceous floras belong to widely ranging groups, while the Middle and Upper Cretaceous (angiosperm) ones are essentially similar to those that occur today in the tropical and subtropical zones of the world (Menéndez, 1969). Freake (1968), however, has recorded that Cretaceous spore-pollen floras from Brazil and Congo-Gabon have 34 out of 39 taxa in common. Likewise those of Nigeria and Colombia also show marked similarities (Hoeken-Klinkenberg, 1964).

By the late Cretaceous the dinosaur faunas of South America bore undeniable North American affinities, only 33 per cent of the families were shared with Africa, compared to 66 per cent with North America; 58 per cent with Europe, and 8 per cent with Australia (Colbert, 1952). Two prominent North American dinosaur types, the ceratopsids and hadrosaurs were, however, conspicuous absentees from South America (Colbert, 1965). This absence indicates, as do the early mammals, a continuing faunal filter.

Mesozoic vertebrate fossil data that might help reveal the spatial relationships of Australia and the other continents in the Cretaceous are poor. What there are suggest, alternatively, a fair degree of isolation, and good contacts with the northern continents. A presumed Lower Cretaceous fauna of freshwater fishes from Victoria contains five genera, two of them endemic (Waldman, 1967). Of the others, *Leptolepis* is known from the Upper Triassic of East Africa, the Jurassic of North America and Europe, the Lower Cretaceous of Mexico, and the Upper Cretaceous of South America; *Coccolepis* from the Jurassic of Europe and Asia, and the Lower Cretaceous of Belgium; and *Liodesmus* from the Upper Jurassic of Bavaria. These facts certainly suggest a continuing contact between Australia and the northern land masses in the middle Mesozoic.

Colbert (1952) recorded that Australia and South America share only 8 per cent of families in the Upper Cretaceous. The Australian dinosaur faunas, however, are only poorly known, and remains are fragmentary and in need of modern taxonomic assessment. The continent is credited with a range of endemic genera—e.g., the Jurassic *Rhaetosaurus, Agrosaurus,* and the Cretaceous *Austrosaurus* (see Romer, 1966; Bartholomai, 1966), but the skeletal remains of these forms are incomplete. Colbert and Merrilees (1967) have described some Cretaceous dinosaur footprints from near Broome, northwestern Australia, which apparently belong to *Megalosauropus,* one of a group of Lower Cretaceous iguanodonts known from many localities in Europe, central Asia, North America, and South Africa. Also indicating that the Cretaceous dinosaurs of Australia were related to northern groups is the recent discovery, in central Queensland, of a bipedal herbivorous dinosaur thaat apparently belongs to the European genus *Iguanodon* (Bartholomai, 1966).

Some of the giant dinosaurs of the Late Cretaceous were apparently very widely ranging. Thus, *Antarctosaurus* has been recorded from Patagonia, Argentina, India, and probably Kazakhstan, U.S.S.R. (von Huene in Van Valen, 1969). *Laplatosaurus* is known from South America, east Africa, Madagascar, and India (Colbert, 1952). *Titanosaurus* has been recorded from England, central Europe, Madagascar, India, and South America (von Huene and Matley, 1933). At the same time, some of these generic identifications are dubious, new taxonomic studies being badly needed (B. Patterson, pers. commun.).

In considering the latitudinal position of Australia in the Cretaceous relative to the occurrence of dinosaurs, the demonstration by Brown (1968) that Mesozoic tetrapods were latitude-dependent and that a disproportionate percentage of fossils occurs at the lower latitudes ($0°$ to $30°$ S) should be noted.

THE MESOZOIC FOSSIL RECORD AND THE POSITIONS OF THE
SOUTHERN CONTINENTS DURING THE MESOZOIC

The Mesozoic fossil data just reviewed suggest the following:

(1) Up until Lower (or Middle) Triassic times the continents of Antarctica, Africa, South America, India and, presumably, Australia were clustered together as members of a southern supercontinent (Gondwanaland). This contrasted with a northern supercontinent (Laurasia).

(2) In the Jurassic this "exclusive" southern relationship was reduced and there was increasing exchange with the north, as suggested by the plants and dinosaurs taking on a "more cosmopolitan" image.

(3) Cretaceous floras and faunas are also somewhat cosmopolitan. But the relatively more complete Cretaceous data do suggest certain specific positional relationships between the continents during this period. Thus, possibly, West Africa and Brazil lay close together, or were joined, in the Lower Cretaceous; presumably there was a loss of this affinity, and closer links between South America and North America in the Upper Cretaceous. To judge from the incomplete interchange of dinosaurs and mammals in the Upper Cretaceous, however, this did not amount to an actual land junction. There is geological evidence that South America and North America were separated by a marine barrier in the Late Cretaceous (Jacobs, Burgl, and Conley, 1963; Lloyd, 1963; Haffer, 1970).

Postulated reconstructions of the distribution of the southern continents at different times during the Mesozoic, such as those of Dietz and Holden (1970), shown in Fig. 1, suggest the following relationships:

(1) In the mid-Triassic, Africa and South America (West Gondwana) split off from Australia and Antarctica (East Gondwana). India broke free and commenced to move northward. North America split free from northwest Africa, initiating the Caribbean Sea, and moved northwest with respect to South America.

(2) In the late Jurassic, Africa and South America, which were drifting northward, commenced to split apart in the south. India was now isolated and moving northward. Australia was still attached to Antarctica.

(3) By the Late Cretaceous, Africa and South America, which had remained joined for some time in the middle regions (West Africa and Brazil)—see Fig. 1C—became widely separated. Australia now broke free and began to rift away from Antarctica. India was isolated in the middle of the Indian Ocean perhaps two-thirds of the way toward the Asian continent.

The fossil data, it will be seen, are compatible with the postulated distribution of the continents in the Lower Triassic. Likewise, they are compatible with the postulated continuing junction, or proximity, of west Africa and Brazil in the Lower Cretaceous, the increased isolation of Africa and South America during the Cretaceous, and the proximation of the latter to North America at the end of the Cretaceous.

The rest of the fossil data are in conflict with the Dietz-Holden and other reconstructions in varying degrees. The partial break-up of Gondwana in the Triassic would be consistent with reduced relationships in the floras and faunas of the southern continents in the Jurassic. Their "more cosmopolitan" status, one would anticipate, should be associated with greater spatial proximity of the southern and northern continents. This was apparently not the case, however; the Tethys Sea still formed an extensive barrier (Fig. 1C). Presumably, then, the postulated northwest Africa land bridge (Colbert, 1971) must have been adequate to permit a fair amount of biotic flow. As noted, Colbert (1971) has invoked this land bridge to explain the occurrence of southern *Lystrosaurus* Zone and *Cynognathus* Zone fossils in China.

Possibly, however, other factors were involved in the creation of "more cosmopolitan" biota in the Jurassic. Climatic changes might have encouraged greater faunal interchanges by creating comparable habitats in the north and south, and the newly evolved Jurassic biota might have been characterized by greater mobility and ecological plasticity than their predecessors. This would certainly seem to have been the case with the dinosaurs (especially the larger ones) relative to the therapsids.

The Tethys Sea has long been regarded as epicontinental. Accordingly, it has been presumed that, as a result of periodic emergence and narrowing, it would not have been such a formidable distributional barrier to land plant and animal distribution as an ocean basin would have been. Recently, Dewey (1971) suggested, however, that it exhibited the oceanic characteristic of sea-floor spreading during the Mesozoic.

A further point of basic biogeographic interest is that there are enough Laurasian elements in Gondwana deposits, and vice versa, during the Late Paleozoic and Early Mesozoic to make some authorities doubt that the two supercontinents were truly isolated at that time. Thus, during the Permian, certain northern plants were prominent in Argentina (Archangelsky and Orrondo, 1969). It is worth noting, also, that certain authorities have regarded the distributions of the Early Triassic *Lystrosaurus* and *Cynognathus* as being so wide as not to offer any evidence one way or the other for direct southern distributions (e.g., Boonstra, 1969; Crompton, 1969). These comments were made, of course, before the discovery of Antarctic deposits of the former. The discoveries still do not necessarily render the theory untenable since *Lystrosaurus* could have entered Antarctica via the Scotia Arc.

The fossil data, and the Deitz-Holden and comparable reconstructions, are clearly irreconcilable when it comes to the Cretaceous faunas of Australia and India. Australia had northern dinosaur types like *Megalopsaurops* and *Iguanodon* in the Cretaceous, at a time when it was supposed to be just breaking free from Antarctica. Yet Antarctica is alleged to have become isolated from South America by the Middle Triassic, when archosaur development and radiation were only beginning. There can be only two alternative explanations. Either the Australian dinosaurs developed independently from ancestral types in the Triassic, producing, by the late Cretaceous, large-bodied types that bore a striking resemblance to northern genera; or else, Australia was *not* isolated from the other continents (including the northern ones) throughout the Mesozoic. The late Mesozoic freshwater fishes of Australia, it has been noted, also include northern genera; this may not mean anything, however, since *Leptolepis* is ancient, as the others may well be, extending as far back as the Upper Triassic (in Africa).

Equally great problems surround India. This is supposed to have been an isolated land mass, drifting northward across the Indian Ocean from the mid-Triassic onward. Despite this, as Colbert (1971) has noted, India has both Jurassic and Cretaceous dinosaur faunas—see also von Huene and Matley (1933), Darlington (1957) and Robinson (1971). Hence, like Australia, it must have been at least intermittently in contact with other continents during this time, and the Dietz and Holden (1970) reconstruction must be wrong.

The wide distribution of certain dinosaurs has, of course, long been a topic for speculation. Matthew (1915), for example, argues that they could well have become world-wide by means of such continental connections as occur today. Von Heune and Matley (1933), however, felt it necessary to postulate the former existence of a series of land bridges to account for them.

It is obvious, therefore, that Australia and India could not have been isolated relative to other land masses during the Middle and Late Mesozoic, as Dietz and Holden (1970) and others have suggested. Their Cretaceous dinosaur faunas must somehow be explained. It is a problem both the advocates of drift and the taxonomists must face in the future for the Indian evidence casts grave doubts on the whole notion of drift.

THE CONTEMPORARY BIOLOGICAL AFFINITIES OF THE
SOUTHERN CONTINENTS

Africa and South America

The contemporary faunas of Africa and South America are very distinct. Among vertebrates, however, the two continents share several orders of birds (including the ratites), pelomedusid turtles, pipid frogs, and several families of freshwater fishes. A few of the bird groups that are today predominantly South American and African (or South American, African, and Asian) tend to be widely distributed as fossils. Thus, the Trogonidae are known from the Eocene, Oligocene, and Miocene of Europe, just as the Psittacidae (best developed in South America and Australia today) are known from the Miocene of both Europe and North America (Romer, 1966). The Capitonidae (barbets), with contemporary centers of abundance in South America, Africa, and southeast Asia, are unknown as fossils. Ratites go back to the Lower Eocene in South America and the Upper Eocene in Africa (Brodkorb, 1963). Recent egg-white protein studies suggest that the large ratites of the southern continents are closely related biochemically and immunologically (Osuga and Feeney, 1968).

The South American and African fishes present a different problem, for both faunas are dominated by characoids, a group unknown elsewhere. It has commonly been argued that both faunas must have been derived from common ancestral types that entered from the north (Darlington, 1957). No family of South American fishes can be derived from any North American one (Darlington, 1957), however, and true or "primary division" North American freshwater fishes do not reach South America. These facts testify to the difficulties of colonizing the southern continent from the north along an isthmus deficient in freshwater streams. The characoids consist of about 16 families and probably over 1100 species (Myers, 1967). They are the most primitive of the cypriniform fishes, are entirely freshwater, and have osmoregulatory limitations that prevent their entrance into the sea. Unfortunately, the origin and radiation of the ostariophysan fishes have not been traced, virtually nothing is known of Jurassic freshwater fishes, while only one assemblage of freshwater fishes is known from the Triassic of Africa, and the several known from Argentina are in need of critical evaluation (B. Schaeffer, pers. commun.). Accordingly, Schaeffer (1952) felt that the characoid fishes could not be used as an argument either for or against former South American-African connections. Recently, however, Myers (1967) and Gery (1969) have reiterated the view that these faunal similarities can only be explained by a former junction of the two continents.

The contemporary invertebrates provide many examples of exclusively Southern Hemisphere distributions, and du Toit (1937) and others have drawn extensively on these examples to support their arguments for former direct junctions of the southern continents. While some of these alleged examples have not withstood subsequent taxonomic scrutiny, many have been fully corroborated by later workers. Thus, among the terricolous oligochaetes two genera, *Chilota* and *Parachilota,* are confined to South America and Africa and two others, *Microscolex* and *Eodrilus,* are restricted to these two continents plus Australia (Omodeo, 1963). Plecoptera distributions include a "Gondwanian type" (South America, Africa, Australia), as seen in the Notonemourinae, and an "Amphinotic type" (Australia, New Zealand, the subantarctic islands, and cold temperate South America). Examples of the latter are to be found in the Archiperlaria, with the Eustheniidae (already differentiated in the Permian of Victoria) forming, with the Australoperlidae and Gripopterydidae, a distinctive group (Illies, 1965, 1969). The occurrence of a distinct series of Southern Hemisphere chironomid dipterans has now been well documented by Brundin (1966). One major subfamily (Podonominae) shows well-marked South American-Tasmanian-Australian relationships, while the New Zealand members are rather markedly independent and the southern African ones are strongly independent. The Diamesinae, by contrast, show very close South American-New Zealand relationships, weak

South American-Australian ones, and very weak South American-African and New Zealand-Australian ones.

Certain plant groups are of course shared by Africa and South America, as well as the other southern continents. These include the Proteaceae and three genera of podocarps. *Nothofagus,* however, is unknown from Africa.

The mammals of Africa and South America, contemporary and fossil, are quite distinct. They obviously represent lineages that have had long histories of evolution in isolation. The earliest African deposits (Upper Eocene–Lower Oligocene) are dominated by endemic orders like the Hyracoidea, Embrithopoda, and Proboscidea, quite distinct from marsupials, Xenarthra, condylarths, and notoungulates of the South American Paleocene (Cooke, 1968; Patterson and Pascual, 1968; and Chapters III and VI). The latest sea-floor spreading and paleomagnetic data, it will be noted, suggest that there was no direct junction between Africa and South America after the Lower Cretaceous. (See p. 70 for a discussion of the relationships of the monkeys of these two continents.) The mammals, certainly, argue against any direct connection much after that time.

South America and Australia

Analysis of the contemporary faunas and floras of Australia and South America shows a range of groups that are common, and exclusive, to the two continents. These similarities must not, of course, obscure the fundamental and striking floristic and faunistic differences between them. The groups that have long been used in arguments to support a former direct southern connection between South America and Australia include parastacid crayfish, leptodactylid and hylid frogs, chelydid turtles, extinct meiolanid turtles, lungfishes (also in Africa, but world-wide in the Mesozoic), the semiparasitic (on crayfish) flatworm *Temnocephala,* galaxiid fishes, and marsupials (cf. Harrison, 1924). Later authorities were able to dismiss many of these presumed examples on the ground that they were not really as closely related as claimed, or that they merely represented relics of formerly more widely ranging groups. Simpson (1940a) has presented a cogent argument in the case of the vertebrates. For example, *Galaxias* is readily dispersed by sea (see also the latest account by McDowell, 1964); the leptodactylid amphibians do *not* constitute a distinct Southern Hemisphere group; and the "meiolanid" turtles of the two continents are not only unrelated, but one of them existed during the Eocene and the other during the Pleistocene. Simpson's argument that the ratite birds are probably polyphyletic and may have arisen independently on each continent is now, however, less readily accepted, there being evidence that they are monophyletic (Osuga and Feeney, 1968). Riek (1959), arguing in similar fashion to Simpson, has suggested that the parastacid crayfishes could have arisen independently in the two continents from a marine ancestor. It has long been appreciated, of course, that the South American and Australian marsupials are relics of a formerly much more widely ranging group; there were, for example, at least five genera and 13 species in North America during the late Cretaceous (Clemens, 1968).

Notwithstanding the above objections, there exists a range of primitive, exclusively southern temperate groups of invertebrates common to Australia, New Zealand, and South America. Examples are given from a wide range of insect orders, including members of flightless groups, by Evans (1958, 1959), who stresses the archaic nature of the various groups concerned. Other examples occur in the Plecoptera (Illies, 1965, 1969); chironomids (Brundin, 1966); earthworms (Omodeo, 1963); and others. A significantly large number of these indicate that the Australasian and South American members are more closely related than either group is to the African ones. Brundin (1966) has brought out these different levels of relationship in the chironomids: those of South America and New Zealand are closely related, as are those of South America and Australia; those of Australia and New Zealand are fairly distinct; those of Africa are quite distinct. Likewise Besch (1969, p. 727) has written respecting one group of spiders, the Migidae, within the primitive Mygalomorphes, as follows: "That the disjunction between Africa (Madagascar) and South America is found on the subfamily level and that the disjunction between South America and Australia (New Zealand) is found on the genus level is an indication that a connection existed for a longer time between the southern continents of South America and Australia-New Zealand than between South America and Africa. Corresponding disjunctions for the southern hemisphere exist also in many other groups (e.g., Opiliones)."

Much of the botanical evidence also suggests closer relationships between Australasia and South America than between either one and Africa. This was brought out by Hooker (1860), and can be seen in the works of Florin (1940, 1963) and du Rietz (1940). Hooker provided a series of determinations of the origin of the New Zealand flora. Eighty-nine species (one-eighth of the total) are shared with South America, 77 species (one-tenth) with Australia and South America. The remaining species are shared with Australia (193, or one-fourth of the whole), Antarctic islands (50), are "European" (60), or are endemic (half the total). Australian botanists have long allowed a special term, "Andean," for southern plants of apparent South American origin. Lastly, as noted, although extensive fossil podocarp floras are shared by all the southern continents, as is the case with the Proteaceae, *Nothofagus* is unknown from Africa. Cranwell (1964, p. 389) points out that if, in fact, *Nothofagus* never lived there the fact would be "profoundly significant for estimating the time and nature of earlier land connections and severances in the Africa-Australasia-Antarctic-South America rhomboid." [It might be noted, in passing, that *Nothofagus* pollen has recently been recorded in eastern Asia as a constituent of an otherwise wholly Arctic Late Mesozoic flora—see Vakhrameev, et al. (1970). It has also been recorded from the London clay in Eocene deposits (Sein, 1961). If correct, this indicates a wide range extension for this tree. But see remarks in Cranwell (1964).]

Lined up against Hooker and the later advocates of former direct South American-Australasian connections were personages as formidable as Charles Darwin and A. R. Wallace, who challenged Hooker's interpretations right from the beginning. They preferred to interpret the southern disjunct populations as relics of forms that were originally dispersed by way of the northern continents.

Among recent botanists Burbidge (1960) is somewhat uncommitted as to the necessity for continental drift to explain affinities, and notes that even the early Tertiary flora of Australia included taxa with northern, as well as Antarctic affinities. She concluded: "There is no palaeobotanical evidence which might unequivocally support a view that the continent has not been in its present position throughout the period over which angiosperms have shown their chief development. In particular there is nothing to suggest that the continent has drifted eastwards from a position near southern Africa . . ." (p. 163). Skottsberg (1957) and Gordon (1949) both feel that continental drift is unnecessary to explain Pacific plant distribution, although certain Australian plants are regarded as Antarctic in origin.

More recently, van Steenis (1963) and van Steenis and van Balgooy (1966), have produced distribution maps of 173 Pacific plant genera. These show just about every kind of distribution pattern. About ten genera have Australian-South American, or Australian-New Zealand-South American distributions. Southeast Asia-New Guinea-Australia, and purely Pacific island distribution patterns, however, prove to be much more common than "Gondwana" ones. Viewed as a group, van Steenis' maps bring out clearly that distributional patterns cannot be explained without taking into full account such things as the geological history of a group, its dispersal mechanisms, and its particular ecological requirements.

Apart from marsupials, the mammal faunas of South America and Australia are of course distinct. Australia has the endemic Monotremata, while South America, right from the very beginning (Paleocene), had placental herbivores and edentates, in addition to marsupials. The marsupials of the two continents are, as far as present knowledge goes, relatively distinct. Forms that were formerly regarded as being closely related (e.g., South American *Borhyaena* and the Australian *Thylacinus*) are now regarded as examples of convergent evolution. Recent serological data, however, "does not seem to support a separation of living marsupials into Australasian and American stocks, but suggests that the caenolestoids diverged from the principal line of marsupial evolution before the separation of didelphoids and Australasian marsupials" (Hayman, Kirsch, Martin, and Waller, 1971, p. 195).

Africa and Australia

Affinities between Africa and Australia are less marked than between South America and Australia. Certain plant groups, notably the Proteaceae, occur in both Africa and Australia. The vertebrate faunas are quite distinct. Groups that are shared, such as varanid lizards, turnicid quail, and estrildid finches, apparently represent a recent interchange along the Indonesian island arc. The varanids had an extensive northern hemisphere distribution in the Tertiary. The mammals of these two continents, both fossil and contemporary, are quite unrelated.

The Antarctic Continent as a Former Biotic Environment

A prerequisite to the role of the Antarctic continent as a "stepping stone" in the dispersal of mammals between the southern continents is that it had a mild climate and was suitably vegetated in the late Mesozoic and early Tertiary. Oxygen isotope data for the early Tertiary confirms that climates were not severe at the higher latitudes. Margolis and Kennett (1970), however, produce evidence of glaciation in Antarctica during the Lower Eocene, upper Middle Eocene, and Oligocene. The evidence consists of sand grains from deep sea cores with etch-marks that can be attributed to ice rafting, and reduced foraminiferal diversity at these times, confirming lowered temperatures. The glaciers, they suggest, might have been of the montane variety. Not all workers, however, agree that sand grains with such surface characteristics indicate ice action (e.g., Fitzpatrick and Summerson, 1971).

No Tertiary vertebrate fossils are known from Antarctica but in the Early Triassic the continent supported vertebrate faunas, as shown by the discovery of part of a jaw of a Triassic labyrinthodont near the Beardmore Glacier (Barrett, Baillie, and Colbert, 1968), and by the finding of a bed of Lower Triassic tetrapods at Coalsack Bluff in the Transantarctic Mountain Range (Elliott et al., 1970). Other finds have been made in the McGregor Glacier area (D. H. Elliot, pers. commun.). The assemblages include labyrinthodont amphibians, the therapsid reptiles *Lystrosaurus* and *Thrinaxodon*, the cotylosaur *Procolophon*, and a variety of prolacertids (Colbert, 1971). Early Tertiary pollen of both *Nothofagus* and of Proteaceae is also now known from McMurdo Sound (Cranwell, Harrington, and Speden, 1960; Cranwell, 1964). Moreover, it is now acknowledged that a forest containing the pine *Araucaria* and three groups of *Nothofagus* apparently existed on the Antarctic Peninsula from the Upper Cretaceous through much of the Tertiary (Darlington, 1965). This forest apparently persisted until at least the Miocene. While the McMurdo pollen belongs to types that are commonly wind-blown and its occurrence, accordingly, is not proof that forests grew in this particular area, it "does suggest the presence of forest including *Nothofagus* on the mainland of Antarctica" (Darlington, 1965, p. 117-118).

J. M. Schopf (pers. commun.) has confirmed that interpretations about past climates based on the distribution of *Nothofagus* pollen should be conservative. Thus, he stresses that the good fossil record of *Nothofagus* from the tip of the Antarctic Peninsula can readily be related to modern occurrences of that tree in Patagonia. *Nothofagus* produces abundant pollen, and stray grains may be carried over long distances (Patagonia to Juan Fernandez, for example). The "meager record" of *Nothofagus* pollen near McMurdo Sound in Antarctica can, he feels, probably be explained in this manner.

The above, taken in conjunction with paleoclimatic data, implies that Antarctica was partly vegetated, and hence presumably could have supported mammals in the early Tertiary. The chances, of course, would have been better still if part of the continent lay further north than it does now. Notwithstanding this, for Antarctica to have functioned as a "stepping stone," either a direct connection or close proximity to both South America and Australia at the right times would have been necessary.

In this regard the recent reconstruction of Dalziel and Elliot (1971) and Elliot (1972), developed following a review of the geology of the Scotia Arc area is significant (Fig. 3). It suggests the possibility of a continued junction of South America and the Antarctic Peninsula as late as the Late Cretaceous-Early Tertiary.

New Zealand, A Biogeographic Riddle

New Zealand lacks mammals, other than bats. Apart from this its whole biota is anomalous, depauperate, and rather different from that of Australia. Dinosaurs are unknown. It had a rich early Tertiary flora of fossil palms; palms are unknown from Australia at this time, although India had them (Kremp, 1964). Turtles and snakes are absent from the contemporary fauna, yet primitive frogs (*Leiopelma*) and Rhyncocephalia are present. The contemporary vegetation is fundamentally different from that of Australia. The dominant terrestrial vertebrates in historic times were the now extinct moas, some 27 species of which have been described, and which ranged in size up to giants with an estimated height of 12 feet. Ecologically, these undoubtedly filled the role of grazing mammals elsewhere.

These deficiencies and marked floristic and faunistic differences between Australia and New Zealand are just as puzzling today as they were to earlier workers like Benham (1902, in Hedley, 1912), a student of earthworms, and Hedley (1912). Benham, for example, argued that marked dissimilarities in the acanthrodrilid faunas indicated that Australia and New Zealand were connected with Antarctica at different times. Hedley (1912) suggested three possible explanations: that Australia and New Zealand were connected with Antarctica at different times (actually different "interglacial periods"); that Antarctica was actually an archipelago, and that Australia and New Zealand were connected to different parts of it; and that the one received only highland floras and faunas, and the other only lowland forms from the Antarctic continent.

As noted, it is now suggested by one author (Le Pichon, 1968) that New Zealand may have broken free from Antarctica in the Cretaceous, but

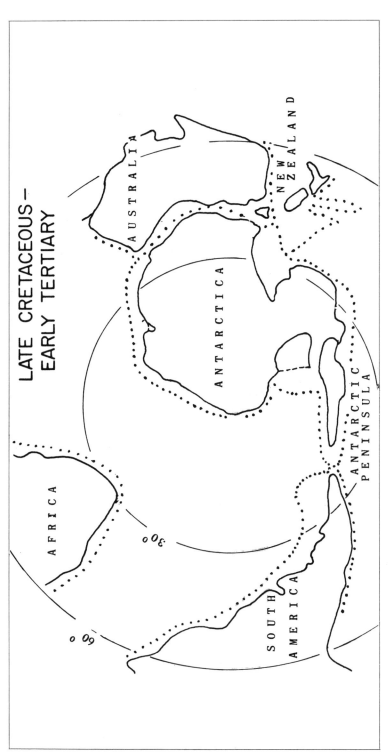

FIG. 3. ELLIOT'S (1972) RECENT RECONSTRUCTION OF THE RELATIONSHIPS OF SOUTH AMERICA AND THE ANTARCTIC PENINSULA IN THE LATE CRETACEOUS

The reconstruction is based on that in Dalziel and Elliot (1971), which stemmed from a detailed review of the geology of the Scotia Arc region. Dotted lines indicate the continental margins (1000 fathom contours).

The existence of a land connection or minimum water gap between South America and Antarctica in the Late Cretaceous or Early Tertiary could have profound implications with respect to floral and faunal interchange between these continents.

Australia not until the Eocene. Could this explain the occurrence of ratites in New Zealand and the absence of marsupials there? Ratites were already widely distributed, and presumably already flightless, in the early Tertiary. Thus, Rheiformes (Opisthodactylidae) are known from the Lower Eocene of Argentina, Aepyornithiformes from the Upper Eocene of Egypt, and Struthioniformes (Eleutherornithidae) from the Lower Middle Eocene of Switzerland (Brodkorb, 1963). The fossil record of ratites in New Zealand and Australia unfortunately extends no farther back than the Miocene (Fleming, 1962; Stirton et al., 1968). A long history on both is indicated. For New Zealand to have acquired ratites but not the equally old, or older, mammals is anomalous. Presumably, it can only be explained on the basis of differing abilities of the ancestors of the two groups to cross water gaps, different distribution patterns at the time of New Zealand's separation, the severance of the islands at a different time from Australia, or by secondary extinction. We are unable to take the matter any farther than did Hedley in 1912.

The alternative hypothesis to account for the origin of the New Zealand fauna and flora is that it drew a nucleus from Australia early in the Mesozoic, and became isolated prior to the radiation of the dinosaurs and origin of the mammals. This hypothesis is equally, if not more, fraught with unexplained problems.

Much of the difficulty in assessing the past history of separation of Australia and New Zealand stems from the fact that the history and age of the Tasman Sea have yet to be determined. With regard to the latter, however, Jones (1971, p. 238) writes that "the small amount of data favours a late Eocene age for the onset of Tasman dilation." Seismic refraction studies, it might be noted, demonstrate that the whole Australia-New Zealand-Tonga area shows extreme diversity of crustal structure (Shor, et al., 1971). These authors write (p. 2562): "All the features are compatible with the hypothesis that the area has been disrupted and fragments of continental material have been separated from the Australian mass." A newer speculative model (Griffiths, 1971; Griffiths and Varne, 1972) for the evolution of the Tasman Sea does not help elucidate the spatial history of New Zealand relative to Australia.

The Indian Subcontinent Relative to the Other Gondwana Continents

Biological data that might throw light on the position of India relative to the other southern continents subsequent to the Triassic is lacking. As noted, since India had dinosaurs in the Jurassic and Cretaceous it could hardly have been as isolated as some of the new "reconstructions" claim. Apart from the dominant faunal relationships with the rest of Asia, the contemporary biotic relationships of India are largely with Africa, as would be expected from the adjacent position of these two land masses. The occasional narrowings of the Tethys Sea during the Tertiary obviously encouraged an accelerated interchange of faunas between Africa and Asia at these times (Cooke, 1968). This interchange was doubtless also periodically increased in the Pleistocene by the climatic oscillations that initiated north-south shifts in the major vegetation belts. The relationships between the contemporary vertebrates of Australia and India are slight, and are also exactly about what would be expected from the degree of isolation involved.

The striking cases of disjunct distributions in "archaic" groups, discussed in detail for South America and Australia, rarely involve India. Evans (1959), however, in his reconstruction of the origins of the Australian insect fauna postulated an initial stratum of Indian origin; he indicated that this stratum antedates an "Antarctic" one.

If, in fact, India did have a "southern" biota early in the Tertiary, it is not surprising that the contemporary flora and fauna show scant traces of it, for it would long since have been overrun and eliminated by the advanced continental forms of Asia. Unfortunately, the Tertiary fossil vertebrate record from India is scant. Interestingly, however, an admittedly scrappy mid-Eocene deposit from the northwest frontier district, from which 16 mammal species have been identified, contains only holarctic and palearctic elements (Dehm and Oettingen-Spielberg, 1958). This segment should have been towards the leading edge of the isolated Indian plate.

Geological evidence on the Mesozoic and Tertiary spatial history of India is highly controversial. Paleomagnetic, sea-floor spreading, and stratigraphic data, all skimpy, are in conflict to the extent that several quite different "models", or reconstructions, have been postulated—see Le Pichon and Heirtzler (1968), Crawford (1969), Dietz and Holden (1970), Smith and Hallam (1970), Creer (1970), Tarling (1971), and Veevers, et al. (1971). Le Pichon and Heirtzler (1968) provide a detailed summary of magnetic anomaly and sea-floor spreading data for the Indian Ocean.

Dietz and Holden (1969, 1970), as noted, suggest a mid-Triassic split of West Gondwana (Africa and South America), from an East Gondwana, with India splitting off from the latter about the same time, or soon thereafter. India then "drifted" northward across the Indian Ocean, finally abutting against Asia in the Eocene (Heirtzler et al., 1968). An alternative reconstruction is that India remained close to Africa in the early stages of drift (du Toit, 1937; Schopf, 1970a; Smith and Hallam, 1970). This kind of configuration is shown in Fig. 4A,B. The paleomagnetic data indicate this (Creer, 1970). McElhinny (1970) feels, however, that the paleomagnetic evidence suggests that the India-Madagascar-Antarctica block broke away from Africa between the mid-Jurassic and mid-Cretaceous, prior to the separation of the first two land masses from Antarctica.

Stratigraphers, by contrast, argue for an eastern position for India, adjacent to Australia, in the Mesozoic—see Crawford (1969), Veevers, et al. (1971), and Tarling (1971). This kind of configuration is shown in Fig. 4C. Crawford (1969), using the rubidium-strontium dating technique,

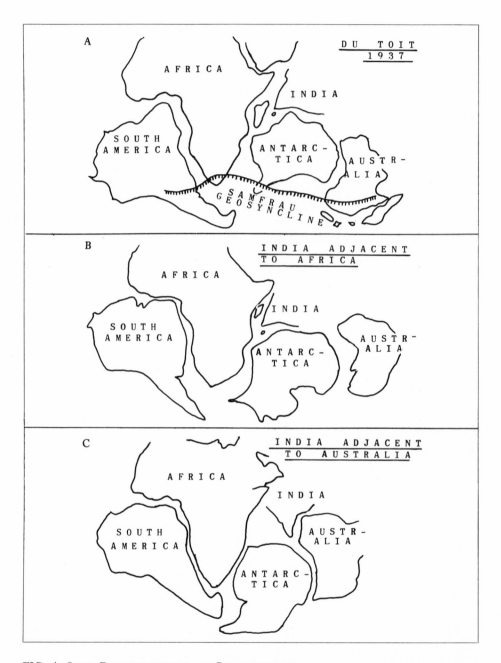

FIG. 4. SOME RECONSTRUCTIONS OF GONDWANALAND

   A, the early reconstruction of du Toit (1937), based on a variety of data.

   B, India placed adjacent to Africa; various workers have followed this configuration —e.g., Schopf (1970a), Smith and Hallam (1970). Redrawn from McElhinny (1970), whose reconstruction is based on mean paleomagnetic poles.

   C, India placed adjacent to Australia, a configuration adopted by various stratigraphers and others—e.g., Carey (1958), Crawford (1969), Tarling (1971). Redrawn from Veevers, Jones, and Talent (1971).

finds that both land masses have rock strata of the following ages: 3000 million years, 2700-2550 m.y., 1150-1000 m.y., and 750-590 m.y. Veevers, Jones, and Talent (1971) match Permian, Triassic, and Jurassic rock sequences in Australia and India. They suggest, on this basis, that India and Australia ruptured in the latest Jurassic or earliest Cretaceous, and that this is marked by basaltic extrusions, tuff depositions, and marine sediments in Western Australia. In weighing these data note should be taken of the paper by Robinson (1967) concerning paleocurrents flowing from ESE to ENE in the interior of the Gondwana cratonic area during the Triassic, and inferring land where Veevers et al. (1971) place an arm of the sea.

Francheteau and Sclater (1969) advance a model, based on paleo-magnetic data, that entails an east to west motion between Australia and India between the Middle Cretaceous and the Cretaceous-Tertiary boundary.

Just as there is marked conflict between the suggested positions for India in the Mesozoic, so authorities differ widely as to its supposed time for breaking free from Antarctica—Triassic (Dietz and Holden, 1970), middle to late Cretaceous (Le Pichon and Heirtzler, 1968; Hallam and Smith, 1970), and post-Tertiary (Creer, 1970). The time of "collision" between India and southern Asia is postulated to be Eocene by Dietz and Holden (1970), the end of the Eocene by Veevers, Jones, and ·Talent (1971), Early Miocene by McElhinny (1970) and Fisher et al. (1971), and possibly as recently as 10,000,000 years ago by Larson and La Fountain (1970).

The Fauna of Madagascar and Its History

The mammal fauna of insular Madagascar is dominated by primitive insectivores, lemuroids, and viverrids, plus rodents and bats. The "old" character of the fauna, its largely African affinities, and the high degree of endemism, suggest very early colonization by a few ancestral types across a temporarily narrowed channel (Millot, 1952; Bigalke, 1968). This affinity with Africa also extends to other groups (Millot, 1952; Darling-ton, 1957). There is a very limited affinity with Asia—e.g., some frogs, some bats, and four avian genera (Darlington, 1957).

In the past it has generally been believed either that Madagascar was joined to Africa until the early Tertiary (e.g., du Toit, 1937), or that, at least, it formerly lay closer to this continent. The opposite view, that there has been no direct contact and that the fauna was built up by adventitious means across the 250 mile water-gap, has been convincingly argued by Simpson (1940b, 1943), and Darlington (1957). As well as drawing attention to the fact that the mammalian groups present would be those most likely to be able to make the transoceanic journey, these authorities place great weight on the absence of most of the more success-ful African groups. More difficult to explain, possibly, is the presence of dinosaurs on Madagascar during the Jurassic and Cretaceous. Von Heune and Matley (1933) postulated a land bridge to account for them, although it is known that certain dinosaurs could swim.

It is of very considerable importance to the biologist to learn more of the past spatial history of Madagascar. Unfortunately, here too, the newer geological thinking is very confusing. Dietz and Holden (1970), for example, postulate that Madagascar broke free from Africa in the Cretaceous. Dixey (1956), Flower and Strong (1969), and Tarling (1971) disagree, pointing out that the western Indian Ocean, and the Mozambique Channel in particular, is underlain by nonoceanic crust, and hence could not have arisen by sea-floor spreading. The evidence is that the Mozambique Channel is part of a giant geosyncline and is underlain by perhaps 14 kms of Karoo (Late Carboniferous) and post-Karoo sediments, showing that it extends back at least as far as the Late Carboniferous. The isolation could, however, extend back to the Precambrian (Flower and Strong, 1969). Africa and Madagascar, on this basis, have been isolated since before the beginning of the Age of Reptiles.

Equally puzzling as the past history of Madagascar is that of the surrounding features, the Seychelles to the north, the Comoros to the west, and the Saya de Malha Ridge to the east. Recent evidence has confirmed that these are continental relicts and contain continental rocks such as granite, and sandstone intrusives—see Flower and Strong (1969) and references contained therein. The term "Indian Ocean Microcontinents" has been coined for these features, which are believed to lie on distinct subplates.

Several recent workers have postulated a former close spatial connection of Madagascar or the "microcontinents", or both, with India. Fisher, Engel, and Hilde (1968), on the basis of oceanographic studies, suggest that Madagascar was formerly twenty degrees further to the north. Davies (1968) has suggested that the Seychelles "left" India in the Early Paleocene. Le Pichon and Heirtzler (1968) believe that the separation of India, Madagascar, and the island "microcontinents" took place at the end of the Cretaceous. Newer data on magnetic pole positions convinces McElhinny (1970, p. 978), that "the proximity of India and Madagascar was maintained at least up to the latter part of the Late Cretaceous (say 70 to 80 m.y. ago.)."

If Madagascar formerly lay closer to India than Africa it could have acquired its Early Tertiary fauna from there. On the basis of the present evidence, however, this seems unlikely.

Tropical Disjuncts and Continental Drift

Continental drift, if substantiated, is potentially capable of helping explain certain puzzling facets of biogeography. Included is the problem of "tropical disjuncts," the various cases of related plants and animals distributed from east to west through the world's tropical regions, but with a range broken up by the oceanic barriers separating South America, Africa, the Oriental Region, and Australia. These groups are confined to the narrow equatorial climatic belt, so that any interchange through the temperate regions of the north is obviously impossible, under present-day climatic conditions. Examples of such disjunct distributions in the higher vertebrates include tapirs (Oriental Region and Neotropica), trogons and barbets (Ethiopian, Oriental, and Neotropical Regions), and parrots (Australian and Neotropical regions mainly). Invertebrate examples are to be found in the copepods (Sewell, 1956), scorpions (du Toit, 1937), and other groups.

Tropical disjuncts are particularly marked among the plants. Thus, Axelrod (1970, p. 292-293) summarized the situation in angiosperms as follows:

> There are 54 large pantropical families that attain optimum development and diversity in tropical areas and scarcely extend out of the region; 36 additional families are discontinuous in the inner tropics, linking America with Africa-Madagascar (12), and Africa-Madagascar with the Indo-Australasian region (16), or the latter area and America (8 families); and 125 other families attain optimum development and diversity in the tropics, are largely pantropic, and have generally derived comparatively few taxa in extratropic regions. Furthermore some of the 80-odd families that are now endemic to tropical regions (25 America, 23 Africa, 40-plus Australasia) occurred earlier on other continents (e.g., Cyclanthaceae in India). Of the inner tropical links, it is noteworthy that 287 genera are pantropic, 91 are common to America and Africa-Madagascar, 289 link the latter area and the Indo-Australasian region, and 37 are common to the Indo-Australasian area and the Americas.

It has hitherto been widely accepted by most zoologists that tropical disjuncts are to be explained by dispersal through the higher latitudes of the Holarctic during the Tertiary, when world climates were milder. The fossil record, moreover, provides many examples that such forms were more widely distributed formerly. Tapirs, for example, were formerly widespread in North America, and during the Miocene trogons occurred in southern France (Romer, 1966).

While some botanists (e.g., Sharp, 1966; MacGinitie, 1969) agree with this northern dispersal theory, others (e.g., Hutchinson, 1946; Camp, 1947; Good, 1964) have argued that these east-west distributions can only be explained by former direct connections within the tropical belt. As Axelrod (1970) notes, land bridges, "island stepping stones," and continental drift have been invoked to explain the patterns. Axelrod (1970), the most recent writer on the subject, feels that tropical disjuncts can only be explained by continental drift, for (1) the so-called "tropical" and "subtropical" plants that occurred at middle to high latitudes in the Early Tertiary, and that have been used to prove a former more northward extension of the tropical belts, although they did live under conditions of high equability, were members of mixed temperate, not tropical, forests; and (2) tropical taxa are highly sensitive to frost. Axelrod, accordingly, argues for continental drift as an explanation.

Axelrod's reasoning is interesting. Contemporary "tropical disjuncts", however, like the disjunct plants and animals of the southern continents, can only, by themselves, provide supporting evidence of continental drift. Tropical floras are combinations of plant groups of different ages and origins, of different ecological tolerances, and of different dispersive capacities. Some groups are relictual in the tropics and formerly ranged more widely. The telling argument against drift as the major explanation, however, is that it requires early Tertiary junctions where these could not have occurred—e.g., between the Indo-Australian and American tropics.

Diversity in Mesozoic Reptiles and Tertiary Mammals and the Distribution of the World's Major Land Masses

Kurtén (1969), in a speculative paper, has suggested that the limited original diversity of Mesozoic reptiles (20 orders), compared to Tertiary and modern mammals (30 orders), can be explained in terms of the different degrees of isolation of the world's major land masses at the two times. He suggests that, since the world's land was grouped into the two southern and northern supercontinents, Gondwanaland and Laurasia, during the Mesozoic, there were only two centers available for evolution and differentiation. This compares to the five major continental areas of the Tertiary. On the basis of first occurrences in the fossil records, and to some extent centers of abundance, Kurtén argued that three of the groups of reptiles existing in the Cretaceous originated in Gondwana: Crocodilia, Saurischia (possibly), and Ornithischia; and four in Laurasia: Pterosauria, Chelonia, Squamata—although prolacertids were abundant in the Lower Triassic in Antarctica—and Choristodera (champsosaurs). Kurtén points out, by contrast, that the isolated continents of the Tertiary permitted considerable replication of mammalian types from ecological and morphological standpoints; e.g., the Proboscidea, Hyracoidea, Embrithopoda, Tubulidentata, and possibly the aquatic Sirenia and Demostylia arose in Africa; the Edentata, Notoungulata, Paucituberculata, Pyrotheria, Litopterna, and Astrapotheria, in South America; and the Peramelina, Diprotodonta, and Monotremata, in Australia.

Kurtén's ideas are dubiously sound. They are, moreover, greatly oversimplified. As coming from later deposits, and being a contemporary group, the mammals are much better known than the reptiles. Again, the classifications are not truly equivalent. The mammals have been rather more finely divided up ordinally than have reptiles, although not as finely as birds. Finally, Kurtén's "Gondwanan" and "Laurasian" reptile groups are not true morphological and ecological "equivalents" of each other, as are many of the above mammalian orders, but are "uniques".

Contemporary Biota, Continental Drift, and Order of Break-Up of the Continents

The contemporary biota cannot prove or disprove continental drift; at most, it can only supply suggestive evidence that may render the whole concept more plausible. There is obviously a real need for a new look at many of the Southern Hemisphere (and tropical) disjuncts that some authorities have used as "proofs" of former continental connections. These analyses should take into account, in addition to taxonomics, the relative ages, dispersal capacities, and ecological tolerances of these groups.

Analysis of the contemporary biota of the southern continents shows different degrees and levels of relationships which might be interpreted as indicating that they separated at different times. The differences between Australia and New Zealand, for example, are fairly marked; the absence of terrestrial mammals in New Zealand suggests its longer isolation. In that the Australian and South American floras and faunas seem to be more alike than either one is to the African (although the fishes are a striking exception), Africa *should* have been isolated earlier. This accords with the reconstructions of Dalziel and Elliot (1971) but not those of Dietz and Holden (1970) and others.

CONTINENTAL DRIFT AND THE ORIGIN OF THE MAMMALIAN FAUNAS OF THE SOUTHERN CONTINENTS

As a result of the developments of the last few years, most geologists now accept the view that some form of continental movement has occurred in geologic time; this is not uniformly accepted, as previously noted, and the postulated mechanisms and time-scale remain speculative. The changed thinking, however, has wide implications for biologists, and many interpretations and hypotheses must be reexamined in the light of it. At the same time the biological record ultimately has a considerable role to play by way of determining if, when, and where continental disjunctions and junctions have occurred.

On the basis of the latest biological information, the following general statements regarding past continental connections may be made.

(1) Evidence for a clustering of the southern continents around Antarctica in the Permian is good. The latest work on the Permian floras not only confirms "the exclusively southern" nature of the *Gangamopteris* and *Glossopteris* associations, but actual species were common to the various continents (Schopf, 1970b). It should be noted, of course, that isolation does not prevent all species from spreading; e.g., New Zealand and South America have some species in common. Hence Schopf's findings only infer contiguity; they do not prove it. The common Permo-Carboniferous glaciations of the southern continents also indicate clustering in the south (Hamilton and Krinsley, 1967); note, however, the recent assertion of Meyerhoff and Teichert (1971) that the precipitation necessary for the laying down of glaciers would not have been available had the southern continents all been part of a giant continuous land mass.

(2) The newly discovered fauna of Lower Triassic reptiles and amphibians on the mainland of Antarctica not only proves that this continent supported vertebrate life early in the Mesozoic, but also that it was prob-

ably important in floristic and faunistic interchanges between the southern continents at this time.

(3) These Antarctic fossils largely duplicate those of the *Lystrosaurus* Zone of the Early Triassic of Africa, bear good resemblances to an equivalent Indian fauna, and have fair resemblances to a fauna in China (Colbert, 1971). Overlying the *Lystrosaurus* Zone in Africa is a *Cynognathus* Zone, dominated by reptiles belonging to that genus. This assemblage bears striking relationships to a counterpart in South America which also includes the genus *Cynognathus*. There are also counterparts in India and China (Colbert, 1971). This pair of Lower Triassic faunas is persuasive evidence for a continuing cluster of southern continents at this time. Its anomalous extension to China (which was not part of Gondwanaland) can possibly be explained by a northward penetration along a landbridge joining Gondwanaland and Laurasia (Colbert, 1971). The occurrence of these faunas in China is, of course, disharmonious with the concept that Gondwanaland was *completely* isolated from Laurasia at that time. Interestingly, it also raises the possibility that the marked development of the *Lystrosaurus* and *Cynognathus* faunas in the south may have been as much a function of climate and suitable environment as of isolation. Alternatively, it might reflect the fact that the right depositional environment was available at this time.

(4) Work on the Triassic floras of South America shows the persistence there at that time of a flora closely related to the Triassic floras of South America, Australia, and India (Menéndez, 1969). However, as noted, some northern elements were also present at this time.

(5) By the Late Jurassic the picture of "exclusive," or nearly exclusive, southern floras and faunas became obscured in favor of dominance by more "cosmopolitan" types. This applies both with respect to plants and to dinosaurs. It possibly also applies to the early mammals, e.g., the African Triassic *Erythrotherium* resembles the morganucodontids of Europe (Clemens, 1970). What this new pattern means from the viewpoint of continental junctions during the Jurassic is obscure. It would seem to indicate: (1) a loss of the "exclusively southern" relationships; (2) increased opportunities for the entry of forms from the north; and (3) the appearance of a new biota, more mobile, possibly more ecologically plastic, and fitted for a changed environment. The observations would conform with the view that Gondwanaland had been disrupted (Fig. 1) but not with the other seeming prerequisite—i.e., that the southern and northern continents had drawn closer. Thus, the postulated reconstructions suggest that North America and South America were isolated from each other and Africa and Eurasia, at most, were only tenuously connected by a land bridge. This suggests that the appearance of a new ecologically plastic biota, with better dispersive capacities may be the explanation of the "cosmopolitan" nature of the Jurassic plants and animals.

(6) The Cretaceous fossil data are more complete than the Jurassic data. Some of these suggest certain things about the spatial relationships

of land masses, but corroborative evidence is still lacking. Other data (specifically the dinosaurs of India and Australia) seem flatly to deny aspects of the Dietz-Holden postulations. Note, however, the recent paper of Veevers, Jones, and Talent (1971) arguing for a continued junction of India and Australia as late as the Late Jurassic or earliest Cretaceous.

(7) The Lower Cretaceous freshwater ostracod faunas (Krommelbein, 1965a,b), and certain spore-pollen floras (Freake, 1966) suggest a junction or near junction of west Africa and Brazil at that time. This fits the sea-floor spreading data. The suggested similarity between the Late Cretaceous dinosaur faunas of South America and North America, rather than between those of South America and Africa, would also fit the Dietz-Holden deductions that the Atlantic by that time formed an effective water barrier. It also supports the inference of increased opportunities for north-south interchange between the two Americas. The newer writers on sea-floor spreading and plate tectonics have not yet focussed on the finer details of the spatial relationships of these two continents in the later Mesozoic. They are believed to have drawn closer together. There is, of course, ample other geological evidence that they were not actually joined (Jacobs et al., 1963; Lloyd, 1963; Haffer, 1970). (In partial conflict with the concept of reduced South American-African relationships and replacement by increased South American ones is the distribution of the dinosaur *Laplatosaurus* which is recorded from east Africa, Madagascar, South America, and India.)

The Upper Cretaceous flora of South America reveals virtually nothing about the spatial relationships of that continent relative to others. Angiosperms appeared and "they form a flora with elements similar to those which today occur in tropical and subtropical zones; although there are also enough plants of southern origin which indicate an evident relation to the floras of Australia and New Zealand" (Menéndez, 1969, p. 559).

As noted, the anomalous situation that India had dinosaurs, when it is supposed to have been in the middle of the Indian Ocean during the Cretaceous, certainly requires explanation. So does the presence of dinosaurs in Australia, since Australia, together with Antarctica, is supposed to have been isolated from the other continents since the Triassic. Dalziel and Elliot (1971) and Elliot (1972), as noted, indicate a continuing link between South America and Antarctica by means of the Antarctic Peninsula as late as the Late Cretaceous; presumably, therefore, dinosaurs could have reached Australia in this way. However, the route is very circuitous.

(8) It will be seen from the above that plant, invertebrate, and reptile fossils help very little, at the present stage, in tracing out the pre-Tertiary distributional history of the mammals. They tell no more, really, than do the mammals themselves.

(9) The contemporary biota of the southern continents confirms the existence of a range of "exclusively southern" plants and animals. This applies even when all the dubious cases have been excluded.

Numerically, of course, these so-called "old southern" elements make up only a very minor percentage of the floras and faunas of each continent today. An important point, however, is that many of them can clearly be thought of as being, or demonstrated to be, archaic. The plecopteran family Eustheniidae, for example, is known from Permian deposits in Victoria. Most of these "old southern" elements are confined to the cold temperate south of each continent. The fact that a few, like the Proteaceae, have marginally entered the Northern Hemisphere, does not invalidate their southern status. More complex is the question of survival. When no fossil record is available, one cannot tell whether an "old" form has always been confined to its present area of distribution or is simply relictual there.

Circum-Antarctic distribution patterns cannot, of course, in any way prove continental drift. They can only supply inferential or corroborative evidence for it.

(10) Are the successive stages in the break-up of the southern continents, as suggested by the sea-floor spreading and marine geomagnetic data, discernible in their faunas and floras? If the biotas of Australia and South America are more similar to each other than either is to Africa, does this not suggest a shorter isolation of the former? Does the newer geological evidence help explain the marked biotic differences between New Zealand and Australia?

It is obvious that when it comes to South American-Australian-African relationships, the biological evidence and Dietz-Holden disagree. Australia is supposed to have separated from the other two continents in the Triassic. They, in turn, started to separate during the Jurassic but did not finally part company until the Cretaceous. There could be various explanations for this incongruity: (1) the geological time-scale might be wrong; (2) despite early initial separation, South America, Antarctica, and Australia may have remained close to each other (see Dalziel and Elliot, 1971), permitting a fair interchange of biotas; (3) the temperate elements of Africa and South America were really separated quite early, with the formation of the South Atlantic in the Jurassic; the continuing tropical junction of west Africa and Brazil had no relevance for them; and (4) the majority of the archaic southern forms have been eliminated without trace from Africa as a secondary result of climatic or other changes. Thus, southern Africa is today perceptibly drier than either southern South America, or southern Australasia (Tasmania, New Zealand, Victoria). Some support for this final possibility would seem to come from the freshwater fishes; those of Africa and South America are very similar. Australia, a dry continent today, very deficient in large permanent freshwater streams, has virtually no true freshwater fishes; those it has (with the conspicuous exception of the lungfish and *Scleropages*) are secondarily derived from the sea. The original freshwater fish fauna of Australia has been lost. (There is, of course, no evidence of characoids ever reaching Australia.)

It is obvious from the above that an extensive series of new taxonomic analyses will have to be undertaken before any more can be deduced from the contemporary biota about the possible order of separation of the southern continents. Likewise, the sea-floor-spreading data are not yet refined enough to discriminate between the conflicting theories as to the past history of New Zealand.

The new data on continental drift are of little or no significance yet, in helping to explain or interpret early patterns of mammalian distribution in the southern continents. They do nothing to shake earlier convictions (e.g., Simpson, 1966) that both South America and Africa obtained their Tertiary faunas from the north. Only in the case of Australia do they necessitate rethinking.

The Origin of South American Mammals

Mammals first appear in the South American fossil record in the Cretaceous on the basis of fragmentary remains of a presumed condylarth and remains of marsupial species (Patterson and Pascual, 1968; Chapter VI). In the Paleocene there are the remains of early marsupials, edentates, and primitive ungulates (Simpson, 1950). Colonization is presumed to have occurred from North America in the Upper Cretaceous, the North American Cretaceous stocks apparently being ancestral (although the edentates were autochthonous). These two continents were possibly only separated by a narrow water gap at the time (see maps in Harrington, 1962), but later became more widely separated.

Subsequent to the initial colonizations, Simpson (1950), Patterson and Pascual (1963, 1968), and others recognized a Late Eocene colonization of South America by primates and caviomorph rodents, which suddenly appear in the fossil record there in the early Oligocene. This abrupt appearance is presumed to have been by "island-hopping," since Central America was a peninsula and series of islands at this time (Woodring, 1954; Eardley, 1951; Mayr, 1946). A third major invasion of South America occurred with the formation of the Panamanian Isthmus in the Pliocene, marked by a striking interchange of faunas between the two continents.

The early South American mammal fauna is strikingly different from the earliest African one (Upper Eocene). There is hence no indication of any direct interchange of faunas between these continents.

The possibility must be considered, however, that the rodents and primates that reached South America in the Late Eocene (Patterson and Pascual, Chapter VI), could have come from Africa rather than North America. Several workers have recently suggested this (Lavocat, 1969; Hoffstetter and Lavocat, 1970, for rodents; Sarich, 1970, for the primates; and Brundin, 1966, on more general grounds). Hershkovitz (Chapter VII) is also inclined to favor a trans-Atlantic origin for these two groups. Both rodents and primates have, of course, repeatedly demonstrated their ability to "raft" across water-gaps. At the calculated sea-floor spreading rate of 2 cm per year, or 200 kms in 10 million years, these two continents may still have been only 400 kms apart by the beginning of the Oligocene.

Wood and Patterson (1970) have discussed the relationships of the African and South American rodents in some detail. They hold that, despite various anatomical features in common, as pointed out by Lavocat (1969), there are differences that make a direct relationship unlikely. Moreover, the living African hystricomorphs which so resemble some of the South American stocks, are clearly descended from the early Oligocene African Phiomyidae. (The Hystricidae are unknown before the late Miocene or early Pliocene.) They quote Dingle and Klinger (1971) as authority for believing that the South Atlantic was relatively wide by the later Eocene (i.e., wider than the 400 kms suggested by the writer above).

The monkeys of Africa and South America, the Catarrhini and Platyrrhini, respectively, obviously represent interesting parallel radiations. A wide range of recent work on blood proteins indicates that the two groups are more closely related than either group is to the lemuroids. Data are now available for blood albumin (Sarich, 1970), hemoglobin (Boyer et al., 1969), transferrin (Wang et al., 1968), and DNA (Kohne, 1970). These data have led Sarich (1970) to argue that the two groups must stem from a common ancestor that succeeded in crossing the South Atlantic.

In the cases of both monkeys and rodents there is an alternative explanation that does not require a southern crossing: an ancestor already having the shared attributes may have become dispersed by way of the northern continents.

Northern trans-Atlantic links between Europe and North America apparently occurred during the Eocene, for many forms (e.g., primitive horses) were common to both continents. It is presumed that the ancestors of both the South American monkeys and the rodents passed through North America. Possible ancestral types there have been discussed both by Simpson (1950), and Patterson and Pascual (1968, Chapter VI).

The Origin of African Mammals

The earliest African Tertiary fossil mammals are exclusively placental, and the faunas (Upper Eocene and Lower Oligocene) are dominated by endemic orders such as the Proboscidea, Embrithopoda, and Hyracoidea (Cooke, 1968). The subsequent history of Africa is one of long periods of isolation during which diversification and evolution took place. The Tethys Sea was the main barrier isolating the continent from Eurasia. Faunal interchanges were limited to brief periods in the late Oligocene, late Miocene, and late Pliocene, and these were with Eurasia (Cooke, 1968, Chapter III).

The Origin of Australian Mammals

The initial Australian mammal fauna was apparently exclusively monotreme and marsupial. Bats and rodents represent later waves of colonization late in the Tertiary (Simpson, 1961). The Australian fauna today differs strikingly from the Asian one to the west of Wallace's line (see Raven, 1935). In recent decades it has generally been accepted that marsupials must have reached Australia from the north (see chapter on Australian mammals), presumably by "island hopping" in the late Cretaceous or early Tertiary. The alternative hypothesis is, as noted, the older one of southern entry.

Recently three new hypotheses have been advanced to account for the facts of marsupial distribution. Martin (1970) has postulated that the group originated on a former land mass situated over the Darwin Rise in the central Pacific, and that this land mass broke up into two segments that drifted, each with its cargo of marsupials, to North America and Australia, respectively. Cox (1970) rightly criticizes Martin's hypothesis not only for being unrealistic, but also for being at complete variance with current data and concepts on continental movements. He suggests instead that marsupials arose in Africa and entered Australia via Antarctica. He has discounted the possibility that they could have entered Australia from the north down the Indonesian island chain because no trace of marsupials remain on those islands other than obviously recent colonizers (like *Phalanger* on the Celebes).

Cox's arguments, like Martin's, are unconvincing. The eastern Indonesian islands are relatively recent geologically, and the whole area has been, throughout the Tertiary, one of great tectonic instability. Islands have seemingly appeared and disappeared. Marsupials would hardly be expected to have persisted under these circumstances. Farther west, on Borneo, Java, and the other islands of the Asian continental shelf, any marsupial present would have been subjected to repeated competition from advanced placentals and, as in Europe and North America, would presumably have been exterminated relatively early. The mammalian fossil record in Indonesia is insignificant. Secondly, there is no evidence that marsupials have ever occurred in Africa. In the absence of an early Tertiary fossil record from Africa and Madagascar, however, no conclusions can be drawn from this.

Hoffstetter (1970) suggests a third hypothesis, that placental mammals arose in Europe and Africa, and marsupials in the Americas. Colonization of Australia by marsupials would then have been from South America. Lillegraven (1969) and Clemens (1970) have also postulated separate areas of origin for placentals and marsupials in the Northern Hemisphere. Late Cretaceous distributions suggest that placentals originated in Asia, and marsupials in North America. This idea has an attractive feature: it would explain how two potentially competitive mammalian evolutionary lines could evolve and radiate simultaneously.

If, as the new paleomagnetic data suggest, Australia occupied much higher latitudes at the beginning of the Tertiary, a northern entry by marsupials at this time would obviously have been impossible.

The newer geological reconstructions based on plate movements give a Cretaceous (or Eocene) date for the separation of Australia from Antarctica. In the absence of fossil evidence as a means of dating, this must remain speculative. Equally important to the migrations of plants and animals are the spatial relationships of South America and Antarctica in the late Mesozoic—early Tertiary. Proximity would be required if an ancestral marsupial type were to reach Antarctica, thence subsequently to colonize Australia. Work on the geological history and magnetic profiles of the Scotia Sea region, which might be enlightening on the point, has only recently begun, however (Barker, 1970). The most significant structural feature of the region, "the series of flat-topped, steep-sided, shallow submarine ridges that make up the Scotia Ridge," abound "with geological structures inconsistent with their present isolated situation and truncated by present 'continental' margins, suggesting the fragmentation of a previously continuous continental area" (Barker, 1970, p. 1296). "The structure of component blocks of the south Scotia Ridge indicate that it too should be made more compact, and seemingly the entire Scotia Ridge becomes a continuous continental connection between West Antarctic and South America" (p. 1296). The age of the geological structures is said to argue for a post-Cretaceous fragmentation. It is suggested that separate East and West Antarctic plates joined in the Middle Tertiary, about the same time as the latter began to separate from South America; and that the Scotia Sea has a post-Middle Tertiary age.

A still later review of the geology of the southern Andean-Scotia Arc-Antarctic Peninsula region by Dalziel and Elliot (1971) and Elliot (1972) corroborates possible land continuity through this section until the Late Cretaceous–Early Tertiary (Fig. 3).

For Antarctica to be a stepping stone in marsupial distribution it would also be necessary, as noted, for it to have had a mild climate and be partly vegetated at the appropriate time. There is evidence that this was possibly the case.

For both the northern and southern entry theories, there still remains the problem of explaining why placental mammals failed to reach Australia. Placentals were widespread in Asia before the end of the Mesozoic. The group was well established in South America in the Paleocene, and the oldest described mammal, *Perutherium*, which is apparently late Cretaceous in age (Patterson and Pascual, 1968), is a condylarth. Hence the older theory, that placentals evolved after marsupials and failed to reach Australia because it had in the interim become an island, cannot be invoked. A barrier that selectively permitted the passage of one or more types of ancestral marsupials, but screened out the placentals, seems the only logical explanation. A small arboreal mammal, which we assume the earliest Australian marsupial may have been, would have been well equipped for being rafted across a water gap, for example.

Whether the first marsupial "propogules" to reach Australia came from the north or south must remain an open question at present.

SUMMARY

That some form of continental movement occurred during the Mesozoic Era is now generally accepted by geologists, although there is wide disagreement as to the timing and details. It is essential to investigate how continental movement may have affected the distribution and evolution of the early mammals, and their late Mesozoic and Tertiary successors. The present state of the literature on continental drift, however, is confusing, and it is difficult to separate fact, theory, and speculation.

The newer geological studies of sea-floor spreading, dated by means of marine paleomagnetism, suggest the existence, in the Permian and Early Triassic, of a southern supercontinent, Gondwanaland—a clustering of the present land masses of Africa, South America, Australia, New Zealand, and India around Antarctica. Most of the reconstructions envision a break-up starting in the later Triassic, followed by a successive separation of the various component parts.

If these reconstructions accurately reflect geological history, tetrapods, including the evolving mammals, must have been affected in specific ways. Broadly speaking, however, the plant and animal fossil record is far too incomplete to enable judgment to be passed on them. What there is, however, tends to support parts of them and to deny other parts. Thus, the proximity of the southern continents in the Permian is suggested by their common *Glossopteris-Gangamopteris* floras, and in the Early Triassic by two fossil reptile associations, the *Lystrosaurus* zones of Antarctica, Africa, and India, and the *Cynognathus* zones of Africa and South America. *Cynognathus* is unknown from India but some of the groups with which it occurs in southern Africa occur there (Colbert, 1971, p. 264). However, the significance of the lower Triassic reptile assemblages from the viewpoint of indicating the existence of a semi-isolated southern supercontinent at this time is materially weakened by the occurrence of *Lystrosaurus* in China. The recent discovery of Early Triassic fossil reptiles and labyrinthodonts in Antarctica is, however, of tremendous importance in proving that vertebrate life occurred on this continent and that it could have been involved in the movements of vertebrates among the other southern land masses.

After the mid-Triassic the fossil record indicates little about the position of the continents. A loss of "special southern" relationships is noted, as would be expected if Gondwanaland was breaking up, and floras and faunas, generally speaking, are described as taking on a "more cosmopolitan" appearance. There is some fossil evidence to support a continued junction, or at least a close proximity, of west Africa and Brazil in the Lower Cretaceous, and for a close approach of the two Americas toward the end of that period (similarities in dinosaur faunas; apparently some colonization of South America by northern mammals). Anomalous, from the viewpoint of the postulated isolated positions of India and Australia during the Cretaceous, is the presence of dinosaurs on each.

Mesozoic mammals are known only from the Southern Hemisphere from the Upper Triassic and Jurassic (Africa) and the Cretaceous (South America). Deficiencies in the total fossil record during the Jurassic and Cretaceous, and the virtual absence of mammalian fossils, mean that very little can be deduced about the distributional history of the early mammals. The same is true of the Early Tertiary. While there are some good South American fossil deposits from the Paleocene and after, the earliest known Tertiary mammals from Africa are Upper Eocene, and from Australia, Upper Oligocene.

The contemporary biota of the southern continents has been reviewed in detail in an attempt to determine whether different levels of relationship might confirm hypotheses about the order of separation of the southern continents. The relationships between South America and Australia, and between South America and New Zealand seem distinctly closer than between any one of these and Africa. Of course, there could be explanations for this other than an earlier separation of Africa. While it is still too early to discard the northern entry theory in favor of the southern one for the occurrence of marsupials in Australia, it might be noted that this subclass of mammals occurs in South America and Australia, but is unknown from Africa.

ACKNOWLEDGMENTS

I should like to express my gratitude to R. Price, Department of Geology, Queen's University for helping me with the latest published data on marine geomagnetism, sea-floor spreading, and plate tectonics, and to Warren Hamilton, U.S. Geological Survey, Denver, for various discussions in these areas and their possible biological implications. I was also helped by discussions with Norman Newell, American Museum of Natural History, concerning the weight to be placed on some of the invertebrate fossil data in interpreting past continental movements. J. M. Schopf, U.S. Geological Survey Coal Geology Laboratory, Ohio State University, provided me with counsel on Antarctic paleobotany, read the manuscript, and made many valuable suggestions, as did D. H. Elliot of the Institute of Polar Studies, Ohio State University. The latter also kindly let me see some of his unpublished manuscripts. Again, R. H. Tedford, American Museum of Natural History, helped with many suggestions as did H. B. S. Cooke and J. Cracroft. Lastly, B. Patterson was kind enough to read this manuscript in toto and has made numerous helpful suggestions.

The work was carried out while I held a research grant from the National Research Council of Canada and I should also like to thank that body for its support.

LITERATURE CITED

ADIE, R. J. 1963. Geological evidence on possible Antarctic land connections. In J. L. Gressitt (ed.), *Pacific Basin Biogeography*, p. 455-463. Bishop Museum, Hawaii.

ALLARD, G. A., and V. J. HURST. 1969. Brazil-Gabon geologic link supports continental drift. *Science*, 163: 528-532.

AMOS, A. J., and N. SABATTINI. 1969. Upper Palaeozoic faunal similitude between Argentina and Australia. In *Gondwana Stratigraphy*, p. 235-248. I.U.G.S. Symposium, Buenos Aires, 1-15 October, 1967. UNESCO, Paris.

ARCHANGELSKY, S., and O. G. ORRONDO. 1969. The Permian taphofloras of Argentina with some considerations about the presence of "northern" elements and their possible significance. In *Gondwana Stratigraphy*, p. 71-85. I.U.G.S. Symposium, Buenos Aires, 1-15 October, 1967. UNESCO, Paris.

AUDLEY-CHARLES, M. G. 1966. Mesozic paleogeography of Australasia. *Palaeogeogr., Palaeoclimatol., Palaeoecol.*, 2: 1-25.

AXELROD, D. I. 1970. Mesozoic paleogeography and early angiosperm history. *Bot. Review*, 36: 277-319.

BARAZANGI, M., and J. DORMAN. 1969. World seismicity maps, compiled from Essa Coast and Geodetic Survey Epicenter Data, 1961-1967. *Bull. Seismol. Soc. Am.*, 59: 369-380.

BARKER, P. F. 1970. Plate tectonics of the Scotia Sea region. *Nature*, 228: 1293-1296.

BARRETT, P. J., R. J. BAILLIE, and E. H. COLBERT. 1968. Triassic amphibian from Antarctica. *Science*, 161: 460.

BARTHOLOMAI, A. 1966. Fossil footprints in Queensland. *Austral. Natur. Hist.*, March, 1966: 147-150.

BARTHOLOMAI, A., and A. HOWIE. 1970. Vertebrate fauna from the Lower Trias of Australia. *Nature*, 225: 1063.

BELOUSSOV, B. B. 1967. Against continental drift. *Science J.*, January, 1967: 2-7.

BESCH, W. 1969. South American Archnida. In E. J. Fittkau, J. Illies, H. Klinge, G. H. Schwabe, and H. Sioli (eds.), *Biogeography and Ecology in South America*, Vol. 2, p. 723-740. W. Junk, The Hague.

BIGALKE, R. C. 1968. The contemporary mammal fauna of Africa. *Quart. Rev. Biol.*, 43: 265-300.

BONAPARTE, J. F. 1967. New vertebrate evidence for a southern Transatlantic connection during the Lower and Middle Triassic. *Palaeontology*, 10: 554-563.

BONATTI, E., M. BALL, and C. SCHUBERT. 1970. Evaporites and continental drift. *Naturwissenschaften*, 57: 107-108.

BOONSTRA, L. D. 1969. The terrestrial reptile fauna of *Tapinocephalus* zone age and Gondwanaland. In *Gondwana Stratigraphy*, p. 327-328. I.U.G.S. Symposium, Buenos Aires, 1-15 October, 1967. UNESCO, Paris.

BOYER, S. H., E. F. CROSBY, T. F. THURMAN, A. N. NOYES, G. F. FULLER, S. E. LESLIE, M. K. SHEPARD, and C. N. HENDERSON. 1969. Hemoglobins A and A$_2$ in New World primates. *Science*, 166: 1428-1431.

BRODKORB, P. 1963. Catalogue of fossil birds. *Bull. Florida State Museum*, 7: 179-293.

Brown, D. A. 1968. Some problems of distribution of late Palaeozoic and Triassic terrestrial vertebrates. *Austral. J. Sci.,* 30: 434-445.

Brundin, L. 1966. Transantarctic relationships and their significance, as evidenced by chironomid midges with a monograph of the subfamilies Podonominae and Aphroteniinae and the austral Heptagyiae. *Kungl. Sv. Vet. Akad. Handl.,* 11: 1-472.

Bullard, E., J. E. Everett, and A. G. Smith. 1965. The fit of the continents around the Atlantic. *Phil. Trans. Roy. Soc. London,* A, 1088: 41-51.

Burbridge, N. T. 1960. The phytogeography of the Australian Region. *Austral. J. Bot.,* 8: 75-211.

Burckle, L. H., J. Ewing, T. Saito, and R. Leyden. 1967. Tertiary sediment from the east Pacific rise. *Science,* 157: 537-540.

Camp, W. H. 1947. Distribution patterns in modern plants and the problems of ancient dispersals. *Ecol. Monogr.,* 17: 159-183.

Carey, S. W. 1958. A tectonic approach to continental drift. In S. W. Carey (ed.), *Continental Drift, A Symposium,* p. 177-355. Univ. Tasmania Press, Hobart.

Carozzi, A. V. 1970. New historical data on the origin of the theory of continental drift. *Geol. Soc. Amer. Bull.,* 81: 283-285.

Casamiquela, R. M. 1961. Sobre la presencia de un mamifero en el primer elenco (Icnologico) de vertebrados del Jurasico de la Patagonia. *Physis,* 22: 225-233.

Christoffel, D. A., and D. I. Ross. 1970. A fracture zone in the southwest Pacific basin south of New Zealand and its implications for sea floor spreading. *Earth Planet. Sci. Letters,* 8: 125-130.

Clemens, W. A. 1968. Origin and early evolution of marsupials. *Evolution,* 22: 1-18.

——. 1970. Mesozoic mammalian evolution. *Ann. Rev. Ecol. System.* 1: 357-390.

Colbert, E. H. 1952. The Mesozoic tetrapods of South America. *Bull. Am. Museum Natur. Hist.,* 99: 237-249.

——. 1962. *Dinosaurs: Their Discovery and Their World.* Hutchinson, London.

——. 1965. *The Age of Reptiles.* W. W. Norton, New York.

——. 1971. Tetrapods and continents. *Quart. Rev. Biol.,* 46: 250-269.

Colbert, E. H., and D. Merrilees. 1967. Cretaceous dinosaur footprints from Western Australia. *J. Roy. Soc. West Austral.,* 50: 21-25.

Cooke, H. B. S. 1968. The fossil mammal fauna of Africa. *Quart. Rev. Biol.,* 43: 234-264.

Cosgriff, J. W. 1967. Triassic labyrinthodonts from New South Wales. *Austral. N. Z. Assoc. Adv. Sci. Meeting, 39th Congress, Melbourne,* January, 1967, Section C, p. k4-k5 [Abstract].

Cox, A., R. F. Doell, and G. B. Dalrymple. 1968. Time scale for geo-magnetic reversals. In T. A. Phinney (ed.), *The History of the Earth's Crust*, p. 101-108. Princeton Univ. Press, Princeton.

Cox, C. B. 1965. New Triassic dicynodonts from South America, their origins and relationships. *Roy. Soc. Philos. Trans. (B)*, 248: 457-516.

———. 1967. Changes in terrestrial vertebrate faunas during the Mesozoic. In W. B. Harland et al. (eds.), *The Fossil Record*, p. 77-89. Geol. Soc. Lond.

———. 1970. Migrating marsupials and drifting continents. *Nature*, 226: 767-770.

Cranwell, L. M. 1964. *Nothofagus:* living and fossil. In J. L. Gressitt (ed.), *Pacific Basin Biogeography*, p. 387-400. Bishop Museum Press, Honolulu.

Cranwell, L. M., H. J. Harrington, and I. G. Speden. 1960. Lower Tertiary microfossils from McMurdo Sound, Antarctica. *Nature*, 186: 700-702.

Crawford, A. R. 1969. India, Ceylon and Pakistan: new age data and comparisons with Australia. *Nature*, 223: 380-384.

Creer, K. M. 1964. Palaeomagnetic data and du Toit's reconstruction of Gondwanaland. *Nature*, 204: 369-370.

———. 1970. A review of palaeomagnetism. *Earth Sci. Rev.*, 6: 369-466.

Creer, K. M., B. J. J. Embleton, and D. A. Valencio. 1970. Triassic and Permo-Triassic palaeomagnetic data for S. America. *Earth Planet Sci. Letters*, 8: 173-178.

Crompton, A. W. 1964. A preliminary description of a new mammal from the Upper Triassic of South Africa. *Proc. Zool. Soc. Lond.*, 142: 441-452.

———. 1969. The Late Triassic terrestrial fauna of South Africa. In *Gond-wana Stratigraphy*, p. 331. I.U.G.S. Symposium, Buenos Aires, 1-15 October, 1967. UNESCO, Paris.

Crompton, A. W., and F. A. Jenkins. 1968. Molar occlusion in the late Triassic mammals. *Biol. Rev.*, 43: 427-458.

Cullen, D. J. 1967. Mantle convection and sea-floor spreading in the south-west Pacific. *Nature*, 216: 356-357.

Dalziel, I. W. D., and D. H. Elliot. 1971. Evolution of the Scotia Arc. *Nature*, 233: 246-252.

Darlington, P. J. 1957. *Zoogeography: The Geographical Distribution of Animals*. John Wiley, London.

———. 1965. *Biogeography of the Southern End of the World*. Harvard Univ. Press, Cambridge.

Davies, D. 1968. When did the Seychelles leave India? *Nature*, 220: 1225-1226.

Dehm, R., and T. zu Oettingen-Spielberg. 1958. Paläontologische und

geologische Untersuchunden im Tertiär von Pakistan. II. Die mit-
teleocänen Zäugetiere von Ganda Kas bei basal nordwest Pakistan.
Abh. Bayers. Akad. Wiss. Math.-Naturw. Kl., N.F., 91: 1-54.

DEL CORRO, G. 1968. La presencia de Madtsoa Simpson (Boidae) en el
Eocene de Patagonia y en el Cretacio de Madagascar y algunos
ejemplos de distribucion disjunta. *Com. Museo Argentino Cien.
Nat. "Bernardino Rivadavia,"* Paleo., 1: 21-26.

DEWEY, J. F. 1971. Plate models for the evolution of the Alpine fold
belt. 17th Annual Meeting Geol. Soc. Amer., Washington, D. C.,
p. 543 [abstract]. Geological Society of America, Boulder, Colorado.

DIETRICH, W. O. 1928. *Brancatherulum* n.g.—ein Proplacentalier aus dem
obersten Jura des Tendaguru in Deutsch-Ostafrika. *Zentr. Mineral
Geol. Palaeontol.,* 1927B: 423-426.

DIETZ, R. S., and J. C. HOLDEN. 1969. The breakup of Pangaea. *Sci. Am.,*
233: 30-41.

——, and ——. 1970. Reconstruction of Pangaea: breakup and dispersion
of continents, Permian to present. *J. Geophys. Res.,* 75: 4939-4956.

——, and ——. 1971. Pre-Mesozoic oceanic crust in the eastern Indian
Ocean (Wharton Basin). *Nature,* 229: 309-312.

DIETZ, R. S., and W. P. SPROLL. 1970. Fit between Africa and Antarctica, a
continental drift reconstruction. *Science,* 167: 1612-1614.

DINGLE, R. V., and H. C. KLINGER. 1971. Significance of Upper Jurassic
sediments in the Knysna outlier (Cape Province) for timing of the
breakup of Gondwanaland. *Nature,* 232: 37-38.

DIXEY, F. 1956. The East African Rift System. *Col. Geol. and Min.
Resources Supp.,* Ser. 1: 71.

DORMAN, F. H. 1966. Australian Tertiary paleotemperatures. *J. Geol.,*
74: 49-61.

DU RIETZ, G. E. 1940. Problems of bipolar plant distribution. *Acta Phyto-
geogr. Svec.,* 13: 215-282.

DU TOIT, A. L. 1937. *Our Wandering Continents: An Hypothesis of
Continental Drifting.* Oliver and Boyd, London.

EARDLEY, A. J. 1951. *Structural Geology of North America.* Harper, New
York.

ELLIOT, D. H. 1972. Antarctic geology and drift reconstructions. SCARI-
IUGS Symposium on Antarctic Geology and Solid Earth Geophysics,
Oslo, August, 1970. In press.

ELLIOT, D. H., E. H. COLBERT, W. J. BREED, J. A. JENSEN, and J. S.
POWELL. 1970. Triassic tetrapods from Antarctica: evidence for continental drift. *Science,* 169: 1197-1201.

EVANS, J. W. 1958. Insect distribution and continental drift. In S. W.
Carey (ed.), *Continental Drift, A Symposium,* p. 134-161. Univ. of
Tasmania Press, Hobart.

———. 1959. The zoogeography of some Australian insects. In A. Keast, I. I. Crocker, and C. S. Christian (eds.), *Biogeography and Ecology in Australia*, p. 150-163. W. Junk, The Hague.

FAIRBRIDGE, R. W. 1965. The Indian Ocean and the status of Gondwanaland. *Progr. in Oceanogr.*, 3: 83-136.

FELL, H. B. 1967a. Resolution of Coriolis parameters for former epochs. *Nature*, 214: 1192-1198.

———. 1967b. Cretaceous and Tertiary surface currents of the oceans. *Oceanogr. Mar. Biol. Ann. Rev.*, 5: 317-341.

FISCHER, A. G., B. C. HEEZEN, R. E. BOYCE, D. BUKRY, R. G. DOUGLAS, R. E. GARRISON, S. A. KLING, V. KRASHENINNIKOV, A. P. SISTZIN, and A. C. PIMM. 1970. Geological history of the western North Pacific. *Science*, 168: 1210-1214.

FISHER, R. L., C. G. ENGEL, and T. W. C. HILDE. 1968. Basalts dredged from the Amirante Ridge, Western Indian Ocean. *Deep Sea Res.*, 15: 521-534.

FISHER, R. L., J. G. SCLATER, D. P. MCKENZIE. 1971. Evolution of the Central Indian Ridge, western Indian Ocean. *Bull. Geol. Soc. Am.*, 82: 553-562.

FITZPATRICK, K. T. and C. H. SUMMERSON. 1971. Some observations on electron micrographs of quartz sand grains. *Ohio J. Sci.*, 71: 106-119.

FLEMING, C. A. 1962. New Zealand biogeography. A paleontologist's approach. *Tuatara*, 10: 53-108.

FLORIN, R. 1940. The Tertiary fossil conifers in South Chile and their phytogeographical significance, with a review of the fossil conifers of southern lands. *Kungl. Sv. Vet. Akad. Handl.*, 19: 1-107.

———. 1963. The distribution of conifer and taxad genera in time and space. *Acta Horti Bergiani* (Uppsala), 20: 121-312.

FLOWER, M. F. J., and D. F. STRONG. 1969. The significance of sandstone inclusions in lavas of The Comores Archipilago. *Earth Planet Sci. Letters*, 7: 47-50.

FOX, P. J., B. C. HEEZEN, and G. L. JOHNSON. 1970. Jurassic sandstone from the tropical Atlantic. *Science*, 170: 1402-1404.

FRANCHETEAU, J., and J. G. SCLATER. 1969. Paleomagnetism of the southern continents and plate tectonics. *Earth Planet Sci. Letters*, 6: 93-106.

FREAKE, J. R. 1968. Palynology. A summary of results obtained during the 2nd W. African Micropaleontological Colloquium, 1966. In J. E. Van Hinte (ed.), *Second W. African Micropal. Colloquium Proc.* (Ibadan), p. 269. E. J. Brill, Leiden.

FUNNELL, B. M., and A. G. SMITH. 1968. Opening of the Atlantic Ocean. *Nature*, 219: 1328-1333.

GERY, J. 1969. The fresh-water fishes of South America. In E. J. Fittkau,

J. Illies, H. Klinge, G. H. Schwabe, and H. Sioli (eds.), *Biogeography and Ecology in South America,* Vol. 2, p. 828-848. W. Junk, The Hague.

GILLULY, J. 1971. Plate tectonics and magmatic evolution. *Geol. Soc. Am. Bull.,* 82: 2383-2396.

GLAESSNER, M. F. 1962. Isolation and communication in the geological history of the Australian fauna. In G. W. Leeper (ed.), *The Evolution of Living Organisms,* p. 242-249. Melbourne Univ. Press, Melbourne.

GOOD, R. D. 1964. *The Geography of Flowering Plants.* 3rd edition. Wiley, New York.

GORDON, H. D. 1949. The problem of sub-Antarctic plant distribution. *Austral. Assoc. Adv. Sci. Meeting Hobart:* 142-149.

GOUGH, D. I., N. D. OPDYKE, and M. W. MCELHINNY. 1964. The significance of paleomagnetic results from Africa. *J. Geophys. Res.,* 69: 2509-2519.

GRAHAM, K. W. T., C. E. HELSLEY, and A. L. HALES. 1964. Determination of the relative positions of continents from paleomagnetic data. *J. Geophys. Res.,* 69: 3895-3900.

GRIFFITHS, J. R. 1971. Reconstruction of the southwest Pacific margin of Gondwanaland. *Nature,* 234: 203-207.

GRIFFITHS, J. R., and R. VARNE. 1972. Evolution of the Tasman Sea, Macquarie Ridge, Alpine Fault. *Nature, Phys. Sci.,* 235: 83-85.

HAFFER, J. 1970. Geologic climatic history and zoogeographic significance of the Uraba region in northwestern Colombia. *Caldasia,* 10: 603-636.

HALLAM, A. 1967. The bearing of certain palaeozoogeographic data on continental drift. *Palaeogeogr., Palaeoclimatol., Palaeoecol.,* 3: 201-241.

HALPERN, M. 1968. Ages of Antarctic and Argentine rocks bearing on continental drift. *Earth Planet Sci. Letters,* 5: 159-167.

HAMILTON, W. 1967. Tectonics of Antarctica. *Tectonophysics,* 4: 555-568.

———. 1971. Plate tectonic evolution of Indonesia. 17th Annual Meeting Geol. Soc. Am., p. 589-590 [abstract]. Geol. Soc. Am., Boulder, Colorado.

HAMILTON, W., and D. KRINSLEY. 1967. Upper Paleozoic glacial deposits of South Africa and southern Australia. *Bull. Geol. Soc. Am.,* 78: 783-799.

HARRINGTON, H. J. 1962. Paleogeographic development of South America. *Bull. Am. Assoc. Petrol. Geol.,* 46: 1773-1814.

HARRISON, L. 1924. The migration route of the Asutralian marsupial fauna. *Austral. Zool.,* 3: 247-263.

HAYMAN, D. L., J. A. W. KIRSCH, P. G. MARTIN, and P. F. WALLER. 1971. Chromosomal and serological studies of the Caenolestidae and their implications for marsupial evolution. *Nature,* 231: 194-195.

HEDLEY, C. 1912. The palaeogeographical relations of Antarctica. *Proc. Linn. Soc. London*, 24: 80-90.

HEIRTZLER, J. R. 1968. Evidence for ocean floor spreading across the ocean basins. In T. A. Phinney (ed.), *The History of the Earth's Crust*, p. 90-100. Princeton Univ. Press, Princeton.

HEIRTZLER, J. R., G. O. DICKSON, E. M. HERRON, W. C. PITMAN, III, and X. LE PICHON. 1968. Marine magnetic anomalies, geomagnetic field reversals, and motions of the ocean floor and continents. *J. Geophys. Res.*, 73: 2119-2136.

HOEKEN-KLINKENBERG, P. M. 1964. A palynological investigation of some Upper Cretaceous sediments in Nigeria. *Pollen et Spores*, 6: 209-231.

HOFFSTETTER, M. R. 1970. L'histoire biogeographique des marsupeaux et la dichotomie marsupeaux-placentaires. *Comptes Rend. Acad. Sci. (Paris)*, 271: 388-391.

HOFFSTETTER, M. R., and R. LAVOCAT. 1970. Découverte dans le Déséadien de Bolivie de genres pentalophodontes appuyant les affinités africaines des rongeurs caviomorphes. *Comptes Rend. Acad. Sci. (Paris)*, 271: 172-175.

HOLMES, A. 1965. *Principles of Physical Geology*. Thomas Nelson, London.

HOOKER, J. D. 1860. *Botany of the Antarctic Voyage of H. M. Discovery Ships* Erebus and Terror *in the Years 1839-1843. Part III: Flora Tasmaniae, Vol. 1. Introductory Essay*. Lovell Reeve, London.

HOPSON, J. A., and A. W. CROMPTON. 1969. Origin of mammals. In T. Dobzhansky, M. K. Hecht, W. G. Steere (eds.), *Evolutionary Biology*, Vol. 3, p. 15-72. Appleton-Century Crofts, New York.

HOWIE, A. 1971. A branchopid labyrinthodont from the lower Trias of Queensland. *Proc. Linnean Soc. N. S. Wales*, October, 1971, p. 3 [abstract].

HURLEY, P. M. 1968. The confirmation of continental drift. *Sci. Am.*, 218: 53-64.

HURLEY, P. M., and J. R. RAND. 1968. Review of age data in west Africa and South America relative to a test of continental drift. In T. A. Phinney (ed.), *The History of the Earth's Crust*, p. 153-160. Princeton Univ. Press, Princeton.

HURLEY, P. M., F. F. M. DE ALMEIDA, G. C. MELCHER, U. G. CORDANI, J. R. RAND, K. KAWASHITA, P. VANDOROS, W. H. PINSON, JR., and H. W. FAIRBAIRN. 1967. Test of continental drift by comparison of radiometric ages. *Science*, 157: 495-500.

HUTCHINSON, J. 1946. *A Botanist in Southern Africa*. P. R. Gawthorn Ltd., London.

ILLIES, J. 1965. Phylogeny and zoogeography of the Plecoptera. *Ann. Rev. Entomol.*, 10: 117-140.

———. 1969. Biogeography and ecology of Neotropical freshwater insects, especially those from running waters. In E. J. Fittkau, J. Illies, H.

Klinge, G. H. Schwabe, and H. Sioli (eds.), *Biogeography and Ecology in South America*, Vol. 2, p. 685-708. W. Junk, The Hague.

IRVING, E., W. A. ROBERTSON, and P. M. STOTT. 1963. The significance of the paleomagnetic results from Mesozoic rocks of Eastern Australia. *J. Geophys. Res.*, 68: 2313-2317.

ISACKS, B., J. OLIVER, and L. R. SYKES. 1968. Seismology and the new global tectonics. *J. Geophys. Res.*, 73: 5855-5899.

JACOBS, C., H. BURGL, and D. L. CONLEY. 1963. Backbone of Colombia. *Am. Assoc. Petrol. Geol. Mem.*, 2: 62-72.

JEFFRYS, H. 1970. Imperfections of elasticity and continental drift. *Nature*, 225: 1007-1008.

JONES, J. G. 1971. Australia's Caenozoic drift. *Nature*, 230: 237-239.

JUST, T. 1952. Fossil floras of the southern hemisphere and their phyto-geographical significance. *Bull. Am. Museum Natur. Hist.*, 99: 189-203.

KEAST, A. 1968. Australian mammals: zoogeography and evolution. *Quart. Rev. Biol.*, 43: 373-408.

KERMACK, K. A., and F. MUSSETT. 1958. The jaw articulation of the Docodonta and the classification of Mesozoic mammals. *Proc. Roy. Soc. London*, B., 148: 204-215.

KOHNE, D. E. 1970. Evolution of higher organism DNA. *Quart. Revs. Biophysics*, 3: 327-375.

KREMP, G. O. W. 1964. Antarctica, the climate of the Tertiary and a possible cause of our ice age. In R. J. Adie (ed.), *Antarctic Geology*, p. 736-747. Proc. 1. Internat. Symp. on Antarctic Geology. North-Holland, Amsterdam.

KROMMELBEIN, K. 1965a. Neue, fur Vergleiche mit Westafriki wichtige Ostracoden-Arten der brasilianischen Bahia-Serie (Ober-Jura/Unter-Kreide in Welden-Fazies). *Senckenberg. leth.* 46a: 177-213.

——. 1965b. Ostracoden aus der nicht-marinen Unter-Kreide (Westafrikanischer Wealden) des Congo-Kustenbeckens. *Meyniana*, 15: 59-74.

KUMMEL, B. 1961. *History of the Earth. An Introduction to Historical Geology.* W. H. Freeman, San Francisco.

KURTÉN, B. 1969. Continental drift and evolution. *Sci. Am.*, 220: 54-64.

LARSON, E. E. and L. LA FOUNTAIN. 1970. Timing of the breakup of the continents around the Atlantic as determined by paleomagnetism. *Earth Planet. Sci. Letters*, 8: 341-351.

LAVOCAT, R. 1969. La systématique des rongeurs hystricomorphes et la dérive des continents. *Comptes Rend. Acad. Sci. (Paris)*, 269: 1496-1497.

LE PICHON, X. 1968. Sea-floor spreading and continental drift. *J. Geophys. Res.*, 73: 3661-3697.

LE PICHON, X. and J. R. HEIRTZLER. 1968. Magnetic anomalies in the Indian Ocean and sea-floor spreading. *J. Geophys. Res.,* 73: 2101-2117.

LILLEGRAVEN, J. 1969. The latest Cretaceous mammals of the upper part of the Edmonton Formation of Alberta, Canada, with a review of the marsupial-placental dichotomy in mammalian evolution. Univ. Kansas Paleontol. Contrib. Vertebrata, No. 12, Art. 50.

LLOYD, J. J. 1963. Tectonic history of the south Central-American orogen. *Am. Assoc. Petrol. Geol. Mem.,* 2: 88-100.

MACGINITIE, H. D. 1969. The Eocene Green River flora of northwestern Colorado and northeastern Utah. *Univ. Calif. Publ. Geol. Sci.,* 83: 1-140.

MARGOLIS, S. V., and J. P. KENNETT. 1970. Antarctic glaciation during the Tertiary recorded in sub-Antarctic deep-sea cores. *Science,* 170: 1085-1087.

MARTIN, H. 1968. A critical review of the evidence for a former direct connection of South America and Africa. In E. J. Fittkau, J. Illies, H. Klinge, G. H. Schwabe, and H. Sioli (eds.), *Biogeography and Ecology in South America,* Vol. I, p. 25-53. W. Junk, The Hague

MARTIN, P. G. 1970. The Darwin Rise hypothesis of the biogeographical dispersal of marsupials. *Nature,* 225: 197-198.

MATTHEW, W. D. 1915. Climate and evolution. *Ann. N.Y. Acad. Sci.,* 24: 171-318.

MAXWELL, A. E., R. P. VON HERZEN, K. J. HSÜ, J. E. ANDREWS, T. SAITO, S. F. PERCIVAL, E. D. MILOW, and R. E. BOYCE. 1970. Deep sea drilling in South Atlantic. *Science,* 168: 1047-1059.

MAYR, E. 1946. History of the North American bird fauna. *Wilson Bull.,* 58: 3-41.

——. 1952. The problem of land connections across the South Atlantic, with special reference to the Mesozoic. *Bull. Am. Museum Natur. Hist.,* 99: 81-258. [A symposium.]

MCDOWELL, R. M. 1964. The affinities and derivation of the New Zealand fresh-water fish fauna. Fisheries Laboratory, Marine Dept., Wellington; Lab. Publ. No. 65. p. 59-67.

MCELHINNY, M. W. 1970. Formation of the Indian Ocean. *Nature,* 228: 977-979.

MCELHINNY, M. W., and J. C. BRIDEN. 1971. Continental drift during the Palaeozoic. *Earth Planet. Sci. Letters,* 10: 407-416.

MCELHINNY, M. W., and P. WELLMAN. 1969. Polar wandering and sea-floor spreading in the southern Indian Ocean. *Earth Planet. Sci. Letters,* 6: 198-204.

MELVILLE, R. 1969. Leaf venation patterns and the origin of Angiosperms. *Nature,* 224: 121-125.

MENARD, H. W. 1964. *Marine Geology of the Pacific*. McGraw Hill, New York.

MENÉNDEZ, C. A. 1969. Die fossilen Floren sudamerikas. In E. J. Fittkau, J. Illies, H. Klinge, G. H. Schwabe, and H. Sioli (eds.), *Biogeography and Ecology in South America*, Vol. 2, p. 519-561. W. Junk, The Hague.

MEYERHOFF, A. A. 1970a. Continental drift; implications of paleomagnetic studies, meteorology, physical oceanography, and climatology. *J. Geol.*, 78: 1-51.

——. 1970b. Continental drift, II. High-latitude evaporite deposits and geologic history of Arctic and North Atlantic oceans. *J. Geol.*, 78: 406-444.

MEYERHOFF, A. A. and C. TEICHERT. 1971. Continental drift. III: Late Paleozoic glacial centers, and Devonian-Eocene coal distribution. *J. Geol.*, 79: 285-321.

MILLOT, J. 1952. La faune malagache et le mythe gondwanien. *Mem. Inst. Sci. Madagascar*, Ser. A, VII (1): 1-36.

MORGAN, W. J. 1968. Rises, trenches, great faults, and crustal blocks. *J. Geophys. Res.*, 73: 1959-1982.

MYERS, G. S. 1967. Zoogeographical evidence of the age of the South Atlantic Ocean. *Stud. Trop. Oceanog., Miami*, 5: 614-621.

NEUMAYR, M. 1887. Erdgeschichte. *Bibliogr. Inst. Leipzig*, 1: 653; 2: 879.

OMODEO, P. 1963. Distribution of the terricolous oligochaetes on the two shores of the Atlantic. In A. Löve and D. Löve (eds.), *North Atlantic Biota and their History*, 127-151. Pergamon Press, New York.

OPDYKE, N. D. 1968. The paleomagnetism of oceanic cores. In T. A. Phinney (ed.), *The History of the Earth's Crust*, p. 61-72. Princeton Univ. Press, Princeton.

OSUGA, D. T., and R. E. FEENEY. 1968. Biochemistry of the egg-white proteins of Ratites. *Arch. Biochem. Biophys.*, 124: 560-574.

PATTERSON, B., and R. PASCUAL. 1963. The extinct land mammals of South America. *Proc. 16. Intern. Congr. Zool.*, Program Vol., App: 138-148.

——, and ——. 1968. The fossil mammal fauna of South America. *Quart. Rev. Biol.*, 43: 409-451.

RAVEN, H. C. 1935. Wallace's line and the distribution of Indo-Australian mammals. *Bull. Am. Museum Natur. Hist.*, 68: 179-293.

REYMENT, R. A. 1967. Review of non-paleomagnetic evidence for continental drift for West Africa and Brazil. In *Symposium on Continental Drift, UNESCO, Montevideo* [unpublished].

——. 1969. Ammonite stratigraphy, continental drift and oscillatory transgressions. *Nature*, 224: 137-140.

RIDE, W. D. L. 1964. A review of the Australian fossil marsupials. *J. Roy. Soc. West. Austral.*, 47: 97-131.

RIEDEL, W. R. 1967. Radiolarian evidence consistent with spreading of the Pacific floor. *Science,* 157: 540-542.

RIEK, E. F. 1959. The Australian freshwater Crustacea. In A. Keast, R. L. Crocker, and C. S. Christian (eds.), *Biogeography and Ecology in Australia,* p. 246-258. W. Junk, The Hague.

——. 1970. Lower Cretaceous fleas. *Nature,* 227: 746-747.

ROBINSON, P. L. 1967. The Indian Gondwana formations—a review. In *First IUGS Symposium on Gondwana Stratigraphy, Mar del Plata,* p. 202-268. International Union of Geological Sciences, Haarlem.

——. 1971. A problem of faunal replacement on Permo-Triassic continents. *Paleontology,* 14: 131-153.

ROMER, A. S. 1952. Discussion of paper by E. G. Colbert. *Bull. Am. Museum Natur. Hist.,* 99: 250-254.

——. 1966. *Vertebrate Paleontology.* 3rd ed. Univ. Chicago Press.

——. 1967. The Chañares (Argentina) Triassic reptile fauna. III. Two new gomphodonts, *Massetognathus pascuali* and *M. teruggii. Breviora, Mus. Comp. Zool., Harvard,* 264: 1-25.

——. 1969. Reptiles of Gondwanaland. *Nature,* 224: 1059.

RUNCORN, S. K. 1962. Palaeomagnetic evidence for continental drift and its geophysical cause. In S. K. Runcorn (ed.), *Continental Drift,* p. 1-40. Academic Press, London.

SARICH, V. M. 1970. Primate systematics with special reference to Old World monkeys, a protein perspective. In J. R. Napier and P. H. Napier (eds.), *Old World Monkeys, Evolution, Systematics, and Behaviour,* p. 175-226. Academic Press, New York.

SCHAEFFER, B. 1952. The evidence of the freshwater fishes. *Bull. Am. Museum Natur. Hist.,* 99: 227-234.

SCHOPF, J. M. 1970a. Relation of floras of the Southern Hemisphere to continental drift. *Taxon,* 19: 657-674.

——. 1970b. Gondwana paleobotany. *Antarctic J. U. S.,* 5: 62-66.

SEIN, MA KHIN. 1961. *Nothofagus* in the London Clay. *Nature,* 190: 1030-1031.

SERVENTY, D. L. 1972. Causal Zoogeography in Australia. *Proc. XIV Intern. Ornith. Congr.,* The Hague, 1970. In press.

SEWELL, R. B. S. 1956. The continental drift theory and the distribution of Copepoda. *Linn. Soc. London Proc.,*166: 149-177.

SHARP, A. J. 1966. Some aspects of Mexican phytogeography. *Ciencia Mex.,* 24: 229-232.

SHOR, G. G., JR., H. K. KIRK, and H. W. MENARD. 1971. Crustal structure of the Melanesian area. *J. Geophys. Res.,* 76: 2562-2586.

SILL,W. D. 1969. The tetrapod-bearing continental Triassic sediments of South America. *Am. J. Sci.,* 267: 805-821.

SIMPSON, G. G. 1928. Mesozoic mammalia XI. *Brancatherulum tendaguruense* Dietrich. *Am. J. Sci.,* (ser. 5), 15: 303-308.

——. 1940a. Antarctica as a faunal migration route. *Proc. 6. Pacific Sci. Congr.:* 755-768.

——. 1940b. Mammals and land bridges. *J. Wash. Acad. Sci.,* 30: 137-163.

——. 1943. Mammals and the nature of continents. *Am. J. Sci.,* 241: 1-31.

——. 1950. History of the fauna of Latin America. *Am. Sci.,* 38: 361-389.

——. 1959. Mesozoic mammals and the polyphyletic origin of mammals. *Evolution,* 13: 405-414.

——. 1961. Historical zoogeography of Australian mammals. *Evolution,* 15: 431-446.

——. 1966. Mammalian evolution on the southern continents. *Jahrb. f. Geol. u. Palaeontol.,* 125: 1-18.

——. 1970. Drift theory: Antarctica and central Asia. *Science,* 170: 678.

——. 1971. Recent literature on Mesozoic mammals. *J. Paleontol.,* 45: 862-868.

SKOTTSBERG, C. 1957. *The Natural History of Juan Fernandez and Easter Island. Derivation of the Flora and Fauna of Juan Fernandez Island.* Almquist and Wiksells, Uppsala.

SMITH, A. G., and A. HALLAM. 1970. The fit of southern continents. *Nature,* 225: 139-144.

SPROLL, W. P., and R. S. DIETZ. 1969. Morphological continental drift fit of Australia and Antarctica. *Nature,* 222: 345-348.

STEHLI, F. G., and C. E. HELSLEY. 1963. Paleontologic technique for defining ancient pole position. *Science,* 142: 1057-1059.

STIRTON, R. A., R. H. TEDFORD, and M. O. WOODBURNE. 1968. Australian Tertiary deposits containing terrestrial mammals. *Univ. Calif. Pubs. Geol. Sci.,* 77: 1-30.

SUESS, E. 1906. *The Face of the Earth.* Vol. 2. Clarendon Press, Oxford.

TARLING, D. H. 1971. Gondwanaland, paleomagnetism and continental drift. *Nature,* 229: 17-21.

TEICHERT, C. 1941. Upper Paleozoic of Western Australia: correlation and paleogeography. *Bull. Am. Assoc. Petrol. Geol.,* 25: 371-415.

TRIPATHI, C. and P. P. SATSANGI. 1963. *Lystrosaurus* fauna from the Panchet Series of the Raniganj coalfields. *Palaeontol. Indica* (N.S.), 37: 1-53.

VAKHRAMEEV, V. A., I. A. DOBRUSKINA, E. D. ZAKLINSKAJA, and S. V. MEYEN. 1970. Paleozoic and Mesozoic floras of Eurasia and phytogeography of this time. *Trans. Acad. Sci. U.S.S.R.,* 208.

VALENCIO, D. A., and J. F. VILAS. 1969. Age of the separation of South America and Africa. *Nature,* 223: 1353-1354.

VAN ANDEL, T., and T. C. MOORE, JR. 1970. Magnetic anomalies and seafloor spreading rates in the northern South Atlantic. *Nature,* 226: 328-330.

VAN STEENIS, C. J. 1963. *Pacific Plant Areas, Vol. 1.* Netherlands Organ. Adv. Pure Res., Leyden.

VAN STEENIS, C. J., and M. VAN BALGOOY. 1966. *Pacific Plant Areas, Vol. 2.* Bloomea Supplement 5. Netherlands Organ. Adv. Pure. Res., Leyden.

VAN VALEN, L. 1969. What was the largest dinosaur? *Copeia,* 1969, No. 3: 624-626.

VEEVERS, J. J. 1969. Palaeogeography of the Timor Sea region. *Palaeogeogr., Palaeoclimatol., Palaeoecol.,* 6: 125-140.

VEEVERS, J. J., J. G. JONES, and J. A. TALENT. 1971. Indo-Australian stratigraphy and the configuration and dispersal of Gondwanaland. *Nature,* 229: 383-388.

VILAS, J. F., and D. A. VALENCIO. 1970. Palaeogeographic reconstructions of the Gondawnie continents based on palaeomagnetic and sea-floor spreading data. *Earth Planet. Sci. Letters,* 7: 397-405.

VINE, F. J. 1966. Spreading of the ocean floor: new evidence. *Science,* 154: 1405.

VON HUENE, F., and C. A. MATLEY. 1933. The Cretaceous Saurischia and Ornithischia of the Central Provinces of India. *Mem. Geol. Surv. India, Pal. Indica, N.S.,* 21 (1): 1-74.

VON KOENIGSWALD, G. H. R. 1967. An upper Eocene mammal of the family Anthracotheriidae from the island of Timor, Indonesia. *Proc. Koninkl. Ned. Akad. Wetenschap.,* Ser. B. (Phys. Sci.), 70: 529-533.

WALDMAN, M. 1967. Mesozoic fish from Koonwarra, Victoria. *Austral. N. Z. Assoc. Adv. Sci. Meeting, 39th Congress, Melbourne,* January 1967, Section C, p. K2-K3 [Abstract].

WANG, A. C., J. SHUSTER, A. EPSTEIN, and H. H. FUDENBERG. 1968. Evolution of antigenic determinants of transferrin and other serum proteins in primates. *Biochem. Genet.,* 1: 347-358.

WEGENER, A. 1924. *The Origin of Continents and Oceans.* 3rd ed. Methuen, London.

WOOD, A. E., and B. PATTERSON. 1970. Relationships among hystricognathous and hystricomorphous rodents. *Mammalia,* 34: 628-639.

WOODRING, W. P. 1954. Caribbean land and sea through the ages. *Bull. Geol. Soc. Am.,* 65: 719-732.

III

The Fossil Mammal Fauna of Africa

by H. B. S. Cooke

INTRODUCTION

For more than a century biologists have followed the general scheme for the zoogeographic division of the land masses of the earth that was proposed by Sclater (1858), consolidated by Wallace (1876) and recently refined by Schmidt (1954). It would be futile to deny the realities of the existing faunal differences which make it possible for such geographic boundaries to be drawn but, as a number of eminent authorities have pointed out (Mayr, 1946; Simpson, 1953), these divisions in space break down seriously when any attempt is made to apply them to former geological times. In the cases of Australia and South America, physical isolation of long duration led to genetic isolation which allowed the early inhabitants of these continents great freedom for development along lines largely unaffected by the march of events elsewhere. In Australia the isolation has remained almost complete while in South America contact with the northern continents has been slender enough to allow a large part of the autochthonous (indigenous) fauna to survive without being swamped completely. Although the wild life of Africa at the present day constitutes a characteristic assemblage which warrants separation of the Ethiopian region as a zoogeographic entity, the fossil record shows that many African mammals existed in Eurasia in geologically very recent times, and it is clear that the boundaries between the faunistic regions would have had to be drawn quite differently in the past. Intermittent contacts between Africa and Eurasia during the Cenozoic have tended to diminish the distinctiveness of their respective faunas and to obscure the contribution that evolution in Africa may well have made to the total complex.

The presence of fossil mammals of Ethiopian type in Eurasia and their subsequent extinction there have also led to the widespread belief that Africa possesses its present character primarily because it has served as a "refuge" for the survival of archaic forms of life. W. D. Matthew's classic study, *"Climate and Evolution"* (1915), did much to foster a vision of Asia as the major center from which the various groups dispersed, and the views of such workers as Pilgrim (1941) in favor of Africa as an important evolutionary center and a source for diffusion *into* the Palearctic region have received scant approval or acceptance. Further paleontological discoveries are needed before the extent of the interchanges between the Palearctic and Ethiopian regions can be fully evaluated, but in the last few years new evidence has accumulated which emphasizes the essentially indigenous nature of much of the living and extinct African mammalian fauna.

The living terrestrial mammals of Africa belong to twelve orders and comprise about 750 species divided into 230 genera, representing 52 families. Although it is now out of date, Simpson's 1945 census listed a world total of only 197 living families of terrestrial placental mammals, so that the extent to which Africa is involved in the world fauna is obvious; but the world total of 835 genera in these families suggests that the living African fauna is somewhat less diversified than is the case in many other regions. This is particularly true of the Chiroptera (25 genera out of 118) and the Rodentia (85 out of 344). Africa lacks Dermoptera and Edentata, and no monotreme or marsupial has been found either living or fossil (a supposed fossil marsupial from South-West Africa is a macroscelidid insectivore). On the other hand Africa (including Madagascar) has eight unique families of insectivores and primates, one of bats, and four among the rodents.

Although the ungulates represent only some 50 genera and about 120 species, they are numerically abundant and constitute a major part of the animal life of the continent. In the three main game sanctuaries in east Africa the ungulate biomass ranges between 15 and 25 metric tons/km² (Bourlière, 1963); even in the drier thornbush savannas of southern Africa the corresponding figures are 2 to 5 metric tons/km². By contrast, the dense tropical forest environment of west Africa has only an insignificant ungulate population so that the major part of the mammal fauna there is comprised of primates, rodents, and insectivores whose combined biomass is no more than 0.1 metric ton/km²—a figure comparable with that for the ungulates in the near-desert steppes! The large carnivores (lions and leopards) and the scavenging hyenas amount only to about 2 per cent of the number of ungulates. It is thus clear that the Ethiopian region is one in which the ecological conditions for ungulate survival are now particularly favorable. To what extent this is true for earlier geological periods has yet to be evaluated.

MESOZOIC PALEOGEOGRAPHY: THE SHAPING OF AFRICA

It is obvious that the evolution of the terrestrial life of a continent is intimately involved with the morphological evolution of the land itself, not only on account of the importance of physical connections with other continents as far as migration is concerned, but also because of the effects that physiographic changes have upon the climatic and ecological environments. The literature on the paleogeography of Africa is scanty, scattered, and incomplete; almost the only synthesis is that of Moreau (1952) in his important consideration of the development of the avifauna of the continent. Most of his thesis is unaffected by later studies, but there is enough new information to make it seem worthwhile to reconstruct the paleogeographic picture.

Although Africa is now separated from southwest Asia by the Red Sea trench and the Gulf of Aden, the Arabian block has been essentially a unit in the structure of Africa through most of geological time. On many occasions, the persistent Tethys Sea extended across the northern fringe of Africa through the Persian Gulf, and the northwestern part of the continent was invaded extensively by the ocean during portions of the Paleozoic and Mesozoic eras. In Triassic times the African continent was the site of widespread continental deposition, but during this time an arm of the sea extended from Pakistan down to western Madagascar along the general trend of the subsiding Madagascar channel (or geosyncline).

During the Permian and Triassic periods, southern Africa supported a large population of diverse mammal-like reptiles, the Therapsida, which bridged the morphological gap between primitive reptiles and early mammals, including the possible acquisition of warm blood, hair and skin glands (Brink 1957). Van Valen (1960) and others have actually suggested that the therapsids should be included in the Mammalia but Simpson (1961) has advanced cogent reasons for retaining the existing nomenclature. The most mammal-like forms occur in the upper Triassic beds of South Africa and recently two tiny skulls of undoubted true mammals have been found in the late Triassic "Red Beds" in Basutoland (Crompton, 1964, 1968).

In the Jurassic, marine conditions encroached upon the present continent on its east side and the sea broke across Arabia and Ethiopia for the first time since the Precambrian, forming a "trans-Erythraean trough" (Lamare, 1936), but leaving an "Arabo-Somali massif" which was not submerged (Picard, 1939). During this period southern Africa was apparently undergoing general erosion but a substantial basin of deposition existed in the western half of the equatorial belt, in which fresh and brackish-water fossils occur; one upper Jurassic unit in the Stanleyville area of the eastern Congo contains an intercalation of limestones with fossil fish that are believed to be marine (Saint-Seine, 1955) and this may imply a temporary link with the trans-Erythraean trough. An indication of the paleogeography of Africa during the later Jurassic is given in Figure 1.

During the Cretaceous, general warping of the whole continent took place. In the south there was broad uplift accompanied by marginal monoclinal flexing which permitted the seas to invade the ancient landmass, first on the east side and later on the west. In east Africa there was

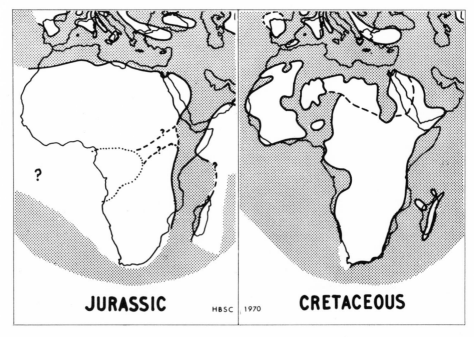

FIGS. 1 and 2. PALEOGEOGRAPHY OF THE JURASSIC AND THE CRETACEOUS

In the Jurassic a temporary link may have existed between the eastern ocean and a non-marine basin in the Congo region. In the Cretaceous, the area to the north of the dashed line is that occupied by the Nubia sandstone and "continental intercalaire."

only minor change in the Jurassic shoreline, but the sea withdrew from the Somali-Yemen area. The Atlantic margin of the present continent began to take shape and by mid-Cretaceous times the Atlantic and Tethys Seas became united across an area which stretched from the Gulf of Guinea to Algeria, separating the main mass of Arabo-Africa from the west African shield area (Fig. 2). In a broad belt between latitudes 10° and 30° N deposition took place of a complex of sandy sediments known in Egypt and Arabia as the Nubia (or Nubian) sandstone, and in the former French territories as the "continental intercalaire." Although partly continental in origin and frequently cited as evidence for an extensive and persistent pre-Saharan desert zone, these deposits are often fluvio-marine or lacustrine in character and are largely the product of deposition upon a slowly sinking peneplained surface (Shukri and Said, 1944, 1946). In Egypt the progressive southward advance of the shoreline during the Cretaceous, followed by regression of the sea in the Paleocene, have been demonstrated by Nakkady (1957) and Said (1961).

The continent as a whole was subjected to extensive denudation during the Jurassic and much of the Cretaceous, with the result that it was reduced to a land mass of low relief (the "Gondwana" and "post-Gond-wana" surfaces of King, 1951, 1962). The planed-off landscape has since been warped extensively but remnants are still traceable in strongly uplifted areas where they have escaped subsequent destruction.

Continental deposits with identifiable dinosaur remains do exist in the interior but the most important locality is near Tendaguru in southern Tanzania, where marine and continental deposits interdigitate and form an unbroken sequence astride the Jurassic-Cretaceous boundary. From a high Jurassic horizon in this deposit a single toothless jaw of a mammal was recovered in 1911. Dietrich (1927) named it *Brancatherulum tendaguruense* and Simpson (1928) regards it as a paurodontid pantothere resembling *Peramus* of the English Purbeckian. It is particularly un-unfortunate that no Cretaceous mammals have yet been found in the continent.

TERTIARY PALEOGEOGRAPHY

Early in the Paleocene, mountain building in the Tethys area and general uplift to the south led to the withdrawal of the invading seas, leaving only a large embayment in Nigeria and small areas in Morocco and Algeria still inundated. The Tethys was drastically reduced in size and there were broad land connections through Arabia to India, and through the Balkan region to Europe; tenuous links may also have existed between northwestern Africa and the Iberian peninsula and between Madagascar and the African mainland (Fig. 3). This Paleocene uplift initiated the dissection of the newly-elevated Gondwana and post-Gondwana surfaces and a fresh cycle of planation began.

In the Eocene the seas advanced once more and Arabo-Africa was again virtually isolated, although the marine invasions were less extensive than those of the late Cretaceous (Fig. 4). Except in Tanzania, where the lower Oligocene was transgressive, the maximum advance of the sea usually occurred in the later Eocene. In north Africa, in particular, the lower Oligocene was marked by a gradual withdrawal of the sea. Uplift became general and mountain-building activity associated with the folding of the Alpine chain reduced the size of the Tethys Sea very substantially. Towards the end of the Oligocene (Fig. 5) there was also folding and elevation of the Atlas region, resulting in the complete emergence of Tunisia, Algeria and Morocco (Choubert, 1952).

From the middle Eocene until the end of the Miocene, the western trough of the Tethys between north Africa and Spain was divided into two parts, separated by an upfolded land mass known as the "Betic massif," remnants of which occur in southeastern Spain and in the Kabylie range of the Algerian coast. The northern arm of the sea is the Betic trough and the southern is the Rifian (or South Tellian) trough (see Furon, 1959; Brinkmann, 1960). At times the Betic massif was reduced to a string of islands but at the end of the Oligocene it must have been fully emergent. At this time there was almost certainly some kind of land connection between north Africa and emergent Europe even if it was not a continuous

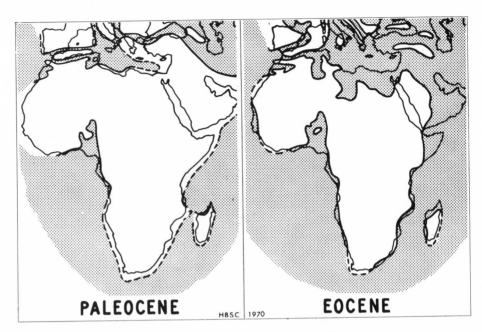

FIGS. 3 and 4. PALEOGEOGRAPHY OF THE PALEOCENE AND THE EOCENE

one. The floors of both troughs were again fully submerged in the early Miocene.

In the Arabian region the emergence which began in the late Eocene became much more pronounced in the Oligocene. Tectonic movements, slumping, and marginal elevation created the elongate trench that was subsequently to form the Red Sea. At this stage the trench was almost certainly not occupied by marine waters but formed a feature resembling the better developed portions of the east African rift valleys, doubtless strung with saline lakes. The Gulf of Aden was not formed until the end of the Oligocene, or early in the Miocene (Swartz and Arden, 1960; Said, 1961, 1962). The situation in the area between Arabia and India is uncertain but marine Oligocene beds are lacking in northern Pakistan and there is a high probability that uplift was sufficiently general to provide some kind of land link across this region in the late Oligocene.

The Miocene was characterized by renewed marine invasion of the borders of the African continent and of the fringes of an uplifted Arabian massif (Fig. 6). The Tethys/Mediterranean Sea was also able to flow through the Gulf of Suez and flooded the Red Sea trench as far south as the Farsan Islands, while the waters of the Indian Ocean extended into the Gulf of Aden (Beydoun, 1960). Arabia thus became partially isolated from Africa for the first time in its geologic history, but the severance was incomplete as a fairly wide belt of land remained between Yemen and Ethiopia (the Arabo-Somali massif of Picard, 1939); although there was a marine incursion from the Gulf of Aden in the middle Miocene, the

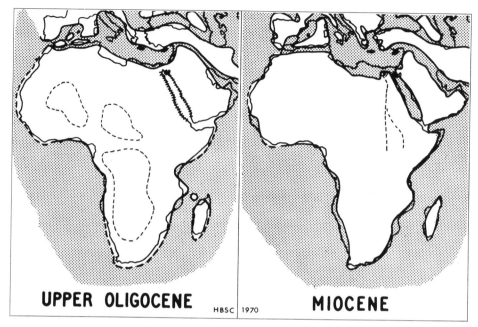

FIGS. 5 and 6. PALEOGEOGRAPHY OF THE UPPER OLIGOCENE AND THE MIOCENE
In Fig. 5 the areas outlined by dashed lines represent inland basins; hachures indi-cate the rifting in the Red Sea area.

land connection was not cut finally until fairly late in the Miocene. It is possible that a tenuous link existed between the Arabian block and Turkey or Iran during some part of the Miocene, but this is speculative.

In the interior of Africa the 25 million years that elapsed between the major Paleocene uplift and that of the late Oligocene were occupied in extensive planation which resulted in the development of the "African" peneplain (or pediplain) which is so prominent a feature of the landscape of the continent (King, 1962). Warping during the late Oligocene emergence of the continent was followed by dissection, so that by lower Miocene times quite considerable relief had been produced in the east African region. Here deposits containing fossil mammals occur, some resting on the erosion surface itself but mostly interbedded within volcanic deposits that overlie it. Because of the existence of these deposits, Shackleton (1951) has referred to the surface as the "sub-Miocene surface."

In the late Miocene uplift again occurred, causing the seas to withdraw from the margins of the continents. Orogenic movements finally closed off the Betic and Rifian troughs, producing a temporary land link; but a new channel soon developed through the Strait of Gibraltar as a result of faulting and warping so that this land connection between Morocco and Spain was of short duration. Uplift closed off the northern end of the Red Sea, creating the narrow isthmus of Suez, and faulting formed the Gulf of Aqaba. At about the same time, the southern end of the

Red Sea broke through the Strait of Bab el Mandeb to connect up with the Indian Ocean. This brought about the virtual isolation of Arabia from Africa, although partial isolation must have resulted from the earlier Miocene rifting. On the other hand, draining of the Tethys-Persian Gulf channel at about the same time led to the development of a continuous land connection between Arabia and India along the southern side of the upfolded Himalayan chain (Kaufman, 1951). It would appear that during the later Miocene Arabia may well have had intermittent links with Asia before there occurred the more drastic geographical changes which isolated it from its parent continent of Africa and linked it firmly to Asia.

Pliocene events are not well known (see p. 110 for definition of terms used here); towards the close of the Pliocene, however, uplift affected most areas and temporary island connections may have been established both across the Strait of Bab el Mandeb and the Strait of Gibraltar. Thereafter, during the Pleistocene, it would seem that the only land connnection between Africa and Eurasia was the narrow and rather inhospitable Isthmus of Suez, whose dimensions varied considerably with fluctuations of sea level; it was even cut through completely at times (Avnimelech, 1962). Post-Miocene uplift, volcanicity and faulting together greatly modified the interior of the continent, producing the relief and form with which we are now familiar.

THE TERTIARY FAUNAS

Although fossil mammals of Tertiary age have been described over a period of almost a century, the whole vast continent of Africa has so far yielded only some three dozen sites of reasonable significance (Fig. 7). The entire Tertiary fauna so far recorded comprises only 150 genera of terrestrial mammals, totalling fewer than 250 species, and it is clear that our knowledge is extremely limited. Very few Eocene fossils are known. All the Oligocene collections have come from the Fayum area of Egypt or elsewhere in north Africa, and a very high proportion of the Miocene specimens have been found in the region around the Kavirondo Gulf of Lake Victoria in east Africa. The Pliocene has been poorly represented until fairly recently, when new discoveries in east Africa have added substantially to the fauna, particularly for the upper Pliocene. The relative ages of the main sites are indicated in Table 1. Figures 15, 16, and 17 show attempted restorations of the main morphological types found in the Oligocene, Miocene, and early Pleistocene of Africa.

Eocene—Oligocene

Fossil bones of the primitive cetacean *Dorudon* were found in the Fayum area in 1879 by Schweinfurth (1886) who gave the first account of the geology of these deposits. Beadnell surveyed the region more thoroughly at the turn of the century and found terrestrial mammals which formed the subject of a series of accounts by Andrews (see Beadnell, 1905; An-

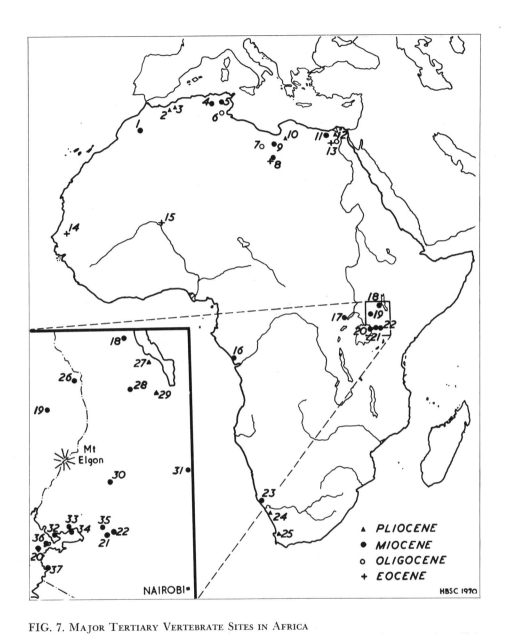

FIG. 7. MAJOR TERTIARY VERTEBRATE SITES IN AFRICA

The inset shows the east African localities on an enlarged scale. 1, Beni Mellal; 2, Wadi el Hammam; 3, Mascara; 4, Kouif; 5, Thala; 6, Gebel Bon Gobrine; 7, Zella; 8, Gebel Coquin and Dor el Talha; 9, Gebel Zelten; 10, Gasr-es-Sahabi; 11, Moghara; 12, Wadi Natrun; 13, Fayum; 14, M'Bodione Dadere; 15, In Tafidet; 16, Malembe; 17, Karugamania; 18, Losodok; 19, Napak; 20, Mfwanganu; 21, Koru; 22, Fort Ternan; 23, Namib; 24, Klein Zee; 25, Langebaanweg; 26, Moroto; 27, Lothagam; 28, Loperot; 29, Kanapoi and Ekora; 30, Tambach; 31, Kirimon; 32, Chianda Uyoma; 33, Ombo; 34, Maboko; 35, Songhor; 36, Rusinga; 37, Karungu.

TABLE 1

Main tertiary fossil mammal sites

	NORTHWEST AFRICA	LIBYA	EGYPT	EAST AFRICA	SOUTHERN AFRICA
PLIOCENE	Fouarat Mascara Wadi-el-Hammam Beni Mellal	Gasr-es-Sahabi	Wadi Natrun	Lower Shungura Kaiso Kanapoi Lothagam	Langebaanweg I Chiwondo Klein Zee
MIOCENE		Gebel Zelten	Wadi Faregh Moghara	Fort Ternan Maboko Kavirondo Gulf region and Napak Karungu, Bukwa	Malembe Namib
OLIGOCENE	Gebel Bon Gobrine	Zella	Gebel Qatrani formation	(no upper Oligocene sites known)	
EOCENE	In Tafidet M'Bodione Dadere	Dor el Talha Gebel Coquin	Qasr el-Sagha formation Birket Qurun formation		

FAYUM SERIES (label spanning the Oligocene–Eocene Egypt column)

drews, 1906). Many scientific expeditions subsequently worked in the area and major additions to the fauna were made by Schlosser (1911), Osborn (1908, 1909) and Simons (1960, 1962; Simons and Wood, 1968). The mammals occur in two series of fluviomarine beds which overlie the entirely marine Birket Qurun formation, which is most probably of Bartonian age. The succeeding Qasr el-Sagha formation comprises fossiliferous marine shales and limestones, which become sandy in the upper portion and then contain fossil remains of marine and terrestrial vertebrates. The marine fauna indicates an upper Bartonian to Ludian (uppermost Eocene) age. The vertebrates include fish and creatures of aquatic habit such as the primitive whales *Dorudon* and *Prozeuglodon,* the early dugong *Eotheroides* and the crocodile *Tomistoma,* but there are also bones and teeth of the oldest known proboscidians, assigned to four species of *Moeritherium* and one of *Barytherium* (B. *grave*). The remains of terrestrial animals, and also the occurrence in these beds of shales crowded with plant debris, suggest that the environment of deposition was an embayed shoreline area fed by a river system which swept terrestrial organisms into the ocean.

Somewhat similar conditions must have prevailed during the deposition of the overlying Gebel Qatrani formation, but the abundant crossbedded variegated sands and sandstones and very subordinate shales, marls and calcareous grits suggest a shift towards an estuarine-deltaic environment. Marine invertebrates are rare but occasional horizons of freshwater mollusks occur and there is very little doubt that the deposits are lower Oligocene in age. Land vertebrates are moderately plentiful in the sandy horizons, occurring in patches of relatively greater concentration and often associated with fossil wood. Remains of snakes, turtles, tortoises, and crocodiles are found, and parts of flightless birds have been recovered. The principal interest centers in the mammals, of which 73 species have been described, assigned to 35 genera, 16 families, and 9 orders.

None of the four Eocene species of *Moeritherium* is present in the Oligocene beds but there is one additional species of this genus, M. *andrewsi; Barytherium grave* persists and there are two further proboscidian genera, *Palaeomastodon* and *Phiomia,* each with four species, making a total of 9 proboscidians in the lower Oligocene, presently assigned to three different families and thus clearly possessing a long evolutionary history. The dominant element in the fauna consists of hyracoids, of which 6 genera and 24 species are recognized (Matsumoto, 1926). The hyracoids are varied in size and character, the largest *(Titanohyrax)* being considerably bigger than a domestic pig and about as large as the contemporary *Moeritherium,* while the smallest *(Saghatherium)* is much the same size as the living *Procavia* or a large domestic cat. The cleavage of the hyracoids into two quite distinct families reflects a long period of evolution and adaptation to different ecological niches and in some forms the suine structure of the skull, jaw musculature, and teeth may indicate a habit somewhat like that of a river-hog. A lengthy history must also lie behind the unique embrithopod *Arsinoitherium,* of which only two species are known. It was an animal outwardly resembling an African rhinoceros but with a pair of large bony horns whose bases extended from behind the nostrils to the top of the braincase. Its affinities are somewhat uncertain but it is most probably related fairly distantly to the hyracoids. It is certainly not a perissodactyl but perhaps occupied an ecological place similar to that of the Asiatic rhinoceroses. The sole insectivore so far described is apparently macroscelidid.

The groups discussed above are uniquely African at this time, but this is less true of the remaining mammal fauna of the Fayum deposits which are more clearly part of the "world fauna." Two genera of bats are present but are of indeterminate family affinities. Eight species of rodents have been described; they have resemblances to the Theridomyidae of Europe but also have characters reminiscent of the hystricomorph "rats" of Africa itself. Simpson (1945) classified them as "cf ? Theridomyidae" and suggested that further research might result in the various genera being divided between two families. Wood (1955, 1968) has suggested placing these peculiar African genera in a new family, the Phiomyidae; this is a very acceptable proposal and there can be little doubt that the Thryonomyidae are related to them.

The primates are of exceptional interest and have been widely discussed since the first one was found in 1908 and three more species added in 1910. More recently four valuable additions have been made by Simons (1962, 1965), bringing the total number of genera to six; there are eight described species and two more await specific designation (Simons and Wood, 1968). Two of the three families comprise only extinct forms and the genera placed in the Pongidae are important in relation to hominoid evolution in the continent. The carnivores are creodonts referable to four genera (9 species), all of which are identified with genera from contemporary or earlier deposits in Europe; there is also an undescribed proviverrid. The artiodactyls include one paleodont cebochoerid referred to the European Eocene genus *Mixtotherium;* the remainder are anthracotheres placed in *Rhagatherium* (1 species) and *Brachyodus* (5 species), which were also contemporary in Europe.

Deposits of Eocene and Oligocene age containing fossil mammals are known at a few other places in Africa, but most of them have furnished insignificant amounts of material. A sequence of marine beds at M'Bodione Dadere in Senegal yielded some tooth fragments which are regarded by Gorodiski and Lavocat (1953) as belonging to a species of *Moeritherium* smaller and more primitive than those of the Fayum; the age is Lutetian-Bartonian. A site at In Tafidet in the Sudan area of the Mali Republic has also furnished remains of *Moeritherium* from continental beds of uncertain age but probably close to the Eocene-Oligocene boundary (Arambourg, Kikoine, and Lavocat, 1951).

A more significant upper Eocene deposit was reported by Arambourg and Magnier (1961) from an area in Libya which they termed Gebel Coquin, the geological setting of which resembles closely the Fayum sequence. The fauna includes fish, crocodiles, snakes and tortoises, as well as remains of *Barytherium* and *Moeritherium*. R. J. G. Savage has undertaken further work in this area, which he designates Dor el Talha, and considers that the succession ranges up into the lower Oligocene (Savage, 1969). He has found remains of the Fayum proboscideans *Palaeomastodon* and *Phiomia,* as well as hyracoids, creodonts, and a suoid. Two hundred miles north of Gebel Coquin (Dor el Talha) is an undoubted Oligocene deposit at Zella, where the stratigraphy is similar to that in the south (Arambourg and Magnier, 1961). Here the assemblage includes at least two of the Fayum proboscideans, the anthracothere *Brachyodus,* the large hyracoid *Megalohyrax,* and other forms not yet described. (Miocene beds occur at Gebel Zelten, 100 miles to the east, and there is a Pliocene deposit still nearer the coast at Gasr-es-Sahabi.)

The only other Oligocene mammal deposit so far described is at Gebel Bon Gobrine in Tunisia (Arambourg and Burollet, 1962), where a conglomeratic and ferruginous layer in a dominantly sandy sequence has furnished silicified wood and some badly preserved remains referred to the Fayum proboscidean *Phiomia osborni* and to a large unidentified anthracothere. It is thus clear that the Fayum type of deposit occurs fairly extensively in the north African region and the occurrence of even the few Eocene proboscidians known in Mali and Senegal testifies to the wide distribution of the basic fauna.

The paleogeographic interpretations point clearly to a substantial land connection between Africa and Eurasia in the Paleocene and there must have been a fairly free interchange which set Africa up with a sample cross-section of the basic "world fauna" of that time. The structural interrelationships known to exist between the sirenians, proboscidians, hyracoids, and embrithopods are reflected in their grouping by Simpson (1945) under the common Superorder Paenungulata. In the Oligocene fauna these four groups make up close to 40 per cent of the total number of genera represented and more than 50 per cent of the recorded species. The degree of specialization reached indicates that the fundamental splitting took place no later than the early Eocene. It is virtually certain that these groups arose in Africa from a common condylarth ancestor which was present in the Paleocene. The considerable diversity of forms also suggests that the conditions were favorable for evolution and adaptation to a variety of ecological environments, particularly in the case of the hyracoids, and that the rapid decline of these creatures after the lower Oligocene resulted from the development (or arrival) of more successful competitors, or of predators. Although the peculiar tubulidentates are not actually represented in the Oligocene fauna, they occur in the Miocene and are by then so specialized that they certainly existed even in the Eocene. It is likely, as Colbert (1941) has suggested, that *Orycteropus* descended from a condylarth stock and it is reasonable to suppose that

its ancestors were part of the population complex of the African Paleocene. It is not necessary that the same stock should have given rise both
to the African paenungulates and to the tubulidentates, but this is not
impossible.

As far as the primates are concerned, prosimians are found in Paleocene
and Eocene deposits in North America and Europe but the oldest known
anthropoid primates are those of the Fayum. There is thus a strong
implication that they originated in Africa from a Paleocene or early
Eocene stock; the ceboid primates of South America are almost certainly
a parallel but largely independent development (Gidley, 1923; Simpson,
1951). (In like manner, the pantodonts, dinocerates and pyrotheres are
only very remotely related to the African paenungulates.) The solitary
insectivore, the bats and the "phiomyid" rodents could well be African
differentiates from Paleocene or early Eocene immigrants, although this
is uncertain. However, the same does *not* appear to be true for the creodonts and anthracotheres, which are closely allied to contemporary forms
in Europe where, in some cases, the earlier ancestral forms are also present.
The purely geological data do not indicate any suitable land link for
population transfer in the late Eocene but it would seem that the barrier
need not have been absolute—what Simpson (1953) describes as a "sweepstakes route"—and may have permitted some very limited chance dispersal. Henson (1951) indicates in his tables that uplift or slight uplift
was fairly general at the end of the Eocene, but the detailed basis for this
view is not presented. The only other alternatives are either that the
supposed generic identity of the African and European forms is wrong
and the respective genera are the result of improbably close convergence,
or that the evolution of these groups was extremely slow and that parallel
development took place during the Eocene.

It is extremely difficult to reconstruct the physical and ecological environments of Africa during the Eocene-Oligocene and little need be
altered in the pioneer study by Moreau (1952). Prolonged denudation
must have graded the surface so that a landscape of little relief rose gently
from sea level, reaching a general elevation in the far interior that was
probably no more than 2,000 to 3,000 feet above sea level (see also Cooke,
1958). Above this surface rose residual remnants of the earlier peneplain,
becoming more common in the interior and passing into dissected highlands in the vicinity of the continental watershed (whose location is
unknown). The highland areas were probably not above 5,000, but this
also is very uncertain.

Moreau considered the possibility that the equator might have been
further north in the Eocene but rightly regarded this as improbable,
suggesting that the mean temperatures were higher and the climate
belts wider then than they now are, but that the general circulation patterns of the atmosphere were not radically different from those of the
present day. This view is amply supported by more recent work (see
Nairn, 1961). Various lines of evidence also indicate that the climatic

conditions in the early Tertiary were rather more equable than is now the case. The general decline in temperatures after the Eocene has been demonstrated by Durham (1950), Emiliani (1961), Dorman and Gill (1959) and others. The Egyptian and Libyan mammal deposits are associated with abundant plant debris and fossil wood which demand the presence of substantial forests. The trees show well-marked annual growth-rings suggestive of sub-tropical rather than tropical conditions and the remains of crocodiles, turtles and snakes add to the impression of a forest environment traversed by numerous streams. The silty to sandy nature of the deposits, however, may be taken to indicate that the rivers drained areas which did not have too heavy a vegetational cover. Such a setting is compatible with the diversified primate population and with the varied hyracoids, proboscidians, and anthracotheres; carnivores may be expected wherever successful predation is possible. It is thus likely that the Eocene-Oligocene mammals so far known from the African fossil record are drawn from a rather limited kind of habitat and that we remain ignorant of the contemporary population of the savanna and more arid areas of the continent.

Miocene

By comparison with the 30 genera and 63 species recorded from the Eocene-Lower Oligocene, the fauna of the African Miocene is relatively well known with 74 genera and more than 100 described species; much new material awaits detailed study.

About 75 per cent of the species come from the valuable deposits of east Africa, whose localities are shown in the inset in Fig. 7. Fossils were first found in Koru in 1909 and a little later at Karungu (Andrews, 1911). The richest site is Rusinga Island in the entrance to the Kavirondo Gulf of Lake Victoria, from which tens of thousands of individual fossils (mostly fragmentary) have been recovered since the locality was found in 1931. A similar fauna exists on the adjoining island of Mfwanganu, but the sites are not quite as rich as those of Rusinga. Not far from Koru is another important site, that of Songhor, and there are many others. The general history of the discoveries in this region was given by Le Gros Clark and Leakey (1951) and the geology has been described by Kent (1942, 1944), Shackleton (1951) and Whitworth (1953, 1961). In Uganda, 200 miles to the north of the Kavirondo Gulf group of sites, is another important area around Napak (Bishop, 1958, 1963), the faunal content of which indicates approximate contemporaneity with that of the Kavirondo Gulf complex. Similar fossils occur on the west side of Lake Albert, at Karugamania (Hooijer, 1963). The age of these faunas has been regarded generally as "Burdigalian" but this is difficult to assess paleontologically since some forms are considered to have the closest affinities with the Lower Oligocene (Savage, in Bishop, 1963)—though this is very unlikely— whereas other forms are considered as late Miocene. Much of the uncer-

tainty undoubtedly arises from failure to take into account the autochthonous nature of many of the elements in the faunas, which are thus
not necessarily contemporary with "exports" elsewhere. It is highly probable that they are not all contemporary and a lower to mid-Miocene
age is most likely. Precision in dating must await better radiometric age
determinations from the lavas with which the fossil-bearing deposits are
associated. Evernden, Savage, Curtis, and James (1964) give measurements for Rusinga with so wide a range as to be meaningless, although
with probable limits between 15.3×10^6 and 22.2×10^6 years. Van Couvering and Miller (1969) bracket the main fossiliferous beds between an
underlying date of 19.6×10^6 years and overlying beds of 16.5×10^6
years; from rates of deposition they estimate that the fossils have an age
close to 18 million years. Bishop, Miller and Fitch (1969) find the oldest
deposits to be at Karungu, dated at 22.2×10^6 years, while Songhor, Koru,
Napak and Rusinga range from 20 to 18×10^6 years. This would place
the early faunas near the upper limit of the Aquitanian, with the majority
as probably Burdigalian, but some perhaps ranging into the early Vindo-
bonian.

The stratigraphy of the deposits is complex and variable, including
grits and conglomerates, coarse and fine pyroclastic materials (both terrestrial and water-laid) and fine argillaceous and arenaceous sediments.
Volcanic lava normally caps the sedimentary sequence at Rusinga but at
some sites lava occurs below the sediments as well. In general the deposits
lie on or near the sub-Miocene erosion surface and date to a fairly early
stage in the vulcanicity of the east African region. Whitworth (1953)
established that the Mfwanganu rocks formed part of the base of a volcanic cone thrown up around the eruptive center of Rangwa, whose
original volcano has been removed almost completely by subsequent erosion. Rusinga and Karungu apparently lie also within the old Rangwa
cone area. Bishop (1963) has demonstrated a similar relationship for his
fossil sites around the Napak center, 200 miles to the north, and suggests
(1963) that Songhor and Koru are correspondingly related to the Tinderet
volcanic center; the Moroto site, 50 miles northeast of Napak seems to
have had a similar origin. The sites at Losodok, near Lake Rudolph, are
interbedded in lavas that were probably on the flanks of a large volcano
on the site of the present mountain of that name (Arambourg, 1943).
With the exception of Rusinga, and perhaps also of Mfwanganu, the
deposits are not essentially lacustrine and represent chance traps within
an eruptive sequence. Bishop rightly emphasizes that such settings are
particularly favorable for the preservation of fossil material, especially
if the lavas are calcic ones.

The composition of the "Burdigalian" mammal faunas of east Africa is
varied and includes representatives of eleven out of the twelve orders
now living on the continent, only the rare Pholidota being absent. The
Oligocene Embrithopoda do not occur but the Tubulidentata, Lagomorpha, and Perissodactyla make their first appearance in the African

fossil record. The lagomorphs are apparently Ochotonidae, with Eurasiatic affinities. The perissodactyls are rhinoceroses and chalicotheres, but there are no equines. The proboscidians, hyracoids, hyaenodonts and anthracotheres follow naturally from the Oligocene fauna but are diminished in specific variety. Four artiodactyl families are added. The carnivores include an arctocyonid and a teratodontid, as well as a number of creodonts and proviverrids; however, there is also a fissiped canid, a felid referred to the European genus *Metailurus,* and an herpestine viverrid (Savage, 1965, 1967). The varied insectivores include the earliest known chrysochlorid (Butler, 1969), and there are three genera of Tenrecidae (Butler and Hopwood, 1957), a group whose living representatives are almost wholly confined to Madagascar. The rodents include "phiomyids," apparently descended from the Fayum types, but there are also characteristically African Anomaluridae, Pedetidae, and Bathyergidae, as well as undescribed forms. The primates are again of outstanding interest, including several genera of Lorisidae and at least four genera (with seven or more species) of Pongidae; few cercopithecoids have yet been described but they are known to occur.

Other lower Miocene deposits in Africa have furnished small collections but these include some elements not reported in the east African material. In Egypt there are beds of fluviomarine and deltaic character which were laid down under conditions rather like those of the Oligocene; two areas, Moghara oasis and the Wadi Faregh, have provided fossil mammals. From Moghara there is a primate, *Prohylobates tandyi,* long thought to be an ape but recently shown by Simons (1969b) to be a monkey, possibly with colubine affinities. The artiodactyls are anthracotheres referred to two species of *Brachyodus* and to a unique genus *Masritherium.* Perissodactyls are represented by *Brachypotherium* and *Aceratherium,* both Eurasiatic genera. The proboscideans are all referred to two species of *Gomphotherium,* but it is worth recording that the British Museum collections from Moghara include undescribed remains of *Deinotherium,* a genus well represented in east Africa, and it is possible that the species from the two regions may be identical. A carnivore originally regarded by Fourtau (1920) as a hyena has been described by von Koenigswald (1948) as *Hyainailouros fourtaui* and is considered to be a felid of African origin. In Libya the site of Gebel Zelten (Arambourg and Magnier, 1961; Savage and White, 1965) is geologically similar to the Moghara occurrence and has a similar fauna, but the elephant remains are slightly more primitive. Of particular interest is a sivatherine *Prolibytherium* (Arambourg, 1961b) which is the oldest known member of the group. Also new are a large canid, *Afrocyon,* and a suid, *Libycochoerus,* which is more primitive than the Indian genera (Arambourg, 1961a). This site has also produced remains of crocodiles, tortoises, and a giant flightless bird.

Near the southern end of the continent, in the Namib desert area of South-West Africa, fluviolacustrine and continental beds occur which have provided a limited fauna described by Stromer (1926) and Hopwood (1929). Rodents are conspicuous and four genera appear to belong to the peculiar "phiomyids" while two are thryonomyids, one a pedetid "jumping hare" and one a bathyergid. Two species of ochotonid lagomorphs are referred to a genus *Australolagomys,* which is in some respects more primitive than *Kenyalagomys* of east Africa. The insectivores are represented by a macroscelidid probably identical with the east African *Myohyrax oswaldi.* There are no primates recorded, nor are perissodactyls or proboscidians known. Three hyracoids occur, but their relationship to the east African species is uncertain. Two undoubted Bovidae are present and there is a suid, *Diamantohyus,* which resembles some of the later Eurasiatic types. There is only one carnivore, *Metapterodon,* which is an advanced hyaenodont.

At Malembe, just north of the mouth of the Congo river, supposedly Burdigalian marine beds, rich in fish remains, include some terrestrial vertebrate fragments (Dartevelle, 1952; Hooijer, 1963). There are several minor occurrences in the Atlas region, from Morocco to Tunisia, one of the most important of which is a deposit near Beni Mellal in Morocco (Lavocat, 1952) which is described as late Miocene but is more probably early Pliocene. The fauna consists dominantly of rodents but there are also insectivores, bats, and fragments of a ruminant. Some of the remains are identified as belonging to a species of *Cricetodon* closely allied to *C. ibericum* from the upper Miocene of Spain; the other rodents include a new genus, *Myocricetodon,* considered to be derived from *Cricetodon,* but with murid features. In a subsequent account Lavocat (1959) discussed the bearing of these discoveries on the evolution of African murids.

The upper Miocene is not widely known in Africa, only two localities in east Africa being assigned to this period—Maboko island in the eastern part of the Kavirondo Gulf, and Fort Ternan on the mainland, some distance east of the Gulf. Maboko has furnished a mastodont which is regarded as intermediate in character between the lower Miocene trilophodonts and the Plio-Pleistocene *Anancus* of east Africa (Arambourg, 1946). Also present are a cercopithecoid *Victoriapithecus,* and an oreopithecid *Mabokopithecus* (von Koenigswald, 1969), as well as an antlered creature, *Climacoceras,* which MacInnes (1936) described as a cervid but which is more likely a lagomerycid. Fort Ternan yielded an important hominoid primate, *Kenyapithecus wickeri* (L. S. B. Leakey, 1962, 1963), which Simons (1963, 1969a) believes to be inseparable from the early Pliocene *Ramapithecus* of the Indian Siwaliks. There is also an undescribed oreopithecid, as well as pongids belonging to the European genus *Pliopithecus* and the Indian *Dryopithecus* (see Simons, 1969a). The perissodactyls are represented by a rhinoceros placed by Hooijer (1968) in a new genus *Paradiceros.* Remains of small mammals occur and include phyomyids and sciurids, but only a cricetid, *Leakymys* has been described (Lavocat, 1964). There are several carnivores, a few suids and a hippopotamus-like animal that does not seem to be an actual anthracothere. An antler might represent *Climacoceras,* but there is another antler that was not deciduous and represents an unknown form. There are two large giraffids, referred by Churcher (1970) to *Palaeotragus* and *Samotherium,* but there is also a smaller giraffid which might be ancestral to the modern *Giraffa.* A tragulid is present, perhaps *Dorcatherium,* and there are various Bovidae which are discussed fully by Gentry (1970). One abundant species is referred to the Eurasiatic boselaphine genus *Protragocerus* and another plentiful form is placed in the caprine genus *Oioceros,* known from Mongolia, Yugoslavia and the Greek islands; an unnamed species of *Gazella* is also present and there are remains of a form resembling a Siwalik bovid of uncertain affinities. The fauna as a whole is rather remarkably different from that of the Kavirondo Gulf deposits, favoring a substantial time interval between the two. Simpson (1965) suggested that the age is either earliest Pliocene or final Miocene, but the bulk of the evidence seems to favor the latter. The fossil-bearing sediments at Fort Ternan are stratified volcanic tuffs a few feet thick lying within a somewhat thicker pyroclastic sequence which is sandwiched between lava flows (Bishop and Whyte, 1962). Potassium-argon dating of a tuff just below the fossil-bearing horizons gave an age of 14.0×10^6 years (Bishop, Miller and Fitch, 1969), giving an age difference of 4 to 6 million years between Fort Ternan and the other deposits of the Kavirondo Gulf region. If the chronology of Evernden, Savage, Curtis and James (1964) is employed, the Pliocene/Miocene boundary lies at about 12 million years, placing Fort Ternan in the upper Miocene.

As far as the Miocene climate is concerned, it would seem that world temperatures were a little lower than in the Eocene-Oligocene, although still rather higher than at the present day. The planation of the "African" bevel was brought to an end by uplift and some slight warping at the end of the Oligocene, followed by erosion, and the lower Miocene deposits are younger than the "African" surface. The general topographic picture is thus similar to that of the Eocene-Oligocene but rift faulting had begun in north Africa-Arabia and volcanic activity commenced in the east African region. Little can be inferred regarding the environment in the north African region or that of South-West Africa but it is clear that if desert conditions were present, they were not nearly as severe as at the present day.

The east African deposits in the Kavirondo Gulf have furnished a substantial flora, including a large number of fruits and seeds, thorny wood and some leaf fragments. Although the study of the material is incomplete, Chesters (1957) has demonstrated the close resemblance of the flora to that of the tropical part of Africa at the present time. About half of the forms identified are climbers and the remainder are trees of varying size, some of them immense. This proportion is not typical of dense rain forests but is characteristic of damp well-illuminated places such as clearings, the edges of forests, or river banks. Taken in conjunction with the presence in the fauna of savanna elements, this has been regarded as indicative of gallery forests on the fringe of open areas; this type of setting is very common in west Africa today. A small collection of plants from the Bugishu series at Busoba near Mount Elgon in Uganda (see Fig. 7) is of approximately similar age and is inferred by Chaney (1933) to represent a savanna or woodland assemblage like that of central Africa today. It would thus appear that the broad vegetational environment in the Miocene of east Africa was basically similar to that of the present day in the same region. It is very probable that the end-Oligocene elevation of the interior, coupled with a decline in general temperatures, led to more distinct climatic contrast and zonation than in earlier times and thus to some extension of the savanna environment. Such circumstances would favor the expansion of the ungulate fauna and would extend the "forest fringe" environment to which certain African animals are particularly partial.

Whitworth (1958) has remarked upon the difference between the faunal assemblages from various parts of Rusinga and Songhor and suggested that there were synchronous differences in the environment. Bishop (1963) has put forward well-founded arguments for recognizing fully lacustrine, ponded and sub-aerial conditions of deposition. He also suggests that the volcanoes (which are so clearly related to the preserved sites) must have possessed vertical zonation of the vegetation on their cones and were probably clad with dense forests on the upper slopes, even if the plains areas were largely savanna. The influence exerted by the alkaline volcanic products in aiding preservation of the fossils is obvious but Bishop (1963) also points out the possible biological importance of the carbonatitic centers in providing calcium salts and trace elements to the fauna.

A good part of the Miocene fauna is clearly derived from the lower Oligocene and earlier stock, but there are also new elements of uncertain derivation. Among the insectivores the Chrysochloridae and Tenrecidae must surely be of African origin, and so also most probably are the Macroscelididae. The crocidurine Soricidae and Erinaceidae almost certainly came into Africa from Europe at the end of the Oligocene (Butler, 1949), and the tenrecids probably entered Madagascar from Africa at about that time. Bats occur in the east African Miocene (Butler, 1969) but there is no reason to suppose that they are African by derivation. The primates are certainly African in origin, having diverged from the Paleocene prosimian stock; lorisids and various pongids, some of which have hominid features, are important new elements. It is logical to suggest that pongids were exported to Eurasia at the end of the Oligocene and there developed into the diversified Asiatic complex that paralleled their Ethiopian cousins. The cercopithecoids were apparently more conservative and did not leave Africa for Asia and Europe until the latter part of the Miocene. The origin and movements of the lorisids are uncertain.

For the lagomorphs and rodents events are much more speculative. The Miocene ochotonids must have come from Europe at the end of the

Oligocene and did not survive the period. The "phiomyid" rodents are clearly autochthonous and although there are no known post-Miocene descendants, it is highly probable that the Thryonomyidae and Petromuridae are derived from the same stock. The Pedetidae must be of African origin, as also most probably are the Bathyergidae. No fossil Hystricidae are known in the Miocene at present and their origin is obscure. Thryonomyids were exported to Eurasia at the end of the period. The position of the Cricetidae is problematical but if Lavocat's (1959) assessment is correct they entered Africa from Europe at the end of the Oligocene, when some forms reached Madagascar, then evolved in Africa and entered Asia at the end of the Miocene. Lavocat's separation of the Dendromurinae from the Murinae would accord with an African derivation from a local cricetid stock. A ctenodactylid is known from Beni Mellal and probably came from Asia in the late Miocene. Other rodents are presumably subsequent immigrants into Africa.

Among the larger animals, new elements which seem to have originated outside Africa include the Perissodactyla (chalicotheres and rhinoceroses) and a few fissiped carnivores closely allied to European canids and felids. The suggestion by von Koenigswald (1948) that *Hyainailouros fourtaui* from Moghara is a felid of African origin and the recognition by Arambourg (1961a) of a peculiar new genus of canid, *Afrocyon,* from Libya, could be taken to indicate a substantial period of African differentiation before Miocene time. It is likely that an important unspecialized viverrid arrived in time to reach Madagascar in the late Oligocene, and this stock also gave rise in Africa to the varied indigenous forms which abound at the present day, but have so poor a fossil record.

In addition to the anthracotheres, great interest attaches to the other artiodactyls, for the African Miocene includes ruminants which are difficult to separate into their components. Whitworth (1958) refers material to *Palaeomeryx* and regards it as a cervoid and not a giraffoid; *Climacoceras* from the same deposit, which MacInnes (1936) considered cervoid, is placed by Simpson (1945) and by Arambourg (1961a) as a lagomerycid giraffoid; other contemporary remains are more clearly bovoid. On the other hand *Prolibytherium* from Libya (Arambourg, 1961b) is undoubtedly a giraffoid and seems to represent the early branching off of the sivatherines. The most likely explanation seems to be that Africa acquired in the later Oligocene a basic traguloid-pecoran stock from which there developed in Africa both the giraffids and the bovids. The chevrotain occurs in the African Miocene, earlier than it is recorded in Asia, but it is an open question whether it is of African or Asiatic origin. Cervids are alleged to occur in limited numbers in the Miocene, but have not been described; if this is so, then they must have entered Africa with the basic stock but failed in competition with the Bovidae and Giraffidae. It is most unlikely that the Bovidae are directly related to the Antilocapridae of the new world, which probably arose independently from a similar basic pecoran stock. This would imply that giraffids and bovids are essentially of African origin and that the cervids and antilocaprids are parallel developments outside Africa from a common stock of late Oligocene age. The Eurasiatic resemblances manifested by the Fort Ternan bovids are undeniable, and Gentry (1970) has presented an excellent analysis of the situation. There is a distinct dichotomy between Eurasian and African bovids, but the Fort Ternan fauna seems to belong to a period shortly before the typically African forms had begun to diversify and the dichotomy was incipient rather than already achieved. During the later Pliocene and early Pleistocene, some African bovids did exist in the Siwalik region, but this does not imply that they evolved there. However, it does seem probable that there was some faunal interchange between Africa and Eurasia shortly before the time of the Fort Ternan fauna and, until absolute age determinations are available from the Siwaliks or elsewhere in Eurasia, it is difficult to determine where some of the groups may have originated.

At least four genera of Suidae have been found in the Miocene of Africa and some of them are allied to near-contemporary European forms. There is thus an implication that the Suidae entered Africa from Europe at the end of the Oligocene, although this is by no means certain. The known fossil Suidae of Asia are not as old as those of Africa, although some are structurally related to them, and it is possible that such Asiatic forms were derived secondarily from the African types rather than directly from those of Europe. *Bunolistriodon* from Zelten (Arambourg 1961a, 1963) has affinities both with the tetraconodont and with the suine forms of India and could well be a surviving part of the parent stock from which the Indian forms developed. *Nyanzachoerus* of the African Pliocene may be a direct descendant from this stock.

Pliocene

Much recent controversy centers around the Miocene/Pliocene boundary and a good case can be made for placing it about 5 m.y. ago in the marine sequence. Pending resolution of this problem, the author here follows the more "traditional" boundary drawn by the first appearance of *Hipparion* in Europe 12 m.y. ago—the base of the so-called "Pontian."

Although a number of new Pliocene localities have been found recently in east Africa, our knowledge of the faunas is still poor, especially for the earlier part of the period. In 1963 there were recorded only 29 genera and 36 species (many of which were not named because the material was so inadequate); subsequent finds may have doubled these numbers, but most of the new material is still undescribed and only preliminary lists are available.

A number of localities occur in the Atlas region of Morocco and Algeria and some of them were recorded before the beginning of the present century. The occurrence of one or both of two species of *Hipparion* suggests affinities with the typical "Pontian" fauna of Europe. With *Hipparion* are found anthracotheres (cf. *Merycopotamus*), a *Diceros*-like rhinoceros, hyenas, giraffids and bovids. A controversial site is that of Wadi-el-Hammam, south-east of Oran in Algeria. Arambourg (1951, 1954a) has described the deposit as upper Miocene, although it contains a typically Pontian mammal fauna; this is undoubtedly due to differences in usage in France, where the Pontian is often regarded as final Miocene. The mammal bed is intercalated between two marine horizons, the upper one of which carries marine fossils which are generally considered to be Tortonian, and it is on this that Arambourg bases his reference of age. Mongin (1954), however, regards the Sarmatian and Pontian as respectively lagoonal and terrestrial facies of the marine Tortonian in this region and so the age is somewhat in doubt. Furthermore, Tobian (1956) has suggested that the arrival of the "Pontian" *Hipparion* fauna at various points in Europe does not coincide with the apparent base of the Pliocene derived from other criteria. The Wadi-el-Hammam fauna is thus most probably early Pliocene and contains the customary associations but, interestingly, it includes remains of *Orycteropus* not separable from *O. gaudryi* from Samos—indeed the resemblance of the whole fauna to the Greek assemblages is striking. Although *Hipparion* may continue into the lower Pleistocene, a distinctly different hipparionid, *Stylohipparion*, is more characteristic in the Pleistocene and is also found in the Pliocene at Lothagam in east Africa.

The Wadi Natrun in Egypt has furnished scanty fossil remains from a fairly thin fluviomarine sequence of middle to upper Pliocene age. These include a cercopithecid, *Libypithecus*, the oldest African mustelid carnivores, a machairodont felid and a suid referred to the typically Indian *Sivachoerus* (Tobien, 1936), although it more probably belongs to the African genus *Nyanzachoerus*. *Hippopotamus* is recorded and remains of *Hipparion* occur but are apparently undescribed. Other sites in Egypt have also furnished some fossils, the most important of which is the mastodont *Anancus osiris* from the Mena House near Cairo (Arambourg, 1946). In Libya a deposit at Gasr-es-Sahabi has yielded a moderate fauna which may be similar in age to that of the Wadi Natrun. Two species of *Sivachoerus* were described by Leonardi (1952), one of which is very similar to the Wadi Natrun skull and the other close to an undescribed species of *Nyanzachoerus* from Lothagam in east Africa. Also close to a Lothagam form is a gomphothere-like elephant *Stegotetrabelodon* (Petrocchi, 1943) which Maglio (1970a) places as close to the stem of the true Elephantinae. Other remains from Sahabi include mastodonts, dinotheres, rhinoceros, equines, anthracotheres, hippopotamus, bovids and carnivores, but they have not been described.

In east Africa, largely as a result of intensified search for hominid fossils, deposits of Plio-Pleistocene age have been studied and new deposits of middle to upper Pliocene age have been found. A number of the sequences contain volcanic horizons that can be dated by potassium-argon techniques, thus facilitating correlation. Unfortunately, there is as yet no internationally agreed boundary between the Pliocene and the

Pleistocene so that the proper terminology for the east African deposits is open to question. The Villafranchian stage in Europe has been placed by some authorities wholly in the Pleistocene and by others wholly in the Pliocene. The most probable situation is that it lies astride the boundary and it seems best to follow Azzaroli (1970), who places the Lower Villafranchian in the Pliocene, with its top at 2.7 million years (and its base at about 3.5 m.y.). As it is relatively easy to identify this date in the east African sequences, the Plio-Pleistocene boundary used in the following discussions will be taken as close to 2.7 million years.

The most important of the new east African deposits is that at Lotha- gam, on the west side of Lake Rudolf, where two mammal-bearing units (1 and 3) are separated by barren lacustrine clays (2). Two other deposits in the same region, at Kanapoi and Ekora, are faunistically equated with Lothagam-3 (Patterson, Behrensmeyer and Sill, 1970). The older fauna of Lothagam-1 is estimated to have an age of about 5 to 6 million years, and the younger (Kanapoi) fauna of 4.0 to 4.3 million years (Cooke and Maglio, 1971). The Lothagam-1 fauna includes an australopithecine— the oldest so far known—an anomalurid, carnivores, an orycteropodid, the three-toed *Stylohipparion*, a rhinoceros, *Brachypotherium*, two species of hexaprotodont *Hippopotamus*, *Giraffa*, and a number of Bovidae. Most of the latter are typically African, but a few specimens are reminiscent of some of the Fort Ternan forms. The dominant suid is *Nyanzachoerus*, of which there are two typical species allied to those from Sahabi and the Wadi Natrun. The elephants include a *Deinother- ium*, a *Stegotetrabelodon* (*S. orbus*) and the most primitive true elephant so far known, *Primelephas gomphotheroides* (Maglio, 1970b). The Kana- poi fauna also includes an australopithecine, as well as a cercopithecoid, *Parapapio*, previously known only from the cave breccias of South Africa. Rodents are present but so far only a *Hystrix, Lepus,* and the earliest known *Tatera* have been identified. One of the carnivores seems to represent the European mustelid *Enhydriodon*. *Stylohipparion* is accom- panied by an early *Ceratotherium*-like rhinoceros. Another species of hexaprotodont *Hippopotamus* occurs, together with a third new species of *Nyanzachoerus*, and two species of the large extinct suid *Notochoerus*. *Deinotherium bozasi* accompanies the earliest representative of the *Loxodonta* lineage (*L. adaurora*) and the earliest *Elephas* (*E. ekorensis*). The bovids resemble those of the Villafranchian. Elements of this "Kana- poi" fauna are found in the Mursi Formation of the Omo area in southern Ethiopia (Howell, Fichter and Eck, 1969), in the Chemeron Formation, west of Lake Baringo, and in the lower part of the Kaiso Formation in Uganda (Cooke and Coryndon, 1970). The lower part of the Shungura Formation of the Omo area (and the Usno Formation of the same region) is younger than the Mursi Formation and the Kanapoi; it would fall within the Lower Villafranchian (=Upper Pliocene) of Azzaroli's defini- tion. There is a characteristic elephant, *Elephas recki*, represented by an early evolutionary stage in its lineage, which extends right through to the upper Pleistocene. It will be convenient to discuss the Shungura fauna with the Pleistocene, below.

In southern Africa there are no radiometric dates and the exact ages of the deposits are uncertain. In Malawi the Chiwondo Beds have furnished a fauna of Plio-Pleistocene character (Clark, Stephens and Coryndon, 1966) that includes remains of cercopithecoids, proboscideans, *Stylohipparion*, *Hippopotamus*, suids, a small giraffe and several bovids. One of the suids from the lower part of the sequence is the same species of *Nyanzachoerus* as one from Kanapoi, and there is also a *Notochoerus*. The proboscideans include a primitive *Mammuthus*, an early *Elephas*, and an early *Loxodonta* (Maglio, 1970a), all of which suggest an age close to that of the Kanapoi beds, although perhaps a little younger. Perhaps of roughly similar age is a deposit at Langebaanweg, in the south-western Cape, where the lowest strata (Langebaanweg I) have yielded a fauna that includes a chrysochlorid, viverrids, an hyena, a gomphothere, a primitive *Mammuthus*, rhinoceros, *Hipparion*, a suid which may be a *Nyanzachoerus*, the giraffid *Libytherium*, bovids, a leporid and several murids; there is also the first recorded Plio-Pleistocene ursid from Africa (Hendey, 1970). The upper part of the deposit seems to be considerably younger, perhaps Middle Pleistocene. Of uncertain age, but almost certainly upper Pliocene, is a small assemblage from Klein Zee, near the coast a short distance south of the mouth of the Orange River (Stromer, 1932). The collection included the first African Pliocene insectivore to be recorded (a macrosceledid), a mustelid referred to *Enhydriodon*, two viverrids, an hyena, and undetermined remains of rodents and bovids.

As far as the Pliocene environment is concerned, much remains to be learned. Uplift at the beginning of the Miocene initiated the marginal dissection of the extraordinarily perfect "African" peneplain, but the uplift continued during the Pliocene. At the same time, extensive volcanic activity built very high conical mountains in east Africa and Ethiopia, greatly modifying the topography and general relief of this region, with consequent effects also on the climate. Some portions of the continent had not risen as rapidly as others so that a broad "basin and swell" structure had developed, the most important of which is the Kalahari basin. This extensive shallow warp was filled during the Eocene-Oligocene with a few hundred feet of coarse debris, calcareous muds and chemical limestones, until the hollow was built up to accord with the "African" surface. In the Miocene or early Pliocene, minor warping resulted in renewed accumulation in this basin of moderate thicknesses of sandy sediment. These were deposited sub-aerially by water and wind under conditions of strong seasonal variation, yet not completely desertic. Similar conditions apparently prevailed across the Saharan belt and one may infer that the rather equable climate of the early Tertiary gave way in Pliocene times to one of increased seasonality and greater zonal variation from place to place.

Towards the end of the Pliocene widespread uplift occurred in eastern and southern Africa, elevating the interior generally by 2,000 to 4,000 feet. Maximum uplift was not in the interior but along a belt roughly parallel to the coast and about 200 miles inland; along this belt uplift was sometimes as much as 6,000 feet (King, 1962). The margins of the continents were thus tilted sharply seawards and a new cycle of erosion began to cut deep gorges back into the interior. In east Africa rift faulting was active and considerable tectonic changes modified the relief, the most striking example being the elevation of the non-volcanic Ruwenzori massif to a peak height of almost 17,000 feet—about 12,500 feet above the general level of the surrounding countryside! These movements continued into the Pleistocene but on a very much reduced scale. The effects of such profound topographic changes upon the climate and the vegetation must have been considerable but cannot be evaluated at the present state of our knowledge.

As the new Pliocene material is studied, much light should be thrown on mammal evolution in the continent, bridging the gap between the unfamiliar-looking animals of the Miocene fauna and the familiar aspect of the present-day African assemblage. The Pliocene fauna consists almost entirely of extinct genera, but the genera do represent similar kinds of animals to those of the present and the ecological associations are much alike. Compared with the Miocene, the Pliocene fauna differs through the extinction of the anthracotheres, and the flourishing and expanding of the ungulates. New elements which make their first African appearance include leporids, the sciurid rodents, mustelid carnivores, hyenas, hipparionid equines, and hippopotamus. The latter belong to the hexaprotodont division of the hippopotami, previously known only in the Upper Pliocene of Asia, where they are probably later than they appear in Africa and they may have originated in Africa itself. The Pliocene Suidae are peculiar forms which did not survive far into the Pleistocene and their derivation is uncertain as the Miocene suids have not yet been described. The Giraffidae and Bovidae are well represented and are essentially African in character, although there may still be elements with Asiatic resemblances like those of the upper Miocene. The proboscideans, which already had a long African history, evolved the earliest true Elephantidae. These diversified, with astonishing rapidity, to produce the ancestors of the living and fossil elephants of Eurasia, as well as the indigenous African elephant. Both *Elephas* and *Mammuthus* were exported late in the Pliocene.

THE PLEISTOCENE FAUNA

Whereas fewer than one hundred species of fossil mammals are known from the Pliocene of Africa, several hundred have been described from the Pleistocene, some 250 of which certainly represent extinct forms. It is only for the later Pleistocene that sites are numerous, however, and barely two dozen localities have yielded significant collections of fossil

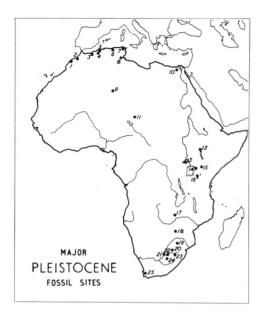

FIG. 8. Major Pleistocene Vertebrate Sites in Africa

1, Sidi Abderrahman; 2, Fouarat; 3, Lac Karar; 4, Ternifine; 5, Bel Hacel; 6, St. Arnaud; 7, Lac Ichkeul; 8, Ain Brimba; 9, Tihoudaine; 10, Wadi Natrun; 11, Koro Toro (Yayo); 12, Omo; 13, Kaiso; 14, Kanam, Rawi, Kanjera; 15, Nakuru-Naivasha Basin; 16, Laetolil, Olduvai; 17, Broken Hill; 18, Chelmer; 19, Makapansgat; 20, Sterkfontein area; 21, Taung; 22, Vaal River gravels; 23, Cornelia; 24, Florisbad, Vlakkraal; 25, Hopefield, Langebaanweg.

mammals of lower and middle Pleistocene age; the more important of these are shown in Fig. 8. With some exceptions, these sites occur in three main areas, the northwest African coastal belt known to the Arabs as the Maghreb, the upland region of east Africa, and the interior plateau of South Africa. The fossil faunas as a whole were reviewed not long ago by this author (Cooke, 1963) and, accordingly, it does not seem necessary to do more here than summarize a few of the most important points. New data are also included and the correlation has been modified slightly (Table 2).

The Pleistocene mammals are so much African in character that it is difficult to compare them adequately with the European forms for correlation and dating. The occurrence of volcanic intercalations in many of the east African sequences, however, does make it possible to relate the faunas to an absolute time scale. Although the paucity of absolute age determinations in the European Pliocene and Pleistocene is still a severe handicap in permitting firm correlations, it is possible to place the African materials within the broad divisions of the Villafranchian proposed by Azzaroli (1970). The *Lower Villafranchian* is late Pliocene and covers a time span from about 3.5 million years to the Pliocene-Pleistocene boundary at 2.7 m.y. The *Middle Villafranchian* is of short duration (perhaps 2.7 to 2.4 m.y.) and the *Upper Villafranchian* has its top boundary at approximately 1.3 m.y. Azzaroli recognizes two divisions in the Upper Villafranchian, designated "a" and "b." In Europe the Upper Villafranchian is followed by the Cromerian. However, in the absence of absolute age data at most of the African localities, the use of the term Villafranchian in this continent is not entirely desirable and it should be replaced

TABLE 2

Tentative correlation of Plio-Pleistocene and Pleistocene deposits in Africa

SOUTH AFRICA Faunal Unit	SOUTH AFRICA Deposit	EAST AFRICA	NORTH AFRICA	Possible Age
'Recent'	Cave and surface sites without extinct faunas	Cave and surface sites without extinct faunas	Cave and surface sites without extinct faunas	'Recent'
FLORISBAD-VLAKKRAAL FAUNAL SPAN	Vlakkraal and other deposits / Florisbad and Chelmer / Cave of Hearths	'Later Gamblian' beds and Eyasi beds / 'Early Gamblian' beds	Deposits with Micoquian and Aterian cultures	'Upper Pleistocene'
	Hopefield	Olduvai Bed IV +	Sidi Abderrahman	'Middle to Upper Pleistocene'
VAAL CORNELIA FAUNAL SPAN	Cornelia	Olduvai Beds III to IV / Semliki Beds	Lac Karar etc / Yayo (Chad)	
	'Younger Gravels' of Vaal river / Langebaanweg II	Olduvai Beds II to III	Ternifine	'Middle Pleistocene'
		Peninj Beds		
		Olduvai Bed II (lower)		
SWARTKRANS FAUNAL SPAN	Kromdraai / Swartkrans / Sterkfontein extension	Olduvai Bed I	Bel Hacel / Ain Hanech	'Upper Villafranchian'
STERKFONTEIN FAUNAL SPAN	Sterkfontein / Taung / Makapansgat	Upper Shungura	Ouadi Derdemi, Koula / Lac Ichkeul / Ain Brimba	'Middle or Lower Villafranchian'
	Langebaanweg I	Upper Kaiso / Lower Shungura	Ain Boucherit / Fouarat	'Lower Villafranchian'

by a term of African definition. In the meantime, it is used in quotation marks in this article to indicate its tentative equivalence.

Because some of the north African localities are close to the Mediterranean, there are places where it has been possible to relate continental mammal-bearing deposits with marine beds or with raised beaches that can be correlated with strand lines of the European coast. The most important is Fouarat on the Atlantic coast of Morocco, where a marine deposit with a Pliocene fauna is overlain by one with an Astian/Calabrian marine assemblage, but including vertebrates as well. If Azzaroli (1970) is correct in equating the Calabrian with his Middle Villafranchian fauna, then the Fouarat fossils must be of an age close to the Pliocene-Pleistocene boundary. The assemblage includes a mastodon, *Anancus osiris,* and the very primitive elephant *Mammuthus africanavus,* which is regarded by Arambourg as a reliable indicator for the "Lower Villafranchian" in Africa. This association parallels the occurrence of *Anancus arvernensis* with a very early *Mammuthus* (pre-*meridionalis* in character) in the Lower Villafranchian of Europe and it seems proper to place Fouarat just below the Pliocene-Pleistocene boundary. Elsewhere in north Africa, *M. africanavus* is replaced by an elephant close to the *M. meridionalis* of the Upper Villafranchian "a" division. Present in both the "Lower" and the "Upper Villafranchian" of North Africa, but particularly in the latter, are the African hipparionid *Stylohipparion,* the large sivatherine *Libytherium,* typical African suids, and various extinct ungulates and carnivores; machairodonts persist in the "Upper Villafranchian." Pebble tools occur in the "Upper," but not in the "Lower Villafranchian."

The middle Pleistocene in north Africa lacks the archaic proboscideans and the characteristic form is *Elephas atlanticus (Loxodonta atlantica).* The ungulate fauna differs substantially from that of the "Villafranchian" but includes a high proportion of extinct species and has an aspect rather more like that of southern Africa than of equatorial or north Africa. Hand ax tools occur widely and at Ternifine, near Casablanca, Arambourg (1954b) found remains of a human mandible described as *"Atlanthropus mauritanicus"*; it is of pithecanthropine type and may be regarded as a variety of *Homo erectus.*

In the Sahara are several important sites, of which the most significant are in the Lake Chad region. In the area near Koro Toro, a broadly "Villafranchian" fauna was reported (Abadie, Barbeau and Coppens, 1959; Coppens, 1960), and elements of "Lower" or "Middle Villafranchian" character have been found at Ouadi Derdemi and Kouala (Coppens, 1967). The nearby site of Yayo furnished a partial skull of an early human, supposedly with australopithecine affinities (Coppens, 1965), although this is questionable. Also in the Sahara are many younger sites with faunas indicative of the existence of more humid conditions at times during the Pleistocene (Monod, 1963); hence the desert was not always a strong barrier to the movement of animals.

In the tectonically disturbed region of east Africa, many local basins formed traps for sediment and, very fortunately, volcanic activity resulted in the extrusion of lavas or the blasting out of volcanic tuff which can be dated by potassium-argon techniques. The most famous of these deposits is that of Olduvai Gorge in Tanzania. A well-exposed sequence of four series was named, from the base upwards, Beds I, II, III, and IV; an unconformable deposit named Bed V is a good deal younger (Reck, 1914; L. S. B. Leakey, 1951, 1965). The fauna of Bed I is "Upper Villafranchian" and that of Bed IV is middle Pleistocene; there is a distinct faunal break in the lower part of Bed II, the fauna below the break belonging with that of Bed I. The stratigraphy has been restudied by Hay (1963, 1967) and some of the volcanic ash layers have been dated radiometrically by Evernden and Curtis (1965). The basaltic lava on which Bed I rests has an age close to 1.9×10^6 years and a tuff just overlying the most important lower layers, which contain hominid remains, is dated at 1.75×10^6 years and another tuff, a little higher in the sequence, is 1.65×10^6 years old. The lower part of Bed II is thus most probably terminal "Upper Villafranchian." The hominids from the lower part of Bed I represent a robust australopithecine, *Paranthropus boisei,* and a larger-brained gracile creature named *Homo habilis* by Leakey, Tobias and Napier (1964) but regarded by some other authorities as a species of *Australopithecus*. In the upper part of Bed II there was found a skull cap which resembles that of *Pithecanthropus* (or *Homo*) *erectus* from Java. Pebble tools occur in Bed I, giving place to hand-axes in Bed II, above the faunal break (M. D. Leakey, 1967). The abundant fauna is at present being reexamined and preliminary conclusions (L. S. B. Leakey, 1965) indicate that many of the previous identifications for the Bed I material are unreliable. The typical elephant is a moderately developed form of *Elephas recki* (Stage 3 of Maglio, 1970a), but the peculiar proboscidean *Deinotherium* also occurs. There is a rhinoceros (Hooijer, 1969), *Equus,* and *Stylohipparion,* a chalicothere (*Ancylotherium*) (Butler, 1965), the sivathere *Libytherium,* and a small giraffe. Bovidae are plentiful and there are several carnivores, including machairodonts. The Suidae include a form of *Mesochoerus* somewhat like a forest-hog, and an ancestral warthog, *Phacochoerus antiquus*. In the upper part of Bed II, and continuing through Bed IV, are a wide variety of Suidae, including a more developed *Mesochoerus* and a number of very large aberrant phacochoerines. The characteristic elephant is a more advanced variety of *Elephas recki* (Stage 4), and *Deinotherium* is absent. *Equus, Stylohipparion,* and *Libytherium* persist, but the rhinoceros and the bovids are mainly different forms. There is a characteristic hippopotamus, *H. gorgops*. The Bed II fauna is represented at another locality in Tanzania in the Peninj beds west of Lake Natron. The Bed IV fauna, although scantily known, resembles that of the hand-ax-rich site at Olorgesailie, in Kenya north of Lake Magadi, and that of Kanjera in the Kavirondo Gulf.

In 1932 the late Professor Arambourg of Paris explored the west side of Lake Rudolf, up into southern Ethiopia, where there are tilted and faulted sediments flanking the Omo river. The fauna recovered from the Omo beds indicated an age comparable with that of the lower part of the Olduvai succession (Arambourg, 1947). In 1966 Arambourg returned to the Omo as a member of an international expedition (Howell, 1968) that has recovered large quantities of fossil material, including some remains of australopithecine hominids, both robust and gracile (Howell, 1969). Volcanic tuffs permit dating of the sedimentary sequence from 3.75×10^6 years near the base to 1.84×10^6 years some distance below the exposed top, and the strata have been designated as the Shungura Formation (Butzer and Thurber, 1969). There is a distinct change in the fauna below a tuff ("D") dated at 2.35×10^6 years and this forms a convenient subdivision into a Lower Shungura, which would be "Lower Villafranchian" (uppermost Pliocene) and an Upper Shungura, which would be largely "Upper Villafranchian" (Arambourg, Chavaillon and Coppens, 1969). In the Lower Shungura the characteristic proboscidean is *Elephas recki*, Stage 1, and in the upper Shungura is Stage 2; *Deinotherium* also occurs. The most characteristic suid is *Mesochoerus limnetes*, showing progressive elongation of the third molars throughout the succession; *Nyanzachoerus* occurs in the Lower division, while a phacochoerine suid "*Pronotochoerus*" occurs in the Upper division; *Notochoerus* is represented by two different species in the Upper and the Lower Shungura (Cooke and Maglio, 1971). A hexaprotodont hippopotamus occurs throughout, showing evolutionary changes in the successive horizons. Perissodactyls are rare, but both black and white rhinoceroses seem to be represented. *Stylohipparion* is present, but *Equus* appears only in the upper beds. Bovidae are varied and abundant throughout, but carnivores are scarce. Somewhat unexpected was the discovery of undoubted camel remains both in the Lower and the Upper Shungura (Howell, Fichter and Wolff, 1969); camel also occur at Marsabit Road in an horizon equivalent to the Upper Shungura, and near the top of Bed II at Olduvai (A. W. and A. Gentry, 1969). Camel had previously been known from the "Lower Villafranchian" in north Africa.

In the Omo area, but not directly connected with the Shungura Formation, is a fairly thin sequence named the Mursi Formation (Butzer and Thurber, 1969) capped by a lava dated at 4.18×10^6 years. It contains a fauna equating it with that of Kanapoi. On the east side of Lake Rudolf, in Kenya, beds of the same general type as those of the Omo area are found around Ileret, Koobi Fora and Kubi Algi (R. E. F. Leakey, 1970; Behrensmeyer, 1970). The Kubi Algi fauna resembles that of Kanapoi, while the deposits at Koobi Fora and Ileret correspond to the Upper Shungura. Fine australopithecine material, together with pebble tools, have come from the Koobi Fora beds (R. E. F. Leakey, 1970).

Kanam, in the Kavirondo Gulf, has furnished a somewhat scanty fauna that includes *Nyanzachoerus*, early *Mammuthus* and *Loxodonta*, *Stegodon*, *Anancus*, *Libytherium* and a hexaprotodont hippopotamus, all of which suggest an age approximately equivalent to Kanapoi. However, some elements of younger aspect occur and it is possible that more than one horizon is involved. A hominid jaw from Kanam West (L. S. B. Leakey, 1933) is not from the horizons with the early fauna for certain, although it may be. Farther west, in Uganda, the Kaiso Formation occurs on the east side of Lake Albert and extends southward past the Kazinga Channel. The thick sequence has yielded fossil material mainly from two zones, respectively near the top and near the bottom of the Formation (Bishop, 1965; Cooke and Coryndon, 1970). The earlier Kaiso assemblage includes *Anancus, Primelephas,* and *Loxodonta,* which do not occur in the later Kaiso assemblage. The latter has an early (Stage 1) *Elephas recki. Stegodon* is present throughout, as also are the suids *Mesochoerus* and *Nyanzachoerus,* both hexaprotodont and tetraprotodont hippopotamus, and *Hipparion.* The later Kaiso assemblage resembles that of the middle of the Shungura Formation, but the earlier Kaiso assemblage is comparable with that of Kanapoi, or may be a little older.

Well south of Lake Rudolf, in the area around Lake Baringo, there are several occurrences of sediments intercalated in lavas. The Chemeron Formation (Martyn, 1967) is probably comparable in age to the Kanapoi and Lower Shungura. Hominid remains have been found in it, and also in other localities of uncertain age in the same region.

In South Africa there are no long series of strata comparable with those of Olduvai and the main fossil-bearing sites comprise restricted and disconnected deposits. The terrace gravels of the Vaal River have yielded hand ax tools in abundance, together with fragmentary fossil mammalian remains of generally middle Pleistocene aspect but with a few derived "Villafranchian" fossils. A pan deposit at Cornelia in the Orange Free State has furnished a fauna resembling that of Bed IV at Olduvai. Interest attaches to an extensive deposit at Hopefield in the southwestern Cape where a somewhat similar fauna is associated with a neanderthaloid human cranium clearly allied to that from the famous Rhodesian site of Broken Hill. Another somewhat neanderthaloid, but sapient, skull was found in a thermal spring deposit at Florisbad in the Orange Free State, accompanied by a fauna of upper Pleistocene aspect; a similar fauna occurs at the nearby Vlakkraal spring. The writer has distinguished these units as representing a "Vaal-Cornelia Faunal Span" and a "Florisbad-Vlakkraal Faunal Span," respectively (Cooke, 1967).

Clearly older than the above are the faunas associated with the South African ape-men, the Australopithecinae. The first fossil of this group was found in a cemented sand-filled cavity in secondary limestone at Taung and was named *Australopithecus africanus* by Dart (1925). Further material belonging to this genus was subsequently discovered in consolidated cave breccias at Sterkfontein and Makapansgat. Fossil remains of a different australopithecine, *Paranthropus robustus* were later unearthed at Kromdraai and Swartkrans, within a few miles of Sterkfontein. At Swartkrans there also occurred a more advanced human type originally named *Telanthropus capensis* but now regarded by Robinson

(1961) as belonging to the genus *Homo* and to be closely allied to the pithecanthropine *Homo erectus*. Approximately 150 species of fossil mammals have been identified from these sites and it is clear that two faunal stages are represented, conveniently termed the "Sterkfontein Faunal Span" and the "Swartkrans Faunal Span" respectively, probably covering a considerable range in time. Unfortunately, because of the peculiar environment of deposition, the important proboscidian "zone fossils" are too rare to be useful, whereas carnivores not known elsewhere in Africa are fairly common. Bovidae are present in profusion and there is a considerable variety of baboons. Both *Libytherium* and hipparionids occur, together with pigs allied to those of east Africa, but correlation is difficult and there are still some uncertainties. A tentative correlation is presented in Table 2.

The "Villafranchian" fauna consists entirely of extinct species and may contain 30 to 40 per cent of extinct genera; yet the general assemblages bear a characteristic Ethiopian imprint. At the order and family level, the composition of the fauna is much like that of the present day. Compared with the Miocene and Pliocene, there is a great expansion in the variety and number of artiodactyls, especially Suidae and Bovidae which must have undergone almost explosive diversification during the late Pliocene. A fossil camel occurs in the "Lower Villafranchian" in the Maghreb but this family is otherwise rare in the rest of Africa. The proboscideans are present in some variety but the Deinotheriidae and Gomphotheriidae are almost at the end of their existence. The Elephantidae, which had diversified in the mid-Pliocene, become less varied through the Pleistocene. Carnivores are present in wide variety, especially sabertoothed cats and archaic autochthonous hyaenids. A chalicothere, although rare, is of Asiatic type and does not seem to have evolved from the African Miocene stock; nor did it survive the "Villafranchian." The rhinoceroses are represented by forms closely allied to the living species, both black and white, but also by some aberrant types now extinct. *Hipparion* occurs in the north African Pliocene, and is also known south of the Sahara, being characterized by an elongate protocone which Arambourg (1959) regards as distinctively African. The hipparion group (Boné and Singer, 1965) is also represented by the genus *Stylohipparion*, which is uniquely African. *Equus* is an obvious immigrant. Many new rodents occur, some indigenous and others clearly immigrants. The primates are varied and the human family well represented in early stages of cultural and physical evolution.

During the middle Pleistocene, more and more living species replace archaic forms until, in the upper Pleistocene, the fauna is essentially that of the present day. The Pleistocene faunas seem to have been rich in variety and the late upper Pleistocene extinctions have left a decidedly impoverished modern fauna. The Suidae and Bovidae, in particular, have been greatly diminished. Compared with four living species from three genera of African pigs, there are at least a dozen valid additional fossil species and half as many additional genera. The alcelaphine Bovidae today comprise three genera with no more than twelve species but the fossil record provides at least fifteen further species and more than eight genera, some of them decidedly aberrant and reflecting a long evolutionary history in Africa. Gazelles are abundant in the Pleistocene and many are found as fossils in south Africa, where they no longer occur, although the springbok and impala occupy similar ecological niches. These two genera (*Antidorcas* and *Aepyceros*), and also the more distantly related gerenuk *Litocranius* of east Africa, demand a long lineage which had branched off from the gazelline stock well back in the Pliocene.

In Europe, the Pleistocene is marked by alternations of glacial and interglacial periods, which caused wide latitudinal shifts in climatic belts and ecological conditions; this is reflected in the "more arctic" or "more tropical" nature of the successive fossil faunas. With the geographical limitations placed on movement, failure to adapt meant failure to survive. Although temperature changes and periods of higher or of diminished rainfall affected Africa, neither the exact chronology nor the ecological effects have been evaluated adequately. Forest areas undoubtedly expanded and contracted, and the desert steppe encroached upon the normal savannas on more than one occasion. It is likely, however, that these Pleistocene fluctuations served mainly to shift the boundaries of the vegetational and ecological zones, allowing the mammals to move with them. There is no evidence for wholesale extinction or gross population transfer, nor is it apparent that climatic change was responsible for inducing abnormal speciation, although it must have resulted in some cases of physical and genetic isolation. Most profound in its effects was the development of the Sahara desert as a continent-wide barrier between sub-Saharan Africa and the northern littoral, which has become "Eurasianized" and includes living camels and cervids not known in the deeply autochthonous fauna below the Sahara.

THE HISTORY OF THE FAUNA

In the account given above, a good deal of attention has been paid to the characteristics of the mammalian faunas as reflected in the fossil record at various geological stages. Fig. 9 presents an analysis to show the variations in composition as reflected in the numbers of genera belonging to various orders, expressed as a percentage of the total fauna. The figures for the Pliocene have a low confidence level and may be a little misleading. The early dominance of the hyracoids and proboscideans and their low rating at the present time, are very apparent, as also is the great growth of the artiodactyls. Indeed, these two factors are the ones most obvious in the evolution of the African fauna as a whole.

An attempt has been made in Figs. 10 to 14 to show diagrammatically an interpretation of the main lines of development of the African mammalian faunas. These diagrams are intended to convey an impression of

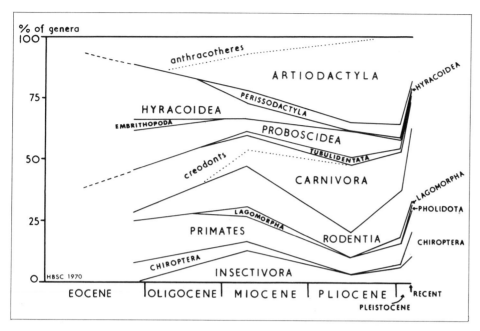

FIG. 9. VARIATION IN COMPOSITION OF THE VERTEBRATE FAUNAS DURING THE TERTIARY-QUATERNARY

The number of recorded genera ascribed to each family is expressed as a percentage of the total number of genera in the fauna of the particular period. The sharp upward kink to the recent fauna is largely due to the paucity of insectivores and bats in the fossil state.

the extent to which the living fauna is indebted to evolution within the continent. The scale in the diagrams is approximately a true time scale from left to right and represents a total duration of about seventy million years. Full lines show the known occurrence in the fossil state of members of the family indicated and dotted lines show inferred existence of the group *in Africa*. Where these lines originate in the Paleocene (Pal.) it is believed that the family belonged to the stock existing in Africa before the continent was isolated from Eurasia. The arrival of new stock is shown by a solid arrow and the possible source of the stock is indicated by E for Europe and A for Asia. The exodus, or "export" of African-evolved forms is shown by hollow arrows and the receiving continent is designated by the same letters; M is used to show transfer of stock to Madagascar. An obelus (†) indicates extinction of the group *in Africa*. Figs. 15, 16, and 17 show the major morphological types found in the Oligocene, Miocene, and Early Pleistocene.

Of course, there is a good deal of speculation involved in the preparation of these very generalized charts, but there is also much that rests on solid observational evidence. It is perhaps of interest to comment that both the geological and the faunal evidence favor the concept of long

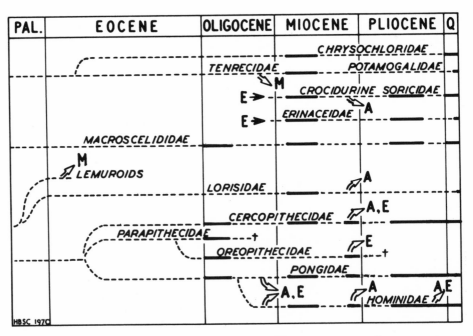

FIG. 10. Reconstruction of the Geological History of the Insectivora and Primates in Africa during the Tertiary

[See text for details.]

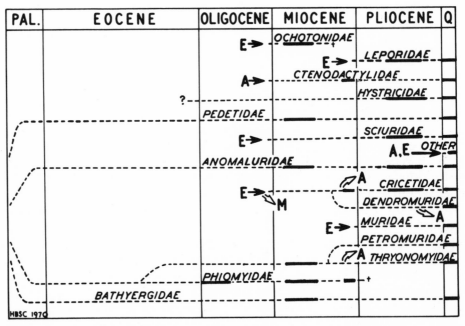

FIG. 11. Reconstruction of the Geological History of the Lagomorpha and Rodentia in Africa during the Tertiary

[See text for details.]

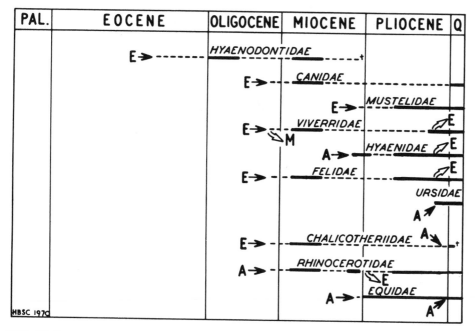

FIG. 12. RECONSTRUCTION OF THE GEOLOGICAL HISTORY OF THE CARNIVORA AND PERISSO-
DACTYLA IN AFRICA DURING THE TERTIARY

[*See text for details.*]

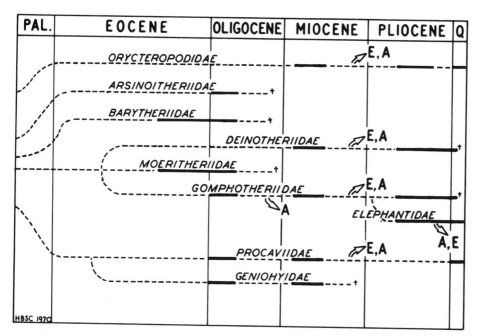

FIG. 13. RECONSTRUCTION OF THE GEOLOGICAL HISTORY OF THE TUBULIDENTATA, EM-
BRITHOPODA, PROBOSCIDEA AND HYRACOIDEA IN AFRICA DURING THE TERTIARY

[*See text for details.*]

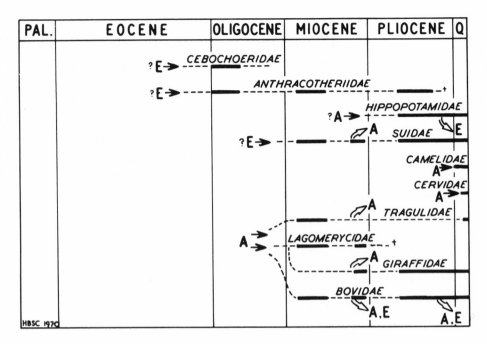

FIG. 14. RECONSTRUCTION OF THE GEOLOGICAL HISTORY OF THE ARTIODACTYLA IN AFRICA DURING THE TERTIARY

[See text for details.]

periods of isolation during which diversification and evolution took place in Africa, separated by a very few rather brief periods during which some faunal interchanges were possible. Both geological and faunal evidence suggests that such exchanges were rare and point to the late Oligocene, late Miocene and late Pliocene as the only ones of general significance; but even then the connections must have been filter bridges or "sweepstakes routes" since the faunas as a whole did not become deeply involved in the interchanges. Had this not been so, it would be expected that more of the characteristic Asiatic animals would have penetrated Africa than is actually the case. As our knowledge of the African faunas grows, case after case comes to light in which the ancestors of supposed Asiatic immigrants into Africa are found in earlier deposits within the latter continent. The so-called "Villafranchian" faunas of Africa are fundamentally African in character and some of the Eurasiatic resemblances are proving to be convergent rather than genetic. The history of the living fauna of Africa is indeed complex and we are still a long way from final evaluation. Nevertheless, the evidence at the present time favors this continent as an important center of evolution with a long history of indigenous development for its wide variety of living mammals. Man himself may perhaps be among the important exports from the African continent.

FIG. 15. MAJOR MORPHOLOGICAL TYPES OF OLIGOCENE MAMMALS IN AFRICA
A, Arsinoitherium; *B*, Saghatherium; *C*, Megalohyrax; *D*, Parapithecus; *E*, Propliopi-
thecus; *F*, Hyaenodon; *G*, Bothriodon; *H*, Mixtotherium; *I*, Phiomia; *J*, Moeritherium;
K, Palaeomastodon.

FIG. 16. MAJOR MORPHOLOGICAL TYPES OF MIOCENE MAMMALS IN AFRICA

A, Proconsul; *B,* Limnopithecus; *C,* Progalago; *D,* Protenrec; *E,* Prochrysochloris; *F,* Parapedetes; *G,* Anasinopa; *H,* Myorycteropus; *I,* Chalicotherium; *J,* Aceratherium; *K,* Prolibytherium; *L,* Dorcatherium; *M,* Deinotherium; *N,* Trilophodon.

FIG. 17. MAJOR MORPHOLOGICAL TYPES OF EARLY PLEISTOCENE MAMMALS IN AFRICA
A, Paranthropus; *B*, Australopithecus; *C*, Dinopithecus; *D*, Papio; *E*, Machairodont;
F, Crocuta; *G*, Phacochoerus; *H*, Notochoerus; *I*, Hippopotamus; *J*, Hipparion; *K*,
Libytherium; *L*, Gazella; *M*, Deinotherium; *N*, Stegodon; *O*, Anancus; *P*, Elephas.

SUMMARY

The African continent has long been regarded as a "refuge" for the survival of archaic forms of life, but in recent years evidence has been accumulating which serves to emphasize the essentially indigenous nature of the living and extinct mammalian faunas. This paper discusses the major fossil localities and their faunas against a background of new paleogeographic studies. The latter show that through most of geological time Arabia has been basically part of the African continent; the Red Sea rift developed as a terrestrial trough in the Oligocene, was invaded from the Mediterranean in the Miocene, and connected through to the Indian Ocean in the Pliocene. The pre-Mediterranean Tethys Sea cut Arabo-Africa off from Eurasia during much of the Mesozoic and Tertiary. Temporary land or island connections occurred during the Paleocene elevation of the Arabo-African block, during the late Oligocene orogenesis in the Atlas and the Alps, and again near the end of the Miocene. At these times there was opportunity for limited faunal interchange between Arabo-Africa and Eurasia. From a Paleocene ferungulate stock, already possessing early anthracotheres and hyaenodonts, the proboscideans, hyracoids, and sirenians developed as new elements in Africa. Insectivores and primates must also have been part of this early fauna. In the late Oligocene there was an export of African stock to Eurasia in exchange for importation of some perissodactyls, fissiped carnivores, and perhaps basic suid, tragulid, and palaeomerycid-bovid elements. Lesser interchanges took place in the later Miocene, contributing African forms to Eurasia and admitting hipparionids to Africa. During the Pliocene great diversification took place among the African Proboscidea, Bovidae and Suidae in particular, but the Ethiopian region was effectively isolated from Eurasia until near the end of the period. However, Arabia became firmly linked to Asia and probably furnished much African material to that continent. An attempt is made to show by means of diagrams the apparent duration of African evolution for each mammalian family and to suggest the time and geographic origin or destination of imports and exports. The role of Africa as an important center of evolution and source for diffusion into the Palearctic region is apparent.

LITERATURE CITED

ABADIE, J., J. BARBEAU, and Y. COPPENS. 1959. Une faune de vertébrés villafranchiens au Tchad. *Comptes Rend. Acad. Sci. (Paris)*, 248: 3328-3330.

ANDREWS, C. W. 1906. A descriptive catalogue of the Tertiary Vertebrata of the Fayûm, Egypt. 342 p. British Museum, London.

———. 1911. On a new species of Dinotherium (*Dinotherium hobleyi*) from British East Africa. *Proc. Zool. Soc. Lond.*, 1911: 943-945.

ARAMBOURG, C. 1943. Contribution à l'étude géologique du bassin du lac Rodolphe et de la basse vallée de l'Omo. Mission Scient. Omo, 1932-1933, 1: Géol. Paléont. Muséum National d'Historie Naturelle, Édition du Muséum, Paris.

——. 1946. *Anancus osiris*, un mastodonte nouveau du Pliocène inférieur d'Egypte. *Bull. Soc. Géol. Fr.*, ser. 5, 15: 479-495.

——. 1947. Contribution a l'étude géologique et paléontologique du bassin du lac Rodolphe et de la basse valée de l'Omo. Deuxième partie, Paléontologie. Mission scient. Omo. Géol.-Anthrop. I: 232-562.

——. 1951. Observations sur les couches a *Hipparion* de la vallée de l'Oued el Hammam (Algerie) et sur l'époque d'apparition de la faune de vertébrés dite "Pontienne". *Comptes Rend. Acad. Sci. (Paris)*, 232: 2464-2466.

——. 1952. Note preliminaire sur quelques éléphants fossiles de Berberie. *Bull. Museum Nat. Hist. Natur. Paris*, ser. 2(24): 407-418.

——. 1954a. La faune a *Hipparion* de l'Oued el Hammam (Algerie). *Comptes Rend. 19. Congr. Géol. Intern.*, 21: 294-302.

——. 1954b. L'hominien fossile de Ternifine (Algerie). *Comptes Rend. Acad. Sci. (Paris)*, 239: 893-895.

——. 1959. Vertébrés continenteaux du Miocène superieur de l'Afrique du Nord. *Mém. Serv. Carte Géol. Algerie*, 4: 1-161.

——. 1961a. Note preliminaire sur quelques vertébrés nouveaux du Burdigalien de Libye. *Comptes Rend. Soc. Géol. Fr.*, 1961 (4): 107-108.

——. 1961b. *Prolibytherium magnieri*, un Velléricorne nouveau du Burdigalien de Libye. *Comptes Rend. Soc. Géol. Fr.*, 1961 (3): 61-62.

——. 1962. Les faunes mammalogique du Pléistocène circummediterranean. *Quaternaria*, 6: 97-109.

——. 1963. Le genre *Bunolistriodon* Arambourg 1933. *Bull. Soc. Géol. Fr.*, ser. 7, 5: 903-911.

ARAMBOURG, C., and P. F. BUROLLET. 1962. Restes de vertébrés oligocènes en Tunisie centrale. *Comptes Rend. Soc. Géol. Fr.*, 1962 (2): 42.

ARAMBOURG, C., and P. MAGNIER. 1961. Gisements de vertébrés dans la bassin tertiare de Syrte (Libye). *Comptes Rend. Acad. Sci. (Paris)*, 252: 1181-1183.

ARAMBOURG, C., J. CHAVAILLON and Y. COPPENS. 1969. Resultats de la nouvelle mission de l'Omo (2e campagne 1968). *Comptes Rend. Acad. Sci. (Paris)*, 268D: 759-762.

ARAMBOURG, C., J. KIKOINE, and R. LAVOCAT. 1951. Découverte du genre *Moeritherium* dans le Tertiaire continental du Soudan. *Comptes Rend. Acad. Sci. (Paris)*, 233: 68-70.

AVNIMELECH, M. 1962. The main trends in the Pleistocene-Holocene history of the Israelian coastal plain. *Quaternaria*, 6: 479-495.

AZZAROLI, A. 1970. Villafranchian correlations based on large mammals. *Giornale di Geol. (Pisa),* (2) 35: 1-21.

BEADNELL, H. J. L. 1905. *The Topography and Geology of the Fayum Province of Egypt.* 101 p. Survey Department, Cairo.

BEHRENSMEYER, A. K. 1970. Preliminary geological interpretation of a new hominid site in the Lake Rudolf basin. *Nature,* 226: 225-226.

BEYDOUN, Z. R. 1960. Synopsis of the geology of East Aden Protectorate. *21. Intern. Geol. Congr., Rept. Session Norden,* part 21: 131-159.

BISHOP, W. W. 1958. Miocene mammalia from the Napak volcano, Karamoja, Uganda. *Nature,* 182: 1480-1482.

——. 1963. The later Tertiary and Pleistocene in eastern equatorial Africa. In F. C. Howell and F. Bourlière (eds.), *African Ecology and Human Evolution,* p. 246-275. Viking Fund Publications in Anthropology No. 36, New York.

——. 1964. More fossil primates and other Miocene mammals from north-east Uganda. *Nature,* 203: 1327-1331.

——. 1965. Quaternary geology and geomorphology of the Albert-Edward Rift Valley. Geol. Soc. Am. Sp. Paper 84: 293-321.

BISHOP, W. W., and F. WHYTE. 1962. Tertiary mammalian fauna and sediments in Karamoja and Kavirondo, East Africa. *Nature,* 196: 1283-1287.

BISHOP, W. W., J. A. MILLER and F. J. FITCH. 1969. New potassium-argon age determinations relevant to the Miocene fossil mammal sequence in East Africa. *Am. J. Sci.,* 267: 669-699.

BONÉ, E. L. and R. SINGER. 1965. *Hipparion* from Langebaanweg, Cape Province, and a revision of the genus in Africa. *Ann. S. Afric. Museum,* 48(16): 273-397.

BOURLIÈRE, F. 1963. Observations on the ecology of some large African mammals. In F. C. Howell and F. Bourlière (eds.), *African Ecology and Human Evolution,* p. 43-64. Viking Fund Publications in Anthropology No. 36, New York.

BRINK, A. S. 1957. Speculations on some advanced mammalian characteristics in the higher mammal-like reptiles. *Palaeontol. Afric.,* 4: 77-96.

BRINKMANN, R. 1960. *Geologic Evolution of Europe.* 161 p. F. Enke, Stuttgart.

BUTLER, P. M. 1949. On the evolution of the skull and teeth in the Erinaceidae, with special reference to fossil material in the British Museum. *Proc. Zool. Soc. Lond.,* 118: 446-500.

——. 1965. East African Miocene and Pleistocene chalicotheres. Fossil Mammals of Africa, No. 20. *Bull Brit. Museum Natur. Hist. Geol.,* 10 (7).

——. 1969. Insectivores and bats from the Miocene of East Africa: new material. *Fossil Vertebrates of Africa,* 1: 1-37.

BUTLER, P. M., and A. T. HOPWOOD. 1957. Insectivora and Chiroptera from the Miocene rocks of Kenya Colony. Fossil Mammals of Africa No. 13. British Museum, London.

BUTZER, K. W. and D. L. THURBER. 1969. Some late Cenozoic sedimentary formations of the lower Omo basin. *Nature*, 222: 1132-1143.

CHANEY, R. W. 1933. A Tertiary flora from Uganda. *J. Geol.*, 41: 702-709.

CHESTERS, K. I. M. 1957. The Miocene flora of Rusinga Island, Lake Victoria, Kenya. *Palaeontographica B*, 161 (1-4): 30-67.

CHOUBERT, G. 1952. Histoire géologique du domaine de l'Anti-Atlas. *19. Congr. Géol. Intern., Monographie Regionales, Géologie du Maroc* 1: 77-194.

CHURCHER, C. S. 1970. Two new upper Miocene giraffids from Fort Ternan, Kenya, East Africa: *Palaeotragus primaevus* n.sp. and *Samotherium africanum* n.sp. *Fossil Vertebrates of Africa*, 2: 1-105.

CLARK, J. D., E. A. STEPHENS and S. C. CORYNDON. 1966. Pleistocene fossiliferous lake beds of the Malawi (Nyasa) rift: a preliminary report. *Am. Anthrop.*, 68: 46-87.

COLBERT, E. H. 1941. A study of *Orycteropus gaudryi* from the island of Samos. *Bull. Am. Museum Natur. Hist.*, 78: 305-351.

COOKE, H. B. S. 1958. Observations relating to Quaternary environments in east and southern Africa. *Trans. Geol. Soc. S. Afric.*, 61 (Annexure): 1-73.

———. 1960. Further revision of the fossil Elephantidae of southern Africa. *Palaeontol. Afric.*, 7: 59-63.

———. 1963. Pleistocene mammal faunas of Africa, with particular reference to southern Africa. In F. C. Howell and F. Bourlière (eds.), *African Ecology and Human Evolution*, p. 65-116. Viking Fund Publications in Anthropology No. 36, New York.

———. 1967. The Pleistocene sequence in South Africa and problems of correlation. In W. W. Bishop and J. D. Clark (eds.) *Background to Evolution in Africa*, p. 175-184. Univ. Chicago Press.

COOKE, H. B. S. and S. C. CORYNDON. 1970. Pleistocene mammals from the Kaiso Formation and other related deposits in Uganda. *Fossil Vertebrates of Africa*, 2: 107-224.

COOKE, H. B. S. and V. J. MAGLIO. 1971. Plio-Pleistocene stratigraphy in East Africa in relation to proboscidean and suid evolution. In W. W. Bishop and J. A. Miller (eds.), *Calibration of Hominid Evolution*, p. 303-329. Wenner-Gren Foundation, New York.

COPPENS, Y. 1960. Le Quaternaire fossilifère de Koro-Toro (Tchad). Resultats d'une première mission. *Comptes Rend. Acad. Sci. (Paris)*, 251: 2385-2386.

———. 1965. L'hominien du Tchad. *Comptes Rend. Acad. Sci. (Paris)*, 260 (10): 2869-2871.

——. 1967. Les faunes de vertebres Quaternaires du Tchad. In W. W. Bishop and J. D. Clark (eds.), *Background to Evolution in Africa,* p. 89-97. Univ. of Chicago Press.

CROMPTON, A. W. 1964. A preliminary description of a new mammal from the Upper Triassic of South Africa. *Proc. Zool. Soc. Lond.,* 142: 441-452.

——. 1968. In search of the "insignificant." *Discovery (Yale),* 3 (2): 23-32.

DART, R. A. 1925. *Australopithecus africanus:* the man-ape of South Africa. *Nature,* 115: 195-199.

DARTEVELLE, E. 1952. Echinides fossiles du Congo et de l'Angola. Première partie, introduction historique et stratigraphique. *Ann. Musee Roy. Congo Belge: Ser. 8, Sci. Géol.,* 12: 1-70.

DIETRICH, W. O. 1928. *Brancatherulum* n.g.—ein Proplacentalier aus dem obersten Jura des Tendaguru in Deutsch-Ostafrika. *Zentr. Mineral Geol. Palaeontol.,* 1927B: 423-426.

DORMAN, F. H. and E. D. GILL. 1959. Oxygen isotope palaeotemperature measurements on Australian fossils. *Proc. Roy. Soc. Victoria,* 71(1): 73-98.

DURHAM, J. W. 1950. Cenozoic marine climates of the Pacific coast. *Bull. Geol. Soc. Am.,* 61: 1243-1264.

EMILIANI, C. 1961. Cenozoic climatic changes as indicated by the stratigraphy and chronology of deep-sea cores of Globigerina-ooze facies. *Ann. N.Y. Acad. Sci.,* 95(1): 521-536.

EVERNDEN, J. F. and G. H. CURTIS. 1965. The potassium-argon dating of late Cenozoic rocks in East Africa and Italy. *Current Anthropology,* 6: 343-364 (with comments 364-385).

EVERNDEN, J. F., D. E. SAVAGE, G. H. CURTIS, and G. T. JAMES. 1964. Potassium-argon dates and the Cenozoic mammalian chronology of North America. *Am. J. Sci.,* 262: 145-198.

FOURTAU, D. 1920. *Contribution a l'etude des vertébrés miocènes de l'Egypte.* 122 p. Government Press, Cairo.

FURON, R. 1959. *La paléogéographie.* 2 ed. 405 p. Payot, Paris.

GENTRY, A. W. 1970. The Bovidae (Mammalia) of the Fort Ternan fossil fauna. *Fossil Vertebrates of Africa,* 2: 243-323.

GENTRY, A. W. and A. GENTRY. 1969. Fossil camels in Kenya and Tanzania. *Nature,* 222: 898.

GIDLEY, J. W. 1923. Paleocene primates of the Fort Union, with discussion of relationships of Eocene primates. *Proc. U.S. Natl. Museum,* 63: 1-38.

GORODISKI, A. and R. LAVOCAT. 1953. Première découverte de Mammifères dans le Tertiare (Lutétien) du Senegal. *Comptes Rend. Soc. Géol. Fr.,* 1953: 315-317.

HAY, R. L. 1963. Stratigraphy of Beds I through IV, Olduvai Gorge, Tanganyika. *Science,* 139: 829-833.

——. 1967. Revised stratigraphy of Olduvai Gorge. In W. W. Bishop and J. D. Clark (eds.), *Background to Evolution in Africa.* p. 221-228. Univ. of Chicago Press.

HENDEY, Q. B. 1970. The age of the fossiliferous deposits at Langebaanweg, Cape Province. *Ann. S. Afr. Museum,* 56 (3): 119-131.

HENSON, F. R. S. 1951. Observations on the geology and petroleum occurrences of the Middle East. *Proc. 3., World Petrol. Congr.,* 118-140.

HOOIJER, D. A. 1963. Miocene Mammalia of Congo. *Ann. Koninklijk Museum Midden-Afrika, ser. 8, 46, Tervuren:* 1-77.

——. 1968. A rhinoceros from the late Miocene of Fort Ternan, Kenya. *Zool. Med. Museum Nat. Hist. Leiden,* 43: 77-92.

——. 1969. Pleistocene East African rhinoceroses. *Fossil Vertebrates of Africa,* 1: 71-98.

HOPWOOD, A. T. 1929. New and little known mammals from the Miocene of Africa. *Am. Museum Novitates,* 344: 1-9.

HOWELL, F. C. 1968. Omo Research Expedition. *Nature,* 219: 567-572.

——. 1969. Remains of Hominidae from Pliocene/Pleistocene formations in the lower Omo basin, Ethiopia. *Nature,* 223: 1234-1239.

HOWELL, F. C., L. S. FICHTER and G. ECK. 1969. Vertebrate assemblages from the Usno Formation, White Sands and Brown Sands localities, lower Omo basin, Ethiopia. *Quaternaria,* 11: 65-88.

HOWELL, F. C., L. S. FICHTER and R. WOLFF. 1969. Fossil camels in the Omo beds, southern Ethiopia. *Nature,* 223: 150-152.

KAUFMANN, G. F. 1951. The tectonic framework of the Far East and its influence on the origin and accumulation of petroleum. *Proc. 3. World Petrol Congr.,* 86-112.

KENT, P. E. 1942. The country around the Kavirondo Gulf of Victoria Nyanza. *Geograph. J.,* 100: 22-31.

——. 1944. The Miocene beds of Kavirondo, Kenya. *Quart. J. Geol. Soc. Lond.,* 100: 85-116.

KING, L. C. 1951. *South African Scenery.* 378 p. Oliver and Boyd, Edinburgh.

——. 1962. *The Morphology of the Earth.* 699 p. Oliver and Boyd, Edinburgh.

LAMARE, P. 1936. *Structure géologique de l'Arabie.* 60 p. Beranger, Paris.

LAVOCAT, R. 1952. Sur une faune de mammifères miocènes découverte a Beni Mallal (Atlas Marocain). *Comptes Rend. Acad. Sci. (Paris),* 235: 189-191.

——. 1959. Origine et affinités des Rongeurs de la sous-famille de Dendromurinae. *Comptes Rend. Acad. Sci. (Paris),* 248: 1353-1377.

———. 1964. Fossil rodents from Fort Ternan, Kenya. *Nature,* 202: 1131.

LEAKEY, L. S. B. 1933. The status of the Kanam mandible and the Kanjera skulls. *Man,* 33: 200-201.

———. 1951. *Olduvai Gorge.* Cambridge University Press.

———. 1959. A new fossil skull from Olduvai. *Nature,* 184: 491-493.

———. 1961. New finds at Olduvai Gorge. *Nature,* 189: 649-650.

———. 1962. A new lower Pliocene fossil primate from Kenya. *Ann. Mag. Natur. Hist., 13 ser.,* 4: 689-696.

———. 1963. Adventures in the search for man. *Natl. Geograph. Mag.,* 123(1): 132-152.

———. 1965. *Olduvai Gorge 1951-1961. Volume 1: Fauna and Background.* Cambridge University Press.

LEAKEY, L. S. B., P. V. TOBIAS, and J. R. NAPIER. 1964. A new species of the genus *Homo* from Olduvai Gorge. *Nature,* 202: 7-9.

LEAKEY, M. D. 1967. Preliminary survey of the cultural material from Beds I and II, Olduvai Gorge, Tanzania. In W. W. Bishop and J. D. Clark (eds.), *Background to Evolution in Africa,* p. 417-446. Univ. of Chicago Press.

LEAKEY, R. E. F. 1970. Fauna and artefacts from a new Plio-Pleistocene locality near Lake Rudolf in Kenya. *Nature,* 226: 223-224.

LE GROS CLARK, W. E. and L. S. B. LEAKEY. 1951. The Miocene Hominoidea of East Africa. Fossil Mammals of Africa, No. 1. British Museum, London.

LEONARDI, P. 1952. I suidi di Sahabi nella Sirtica (Africa Settentrionale). *Rend. Accad. Nazionale dei XL,* Ser. IV, 4: 75-88.

MACINNES, D. G. 1936. A new genus of fossil deer from the Miocene of Africa. *J. Linnean Soc., London, Zool.,* 39: 521-530.

MAGLIO, V. J. 1970a. Early Elephantidae of Africa and a tentative correlation of African Plio-Pleistocene deposits. *Nature,* 225: 328-332.

———. 1970b. Four new species of Elephantidae from the Plio-Pleistocene of northwestern Kenya. *Breviora,* 341: 1-43.

MARTYN, J. 1967. Pleistocene deposits and new fossil localities in Kenya (with a note on the hominid remains by P. V. Tobias). *Nature,* 215: 476-479.

MATSUMOTO, H. 1926. Contribution to the knowledge of the fossil Hyracoidea of the Fayum, Egypt, with descriptions of several new species. *Bull. Am. Museum Natur. Hist.,* 56: 253-350.

MATTHEW, W. D. 1915. Climate and evolution. *Ann. N.Y. Acad. Sci.,* 24: 171-318.

MAYR, E. 1946. History of the North American bird fauna. *Wilson Bull.,* 58: 1-41.

MONGIN, D. 1954. Note prèliminaire sur une faune Miocène saumatre recueille par M. Arambourg, au sud de Mercier-Lecombe (Algerie). *Comptes Rend. 19. Congr. Géol. Intern., fasc. 21:* 303-308.

MONOD, T. 1963. The late Tertiary and Pleistocene in the Sahara and adjacent southerly regions. In F. C. Howell and F. Bourlière (eds.), *African Ecology and Human Evolution,* p. 117-229. Viking Fund Publications in Anthropology No. 36, New York.

MOREAU, R. E. 1952. Africa since the Mesozoic, with particular reference to certain biological problems. *Proc. Zool. Soc. Lond.,* 121: 869-913.

NAIRN, A. E. M. 1961. *Descriptive Palaeoclimatology.* Interscience Publishers Inc., London.

NAKKADY, S. E. 1957. Biostratigraphy and interregional correlation of the upper Senonian and lower Paleocene of Egypt. *J. Paleontol.,* 31: 428-447.

OSBORN, H. F. 1908. New fossil mammals from the Fayûm Oligocene, Egypt. *Bull. Am. Museum Natur. Hist.,* 24: 265-272.

———. 1909. New carnivorous mammals from the Fayûm Oligocene, Egypt. *Bull. Am. Museum Natur. Hist.,* 26: 415-424.

PATTERSON, B., A. K. BEHRENSMEYER and W. D. SILL. 1970. Geology and faunal correlations of a new Pliocene locality in northwestern Kenya. *Nature,* 226: 918-921.

PETROCCHI, C. 1943. I giacimento fossilifero di Sahabi. *Coll. Scient. Docum. a Cura (Min. A. I., IX),* 12.

PICARD, L. 1939. On the structure of the Arabian peninsula. *17. Intern. Geol. Congr., Rept. Vol. 2:* 415-423.

PILGRIM, G. E. 1941. The dispersal of the Artiodactyla. *Biol. Rev.* 16: 134-163.

RECK, H. 1914. Erste verläufige Mitteilung über der Fund eines fossilen Menschenskelets aus Zentral-afrika. *Sitzber. Ges. Naturf. Freunde, Berlin:* 81-95.

ROBINSON, J. T. 1961. The Australopithecines and their bearing on the origin of Man and of stone tool-making. *S. Afric. J. Sci.,* 57: 3-13.

SAID, R. 1961. Tectonic framework of Egypt and its influence on the distribution of foraminifera. *Bull. Am. Assoc. Petrol. Geologists,* 45: 198-218.

———. 1962. *The Geology of Egypt.* Elsevier, Amsterdam.

SAINT-SEINE, P. DE. 1955. Poissons fossiles de l'étage de Stanleyville (Congo Belge). *Ann. Musée Roy. Congo Belge: Ser. 8, Sci. Géol.,* 14: 1-126.

SAVAGE, R. J. G. 1965. The Miocene Carnivora of East Africa. Fossil Mammals of Africa No. 19. *Bull. Brit. Museum Natur. Hist. Geol.,* 10: 239-316.

———. 1967. Early Miocene mammal faunas of the Tethyan region. In

C. G. Adams and D. V. Ager (eds.) *Aspects of Tethyan Biogeography*, 247-282. Systematics Assn. Publ. No. 7.

——. 1969. Early Tertiary mammal locality in southern Libya. *Proc. Geol. Soc. Lond.*, No. 1657: 167-171.

SAVAGE, R. J. G. and M. E. WHITE. 1965. Two mammal faunas from the early Tertiary of central Libya. *Proc. Geol. Soc. Lond.*, No. 1623: 89-91.

SCHLOSSER, M. 1911. Beiträge zur Kentniss der Oligozänen Landsäugetiere aus Fayum: Aegypten. *Beitr. Palaeontol. Geol. Österreich-Ungarns und des Orients (Wien)*, 24: 51-167.

SCHMIDT, K. P. 1954. Faunal realms, regions, and provinces. *Quart. Rev. Biol.*, 29: 322-331.

SCLATER, P. L. 1858. On the general geographic distribution of the members of the class Aves. *J. Linnean Soc. Lond., Zool.*, 2: 130-145.

SCHWEINFURTH, G. 1886. Reise in das Depressionsgebiet im Umkreise des Fayum. *Z. Ges. Erdkunde Berlin*, 21: 96-149.

SHACKLETON, R. M. 1951. A contribution to the geology of the Kavirondo Rift valley. *Quart. J. Geol. Soc. Lond.*, 106: 345-389.

SHUKRI, N. M. and R. SAID. 1944. Contributions to the geology of the Nubian Sandstone. Part I: Field observations and mechanical analysis. *Bull. Fac. Sci. Cairo*, 25: 149-172.

——. 1946. Idem. Part 2: Mineral analysis. *Bull. Inst. Egypte*, 27: 229-264.

SIMONS, E. L. 1960. New fossil primates: a review of the past decade. *Am. Scientist*, 48: 179-192.

——. 1962. Two new primate species from the African Oligocene. *Postilla, Yale*, 64: 1-12.

——. 1963. Some fallacies in the study of Hominid phylogeny. *Science*, 141: 879-889.

——. 1965. New fossil apes from Egypt and the initial differentiation of Hominidae. *Nature*, 205: 135-139.

——. 1969a. Late Miocene hominid from Fort Ternan, Kenya. *Nature*, 221:448-451.

——. 1969b. Miocene monkey (*Prohylobates*) from northern Egypt. *Nature*, 223: 687-689.

SIMONS, E. L. and A. E. WOOD (eds.). 1968. Early Cenozoic mammalian faunas, Fayum Province, Egypt. *Bull. Peabody Museum Natur. Hist. Yale*, 28: 1-105.

SIMPSON, G. G. 1928. Mesozoic Mammalia XI. *Brancatherulum tendaguruense* Dietrich. *Am. J. Sci.* (ser. 5), 15: 303-308.

——. 1945. The principles of classification and a classification of mammals. *Bull. Am. Museum Natur. Hist.*, 85: 1-350.

——. 1951. History of the fauna of Latin America. In G. A. Baitsell (ed.), *Science in Progress*, 369-408. Yale University Press, New Haven.

——. 1953. *Evolution and Geography.* 64 p. Condon Lecture, University of Oregon Press, Corvallis.

——. 1961. Evolution of Mesozoic mammals. In G. Vandebroek (ed.), *International Colloquium on the Evolution of Mammals,* p. 57-95. Kon. Vlaamse Acad. Wetensch. Lett. Sch. Kunsten Belgie, Part 1. Brussels.

——. 1965. Note on the Fort Ternan beds of Kenya. *Am. J. Sci.,* 263: 922.

STROMER, E. 1926. Reste land- und süsswasserbewohnender Wirbeltiere aus den Diamantenfelden Deutsch-Südwestafrikas. In E. Kaiser (ed.), *Die Diamantenwüste Südwestafrikas,* p. 107-153. D. Reimer, Berlin.

——. 1932. Reste süsswasser- und landbewohnender Wirbeltiere aus den Diamantfelden Klein-Namaqualandes (Südwestafrika). *Sitz.-Ber. Math.-Naturw. Kl. Bayer. Akad. Wiss., Muenchen,* 1931: 17-47.

SWARTZ, D. H. and D. D. ARDEN. 1960. Geologic history of the Red Sea area. *Bull. Am. Assoc. Petrol. Geologists,* 44: 1621-1637.

TOBIEN, H. 1936. Mitteilungen über Wirbeltierreste aus dem Mittelpliocän des Natrontales (Ägypten). 7. Artiodactyla: A. Bunodontia: Suidae. *Z. deutsch. geol. Gesell, Berlin,* 88: 42-53.

——. 1956. Zur Ökologie der jungtertiären Säugetiere von Höwenegg/Hegan und zur Biostratigraphie der europäischen Hipparion-Fauna. *Schriften Verein Gesch. Naturgeschicht, Donaueshingen,* 24: 208-223.

VAN COUVERING, J. A. and J. A. MILLER. 1969. Miocene stratigraphy and age determinations, Rusinga Island, Kenya. *Nature,* 221: 628-632.

VAN VALEN, L. 1960. Therapsids as mammals. *Evolution,* 14: 304-313.

VON KOENIGSWALD, G. H. R. 1948. Ein Hyaenaelurus aus der Miocene Nordafrikas. *Eclogae Geol. Helv.,* 40: 292-294.

——. 1969. Miocene Cercopithecoidea and Oreopithecoidea from the Miocene of East Africa. *Fossil Vertebrates of Africa,* 1: 39-52.

WALLACE, A. R. 1876. *The Geographical Distribution of Animals.* 2 vols. Macmillan, London.

WHITWORTH, T. 1953. A contribution to the geology of Rusinga Island, Kenya. *Quart. J. Geol. Soc. Lond.,* 109: 75-96.

——. 1958. Miocene ruminants of East Africa. Fossil Mammals of Africa No. 15. British Museum, London.

——. 1961. The geology of Mfwanganu Island, Western Kenya. *Overseas Geol. Mineral Resources (Gt. Brit.),* 8(2): 150-190.

WOOD, A. E. 1955. A revised classification of the rodents. *J. Mammal.,* 36: 165-187.

——. 1968. The African Oligocene Rodentia. In E. L. Simons and A. E. Wood (eds.), *Early Cenozoic Mammalian Faunas, Fayum Province, Egypt,* p. 23-105. Bull. Peabody Museum Natur. Hist. Yale, No. 28, New Haven.

IV The Contemporary Mammal Fauna of Africa

by R. C. Bigalke

FAUNISTIC ORIGINS AND BASIC ZOOGEOGRAPHY

Africa and the Oriental region are the two main regions of the Old World tropics. Both are less limited by climate and barriers than are the other faunal regions and Darlington (1957) believes that they have probably been the main centers from which vertebrates have radiated into the rest of the world.

Where exactly the boundary between the Ethiopian faunal region and its neighbor, the Palearctic, should be placed, is almost a matter of choice. From many points of view it is convenient to regard the Tropic of Cancer as the dividing line. Northern Africa (with its limited mammalian fauna which is in part related quite strongly to that of Eurasia) and southwestern Arabia (a transitional area which is traditionally included in the Ethiopian Region) are thereby omitted. This treatment has the advantage of showing up the peculiarities of the "proper" African fauna very clearly. The complex relationships of the mammals inhabiting the northern deserts are, however, of quite considerable interest. For the purposes of this work, therefore, the Ethiopian region will be considered to be the whole of the continent of Africa without the extreme northwest corner. [See Fig. 1 for convenient reference to the political equivalents of the zoogeographic boundaries discussed in this paper.]

The area which is excluded lies to the north of the Atlas mountains. It is known as Barbary and comprises the northern parts of Morocco and Algeria. This region has a "depauperate fauna which is European in most of its relationships" (Darlington, 1957). For example, the only cervids and ursids (each group represented by a single species) occurring on the continent of Africa are found in Barbary. As Cooke (1963) has pointed out, however, the Pleistocene fossils and even historical records show that the Barbary fauna was until quite recently neither as depauperate nor as European as Darlington suggests. About two-thirds of the

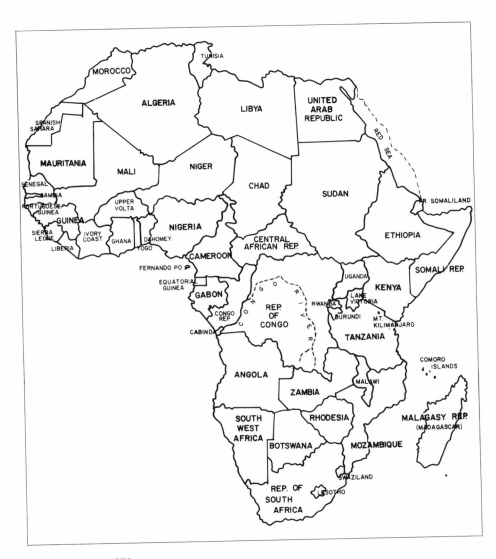

FIG. 1. Africa, 1971

mammals were African types which formed the basic stock. Nevertheless, the fauna does have stronger affinities with that of Europe than any other part of Africa, and indeed the region is often referred to as Palearctic Africa. This region will be disregarded in this paper, and "Africa" will be used to mean Ethiopian Africa.

[Note: Wherever practicable, nomenclature has been arranged to conform with the classification adopted in the *Preliminary Identification Manual for African Mammals* to be published shortly by the Smithsonian Institution, Washington. Any deviations from this practice are noted in the text.]

In Africa 52 families of mammals occur, a greater variety than in any other zoogeographic region. All are placental mammals; monotremes and marsupials are absent. Endemism at the family level is quite high. Twelve families, almost one-quarter of the total number, are strictly confined to the region. They are: Potamogalidae (see notes below Table 1), Chrysochloridae, Galagidae, Anomaluridae, Pedetidae, Thryonomyidae, Petromyidae, Bathyergidae, Protelidae, Orycteropodidae, Hippopotamidae, and Giraffidae. In addition, two subfamilies of the Cricetidae, the Dendromurinae and the Otomyinae, are also endemic.

Another three families are virtually limited to this region. Two of them, the Macroscelididae and the Ctenodactylidae, extend only into Palearctic Africa. A third, the Procaviidae, is represented outside Africa by only one species which is found in Arabia, Israel, Jordan, the Sinai Peninsula and Syria.

Of these 15 families and two subfamilies which have fossil representatives, only five are known to have occurred outside Africa in the past. They are the Thryonomyidae, Orycteropodidae, Procaviidae, Hippopotamidae and Giraffidae. In no case have fossils been found further afield than Europe and Asia.

Another striking feature of the African mammal fauna is its strong affinity with that of the Oriental region. Ten families are shared with that area only. They are: Lorisidae, Cercopithecidae, Pongidae, Manidae, Rhizomyidae, Hystricidae, Viverridae, Elephantidae, Rhinocerotidae and Tragulidae (but the Hystricidae and Viverridae each have one species which extends into southern Europe). Most of the groups have fossil representatives from no further afield than Europe.

Another 17 families are shared in varying degrees with Eurasia, and in a few cases with other regions. No purpose would be served by analyzing these mixed relationships in detail, but the degree of sharing with the continents farthest away must be mentioned. It is not great; at the present time only one family, the Bovidae, occurs in Africa, Europe, Asia and North America. The Equidae, too, were originally as widely distributed. The bat families Pteropodidae, Megadermatidae, Rhinolophidae and Hipposideridae and the murid subfamily Murinae are shared with Eurasia, Australia and several islands. The one African species of Trichechidae is endemic; other representatives of the family are found in South American waters. One bat family, the Emballonuridae, lives in both the Old and the New World tropics. The genera *Thryonomys* and *Petromus* must also be mentioned here. We follow Simpson (1945) in placing each in its own family endemic to Africa. These creatures are "morphologically octodontoid," however, and have been referred by some authors to Neotropical families and subfamilies.

Eight families remain to be considered. These, together with the cricetid subfamily Cricetinae, are widespread or worldwide in their distribution. Many of the genera occurring in Africa, however, are endemic (see also below).

Darlington's (1957) summary is apt: he writes that the African mammal fauna "is a diverse mixture of more or less widely distributed families, families shared with the Oriental Region, and exclusive families, and a few families with other relationships."

The point of greatest significance to the present subject is that the contemporary African mammal fauna has very few relationships with the faunas of the other southern continents.

THE CONTEMPORARY FAUNA AND ITS RADIATION

The composition of the contemporary fauna is summarized in Table 1, and representative types are shown in Figs. 3, 4, and 5. The taxonomy of many groups is far from settled so that the numbers of species, and especially of superspecies, must be regarded as provisional.

The fauna is an extraordinarily rich and diverse one. The Insectivora are well represented with many shrews and a number of hedgehogs. The endemic otter shrews (Potamogalidae) are interesting creatures resembling small otters in their adaptations to aquatic life. Also endemic are the subterranean golden moles (Chrysochloridae). The elephant shrews (Macroscelididae), almost endemic to Ethiopian Africa, are smallish long-snouted kangaroo-like creatures.

The bats call for no special comment. Both fruit eaters and insectivorous species are abundant. Among the primates, the cercopithecid monkeys stand out as a group with a large number of species. There are also small primitive forms, the pottos and galagos, as well as the family of the great apes, represented by the chimpanzee and the gorilla.

Two unrelated groups are adapted to a highly specialized diet. The scaly anteaters (Pholidota, Manidae) feed on ants and termites while the endemic aardvark (Tubulidentata, Orycteropodidae) is a large robust termite eater.

Hares are successful cursorial herbivores of the open country which have not speciated to any marked extent. The rodents have a large number of ordinary rat and mouse-like forms, graminivorous, herbivorous or omnivorous key-industry animals. There are many squirrel species. Gigantism is rare among the rodents, the biggest being the cane rats (Thryonomyidae) which weigh up to about 7 kg and the porcupines (Hystricidae) which may weigh 23 kg. There are "flying" rodents (Anomaluridae), kangaroo-like forms (Pedetidae, Dipodidae), two groups of subterranean mole-like creatures (Bathyergidae and Rhizomyidae) and rock dwellers very similar to hyraxes (Ctenodactylidae).

The Carnivora are represented by dogs, jackals and foxes, a variety of cats, hyenas, the aardwolf, a very few kinds of mustelids and a great variety of viverrids.

Well-known members of the African fauna include the elephant, hyraxes (which are virtually endemic to Africa and have arboreal and rock-dwelling forms), the zebras and a wild ass, and two kinds of rhinoceros.

In the tropical waters of the west coast, extending some way into the large rivers, a manatee occurs. A dugong is found in the Red Sea and on the northern Indian Ocean coasts south to Kenya. The Artiodactyla are perhaps the most spectacular group of African mammals. There are pigs, two species of hippopotamus, a chevrotain inhabiting west African forests, the giraffe and the okapi. Finally, there is the great family Bovidae with no fewer than 78 species, ranging from tiny antelope the size of hares to the great eland and buffalo.

In the introductory section it was pointed out that quite a number of mammal families are endemic to Africa. As might be expected, endemicity is much more marked at the level of the genus. In Table 2 the proportion of families and genera in each order which are confined to Ethiopian Africa is shown.

In the small groups, endemism at the generic level varies from nil (Sirenia, Pholidota) to 100 per cent (Tubulidentata, Proboscidea), with some intermediate between these extremes (Lagomorpha, Hyracoidea, Perissodactyla). Among the large groups, the bats have only 41 per cent of the genera endemic. In the Carnivora, two-thirds of the genera are limited to Africa. Endemism is most highly developed in the Insectivora (79%), Rodentia (81%), Artiodactyla (88%) and Primates (100%).

In the section which follows, speciation, radiation and the main features of ecology and geographical distribution will be discussed in each order.

Insectivora

(See Fig. 3)

The otter shrews, Potamogalidae, are endemic aquatic animals of the forest biome which feed on aquatic invertebrates. *Potamogale velox* is widely distributed in the main lowland forest block (the main biotic zones are shown in Fig. 2) and its outliers. Each of the other two species (*Micropotamogale*) is known only from a restricted area of montane forest.

The golden moles (Chrysochloridae) have evolved in Africa and some authors (e.g., Roberts, 1951) consider them distinct enough to merit ordinal rank. They are highly adapted for subterranean life and convergence with other mole-like forms, such as the rodent families Rhizomyidae and Bathyergidae, is marked.

The group is essentially a non-forest one which occurs in the South West Cape, the South West Arid and the Southern and Northern Savanna zones. Speciation has been most active at the southern end of the continent, about two-thirds of the species being confined to southern Africa. Chrysochlorids occupy a considerable range of non-forest habitats. For example, *Eremitalpa granti* extends into the Namib desert while *Chrysospalax villosus* occupies moist grassland. Body sizes range from about 20 cm (*Chrysospalax trevelyani*) to less than half this length. There is little

TABLE 1

Families and approximate numbers of species and superspecies of contemporary mammals of continental Ethiopian Africa

	SPECIES	SUPER-SPECIES
INSECTIVORA		
Potamogalidae (Otter Shrews)	3	3
Chrysochloridae (Golden Moles)	16	7
Erinaceidae (Hedgehogs)	6	3
Macroscelididae (Elephant Shrews)	13	7
Soricidae (Shrews)	56	41
CHIROPTERA		
Pteropodidae (Fruit Bats)	26	22
Rhinopomatidae (Mouse-tailed Bats)	2	2
Emballonuridae (Sheath-tailed Bats)	7	7
Nycteridae (Hollow-faced Bats)	11	7
Megadermatidae (Big-eared Bats)	2	2
Rhinolophidae (Horseshoe Bats)	17	16
Hipposideridae (Leaf-nosed Bats)	14	14
Vespertilionidae (Simple-nosed Bats)	64	?56
Molossidae (Mastiff Bats)	31	26
PRIMATES		
Lorisidae (Pottos)	2	2
Galagidae (Galagos)	6	4
Cercopithecidae (Monkeys)	47	20
Pongidae (Apes)	3	2

	SPECIES	SUPER-SPECIES
Microtinae	1	1
Rhizomyidae (Bamboo rats)	2	2
Muscardinidae (Dormice)	7	5
Dipodidae (Jerboas)	3	3
Hystricidae (Porcupines)	5	3
Thryonomyidae (Cane Rats)	2	2
Petromyidae (Dassie Rats)	1	1
Bathyergidae (Mole Rats)	13	8
Ctenodactylidae (Gundis)	5	5
Spalacidae (Blind Mole Rats)	1	1
CARNIVORA		
Canidae (Jackals, etc.)	11	10
Mustelidae (Weasels, etc.)	7	6
Viverridae (Genets, etc.)	37	32
Hyaenidae (Hyenas)	3	2
Protelidae (Aardwolf)	1	1
Felidae (Cats)	10	10
TUBULIDENTATA		
Orycteropodidae (Aardvark)	1	1

PHOLIDOTA		
Manidae (Scaly Anteaters)	4	3
LAGOMORPHA		
Leporidae (Hares)	10	8
RODENTIA		
Sciuridae (Squirrels)	31	17
Anomaluridae (Scaly Tails)	7	7
Pedetidae (Springhare)	1	1
Muridae		
Murinae	79	54
Cricetidae		
Dendromurinae	14	11
Otomyinae	12	11
Cricetinae	1	1
Gerbillinae	33	26
Lophiomyinae	1	1
Cricetomyinae	5	3
Petromyscinae	3	3

PROBOSCIDEA		
Elephantidae (Elephants)	1	1
HYRACOIDEA		
Procaviidae (Dassies)	11	4
SIRENIA		
Trichechidae (Manatees)	1	1
Dugongidae (Dugongs)	1	1
PERISSODACTYLA		
Equidae (Zebras)	5	4
Rhinocerotidae (Rhinos)	2	2
ARTIODACTYLA		
Suidae (Pigs)	3	3
Hippopotamidae (Hippos)	2	2
Tragulidae (Chevrotain)	1	1
Giraffidae (Giraffe and Okapi)	2	2
Bovidae (Antelopes)	78	67

[Note: The order Insectivora has been retained here, although it has been replaced by the orders Lipotyphla (Tenrecidae, Chrysochloridae, Erinaceidae, and Soricidae) and Menotyphla (Macroscelididae) in the Preliminary Identification Manual for African Mammals (Corbet, 1966, 1968; Meester, 1968). Similarly, the family Potamogalidae has been retained in this text, although it has been submerged in the Tenrecidae, an otherwise endemic Madagascan family, in the same Manual.]

TABLE 2

Endemism in contemporary African mammals

Order	Families Total No.	Families Endemic No.	Families Endemic %	Genera Total No.		Genera Endemic No.	Genera Endemic %
Insectivora	5	3	60	20	*24*	*19*	79
Chiroptera	9	0	0	42	*44*	*18*	41
Primates	4	1	25	17	*11*	*11*	100
Pholidota	1	0	0	1		0	0
Lagomorpha	1	0	0	2	*4*	*3*	75
Rodentia	14	6 *	43	73	*84*	68	81
Carnivora	6	1	17	36		24	66
Tubulidentata	1	1	100	1		1	100
Proboscidea	1	0	0	1		1	100
Hyracoidea	1	0	0	3		2	66
Sirenia	2	0	0	2		0	0
Perissodactyla	2	0	0	3		2	66
Artiodactyla	5	2	40	36		32	88

* *Ctenodactylidae included as endemic*

Numbers of genera in italics represent revisions based on Smithsonian Preliminary Identification Manual of African Mammals.

morphological variation, the most striking difference between species being the enlargement of either one or two foreclaws as digging implements. Some forms burrow deeply and throw up mounds (*Amblysomus*) while species inhabiting sandy areas (such as *Eremitalpa*) burrow just below the surface and throw up a ridge of sand. The giant forms (*Chrysospalax*) inhabit mounds and feed mainly on the surface. Invertebrates such as earthworms and insects constitute the diet of golden moles.

Hedgehogs (Erinaceidae) are medium-sized terrestrial insectivores with a covering of spines. *Erinaceus* has several species in the arid and savanna zones. *Hemiechinus auritus* is the common Egyptian hedgehog (Setzer, 1956) and *Paraechinus* is another north African form. All hedgehogs are essentially similar in size and body form. The family is widely distributed in Europe and Asia and may have invaded Africa from outside.

The elephant shrews (Macroscelididae) are endemic creatures which evolved in Africa. Some authors (e.g., Corbet, 1966) place the family in a separate order, the Menotyphla. The range extends into Palearctic Africa. Elephant shrews are saltatorial, kangaroo-like animals ranging in size from that of a small mouse to that of a large rat. They feed on invertebrates. There is little structural variation but the Rhynchocyoninae lack the pollex; the upper incisors are absent or rudimentary and the upper canines are dominant. It is not known whether these features are related to the ecology of this forest group.

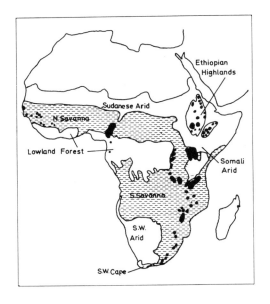

FIG. 2. THE MAIN BIOTIC ZONES
OF AFRICA SOUTH OF THE SAHARA
*Montane forest in black (after
Davis, 1962).*

The body form suggests that the Macroscelididae evolved in open regions, and the present distribution of species supports this view. Only two of the 13 species, the giant forms of the genus *Rhynchocyon*, occur in forests. The other eleven species are distributed in the savanna and arid zones as follows: South West Arid—*Macroscelides proboscideus*, *Elephantulus* (3 spp.), a total of four; Southern Savanna—*Elephantulus myurus*, *Nasilio brachyrhynchus*, *Petrodromus tetradactylus* (also on mountains), a total of three; Southern Savanna and into Somali Arid—*Elephantulus rufescens*; Northern Savanna—*Nasilio fuscipes*; Somali Arid—*Elephantulus revoili*; Mediterranean and subdesert zones of north-western Africa—*Elephantulus rozeti*. It will be seen from this list that speciation has been most active in the southern part of the continent, a situation similar to that described for the Chrysochloridae.

The shrews (Soricidae) are rich in species and widely distributed, as they are elsewhere in the world except in Australia and South America. They occur in all biotic zones, in tropical forests and semi-arid areas, from lowlands to extreme altitudes on the mountains of central Africa.

Shrews fill the niche of small insect-eaters and predators. Apart from some diversity in size and relatively minor morphological differences (Heim de Balsac and Lamotte, 1956, 1957; Meester, 1953, 1954) they are rather similar and generalized types.

The genera *Myosorex* (including *Surdisorex*) and *Sylvisorex*, each with about eight species, are mainly central African, many of the species being confined to isolated mountains. *Suncus* plays a minor role faunistically and there are three monospecific genera (*Scutisorex*, *Praesorex*, and *Paracrocidura*) in the tropics. The genus *Crocidura* is the biggest. It has

FIG. 3. MAJOR MORPHOLOGICAL TYPES OF CONTEMPORARY AFRICAN INSECTIVORES AND PRIMATES

INSECTIVORES: *A*, Erinaceus (*Hedgehog*); *B*, Chlorotalpa (*Golden Mole*); *C*, Elephantulus (*Elephant Shrew*); *D*, Suncus (*Shrew*); *E*, Potamogale (*Otter Shrew*). PRIMATES: *A*, Galago; *B*, Perodicticus (*Potto*); *C*, Cercopithecus (*Vervet Monkey*); *D*, Colobus (*Colobus Monkey*); *E*, Gorilla.

a large number of species, the status of many of which is far from clear. Representatives of this genus are found in all biotic zones.

Chiroptera

The bats are second only to the rodents in the number of species which occur in Africa. The majority are insectivorous but there are a number of fruit-, nectar-, and pollen-eating species which are essentially tropical in distribution. Bats vary considerably in size, from the largest fruit eating species (Pteropodidae) to dwarf forms only a few inches across. The order is found in all biotic zones but the number of species decreases northward and southward from the tropics. A large proportion of the genera found in Africa are not endemic (Table 2).

Primates

(See Fig. 3)

Arboreal specialization is marked in the Primates, which are primarily inhabitants of forests, where they constitute a dominant group.

The Lorisidae are highly adapted little creatures whose slow movements and strong grasping reflexes are reminiscent of the sloths. Indeed they resemble this group in some adaptive skeletal features (Hill, 1953). The two forms occupy the lowland forest zone and have presumably been isolated there for a long period. Other members of the family occur in Asia. The pottos appear to be mainly carnivorous and are thus ecologically separated from monkeys and galagos of similar size. They are nocturnal and largely arboreal.

The Galagidae are endemic, quick and agile primates, ranging between a mouse and a rabbit in size. *Galagoides, Euoticus* and one species of *Galago* occur in the forest blocks and all are mainly arboreal. Two other species of *Galago* inhabit the savanna zones and are partly terrestrial, using their tails as balancing aids when on the ground.

The galagos are omnivorous and non-social; most are nocturnal in habit. In contrast to the Lorisidae, in which forelimbs and hindlimbs are approximately equal in length, the Galagidae have elongated hind limbs.

Monkeys of the family Cercopithecidae (4 gen., 47 spp., ?27 superspp.) are the most characteristic primates. They are diurnal and social and feed on leaves, fruit, flowers, and some to a limited extent, on eggs and other animal foods. Tappen (1960) has studied distribution and adaptation in African monkeys. They are essentially a group of the west and central African forest blocks where speciation has been active. The few species adapted to life outside the forest borders are ecologically tolerant and, for the most part, widely distributed.

The non-forest block monkeys comprise eleven species. The common baboons, *Papio (Papio)* [excluding *P. (P.) hamadryas*—taxonomy after Dandelot, 1968], are large terrestrial omnivores, widely distributed in the savanna and arid zones. Freedman (1963) suggests that all named forms constitute one superspecies. *P. (P.) hamadryas* is restricted to Ethiopia where it occurs at all altitudes. It would be of interest to establish its relationship with another baboon, *Papio (Theropithecus) gelada.* This is also confined to Ethiopia but is apparently restricted to high altitudes. The patas monkey, *Cercopithecus (Erythrocebus) patas,* is a large (30 kg) long-legged, almost purely terrestrial species of the Northern Savanna. *Cercopithecus (aethiops)* (a superspecies with five recognized species—Dandelot, 1959, and 1968) is a much smaller monkey which occurs widely outside the forest blocks. It is absent only from very arid areas, although it penetrates even these along tree-lined rivers.

The forest monkeys comprise two large genera of the subfamily Cercopithecinae, *Cercocebus* (4 spp., 2 superspp.) and *Cercopithecus* (18 forest spp., 14 superspp.); the three subgenera of the subfamily Colobinae, *Colobus* (4 spp.), *Piliocolobus* (approx. 4 spp.), and *Procolobus* (1 sp.); and two terrestrial baboons, the mandrill, *Papio (Mandrillus) mandrillus,* and the drill, *P. (M.) leucophaeus.* Most species are very variable geographically and many subspecies have been described. For example, the superspecies *Cercopithecus (mitis)* has a scattered distribution from the Guinea and Congo forest blocks themselves, eastwards through the forest outliers and densely wooded savannas of eastern and southern Africa. *C. (mitis)* overlaps *C. (aethiops)* but is in general confined to more moist, more densely wooded areas, in those parts of its range outside the major forest blocks. It is also more strictly arboreal.

The distribution of the forest monkeys is summarized by Tappen (1960) as follows: endemic to Guinea forest block, 3 species; occurring on both sides of the Dahomey gap, 7 to 11 species; found only east of the Dahomey Gap and in outlying forests east of the Congo Basin, 9 to 11 species. Some of the prolific speciation is perhaps explicable by the fragmentation of the main forest blocks which appears to have taken place in the past (see below). In some cases rivers can be shown to constitute barriers.[Note: Tappen's classification included fewer species than that of Dandelot (1968), but the distribution patterns are essentially similar.]

The coexistence of many species in the same area at the present time poses some interesting problems. Booth (1956) has studied the synecology of forest primates in Ghana. The species which are sympatric there are all diurnal and gregarious, tend to be socially organized and are to a greater or lesser extent arboreal. They also overlap largely in size and weight. It is therefore inevitable that there should be some degree of ecological overlap. An indication of the extent of overlap is the occurrence of mixed feeding parties where different species take identical food at the same spot. Nevertheless Booth was able to establish some basic differences in diet and to work out the preferences of different species for different levels in the tree layer. This information is presented in Table 3.

Klopfer (1962) has shown that enhanced diversity of the faunas of tropical regions can be explained by assuming a reduction in size of the

TABLE 3

Vertical range of monkeys in forests of southwest Ghana

	Sleeping			Travelling				Feeding				Food	
	Upper	Middle	Lower	Upper	Middle	Lower	Ground	Upper	Middle	Lower	Ground	Fruit	Leaves
Colobus (Piliocolobus) badius	x	—	—	xx	x	—	—	xx	x	(x)	—	—	x
Colobus (Colobus) polykomos	x	x	—	x	x	—	—	(x)	x	x	—	—	x
Colobus (Procolobus) verus	—	x	x	—	x	x	—	—	(x)	x	—	—	x
Cercopithecus (Cercopithecus) diana	x	x	—	x	x	—	—	x	x	(x)	—	x	—
Cercopithecus (mona) campbelli	—	x	(x)	(x)	x	x	(x)	—	x	x	—	x	—
Cercocebus torquatus lunulatus	—	x	x	—	x	x	xx	—	—	x	x	x	—
Cercopithecus (Cercopithecus) petaurista	—	x	x	—	x	xx	(x)	—	(x)	xx	—	x	x

Adapted from Booth, 1956.

x, *activity in this level of forest canopy.*

xx, *activity mainly in this level of forest canopy.*

(x), *activity occasionally in this level of forest canopy.*

niches occupied by each species. Put in another way, the tropics are populated by many specialized, primitive species with a high degree of behavioral stereotypy, whereas the extratropical areas support fewer more recently evolved species which are adaptable and occupy large niches.

Booth's primate data fit these concepts quite well but Tappen gives several examples of great adaptability in the forest monkeys. Thus, the black and white colobus, *Colobus (C.) polykomos,* will move into new layers of forest if *Colobus (Piliocolobus) badius* and *Colobus (Procolobus) versus* are absent. The latter species, however, will not leave its thickets, even if there are no other colobines about. *Cercopithecus (mitis) nictitans* is restricted to primary forest in the Ivory Coast, but in Nigeria it lives in all levels of secondary forest and in bush country around farms. In Uganda, *C. ascanius* moves into all levels of primary forest when competing species are absent.

The fact that the forests have many more monkey species than do the savannas, does, of course, support Klopfer's main thesis, but it would seem that the behavior of the forest forms is not necessarily as stereotyped as his arguments would lead one to expect. Strong interspecific competition may be the root cause of the usual occupation of small niches by at least some species. When the competition is removed they enlarge their niches. This is what Simpson (1944, cited in Tappen, 1960) calls shifts in adaptive zone, and he regards it as one of the most important evolutionary processes. Tappen notes that some species seem to be equipped to make these shifts more readily than others.

The largest primates are the well-known chimpanzees and gorilla (Pongidae). All dwell in forests and spend much time on the ground. The chimpanzees, perhaps because of their smaller size, tend more towards an arboreal habit than the gorilla.

Pholidota

The pangolins or scaly anteaters (Manidae) have a body covering of horny scales and are able to roll up into a ball. They are edentate, have a long retractable tongue, dig with strong claws, and feed on ants and termites. It is interesting that animals occupying such a specialized niche should have radiated to any extent.

There are four species. Two are arboreal and occur in the lowland forest zone; their areas of distribution appear to overlap almost completely. One is nocturnal, whereas the other tends to be diurnal and less widespread (Rahm, 1960; Booth, 1960). Two species are terrestrial. One occurs in the Southern Savanna and extends slightly into the Northern Savanna; the second is a giant form distributed in the forest blocks and adjacent savannas.

Tubulidentata

The single family of this group contains one well-known monotypic genus, *Orycteropus,* the aardvark. It is widely distributed in the savanna zones. The group bears no relationship to the Pholidota but shows some interesting convergent features in adaptation to a similar diet. The aard-vark is generally believed to be mainly termitophagous but is also de-scribed as eating ants and tubers (Verschuren, 1958). It is a heavily built pig-like creature with bristly hair and hoof-like feet. Like the pangolins, the aardvark has a long, extrusible sticky tongue.

Lagomorpha

The hares (Leporidae) are successful and abundant cursorial herbivores of the savanna and arid zones. Rock hares of the endemic genus *Prono-lagus* (3 spp.) occupy hilly and mountainous country in the Southern Savanna and South West Arid zones, in some cases living among rocks like hyraxes. The isolated "Bunyoro rabbit" *Poelagus marjorita* occupies a "forest-type habitat" (Setzer, 1956) in mountainous areas of the north-east Congo, Uganda, and the southern Sudan. It is a small burrowing rabbit unique in Africa. The Bushman hare, *Bunolagus monticularis,* is apparently restricted to a small area of the South-West Arid zone in Cape Province, South Africa.

All other hares belong to the genus *Lepus* (5 spp.). Two species range across most of nonforested Africa and into Europe and Asia. They are largely sympatric but one species tends to favor more open habitats. The remaining three species, not markedly differentiated, occupy fairly restricted ranges (Petter, 1967).

Rodentia

(See Fig. 4)

The rodents, with approximately 227 species (?166 superspp.), are repre-sented by more taxa than any other group. Africa "must surely be con-sidered the present headquarters of the order so far as variation in char-acter goes" (Ellerman, 1940-41). The richness and diversity of the rodent fauna is the result partly of the evolution in Africa of a number of fami-lies and subfamilies, and partly of active speciation in families not con-fined to the continent.

The closely related Muridae and Cricetidae constitute the dominant groups and will be considered together here. The subfamily Cricetinae, so conspicuous in the New World, is represented only by the monotypic genus *Mystromys* and possibly also by the peculiar maned rat *Lophiomys,* which is, however, referred to the Lophiomyinae by Misonne (1968). The Microtinae, which are the dominant cricetids of the Holarctic, reach North Africa with but one, otherwise Palearctic, species.

The murids and cricetids have not radiated to any extent in the forest biomes of Africa, probably because they arrived late (Misonne, 1963). Those few species that are found in forests have evolved relatively recently from savanna lines. The fact that the families Galagidae, Anomaluridae and Sciuridae contain several mouse-sized species living in forests seems to indicate that the "mouse niche" in that biome had already been filled by radiation within these families when the murids and cricetids reached Africa.

The Murinae are represented by some 22 genera, all but two of which are endemic. Most are generalized forms similar to rats and mice, and are graminivorous, herbivorous or omnivorous key-industry animals. The genera *Thamnomys, Aethomys,* and *Thallomys* exhibit some degree of adaptation to arboreal life, and have short, broad feet. *Dasymys* is a soft-furred rat which is partly aquatic. *Malacomys* and *Colomys* possess long, narrow, hindfeet which provide support on swampy ground. The coat of *Acomys* and, to a lesser extent of *Uranomys,* is a specialized spiny covering.

The Cricetomyinae (3 gen.) include *Cricetomys,* a giant rat (head-and-body length, 380 mm; tail length, 430 mm); this noticeably aberrant form of cricetid has a wide distribution from Senegal to South Africa. *Beamys,* on the other hand, has a restricted distribution in the relic forests of Kenya and Malawi.

The Otomyinae are endemic, generalized ratlike forms which are separated mainly because of their curious, broad, hypsodont teeth. They occur in the South West Arid and Southern Savanna zones and some forms are found on mountains up to the equator.

The Dendromurinae or African climbing mice are also endemic. *Dendromus* and *Dendroprionomys* are specialized for arboreal life; the former has only three functional fingers on the hand, and a prehensile tail, while the latter (monospecific) genus, known only from four specimens from the Congo, possesses four functional fingers. *Dendromus* is quite widely distributed, with five species which occur mainly in the Southern Savanna.

Steatomys is a peculiar, corpulent, burrowing form with a number of species in the Northern and Southern Savanna zones. The extremely aberrant monospecific genus *Malacothrix* has an abnormal skull structure, and is essentially confined to the South West Arid zone. Only two forms occur in the forest blocks; *Prionomys,* which is modified for arboreal life, and *Deomys,* with a peculiar skull structure. The closely related subfamily Petromyscinae is represented by two genera, *Petromyscus* and *Delanymys,* the latter being monospecific. The two species of *Petromyscus* are confined to the South West Arid zone while, in contrast, *Delanymys* is apparently confined to peaty swamps in the bamboo forests around the Kivu volcanoes.

The subfamily Gerbillinae is widely distributed in the savanna and arid zones of the continent. Within the group there is some development of the special features associated with bipedal saltatorial life—a kangaroo-like form, elongated hindlimbs and tail, a broad skull with enlarged bullae. Genera such as *Gerbillus* and *Tatera* tend to be more generalized and are widely distributed with many named forms. The genera *Pachyuromys, Meriones* and *Psammomys,* which occur in north Africa and beyond, contain the most specialized forms.

The dormice (Muscardinidae) are represented in Africa by the subfamily Graphiurinae. The genus *Graphiurus*, with about 5 species, occurs in the forest and savanna zones and even extends into arid areas. These small, slow-moving, squirrel-like rodents are omnivorous or perhaps mainly carnivorous. The tail is thick and bushy and the feet are of an arboreal type.

The largest African rodents are the porcupines (Hystricidae). The crested porcupine *Hystrix* attains a weight of up to 23 kg. There are two species, one in the Southern Savanna extending into the adjacent arid zone and marginally into forest, and one in the Northern Savanna and adjoining arid and forested regions. *Hystrix* has an unusually wide range which includes southern Europe. It has a well developed covering of stout spines, is nocturnal, partly fossorial and feeds on coarse vegetable matter. The brush-tailed porcupine *Atherurus* is a much smaller form with poorly developed spines; it is common in the main forest blocks and their outliers. The genus contains three species.

The Thryonomyidae are an endemic group of large hystricomorph rodents (up to 7 kg). There are two species of the genus *Thryonomys*, widely distributed in the savanna zones and extending into forest, perhaps secondarily. Cane rats feed on coarse grasses, reeds and cultivated crops.

There is yet another endemic hystricomorph family, the Petromyidae, which contains *Petromus typicus* of the South West Arid zone. This is a small squirrel-like rat which lives in crevices among rocks and feeds on vegetable matter.

The Bathyergidae, also endemic to Africa, are an extremely isolated group of rodents of obscure affinities. They may possibly be hystricomorph. The peculiar structure of the jaw muscles and the great variability in the number of cheek teeth set the group apart. Mole rats are adapted to subterranean life. The body is compact, the legs and tail short, the eyes are small and the ear pinnae reduced. There is a tendency for reduction of the pelage, culminating in the extraordinary form *Heterocephalus* which is practically naked. The foreclaws are enlarged for digging in *Bathyergus;* they are relatively small in the other forms which use their deeply rooted upper incisors to move soil. The mole rats feed on vegetable matter and are a non-forest group.

Cryptomys with seven species is widely distributed in the Northern and Southern Savanna zones, the South West Arid and the South West Cape. It is closely allied to *Georhychus* (one sp.), a South West Cape form. One species of *Bathyergus* has a similar distribution, while the other extends into the South West Arid. *Heliophobius* is represented by two species, one with quite a wide range in the Southern Savanna and one restricted to the vicinity of Mt. Kilimanjaro. *Heterocephalus* is monospecific and occurs mainly in the Somali Arid zone.

A second group of subterranean rodents is represented in Ethiopian Africa. This is the myomorph family Rhizomyidae (bamboo rats) which occurs also in Asia. The single endemic genus *Tachyoryctes* is mole-like but not extremely so. A larger species is found in southern Ethiopia. All the other named forms, occurring (mainly in highland areas) from Tanzania through Kenya, eastern Congo, and Uganda to Somalia and Ethiopia, may be referable to a single species.

The basically Palearctic myomorph family Spalacidae (blind mole rats), which contains the most extremely modified subfossorial rodents, only just reaches Africa. One species extends into northern Egypt and Libya.

Two unrelated families are kangaroo-like in form. The Dipodidae (jerboas) are a Holarctic group extending only into northern Africa. They are more specialized for saltatorial life than any other rodents, with elongation of the hindlimbs and a reduction in the number of functional digits, fusion of the central metatarsals into a cannonbone, and a tendency towards fusion of the cervical vertebrae. The family is represented by one species of *Allactaga* and two of *Jaculus*.

The endemic family Pedetidae comprises the archaic monotypic genus *Pedetes* (the spring hare) which resembles a rabbit-sized jerboa. It is a nocturnal vegetarian which spends the day in burrows dug with the aid of strong, hoof-like claws. The distribution pattern is an interesting one found in a number of dry country forms. Spring hares occur in the South West Arid zone and adjacent parts of the Southern Savanna. There is a gap, beyond which the species occurs again in the northern part of the Southern Savanna (Tanzania, Kenya, southeast Congo). The significance of this interrupted distribution will be discussed below under Regional Faunas.

The Ctenodactylidae are a north African group extending beyond the bounds of Ethiopian Africa into the Palearctic region of the continent and hence not strictly endemic to Africa as defined for the purposes of this paper. Fossils are known from southern Europe and from India (Ellerman, 1940-41). Whether the group evolved in Africa and radiated outwards, or evolved outside the continent, invaded it and subsequently became extinct, leaving the living forms as African relicts, is not known. The gundis are interesting rodents of uncertain affinities which resemble the hyraxes both in form and ecology. *Pectinator* (one sp.) occurs in the Somali Arid, *Massoutiera* (one sp.) in the Sudanese Arid from Chad to Algeria, and *Felovia* (one sp.) from Senegal to Mauritania. *Ctenodactylus* (2 spp.) is a genus of extreme north and northwestern Africa. All are stoutly built, short-tailed animals about the size of a cat and live among rocks. They are vegetarian and in many areas occur together with hyraxes, apparently occupying a very similar if not identical niche.

Two rodent families have still to be discussed. Both are essentially arboreal groups of the forest biome. The Anomaluridae ("flying squirrels") show convergence with the flying squirrels, such as *Pteromys*, of the Holarctic and Nearctic, but probably have no close affinities with the Sciuridae (Simpson, 1945). The genus *Zenkerella* (one sp.) is peculiar in

FIG. 4. MAJOR MORPHOLOGICAL TYPES OF CONTEMPORARY AFRICAN RODENTS AND CARNIVORES

RODENTS: *A*, Pedetes (*Spring Hare*); *B*, Anomalurus (*Scaly Tail*); *C*, Petromus (*Rock Rat*); *D*, Cryptomys (*Mole Rat*); *E*, Graphiurus (*Dormouse*); *F*, Xerus (*Ground Squirrel*); *G*, Jaculus (*Kangaroo Rat*); *H*, Thryonomys (*Cane Rat*). CARNIVORES: *A*, Canis (*Jackal*); *B*, Crocuta (*Spotted Hyena*); *C*, Mungos (*Mongoose*); *D*, Proteles (*Aardwolf*); *E*, Felis (*Wild Cat*); *F*, Mellivora (*Ratel*).

lacking gliding membranes. It is a small form which occurs in the central forest block. All other members of the group have a membrane stretched between the forelimbs and hindlimbs and between hindlimbs and tail, which enables them to glide from tree to tree. Sharp claws and a row of sharp, horny scales on the underside of the tail aid the animals in running up tree trunks.

Idiurus (2 spp.) is a pigmy form (head-and-body length, 100 mm; tail length, 125 mm) living colonially in hollow trees and under bark. It is nocturnal and feeds on fruit and perhaps also on insects (Booth, 1960; Sanderson, 1940). The area of distribution includes both the central and western forest blocks. *Anomalurus* has one large species, about the size of a large squirrel, which occurs in the western forest block. It is nocturnal and feeds on leaves and flowers. A smaller form occurs in the central forest zone. Another species of about the same size is found in both forest blocks, ranging into quite dry forest; it is diurnal. The fourth form of *Anomalurus* is the typical nocturnal flying squirrel of most of the lowland forest zone and extends into outlying forest patches as far south as Zambia. It spends the day lying up in dense foliage.

The squirrels (Sciuridae) are a dominant group in the African forests. Like the cercopithecid monkeys, they have speciated to a much greater extent in the forest zones than elsewhere. Most species are restricted to these zones, relatively few occurring elsewhere. Amtmann (1966) recognizes 31 species, which may perhaps comprise 17 superspecies, grouped into seven genera.

The ground squirrels (*Xerus*) are largely or entirely vegetarian, feeding on seeds, plants, and bulbs. The arboreal forms appear to resemble each other rather closely in their dietary habits, taking fruits, seeds and nuts (some have become a nuisance through feeding on cocoa beans in west African plantations) and animal matter such as bird eggs and insects. Ansell (1960) has a record of *Heliosciurus lucifer* (now *Paraxerus lucifer*) eating ants. The little information on record about squirrel feeding habits does not suggest that sympatric species separate out ecologically by eating different kinds of food. Some alimentary separation is to be expected, however, as a result of differences in body size.

Tropical forest squirrels can be arranged in order of size from the pigmy form *Myosciurus* (head-and-body length, 70 mm; tail length, 60 mm) to the giant *Protoxerus stangeri* (head-and-body length, 250 mm; tail length, 330 mm). On the other hand the arboreal savanna species and the ground squirrels, most of which are extra-tropical in distribution, are all rather similar in size. A study of jaw sizes might well produce results in agreement with Klopfer's (1962) finding that tropical avifaunas show a greater bill-size diversity than do those of extra-tropical regions. From this and other evidence he argues that the enhanced faunal diversity of the tropics is largely to be accounted for by a reduction in the size of the niches which tropical species, as distinct from non-tropical ones, occupy.

The genus *Xerus* comprises four species of ground squirrels. One is a South West Arid form encroaching into the Southern Savanna. A second is partly sympatric in the South West Arid but appears to be ecologically separated from the first (Shortridge, 1934; Roberts, 1937). The other two species occur north of a gap running across Rhodesia and Zambia. One is essentially a Northern Savanna form while the other, with a partly overlapping range, is typically a Somali Arid species.

Myosciurus (one sp.) is the pigmy squirrel of parts of the central forest block. *Heliosciurus* has three species, one ranging from Rhodesia to the Sudan and Senegal in high forest; one quite widely distributed over a similar range but occupying savanna woodland and secondary forest; and one with a restricted range in montane forests of the eastern Congo and adjoining regions. *Protoxerus* comprises two giant forest species. *Epixerus* is another giant form of the lowland forest zone. The genus *Funisciurus* consists of nine species, eight of them occurring in the lowland forest zone and some of its montane outliers. The remaining species extends into forest outliers down through Angola to southwest Africa. *Paraxerus* with eleven species, includes a predominantly savanna species (*P. cepapi*) which extends down to the Transvaal, as well as lowland and montane forest forms and a species of forest outliers southward to Natal.

Carnivora

(See Fig. 4)

With about 69 species (61 superspp.) the Carnivora are a large and diverse group. All but one of the families, and many genera, are not peculiar to the continent and there is a good deal of sharing with Europe and Asia. The most interesting feature of the order in Africa is the extensive speciation which has taken place in the Viverridae.

The endemic family Protelidae contains the monotypic genus *Proteles* (aardwolf), a curious creature with the appearance of a small hyena and few rudimentary cheek teeth. It feeds mainly on termites and occurs in the South West and Somali Arid zones and adjacent regions of the Southern Savanna, extending northward to Egypt. There is a gap separating the southwestern and northeastern regions of distribution.

The Canidae (5 gen., 11 spp.) are distributed over the arid and savanna zones but are absent from the forest, as one might expect of a group adapted for running. There are two endemic genera. *Otocyon* is a small fox-like form with supernumerary cheek teeth. It is diurnal, lives in pairs or family groups and feeds on invertebrates, small vertebrates and plant matter. The distribution is very similar to that of *Proteles*.

Lycaon, originally with a wide distribution outside the forest zones, fills the wolf niche. It hunts in packs and kills antelopes of various kinds.

Foxes of the genus *Vulpes* are solitary or live in small family groups. They are mostly nocturnal and feed on invertebrates, small vertebrates, berries and other vegetable food and, to a limited extent, carrion. One species, *V. chama,* is endemic to the South West Arid and adjacent grassland zones of the Southern Savanna. Two are known as sand foxes. *V. pallida* occurs in the Sudanese Arid zone and the southern Sahara. The other, *V. rüppellii,* is found in Ethiopia, the Somali Arid and throughout north Africa, possibly overlapping *pallida* to some extent. It ranges beyond the bounds of the continent into southern Arabia and Afghanistan.

The European red fox *V. vulpes* extends into northeastern Africa, being common in Egypt and occurring down the Nile valley to northern Sudan.

Fennecus (one sp.) is a small north African desert form living especially in dune areas. It occurs throughout the Sahara and southwards to the southern edge of the Saharan savannas.

The genus *Canis* is represented by four species of jackal, three of them endemic. Jackals are omnivorous and probably differ ecologically from the foxes mainly in being able to kill larger prey and in eating more carrion. *C. simensis* is an Ethiopian highland form. *C. adustus* is distributed over the Southern and Northern Savanna. *C. mesomelas* occurs in the South West Arid and adjacent parts of the Southern Savanna and, after a break in distribution, in the Somali Arid and Ethiopia. The Asiatic jackal *C. aureus* extends into Palearctic and northern Ethiopian Africa as far south as northern Kenya and Somalia.

The Mustelidae are faunistically unimportant in Africa. Of the Mustelinae, three European and Asiatic species of *Mustela* extend into the extreme north of the continent and are not here reckoned to the fauna. In addition there are three endemic forms with black and white aposematic coloration. Two are small and weasel-like. *Poecilogale* is a Southern Savanna species, while *Poecilictis* (one sp.) occurs in north Africa, southward to the Sudanese Arid. *Ictonyx* (one sp.) is larger and skunk-like in ecology and behavior. It has an extremely wide distribution through the arid and savanna zones and into north Africa.

Mellivora, the honey badger, is the only living member of the Mellivorinae. It is a stoutly built omnivore about the size of a small dog, with a wide distribution outside the forest zones. *Mellivora* is also found beyond the bounds of the continent, as far as India. Two genera of otters (Lutrinae) exist in Africa. The widespread *Lutra* has an endemic species *maculicollis* distributed in most streams and rivers of sub-Saharan Africa. The common Palearctic and Oriental *L. lutra* extends into the palearctic region of the continent. An endemic genus, *Aonyx,* has two species, one with a range similar to that of *L. maculicollis* and another which tends to replace it in the lowland forest biome.

We have already noted that the Viverridae have speciated to a remarkable extent in Africa. There are about 37 species, compared with only eleven species of Canidae, ten of Felidae and seven of Mustelidae. This richness results mainly from the evolution of endemic forms, 15 of the 18 genera being confined to the continent. The family is an old one which includes many different lines of specialization. In Africa the subfamilies Nandiniinae, Viverrinae and Herpestinae are represented.

Nandinia binotata, the two-spotted palm civet or tree civet, is the only member of the Nandiniinae in Africa. It is a nocturnal, largely arboreal, creature, about 60 cm long with a tail of equal length. *Nandinia* is a forest species and is found throughout the Guinea and Congo forest blocks, in lowland, montane, and gallery forests. It extends, in outlying forest islands, to east Africa and ranges southwards to eastern Rhodesia and northwards to the southern Sudan. Malbrant and Maclatchy (1949) regard it as the commonest viverrid in French Equatorial Africa. Like many carnivores it takes a good deal of vegetable food in addition to small rodents and other animal matter. According to the observations of Mitchell and Bates (quoted in Roberts, 1951) and the remarks of Malbrant and Maclatchy (1949) and of Sanderson (1940), it may indeed be mainly vegetarian. *Nandinia* appears to be an ancient, stable form.

The Viverrinae have four African genera with about 14 species (11 superspp.). *Poiana richardsoni* is a small genet (head-and-body length, 340 mm; tail length, 420 mm) with a long tail. Booth (1954), Malbrant and Maclatchy (1949) and Schouteden (1944/46) all state that it is rare. It is confined to forests and is found in the Congo, Gabon and Cameroons; after a gap it appears again in Ghana, ranging westwards into Sierra Leone. Booth (1954) suggests that this and other species, which have a similar scattered distribution in west Africa and are all quite rare, may represent stable "end-forms" of evolutionary lines which had reached a climax before the Dahomey Gap appeared. *Poiana* may thus be an ancient stable forest species which has suffered from competition with ecologically similar but more vigorous evolutionary lines—e.g., *Genetta.* Details of its ecology have not been recorded. One may assume the feeding habits of *Poiana* to be similar to those of other genets.

The taxonomy of the genus *Genetta* is confused. It seems likely that eleven species can be distinguished (Coetzee, 1967). There is no indication in the literature that the *Genetta* species are ecologically separated according to diet. As far as their feeding habits are known, all seem to be essentially or entirely carnivorous. They prey upon any small animals available, not infrequently raiding poultry yards, and live very largely on small rodents. They also climb trees to rob birds' nests and capture roosting birds, and possibly to take berries and other vegetable material on occasion. All species appear to be nocturnal in the main, to be both terrestrial and arboreal, and to overlap largely in weight and size.

Genetta (Pseudogenetta) villiersi occurs in the western part of the Northern Savanna while *G. (P.) abyssinica* is restricted to the Ethiopian Highlands. *G. (Paragenetta) johnstoni* is a forest form known only from skulls collected at one locality in Liberia.

G. (Genetta) genetta is extremely widely distributed outside the forest blocks and is found in northern Africa, southern Europe and southwest Asia. In many areas it overlaps the ranges of other species in this subgenus, but in general tends to prefer drier habitats. The three species with which it may be sympatric are *angolensis,* found in a restricted area of the Southern Savanna; *pardina* from the forest fringes and guinean savannas of west Africa; and *tigrina* (with *rubiginosa* and *mossambica*—species or subspecies?) which has a range in Africa almost as wide as that of *genetta*.

Two species of this subgenus remain. *G. (G.) victoriae* is a giant forest genet from the eastern part of the central forest block; *servalina* occurs mainly to the west but there are records from savanna country and also as far east as central Kenya.

The extremely rare and little known aquatic civet *Osbornictis piscivora* is endemic to deep forests of northeastern Congo. It is semi-aquatic or at least confined to the vicinity of water and feeds in part if not entirely on fish. The largest member of the Viverrinae is the civet *Viverra civetta* (head-and-body length, 900 mm; tail length, 550 mm) with a wide distribution in the Northern and Southern Savanna zones and in both forest blocks. It appears to be absent from primary high forest but is in other respects ecologically quite tolerant. It occurs in secondary forest and various kinds of savanna vegetation, and Moreau (1944) remarks that it wanders onto the moorland of Mount Kilimanjaro, dung having been found as high as 15,000 ft. Like the genets it is nocturnal, but it is slow-moving and far less agile than they. The civet is terrestrial and feeds on a wide variety of invertebrate and small vertebrate animals as well as eggs, fruits, berries and young shoots. It seems unlikely that there is much overlap between the niche occupied by the civet and those of other members of the subfamily.

The Herpestinae (mongooses) are extremely well represented, with about 22 species (about 20 superspp., 13 gen.). The biggest mongoose *Herpestes ichneumon* (head-and-body length, 500-650 mm; tail length, 450-500 mm) approaches the genets in size and is about twice the size of the dwarf mongoose *Helogale parvula* (head-and-body length, 200-250 mm; tail length, 150-200 mm). Two species have a very wide distribution on the continent. *Herpestes (Galerella) sanguineus* is found throughout the arid and savanna zones, south of the Sahara. The water mongoose *Atilax paludinosus* has the same geographical range but is limited in the habitats occupied by its semi-aquatic habits.

Savanna species which inhabit both northern and southern zones and encroach marginally into the Somali Arid are *Mungos mungo, Ichneumia albicauda* and *Herpestes (Herpestes) ichneumon*. The two latter species also range into north Africa and beyond the borders of the continent. Southern Savanna forms are *Helogale parvula* (also in Somali Arid); two apparently rare species, *Bdeogale crassicauda* (only as far south as Zambia) and *Rhynchogale melleri;* and *Paracynictis selousi* (only as far north as Zambia and Angola). *Helogale hirtula* represents *H. parvula* in Ethiopia and the Somali Arid. *Mungos gambianus* is found in the western part of the Northern Savanna. *Dologale dybowskii* has a restricted distribution in the east.

Three mongooses are endemic to the South West Arid, encroaching slightly into the adjoining parts of the Southern Savanna. They are *Suricata suricatta, Herpestes (Galerella) pulverulentus* and *Cynictis penicil-*

lata. All are common and successful and the last-named is probably the commonest southern African mongoose.

There are not many forest mongooses. *Crossarchus* has two allopatric species which collectively range throughout the lowland forest zone; a third has a restricted distribution in northern Angola. *Bdeogale (Galeriscus) nigripes* is found in the western part of the Congo forest block; the related *jacksoni* occurs in central Kenya and southeastern Uganda. *Herpestes (Xenogale) naso* is a Congo forest block representative of the widespread *H. (H.) ichneumon* mentioned above. The rather mysterious *Liberiictis kuhni,* known only from skulls collected at a single locality in Liberia, is a large, high forest form.

To summarize, the Herpestinae are essentially inhabitants of the arid and especially the savanna zones with relatively few species inhabiting the forests. Adaptive morphological specializations for life in any of the variety of habitats they occupy are conspicuous by their absence. As Shortridge (1934, vol. 1, p. 130) has pointed out, *Atilax paludinosus,* which is more completely at home in the water than any other species, is the only mongoose which has toes entirely destitute of webs. His implication that this feature may really be an adaptation enabling the animals to probe delicately in the mud for aquatic prey in the manner of a raccoon, rather than the absence of an adaptation for swimming, may have some foundation. In any event the specialization, if it is one, is of a minor nature. The African mongoose species differ from one another only in size, color and other relatively unimportant characteristics and all are basically very similar.

Differences in feeding habits are partly a function of size. The two largest mongooses *Herpestes ichneumon* and *Ichneumia albicauda* are able to tackle vertebrate prey up to about the size of hares and guineafowl and must be presumed to compete with sympatric species of *Genetta.* Verschuren (1958) examined stomachs of *G. tigrina* and *H. ichneumon* in the Garamba Park and found them both to contain only murids. Most of the mongooses, however, are much smaller than the genets and subsist on insects and other invertebrates and to a limited degree on small reptiles, birds and their eggs, and small rodents. There are records of several species feeding on fruits and other plant matter, and it is likely that most of them do so to some extent. Although none is strictly arboreal, many species climb trees with ease. In the Garamba Park where both *Mungos mungo* and *Herpestes (Galerella) sanguineus* are common, the former is almost exclusively insectivorous and the latter carnivorous (rodents) according to Verschuren (1958). Other sympatric species may be ecologically separated in the same way—e.g., *Suricata* and *Cynictis.* *Dologale dybowskii* is much rarer than *Mungos mungo* in the Garamba Park; both are insectivorous (Verschuren, 1958).

The majority of mongooses are diurnal. Some half dozen species exhibit quite well-developed social behavior patterns. *Suricata suricatta* is one such, living colonially in burrows which the animals dig for themselves.

They also use burrows made by ground squirrels and *Cynictis penicillata*, and all three animals sometimes inhabit the same warrens simultaneously. All the members of a *Suricata* colony, which may number 20 or more individuals, hunt together for food and contact is maintained by frequent grunting. When disturbed, all members of the group run off to the burrows together. The method of feeding is typical for all social species and is best described as fossicking. Shortridge (1934) has sketched it as follows: "*Suricata* is less active than *Cynictis* and does not as a rule wander very far from its burrows, around which it spends most of its time busily and restlessly scratching in the sand for insects, grubs, etc." (vol. 1, p. 147). The groups or packs of this and other social species appear to be quite nomadic and move their quarters fairly frequently, presumably to find new food sources. A common feature is that contact is maintained by incessant vocal signals, described in the various species as "low grunts," "chattering," and "chirruping."

The hyenas (Hyaenidae) are large, robust scavengers and, to a lesser extent, hunters, with exceptionally powerful jaws and teeth. Bones form an important constituent of their diet. Adaptive features in the dentition are described by Ewer (1954). The indigenous genus *Crocuta* (one sp.) occurs widely outside the forested areas of sub-Saharan Africa. *Hyaena brunnea* occupies the South West Arid zone and part of the Southern Savanna. The distribution of the genus is interrupted and a second species, *H. hyaena*, replaces the first from Tanzania northward through north Africa to Asia.

The final family to be discussed is the Felidae (3 gen., 10 spp.). Most African forms are shared with the Oriental region. Differentiation is mainly by size, all but one species (the cheetah) being typical cats in form and behavior. *Felis nigripes* is the smallest member of the family, an endemic of the South West Arid and nearby parts of the Southern Savanna. Forms the size of a tabby-cat comprise an endemic forest species, a very widely distributed savanna and arid zone representative and three European/Asiatic species which just enter north Africa. These smaller cats prey largely on small rodents and birds.

The caracal (*F. caracal*) is one of two medium-sized cats. It is common to Asia and most drier parts of Africa and takes prey up to the size of small antelopes. The other is the serval (*F. serval*) an endemic savanna species with a preference for moister areas and denser vegetation. It is a less aggressive predator, feeding mainly on birds and rodents.

The leopard (*Panthera pardus*) occurs throughout the continent and takes a variety of small to medium-sized prey.

The lion (*Panthera leo*) was originally distributed over all the savanna and arid regions. It is able to cope with the largest antelope, but preys mostly on medium-sized animals (100 to 300 kg) and also takes small ones (20 to 100 kg) (Kruuk and Turner, 1967). Lions catch their prey by stalking and running. Smithers (1968) places both lion and leopard in the genus *Panthera* but some authorities prefer to include both in the genus *Felis*.

Finally there is the cheetah, *Acinonyx jubatus,* a rather dog-like cursorial animal of open habitats which is exceptional in coursing its prey, mainly small or medium-sized antelopes.

Proboscidea

The elephants, a family shared with Asia, have one endemic representative, *Loxodonta,* in Africa. It is the largest herbivore on the continent, widely distributed, ecologically tolerant and successful.

Hyracoidea

These are small herbivorous hoofed mammals which are very similar to some rodents in body form and have rhinoceros-like teeth. They are probably distantly related to the Proboscidea. The hyraxes are an African group which extends only into adjacent areas of the Middle East and has apparently always been so distributed. The latest revision is that of Bothma (1966). The three genera are rather similar. Two of them, *Procavia* and *Heterohyrax,* are social rock dwellers and mainly diurnal. *Dendrohyrax* comprises tree-living forms which are non-social and nocturnal.

Procavia (5 spp.) occurs throughout the arid and savanna zones, in Ethiopia and in northern Africa; one species extends to Arabia. *Heterohyrax* (3 spp.) has a similar but rather more restricted distribution; there is a suggestion that it may prefer moister habitats. *Dendrohyrax* (3 spp.) has a Lowland Forest species, one in the forest outliers down to South Africa, and one with a restricted distribution in Tanzania and the off-shore islands.

Sirenia

Two families occur in African waters. An endemic manatee (Trichechidae) inhabits the tropical Atlantic coast and extends some distance up the major rivers. A dugong is found off-shore in the Red Sea and adjacent areas of the Indian Ocean, south to Kenya (Jarman, 1966).

Perissodactyla

There has not been a great deal of diversification in this order but it is nonetheless a widespread and successful group. The Equidae are large grazers which compete directly with some bovids (Lamprey, 1963). The uniquely striped zebras are endemic members of the genus *Equus.* The mountain zebra inhabits the arid ranges of southwestern Africa and South Africa. The extinct quagga occurred in the open plains of central South Africa. *E. burchelli* is the Southern Savanna form. The larger *E. grevyi* is restricted to parts of the Somali Arid zone. The fifth species is the (unstriped) north African wild ass which is now extremely rare.

The two members of the family Rhinocerotidae are the largest herbivores after the elephant. *Ceratotherium* is a grazer of open habitats, originally quite widely distributed in the savanna zones. *Diceros,* a slightly smaller form, formerly had a somewhat wider range which included the arid areas. It is essentially a browsing rhinoceros and occupies country more wooded than that tolerated by *Ceratotherium.*

Artiodactyla

The three living genera and species of pigs (Suidae) are the remnants of a diverse suid fauna well represented in the fossil record. *Phacochoerus* occurs in the Southern and Northern Savanna zones; *Potamochoerus* is widespread in the main forest blocks and their outliers down to South Africa. The third member of the family is the giant forest hog *Hylochoerus* which is restricted to high forest in parts of the main lowland blocks and on some east African mountains. The adaptive features of their skulls, teeth, and head musculature which fit *Phacochoerus* for grazing and the other two genera for rooting have been analyzed by Ewer (1958).

Hippopotamidae were present in Europe and Asia during the Pliocene and Pleistocene but are now purely an African group. The large *Hippopotamus* is widely distributed in lakes and rivers. It is a successful coarse grazer with a number of interesting adaptations to its amphibian habits. *Choeropsis* is a dwarf form of the western forests which is not as aquatic as its large relative.

The Giraffidae contains the bizarre long-necked browser, *Giraffa,* with a range covering much of arid and savanna Africa. The shorter-necked *Okapia* has a limited distribution in the dense forests of the northeastern Congo.

The Tragulidae are represented by only a single species of *Hyemoschus,* the water chevrotain of the west African forests. This small semi-aquatic herbivore is separated by a very great distance from its Asiatic relatives.

We come finally to the large and spectacular family Bovidae (about 78 spp., ?67 superspp.), so dominant a feature of the African fauna (see Fig. 5). There is no general agreement about the classification of the 27 genera. Simpson's (1945) arrangement into subfamilies and tribes is not regarded as a natural one by Ellerman, Morrisson-Scott, and Hayman (1953). These authors list no subdivisions, but this cautious attitude is not adopted here. It is convenient to discuss speciation and radiation by groups and Simpson's system of tribes, with one or two minor modifications, is followed.

Wells (1957) has adduced evidence for the existence of two bovine strata, an older "African" (i.e., those forms which probably evolved in Africa: Cephalophini, Neotragini, and Alcelaphini) and a younger "Afro-Eurasiatic" (Antilopini, Tragelaphini, Hippotragini and Reduncini). The peculiar isolated endemic *Pelea,* considered to constitute a tribe on its own (Ansell, 1968) should presumably be reckoned to the African stratum.

The Bovini, which include oxen and other large species of Europe, Asia, and North America, are represented by *Syncerus* (one sp.), the African buffalo. There is a large dark form, with a wide distribution in well-watered savanna areas, and a small red forest-and-mountain buffalo (Christy, 1929). Buffalo are primarily grass eaters (Lamprey, 1963) and markedly social animals which sometimes occur in enormous herds (see Pienaar, 1963).

The tribe Tragelaphini includes the largest African antelope *Taurotragus,* the eland, with two species (one supersp.). *T. oryx* (shoulder height, 1.6 m; weight, 750 kg) was originally widespread in the Southern Savanna and adjacent parts of the arid zones, just entering the Northern Savanna in east Africa. The eland ranged from sea level to high altitudes and occupied habitats ranging from treeless savanna to quite well-wooded country. Eland browse and graze (Darling, 1960; Lamprey, 1963) and are social. Extreme nomadism is a feature of their behavior, at least in dry habitats. *T. derbianus* is a Northern Savanna species with large horns which is often described as the giant eland. It is not certain whether this species exceeds *oryx* in weight and size.

Boocercus euryceros, the bongo, is a heavily built antelope (shoulder height, 1.25 m; weight, 220 kg). It is the only species of large bovid confined to forests. The bongo is discontinuously distributed in the Lowland Forest zone and occurs in some of the montane forests of Kenya and the southern Sudan. Its diet includes the shoots of trees, ground herbs, bark, roots and decayed wood (Lydekker, 1926). Bongo may run in small herds, presumed to be family parties, a primitive form of social behavior that is unusual in forest bovids.

Members of the genus *Tragelaphus* exhibit an interesting pattern of radiation. They are medium-sized to large species which inhabit heavily wooded savanna of various kinds. Sexual dimorphism is well marked, females being smaller, hornless, and often differently colored than the males. In their build and mode of progression, these antelope have many "Schlüpfer" attributes (Hediger, no date; see below).

The smallest and most widespread form of *Tragelaphus,* is the bushbuck *T. scriptus* (shoulder height, up to 80 cm; weight, up to 75 kg). It occurs throughout Africa from about 12°N southward, but is absent in the arid zones. In the forested areas it is found mainly in clearings and on forest edges. In the savanna biome it occupies wooded valleys and other moist areas with dense cover. The bushbuck also ranges into the alpine zone on many central African mountains (see Eisentraut, 1957). Mainly a delicate browser, the bushbuck eats grass to some extent (Lamprey, 1963); it is essentially solitary and territorial (Bourlière and Verschuren, 1960), the only member of the genus with this type of social structure.

T. angasi, the nyala (shoulder height, up to 1.5 m; weight, up to 130 kg) is rather like a large bushbuck. It is mainly confined to the lowlying Mozambique coastal plain in the Southern Savanna and inhabits thicket vegetation, especially riparian forest. The nyala probably occupies much the same niche as the bushbuck but its greater size enables it to browse at a higher level. Nyala occur in small herds.

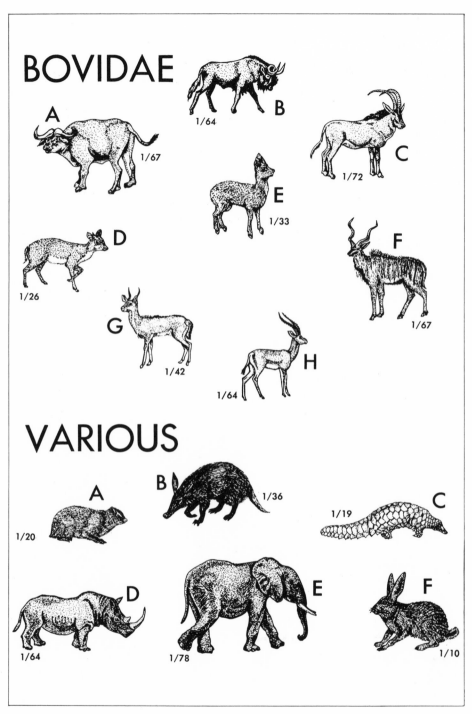

FIG. 5. MAJOR MORPHOLOGICAL TYPES OF CONTEMPORARY AFRICAN BOVIDAE AND VARIOUS OTHER MAMMALS

BOVIDAE: *A*, Syncerus (*Buffalo*); *B*, Connochaetes (*Wildebeest*); *C*, Hippotragus (*Sable Antelope*); *D*, Cephalophus (*Red Duiker*); *E*, Oreotragus (*Klipspringer*); *F*, Tragelaphus (*Kudu*); *G*, Redunca (*Reedbuck*); *H*, Gazella (*Grant's Gazelle*). VARIOUS: *A*, Procavia (*Hyrax*); *B*, Orycteropus (*Aardvark*); *C*, Manis (*Scaly Anteater*); *D*, Ceratotherium (*White Rhinoceros*); *E*, Loxodonta (*Elephant*); *F*, Lepus (*Hare*).

Another large form with an even more restricted distribution is the mountain nyala, *T. buxtoni* (shoulder height up to 1.3 m). It is restricted to the tree-heath zone above the forest line in high mountains of Ethiopia. The social structure is similar to that of *T. angasi,* but the feeding habits must be somewhat different in the peculiar habitat occupied.

T. spekei, the sitatunga, is a markedly semiaquatic member of the genus. It is fairly small (weight of females, 41 kg, weight of males, 70 kg —Robinette, 1963) with extraordinarily long hoofs and shaggy hair. Sitatunga submerge entirely except for the nostrils when pursued. The distribution is discontinuous, in swamp and marshes over most of Africa.

The kudus, placed in the subgenus *Strepsiceros,* are essentially animals of dry bush country. The large *T. strepsiceros* (shoulder height, 1.3 m; weight up to 300 kg) has a wide though somewhat patchy distribution in suitable areas of the arid and savanna biomes. The lesser kudu, *T. imberbis* (shoulder height, about 1 m), is smaller and endemic to the Somali Arid. It may be significant that the greater kudu is very successful and abundant in regions where the lesser kudu does not occur—e.g., in parts of South Africa (Bigalke, 1958; Bigalke and Bateman, 1962). Within the range of the lesser kudu, the greater kudu has a scattered distribution and tends to be rather rare (see Stewart and Stewart, 1963). Both species are browsers which also graze (Darling, 1960; Pienaar, 1963; Lamprey, 1963). They run in small herds which are probably extended family groups.

The duikers, tribe Cephalophini (which constitutes the subfamily Cephalophinae according to Simpson), are a distinct and ancient endemic group. They typify the type of ungulate which Hediger (no date) describes as a "Schlüpfer." This term is difficult to translate, but implies slipping between or creeping through. The concept is nevertheless most useful, and is contrasted with that of a "Läufer" or runner. "Schlüpfer" are animals which live among dense vegetation through which they force themselves like a wedge. They all have the forelegs shorter than the hind legs, the latter pushing the animals through the thickets. The horns are small, backwardly directed and simple, not getting in the way. Physiologically they have a relatively small lung and heart capacity and are thus unable to run for long distances. "Schlüpfer" are also characterized by their sedentary territorial behavior.

As a forest group, the duikers exhibit a pattern of distribution and speciation similar to that of the cercopithecid monkeys. Most species occur in the lowland forest blocks and montane forests, a few extend into outlying forest patches and one inhabits the savanna and arid zones. Sociable behavior has not been evolved in the duikers. They are mainly nocturnal and forest species which browse on leaves and shoots, take seeds and fruits, and probably also graze to a limited extent on the forest edges. The only detailed study of diet is Wilson's (1966) work on *Sylvicapra* in Zambia. He found the animal to be almost entirely a browser which very rarely eats grass. Leaves of non-grasses, fruits, and seeds were the most important foods; flowers, cultivated crops, and (in a few cases) animal material were also taken.

The genus *Cephalophus* has about 15 species, ranging in size from the dwarf forms *monticola* and *maxwelli,* weighing less than 10 kg to the giant yellow-backed duiker *sylvicultor,* which weighs up to 75 kg. The two dwarf species constitute a superspecies, with *maxwelli* in the Guinea forest block and adjacent forest-savanna mosaic, and *monticola* in the remaining areas of Lowland Forest and outlying forests down to South Africa.

C. sylvicultor is the most widespread of the big duikers. It occupies the Lowland Forest zone, and outlying forests eastward to Kenya and extends southward to Zambia, where it is found mainly in forests and thickets but occasionally in more open bush (Ansell, 1960). *C. spadix* is an east African montane forest duiker which probably forms a superspecies with *sylvicultor.* The third large duiker, *jentinki,* is confined to a small part of the Guinea forest block (Liberia and Ivory Coast) where it is sympatric with *sylvicultor.*

Of the medium sized duikers, *C. zebra,* with a bizarre striped coat, has a restricted range similar to that of *jentinki.* The almost black *C. niger* ranges more widely in the Guinea forest block and is also found east of the Dahomey Gap to the Niger River. *C. nigrifrons* has long hooves and in at least some regions is found in marshy areas within the forest (Malbrant and Maclatchy, 1949). It has been recorded in most of the Congo forest block and on several central and east African mountains. Bourlière and Verschuren (1960) found this duiker to be the commonest ungulate in the montane forests of the eastern Congo volcanoes. *C. dorsalis* has a wide range in the forest blocks; it is sympatric with *leucogaster* which may be merely a color phase (Ansell, 1968). One other form, *ogilbyi,* found on the island of Fernando Po, and on adjacent areas of the mainland, may also be conspecific with *dorsalis* (Ansell, 1968).

Three red duikers can probably be considered a superspecies (Ansell, 1968). They are *callipygus* from the western Congo forest block, *adersi* from the island of Zanzibar, and a widely distributed species *natalensis.* This has a pattern of distribution rather similar to that of *C. monticola,* the two being the only representatives of *Cephalophus* extending to South Africa. *C. natalensis* ranges from the eastern Congo forest block through most of the isolated montane and lowland forest patches in east Africa and southward to Natal.

The one remaining species of *Cephalophus* is *rufilatus.* It is a duiker of gallery forest, forest edges and thickets occurring on the northern fringes of the forest blocks and extending a little into the Northern Savanna. This duiker is less strictly a forest animal than the other members of the genus and so resembles to a limited degree the one true savanna duiker and sole representative of the second genus, *Sylvicapra grimmia.* The grey duiker occurs throughout the Northern and Southern Savannas and also in the arid zones, being restricted in its range only by the requirement for quite dense cover (see Bigalke and Bateman, 1962).

Pelea capreolus, placed on its own in the tribe Peleini and perhaps related to the following group, is an ancient form evolved in South Africa.

It is a small antelope which occupies rocky hills and mountain ranges in the grassland zone of the Southern Savanna and neighboring parts of the South West Arid biotic zone. The social structure is simple, small groups of about a half-dozen animals being the rule.

The reedbucks, waterbucks, and their allies are grouped together in the tribe Reduncini. *Redunca fulvorufula*, the mountain reedbuck, is discontinuously distributed in South Africa, east Africa, and in the northern Cameroons. It inhabits grassy hills and mountains and probably competes to some extent with *Pelea* in South Africa. The two other species of the genus *Redunca* live in grassland, often along rivers and on flood plains. The larger southern *R. arundinum* (shoulder height, up to 93 cm) is found in suitable parts of the Southern Savanna from the eastern Cape Province to Tanzania. *R. redunca* (shoulder height up to 75 cm) is distributed in the savanna from Tanzania north to Ethiopia and the Sudan, and in the Northern Savanna westward to Senegal. It is the second most abundant antelope on the flood plains of the Rukwa Valley (Vesey-Fitzgerald, 1960). Reedbuck live in small groups (Bourlière and Verschuren, 1960) and are mainly or entirely grasseaters (Lamprey, 1963).

The largest member of the genus *Kobus* is the waterbuck, *K. ellipsiprymnus,* now regarded as conspecific with *defassa* (Ansell, 1968). It is a heavily built antelope weighing up to 270 kg (Robinette, 1963) which occurs in the vicinity of rivers in much of the Southern and Northern Savanna. Waterbuck are grass-eaters (Verschuren, 1958) and live in herds of various kinds (Bourlière and Verschuren, 1960).

Two smaller species of the subgenus *Adenota* constitute a superspecies. *K. vardoni,* the puku, has a restricted distribution in the Southern Savanna, from northern Botswana to southwestern Tanzania and the southern Congo. The preferred habitat is "dry open grassland adjacent to swamps, rivers, vleis or flood plains, or on the fringes of woodland adjacent to these areas, always associated with water" (Smithers, 1966, p. 111). Puku are largely grazers (Darling, 1960) and are gregarious in small to large herds (Ansell, 1960).

K. kob, the kob, is a little larger than the puku and replaces it in the Northern Savanna. It resembles the puku ecologically and feeds selectively on short grass and a few species of associated herbs (Verschuren, 1958; Bourlière and Verschuren, 1960). Buechner (1961) discovered the existence of a well-defined pattern of territorial behavior. Males defend small, fixed territories with a central area of concentrated activity.

The tendency to be associated with riverine habitats seen in this group of antelope reaches its peak in the subgenus *Hydrotragus*, the lechwes. The southern *K. leche* is confined to much the same area as the puku. *K. megaceros* occupies the swamps bordering the White Nile in the southwestern Sudan, 1000 miles further north. Both species are characteristic of shallowly inundated plains where they graze. They are semi-amphibious and have long hooves. Lechwe are markedly social animals. Ansell (1960) and Allen (1963) deal with subspeciation and ecology.

The Hippotragini are large antelope. *Hippotragus niger* (sable antelope) lives in the Southern Savanna almost up to the Equator while *H. equinus* (roan; average weight of males, 145 kg—Robinette, 1963) is widespread over both the Southern and Northern Savannas. They overlap a good deal, *niger* being more selective in its choice of habitat ("woodlands not too dense nor at too high an elevation"—Darling, 1960) than *equinus*, which tolerates drier country. The extinct *H. leucophaeus* was a curiously isolated South West Cape form.

Two hippotragine genera are adapted to live in desert areas. *Oryx gazella* occupies the South West and Somali Arid zones. The smaller white or scimitar-horned oryx, *O. dammah*, ranges throughout the Sudanese Arid zone and to a limited extent into the Sahara. The characteristic large antelope of the Sahara, where it is endemic, is the heavily built *Addax nasomaculatus*.

The Alcelaphini are antelopes of medium and large size; they are grouped into three genera. *Damaliscus* comprises three medium-sized species. The nominate race of *D. dorcas*, the bontebok, is confined to the South West Cape. The other subspecies, *D. d. phillipsi*, the blesbok, is an animal of the grassland plateau of the Southern Savanna. *D. lunatus* (tsessebe, tiang, topi, korrigum) extends in various races from the Southern Savanna (Transvaal, although originally south to the Orange River —Bigalke and Bateman, 1962), through northern Zambia and the southeastern Congo, to the Somali and part of the Sudanese Arid zones, Ethiopia, and the Northern Savanna. The third species, *D. hunteri*, has a very restricted distribution in northeastern Kenya and adjoining parts of Somaliland, occupying "desert grassbush" (Stewart and Stewart, 1963). The damaliscids are inhabitants of short grass plains or grassy areas in wooded country and appear to be selective grazers (Vesey-Fitzgerald, 1960; Bourlière and Verschuren, 1960; Talbot, 1962; Van Zyl, 1965). They are social in habit.

The hartebeests, genus *Alcelaphus*, are somewhat larger than the damaliscids. *A. buselaphus* was originally widespread in the Savanna and Arid zones and extended into north Africa. The southern form is separated from the many named races occurring elsewhere in Africa by a very distinct Brachystegia woodland species *A. lichtensteini*. Hartebeest inhabit plains and savanna and are probably largely grass-eaters (see Lamprey, 1963). Backhaus (1959) has described the social behavior of *A. buselaphus lelwel;* he found the herds to be small, up to 15 head.

The third alcelaphine genus is *Connochaetes*. It has a very distinct southern species *C. gnou*, the black wildebeest, which originally occupied a range similar to that of the blesbok. *C. taurinus* (blue wildebeest or brindled gnu; white-bearded gnu in east Africa) occurs in a variety of open habitats (plains and savannas) in the Southern Savanna, from the Orange River (originally) to southern Kenya. In South Africa there was in historical times only a very narrow zone of overlap between the two wildebeest species. *C. gnou* occupied the open, treeless karoo and highveld, while *C. taurinus* was restricted to wooded savanna (Bigalke, unpubl.).

It is therefore of interest to note that in the absence of other wildebeest species *C. taurinus* inhabits both open grasslands and savanna (e.g., in southwest Africa—Bigalke, 1961); indeed Lamprey (1963) classifies it as a plains species in Tanzania. Both species are gregarious. *C. taurinus* is well known as a spectacular migrant in several parts of its range (Grzimek and Grzimek, 1960; Bigalke, 1961) and enormous aggregations have been recorded.

The Antilopini are bovids of small to medium size, with many species, most of them cursorial inhabitants of dry plains. The impala, *Aepyceros melampus,* perhaps not very closely related to other members of the group, is a common and widespread species of the Southern Savanna. It is a mixed feeder which browses and takes grass (Lamprey, 1963; Van Zyl, 1965). Impala are gregarious.

There are two morphologically aberrant antelope species with enormously elongated necks which are the ecological equivalents of a small giraffe. *Ammodorcas clarkei,* the dibatag, has a restricted distribution in the very arid scrub savanna of Somaliland (Meester, 1960). *Litocranius walleri,* the gerenuk, is also a Somali Arid species but it is found as far south as Tanzania (Schomber, 1963). There it occupies arid *Commiphora* and *Acacia mellifera* woodland and subsists largely on the foliage of the latter tree species (Lamprey, 1963). Backhaus (1960) has described some features of the adaptation to life in arid regions, including the habit of drinking urine. There appears to be little overlap between these two odd species.

The genus *Gazella* consists of a remarkably large number of species (10, 2 of which are strictly Palearctic) which occupy arid areas in the northern half of the continent. The small form, *G. thomsonii* (shoulder height 65 cm; weight, up to 20 kg), occupies the short-grass plains of northern Tanzania and Kenya. Related forms which are probably conspecific (Brooks, 1961) occur in the southern Sudan and Somalia. The red-fronted gazelle, *G. rufifrons* (shoulder height, up to 80 cm; weight, up to 30 kg), has a wide distribution across the northern fringe of the Northern Savanna and the Sudanese Arid. *G. spekei* is about the same size and occupies the high plateau of Somalia. This curious animal has an inflatable nasal protuberance. All three small gazelles live in arid and mainly treeless country.

G. leptoceros (white gazelle, rhim) is a little larger than the foregoing (shoulder height, up to 70 cm; weight, up to 25 kg) and inhabits more arid country. It is a Sahara form with the light coloring of many desert animals. *G. dorcas* has a similar range but it is found also to the south, in the Northern Savanna zone, and beyond the bounds of Africa in Israel, Jordan, and Syria. This is the smallest African gazelle (shoulder height, up to 60 cm; weight, up to 18 kg). *G. cuvieri* is confined to the Atlas mountains of northwestern Africa and should not, strictly speaking, be listed with the fauna of Ethiopian Africa. *G. rufina* appears to be an extinct form from Palearctic Africa (Gentry, 1968).

Three large gazelles are grouped in the subgenus *Nanger*. *G. (N.) granti* (shoulder height, up to 85 cm; weight, up to 75 kg) is distributed from central Tanzania to Ethiopia, eastward to the coast and westward to northern Uganda. It is a plains species and eats grass, shrubs, and the leaves of trees. *G. (N.) dama* is a little larger and occurs throughout the Sudanese Arid and into the Northern Savanna. It may constitute a superspecies with *granti*. *G. (N.) soemmerringi* is an equally large gazelle found in Ethiopia, Somaliland and the eastern Sudan.

The southern and rather distinct *Antidorcas marsupialis* (springbok; shoulder height, 75 to 85 cm; weight, 40 to 60 kg) is a South West Arid endemic which has evolved in isolation. The springbok is well known for the spectacular mass eruptions or "treks" which took place in historic times.

A proposed regrouping of some genera described above (Ansell, 1968), places the two species of *Aepyceros* in a separate subfamily (Aepycerotinae), and the dibatag, *Ammodorcas clarkei*, in a monospecific tribe (Ammodorcini).

A number of small bovids are grouped together in the tribe Neotragini. *Oreotragus*, the klipspringer, has become specialized for life on rocky hills and mountains which it occupies in the arid and savanna zones. It walks on the tips of hooves of peculiar shape and is an extremely agile jumper. The other small antelope are of solitary habit and most occupy dense vegetation. *Raphicerus* has 3 species: *campestris* (steenbok) in the Southern Savanna and South West Arid, a delicate grazer and browser; *melanotis* (grysbok) a South West Cape form which encroaches into the Southern Savanna; and *sharpei* which replaces it from Natal to Tanzania in the savanna. In parts of its range *R. campestris* is sympatric with *melanotis* or *sharpei*. These two species appear to be ecologically separated from *campestris* by a preference for denser cover. *Ourebia ourebi* is a slightly larger animal typical of open and lightly wooded grasslands from the Cape to Ethiopia and across to Senegal. *Dorcotragus megalotis* is a steenbok-like animal endemic to the northern part of the Somali Arid and inhabiting dry rocky hills.

Two genera of pigmy antelopes remain to be discussed. The dik-diks (*Madoqua*—shoulder height, 35 cm) are discontinuously distributed in the South West and Somali Arid regions. There are about five species; they occupy dense thickets. *Neotragus* includes *moschatus*, an inhabitant of thickets on the southeastern coastal plain; *batesi*, an east African forest species; and *pygmaeus* of some west African forests, said to be the smallest African antelope.

The last bovid group is the tribe Caprini. *Ammotragus lervia*, the maned sheep, is found in the desert mountain ranges of north Africa, as far south as the Sudan. The endemic Ethiopian ibex, *Capra walie*, and a subspecies of the Palearctic *Capra ibex*, which also extends into the Ethiopian Highlands, are the only two wild goats in Africa.

The very considerable ecological separation of a spectrum of bovids and other ungulates occupying the same environment, noted and commented on by many authors, has been objectively demonstrated by Lamprey (1963). In many cases the same kinds of food are eaten, or the animals eat food that is available; separation is achieved by different habitat preferences or by other means. From work of this kind we see the large number of niches which exist in the African savanna environment and which have been filled by the remarkable radiation of the African bovids.

REGIONAL FAUNAS

Many attempts have been made to subdivide Africa into faunal districts, subregions or provinces. The history of these ideas has been fully treated by Chapin (1932). There is fairly general agreement about the fundamental distinction between forest and non-forest facies, the former occurring in the West African Subregion and the latter in the East and South African Subregion, which includes the savanna belt west to Senegal. This scheme leaves out north Africa, which will be considered below.

Beyond the basic differentiation of forest and non-forest zones, most workers have followed to a greater or lesser extent the subdivisions proposed by Chapin (1932), which he based on the distribution of birds and plants. They have not, however, always been found satisfactory for mammals (Setzer, 1956; Ansell, 1960). Moreau (1952) simplified Chapin's scheme and Davis (1962) has slightly modified Moreau's zonal boundaries to bring them into line with Keay's (1959) recent vegetation map. This end product, "the simplest classification of biotic zones based on the major vegetational types" (Davis, 1962) is illustrated in Fig. 2. The scale is too small to show all the montane and lowland forest outliers which extend down to southern South Africa.

Forest

Writing of birds, Moreau (1952) has concluded that "it might be inferred that the differentiation of the lowland forest biome from the savanna biome is probably the oldest on the continent (at least as old as the Miocene)" (p. 903). Data from mammals confirms this view.

Three mammal families (Potamogalidae, Pongidae, and Tragulidae) and one subfamily (Colobinae) are confined to the Lowland Forest zone, including outlying and, in some cases, montane forest. In another two families (Lorisidae, Anomaluridae) and one subfamily (Cercopithecinae) nearly all species are thus confined.

Misonne (1963) has pointed out that since the Indian and African representatives of forest-dwelling mammal families common to the two areas (Pongidae, Cercopithecidae, Lorisidae, Sciuridae) are so different, the forest environments of these two continents are not likely to have been in contact since the Oligocene. He believes that since the Oligocene-Miocene there has been no faunal exchange between the west African and other forested areas, except for a slight exchange with the forests of

Ethiopia. The endemicity of the Potamogalidae, Anomaluridae and the duikers (Cephalophini) in west Africa is cited in support. So, too, is the fact that the Muridae and Cricetidae, which seem to have arrived in Africa only in the Pliocene, have not radiated in the forest biome to any extent. What adaptation to forest conditions has taken place in this family has been by way of recent evolution in savanna genera.

These and other arguments suggest that the lowland forests of west and central Africa have provided a relatively stable environment for a very long time, resulting in the development of a distinct and highly adapted fauna of mammals as well as of birds and other groups. Moreau (1952) has shown that 94 per cent of the bird species occurring there are endemic. An analysis of mammals, handicapped though it is by confused taxonomy and inadequate distributional data, gives a value of approximately 70 per cent, which is much higher than that for any other major biome.

Throughout their extent the forests provide a substantially homogeneous environment at the present day. They are, however, by no means faunistically uniform. Misonne (1963) has calculated that only 30 per cent of the mammals are found throughout, while 32 per cent are very localized in their distribution. From his detailed studies of the zoogeography of west African forest mammals, Booth (1954, 1956) adduces evidence for the existence of three important refuges during the period when contemporary species were differentiating. They are thought to have provided suitable habitats for forest dwelling species when severe dry periods caused the forest vegetation to retreat, possibly several times, from areas to which it has for the most part since returned. Isolation in these refuges, for the first time in the latest Pliocene perhaps, or at the beginning of the Quaternary, resulted in some independent evolution within each one. The subsequent restoration of forest links, partial only in the case of "Liberia," has not erased the marks of isolation and the refuges are now recognizable as three centers of endemism.

The first of these is "Liberia," the term used by Booth for Liberia and the High Forest areas of the adjacent territories (western Ivory Coast, southeastern French Guinea and southern Sierra Leone). It is the most distinct. It is separated from the main Congo forest block by the well-known Dahomey Gap (in the territories of Togo and Dahomey) in which High Forest does not anywhere form a solid, continuous block at the present time. Booth has shown that the width of the Dahomey Gap must have fluctuated considerably during the Quaternary but that it always served to keep "Liberia" in greater isolation than the other two refuge areas. Misonne (1963), notes that 52 per cent of the 84 mammal species recorded from the forests as a whole, are found in "Guinea-Liberia" (the same area as Booth's "Liberia") and that this domain has a higher proportion of peculiar species (20% endemism) than the other two. For convenience the accepted term "Guinea forest block" will be used when referring to this zone in the rest of the paper.

The High Forest in the territories of Gabon, Spanish Guinea, and the Cameroons south of the Sanaga river constitutes the second center of endemism, Booth's "Gaboon" (the "Forêts du Gabon-Cameroun" of Misonne). Sixty-nine per cent of all the forest mammals have been recorded there and endemism is marked (13%), albeit less so than in "Liberia." Thirdly, there is the northeastern or Upper Congo, which Misonne calls "Forêts du Ituri-Maniema," with 70 per cent of the forest mammal species and 15 per cent endemism.

Beyond the confines of the three blocks of continuous evergreen lowland forest, vegetation of this kind occurs, on the one hand as isolated relict patches at low altitudes, and on the other as equally isolated montane forests. The lowland forest isolates are best represented in east Africa but are found also in Angola and Zambia and in patches near the east coast to South Africa. Misonne (1963) has shown that the number of species of forest mammals decreases regularly from the Ituri River eastward to the Indian Ocean. If the Ituri fauna is considered as 100 per cent, the lowland forest islands of the Usambara Mountains in Tanzania and on the lower Tana River in Kenya have only 9 per cent and those of Mt. Kilimanjaro a mere 3 per cent. No mammals are endemic to any of the relict lowland forests. Misonne's interpretation is that the relicts can only have been in contact with the main body of forest for short times during the Pleistocene. It seems clear that the relict forests have been colonized from the west by adaptable species.

The patterns of bird distribution are in some important respects quite different from those of mammals. Fourteen of the 22 species of mammals in the eastern forest relicts are species which also occur in all three of the western blocks. No eastern forest mammals are known which do not also live in the west. On the other hand Moreau (1952) has established the existence of a distinct eastern relict forest avifauna with 50 species, of which only 18 occur also in the main forest blocks.

From his ornithological studies Moreau (1952) has further established that the lowland and montane evergreen forest islands of east Africa have 55 per cent of the bird genera, but only 10 per cent of the species, in common. He concludes that the differentiation of lowland from montane forest must be almost as old as the basic differentiation of the lowland forest biome from the savanna. The facts of mammal distribution give practically no support to this opinion.

Misonne (1963) has tabulated and compared the rodent faunas of the five most important tropical African montane areas, Mount Cameroon, the Ruwenzori, Mount Elgon, Mount Kenya and the Aberdares, and Mount Kilimanjaro. He lists 70 species. A thorough examination of their distribution, as far as it is known, shows that only eight at most might be described as montane forms, i.e., forms which do not occur in the lowlands, whether surrounding the bases of the mountains or elsewhere. Four of them are apparently restricted to the montane forest zone (*Heliosciurus ruwenzorii, Funisciurus carruthersi, Lophuromys woosnami, Thamnomys rutilans*) and are endemic in the northeastern Congo (in some cases extending also to the Uganda side of Ruwenzori). *Funisciurus isabella* (montane forest, Mt. Cameroon, endemic) may be merely a subspecies of *F. lemniscatus* and although *Paraxerus byatti* has been considered to be a purely montane forest species on Mount Kilimanjaro, it is probably only a subspecies, *Paraxerus vexillarius byatti* (Amtmann, 1966). *Otomys denti* and *O. typus* are non-forest species which are known only from central African mountains, although other species of the genus are found in a variety of habitats in South Africa (a point which has been used as an argument for the South African origin of the Otomyinae).

Eisentraut (1957) describes *Dendromus oreas* and *Otomys burtoni* as endemic to the montane grassland and savanna of Mount Cameroon, but neither species is recognized by Misonne (1968). Only a very few members of other families are restricted to montane biomes (Chrysochloridae, ?one sp.; Soricidae, a few spp.; Cercopithecidae, *Papio (Theropithecus) gelada;* Bovidae, *Tragelaphus (T.) buxtoni* and *Capra walie*). Thus while the high mountains, particularly those of central Africa, are not poor in mammal species, by far the greatest number of these species is found in the lowlands as well. It can be concluded that there is no clearly differentiated montane mammal fauna in Africa.

Savanna

This extensive biome includes a diversity of vegetation types, from the treeless grasslands of the South African Highveld to densely wooded savanna. It covers about half the surface of the continent and has more mammal species than any other biotic zone. The only meaningful faunistic subdivision is into Northern and Southern Savanna, which meet at what Davis (1962) calls the Sclater Line, running from the fringes of the Congo Basin in the northwest to the Tana watershed, just north of the equator. This marked the northern boundary of Sclater's (1896) Cape Subregion. The differentiation of the savanna mammals into southern and northern groups, however, is by no means absolute. There is also a good deal of encroachment of savanna forms into the adjoining arid zones (South West, Somali and Sudanese) and vice versa. An interruption of the savanna belt by eastward extension of the forest zone, perhaps repeatedly, coinciding with climatic fluctuations during the Quaternary, would explain the evolution of southern and northern faunas. We have already mentioned the necessity to assume such changes in connection with the present distribution of forest forms. A great deal has been written about past climatic and vegetational changes in Africa and no attempt will be made here to review the literature; van Zinderen Bakker (1962) and Cooke (1963, 1968; Chapter III) may be consulted.

South West Cape

Usually included within the Southern Savanna, the small South West Cape winter rainfall area, with its distinctive and well-known flora (Cape

Macchia), is retained as a separate biotic subregion by Moreau (1952) and also by Davis (1962). Poynton (1960) has found that the South African amphibian fauna contains two major constituents, one of them centered on the South West Cape. Winterbottom (1962) finds some evidence from his ornithological studies for isolation of this area, but does not think it of much importance as a center of evolution of South African birds. Of the 21 species of Muridae which have been recorded from the South West Cape, three are endemic, six are represented by isolated subspecies or populations, and the remainder encroach marginally from the surrounding South West Arid zone (Davis, 1962). No analysis of the other mammal groups present in this zone has yet been undertaken. A few well known large mammals, e.g., *Damaliscus dorcas dorcas* (the bontebok) and the long extinct *Hippotragus leucophaeus,* evolved as distinct forms in the South West Cape. The zone can be considered a minor center of endemism for mammals.

Arid

Of the three arid zones delimited in Fig. 2, the South West Arid has the most distinctive fauna. Endemicity is high in birds (Moreau, 1952) as well as in several other groups, vertebrate and invertebrate (Balinsky, 1962). Of the mammals, almost half of the 24 species of Muridae and Cricetidae which Davis (1962) lists for the region are confined to it. Meester (1965) gives a number of examples of endemic mammals, some of which occur both in the South West Arid and in the adjacent grassland zone of the Southern Savanna. They include the rock rat, *Petromus typicus,* sole representative of the Petromyidae; two monotypic genera of Chrysochloridae and one of Macroscelididae; the hare *Bunolagus monticularis;* two species of ground squirrels (*Xerus*); the mongooses *Suricata suricatta* and *Cynictis penicillata; Hyaena brunnea;* the smallest African cat *Felis nigripes;* two zebras *Equus zebra* and *E. quagga;* and among the Bovidae, *Oryx gazella* and *Antidorcas marsupialis.* This zone must be presumed to have been isolated for a considerable period for such a distinctive mammal fauna to have evolved.

The relationships between the mammals of the South West, Somali, and Sudanese Arid zones brings us to a consideration of the phenomenon of discontinuous distribution. It has long been recognized and attention has been re-focussed on it by Ansell (1960), and by Benson and White (1960). It provides another example of the fundamentally different conclusions resulting from a study of the distribution of birds and mammals.

Moreau (1952) found the Somali and South West Arid avifaunas to be highly specialized with about half the species in each endemic. The birds of the Sudanese Arid were far less restricted. But Moreau goes on to say, "There is no reason to postulate direct interchange between any of the three arid districts except between Sudanese and Somali" (p. 894). On the other hand the facts of mammalian distribution, and indeed some

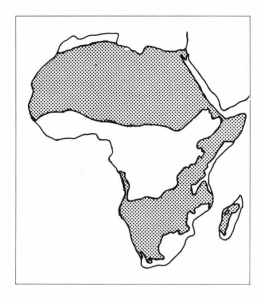

FIG. 6. Map of Africa Showing
the "Drought Corridor"
*Stipples indicate areas in which
the rainfall is less than 10 mm per
month in at least three consecutive
months (after Balinsky, 1962).*

ornithological evidence (Benson and White, 1960), make it essential to assume a direct connection between the Somali and South West Arid zones in the not too distant past. Examples of mammals with a discontinuous distribution in southwestern and northeastern Africa have been mentioned elsewhere in this paper and a list is given by Meester (1965).

Balinsky's (1962) concept of a "drought corridor" (Fig. 6) reaching across the continent from the southwest to the northeast offers a simple and satisfying way of unifying our ideas on discontinuous distribution and the historical events of which it is the result. "During cold and wet periods the rain forests must have expanded and closed the 'drought corridor' completely or at least narrowed it still further, enabling the animals of the wet tropics to migrate from west to east (and from east to west). During hot and dry periods, the drought corridor would have expanded allowing Kalahari and even desert conditions to surge in, linking more closely the arid south-west with the Somaliland arid area, thus accounting for the close links in the fauna of these areas . . ." (p. 306). "Geographically the Kalahari is usually taken to be that portion of the sand-covered Kalahari System which lies between the Orange and the Zambesi Rivers" (Leistner, 1967, p. 3). It is an arid area, the southern part being a semi-desert, and supports savanna vegetation.

The mammal fauna of the Somali Arid zone is rather less distinct than that of the South West Arid. Conspicuous and obvious endemics are a hedgehog *Erinaceus sclateri;* two elephant shrews of the genus *Elephantulus;* a ground squirrel, *Xerus rutilus; Lophiomys imhausi* (maned rat); a number of species of Gerbillinae; the singular hairless bathyergid, *Heterocephalus glaber;* a monotypic ctenodactylid genus *Pectinator;* a zebra, *Equus grevyi;* the bovids, *Tragelaphus imberbis, Damaliscus hun-*

teri, Dorcotragus megalotis, the long-necked *Litocranius walleri* and several species of *Gazella.*

The Sudanese Arid is much less well defined than the other arid zones and is mainly a transitional area between the Northern Savanna and the deserts of north Africa.

Abyssinian Highlands

The last of the major subdivisions is the Abyssinian Highland zone. Published information on the mammals is scarce, the most recent contribution being that of Glass (1965). The region is an important center of endemism, with mammals such as the rodent *Muriculus;* the hamadryas and gelada baboons; the Simenian fox, *Canis simensis;* a genet, *Genetta abyssinica;* the mountain nyala, *Tragelaphus (T.) buxtoni;* and the Ethiopian ibex, *Capra walie.*

North Africa

This is the region between the northern boundary of the Sudanese Arid and the southern boundary of Palearctic Africa. Heim de Balsac (1936, quoted in Moreau, 1952) has contended that most of the mammals as well as the birds of the Sahara are of Ethiopian affinities. Moreau, however, does not agree with Heim de Balsac's statement that the Sahara is faunistically "le stade ultime de dégradation désertique de la savane africaine" (p. 886).

Paleontological evidence for climatic change in the Sahara is reviewed by Cooke (1963). "It is tempting to suggest that the presence of a tropical fauna, including such moisture-loving species as the hippopotamus, demands a very different climatic setting from that of the present day and, indeed, many authorities have suggested that the Sahara region was not a desert during at least portions of Pleistocene and post-Pleistocene time. The extinctions of the faunas are then ascribed to phases of severe climatic deterioration" (p. 71). Cooke, however, cites geological evidence for the existence of arid conditions in the Sahara desert belt also in Tertiary and Cretaceous times, stressing that the existence of the arid zone in and about these latitudes is a direct result of fundamental features of the atmospheric circulation. He concludes, "It is probable that, during the Pleistocene, aridity was the normal condition, offering a barrier to free migration across the desert, and that the periods of higher rainfall did not eliminate the barrier but merely opened up a small number of possible routes across it" (p. 75). At the present time the Sahara is a very harsh environment indeed and consequently it does not support a rich fauna of mammals.

The insectivores are represented by the Erinaceidae (about 4 spp.), Macroscelididae (one sp.) and Soricidae (about 2 spp.). The murid rodents are dominated by the Gerbillinae (about 15 spp.) but the Murinae (about 5 spp.) are also present. Muscardinidae (one sp.), Dipodidae (3 spp.) and

Ctenodactylidae (about 5 spp.) complete the list of rodents. There are three hare species of the genus *Lepus* and two species of Procaviidae. Four families of carnivores occur, the Canidae and Felidae with six species each, and the Mustelidae and Viverridae each with two species. The wild ass (Equidae, one sp.), two large hippotragine bovids (*Addax nasomaculatus* and *Oryx dammah*) and about five species of *Gazella* constitute the large herbivores of the desert.

It is instructive to consider an analysis, by Hoogstraal, Wassif, and Kaiser (1957), of the mammal fauna of one area of the Sahara, viz., southeastern Egypt, which is the country surrounding the Elba mountain mass. They note that the few publications available refer to the Gebel Elba as "the outermost stronghold of Ethiopian faunal elements on continental Africa" (p. 70). Their studies have shown, however, that it is the coastal plains and foothills, with their climatic and physical environment modified by the proximity to the mountains, that harbor Ethiopian components. "Only the more primitive hyrax and the more mobile hare, bat, and a few carnivores encroach into Southeastern Egypt from the south. . . . Significant zoogeographical indicators such as insectivores and rodents are entirely Near Eastern-North African in origin" (p. 70).

The mammals of the area in question comprise a bat, a mustelid (*Ictonyx*), a genet, the aardwolf (*Proteles*), a hyrax (*Procavia capensis* subsp.) and a hare (*Lepus capensis* subsp.), all of Ethiopian affinities. The Near Eastern-North African components are a hedgehog (*Paraechinus*), two species of fox (*Vulpes*—including the European *V. vulpes*), the caracal (*F. caracal* subsp.), *Gazella dorcas*, a dipodid (*Jaculus*) and four species of Gerbillinae. As Near Eastern components they list the mouse *Acomys cahirinus* and the gerbil *Gerbillus calurus* (syn. *Sekeetamys calurus*).

It is not possible to generalize about the Saharan fauna from the findings in one small area. In view of the conclusion of Heim de Balsac stated above (1936, quoted in Moreau, 1962), which is in direct contradiction to that of Hoogstraal, Wassif, and Kaiser (1957), a reexamination of Saharan zoogeography using the new material now available (see Hoogstral, Wassif, and Kaiser, 1955; Setzer 1957a, b, c, 1959; Wassif and Hoogstraal, 1954) is indicated.

Mammals of the Islands

In conclusion, the mammal faunas of the more important islands in the Indian Ocean off the eastern coast of Africa will be briefly described and discussed.

Madagascar

Madagascar is the largest island and has a surface area of approximately 580,000 km^2 (224,000 mi^2). It is almost 250 miles from the African continent and is separated from it by an old and deep channel. The ancient character of the fauna, its largely African affinities and the high degree of endemism, suggest very early colonization by a few ancestral types across a temporarily narrowed channel (Millot, 1952).

The mammal fauna is a typically insular one with few groups, in most of which adaptive radiation has taken place. Only insectivores, primates, rodents, carnivores and bats are present and each order is represented by an extremely limited variety of forms. The total fauna consists of 57 genera and 94 species (including three introduced forms). The African bush pig *Potamochoerus,* now the sole ungulate (with the exception of feral deer introduced quite recently), was almost certainly introduced from Africa in historic times. A pigmy hippopotamus (closely allied to the contemporary west African *Choeropsis*) is, however, a common Pleistocene fossil.

Two families of insectivores occur. The Soricidae are represented only by two species of *Suncus,* one of which is endemic but of doubtful systematic status (Paulian, 1961). These are of little significance faunistically or zoogeographically. It is the second family, the Tenrecidae, which constitutes such an interesting element in the fauna of Madagascar. This basically endemic group (the continental Potamogalidae are now tentatively included by some authors) consists of two subfamilies, 13 genera and 29 species. The largest is *Tenrec* (head-and-body length, up to 34 cm), possibly the biggest living insectivore, with a coat of hair and spines. It is rather opossum-like (Walker, 1964), is nocturnal and dwells in burrows, taking insects, worms, and reptiles. *Setifer* and *Echinops,* each with one species, are the hedgehog tenrecs. They are very similar to hedgehogs in appearance. *Hemicentetes* (one sp.) has a distinctive pattern of dark and light stripes, and a spiny coat. *Dasogale* (one sp.) is a little known genus with short spines. *Oryzorictes* (2 spp.) is mole-like with soft fur, strong claws, and weak eyes. They are known as rice tenrecs from their habit of burrowing in the banks of rice paddies. *Microgale* (14 spp.—Genest and Petter, 1968) contains miniature creatures, similar to shrews and their ecological counterparts. *Limnogale* (one sp.) is the aquatic or web-footed tenrec found in marshes and along water courses. It is a rare form which takes insects, shrimps, and crawfish (Gould and Eisenberg, 1966). The five remaining genera, *Geogale, Nesoryctes, Leptogale, Paramicrogale* and *Nesogale,* contain seven species which are little known, and possibly rare.

The lemurs are perhaps the best known members of the Madagascan fauna. There are three endemic families of these primitive primates. Radiation has produced forms ranging from the size of a mouse to that of a small dog, some nocturnal and some diurnal. There are large, slow-moving and small, agile lemurs, eaters of fruit, leaves or insects, some terrestrial and some arboreal.

The family Lemuridae is the largest, with eight living genera and 14 species (Petter and Petter, 1968). *Lemur* comprises four quite large species (head-and-body length, up to 55 cm) with long, grasping arms and legs, long bushy tails, and fox-like faces; they resemble tree kangaroos to some extent. They are diurnal (except for one species), social, and mainly arboreal. *L. catta,* however, is largely terrestrial and lives in rocky areas rather like a baboon. Lemurs feed on plant matter and insects. The two species of the genus *Hapalemur,* the gentle lemurs, and *Lepilemur* (one sp.—sportive or weasel lemur) are active arboreal forest forms. They are nocturnal and feed mainly on plant matter. Most lemurinids are social.

The lesser lemurs (Cheirogaleinae) are active, nocturnal, solitary, arboreal species. *Cheirogaleus* (2 spp.) is rather squirrel-like; *Microcebus* (2 spp.) includes the smallest form, *M. murinus* (head-and-body length, 15 cm). *Phaner* has one species. It is largely insectivorous and rather galago-like in habit and behavior.

The family Indridae contains fairly large forms of monkey-like appearance which are slow-moving vegetarians and fill a niche comparable to that of leaf-eating monkeys. *Avahi* (one sp.) is a smallish, arboreal, nocturnal species of solitary habits.

Propithecus (2 spp.) contains large diurnal forms which walk upright and can perform great leaps. They feed on leaves and bark, and live in small groups. The indri, *Indri indri,* is the largest lemur, a short-tailed mainly arboreal animal of the forest regions.

The third family (Daubentoniidae) contains the single monotypic genus *Daubentonia.* This is the aye-aye or lemur squirrel, with rodent-like incisors and long-clawed digits. The third finger is a specialized tool with an elongated claw, used mainly to tap wood and to extract from it insects located in this way. In this respect *Daubentonia* resembles the Australian striped possum *Dactylopsila.* The diet also includes birds' eggs and some vegetable matter; the animals are nocturnal and arboreal.

Rodents are represented in Madagascar by two cosmopolitan commensal forms, *Mus musculus* and *Rattus rattus* (doubtless introduced), and by an endemic cricetid subfamily, the Nesomyinae. There are seven genera and 10 species (Petter, 1968). These rodents, like the lemurs and tenrecs, vary a good deal in size and form and have radiated to fill a number of niches.

Macrotarsomys resembles the gerbils in form and in some structural characters such as the presence of inflated bullae. *Eliurus* (2 spp.) includes arboreal and terrestrial species. *Hypogeomys* is a very large rat (head-and-body length, up to 35 cm) which builds rabbit-like burrows in forests and feeds on fruit. *Gymnuromys* is rather mole-like in appearance.

The Carnivora of Madagascar are also of great interest. Only members of the family Viverridae occur. Two genera, *Fossa* and *Eupleres,* are placed in the same subfamily (Hemigalinae) as the Asiatic palm civets and otter civet. *Fossa* (one sp.) is the Malagasy civet, a fairly small animal. The genus *Eupleres* (2 spp.) contains animals with the appearance of mongooses and with rather insectivore-like teeth; they feed on invertebrates and small vertebrates.

The endemic subfamily Galidiinae, with four genera and about seven species, contains smallish mongooses about which little is known. *Galidictis* (2 or 3 spp.) has a rather bizarre color pattern with longitudinal black stripes. *Galidia* (one sp.), *Mungotictis* (2 spp.) and *Salanoia* are the other genera.

The largest and most remarkable carnivore is *Cryptoprocta ferox,* the fossa (head-and-body length, up to 75 cm), a primitive cat-like animal placed in a subfamily of its own (Cryptoproctinae). It is plantigrade and has retractible claws. The fossa lives in forested areas, is nocturnal, and takes a variety of vertebrate prey.

The last group of mammals to be dealt with is the bats. Their mobility makes them of little zoogeographic interest. The order is represented by six families (one endemic), 14 genera (one endemic) and about 20 species (6 endemic). The Pteropodidae have the genera *Pteropus* (one endemic sp.), *Eidolon* and *Rousettus* (one sp. each). There are two genera of Emballonuridae: *Taphozous* (one sp.) and *Emballonura* (one sp., the only representative of the genus outside Asia); and two genera of Hipposideridae: *Hipposideros* (one sp.) and *Triaenops* (3 endemic spp.). The Myzopodidae with the monotypic genus *Myzopoda* are endemic. The two remaining families are Vespertilionidae: *Myotis* (one sp.), *Eptesicus* (one sp.), *Scotophilus* (2 spp.), *Miniopterus* (one sp.); and Molossidae: *Otomops* (one sp.), *Tadarida* (5 spp., of which one is endemic).

Comoros

The Comoro Archipelago is situated to the northwest of Madagascar and is nearer to the African coast than that island. The archipelago consists of four islands, Mayotte, Moheli, Anjouan and Grand Comoro with a total area of 2072 km² (800 mi²). They arise from a submarine bank and are faunistically part of Madagascar. The mammalian fauna is, however, a poor one. The lemurs are represented only by a form of *Lemur macaco* on Mayotte and *Lemur mongoz* on the other three islands.

There is a small fauna of bats belonging to two families. The Pteropodidae are represented by two endemic species of *Pteropus*. The genera *Myotis* (one species on Anjouan, also in Madagascar) and *Miniopterus* (one east African and Madagascan species) represent the Vespertilionidae.

Mascarenes

The Mascarenes are three islands situated four hundred miles and more to the east of Madagascar. Reunion is the largest (2,512 km², 970 mi²) and nearest to Madagascar. Mauritius (1,840 km², 710 mi²) is about 100 miles to the northeast of Reunion. The smallest is Rodriguez (107 km², 41 mi²) which lies some 350 miles east of Mauritius.

Bats are the only mammals present and are distributed as shown in Table 4.

Seychelles

The Seychelles are a group of about 45 islands some 600 miles northeast of Madagascar with a total area of 256 km² (99 mi²). Here, too, bats are

TABLE 4

Distribution of bats on the Mascarenes

Pteropus subniger	:	Reunion, Mauritius
Pteropus niger	:	Reunion, Mauritius
Pteropus rodricensis	:	Rodriguez
Taphozous mauritianus	:	Mauritius (and Madagascar)
Scotophilus nigrita	:	Reunion, ?Mauritius (also Africa and Madagascar)
Scotophilus leucogaster	:	Reunion, Mauritius (and ?Madagascar)
Tadarida acetabulosus	:	Reunion, Mauritius (also Africa and Madagascar)

the only mammals, the two species present being *Pteropus seychellensis* and *Coleura seychellensis* (Hayman, 1967).

SUMMARY

The mammals of Africa are a rich and diverse assemblage of placental forms. The fauna is most closely related to that of the Oriental Region and has little in common with the faunas of the other southern continents. About one-quarter of the families are endemic. Approximate numbers of species and superspecies are given for each family. Africa has about one-quarter of the mammal species of the world; rodents, bats, insectivores, artiodactyls, carnivores and primates, in that order, are the largest groups. Endemism at the generic level is high except in the bats. The main features of speciation, radiation, ecology and geographical distribution are discussed for each order. Outstanding features are the radiation of insectivores with the evolution of three endemic families (the aquatic otter shrews, subterranean golden moles and bipedal elephant shrews); the great diversity of rodents, with endemic families resembling "flying" squirrels (anomalurids), moles (bathyergids), hyraxes (ctenodactylids), cavies (thryonomyids), and kangaroos (*Pedetes*); extensive speciation in the Viverridae; and unparalleled radiation in the Bovidae to fill all available herbivorous niches. Regional faunas of the main biotic zones (Lowland Forest; Southern and Northern Savanna; South-West, Somali and Sudanese Arid; and the Abyssinian Highlands) are described. The basic dichotomy is between forest and non-forest forms. A consideration of centers of endemism, mainly in the lowland forest and arid zones, leads to the conclusion that they were isolated as a result of fluctuations in climate and the resulting displacement of vegetation zones during the Quaternary. The faunas of Madagascar and of the Comoro, Seychelle and Mascarene Islands are described. Madagascar has a peculiar, ancient, typically unbalanced island fauna with African affinities. The other islands have small faunas, composed only of bats in the case of the farthest ones.

ACKNOWLEDGMENTS

This work was originally prepared while I was on the staff of the Alexander McGregor Memorial Museum, Kimberley, and I am grateful to the Trustees for the facilities provided. I was enabled to deliver the paper at the XVI International Congress of Zoology by the generous award of a travel grant by the U.S. National Academy of Sciences–National Research Council. My colleagues, Allen Keast, D. H. S. Davis and J. Meester have been most helpful in discussing the manuscript, in lending literature, and in other ways. My wife has borne with me bravely and Mrs. T. Anderson has cheerfully undertaken the labor of typing the manuscript. Mr. J. C. Greig assisted in its final revision.

LITERATURE CITED

ALLEN, L. D. C. 1963. The Lechwe (*Kobus leche smithemani*) of the Bangweulu swamps. *Puku, Occ. Pap. Dept. Game Fish, N. Rhodesia,* No. 1: 1-8.

AMTMANN, E. 1966. *Preliminary Identification Manual for African Mammals. 3. Rodentia: Sciuridae.* Smithsonian Institution, Washington. [In press.]

ANSELL, W. F. H. 1960. *Mammals of Northern Rhodesia.* Government Printer, Lusaka.

——. 1968. *Preliminary Identification Manual for African Mammals. 8. Artiodactyla.* Smithsonian Institution, Washington. [In press.]

BACKHAUS, D. 1959. A hartebeest herd in the Garamba Park. *Afr. Wild Life,* 13: 197-200.

——. 1960. Zur Anpassung der Giraffengazelle *Litocranius walleri* Brooke, 1878, an trockene Lebensräume. *Säugetierk. Mitt.,* 8: 43-45.

BALINSKY, B. I. 1962. Patterns of animal distribution on the African Continent. *Ann. Cape Prov. Museums,* II: 299-310.

BENSON, C. W., and C. M. N. WHITE. 1960. Discontinuous distributions (Aves). *Fed. Sci. Cong., Salisbury,* 1: 195-216.

BIGALKE, R. C. 1958. On the present status of ungulate mammals in South West Africa. *Mammalia,* 22: 478-497.

——. 1961. Some observations on the ecology of the Etosha Game Park, South West Africa. *Ann. Cape Prov. Museums,* I: 49-67.

BIGALKE, R. C., and J. A. BATEMAN. 1962. On the status and distribution of ungulate mammals in the Cape Province, South Africa. *Ann. Cape Prov. Museums,* II: 85-109.

BOOTH, A. H. 1954. The Dahomey Gap and the mammalian fauna of the West African forests. *Rev. Zool. Bot. Afr.,* L, (3-4): 305-314.

——. 1956. The distribution of primates in the Gold Coast. *J. W. Afr. Sci. Assoc.,* 2: 122-133.

——. 1960. *Small Mammals of West Africa.* Longmans, London.

BOTHMA, J. DU P. 1966. *Preliminary Identification Manual for African Mammals. 1. Hyracoidea.* Smithsonian Institution, Washington. [In press.]

BOURLIÈRE, F., and J. VERSCHUREN. 1960. *Introduction á l'Ècologie des Ongulès du Parc National Albert.* 2 Vol. Inst. des Parcs Nat. du Congo et du Ruanda-Urundi, Bruxelles.

BROOKS, A. C. 1961. A study of the Thomson's gazelle (*Gazella thomsonii* Günther) in Tanganyika. Colonial Office Research Publications No. 25, London.

BUECHNER, H. K. 1961. Territorial behaviour in Uganda Kob. *Science,* 133 (3454): 698-699.

CHAPIN, J. P. 1932. The birds of the Belgian Congo. Part I. *Bull. Am. Museum Natur. Hist.,* 65: 1-756.

CHRISTY, C. 1929. The African buffalos. *Proc. Zool. Soc. Lond.,* 1929 (3): 445-462.

COETZEE, C. G. 1967. *Preliminary Identification Manual for African Mammals. 7. Carnivora (Excluding the Family Felidae).* Smithsonian Institution, Washington. [In press.]

COOKE, H. B. S. 1963. Pleistocene mammal faunas of Africa, with particular reference to southern Africa. In F. C. Howell and F. Bourlière (eds.), *African Ecology and Human Evolution,* p. 65-116. Viking Fund Publications in Anthropology No. 36, New York.

——. 1968. The fossil mammal fauna of Africa. *Quart. Rev. Biol.,* 43: 234-264.

CORBET, G. B. 1966. *Preliminary Identification Manual for African Mammals. 2. Menotyphla.* Smithsonian Institution, Washington. [In press.]

——. 1968. *Preliminary Identification Manual for African Mammals. 12. Lipotyphla: Erinaceidae and Potamogalidae.* Smithsonian Institution, Washington. [In press.]

DANDELOT, P. 1959. Note sur la classification des Cercopithèques du groupe *aethiops. Mammalia,* 23: 357-368.

——. 1968. *Preliminary Identification Manual for African Mammals. 24. Primates: Anthropoidea.* Smithsonian Institution, Washington. [In press.]

DARLING, F. F. 1960. *Wild Life in an African Territory.* Oxford University Press, London and New York.

DARLINGTON, P. J. 1957. *Zoogeography: The Geographical Distribution of Animals.* John Wiley & Sons, New York.

DAVIS, D. H. S. 1962. Distribution patterns of Southern African Muridae, with notes on some of their fossil antecedents. *Ann. Cape Prov. Museums,* II: 56-76.

EISENTRAUT, M. 1957. Beitrag zur Säugetierfauna des Kamerungebirges und die Verbreitung der Arten in den verschiedenen Höhenstufen. *Zool. Jb. Syst.,* 85 (6): 501-672.

ELLERMAN, J. R. 1940-41. *The Families and Genera of Living Rodents.* Vols. 1 and 2. British Museum (Natur. Hist.), London.

ELLERMAN, J. R., T. C. S. MORRISON-SCOTT and R. W. HAYMAN. 1953. *Southern African Mammals.* British Museum (Natur. Hist.), London.

EWER, R. F. 1954. Some adaptive features in the dentition of hyaenas. *Ann. Mag. Natur. Hist.* (12), 7: 188-194.

——. 1958. Adaptive features in the skulls of African Suidae. *Proc. Zool. Soc. Lond.,* 131: 135-155.

FREEDMAN, L. 1963. A biometric study of *Papio cynocephalus* skulls from Northern Rhodesia and Nyasaland. *J. Mammal.,* 44: 24-43.

GENEST, H., and F. PETTER. 1968. *Preliminary Identification Manual for African Mammals. 31. Madagascar Lipotyphla.* Smithsonian Institution, Washington. [In press.]

GENTRY, A. W. 1968. *Preliminary Identification Manual for African Mammals. 9. Artiodactyla: Genus* Gazella. Smithsonian Institution, Washington. [In press.]

GLASS, B. P. 1965. The mammals of Eastern Ethiopia. *Zool. Afr.,* 1: 177-179.

GOULD, E., and J. F. EISENBERG. 1966. Notes on the biology of the Tenrecidae. *J. Mammal.,* 47: 660-686.

GRZIMEK, M., and B. GRZIMEK. 1960. A study of the game of the Serengeti plains. *Z. Säugetierk.,* 25: 1-61.

HAYMAN, R. W. 1967. *Preliminary Identification Manual for African Mammals. 11. Chiroptera.* Smithsonian Institution, Washington. [In press.]

HEDIGER, H. (No date.) *Jagdzoologie, auch für Nichtjäger.* Friedrich Reinhardt Verlag, Basel.

HEIM DE BALSAC, H., and M. LAMOTTE. 1956. Evolution et phylogènie des Soricides Africains. *Mammalia,* 20: 140-167.

——, and ——. 1957. Evolution et phylogènie des Soricides Africains (suite et fin). *Mammalia,* 21: 15-49.

HILL, W. C. O. 1953. *Primates. Comparative Anatomy and Taxonomy. I—Strepsirhini.* University Press, Edinburgh.

HOOGSTRAAL, H., K. WASSIF and M. N. KAISER. 1955. New mammal records from the Western Desert of Egypt. *Bull. Zool. Soc. Egypt,* 12: 7-12.

——, ——, and ——. 1957. Observations on nondomesticated mammals and their ectoparasites. *Bull. Zool. Soc. Egypt,* 13: 52-75.

JARMAN, P. J. 1966. The status of the Dugong (*Dugong dugon* Müller); Kenya, 1961. *E. Afr. Wildl. J.,* 4: 82-88.

KEAY, R. W. J. 1959. *Vegetation Map of Africa South of the Tropic of*

Cancer, with Explanatory Notes. L'Association pour l'Étude Taxonomique de la Flore d'Afrique Tropicale, with the assistance of UNESCO. Oxford University Press, London.

KLOPFER, P. H. 1962. *Behavioral Aspects of Ecology.* Prentice-Hall, Inc., Englewood Cliffs, N.J.

KRUUK, H., and M. TURNER. 1967. Comparative notes on predation by lion, leopard, cheetah and wild dog in the Serengeti area, East Africa. *Mammalia,* 31: 1-27.

LAMPREY, H. F. 1963. Ecological separation of the large mammal species in the Tarangire Game Reserve, Tanganyika. *E. Afr. Wildl. J.,* 1: 63-92.

LEISTNER, O. A. 1967. The plant ecology of the southern Kalahari. Botanical Survey, Memoir No. 38. Gov't Printer, Pretoria.

LYDEKKER, R. 1926. *The Game Animals of Africa.* Rowland Ward, London.

MALBRANT, R., and A. MACLATCHY. 1949. *Faune de l'Équateur Africain Francais.* 2 vols. Paul Lechevalier, Paris.

MEESTER, J. 1953. The genera of African shrews. *Ann. Tvl. Museum,* 22: 205-214.

——. 1954. On the status of the shrew, genus *Myosorex. Ann. Mag. Natur. Hist.* (12), 7: 947-950.

——. 1960. The dibatag, *Ammodorcas clarkei* (Thos.) in Somalia. *Ann. Tvl. Museum,* 14: 53-59.

——. 1965. The origins of the Southern African mammal fauna. *Zool. Afr.,* 1: 87-95.

——. 1968. *Preliminary Identification Manual for African Mammals. 23. Lipotyphla: Chrysochloridae.* Smithsonian Institution, Washington. [In press.]

MILLOT, J. 1952. La faune malagache et le mythe gondwanien. *Mém. Inst. Sci. Madagascar, ser. A,* VII (1): 1-36.

MISONNE, X. 1963. Les Rongeurs du Ruwenzori et des règions voisines. Exploration du Parc National Albert (Deuxième Sèrie), Fasc. 14. Institut des Parcs Nationaux du Congo et du Rwanda, Bruxelles.

——. 1968. *Preliminary Identification Manual for African Mammals. 19. Rodentia: Main Text.* Smithsonian Institution, Washington. [In press.]

MOREAU, R. E. 1944. Kilimanjaro and Mount Kenya: some comparisons with special reference to mammals and birds and with a note on Mount Meru (with a Bibliography of Kilimanjaro by C. Gillman). *Tanganyika Notes Rec.,* 18: 28-68.

——. 1952. Africa since the Mesozoic: with particular reference to certain biological problems. *Proc. Zool. Soc. Lond.,* 121: 869-913.

PAULIAN, R. 1961. *La Zoogéographie de Madagascar et des Iles Voisines.* L'Institut de Recherche Scientifique, Tananarive—Tsimbazaza.

PETTER, A., and J. J. PETTER. 1968. *Preliminary Identification Manual for African Mammals. 26. Primates, Prosimii: Lemuriformes.* Smithsonian Institution, Washington. [In press.]

PETTER, F. 1967. *Preliminary Identification Manual for African Mammals. 10. Lagomorpha.* Smithsonian Institution, Washington. [In press.]

——. 1968. *Preliminary Identification Manual for African Mammals. 15. Rodentia of Madagascar.* Smithsonian Institution, Washington. [In press.]

PIENAAR, U. DE V. 1963. The large mammals of the Kruger National Park—their distribution and present-day status. *Koedoe,* 6: 1-37.

POYNTON, J. C. 1960. Preliminary note on the zoogeography of the Amphibia in Southern Africa. *S. Afr. J. Sci.,* 56: 307-312.

RAHM, U. 1960. The Pangolins of West and Central Africa. *Afr. Wild Life,* 14: 271-275.

ROBERTS, A. 1937. The old surviving types of mammals found in the Union. *S. Afr. J. Sci.,* 34: 73-88.

——. 1951. *The Mammals of South Africa.* Central News Agency, Johannesburg.

ROBINETTE, W. L. 1963. Weights of some of the larger mammals of Northern Rhodesia. *Puku, Occ. Pap. Dept. Game Fish, N. Rhodesia,* No. 1: 207-215.

SANDERSON, I. T. 1940. The mammals of the North Cameroons. *Trans. Zool. Soc. Lond.,* 24 (7, No. 1): 623-725.

SCHOMBER, H. W. 1963. Beiträge zur Kenntnis der Giraffengazelle (*Litocranius walleri* Brooke, 1878). *Säugetierk. Mitt.,* 11 Sonderheft 1: 1-44.

SCHOUTEDEN, H. 1944/46. De Zoogdieren van Belgisch-Congo en van Ruanda-Urundi. *Ann. Musée Roy. Congo Belge Zool., Ser.* 2, 3: 1-576.

SCLATER, W. L. 1896. The geography of mammals. IV. The Ethiopian region. *Geogr. J:* 282-296.

SETZER, H. 1956. Mammals of the Anglo-Egyptian Sudan. *Proc. U.S. Nat. Museum,* 106: 447-587.

——. 1957a. The hedgehogs and shrews (Insectivora) of Egypt. *J. Egypt. Pub. Health Assoc.,* 32: 1-17.

——. 1957b. A review of Libyan mammals. *J. Egypt. Pub. Health Assoc.,* 32: 41-82.

——. 1957c. The jerboas of Egypt. *J. Egypt Pub. Health Assoc.,* 32: 265-271.

——. 1959. The spiny mice (*Acomys*) of Egypt. *J. Egypt. Pub. Health Assoc.,* 34: 93-101.

SHORTRIDGE, G. C. 1934. *The Mammals of South West Africa.* 2 vols. William Heinemann Ltd., London.

SIMPSON, G. G. 1945. The principles of classification and the classification of mammals. *Bull. Am. Museum Natur. Hist.,* 85: 1-350.

SMITHERS, R. H. N. 1966. *The Mammals of Rhodesia, Zambia and Malawi.* Collins, London.

——. 1968. *Preliminary Identification Manual for African Mammals. 25. Carnivora: Felidae.* Smithsonian Institution, Washington. [In press.]

STEWART, D. R. M., and J. STEWART. 1963. The distribution of some large mammals in Kenya. *J. E. Afr. Natur. Hist. Soc.,* 24: 1-52.

TALBOT, L. M. 1962. Food preferences of some East African wild ungulates. *E. Af. Agr. For. J.,* 27(3): 131-138.

TAPPEN, N. C. 1960. Problems of distribution and adaptation of the African monkeys. *Current Anthropol.,* 1: 91-120.

VAN ZINDEREN BAKKER, E. M. 1962. Botanical evidence for quaternary climates in Africa. *Ann. Cape Prov. Museums,* 2: 16-31.

VAN ZYL, J. H. M. 1965. The vegetation of the S. A. Lombard Nature Reserve and its utilisation by certain antelope. *Zool. Afr.,* 1: 55-71.

VERSCHUREN, J. 1958. Écologie et biologie des grands mammifères. Exploration du Parc National de Garamba, fasc. 9. Inst. des Parcs Nat. du Congo Belge, Bruxelles.

VESEY-FITZGERALD, D. F. 1960. Grazing succession among East African game animals. *J. Mammal.,* 41: 161-172.

WALKER, E. P. 1964. *Mammals of the World.* 2 vols. Johns Hopkins Press, Baltimore.

WASSIF, K., and H. HOOGSTRAAL. 1954. The mammals of South Sinai, Egypt. *Proc. Egypt. Acad. Sci.,* 9: 63-79.

WELLS, L. H. 1957. Speculations on the palaeogeographic distribution of antelopes. *S. Afr. J. Sci.,* 53: 423-424.

WILSON, V. J. 1966. Notes on the food and feeding habits of the Common Duiker *Sylvicapra grimmia* in Eastern Zambia. *Arnoldia,* 2(14): 1-19.

WINTERBOTTOM, J. M. 1962. A note on zoogeographical limits in South-East Africa, as suggested by the avifauna. *Ann. Cape Prov. Museums,* II: 152-154.

V Australian Mammals: Zoogeography and Evolution

by Allen Keast

INTRODUCTION

Australia, with a surface area of 2,900,000 mi^2, is the smallest and the most isolated of the continents. Its isolation extends back at least to the beginning of the Tertiary (Fig. 1). New Guinea to the north lies on the Australian continental shelf. It was probably in broad contact with Australia at the end of the Tertiary and repeatedly during the Pleistocene.

The original mammal fauna was presumably exclusively monotreme and marsupial; placentals did not colonize it until the mid- or later Tertiary. The failure of placentals to reach Australia in the beginning is one of the more puzzling facts of zoogeography, since they are now known to have originated contemporaneously with the marsupials. The Australian situation contrasts with the South American one, where the early colonizing fauna was mixed—marsupials and herbivorous placentals.

Marsupials apparently originated in North America and placental mammals in Eurasia (Clemens, 1968; 1970; Lillegraven, 1969), or Europe plus Africa (Hoffstetter, 1970). There is no direct or indirect evidence of the presence of marsupials on continents other than North America prior to the latest Cretaceous (Clemens, 1968). Workers differ in opinion, however, as to whether many of the fragmentary Cretaceous remains rightly belong to marsupials or placentals. Nevertheless, there was a significant marsupial radiation in North America during the late Cretaceous; Clemens (1968) records at least five genera and 13 species. Thereafter they fell away to a few genera. The oldest marsupials from South America are late Cretaceous (Patterson and Pascual, Chapter VI). The oldest unequivocal records of marsupials in Europe (*Peratherium*) are in the early Eocene. The group is unknown from the Asian fossil record. Possibly they never reached Asia. Alternatively, the Asian marsupials, like the North American ones, could have been lowland forest forms, a habitat unrepresented in the fossil record there (Clemens, 1968).

The pathway by which marsupials first colonized Australia has long been a subject for debate (see Chapter II). The early continental drift enthusiasts (e.g., Harrison, 1924) argued that they came from South America, via Antarctica, the former being the only other continent in the world that today has an extensive marsupial fauna. Subsequently, however, most writers came to accept a northern entry from Asia by way of the Indonesian islands (Simpson, 1940; Clemens, 1968; Keast, 1968). This theory has suffered from the weakness that, as noted, fossil marsupials are unknown from Asia, and are not known from Europe until the Eocene. The time of entry, it is generally conceded, must have been either Cretaceous or early Tertiary. The northern entry theory is based on the assumption that Australia has maintained its present position relative to Asia since the end of the Mesozoic. Fig. 1 shows the postulated distribution of land between southeastern Asia and Australia at what is assumed to be various critical periods of mammalian colonization: the Cretaceous

---

FIG. 1. NORTHERN ENTRY THEORY TO ACCOUNT FOR THE COLONIZATION OF AUSTRALIA BY MARSUPIALS—POSTULATED SPATIAL RELATIONSHIPS OF AUSTRALIA AND ASIA DURING CRITICAL PERIODS OF MAMMALIAN COLONIZATION (STATIC CONTINENT CONCEPT)

A and B based on Audley-Charles, 1966; C and D based on Umbgrove, 1938; and E based on Veevers, 1967. The cross-hatched areas represent extensions of land.

During the Lower Cretaceous (A), broad tongues of land apparently extended almost to Australia, the intervening areas being covered by shallow seas. Possibly an ancestral marsupial type reached the continent at this time. The proximity of the continents could also account for certain similarities in the Cretaceous dinosaur faunas of Australia and Eurasia. Marine transgressions in the Upper Cretaceous isolated Australia; with geosynclines forming, "one in front of the Australian continent, and the other in front of the Asian continent" (Audley-Charles, p. 21). Deep-water zones now existed between the two continents for the first time since the Permian.

The two continents remained widely separated through the early and middle Tertiary (Umbgrove, 1938). Between the Miocene (C) and (D) Borneo increased greatly in size, the Celebes emerged, and New Guinea became a major land mass (maps taken from Umbgrove, 1938). Initial colonization of Australia and New Guinea by rodents possibly took place at this time as the narrower water gaps would have made rafting relatively easy.

The Pleistocene glacial maxima were marked by a fall in Pacific sea levels of up to 100 m, bringing New Guinea (and Tasmania in the south) into broad contact with the Australian mainland. To the northwest of Australia the Sahul Shelf emerged (E). This map, taken from Veevers (1967), shows the outer limit of submarine quartz distribution and gives some appreciation of the extent of the continental shelf about 19,000 years B.P., at the height of the last glacial maximum. At this time the width of Timor Strait would have been reduced to about 45 miles (Hooijer, 1967). Rodent colonizations probably occurred during each of the Pleistocene emergences and the genus Rattus may have arrived during the last glacial maximum. It might be noted that during the Pleistocene pigmy elephants (Stegodon) extended as far east as Timor (Hooijer, 1967).

The postulated close proximity of Australia and Asia during the Late Mesozoic and early Tertiary is in direct opposition to the continental drift evidence.

The alternative southern entry theory, which is now receiving greater acceptance, is based on Australia having maintained a position adjacent to Antarctica until at least the end of the Mesozoic; it was thus able to obtain its first marsupials from South America (see Fig. 1 and Chapter II). It has been suggested that it reached its present latitude in the Miocene.

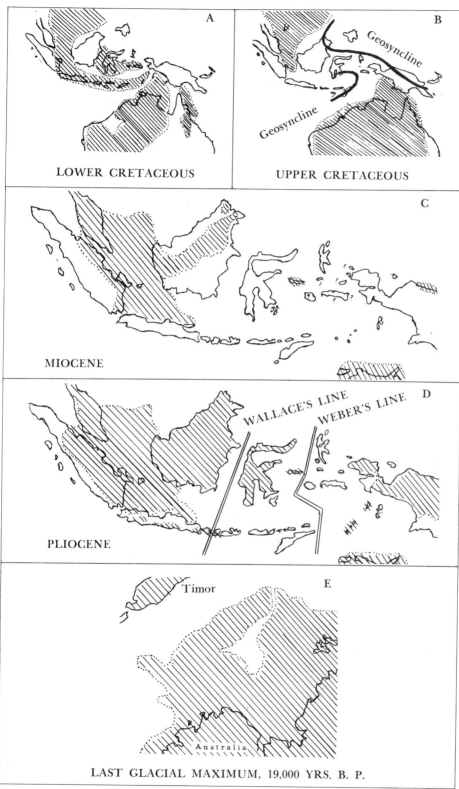

A
LOWER CRETACEOUS

B
Geosyncline
Geosyncline
UPPER CRETACEOUS

C
MIOCENE

D
WALLACE'S LINE   WEBER'S LINE
PLIOCENE

E
Timor
Australia
LAST GLACIAL MAXIMUM, 19,000 YRS. B. P.

FIG. 1.

when marsupials are assumed to have arrived; Miocene, when Simpson (1961) suggests the first rodents arrived; and during the Pleistocene, when the later waves of rodents must have colonized the continent. The Cretaceous reconstructions are based on those of Audley-Charles (1966), and supposes broad land between Asia and Australia in the Upper Cretaceous, followed by marked isolation of Australia in the Upper Cretaceous. Veevers (1967) has demonstrated that the Australian continent extended far to the northwest at times of lowered sea-level during the Pleistocene (Fig. 1).

The southern entry theory of marsupial colonization is based on the assumption that there was once direct land connection between Australia, Antarctica, and South America; or that, at least, Australia formerly lay close enough to South America to render possible adventitious crossing of the intervening water gap. At one time this theory enjoyed wide support (e.g., Harrison, 1924), but then was rejected along with the theory of continental drift (Simpson, 1940). A range of geological developments in the last few years, however, has now given it a solid foundation. Thus, terrestrial paleomagnetism has indicated that the southern continents may have changed latitudinal positions in geologic time (Runcorn, 1962; Irving, Robertson, and Stott, 1963). Sea-floor spreading studies indicate that continents such as Australia and Antarctica are moving apart (Vine, 1966). Marine paleomagnetism provides a basis for determining rates of sea-floor spreading and hence, by inference, continental movements (Heirtzler, 1968). Plate tectonics theory has been introduced to account for continental movement (Morgan, 1968). Finally, the discovery of Lower Triassic reptiles on the mainland of Antarctica (Elliott, et al., 1970) has proven not only that this continent supported vertebrate life during the Mesozoic, but also that obviously it was capable of functioning as a "stepping stone" between continents.

On the basis of this and allied studies various workers have now demonstrated that Australia occupied high latitudes, lying adjacent to Antarctica until the Cretaceous (Dietz and Holden, 1970) or, possibly, as late as the Eocene (Le Pichon, 1968). This would make a southern entry into Australia by early marsupials a distinct possibility and, in turn, rule out a northern entry at that time. Recent mammal paleontologists who have suggested that the ancestral Australian marsupials may have entered from the south include Ride (1964b), Hoffstetter (1970), and Cox (1970).

Continental drift, and its implications for the dispersal of early Southern Hemisphere mammals, is discussed in detail in Chapter II. At the present time, however, little more can be said of the relative merits of the southern and northern entry theories on biological grounds. Biologists are again coming to accept the former. The conflict would finally be resolved by the discovery of fossil marsupials in Antarctica. A few geologists still deny that continental drift has occurred (e.g., Meyerhoff, 1970a,b).

There are at least two good reasons, however, why the northern entry theory of Australian marsupials cannot yet be rejected in favor of the southern one. The Australian Cretaceous dinosaurs include what is apparently the northern (European) genus *Iguanodon* (Bartholomai, 1966), and footprints that apparently belong to the northern genus *Megalosauropus* (Colbert and Merrilees, 1967)—see discussion in Chapter II— and an Upper Eocene anthracothere is known from Timor (von Koenigswald, 1967). [An anthracothere has also been recorded, of course, from Borneo (Stromer, 1931), but this island lies on the Asian continental shelf.]

Recently, two other theories have been advanced to account for the origin of Australian marsupials, that of Martin (1970), who postulates that marsupials arose on a former land mass over the Darwin Rise in the central Pacific; and Cox (1970), who suggests that they reached Australia from Africa, via Antarctica. These hypotheses have already been discussed and rejected (see Chapter II).

There remains the problem of explaining why placental mammals did not colonize Australia in the beginning, along with the marsupials, since both types reached South America prior to the Paleocene. There may be several explanations, including different habitat or ecological specializations and different abilities to cross water gaps (compare, for example, the penetration of the islands to the north of Australia by rodents relative to marsupials at the present time). It is possible, too, despite the absence of a fossil record, that marsupials were the dominant mammals in those parts of Asia or South America closest to Australia during the Cretaceous.

Monotremes, endemic to Australia and New Guinea, have obviously had a long history in Australia and must be pre-Tertiary. They probably evolved in Australia. Fossils representing forms similar to those now living are unknown earlier than the Australian Pleistocene (or possibly late Pliocene). However, some possible monotreme teeth have been recently described from Miocene deposits in South Australia (Stirton, Tedford, and Woodburne, 1968). Three possible origins have been postulated for the monotremes: (1) they are specialized derivatives of a group of early prototherian mammals which subsequently gave rise to the Metatheria and Eutheria; (2) they are secondarily degenerate marsupials (see Gregory, 1947); and (3) they were independently budded off from a line of mammallike reptiles different from that which gave rise to the other mammals. Ride (1959) lists some of the evidence supporting this last view, which is the one accepted by most contemporary biologists.

The first placentals to colonize Australia were presumably bats and they possibly arrived as early as the Eocene (Simpson, 1961). This is based not on the Australian fossil record, for bats are not known prior to the Pleistocene, but rather on the fact that all the Australian bat families were then already differentiated in Europe. Rodents, widely acknowledged to be excellent "island hoppers," obviously arrived in Australia relatively late. Simpson (1961) on the basis of degree of differentiation achieved (two endemic subfamilies) has given the Miocene as the date of the first wave. The earliest fossil, however, is in the middle Pliocene of New Guinea (Plane, 1967) and not until the Pleistocene are there good fossil faunas. Hence a Miocene date of arrival is probably too early. Colonization of Australia by both bats and rodents was certainly progressive, with new waves, and individual species, filtering down the island chain from time to time. This colonization continues today.

The zoogeographic barrier between the Australian and Oriental faunas is, of course, Wallace's Line, which is one of the most striking faunal boundaries in the world. As postulated, it extends from south to north between Java and Bali, and between Borneo and the Celebes (Fig. 1). Between Borneo and the Celebes the strait is only 15 miles wide. Raven (1935) has provided a comprehensive analysis of the influence of Wallace's Line on mammal distribution. Included in the groups that reach it from the west are: insectivores, dermopterans, sciurids, hystricomorphs, lagomorphs, pangolins, tragulids and cervids, tapirs and rhinoceroses, ursids, mustelids, lemuroids, and monkeys. Only shrews, a few squirrels, a couple of monkeys, a porcupine, a suid, and a deer (see later) have crossed to the Celebes, and very few penetrate further east. Fossil hippopotami and giraffes are known from the Pleistocene of Java but not from further east. Fossil Proboscidea (*Stegodon*) are known from the Pliocene of Java; a small elephant did occur, however, on the Celebes (Hooijer, 1951) and even on Timor (Hooijer, 1967) during the Pleistocene. Equally surprising is the record of an Upper Eocene anthracothere, a semi-aquatic artiodactyl resembling a small hippopotamus, from Timor (von Koenigswald, 1967). Such an animal, of course, should not have had any great problem in crossing water gaps. The real significance of this record is that it suggests that Timor lay close to Asia as far back as the Eocene (see Chapter II of this book), a concept at variance with some of the newer ideas concerning continental drift and the positions of various land masses in the Early Tertiary. In an endeavor to further investigate this record D. A. Hooijer (pers. commun.) recently led an expedition to the area. The discoverer of the fossil (a skull fragment) was a member of the expedition. He failed to find the site, however, being able to remember only that it was picked up in a river (D. A. Hooijer, pers. commun.).

Only one Australian marsupial, the cuscus *Phalanger celebensis*, extends to Wallace's Line from the east (Fig. 2) and none penetrates to the west of it.

Various zoogeographers, especially Mayr (1944), have drawn attention to the fact that the island archipelagos northwest of Australia are a "subtraction-addition" area, a filter across which the proportion of species of Oriental and Australian origin changes. Thus, 18 genera of Asian mammals occur on the Celebes, four on Timor, two on Buru and Ceram, and one in the Aru Islands (Fig 2). A gradient is also clearly discernible in birds, reptiles, and other groups. This had led to the suggestion from workers in certain special groups that the line of faunal division is really further east than Wallace's Line (e.g., Weber's Line—Fig. 1). In the case

AUSTRALIAN MAMMALS

201

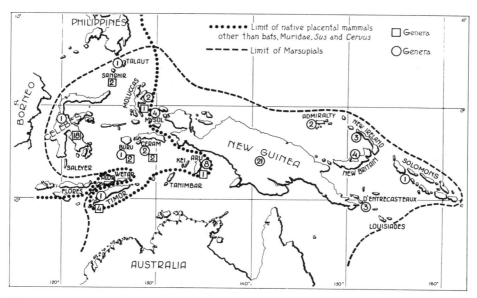

FIG. 2. Islands of the Australian Region to Show Western Limits of Marsupials and Eastern Limits Reached by Oriental Placental Mammals, other than Bats, Muridae, *Sus* and *Cervus*

Numbers of genera of each are indicated for the different islands. From Simpson, 1961.

of bats, Tate (1946) has placed the "50-50" or "faunal balance" line east of the Moluccas rather than west of them.

The reasons for the poor penetration of the island archipelagos by Australo-Papuan mammals are a combination of historic, physiographic, and ecological factors, plus, probably, poorer vagility in some cases. Whereas Borneo and Java, which lie on the Asian continental shelf, were repeatedly joined to the Asian mainland during the Pleistocene, the Australian shelf extends only some three-quarters of the way to Timor. Thereafter the ocean floor drops to between 3000 and 6000 m in the Timor Trough (Klompé, 1957). The sea bottom between New Guinea and the Celebes (Banda Sea) is 3000 to 6000 m deep (Klompé, 1957). Macassar Strait, between Borneo and the Celebes, is 200 to 3000 m deep. The whole area has been tectonically unstable for much of the Mesozoic and Tertiary, with islands appearing and disappearing. The island archipelagos are somewhat impoverished floristically and faunistically (compared to the continents on either side); they do not provide the rich biotic background nor range of living conditions of larger land masses. Broadly speaking, Australian marsupials inhabiting areas closest to Indonesia are adapted to woodlands, grasslands, and rocky outcrops, New Guinea ones to rain forests and montane areas. That their limited penetration of islands is due more to a poor ability to cross water gaps than an inability of the islands to support them can be seen from a comparison of the fairly rich fauna of the Aru Islands, which lie in shallow water and were repeatedly connected with the mainland during the Pleistocene, with those of New Britain (four species) and Solomon Islands (one species), which have remained isolated. The Aru Islands marsupial fauna consists of at least 3 species of dasyurids, one peramelid, and 4 phalangers (Laurie and Hill, 1954).

Authorities are agreed that the isolation of Australia stems from the Cretaceous or Early Tertiary. Audley-Charles (1966), arguing from the static-continent viewpoint, suggests that the deep basin of the Banda Sea and Macassar Strait stem from the Upper Cretaceous. If, however, Australia was located far to the south and adjacent to Antarctica at the end of the Cretaceous, the early history of these seas becomes irrelevant to the present discussion. On this basis, the contorted geology of the eastern Indonesian archipelagos is accounted for as a result of the Australian plate approaching the Asian one (see Chapter II). A Miocene date is suggested for this. If Australia did drift up from the south there is less difficulty in explaining both the marked faunistic differences between Asia and Australia and the late arrival of the rodents in Australia.

THE CONTEMPORARY MAMMAL FAUNA OF THE AUSTRALIAN REGION

The contemporary mammal fauna of the Australo-Papuan Region consists of 4 monotreme species (3 superspp.), about 145 marsupials (about 107 superspp.), and about 214 placental mammals (108 superspp.), a total of about 363 species or 218 superspecies (Tables 1 and 2). Of this total, 188 species are confined to Australia, and 128 species to New Guinea and offshore islands. The number of species common to the two areas is 47. Not included in the totals are a few endemic rodents and bats in the Solomons, Bismarcks, Fiji, and New Zealand (see later section).

One of the striking features of the Australian mammal faunas is its high level of endemicity, as Table 3 (from Simpson, 1961) shows. All families and genera of monotremes and marsupials are endemic, as are 77 per cent of the genera of rodents, and 29 per cent of the genera of bats. Of course, this would be expected from a region that is essentially a zoogeographic cul-de-sac.

All calculations of species numbers are essentially based on the works of Tate (1945a,c; 1946; 1947; 1948a,b; 1951), with minor adjustments from more recent works (e.g., Laurie and Hill, 1954; Ride, 1964a; Troughton, 1965). Tate's works have been used both because of their comprehensiveness and because he critically evaluated the status of allopatric forms in the light of modern taxonomic theory. They thus provide a better comparative basis than older studies such as the Australian Checklist of Iredale and Troughton (1934). Hobart Van Deusen has kindly calculated the numbers of New Guinea bat species and checked calculations for other New Guinea groups based on the latest information. It must be stressed at the outset, of course, that figures for species, and, especially, super-species, can only be "close guesses" since the taxonomy of the smaller mammals, and particularly rodents like *Rattus, Melomys,* and *Pogonomys,* is somewhat in a state of flux.

The best basis for making comparisons between groups, and between the faunas of different continents, is the superspecies concept. Here, strictly allopatric forms, provided they do not meet, are regarded as members of a single species. In doing this, some allowance has to be made for the "status" of the particular form, since some allopatric forms are relatively old and are ecologically quite distinct from the "parental" type (e.g., the rock-dwelling ringtail phalanger *Petropseudes dahli,* of northwestern Australia, would not be included in a superspecies with the arboreal eastern ringtails, *Pseudocheirus*). Another method of zoo-geographic analysis, the use of "species groups" for comparisons (see Tate, 1946, and Simpson, 1961, on bats), is inappropriate here because it does not give proper weight to radiation within groups. In terms of superspecies, the Australo-Papuan mammal fauna is approximately: monotremes, 3; marsupials, 107; placentals, 108 (Table 1).

The numbers of species and superspecies in the various groups of Australian mammals are given in Table 1. For marsupials the system of classification of Ride (1964b) is used. The Australian species are grouped into three Orders: (1) Marsupicarnivora (in which the Australian Dasyuroidea and the South American Didelphoidea and Borhyaenoidea share suborder status); (2) Peramelina (the bandicoots) and (3) Diprotodonta (Phalangeroidea), which include the herbivorous phalangers and kangaroos.

[The term Diprotodonta was introduced by early workers to describe one of the fundamental subdivisions of the marsupials; the other, Polyprotodonta. Subsequently a group of large, terrestrial, quadrupedal herbivores was named the Diprotodontidae, thus introducing possible grounds for confusion. Where the term "diprotodontid" or "diprotodont" is used in the present work it refers to the latter.]

The contemporary marsupial species fall into 7 families and 11 sub-families.

[In reviewing advances in marsupial classification, Ride (1968) has commented upon the gradual change from reliance on osteological and dental data to more sophisticated analyses of hair tracts, blood systems, urogenital systems, spermatozoa, and chromosomes. Recently a detailed comparative serology of the Australian marsupials has been published (Kirsch, 1968). Apart from confirming that marsupials are more similar to placentals than either is to monotremes this indicates that: (1) South American didelphoids and Australian marsupials represent distinct radiations; (2) the honey possum, *Tarsipes,* stands apart from the other phalangers; (3) the koala is closely related to the wombats and is relatively distinct from the phalangers; and (4) the bandicoots are related to the dasyuroids rather than the phalangeroids. Still later serological studies (Hayman, Kirsch, Martin, and Waller, 1971) suggest that there are actually three basic stocks among the contemporary marsupials: the South American caenolestids, the South American didelphids, and the Australian

The mammal fauna of Australia and New Guinea

Order and Family	Genera Total	Total Species	% of Total Fauna	Total Super-species	% of Total Fauna
MONOTREMATA					
Tachyglossidae (spiny anteaters)	2	3	1.0	2	1.0
Ornithorhynchidae (platypuses)	1	1	0.3	1	0.5
MARSUPIALIA					
Order MARSUPICARNIVORA [1]					
Suborder DASYUROIDEA					
Dasyuridae					
Dasyurinae (native "mice" and "cats")	14	41	11.2	30	13.6
Myrmecobiinae (marsupial anteater)	1	1	0.3	1	0.5
Thylacinidae (marsupial wolf)	1	1	0.3	1	0.5
Order PERAMELINA					
Peramelidae (bandicoots)	8	19	5.2	14	6.3
Order DIPROTODONTA (PHALANGEROIDEA)					
Wynyardidae	Early Miocene—extinct				
Phalangeridae					
Phalangerinae (phalangers)	10	21	5.7	14	6.3
Tarsipedinae (honey possum)	1	1	0.3	1	0.5
Phascolarctinae (koala, ringtail possums)	6	14	3.8	9	4.1
Thylacoleoninae (marsupial lion)	Late Oligocene or Early Miocene to Early Recent —extinct				
Macropodidae (wallabies and kangaroos)					
Potoroinae (rat kangaroos)	5	8	2.1	7	3.2
Sthenurinae (short-faced kangaroos)	Late Pliocene to Early Recent—extinct *				
Macropodinae (kangaroos, wallabies)	11–13	34	9.6	27	12.1
Diprotodontidae (diprotodons)	Early Miocene to Recent—extinct				
Vombatidae (wombats)	2	3	1.0	2	1.0
MARSUPIALIA *Incertae sedis*					
Notoryctidae (marsupial mole)	1	2	0.5	1	0.5
PLACENTALIA					
Order RODENTIA					
Muridae					
Hydromyinae (water rats)	11	13	3.4	10	4.6
Pseudomyinae and Murinae (native rats and mice)	20	111	30.1	52	22.9

TABLE 1A—Contd.

Order and Family	Total Genera	Total Species	% of Total Fauna	Total Super-species	% of Total Fauna
Order CHIROPTERA					
Suborder MEGACHIROPTERA					
Pteropodidae					
Pteropodinae	3	13	3.6	10	4.6
(fruit and blossom bats)					
Macroglossinae	2	12	3.3	5	2.3
(blossom bats)					
Suborder MICROCHIROPTERA					
Emballonuridae	2	2	0.6	2	1.0
Megadermatidae	1	1	0.3	1	0.5
Rhinolophidae	1	14	3.8	6	3.0
Vespertilionidae	11	37	10.2	16	7.3
Molossidae	1	10	2.7	5	2.5
Order CARNIVORA					
Canidae	1	1	0.3	1	0.5
(dingo)					
Total MONOTREMATA	3	4	1.3	3	1.5
Total MARSUPIALIA	60	145	39.6	107	47.8
Total PLACENTALIA	53	214	59.1	108	50.7
Total FAUNA	116	363	100.0	218	100.0

* Tedford, 1966
[1] In using the term "Marsupicarnivora" to group the Australian Dasyuroidea and the South American Didelphoidea and Paucituberculata, the classification of Ride (1964b) has been followed. Later serological work, however, indicates that the Paucituberculata represent a different lineage from the Dasyuroidea and Didelphoidea (Hayman, Kirsch, Martin, and Waller, 1971).

TABLE 1B

The mammal fauna of New Guinea

Family	Total Genera	Total Species	Species Exclusively in New Guinea
Tachyglossidae	2	3	2
Dasyuridae: Dasyurinae	8	12	8
Peramelidae	4	8	6
Phalangeridae	7	19	14
Macropodidae	5	11	5
Muridae: Hydromyinae	9	13	10
Murinae	12	42	37
Pteropodidae: Pteropodinae	2	11	8
Macroglossinae	3	10	7
Emballonuridae	2	7	4
Megadermatidae	1	1	—
Rhinolophidae	3	12	7
Vespertilionidae	10	19	15
Molossidae	2	6	5
Canidae	1	1	—
Total MONOTREMATA	2	3	2
Total MARSUPIALIA	24	50	33
Total PLACENTALIA	45	122	93
Total FAUNA	71	175	128

TABLE 2

Comparison of numbers of species of the major groups of mammals found in Australia

	Australia and New Guinea		Australia Total	New Guinea Total	New Guinea, Not Australia
	Species	Superspecies	Species	Species	Species
Monotremata	4	3	2	3	2
Marsupialia	145	107	112	50	33
Placentalia					
Rodentia	124	62	77	55	47
Chiroptera	89	45	43	66	46
Carnivora: Canidae	1	1	1	1	
Total	363	218	234	175	128

marsupials. The inference is that the caenolestids were the first of the three to separate off. It will be noted that, earlier, Simpson (1941) had developed anatomical evidence that primitive borhyaenids like *Patene* approach didelphids and presumably had a common ancestry with them (see discussion in Patterson and Pascual, Chapter VI, page 261).

The supposed relationships of the Australian orders to each other and their fossil history are shown in Fig. 3, redrawn from Ride (1964b). Figures for the number of genera of each group recorded for the different geological periods have been updated by R. H. Tedford (pers. commun.) by the inclusion of data from Stirton, Tedford, and Woodburne (1967, 1968) and other recent sources. No Eocene or Paleocene mammals are known at present.

The major morphological types in the Australian mammal fauna are illustrated in Figs. 4, 7, and 9, which show that the marsupials have radiated into a striking diversity of body forms corresponding to all the major ways of life. The rodents and bats, by contrast, are quite typical of these groups elsewhere. They have developed no novel body structures, other than very minor ones. Notwithstanding this, the numbers of species of rodents and bats is slightly greater than the number of marsupial species. The Australian canid, *Canis familiaris dingo,* is now known to have been introduced by aboriginal man. The earliest published radiocarbon date for it is 3,000 years before the present (B.P.) (Mulvaney et al., 1964).

MAMMALIAN RADIATION WITHIN AUSTRALIA

Monotremata

Both monotreme types, the platypus (*Ornithorhynchus*) and echidna (*Tachyglossus*), while structurally primitive (reptilian reproductive system, persistent coracoid, diffuse mammary glands, incomplete temperature regulation, absence of corpus callosum), are splendidly adapted for

	Families		Genera	
	No.	% En-demic	No.	% En-demic
Monotremata	2	100	3	100
Marsupialia	6	100	47	100
Placentalia				
Chiroptera	7	0	21	29
Rodentia	1	0	13	77
Carnivora	1	0	1	0
Totals	17	47	85	67

TABLE 3

Endemism in Australian native Recent mammals, excluding New Guinea

Groups are counted as endemic if confined to the region east of Wallace's Line; from Simpson (1961).

highly specialized modes of life. Thus, the aquatic platypus has a flattened body, a leathery and ducklike bill, subterminal nostrils, webbed feet, flattened tail, and thick fur (Fig. 4). The bill is used to "nuzzle" worms, crayfish, and other foods from the bottom mud. The quilled echidna is equipped with short, powerful limbs, strong claws, elongated muzzle and sticky tongue for feeding on ants and termites. Both monotremes are relatively free of competition in their respective feeding zones. There are no aquatic marsupials and the specialized water rat (*Hydromys*) takes larger food items, e.g., mussels (McNally, 1960), which it can chew since it has teeth. The marsupial anteater (*Myrmecobius*), which overlaps some-what with *Tachyglossus* in food habits, is restricted to dry areas in the far south of the continent where hollow logs are available for protection.

Monotremes are very versatile in terms of habitat, the platypus inhabit-ing both alpine streams at an altitude of 5,000 feet, and sluggish subtropical Queensland coastal rivers. Echidnas occur in all classes of country from rain-forest to stony areas in the central Australian desert, one of the widest habitat tolerances of any mammal. *Tachyglossus aculeatus,* the Australian echidna, occurs also in the lowlands of New Guinea but is replaced in the highlands by the long-billed genus *Zaglossus* (Fig. 4), and in Tasmania by a more furry form (*Tachyglossus a. setosus*) with less prominent quills.

The contemporary Australian monotremes are obviously the end-products of a very long period of evolution. In this respect it is interest-ing to speculate that they might have enjoyed a Cretaceous or Early Tertiary radiation prior to the ascendancy of the marsupials, as Darling-ton (1957) has suggested. Accounts of the general biology of the Australian monotremes are available in Wood Jones (1923), Troughton (1948) and Ride (1970). The echidna is currently the subject of an intensive study by M. Griffiths (see Griffiths and Simpson, 1966), who has recently pub-lished an extensive review of the biology of this animal (Griffiths, 1968).

Dasyuroidea

The dasyures form a linear sequence from small mouse-sized predomi-nately insectivorous forms (see *Antechinus* and *Sminthopsis,* Fig. 4)

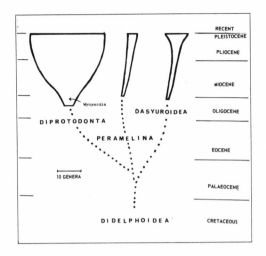

FIG. 3. AUSTRALIAN MARSUPIAL
RELATIONSHIPS AND FOSSIL RECORD
*Breadth of each limb during each
geological period represents the
known number of genera.*
*Redrawn from Ride (1964b), and
revised according to new data on
Australian Tertiary forms presented
by Stirton, Tedford, and Woodburne (1967, 1968).*

through to carnivores the size of a domestic cat (*Dasyurops maculatus*) or
small dog (*Sarcophilus*). The smaller and larger forms were formerly
placed in separate subfamilies (Phascogalinae and Dasyurinae), but Ride
(1964b) has grouped them, pending a proper revision, on the grounds that
there is no real distinguishing feature other than size. The marsupial
wolf, *Thylacinus* (Figs. 4 and 6A), stands apart from the other dasyuroids
and holds family rank (Thylacinidae). The marsupial anteater (*Myrmecobius*) is also aberrant and hence is placed in the Myrmecobiinae.

The marsupial mole (*Notoryctes*), remarkably convergent to the golden
moles of Africa (Chrysochloridae) and the true moles (Talpidae), is so
modified morphologically as to leave few clues about its relationships. It
has been variously regarded as an aberrant dasyuroid and an aberrant
perameloid.

The Dasyuroidea provide a remarkable series of parallel morphological
and ecological forms with placentals elsewhere. Thus, the arboreal *Phascogale tapoatafa* is to all intents and purposes a small weasel (e.g., *Mustela
frenata*). The spotted native cat (*Dasyurus quoll*) and tiger cat (*Dasyurops
maculatus*) are good counterparts of such North American mustelids as
the marten (*Martes americana*) and fisher (*M. pennanti*) or the African
genet (*Genetta tigrina*, Viverridae). The skull form and dentition, however, are less specialized and there is no carnassial (Fig. 5), although all
the molars have carnassial-like shearing action.

The Tasmanian devil, *Sarcophilus*, is a heavy-bodied scavenger, and is
the counterpart in the Australian fauna of the wolverine (*Gulo*) in the
Northern Hemisphere, and the hyenas (*Crocuta*) in Africa. The parallel
adaptations of these three forms to the scavenging way of life include
wide massive skulls with large sagittal crests, heavy jaws, enlarged premolars, high forelimb/hindlimb and scapula/spine ratios, etc. (Keast,
unpubl.). Of the three, however, the hyena is obviously the most efficient

FIG. 4. MAJOR MORPHOLOGICAL TYPES OF AUSTRALO-PAPUAN MAMMALS: MONOTREMATA AND MARSUPIALIA

MONOTREMATA: *A*, Ornithorhynchus anatinus (*Platypus*); *B*, Tachyglossus aculeatus (*Echidna*); *C*, Zaglossus bruijni (*Long-billed Echidna*) (*New Guinea*). MARSUPIALIA (*Dasyuroidea*): *D*, Sminthopsis leucopus (*Narrow-footed Pouched Mouse*); *E*, Antechinomys laniger (*Jerboa Pouched Mouse*); *F*, Dasyurops maculatus (*Tiger Cat*); *G*, Antechinus flavipes (*Yellow-footed Pouched Mouse*); *H*, Dasyurus quoll (*Native Cat*); *I*, Myrmecobius fasciatus (*Banded Anteater*); *J*, Notoryctes typhlops (*Marsupial Mole*); *K*, Phascogale tapoatafa (*Tuan*); *L*, Sarcophilus harrisii (*Tasmanian Devil*); *M*, Thylacinus cynocephalus (*Tasmanian Wolf*).

and *Sarcophilus* the least. A study by Keast of convergent trends in the Australian marsupial carnivores, North American mustelids and canids, and African viverrids, hyaenids, and felids, will be published later. The biology and food ecology of *Sarcophilus* has recently been reviewed by Guiler (1970a,b).

The mouse-sized dasyures partly occupy the niches of shrews, tree-shrews, and small weasels. An interesting feature is that the centralmost incisors are enlarged and project outwards (they are particularly prominent in *Phascogale tapoatafa*, Fig. 5), as in shrews. Shrews, however, show a marked reduction in the rest of their dentition, which dasyures do not. Wood Jones (1923) suggests that "nipping" incisors of this sort have mainly an insect-killing function; there is no denying their lethal qualities, however, from the viewpoint of larger prey.

Several of the genera of small-bodied dasyurids have radiated into half a dozen or more species. The emphasis is usually on the production of allopatric forms (adapted to desert, forest, cold-temperate, or tropical habitats respectively). Commonly no more than two members of a genus occur in a single habitat. The genera tend to be either purely terrestrial or semi-arboreal: the former often have the capacity to stand erect (like a miniature kangaroo), the latter rarely or never do so. This difference, which can be seen in *Sminthopsis*, compared to *Antechinus*, also characterizes *Dasyurus quoll* compared to *Dasyurops maculatus* in the larger forms. (*Dasyurops maculatus* is sometimes included in the genus *Dasyurus*.) *Planigale*, containing the smallest species, is flat-headed, an adaptation permitting it to live in cracks in the dry earth. The desert form, *Antechinomys*, has greatly lengthened legs and has always been regarded as bipedal, saltatory, and convergent with the jumping mice (*Notomys*), some of which share its habitat. Recent studies by Ride (1965) using high speed photography have shown, however, that it is quadrupedal. Several of the smaller Australian dasyures have been the subject of studies in recent years; some of this literature is listed in Ride (1970).

The wolf-like *Thylacinus cynocephalus* (Figs. 4 and 6A), now confined to Tasmania but formerly wide-ranging, was a predator on small macropodids and other animals. It hunted solitarily or in pairs and relied more on tiring the prey than capturing it by speed. In this respect it is notable that the hindlimb/spine ratio in *Thylacinus* averages only 67 per cent compared to 74 per cent in *Canis vulpes;* the forelimb/hindlimb ratios of the two are 81 per cent and 91 per cent (Keast, unpubl.) The placental wolf is obviously the better runner. The strikingly dog-like skull form of *Thylacinus* is apparent in Fig. 6A, as is its unspecialized dasyurid dentition, the molars having both shearing and grinding surfaces, whereas in the dog these functions are borne by separate teeth. *Myrmecobius* approaches the true anteaters in its long muzzle (Fig. 4) and tongue. The number of teeth is large (commonly 50), and they are small and degenerate.

The number of genera in the contemporary Dasyuroidea is 16 (if the various marsupial cats all are grouped under *Dasyurus*); the number of superspecies is 32 and of species 43.

Perameloidea

The Perameloidea (8 gen., 14 superspp., 19 spp.), range from the size and body form of a large rat (most species) to that of a small rabbit (the long-eared *Macrotis*). All are terrestrial and are characterized by somewhat long snouts and strong digging claws (Fig. 7). Insects predominate in the diet (many are obtained by digging), but omnivorous tendencies characterize some species.

Peramelids occur throughout Australia and New Guinea. In many parts of Australia, including the arid interior, a long-snouted species (*Perameles*) and a short-snouted species (*Isoodon*) occur together, usually slightly different habitats being occupied. Dietary differences have yet to be properly investigated. *Macrotis* and *Choeropus* are interior plains and desert dwellers and a couple of distinctive genera (*Echymipera* and *Peroryctes*) are today confined to New Guinea.

The syndactylous foot, in which toes 2 and 3 are united to leave only the terminal portions and claws free (Fig. 5), has been shown by Wood Jones (1924) to be a development for grooming the hair. Interesting variations in the foot structure involve the production of a kangaroo-like type—compare illustrations of the rabbit bandicoot, *Macrotis,* and the wallaby *Thylogale* (Fig. 5). In the cursorial *Choeropus*, by contrast, there is a cleft pig-like manus (all digits but the second and third being reduced), and a "solid-hoofed" foot, in which all but digit 4 are reduced. Wood Jones (1924) points out that the changes are convergent with the hoofs of an artiodactyl and a perissodactyl, respectively. Bandicoots, as a group, have a shuffling, ungainly movement in which the hindlimbs move synchronously. The only description of the gait of *Choeropus,* which now is apparently extinct, is that of G. Krefft, quoted by Wood Jones (1924, p. 170), that it moved like a "broken-down hack in a canter, apparently dragging the hind quarters after it."

Recent papers on the ecology of peramelids include Heinsohn (1966), and Smyth and Philpott (1968). Wood Jones (1924), Troughton (1948), and Ride (1970) provide general accounts of their biology.

Phalangeroidea

The number of contemporary genera in the Phalangeroidea is about 35, superspecies 60, and species 78. The phalangeroids fall into three major series: the somewhat generalized arboreal phalangers, the saltatory macropodids, and the quadrupedal terrestrial wombats. When the fossil record is taken into account, however, there are clearly at least five distinct phyletic lines: (1) Wynyardidae, based on a unique early Miocene fossil (see Ride, 1964b; Quilty, 1966); (2) Phalangeridae, consisting of Phalangerinae (Australian possums, gliders, cuscuses, and pigmy possums; Tarsi-

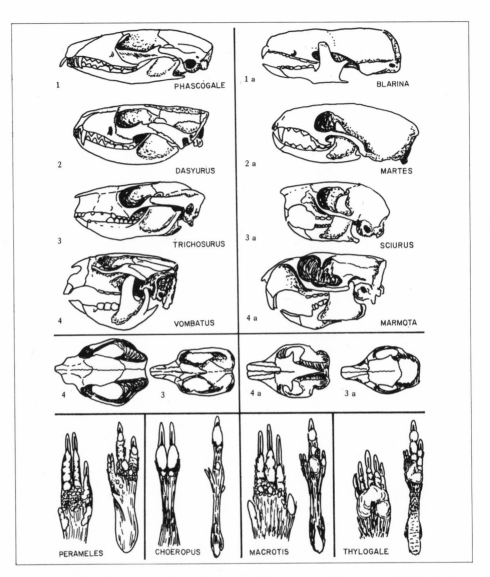

FIG. 5. (Upper) Skulls of Four Pairs of "Ecological Counterparts" Compared; (Lower) Convergence in the Syndactylous Foot of Peramelidae Relative to Other Mammals

UPPER: *Left, marsupials; right, placentals. Note comparable pair of "nipping" median incisors in* Phascogale *and* Blarina, *but reduced dentition of the latter.* Martes *has a more specialized dentition' than* Dasyurus, *including a carnassial.* Sciurus *is again more specialized than* Trichosurus *(rodent incisors permit it to gnaw nuts and other hard substances that are presumably somewhat "unavailable" to the marsupial).* Vombatus *and* Marmota *are convergent in dentition (the marsupial has true "rodent" incisors) and, as semi-fossorial species, they have flattened and somewhat broad skulls. The eyes of* Vombatus *are protected by being sunken, those of* Marmota *by the development of a supraorbital process. Note enlarged cranial cavity of the placentals.*

LOWER: *Note generalized manus (left) and pes (right) of* Perameles *compared to the "hoofs" of* Choeropus, *in which the forelimb has a "cloven hoof" of the artiodactyl type (it is known as "pig-footed bandicoot"); as in the horse, the hindlimb is reduced to a single digit. In the interior rabbit bandicoot,* Macrotis, *by contrast, the foot is convergent with that of a macropodid, as typified by the small wallaby* Thylogale.

pedinae (the unique long-snouted honey possum of southwestern Australia); Phascolarctinae (the koala and, possibly, the ringtail possums and greater glider, with which it shares selenodont molars); Thylacoleoninae (the extinct marsupial lion); (3) Macropodidae, consisting of Potoroinae (rat kangaroos, small-bodied species with a mixture of primitive and specialized features), Macropodinae (kangaroos and wallabies), and Sthenurinae (extinct short-faced kangaroos); (4) Diprotodontidae (extinct giant quadrupeds such as *Diprotodon, Nototherium, Euryzygoma*); and (5) Vombatidae (wombats)—see Ride (1964b).

Great structural diversity is manifested by the Phalangeroidea and each group, apart from *Wynyardia*, about which little is known, and *Tarsipes* which is unique, has undergone interesting and complex radiations. While most of the members are herbivorous, the primitive modern members, such as *Distoechurus* and *Cercartetus* among the Phalangerinae, and *Hypsyprimnodon* among the Potoroinae, are insectivorous. Nectar-feeding is developed in some of the smaller phalangers. A few small forms such as *Bettongia* (Potoroinae), are partly carnivorous.

In terms of ecological equivalence the phalangers can be thought of as occupying the ecological niches of primates and squirrels. The skull and dentition, however, remain generalized with none of the striking specializations in body form, skull, and dentition that characterize these groups (Fig. 5). The koala, *Phascolarctus*, which has become reduced to a "tree-clinger," finds partial counterparts in the South American sloths (Bradypodidae) and Asian slow loris (*Nycticebus*). The long-faced grazing kangaroos are the counterparts of the equids and bovids, and the short-faced forms (especially the extinct *Sthenurus*) correspond to the browsing bovids and cervids. The extinct Pleistocene *Diprotodon* (Fig. 8) had the bulk of a rhinoceros, and *Nototherium* that of a tapir. The extinct *Thylacoleo* (Fig. 8) was a large and striking carnivore.

The terrestrial and semi-fossorial wombats (Figs. 5, 6A, and 7), heavy-bodied and short-limbed, with broad skulls, well-developed nuchal crests, and chisel-like incisors that are continuously growing, represent an interesting parallel with *Marmota* among the Nearctic and Palearctic rodents (Figs. 5 and 6A). On the whole, wombats are better adapted structurally for fossorial life than *Marmota* (Keast, 1963), having more massive frames, skulls, jaws, and limbs; they are also able to consume coarse roots as well as the grasses taken by *Marmota*. The flattened head of both types is presumably an adaptation in part for packing the earth around the top and walls of the burrow (compare the skulls of *Vombatus* and *Marmota* with those of their arboreal counterparts, *Trichosurus* and *Sciurus*, in Fig. 5). The eyes in *Vombatus* are protected by being sunk into the skull, and in *Marmota* by the development of supra-orbital processes.

The Phalangerinae range in size from the tiny pigmy possum (*Cercartetus*), the size of a domestic mouse, to the brush-tailed possum (*Trichosurus*), as big as a large cat (Fig. 7). A wide range of body forms includes the short-faced cuscuses (*Phalanger*), a New Guinea group characterized

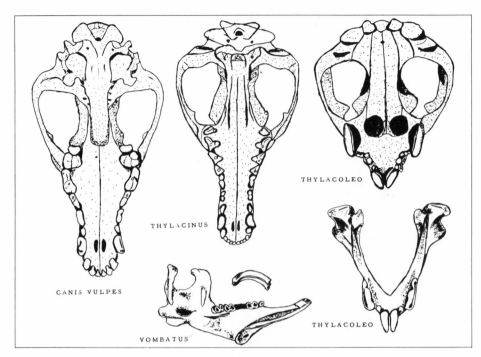

FIG. 6A. SKULLS OF *Canis, Thylacinus,* AND *Thylacoleo* COMPARED

Thylacinus *lacks the individual tooth specialization of the wolf.* Canis *has a well-developed carnassial and a large grinding molar, whereas all the molars of the marsupial have a compound function—a grinding surface combined with a carnassial-like shearing action.*

Thylacoleo *has a greatly foreshortened skull, a pair of pointed incisors and a pair of greatly enlarged and elongated premolars. The molars are lost. There has been much speculation as to how this curious dentition was used.*

The sagittal section of the lower jaw of Vombatus *shows the length of the "open-rooted" gliriform incisor. A molar has been freed to show the length of its root. The Vombatidae are the only Australian marsupials with a true rodent dentition.*

by a semi-erect posture and sluggish movements. The gliding habit has independently been evolved by three genera, the mouse-sized *Acrobates,* the medium-sized *Petaurus* (3 spp.), and the large *Schoinobates* (usually placed in the Phascolarctinae). This last-named species may glide for as much as 120 yards (Troughton, 1948). The gliding membranes of these marsupials are good parallels to those of the gliding squirrels (*Glaucomys* parallels *Petaurus* in size), and the Oriental "flying lemur" (Dermoptera). Prehensile tails characterize a number of phalangers (e.g., the ring-tailed possum, *Pseudocheirus,* Fig. 7).

Tarsipes, the mouse-sized honey possum of southwestern Australia, shows the greatest specialization for nectar-feeding, the lips forming a tube up which the liquid is "pumped" with the aid of a long tongue covered with fine hairs. It is perhaps significant that this specialized nectar-

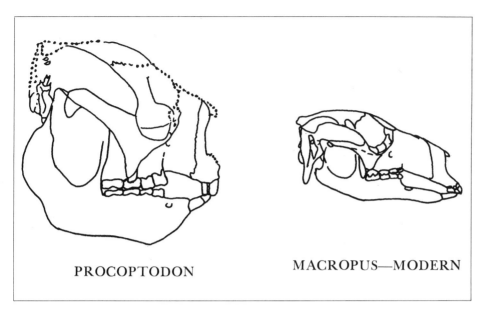

PROCOPTODON   MACROPUS—MODERN

FIG. 6B. SKULLS OF *Procoptodon goliah*, THE GIANT PLEISTOCENE SHORT-FACED KANGA-
ROO, AND THAT OF THE LARGEST OF THE CONTEMPORARY *Macropus* (LONG-FACED) KANGA-
ROOS COMPARED
Redrawn from Tedford, 1966.

feeder occurs in a part of the continent (sand-plain heaths of the southwest) where there is a deficiency in species of nectar-feeding birds (9 meli-
phagids compared to 18 in the eastern forests) and which is exceptionally
rich in endemic flowering shrubs. Lastly, the striped possum, *Dactylopsila*,
of New Guinea, has evolved a device for extracting insects from fissures in
the bark; a greatly elongated phalanx 4 and hooked nail, a parallel structure to that of the Madagascar lemuroid, *Daubentonia*. The most specialized feeder is the koala (*Phascolarctos*, Phascolarctinae), in which the diet
is apparently limited to the leaves of about 10 species of *Eucalyptus*.

The phalangers as a group are arboreal and forest-dwelling. The rain
forests of New Guinea and Australia have a rich fauna, as do the sclerophyll
forests of Australia (see distribution in Fig. 11). There is a marked reduction in species in the woodland areas. Only one member penetrates into
the center of the continent, the brush-tailed possum, *Trichosurus vulpecula*, which lives in hollows in the riverine eucalypts but may, in places,
be terrestrial. On the other hand two distinctive monotypic genera in the
northwest of the continent have become rock dwellers, the scaly-tail possum (*Wyulda*) and the rock ringtail (*Petropseudes*).

The ecology, reproductive biology, and population dynamics of two
phalangers, *Trichosurus vulpecula* and *Pseudocheirus peregrinus*, have
been the basis of extensive study in later years (e.g., Tyndale-Biscoe,

1955; Thomson and Owen, 1964). Some of the papers dealing with recent studies are listed in Ride (1970).

The macropodids provide the most interesting radiation in the Australian fauna, as indicated by Raven and Gregory (1946). Details of evolutionary changes in skull form (especially between dolichocephaly and brachycephaly), dentition, body form, and limb structure are documented by Bensley (1903), Wood Jones (1924), Tate (1948a), and Ride (1964b). In body form the group ranges from thick-set rat-kangaroos (Potoroinae), which are thicket-dwellers, to fleet plains-dwelling Macropodinae like *Megaleia rufa,* old males of which may reach heights of nearly six feet. In relative size, habitat, and way of life, these two subfamilies are good parallels of the skulking duikers (Cephalophinae) and the plains-dwelling antelope (Bovinae) of the African veld. Physiological studies have shown the existence of "pseudorumination" in macropodids, permitting the digestion of cellulose (Moir, Somers, and Waring, 1956), an interesting convergence towards the true ruminants. They also regurgitate food to some extent (Mollison, 1960). An embryological novelty is the occurrence of "embryonic diapause," no development taking place in the fertilized female until the previous young leaves the pouch. This must be of considerable survival value to an animal that can only have one young at a time (Sharman, 1959) and must be especially so in the unpredictable environment of inland Australia.

The most primitive macropodid is *Hypsiprymnodon moschatus* (Potoroinae), the musky rat-kangaroo, in that it provides a link between kangaroos and phalangers. Thus, the hind foot retains the hallux and digital pads while the second and third digits are strongly syndactylous; the posterior upper premolars inherit the prominent vertically high and compressed crowns, with cutting edge and prominent vertical grooves, as in the phalangers; the molars are primitive (quadrituberculate); and the secant premolars are directed sharply outward as in the phalangers (Raven and Gregory, 1946). The alimentary canal is simple and in *Hypsiprymnodon* alone of the Macropodidae both permanent premolars have a brief coexistence in the fully erupted state (Ride, 1964b). The ecology of this species was summarized by its discoverer, as follows: "It inhabits the dense and damp portions of the scrubs (rain forest). . . . Its habits are chiefly diurnal . . . it progresses in much the same manner as the kangaroo rats . . . but procures its food by turning over the debris in the scrubs in search of insects, worms, and tuberous roots, frequently eating the palm berries . . . which it holds in its forepaws after the manner of the phalangers, sitting up on its haunches, or sometimes digging like the bandicoots . . ." (Pierson Ramsay, in Thomas, 1888, p. 124). The other Potoroinae differ from *Hypsiprymnodon* in lacking the hallux but share long, digging foreclaws and many of the dental features, including the grooved vertical premolar which apparently is capable of snipping off quite strong twigs. The brush-tailed rat-kangaroo (*Bettongia penicillata*) (Fig. 9) has the typical squat body form and short legs of the subfamily.

PERAMELOIDEA

PHALANGEROIDEA

FIG. 7. MAJOR MORPHOLOGICAL TYPES OF AUSTRALO-PAPUAN MAMMALS: MARSUPIALIA (continued)

Perameloidea: A, Perameles nasuta (*Long-nosed Bandicoot*); *B*, Macrotis lagotis (*Rabbit-eared Bandicoot*). *Phalangeroidea: C*, Phalanger orientalis (*Cuscus*); *D*, Petaurus breviceps (*Sugar Glider*); *E*, Schoinobates volans (*Greater Glider*); *F*, Tarsipes spenserae (*Honey Possum*); *G*, Pseudocheirus perigrinus (*Ring-tailed Possum*); *H*, Trichosurus vulpecula (*Brush-tailed Possum*); *I*, Cercartetus nanus (*Pigmy Possum*); *J*, Phascolarctos cinereus (*Koala*); *K*, Vombatus hirsutus (*Wombat*).

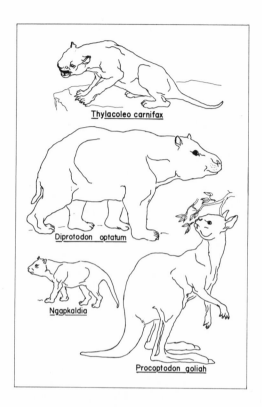

FIG. 8. SOME SPECTACULAR FOSSILS
The Pleistocene cave lion,
Thylacoleo carnifax *(length about
5 ft.); the giant Pleistocene* Diprotodon optatum *(length about 7
ft.); a pig-sized early Miocene
diprotodont,* Ngapkaldia *(Stirton,
1957); and the short-faced* Procoptodon goliah, *which stood about
10 feet high.*

The Macropodinae represent the stem forms of the major macropodid
radiation, lacking the specializations that go with the primitive features
of the Potoroinae. Many retain the sectorial premolars but the small
canines are dropped. The lophodont molars acquire links and folds that
increase their efficiency as grinding surfaces. The large, grazing wallabies
and kangaroos have high-crowned teeth. The number of functional premolars is now reduced. Another adaptation is that the molar tooth-row
moves progressively forward during the life of the animal as the front
teeth wear (Ride, 1964b).

The small to medium-sized wallabies in part occupy the lagomorph
niche of the other continents. The feeding of only a minority of species
has been studied in detail, but the browsing, as distinct from the grazing
habit, has been emphasized in a number of lines and is commonly linked to
the brachycephalic condition. The short-faced browsers par excellence
were the Sthenurinae of the Pleistocene (Tedford, 1966), some of which
reached gigantic sizes (see *Procoptodon,* Fig 8). The rock-dwelling niche of
the chamois, mountain goat, and klipspringer is occupied in Australia by
the rock wallabies (*Petrogale*), which have specially calloused footpads and
in which the tail is used as a balancer during leaps (Fig. 9). Another
interesting group is *Dendrolagus* (the tree-kangaroos), a New Guinea
radiation, which has secondarily reverted to an arboreal existence (Fig.

9). In these relatively short-faced browsers the forelimbs are lengthened, and the soles are much roughened. The tail has not re-acquired a prehensile function, being used only as a balancer. Tree kangaroos climb readily, and are capable of making leaps between branches as well as dropping harmlessly to the forest floor from considerable heights (Troughton, 1948).

The largest contemporary macropodids are the forest and plains kangaroos (*Macropus* and *Megaleia*), old males of which grow to heights of 5.5 to 6 feet (Troughton, 1948; Frith and Calaby, 1968; Ride, 1970). These large grazers have slim forequarters and heavy hindquarters, long powerful hindlimbs, a strong tail that can alternatively function as the third leg of a tripod or as a balancer when leaping; they can achieve leaps of up to 25 feet and speeds, over short distances, of 30 to 35 mi/hr (Wood Jones, 1924; Troughton, 1948; Frith and Calaby, 1968). They are superbly modified for a swift cursorial (saltatory) existence.

Several macropodids have been ecologically and physiologically investigated in recent years, mainly at the University of Western Australia and C.S.I.R.O. Wildlife Division; e.g., see recent papers on *Setonyx* (Dunnet, 1963), the red kangaroo (Frith, 1954; Sharman, 1964; Frith and Sharman, 1964; Newsome, 1966), and the euro (Ealey, 1967). Additional studies are listed in Frith and Calaby (1968) and Ride (1970).

Rodentia

The rodent fauna of Australia and New Guinea totals some 31 genera, 124 species, and 62 superspecies. Of the species, about 69 are endemic to Australia proper and 47 to New Guinea (calculations based on data from Tate, 1951). The two faunas are, accordingly, almost mutually exclusive. If allopatric species be omitted, the Australian list is reduced from about 124 species to 62 superspecies. Each of the endemic subgenera, such as *Pseudomys, Gyomys, Thetomys,* and *Leggadina,* has many species.

When the Australo-Papuan rodent fauna is surveyed from the viewpoint of its distinctness, four different evolutionary levels become apparent (Tate, 1951; Simpson, 1961): (1) The endemic subfamily Hydromyinae (water-rats) are semi-carnivorous rats and are characterized by "basined" cheek teeth and a loss of posterior molars (Fig. 9); this distinctive group has nine genera restricted to New Guinea, some of which are shrewlike, and one to Australia. (2) There is a series of "Old Papuan" genera. (3) The "Pseudomyinae" of Australia (see Fig. 9 for a typical example), are a distinctive and varied group of murids that have undergone a marked adaptive radiation within the continent. (4) There are many typical *Rattus* species.

Simpson (1961) interprets these "levels of difference" as representing about seven different waves of colonization down the "island chain" from Asia. He postulates that the oldest, best-differentiated groups probably arrived in the Miocene, and that there were intermediate waves in the

Pliocene, with later waves in the Pleistocene and Recent. Simpson suggests that all the stocks were murids, the group that succeeded the cricetids in Eurasia. Murids, however, are unknown as fossils before the Pliocene. A late Pliocene fauna of mammals (14 spp.) excavated at Grange Burn, Victoria, by Lundelius and Turnbull (1967) has so far revealed no rodents but a rodent tooth is known from the Pliocene of New Guinea (Plane, 1967). Rodents are numerous in later fossil assemblages, suggesting that Simpson's date for the arrival of rodents is too early, and that they did not reach Australia until at least the Pliocene. The paleogeographic maps of Umbgrove (1938) show a marked narrowing of the watergap between Borneo and New Guinea in the Pliocene (Fig. 1) and this would certainly have favored rodent colonization at this time. The maps of Veevers (1967) demonstrate how, during the Pleistocene, there were periodic narrowings to correspond with the glacial maxima (Fig. 1); presumably later waves of rodent colonization of Australia penetrated at such times. Notwithstanding the difficulties in timing there seems little doubt of the validity of Simpson's broad zoogeographic interpretations.

Rodents occupy a wide range of niches in Australia today, as seen from the accounts in Wood Jones (1925) and Troughton (1948). The morphological diversity, of course, in no way approaches that seen in South America or Africa. There are also no squirrel-like types. There is a rich desert fauna with some species being physiologically adapted to do without exogenous water (MacMillan and Lee, 1967).

Chiroptera

The zoogeography of the Indonesian and Australo-Papuan bats has been reviewed by Tate (1946) and Simpson (1961). A rather different situation from the rodents is involved here—all seven Australian bat families are relatively ancient, being known as fossils as far back as the middle Eocene to middle Oligocene in Europe. "They could, then, have reached Australia at any time since the early Tertiary, and there has been no differentiation of families and comparatively little of genera in the Australian Region" (Simpson, 1961, p. 437). There are, however, a couple of very distinctive types (e.g., the genus *Rhinonicteris*, and the subfamily Nyctophilinae). Bats, accordingly, represent a moderately attenuated sample of the Asian fauna.

About 21 genera, 89 species, and 45 superspecies of bats occur in the Australo-Papuan region. They show a much greater range of morphological types than the rodents. Extreme types are the giant fruit bats or flying foxes (*Pteropus*, Fig. 9), blossom and fruit eaters, the largest of which have a wingspan of four feet, and the bat predator, *Macroderma*, which represents the extreme development of the carnivorous habit in old world bats. Over two-thirds of the species are small insectivorous bats and several families have undergone marked radiations (Table 1). The vespertilionids alone account for about 31 species (16 superspp.). Accounts

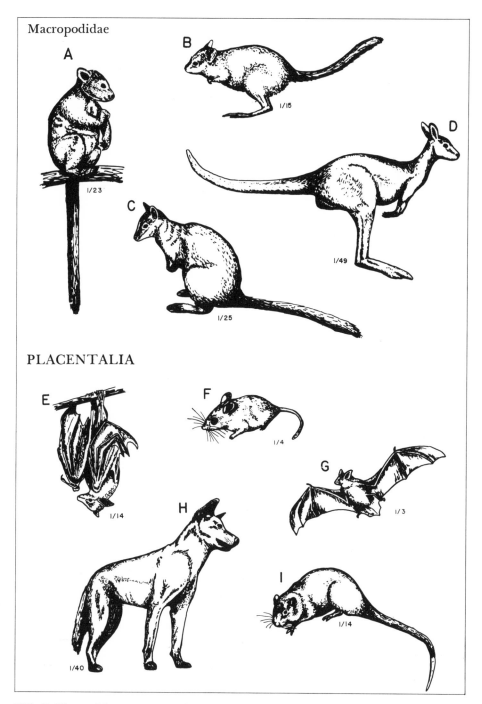

Macropodidae

A

B 1/15

1/23

C 1/25

D 1/49

PLACENTALIA

E 1/14

F 1/4

G 1/3

H 1/40

I 1/14

FIG. 9. Major Morphological Types of Australo-Papuan Mammals: Marsupialia (continued) and Placentalia

Macropodidae: A, Dendrolagus lumholtzi (*Tree Kangaroo*); *B*, Bettongia penicillata (*Brush-tailed Rat Kangaroo*); *C*, Petrogale penicillata (*Rock Wallaby*); *D*, Megaleia rufa (*Red Kangaroo*). placentalia: *E*, Pteropus poliocephalus (*Flying Fox*); *F*, Leggadina delicatula (*Delicate Mouse*); *G*, Hipposideros albanensis (*Horseshoe Bat*); *H*, Canis familiaris dingo (*Dingo*); *I*, Hydromys chrysogaster (*Water Rat*).

of the biology of the various Australian bat species can be found in Wood Jones (1925) and Troughton (1948).

The Dingo

Canis familiaris dingo (Fig. 9) the wild dog of Australia, is now known fairly conclusively to have been brought in by one of the later waves of aboriginal man, the oldest radiocarbon date published so far being 3,000 B.P. for remains at Fromm's Landing, Murray River (Mulvaney et al., 1964). It never reached Tasmania and Kangaroo Island. Its characteristics (a somewhat broad head, bushy tail and commonly reddish coloring) are not sufficient to entitle it to specific distinctness. A small feral dog of the New Guinea mountains, also presumably a camp escapee, has been named *C. hallstromi.*

The above radiocarbon date for the earliest dingo remains is close to those for *Thylacinus* in the same beds, strata immediately below and above the latter being dated at 3895 ± 85 years B.P. and 3770 ± 85 years B.P., indicating temporal overlap between the two. The dingo is believed by some biologists to have eliminated the thylacine on the mainland.

THE FOSSIL HISTORY OF AUSTRALIAN MAMMALS

As is shown in Fig. 3 and Table 4, the fossil history of Australian marsupials is unknown prior to the early Miocene or late Oligocene. This contrasts with South America where there is a comparatively good Tertiary record. Two species of fleas, or flea-like insects, one of the normal pulicid form common on contemporary marsupials, the second with a leg structure that suggests "that this insect lived on a sparsely haired (furred) animal" (Riek, 1970, p. 747), discovered in the Lower Cretaceous of Australia, suggest, however, the presence of furred animals in Australia at this time (Riek, 1970).

By the time they appear in the Pliocene and Pleistocene of Australia most of the modern genera of marsupials are clearly defined. They then occur as members of a richly diversified faunal assemblage, including striking extinct forms (Fig. 8). It is due both to the paucity of outcrops of non-marine Tertiary deposits in Australia and (until recently) a shortage of Australian paleontologists that the search for mammal fossils largely ceased between the 1920's and 1950's. A resurgence of interest is now taking place, stimulated in part by the excavations of R. A. Stirton and his coworkers of late Tertiary deposits of central Australia in the 1950's and early 1960's. A recently published review of this work (Stirton, Tedford, and Woodburne, 1968) is freely drawn upon here.

The main Tertiary fossil sites in Australia are shown in Fig. 10. *Wynyardia* (Fig. 3), the oldest securely dated fossil, is known from a single skeleton from Fossil Bluff, Tasmania. These deposits are now known to be lower Miocene in age (Quilty, 1966, and Table 5). A re-examination by Ride (1964b) of this remarkably complete specimen shows it to have

TABLE 4

Distribution of Australian mammals in the fossil record

Group	Earliest Fossil Record
Tachyglossidae	Pleistocene of Darling Downs, Queensland; Mammoth Cave, southwestern Australia; King Island, Bass Strait; Gulgong, mine shaft (? Pliocene), N.S.W.[a]
Ornithorhynchidae	Pleistocene of Darling Downs; Gulgong (? Pliocene), N.S.W.[a]
Dasyuridae	Late Oligocene or early Miocene (Etadunna formation) of central Australia.[b]
Thylacinidae	Late Miocene (Alcoota fauna).[c]
Myrmecobiinae	Late Pleistocene.[d]
Peramelidae	Middle Miocene[e]; enormous numbers of modern species in Pleistocene cave deposits throughout Australia.[f]
Wynyardidae	Early Miocene (marine) of northern Tasmania; known only from unique specimen.[f]
Phalangeridae	Late Oligocene or early Miocene of Etadunna formation, central Australia *Perikoala palankarinnica*.[b]
Tarsipedinae	Unknown as a fossil.[f]
Thylacoleoninae	Late Oligocene or early Miocene of Etadunna[b]; extinct in early Recent.
Potoroinae	Late Oligocene or early Miocene (Ngapakaldi fauna) of central Australia[b]; also Upper Pliocene of Grange Burn, Victoria[g], wrongly identified as *Phalanger*.[f]
Macropodinae	Late Miocene (Alcoota fauna) of central Australia[e]; alleged Miocene remains from Hamilton, Victoria, were wrongly aged.[h]
Sthenurinae	Late Pliocene[i]; extinct in Early Recent.
Diprotodontidae	Late Oligocene or early Miocene[b]; extinct in Early Recent.
Vombatidae	Middle Miocene of central Australia.[e]
Rodentia	Middle Pliocene of New Guinea.[j]
Chiroptera	Late Pliocene of Victoria.[k]

[a] *Anderson, 1933;* [b] *Stirton, Tedford, and Miller, 1961;* [c] *Woodburne, 1967;* [d] *Tedford, 1967;* [e] *Stirton, Tedford, and Woodburne, 1967;* [f] *Ride, 1964b;* [g] *Stirton, 1957;* [h] *Glaessner, 1964;* [i] *Tedford, 1966;* [j] *Plane, 1967;* [k] *Lundelius and Turnbull, 1967.*

been a primitive diprotodont with distinct marsupicarnivoran characteristics of a didelphid kind. It had a robust build and an erect carriage, the shortness of the distal parts of the limb suggesting that it moved with a slow, deliberate action.

The oldest of the faunas discovered by Stirton is the Ngapakaldi (Etadunna formation) in the Lake Eyre basin (Fig. 10, Table 5). This is dated, by inference, as upper Oligocene or lower Miocene. Recognizable here are two species of Dasyuridae (native cats), Peramelidae (bandicoots), ratkangaroos (Potoroinae), one of which belongs to the contemporary genus

TABLE 5

Temporal relationships of Australian Tertiary faunas

Epoch	Tasmania	Victoria	South Australia	Northern Territory	Queensland	New Guinea
		Hamilton	Palankarinna		Chinchilla	
						Awe
PLIOCENE		Forsyth's Bank				
		Beaumaris				
				Alcoota		
				Bullock Creek (at Camfield)		
			Kutjamarpu			
MIOCENE					Riversleigh	
	Fossil Bluff		Ngapakaldi			
OLIGOCENE						

From Woodburne (1967) and Plane (1967).

Bettongia, a marsupial lion (Thylacoleoninae), and three diprotodonts belonging to the subfamily Palorchestinae, Diprotodontidae (Stirton, Tedford, and Woodburne, 1968). There are no macropodids of the subfamily Macropodinae. A primitive koala, *Perikoala palankarinnica,* proves, however, to be intermediate between the phalangerine and phascolarctine types of phalangers. Among the dasyurids is a form possibly ancestral to *Thylacinus* (Stirton, Tedford, and Miller, 1961), the first molar lacking a metaconid. Ride (1964b), however, is dubious of this since some other dasyurids show a reduction of this feature.

   The Kutjamarpu fauna, also in the Lake Eyre basin, is regarded as mid-Miocene. Included here are what is believed to be monotreme teeth and a marsupial fauna composed of the same families as the Ngapakaldi except that the arboreal Phalangeridae are relatively more diverse and true kangaroos (Macropodinae) occur. There is a wombat (Vombatidae), as large as contemporary forms, whose cheek teeth bear well-developed roots (Stirton, Tedford, and Woodburne, 1968). The Riversleigh fauna, Gulf of

FIG. 10. MAJOR TERTIARY AND
PLEISTOCENE–EARLY RECENT FOSSIL
LOCALITIES IN AUSTRALIA

Carpentaria basin, also younger than the Ngapakaldi, contains Diprotodontidae of the subfamilies Nototheriinae and Zygomaturinae, showing
that differentiation in this quadrupedal, terrestrial group must already
have been well advanced at the beginning of the Miocene (Stirton, Tedford and Woodburne, 1968).

The Alcoota fauna is placed, "by a progressive exclusion of alternatives," at the Miocene-Pliocene junction (Woodburne, 1967, p. 5); see
Table 5. Of interest here is the earliest certain geologic record of the
family Thylacinidae (Tasmanian wolves), the species *Thylacinus potens*
being rather more massive than the contemporary *T. cynocephalus*. Of it
Woodburne (1967, p. 38) writes: "Many of the dimensions . . . could
represent an allometric increase over those of *T. cynocephalus*, but other
features show that the Alcoota fossil has many peculiarities which are different either in proportion or in kind from the Pleistocene and modern
forms." Also present in the deposit are peramelids, vombatids (?), and
macropodids of various sizes, one of which (*Dorcopsoides*) would appear
to be ancestral to the contemporary New Guinea genera *Dorcopsis* and
Dorcopsulus, and another to the Pleistocene Sthenurinae. A feature of
this and some of the other early faunas is the relatively high ratio of four-
footed terrestrial herbivores (Diprotodontidae) to bipedal macropodids.
In the Alcoota fauna four genera of the former and five of the latter occur.
Notwithstanding that the two living macropodid subfamilies, Potoroinae
and Macropodinae, are well differentiated at the beginning of the Miocene, and the Sthenurinae may have appeared in the late Miocene, the
Macropodinae did not begin their major adaptive radiation until
the end of the period (Stirton, Tedford, and Woodburne, 1968).

The recently discovered Bullock Creek fauna on Camfield Station in
the Northern Territory (Plane and Gatehouse, 1968), yet to be described,
would appear, on the stage of evolution of its major zygomaturine diproto-

dontid to be post-Kutjamarpu, pre-Alcoota in age. Included in it is a small thylacoleonid.

Of the Pliocene faunas the Awe fauna of New Guinea is significant, not only in being the earliest fauna so far described from that island, but also in having been rather precisely dated ($5.7\text{-}7.6 \times 10^6$ years B. P.). It is thus mid-Pliocene. Included is a dasyurid of the *Parantechnius* type, two macropodids, and three diprotodontids. A single upper incisor of the murid type represents the earliest fossil record of a placental. One diprotodontid is slightly more primitive than its contemporaries in Australia, suggesting that the island was, to some extent, serving as a tropical refugium at that time.

The Pliocene faunas of the mainland are from various parts of that age. The Beaumaris Fauna is marine but contains a few fossil mammals; on the basis of its marine fossils it is thought to be either lower Pliocene or upper Miocene. The Forsyth's Bank Fauna (Victoria), also a marine deposit, similarly is held to be either middle or upper Pliocene. It contains a single mammalian fossil, a small macropodid. The other Pliocene faunas are probably close to the Pliocene-Pleistocene boundary; these faunas are Palankarinna (South Australia), Chinchilla (Queensland) and Hamilton (Victoria). Of these, Hamilton is most precisely dated; there a basalt overlies the fossil-bearing soil and has a K/A date of 4.35 ± 0.1 million years B.P. (Turnbull, Lundelius and McDougall, 1965). The fossil-bearing soil is underlain by the middle to upper Pliocene Grange Burn coquina which contains the Forsyth's Bank Fauna. Represented in the Hamilton Fauna is a diverse range of forms, many of which belong to contemporary genera —e.g., *Echymipera* and *Peroryctes* (bandicoots), *Trichosurus, Phalanger, Cercartetus, Burramys, Pseudocheirus* (phalangers), *Aepyprymnus, Hypsiprymnodon,* and, in addition, the extinct *Proleopus* and *Palorchestes.* Species of the surviving genera are predominantly woodland forms.

The Palankarinna Fauna of South Australia contains zygomaturine and nototheriine Diprotodontidae, a macropodine, and a bandicoot. The bandicoot was described by Stirton (1955) as possessing characters intermediate between generalized peramelids and rabbit bandicoots, but these characters are now known to lie within the normal range of those of rabbit bandicoots (Ride, 1964b).

The Chinchilla Fauna of Queensland may be slightly younger than that of Palankarinna (Stirton, Tedford and Woodburne, 1968) but it is much more diverse in species. There is a particularly abundant macropodid fauna with Phalangeridae, Vombatidae, Dasyuridae, a distinctive species of *Thylacoleo,* and numbers of different Diprotodontidae including the first record of the Diprotodontinae. There are also abundant crocodilians, turtles, lungfish and birds.

In Victoria, from an unknown, but possibly Pliocene, fauna found in a well at a depth of fifty feet near Ballarat an interesting dasyurid, *Glaucodon ballaratensis,* which is intermediate between *Dasyurus* and *Sarcophilus,* has been described (Stirton, 1957).

Table 4 gives the first record of the major groups of Australian mammals in the fossil record. An approximate date of extinction is given for those groups that did not survive through to the present. All contemporary families, except for the few lacking a fossil record, extend back at least as far as the early Miocene. Their differentiation, accordingly, must have taken place in the middle or early Tertiary. The only family recorded from the early Miocene but not later, is the Wynyardidae. In groups with adequate fossil data there is a progressive change from more primitive to more advanced forms from the early Miocene onward. Most significant in this regard are the Diprotodontidae, in which evolution has been traced in four subfamilies in sufficient detail for them to be used as time markers (Stirton, Woodburne, and Plane, 1967).

THE PLEISTOCENE MARSUPIAL FAUNA

The Pleistocene marsupial fauna of Australia was spectacular, both in its diversity and in that it included giant terminal forms of the now extinct Diprotodontidae, Thylacoleoninae, and Sthenurinae.

The Pleistocene Diprotodontidae included *Diprotodon optatum*, with the dimensions of a hippopotamus (Fig. 8), *Nototherium, Zygomaturus, Euryzygoma, Euowenia,* and *Palorchestes* with large species of the size of a bullock. *Zygomaturus* had a skull broader than it was long.

Thylacoleo, the so-called marsupial "cave lion," long known from only the skull, was in many ways the most spectacular Pleistocene form (Fig. 8). Speculation has long surrounded its unusual dentition which centers on a single pair of pointed incisors and a pair of long sectorial premolars (Fig. 6A). Ride (1964b, p. 118) refers to it as "the supreme diprotodont adaptation to the rapacious habit." Earlier workers, however, were far from agreement as to its diet, Anderson (1929) suggesting that its teeth would have been useless for stripping flesh and that it probably lived partly on wild melons! Almost complete skeletons of *Thylacoleo* have recently been found and the animal proved to have strong forelimbs with grasping paws and sheathed claws (R. A. Stirton and R. H. Tedford, pers. commun.). In his recent studies of the skull, Woods (1956) has drawn attention to several features convergent with the aeluroid carnivores and suggests that the sectorial premolars may have been applied like the carnassials of a cat (to food when the mouth is turned sideways). Gill (1954) has reviewed known information about *Thylacoleo,* and has plotted where fossils have been found, thus showing that the range extended at least throughout eastern and southern Australia during the Pleistocene.

The subfamily Sthenurinae, which includes the largest known kangaroos, has recently been reviewed by Tedford (1966). Typical *Sthenurus* had short faces, deep skulls, deep and thick mandibles, large and complex third premolars, and a monodactyl foot. The striking difference in shape and size between the skull of the largest species, *Procoptodon goliah* and that of one of the largest contemporary *Macropus* is seen in Fig. 6B.

This giant browser must have reached a height of about ten feet. The skull is unique among marsupials because of its remarkable depth and shortness of face. The former results from the elevation of the braincase above the pterygoids and posterior end of the palate, and the latter from the extreme brevity of the preorbital area relative to the condylobasal length (Tedford, 1967). Within *Sthenurus,* both dolichocephalic (subgen. *Sthenurus,* 3 spp.) and brachycephalic (subgen. *Simosthenurus,* 5 spp.) lines occurred in the Pliocene and Pleistocene; these presumably correspond to grazing and browsing subdivisions (Tedford, 1966).

Large body-size also characterized some Pleistocene species in various contemporary groups. Echidnas, represented by the genus *Zaglossus,* were then "twice as large" (Anderson, 1933). *Sarcophilus* had mandibular measurements 15 to 50 per cent larger than the contemporary form (Gill, 1953). By contrast, however, the Pleistocene marsupial wolf, *Thylacinus,* was apparently no larger than the present day one (Ride, 1964b). The largest wombat, *Phascolonus gigas,* was twice the size of existing wombats (Stirling, 1913). Among the typical macropodid kangaroos found in late Pleistocene deposits at Lake Menindee are several large species. No complete skeletons are available for proper comparisons with contemporary forms. Corresponding sections of the tooth row, judging from measurements given in Tedford (1967), would appear, however, to have been 10 to 15 per cent larger in *Macropus birdselli* and *M. titan* than in the largest contemporary species, *M. fuliginosus,* while in *M. ferragus* they may have been 20 per cent larger than in *M. titan.* Within the Potoroinae *Propleopus* had a relatively more massive jaw than its tiny surviving relative *Hypsiprymnodon.*

The richness of the Pleistocene fauna in terms of number of species is demonstrated by such deposits as those of the Wellington Caves, Darling Downs, Lake Menindee, and Mammoth Cave (Fig. 10). Tedford (1967) has recently documented the Lake Menindee deposits which were laid down, according to radiocarbon dates, between $26,300 \pm 1500$ years to $18,800 \pm 88$ years B. P. Represented in them are five dasyurids (*Antechinomys, Dasycercus, Dasyurus, Sarcophilus* and *Thylacinus*), the anteater *Myrmecobius* (apparently), four genera of bandicoots (*Perameles, Isoodon, Choeropus,* and *Macrotis*), the phalanger *Trichosurus,* the koala *Phascolarctos,* the cave lion *Thylacoleo,* the wombats *Vombatus* and *Lasiorhinus,* eighteen different macropodids, a diprotodon, and four genera of rodents. Tedford (1967) attributes the diversity of this assemblage to its having been at the junction of woodland and grassland habitats.

One of the striking features of the late Pleistocene to Recent transition is the curtailment in the ranges of many of the dominant faunal elements. The remains of a small cassowary (*Casuarius lydekkeri*), closely related to the small *C. bennetti* of New Guinea, have been described from the Wellington Caves (Miller, 1962). *Thylacinus* ranged widely, and a lower jaw has been found in New Guinea (Van Deusen, 1964). A radiocarbon determination (sample Y1368) on the beds from which this came (bed 10, approximately 10 ft below the present cave level) has given a date of 9920 ±200 B. P. (Bulmer, 1964; Van Deusen, pers. commun.). A mummy, in excellent state of preservation, recently found in southwestern Australia has been radiocarbon-dated at 4200-4800 years B. P. (Ride, pers. commun.). *Sarcophilus harrisi,* also confined to Tasmania in historic times, has been recorded from aboriginal occupational sites in western Victoria, to which a radiocarbon date of 538±200 years B. P. has been given (Gill, 1953). A recently discovered jaw fragment near Oenpelli in the Northern Territory has been dated at 3120±100 years B. P. (Calaby and White, 1967). Recently an aboriginal skeleton with a necklace of 285 canine teeth of *Sarcophilus,* and of an age estimated at between 3000 and 16,000 years B. P., has been discovered at Lake Nitchie in Victoria (Macintosh, Smith, and Bailey, 1970). Fossil remains are also known from the lower Murray, Kangaroo Island, and southwestern Australia. The koala, *Phascolarctos,* today confined to the eastern forests, is known as a fossil in southwestern Australia (Glauert, 1926) and Lake Menindee, and the arboreal ringtail possum, *Pseudocheirus,* from caves near Eucla at the eastern limits of the southwestern woodland belt (Lundelius, 1957), proving the former existence of scrub or forest there. The writer agrees with Tedford (1967) that only striking climatic shifts can explain such striking distributional changes.

Much interest attends the exact dating of the extinction of the giant marsupials of the Pleistocene. Radiocarbon dates are now on hand for the major fossil sites (list in Tedford, 1967) as follows: Lake Menindee, between 26,300 and 18,800 years B. P. (Tedford, 1967); Lake Calabonna (large numbers of *Diprotodon opatum* remains) more than 40,000 years B. P. (Grant-Taylor and Rafter, 1963; this date, based on plant remains from within a *Diprotodon* skeleton, is now accepted rather than the 6700 years B. P. date based on dentine—see Tedford, 1967); Mowbray Swamp, Tasmania, which contains *Nototherium,* more than 37,380 years B. P. (Gill and Banks, 1956); and Lake Colongulac, near Camperdown in western Victoria, 13,725±350 years B. P. (Gill, 1955). Associated with this last date are remains of *Diprotodon optatum, Thylacoleo carnifax,* and *Procoptodon goliah.* Later dates such as 11,100±130 years B. P. from *Diprotodon* dentine at Yalpara, Flinders Range (Grant-Taylor and Rafter, 1963) require confirmation. The giant marsupials are absent from beds dated at 6020±150 years B. P. (Tindale, 1957—River Murray), and 8500±250 years B. P. (Gill, 1955—Keilor Terrace, Victoria).

REGIONAL FAUNAS AND CONTEMPORARY SPECIATION

Australia is basically an arid land mass, forests and woodlands being peripheral. The rainfall pattern takes the form of a series of concentric zones of increasing precipitation, outward from the desert interior. In the south the chief rains fall in winter while in the north they occur in summer.

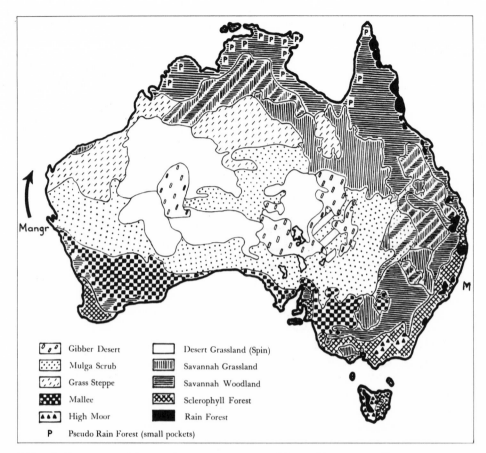

FIG. 11. VEGETATION MAP OF AUSTRALIA SHOWING MAJOR VEGETATION FORMATIONS
Adapted and modified from Wood, 1949.

Vegetation (Fig. 11) mirrors the rainfall pattern. Tropical rain forest is distributed down the east coast of Queensland in a series of small pockets, depending on the right combinations of physiography, high rainfall, and soil. Eucalypt (sclerophyll) forest occurs in a broad strip along the coast in the east and south, and there are outlyers of it in Tasmania, the Mount Lofty region of South Australia, and in the southwest corner. Tropical savannah woodland extends along the north coast, in the summer monsoon belt. Temperate savannah woodland covers the western slopes of the Great Divide in Queensland, New South Wales, and Victoria, penetrating inland along the rivers. It grades into grassland with scattered clumps or individual trees. Mallee, an association of dwarf eucalypts with multiple trunk systems, covers part of the southern inland. Although important to birds this has little influence on mammal distribution. The arid center of the continent is covered either with clumps of spiny porcupine grass (*Triodia*), or tracts of mulga (*Acacia aneura*).

Habitat	% of Total Fauna	
Rain forest	ca 17.0	**TABLE 6**
Sclerophyll forest	ca 35.0	
Savannah woodland	ca 17.0	*Habitat preference in Australian*
Grass plains (savannah grass-		*marsupials, based on the major*
land, mallee)	ca 17.0	*("favored") habitat*
Desert (porcupine grass, etc.)	ca 12.5	*Modified from Keast, 1959.*

Mammal species tend to show a distributional link with vegetation type and, although this is less clear-cut than in birds (Keast, 1959) many species and groups do not extend beyond the limits of a particular formation. Such is the case in Cape York where rain forest and woodland faunas are mutually exclusive (Tate, 1952). On the other hand, a lower level of specificity is characteristic in New South Wales where most species occur in two vegetation formations, e.g., rain forest and sclerophyll forest, or sclerophyll forest and woodland (Marlow, 1958). Table 6, modified from Keast (1959), groups the species of Australian marsupials in terms of their main or "favorite" habitat. It indicates that eucalypt (sclerophyll) forest is the richest zone in numbers of species: it can support both canopy and forest-floor faunas. Rain forest (very small in area), woodland, and savannah grassland all have fairly rich faunas. The number of desert species however, is, somewhat smaller.

These general conclusions are confirmed by a study of regional distributional lists. Thus, on Cape York, Tate (1952) lists 25 marsupials and rodent species as rain-forest dwellers (the rain forests are faunistically richest here, it being on the main colonization route from New Guinea), and 21 as woodland dwellers. In the Dawson River Valley, Queensland, somewhat mixed terrain with woodland and grassland predominant, Finlayson (1931, 1934) records 24 marsupial species. For New South Wales, Marlow (1958) lists 11 species as not uncommon in rain forest (which is impoverished at these latitudes), 26 in sclerophyll forest, 17 in woodland (plus four extinct species), and four grassland species (plus nine that are extinct). Figures for the arid porcupine grass and mulga desert of central Australia are given by Finlayson (1961). They come to 22 species of marsupials, plus seven that are marignal, and 17 rodents. The list, however, includes all species that have ever been recorded. A number have only been trapped on one or two occasions. Most desert species have very patchy distributions. Moreover, from Finlayson's synthesis there appears to be a degree of distinctness between the mammal fauna of the Lake Eyre basin and that of the western desert. This would bring the number of species in any one area down to perhaps a dozen, and more in line with expectations.

Many mammals species have only a limited regional distribution today. Thus, *Hypsiprymnodon* is limited to rain forests of the Capetown-Atherton segment, and *Caloprymnus* to a small part of the central desert. Wombat distribution is disjunct; e.g., there is an isolated population in the St. George district of central Queensland. The large dasyuroids *Sarcophilus* and *Thylacinus,* and the pigmy possum *Eudromicia lepida,* are today confined to Tasmania. As the fossil record shows, these species formerly had much wider mainland ranges and hence are now relicts. Such shrinkages of range certainly antedate settlement by Europeans.

The Geographic Subregion Concept in Australia

As distinct from the analysis of mammal distribution on the basis of vegetation, some Australian zoologists have based their distributional analyses on zoogeographic subregions. These, however, are less clear-cut in Australia than in some of the other continents. The most natural scheme is that of Baldwin Spencer, adapted by Serventy and Whittell (1958), in which three subregions are allowed: (1) Bassian, corresponding broadly to the distribution of the sclerophyll forests in eastern and southern Australia; (2) Eyrean, representing the interior regions; and (3) Torresian, corresponding broadly to the tropical savannah woodland and rain-forest regions of the north.

From the mammalian viewpoint a good proportion of species can be broadly allocated to one or another of these zones. Thus, Bassian species are commonly cold-adapted, inhabit forests, or have persisted through the arid period in the montane forest refuges of southeastern Australia. Eyrean mammal species are adapted to grasslands or desert, and dry conditions with uncertain rainfall. Torresian species are adapted to subtropical woodland or rain-forest conditions, or are recent colonizers from New Guinea.

Ride (1968) has traced the development of the subregion concept from a historical one that purported to explain places of origin to the ecological concept outlined above. He points out that the former has been effectively disproven by recent paleontological discoveries which show that many genera had a much wider range in the past. Furthermore, as our knowledge of ranges increases it is becoming clear that many species are not limited to a single subzone (or, for that matter, vegetation formation). Ride (1968) stresses that distributional patterns cannot be understood properly without much fuller information on paleontology, ecology, and physiology of individual species. He makes the very good point (pers. commun.) that to attempt to explain distributions on the basis of vegetation alone is wrong since all that is being described may be a correlation, not the basic reason.

The present writer's reservations about the zoogeographic subregion concept include objections to its static nature, its limited validity in the case of many groups, and difficulties in delimiting the borders of the zones. Thus the Eyrean region as currently defined artificially embraces somewhat distinct southern woodland, grassland, and interior desert faunas (Keast, 1961).

Contemporary Speciation Patterns

A study of the distribution of geographically representative species and forms in the Australian marsupials showed that active speciation is occurring in the Australian marsupials today (Keast, 1959). It is estimated that there are 35 to 40 isolated forms (1 per 3 spp.) that have reached or are approaching the stage of morphological differentiation typical of species; in addition there is a range of minor isolates (Keast, 1959). Most of this speciation is occurring in "refuge areas," segments of the country protected against increasing desiccation by some physiographic feature (discussion in Keast, 1961). Important refuges are the southeast, southwest, northeast, and northwest corners of the continent. Rain forest and sclerophyll forest mammals are particularly prone to develop isolates, since each of these habitats is broken up into a series of disconnected tracts by tongues of dry or arid country that extend through to the coast from the center of the continent. Forest mammals, dependent on trees and cover, cannot cross such barriers. Hence, they will remain isolated until a further climatic shift reunites the forests. Differentiation is also taking place between New Guinea and Australia (across the Torres Strait water barrier), and to some extent between Australia and Tasmania (across Bass Strait). Both islands were united to the mainland at least three times during the Pleistocene, when ocean levels were lower.

An example of evolution and speciation in a group of arboreal, forest-dwelling marsupials, the ring-tailed phalangers, genus *Pseudocheirus,* is given in Fig. 12. The data are derived largely from the review by Tate (1945b). *Pseudocheirus* shows the full range of intermediate stages in the speciation process. There are four subgenera: *Pseudocheirus* (5 New Guinea and 2 Australian spp.), *Pseudochirops* (3 New Guinea and 1 Australian spp.), *Petropseudes* (monotypic, endemic to northwest Australia), and *Hemibelideus* (monotypic, endemic to the rain forest segment of northeastern Australia). While the last two are quite distinctive (Tate, 1945b), *Pseudochirops* may yet not prove, taxonomically, to warrant subgeneric status (W. D. L. Ride, pers. commun.).

Although it cannot be said whether the ringtailed phalangers are of Australian or New Guinean origin, both *Pseudocheirus* and *Pseudochirops* have radiated very effectively on the island; the species, which occupy a range of different climatic and altitudinal zones there, are distinctive both morphologically and on the basis of color. Speciation has taken place between New Guinea and Australia (or vice versa) in both of these subgenera. The two species of *Pseudocheirus* in the Cairns-Atherton rain forest segment could possibly be an example of a secondary New Guinea invader coming to live alongside a long-established local species, although this needs studying. At any event, in north Queensland, as in New Guinea, two species coexist side by side in slightly different habitats, demonstrating that reproductive isolation has been achieved.

Petropseudes dahli, the aberrant rock-dwelling species of northwestern

234

ALLEN KEAST

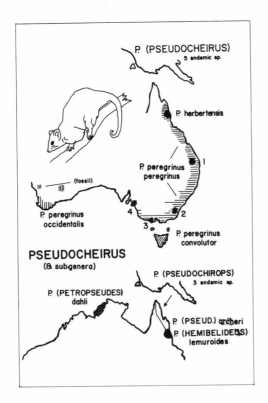

FIG. 12. Isolation and Speciation in the Forest-Dwelling Ring-Tailed Phalangers (Genus *Pseudocheirus*)

This genus, with 3 to 4 subgenera shows the full range of intermediate stages in the speciation process. Distributional barriers are areas of open treeless terrain (where these arboreal species cannot occur) and Torres and Bass Straits. This pattern of distributional break-up and evolution is partly duplicated in various other forest mammals, including the pigmy phalangers (Cercartetus). Modified from Keast, 1959.

Numbers 1 to 4 indicate areas from which regional color forms have been described.

Australia, is the distributional counterpart of the eastern ringtails. It is now so modified morphologically, however, as to be given subgeneric status.

Pseudocheirus peregrinus of the eastern and southern forests of Australia is the most widely ranging species. Isolated geographic races occur in southwestern Australia (*P. peregrinus occidentalis*) and Tasmania (*P. peregrinus convolutor*). The latter of these has presumably been isolated since the last glacial maximum when Tasmania was connected to the mainland; the island probably became isolated about 13,500 years B. P. The western race could have been isolated a shorter, or a longer, period. Coastal forest or scrub must formerly have extended across the now arid thousand-mile-wide Nullarbor Plain that today isolates it from the eastern populations. Fossils of the species have been found in a cave at Eucla, at the eastern limits of the woodland belt in southwestern Australia and a couple of hundred miles to the east of its present range limits (Lundelius, 1957).

A series of regional or local forms of *P. peregrinus* have been described in eastern Australia. These, which partly have an altitudinal basis, are known from the Bunya Mountains in southern Queensland, Mount Koskiusko, the Otway Ranges to the west of Port Philip, Victoria, and in the Mount Lofty Ranges near Adelaide (see numbers 1-4 in Fig. 12).

ONYCHOGALEA
(nail-tail wallabies)

FIG. 13. GEOGRAPHIC REPLACEMENT
IN THE PLAINS-DWELLING NAIL-TAIL
WALLABIES (*Onychogalea*)
*The three species replace each
other geographically. They probably arose in the southwest, northwest, and southeast segments of
the continent respectively, and
spread subsequently to occupy the
intermediate areas. Interestingly,
the two southern species were
sympatric in the Lake Menindee
area in the late Pleistocene. Modified from Keast, 1959.*

The genetic basis of these minor variants needs testing but, since similarly colored individuals crop up in other populations, they are presumably of little evolutionary significance. A measure of isolation, however, may have been involved in their production; this is especially true of the Mount Lofty range population which is restricted to a few square miles of sclerophyll forest isolated from the nearest eastern forests in the Millicent area of eastern South Australia by the hundred-mile wide Coorong arid belt.

The isolation and speciation patterns in *Pseudocheirus* are duplicated in varying degrees by a number of other forest and woodland genera (Keast, 1959). Attention is drawn to a recent review of the pigmy possums, *Cercartetus*, by Wakefield (1963), and to the serological demonstration that the rather similar western (*fuliginosus*) and eastern (*giganteus*) forms of the grey or forester kangaroo (*Macropus giganteus*), which now secondarily overlap in western New South Wales, are reproductively distinct (Kirsch and Poole, 1967). Isolation and differentiation here presumably occurred in the western and eastern forest-mallee belts, respectively.

Figure 13 shows the allopatric distributions of the three species of plains-dwelling wallabies belonging to the genus *Onychogalea* (nail-tail wallabies). The three are morphologically quite distinct. *O. unguifer* occupies the open savannah plains of the north; *O. lunata* inhabits the heath and sandridge desert in the southwest and center of the continent (W. D. L. Ride, pers. commun.); *O. fraenata* inhabits the grassy plains of southeastern Australia. Allopatry is complete today. *O. unguifer* and *O. lunata* approach no closer than about 200 miles of each other in central Australia (Finlayson, 1961). *O. lunata* and *O. fraenata* in the south may have approached each other closely in the recent past, if collections of the naturalist Blankowski, made a century ago near the Murray-Darling junction, are any indication. In Keast (1959) *Onychogalea* was cited as an interesting demonstration of contemporary isolation and speciation in a woodland-grassland group of marsupials, in which the allopatric forms, though distinct, had not had the opportunity to "test" their genetic distinctness because of isolation. Significantly, a recent study of the Lake Menindee fossil fauna by Tedford (1967), however, has shown that *O. lunata* and *O. fraenata* were sympatric in western New South Wales in the late Pleistocene. Speciation in the group, accordingly, was an early or middle Pleistocene event, and not a recent one.

MAMMAL FAUNAS OF THE ISLANDS ADJACENT TO AUSTRALIA

Figures for the number of genera of Australian marsupials and Asian placentals (excluding rodents, bats, and species introduced by man) occurring on the major islands between Borneo and Australia, are given in Fig. 2, taken from Simpson (1961). Details of these faunas, and those of the major islands to the north of Australia, have been extracted from Laurie and Hill (1954) and, for *Phalanger,* from Tate (1945a). They are as follows:

Celebes: *Phalanger celebensis,* regarded as specifically distinct from the widely-ranging *P. orientalis* (Tate, 1945a), occurs here and on Talaut. There is an extensive placental fauna, including shrews (7 spp.), squirrels (8 spp.), a porcupine, *Tarsius* (one sp.), cercopithecid monkeys (2 spp.), Viverridae (3 spp.), a pig (*Babyrousa babyrousa*), a bovid (*Anoa depressicornis*), and a deer (*Cervus timorensis*).

Timor: *Phalanger orientalis* is the only marsupial. Three species of shrews occur, along with a cercopithecid monkey (possibly introduced by man), a palm civet, and a deer.

Aru Islands: These islands have a shrew (the house shrew, a cohabitor of man), and a palm civet. The relatively rich marsupial fauna, composed of 3 species of dasyurids, a peramelid, and 4 phalangers (Laurie and Hill, 1954), has New Guinea origins.

New Guinea: This island has 19 species (14 endemic) of Phalangeridae, 11 Macropodidae (5 endemic), 55 rodent species (47 endemic), and 66 species of bats (46 endemic); see Table 1.

Bismarcks (New Britain and New Ireland): Four marsupials occur: *Phalanger orientalis,* the glider *Petaurus breviceps,* the bandicoot *Echymipera kalubu* (=*doreyana*), and the wallaby, *Thylogale bruijni.*

Solomon Islands: There is only one marsupial species, *Phalanger orientalis.*

Eastward from the Bismarcks and Solomons only bats and rodents occur. There is a rapid falling off in the numbers of these forms east of New Guinea: New Guinea, 66 species of bats, 55 rodents (see above); Bismarcks, 19 bats, 5 rodents (Laurie and Hill, 1954); Solomons, 27 bats (Tate, 1946), 10 rodents (Laurie and Hill, 1954); only a few species of bats reach Fiji and Tonga. Two species of insectivorous bats are New

Zealand's only mammals. One of these constitutes a monotypic family and the other is a recently arrived, undifferentiated Australian species.

A clearcut picture emerges from the above relative to the ability to cross water-gaps. Only one marsupial (*Phalanger orientalis*) has succeeded in spreading widely through the island archipelagos. Presumably this has been achieved by drifting on logs, but the assistance of man (the animal is a favorite food item in Melanesia) cannot be completely ruled out. Of the three other marsupials occurring in the Bismarcks, the small glider, *Petaurus breviceps,* is a common inhabitant of the coastal areas of northern New Guinea, including the coconut plantations. It would, accordingly, be in a very favorable position for drifting on logs.

The relatively great ability of rodents to cross water barriers (on logs, in native canoes) is amply borne out by their penetration of Oceania, attenuated as this may be. The still greater penetration of the region by bats is as expected and emphasizes the advantages of flight.

SUMMARY

(1) The contemporary mammal fauna of the Australo-Papuan region is made up of four monotreme species (3 superspp.), about 145 marsupials (107 superspp.), and about 214 placentals (108 superspp.). Endemism is exceptionally high in every group but bats. Australia provides spectacular demonstrations of evolution and radiation in a fauna with a high degree of isolation, and the progressive development of life-forms convergent with those found elsewhere.

(2) Monotremes, unknown as fossils anywhere prior to the Australian Miocene, possibly originated on the continent. Marsupials presumably arrived prior to, or early in, the Tertiary. Bats possibly arrived as early as the middle Tertiary, but rodents probably not until the Pliocene.

(3) The Australian marsupial fossil record is a blank prior to the early Miocene or late Oligocene. By this time the major contemporary families had already differentiated. We now have some knowledge of Miocene and Pliocene faunas. The Pleistocene is the best known of the fossil faunas.

(4) Whereas the Oriental fauna extends to the western limits of Wallace's Line, the Australo-Papuan one extends little beyond the continental limits. Only one marsupial, a cuscus (*Phalanger celebensis*), reaches the eastern edge of Wallace's Line in the Celebes.

(5) The dasyures display a wide variety of ways of life, ranging from that of a shrew and weasel to a martin or genet and, finally, a scavenger (the counterpart of *Gulo* and *Crocuta*) and a canid. The phalangeroids have undergone a wide range of spectacular radiations. They fill every way of life from the arboreal herbivore to the large terrestrial herbivore (macropodids, wombats). Some of the more primitive members, however, are insectivorous. *Thylacoleo,* a striking carnivore, survived until the early Recent. The rodents include the endemic subfamily Hydro-

myinae (water-rats) and the Pseudomyinae. They too have undergone marked radiations.

(6) A review of the many spectacular cases of structural convergence between Australian marsupials and placental counterparts in other faunas shows every grade from basic body form to single structures. Within the limits of the genetic potential the "closeness of the match" in any case must, in part, reflect the rigorousness of the selective pressures associated with entering that particular way of life. Thus, the mole-like body form approaches the ideal one for its role and, apart from *Notoryctes*, it has been approached independently many times in mammalian evolution. The large terrestrial grazer is not so limited; accordingly, kangaroos are only convergent with ungulates in their lengthened muzzle, dentition, and alimentary structures. At the other extreme, generalized arboreal herbivores, such as *Trichosurus*, and primitive carnivores, such as some of the dasyures, show few truly convergent trends toward ecological equivalents in the placentals. Each organism is, in effect, a mosaic of semi-independent characters; in view of their different genetic heritages the pattern of convergent trends seen in the Australian marsupials is as expected.

Analysis indicates that, usually, where an Australian marsupial and a non-Australian placental are convergent in structure, or else duplicate structures, the latter is functionally superior. This is not the case in *Vombatus* or *Notoryctes*, to give two examples. The placentals, moreover, have produced a considerable array of body forms and morphological structures never achieved by the Australian marsupials.

(7) Within the Australian continent the distribution of individual mammal species is commonly linked to one or another of the major vegetation formations: thus, there are series of rain forest, sclerophyll forest, woodland, grassland, and desert species.

(8) Speciation is actively occurring among the marsupials, the isolating barriers being extensive gaps in the required habitat (e.g., tongues of dry open country, in the case of forest species). Differentiation is also occurring between the mainland and New Guinea and Tasmania.

(9) The marsupials appear to be quite poor colonizers of islands. Although the small islands close to New Guinea have moderately good faunas, only four species occur in the Bismarck Archipelago and one in the Solomons. There has been ample time to achieve a better spread. Only rodents and bats penetrate Oceania, and there is a marked falling off (attenuation) of the number of species with distance from Australia and New Guinea. The only mammals in New Zealand are two species of bats, one representing a unique family and the other a typical Australian species.

ACKNOWLEDGMENTS

The present chapter was compiled in part while the writer held a Senior Research Fellowship from the National Research Council of Canada, and I should like to express thanks to that body for its support.

I am greatly indebted to R. H. Tedford, American Museum of Natural History, for help when assembling the review of the Australian fossil record. His assistance has included making literature available ahead of publication and various fruitful discussions. W. D. L. Ride has extended many courtesies and suggestions. Hobart Van Deusen has provided revised figures for the numbers of New Guinea mammals in the various groups. R. H. Tedford recalculated, on the basis of the latest information, the numbers of genera of Diprotodonta, Peramelina, and Dasyuroidea recorded at different times during the Tertiary and Pleistocene, (see Fig. 3). These three workers, B. Patterson, and E. Horner also read drafts of the manuscript and made numerous helpful suggestions.

The diagrams were drawn by Joanna Young, Brian Bertram, Linda Hobbet, Deirdre Webb, and the author.

LITERATURE CITED

ANDERSON, C. 1929. Palaeontological Notes, No. 1. *Macropus titan* Owen and *Thylacoleo carnifex* Owen. *Rec. Austral. Museum,* 17: 35-49.

——. 1933. The fossil mammals of Australia. *Proc. Linnean Soc. N. S. Wales,* 58: 9-25.

AUDLEY-CHARLES, M. G. 1966. Mesozoic palaeogeography of Australasia. *Palaeogeogr., Palaeoclimatol., Palaeoecol.,* 2: 1-25.

BARTHOLOMAI, A. 1966. Fossil footprints in Queensland. *Austral. Natur. Hist.,* March, 1966: 147-150.

BENSLEY, B. A. 1903. On the evolution of the Australian Marsupialia: with remarks on the relationships of the marsupials in general. *Trans. Linnean Soc. Lond., Zool.,* 9: 83-217.

BULMER, S. 1964. Radiocarbon dates from New Guinea. *J. Polynesian Soc.,* 73: 327-328.

CALABY, J. H., and C. WHITE. 1967. The Tasmanian devil (*Sarcophilus harrisi*) in Northern Territory in recent times. *Austral. J. Sci.,* 29: 473-475.

CLEMENS, W. A. 1968. Origin and early evolution of marsupials. *Evolution,* 22, 1-18.

——. 1970. Mesozoic mammalian evolution. *Ann. Rev. Ecol. System.,* 1: 357-390.

COLBERT, E. H., and D. MERRILEES. 1967. Cretaceous dinosaur footprints from Western Australia. *J. Roy. Soc. W. Austral.,* 50: 21-25.

COX, C. B. 1970. Migrating marsupials and drifting continents. *Nature,* 226: 767-770.

DARLINGTON, P. J. 1957. *Zoogeography: The Geographical Distribution of Animals.* 675 p. John Wiley, London.

DIETZ, R. S., and J. C. HOLDEN. 1970. Reconstruction of Pangaea: breakup and dispersion of continents, Permian to present. *J. Geophys. Res.,* 75: 4939-4956.

Dunnet, G. M. 1963. A population study of the quokka, *Setonix brachyurus* Quoy and Gaimard (Marsupialia). *J. C.S.I.R.O. Wildlife Res.* 8: 78-117.

Ealey, E. H. M. 1967. Ecology of the euro, *Macropus robustus* (Gould), in north-western Australia. Parts I-IV. *J. C.S.I.R.O. Wildlife Res.,* 12: 9-80.

Elliott, D. H., E. H. Colbert, W. J. Breed, J. A. Jensen, and J. S. Powell. 1970. Triassic tetrapods from Antarctica: evidence for continental drift. *Science,* 169: 1197-1201.

Finlayson, H. H. 1931. On the mammals from the Dawson Valley, Queensland. Part I. *Trans. Roy. Soc. S. Austral.,* 55: 67-89.

——. 1934. On the mammals from the Dawson Valley, Queensland. Part II. *Trans. Roy. Soc. S. Austral.,* 58: 218-231.

——. 1961. On central Australian mammals. Part IV. The distribution and status of central Australian species. *Rec. S. Austral. Museum,* 14: 141-191.

Frith, H. J. 1954. Mobility of the red kangaroo, *Megaleia rufa. J. C.S.I.R.O. Wildlife Res.,.* 9: 1-19.

Frith, H. J., and J. H. Calaby. 1968. *Kangaroos.* F. W. Cheshire, Melbourne.

Frith, H. J., and G. B. Sharman. 1964. Breeding in wild populations of the red kangaroo, *Megaleia rufa. J. C.S.I.R.O. Wildlife Res.,* 9: 86-114.

Gill, E. D. 1953. Distribution of the Tasmanian Devil, the Tasmanian Wolf and the Dingo in S. E. Australia in Quaternary time. *Victorian Natur.,* 70: 86-90.

——. 1954. Ecology and distribution of the extinct giant marsupial, "Thylacoleo." *Victorian Natur.,* 71: 18-35.

——. 1955. Radiocarbon dates for Australian archaeological and geological samples. *Austral. J. Sci.,* 18: 49-52.

Gill, E. D., and M. R. Banks. 1956. Cainozoic history of Mowbray Swamp and other areas of northwestern Tasmania. *Rec. Queen Victoria Museum, Launceston,* 6: 1-41.

Glaessner, M. F. 1964. Miocene kangaroo from Hamilton, Victoria. *Austral. J. Sci.,* 25: 411.

Glauert, L. 1926. A list of Western Australian fossils. *Bull. Geol. Surv. Western Austral.,* 88: 36-72.

Grant-Taylor, T. L., and T. A. Rafter. 1963. New Zealand natural radiocarbon measurements, I-V. *Radiocarbon,* 5: 118-162.

Gregory, W. K. 1947. The monotremes and the palimpsest theory. *Bull. Am. Museum Natur. Hist.* 88: 1-52.

Griffiths, M. 1968. *Echidnas.* Pergamon Press, Oxford.

GRIFFITHS, M., and K. G. SIMPSON. 1966. A seasonal feeding habit of spiny anteaters. *J. C.S.I.R.O. Wildlife Res.*, 11: 137-144.

GUILER, E. 1970a. Observations on the Tasmanian devil, *Sarcophilus harrissi* (Marsupialia, Dasyuridae). I. Numbers, home range, movements, and food, in two populations. *Austral. J. Zool.*, 18: 49-62.

——. 1970b. Observations on the Tasmanian devil, *Sarcophilus harrissi* (Marsupialia, Dasyuridae). II. Reproduction, breeding, and growth of pouched young. *Austral. J. Zool.*, 18: 63-70.

HARRISON, L. 1924. The migration route of the Australian marsupial fauna. *Austral. Zool.*, 3: 247-263.

HAYMAN, D. L., J. A. W. KIRSCH, P. G. MARTIN, and P. F. WALLER. 1971. Chromosomal and serological studies of the Caenolestidae and their implication for marsupial evolution. *Nature*, 231: 194-195.

HEINSOHN, G. E. 1966. Ecology and reproduction of the Tasmanian bandicoots (*Perameles gunni* and *Isoodon obesulus*). *Univ. Calif. Publ. Zool.*, 80: 1-96.

HEIRTZLER, J. R. 1968. Evidence for ocean floor spreading across the ocean basins. In T. A. Phinney (ed.), *The History of the Earth's Crust*, p. 90-100. Princeton Univ. Press, Princeton.

HOFFSTETTER, M. R. 1970. L'histoire biogeographique des marsupeaux et la dichotomie marsupeaux-placentaires. *Comptes Rend. Acad. Sci. (Paris)*, 271: 388-391.

HOOIJER, D. A. 1951. Pygmy elephant and giant tortoise. *Sci. Monthly*, 72: 3-8.

——. 1967. Indo-Australian insular elephants. *Genetica*, 38: 143-162.

IREDALE, T., and E. TROUGHTON. 1934. *A Checklist of the Mammals Recorded from Australia.* Memoir VI, The Australian Museum, Sydney.

IRVING, E., W. A. ROBERTSON, and P. M. STOTT. 1963. The significance of the paleomagnetic results from Mesozoic rocks of Eastern Australia. *J. Geophys. Res.*, 68: 2313-2317.

JONES, F. WOOD. 1923. *The Mammals of South Australia. Part I: The Monotremes and the Carnivorous Marsupials.* Government Printer, Adelaide.

——. 1924. *The Mammals of South Australia. Part II: The Bandicoots and the Herbivorous Marsupials.* Government Printer, Adelaide.

——. 1925: *The Mammals of South Australia. Part III: The Monodelphia.* Government Printer, Adelaide.

KEAST, A. 1959. Vertebrate speciation in Australia: some comparisons between birds, marsupials, and reptiles. In C. W. Leeper (ed.), *Evolution of Living Oragnisms*, p. 380-407. Symp. Royal Soc. Victoria, Melbourne University Press.

——. 1961. Bird speciation on the Australian continent. *Bull. Museum Comp. Zool. Harvard Coll.,* 123: 305-495.

——. 1963. The mammal fauna of Australia. *Proc. 16. Intern. Congr. Zool.,* 4: 56-62, 149.

——. 1968. Australian mammals: zoogeography and evolution. *Quart. Rev. Biol.,* 43: 373-408.

KIRSCH, J. A. W. 1968. Prodromus of the comparative serology of Marsupialia. *Nature,* 217: 418-420.

KIRSCH, J. A. W., and W. E. POOLE. 1967. Serological evidence for speciation in the grey kangaroo, *Macropus giganteus Shaw* 1790 (Marsupialia: Macropodidae). *Nature,* 215: 1097-1098.

KLOMPÉ, TH. H. F. 1957. Pacific and Variscian orogeny in Indonesia: a structural synthesis. *Indonesian J. Natur. Sci.,* 113: 43-87.

LAURIE, E. M. O., and J. E. HILL. 1954. *List of Land Mammals of New Guinea, Celebes and Adjacent Islands* 1758-1952. 175 p. British Museum (Natur. Hist.), London.

LE PICHON, X. 1968. Sea-floor spreading and continental drift. *J. Geophys. Res.,* 73: 3661-3697.

LILLEGRAVEN, J. 1969. The latest Cretaceous mammals of the upper part of the Edmonton Formation of Alberta, Canada, and a review of the marsupial-placental dichotomy in mammalian evolution. Univ. Kansas Paleontol. Contrib. Vertebrata, No. 12: Art. 50; Lawrence, Kansas.

LUNDELIUS, E. L. 1957. Additions to the knowledge of the ranges of Western Australian mammals. *Western Austral. Natur.,* 5: 173-182.

LUNDELIUS, E. L., and W. D. TURNBULL. 1967. Pliocene mammals from Victoria, Australia. *39. Congr., Austral. N.Z. Assoc. Adv. Sci.:* K9. [Abstr.]

MACINTOSH, N. W. G., K. N. SMITH, and A. B. BAILEY. 1970. Lake Nitchie skeleton—unique aboriginal burial. *Archaeol. Physical Anthropology in Oceania,* 5: 85-101.

MACMILLEN, R. E., and A. K. LEE. 1967. Australian desert mice: independence of exogenous water. *Science,* 158: 383-385.

MARLOW, B. J. 1958. A survey of the marsupials of New South Wales. *J. C.S.I.R.O. Wildlife Res.,* 3: 71-114.

MARTIN, P. G. 1970. The Darwin Rise hypothesis of the biogeographical dispersal of marsupials. *Nature,* 225: 197-198.

MAYR, E. 1944. Wallace's Line in the light of recent zoogeographic studies. *Quart. Rev. Biol.,* 19: 1-14.

McNALLY, J. 1960. The biology of the water rat. *Hydromys chrysogaster* Geoffroy (Muridae: Hydromyinae) in Victoria. *Austral. J. Zool.,* 8: 170-180.

MEYERHOFF, A. A. 1970a. Continental drift: implications of paleomagnetic studies, meteorology, physical oceanography, and climatology. *J. Geol.*, 78: 1-51.

———. 1970b. Continental drift, II: high-latitude evaporite deposits and geologic history of Arctic and North Atlantic oceans. *J. Geol.*, 78: 406-444.

MILLER, A. H. 1962. The history and significance of the fossil *Casuarius lydekkeri. Rec. Austral. Museum,* 25: 235-237.

MOIR, R. J., M. SOMERS, and H. WARING. 1956. Studies in marsupial nutrition. I. Ruminant-like digestion in a herbivorous marsupial, *Setonix brachyurus* Quoy and Gaimard. *Austral. J. Biol. Sci.,* 9: 293-304.

MOLLISON, B. C. 1960. Food regurgitation in Bennett's wallaby, *Protemnodon rufogrisea* (Desmarest), and the scrub wallaby, *Thylogale billardieri* (Desmarest). *J. C.S.I.R.O. Wildlife Res.,* 5: 87-88.

MORGAN, W. J. 1968. Rises, trenches, great faults, and crustal blocks. *J. Geophys. Res.,* 73: 1959-1982.

MULVANEY, D. J., G. H. LAWTON, C. R. TWIDAIE, N. W. G. MacINTOSH, J. A. MAHONEY, and N. A. WAKEFIELD. 1964. Archaeological excavation of rock shelter No. 6, Fromm's Landing, South Australia. *Proc. Roy. Soc. Victoria,* 77: 479-516.

NEWSOME, A. E. 1966. The influence of food on breeding in the red kangaroo in central Australia. *J. C.S.I.R.O. Wildlife Res.,* 11: 187-196.

PLANE, M. D. 1967. Stratigraphy and vertebrate fauna of the Otibanda formation, New Guinea. *Bull. Bur. Min. Res., Canberra,* 86: 1-64.

PLANE, M., and C. G. GATEHOUSE. 1968. A new vertebrate fauna from the Tertiary of northern Australia. *Austral. J. Sci.,* 30: 272-273.

QUILTY, P. G. 1966. The age of Tasmanian marine Tertiary rocks. *Austral. J. Sci.,* 29: 143-144.

RAVEN, H. C. 1935. Wallace's Line and the distribution of Indo-Australian mammals. *Bull. Am. Museum Natur. Hist.,* 68: 179-293.

RAVEN, H. C., and W. K. GREGORY. 1946. Adaptive branching of the kangaroo family in relation to habitat. *Am. Museum Novit.,* 1309. 1-33.

RIDE, W. D. L. 1959. On the evolution of Australian marsupials. In C. W. Leeper (ed.), *The Evolution of Living Organisms,* p. 281-306. Symp. Royal Soc. Victoria, Melbourne University Press.

———. 1964a. *Antechinus rosamondae,* a new species of Dasyurid marsupial from the Pilbara district of Western Australia; with remarks on the classification of *Antechinus. Western Austral. Natur.,* 9: 58-65.

———. 1964b. A review of the Australian fossil marsupials. *J. Roy. Soc. Western Austral.,* 47: 97-131.

——. 1965. Locomotion in the Australian marsupial *Antechinomys*. *Nature*, 205: 199.

——. 1968. The past, present, and future of Australian mammals. Presidential address, Section D. Zoology, A.N.Z. A.A.S. *Austral. J. Sci.*, 31: 1-11.

——. 1970. *A Guide to the Native Mammals of Australia*. Oxford Univ. Press, Melbourne.

RIEK, E. F. 1970. Lower Cretaceous fleas. *Nature*, 227: 746-747.

RUNCORN, S. K. 1962. Palaeomagnetic evidence for continental drift and its geophysical cause. In S. K. Runcorn (ed.) *Continental Drift*, p. 1-40. Academic Press, London.

SERVENTY, D. L., and H. M. WHITTELL. 1958. *Birds of Western Australia*. 345 p. Paterson Brokensha, Perth.

SHARMAN, G. B. 1959. Marsupial reproduction. In A. Keast, R. L. Crocker, and C. S. Christian (eds.), *Biogeography and Ecology in Australia*, p. 332-368. Junk, The Hague.

——. 1964. The female reproductive system of the red kangaroo, *Megaleia rufa*. *J. C.S.I.R.O. Wildlife Res.*, 9: 20-57.

SIMPSON, G. G. 1940. Antarctica as a faunal migration route. *Proc. 6. Pacific Sci. Congr.*, 755-768.

——. 1941. The affinities of the Borhyaenidae. *Am. Museum Novit.*, No. 1118: 1-6.

——. 1961. Historical zoogeography of Australian mammals. *Evolution*, 15: 431-446.

SMYTH, D. R., and C. M. PHILPOTT. 1968. A field study of the Rabbit Bandicoot, *Macrotis lagotis*, Marsupialia, from central Western Australia. *Trans. R. Soc. South Austral.*, 92: 3-14.

STIRLING, E. C. 1913. On the identity of *Phascolomys (Phascolonus) gigas*, Owen, and *Sceparnodon ramsayi*, Owen: with a description of some parts of its skeleton. *Mem. Roy. Soc. S. Austral.*, 1: 127-178.

STIRTON, R. A. 1955. Late Tertiary marsupials from South Australia. *Rec. S. Austral. Museum*, 11: 247-268.

——. 1957. Tertiary marsupials from Victoria, Australia. *Mem. Nat. Museum Victoria*, 21: 121-134.

STIRTON, R. A., R. H. TEDFORD, and A. H. MILLER. 1961. Cenozoic stratigraphy and vertebrate paleontology of the Tirari Desert, South Australia. *Rec. S. Austral. Museum*, 14: 19-61.

STIRTON, R. A., R. H. TEDFORD, and M. O. WOODBURNE. 1967. A new Tertiary formation and fauna from the Tirari Desert, South Australia. *Rec. S. Austral. Museum*, 15: 427-462.

——, ——, and ——. 1968. Tertiary deposits in the Australian region, containing terrestrial mammals. *Univ. Calif. Publs. Geol. Sci.*, 77: 1-30.

STIRTON, R. A., M. O. WOODBURNE, and M. D. PLANE. 1967. Tertiary

Diprotodontidae from Australia and New Guinea. *Bull. Bur. Min. Res., Canberra,* 85: 1-159.

STROMER, E. 1931. Die ersten alt-tertiaren Saugetier-Reste aus den Sundainseln. *Wetensch. Nedeleal. Batavia,* No. 17: 11-14.

TATE, G. H. H. 1945a. The marsupial genus Phalanger. *Am. Museum Novit.,* 1283: 1-41.

———. 1945b. The marsupial genus *Pseudocheirus* and its sub-genera. *Am. Museum Novit.,* 1287: 1-24.

———. 1945c. Notes on the squirrel-like and mouse-like possums (Marsupialia). *Am. Museum Novit.,* 1305: 1-12.

———. 1946. Geographic distribution of the bats in the Australasian archipelago. *Am. Museum Novit.,* 1323: 1-21.

———. 1947. On the anatomy and classification of the Dasyuridae (Marsupialia). *Bull. Am. Museum Natur. Hist.,* 88: 102-155.

———. 1948a. Studies on the anatomy and phylogeny of the Macropodidae (Marsupialia). *Bull. Am. Museum Natur. Hist.,* 91: 239-351.

———. 1948b. Studies in the Peramelidae (Marsupialia). *Bull. Am. Museum Natur. Hist.,* 92: 317-346.

———. 1951. The rodents of Australia and New Guinea. *Bull. Am. Museum Natur. Hist.,* 97: 189-430.

———. 1952. Mammals of Cape York Peninsula, with notes on the occurrence of rain forest in Queensland. *Bull. Am. Museum Natur. Hist.,* 98: 567-616.

TEDFORD, R. H. 1966. A review of the macropodid genus *Sthenurus. Univ. Calif. Publ. Geol. Sci.,* 57: 1-72.

———. 1967. The fossil Macropodidae from Lake Menindee, New South Wales. *Univ. Calif. Pub. Geol. Sci.,* 64: 1-156.

THOMAS, O. 1888. *Catalogue of the Marsupialia and Monotremata in the Collection of the British Museum (Natural History).* British Museum (Natur. Hist.), London.

THOMSON, J. A., and W. H. OWEN. 1964. A field study of the Australian ringtail possum *Pseudocheirus peregrinus* (Marsupialia: Phalangeridae). *Ecol. Monogr.,* 34: 27-52.

TINDALE, N. B. 1957. Culture succession in southwestern Australia from late Pleistocene to the present. *Rec. S. Austral. Museum,* 13: 1-49.

TROUGHTON, E. 1948. *Furred Animals of Australia.* 376 p. Angus and Robertson, Sydney.

———. 1965. A review of the marsupial genus *Sminthopsis* (Phascogalinae) and diagnosis of new forms. *Proc. Linnean Soc. N. S. Wales,* 89: 307-321.

TURNBULL, W. D., E. L. LUNDELIUS, and K. McDOUGALL. 1965. A potassium-argon dated Pliocene marsupial fauna from Victoria, Australia. *Nature,* 206: 816.

TYNDALE-BISCOE, C. H. 1955. Observations on the reproduction and ecology of the Brush-tailed Possum, *Trichosurus vulpecula* Kerr (Marsupialia), in New Zealand. *Austral. J. Zool.,* 3: 162-184.

UMBGROVE, J. H. F. 1938. Geological history of the East Indies. *Bull. Am. Assoc. Petrol. Geol.,* 22: 1-70.

VAN DEUSEN, H. M. 1964. First New Guinea record of *Thylacinus. J. Mammal.,* 44: 279-280.

VEEVERS, J. J. 1967. The phanerozoic geological history of northwest Australia. *J. Geol. Soc. Austral.,* 14: 253-271.

VINE, F. J. 1966. Spreading of the ocean floor: new evidence. *Science,* 154: 1405.

VON KOENIGSWALD, G. H. R. 1967. An upper Eocene mammal of the family Anthracotheriidae from the island of Timor, Indonesia. *Proc. Koninkl. Ned. Akad. Wetenschap., Ser. B (Phys. Sci.),* 70: 529-533.

WAKEFIELD, N. A. 1963. The Australian pigmy-possums. *Victorian Natur.,* 80: 99-116.

WOOD, J. G. 1949. Vegetation of Australia. *The Australian Environment.* 151 p. C.S.I.R.O., Melbourne.

WOODBURNE, M. O. 1967. The Alcoota fauna, central Australia. An integrated palaeontological and geological study. *Bull. Bur. Min. Res., Canberra,* 87: 1-187.

WOODS, J. T. 1956. The skull of *Thylacoleo carnifex. Mem. Queensland Museum,* 13: 125-140.

——. 1962. Fossil marsupials and Cainozoic continental stratigraphy in Australia: a review. *Mem. Queensland Museum,* 14: 41-49.

VI The Fossil Mammal Fauna of South America

by Bryan Patterson
and Rosendo Pascual

INTRODUCTION

South America, the best known of the southern continents as far as mammalian history is concerned, was more isolated than Africa, but less isolated than Australia during the Cenozoic era. The earliest mammals recorded there comprised only a small fraction of the groups known or confidently inferred to have been in existence in the northern continents at the start of Cenozoic time. From small beginnings an extraordinary indigenous fauna arose and was enriched by the descendants of a few later immigrants that reached the continent across a water barrier at times during the Tertiary. During the course of their evolution some South American mammal groups came to converge, while others came to parallel mammals in other parts of the world. The isolation of South America ended only a few million years ago when the Panama bridge came into existence. Thereafter the record reveals an intermingling of the long separated North and South America faunas. The South American fauna does not support any hypotheses of Cenozoic or late Cretaceous connections with either of the other southern continents, whether by land bridge or by continental drift. Brundin (1966) has recently advocated such connections, but we do not find his arguments convincing.

So complex and comparatively well documented a story cannot be treated adequately in a single chapter. Accordingly, as much information as possible concerning geologic ranges, phyletic relationships and other matters is condensed in the figures and tables that follow. Since verbal descriptions of animals that nobody has seen in the flesh are both difficult and word consuming, and not too useful, we trust that the accompanying restorations of a number of the better known forms will be helpful.

This account, save for passing mention of bats, is confined to terrestrial mammals. Remains of whales are known, especially from the early Miocene Patagonian group, but we do not discuss them. An extinct trichechid

TABLE 1

Cenozoic epochs and corresponding Provincial Ages, with major events affecting South American mammal evolution

EPOCHS		PROVINCIAL AGES	MAJOR EVENTS
Pleistocene	L	Lujanian	Notable extinction of large mammals
	M	Ensenadan	
	E	Uquian	
Pliocene	L	Montehermosan	Beginning of faunal interchange with North America
	M	Huayquerian	
	E	Chasicoan	Appearance of procyonids of the Cyonasua group
Miocene	L	Friasian	Phase of Andean elevation leading to change in southern South America from savanna – woodland to pampas
	M	Santacruzian	
	E	(Marine Invasion)	
Oligocene	L	Colhuehuapian	
	M	(Hiatus)	
	E	Deseadan	Appearance of caviomorph rodents and platyrrhine primates
Eocene	L	(Divisaderan)	
	M	Mustersan	
	E	Casamayoran	
Paleocene	L	Riochican	
	M		
	E		Arrival(s) of the "ancient inhabitants"
Cretaceous			

(L = late, M = middle, E = early)

sirenian, *Ribodon,* occurs in the late Miocene of Colombia and the mid-Pliocene of Argentina (Reinhart, 1951; Pascual, 1953).

THE FOSSIL RECORD IN SOUTH AMERICA

In comparison to other areas of the globe, the record of mammalian life in South America is very good; it is much more complete than those of the other southern continents and not very far behind those of North America and Europe. Faunistic assemblages, a number of them large and containing a good representation of the smaller as well as of the larger mammals, are known for every epoch of the Cenozoic era. From these assemblages, and building on the work of many investigators, it has been possible to set up a sequence of Provincial Ages (Simpson, 1940; Pascual, et al., 1967), based on the Argentinian succession that was so largely established by the devoted labors of the Ameghinos, and which is applicable to the continent as a whole (Table 1). Oddly enough, this record has been described as "meager" (Hershkovitz, 1969, p. 1); as fossil records go, it is quite the reverse.

Because of the unique nature of the South American Tertiary mammalian faunas, consensus on dating has been slow in coming, but there is now general agreement on it. Uncertainties, of course, remain. For example, did the Riochican really terminate at the end of the Paleocene as that epoch is understood in the northern continents? Did the Montehermosan perhaps transgress the Pliocene-Pleistocene boundary? These and other questions cannot be answered at present, but the point to be stressed is that the questions are relatively precise ones; the areas of ignorance concerning dating are being progressively narrowed. A potassium/argon date of 21.7×10^6 years for the Santa Cruz formation has been obtained. This indicates an age corresponding to that of the middle Miocene Burdigalian of the European sequence (Evernden et al., 1964) and supports correlations suggested earlier on other grounds. (Since this was written and Table 1 prepared, J. A. Van Couvering has very kindly informed us that he has evidence (1972) indicating a spread of 22.5 to 18.6×10^6 years for the early Miocene Aquitanian, which would place the Santacruzian in this segment of time.) More radioactive dating is urgently needed in South America.

The record has one great deficiency: it is very largely restricted to the southern parts of the continent. As Fig. 1A shows, only a few Tertiary localities are known outside Argentina. We are thus very largely ignorant of the life of the northern—and greater—portion of the continent. New northern localities are beginning to turn up but unfortunately most of them have so far yielded only one or a few specimens. An exception is Salla, Bolivia (Baird, Woodburne, and Lawrence, 1966; Hoffstetter, 1968a), from which a rather good Deseadan fauna has been obtained. Certain groups, judging from their sudden appearances or poor representation in the southern faunas, may have had their evolutionary centers in the north. On the other hand, the extensive late Miocene La Venta fauna of Colombia shows that some groups survived in the north after their disappearance in the south. The northern localities demonstrate one all-important fact: Tertiary South America was a faunal unit; no major groups of mammals unknown in the south are present in the north.

For the Pleistocene, as for the Tertiary, the principal localities and the only good sequences are Argentinian (Fig. 1B). With two possible exceptions, the northern South American localities appear to be of late Pleistocene (Lujanian) age. The exceptions are the Chichean local fauna of Ecuador and the Ñuapuan of Bolivia, which may be of middle Pleistocene (Ensenadan) age (Hoffstetter, 1952, 1968b). The date is of some importance because, if middle Pleistocene, these faunas furnish the earliest records of *Equus* in the continent. Important northern faunas are few. Scattered finds yielding one or a few forms are very numerous, but no attempt has been made to map them. Some idea of their number may be had from Simpson and Paula Couto's (1957) map showing the distribution of finds of proboscideans in Brazil, or Hoffstetter's (1968b) showing

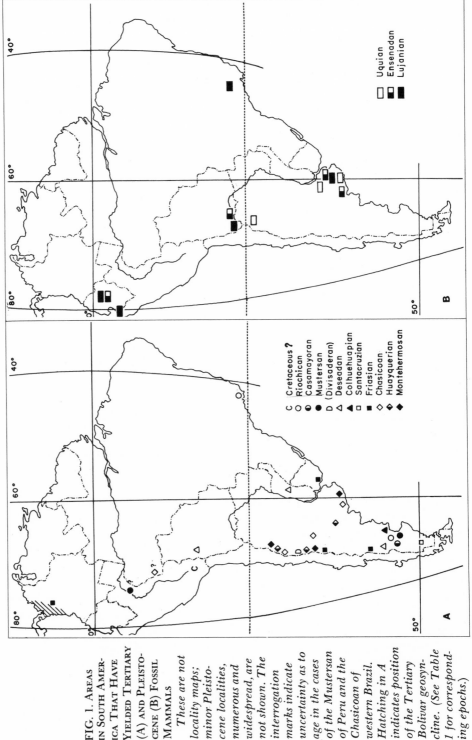

FIG. 1. AREAS IN SOUTH AMERICA THAT HAVE YIELDED TERTIARY (A) AND PLEISTOCENE (B) FOSSIL MAMMALS

These are not locality maps; minor Pleistocene localities, numerous and widespread, are not shown. The interrogation marks indicate uncertainty as to age in the cases of the Mustersan of Peru and the Chasicoan of western Brazil. Hatching in A indicates position of the Tertiary Bolivar geosyncline. (See Table 1 for corresponding epochs.)

Pleistocene localities in Bolivia. Without exception, all Pleistocene localities containing any appreciable number of specimens include mammals of both North and South American ancestry.

The Tertiary record is unfortunately not complete in its earlier part. We have no knowledge of the early and middle Paleocene, and there are major gaps between Mustersan and Deseadan, and between Deseadan and Colhuehuapian. At least one, and in the case of the former possibly two, Provincial Ages are missing in each of these hiatuses. There is one small fauna, the Divisadero Largo, that is post Mustersan and pre-Deseadan. It is of very peculiar facies (Simpson, Minoprio and Patterson, 1962). One of us (Patterson) believes that for this reason it should not serve as the basis for a Provincial Age, while the other (Pascual) has so designated it (Pascual et al., 1967). As a compromise we include it—within parentheses. Not all Provincial Ages are equally well known; knowledge of the Friasian is particularly inadequate in Argentina (Pascual doubts the validity of this age); this is the more unfortunate because the only well-known late Tertiary northern fauna, the La Venta, falls within it.

For all its imperfections, the fossil record reveals a very great deal. Something, often a very considerable amount, is known of the history of a large majority of the South American families. The major faunal and climatic events are recorded in it. The mammals of southern Patagonia, through the Miocene, suggest a climate sufficiently genial to permit such now mainly tropical animals as porcupines, echimyids, dasyproctids, anteaters and primates to flourish there. The molluscs of the Patagonian Miocene are in accord on this point. The environment suggested by the mammalian faunas throughout much of this stretch of time is a woodland and savanna one that graded northward into the rain forest, woodland, and savanna of the tropical zone, then no doubt more extensive than at present. We do not, of course, imply monotonous uniformity. Changes and fluctuations there undoubtedly were, but they occurred within this general environment. At the beginning of the Pliocene a change began in the southern part of the continent. The sedimentation center shifted from Patagonia to the Pampas region and to northwestern Argentina, and the sediments themselves changed from predominantly pyroclastic to predominantly clastic (Reig, 1957; Pascual, 1961, 1965). All of this coincided with a phase of Andean uplift that was to result in elevation of the Main Cordillera (Herrero-Ducloux, 1963). It had a marked ecological effect, largely by acting as a barrier to moisture-laden Pacific winds. The Pampas probably came into prominence at about this time, many of the subtropical savanna-woodland forms retreated northward, and new opportunities arose for those mammals able to adapt to a plains environment.

As Simpson has stressed (1966), the Andes in their present form are a new addition to the South American scene. The last major uplift began at the end of the Tertiary, as is demonstrated by Montehermosan sediments which were involved in it (Riggs and Patterson, 1939). The enduring part

252 BRYAN PATTERSON AND ROSENDO PASCUAL

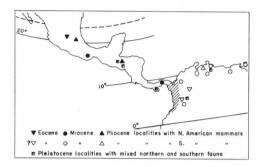

FIG. 2. Fossil Mammal Localities in Central America and Northwestern South America

Hatching indicates position of the Tertiary Bolivar geosyncline. See Table 2 for sources of data; also Schaub, 1935; Stirton and Gealey, 1949; Stirton, 1953a; van Frank, 1957; Gazin, 1957; Pascual and Diaz de Gamero, 1969; Hoffstetter, 1970a.

of South America is and has been the great rain-forest–woodland–savanna complex that today embraces nearly all the tropical and subtropical portions of the continent east of the Andes. It was in this environment that the greater part of South American mammalian evolution probably took place. The area has always been large; there is no good evidence that epicontinental seas ever covered extensive parts of it during the Cenozoic.

The major fact that emerges from the record is that South America was an island continent throughout practically all of Tertiary time. The main water barrier between the two Americas during the period was a seaway, frequently called the Bolivar geosyncline, between Panama and the northwestern corner of the continent (Figs. 1A, 2) that lasted into the Pliocene. During the later Mesozoic, from late Jurassic to Tertiary, even more extensive marine deposition was going on in this general area (Harrington, 1962). The faunal evidence is in agreement. Prior to formation of the Panamanian land bridge the mammals that reached South America could, and we think did, arrive as waif immigrants (see pp. 258-259). In further anticipation of later discussion, we believe available evidence suggests that they came from the north, which is to say from Central America.

TERTIARY CENTRAL AMERICA AND THE NORTH AMERICAN TROPICS

Central America, as the land area nearest to South America, has obviously played a most important part in the South American story. It is therefore all the more regrettable that its fossil record of mammals is so poor. Few as they are, however, the known fossil mammals of the region are consistent with one, and only one, of the principal hypotheses that have been advanced concerning Tertiary Central America, which are:

(1) The region was of far greater extent, reaching eastward to include the Greater Antilles (e.g., Schuchert, 1935);

(2) Part of Central America was an island throughout much of the Cenozoic, being separated from North America by a seaway at the present Isthmus of Tehuantepec as well as from South America, receiving waif immigrants from both north and south, and serving as the departure area

TABLE 2

The Tertiary Mammalia of tropical North America

	Guanajuato, Mexico (late Eocene, Uinton, or earliest Oligocene, Chadronian)	Eastern Panama (middle Miocene, early Hemingfordian)	Oaxaca, Mexico (late Miocene, Barstovian)	Western Honduras (Pliocene, Clarendonian)	Hidalgo, Mexico
Rodentia	Floresomys guanajuatoensis			Fragments, indet.	
Carnivora				Osteoborus cynoides Amphicyon sp.	
Proboscidea				Rhynchotherium sp., cf. R. blicki	
Perissodactyla	Tapiroidea, indet.	Anchitherium sp. Archaeohippus sp. Diceratherium sp.	Merychippus sp.	Pliohippus hondurensis Neohipparion montezumae Brachypotheriinae, indet.	Neohipparion montezumae N. otomii, N. monias
Artiodactyla		Merycochoerus sp. Brachycrus sp. Protoceratidae, indet.	Oxydactylus ? sp.	Cervidae, indet.	

(*Data from Leidy, 1882; Olson and McGrew, 1941; McGrew, 1944; Stirton, 1954; Fries, Hibbard and Dunkle, 1955; Mooser, 1959, 1963; Whitmore and Stewart, 1965*)

for waif emigrants to the Greater Antilles (Darlington, 1957, esp. p. 279-286, 514-517);

(3) Central America has been a peninsula of the North American continent until very late in the Tertiary, when a connection with South America was established.

The first of these hypotheses can be disposed of summarily. There is no compelling faunal evidence to indicate that the Greater Antilles have even been connected with each other, let alone with any part of the neighboring mainlands at any time in the Cenozoic. Hershkovitz (1969) seems inclined to favor a land bridge to Central America in the early Tertiary. Had such a connection existed, the Greater Antillean mammalian faunas would have contained more indigenous forms of northern ancestry than they do. As it is and—so far as known—was, the only terrestrial mammals of North American origin are the solenodontid and nesophontid insectivores and the recently arrived *Oryzomys* in Jamaica. All the rest are of South American ancestry and reached the islands from that continent. The Antillean faunal elements, both Greater and Lesser, arrived as waif immigrants (e.g., Simpson, 1956). The relative success of South American waif emigrants there contrasts with their apparent poor success in Central America. In the islands they would have encountered much less competition. The second hypothesis was put forward in the belief that distribution of at least parts of the faunas of the larger islands indicated an orderly, west to east dispersal pattern that would require a source area separate from North and South America yet containing a fauna derived from both. Arguing strongly against it is the lack of any evidence of a past seaway at Tehuantepec (Durham, Arellano and Peck, 1955), and the presence, at or south of this isthmus, of characteristically North American Miocene and Pliocene mammals of kinds (mostly large) that were not raft-prone. Central American Tertiary mammals are listed in Table 2 (for additional records see Alvarez, 1965). All are northern. The presence of these forms, a number of them referable to genera common in temperate North America, is sufficient evidence that the Madro-Tertiary geoflora (Hershkovitz, 1969, p. 12) was not a major barrier between the temperate and tropical parts of the continent as far as mammals were concerned. That some South American forms were rafted to Central America during the Tertiary is likely—there is indirect evidence that the ancestry of the North American ground sloth *Megalonyx* arrived in this manner (p. 269)—but those that may have done so evidently made no great faunal impact. In sharp contrast to the small, purely North American Tertiary local faunas in Panama and Honduras are the comparably small or even smaller Pleistocene faunules known from Costa Rica, Honduras, Panama, Colombia and Venezuela, which contain mammals of both northern and southern ancestry (Fig. 2). The Colombian and Venezuelan Tertiary localities, one of which, La Venta, has yielded a rich and diversified fauna, contain without exception mammals of southern ancestry. The factual evidence so far as it goes is fully consistent with the third hypothesis, which is now the generally accepted view.

We discuss Central America at greater length than would otherwise be necessary because Hershkovitz (1966b) has claimed that the Bolivar geosyncline was not a serious barrier to faunal interchange: "Evidently, many northern families which spread through the Isthmus to the edge of the gap crossed it opportunely. Herds of wandering mastodons, tapirs, horses, peccaries, camels and deer would cross such bodies of water easily and routinely. . . . Despite the absence of fossil evidence, there is no reason to assume that many more families [than of ground sloths and monkeys] of contemporaneous mammals, some better adapted to water than others, were not doing the same. The traffic was both active and passive and from either continent to the other. . . . Closure of the Panamanian portal may have facilitated the crossing of some species but there is no evidence that it resulted in a spectacular increase in the volume of faunal interchange" (pp. 730, 732). The paper on the geology of the area cited with approval by Hershkovitz is a short contribution by Nygren (1950) on the Bolivar geosyncline in which the following statement is made: "Migrations of terrestrial animals could have taken place through this area during the periods from upper Cretaceous to middle Eocene, middle Oligocene, lower Miocene, middle Miocene and from upper Miocene to Recent"—in other words throughout most of the Tertiary. Later studies (e.g., Woodring, 1954, 1966; Harrington, 1962; Jacobs, Bürgl, and Conley, 1963; Lloyd, 1963; Haffer, 1970) make no such point. The acid test of any suggested land connection is of course provided by the terrestrial faunas of the areas supposedly connected. In the present case

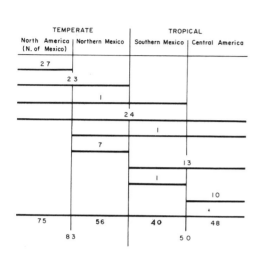

TEMPERATE		TROPICAL	
North America (N. of Mexico)	Northern Mexico	Southern Mexico	Central America
27			
2 3			
	1		
2 4			
		1	
	7		
		13	
		1	
			10
			4
75	56	40	48
83		50	

TABLE 3

Latitudinal distribution of genera of Recent land mammals of northern origin in North America

Data mainly from Hershkovitz, 1958, and Hall and Kelson, 1959.

Confined to temperate North America 57
Confined to tropical North America 24

In common 26

$$\frac{100C}{N_1} = 52 = \text{measure of faunal similarity}$$

(*C = number of genera common to temperate and tropical North America; N_1 = number of genera occurring in tropical North America; see Simpson, 1947.*)

all available facts combine to indicate that the geosyncline was a very real barrier between the two Americas and that it did not go out of existence until very late in geologic time. No member of any of Hershkovitz's herds appears in any South American deposit before the Pliocene-Pleistocene transition, after which an extensive faunal interchange is abundantly documented. Quite simply, his views cannot be reconciled with the evidence. The distribution of cricetine rodents in the New World seems to have played some part in his thinking; this distribution is discussed below (p. 294).

There has been a wholly North American tropical area throughout practically all of Cenozoic time. The North American tropics, which today occupy only a small fraction of the continent, were certainly more extensive in the past (at times in the Pleistocene, perhaps, they were even more restricted than now) and almost surely served as "an important center of regional faunal differentiation" (Simpson, 1951, p. 407). This view has recently been questioned by Whitmore and Stewart (1965), who see no evidence for it in the scanty Tertiary faunas of Central America. A brief comment is accordingly necessary. Table 3 shows that among Recent North American mammals of northern origin well over half of the genera are represented in the tropics, and 24 of them, nearly a quarter of the whole, do not occur in the temperate zone. For so small a portion of the continent this percentage is impressive. [If the Recent forms of South American origin are added the number of genera limited to the tropics rises to 50, over a third of the North American total.]

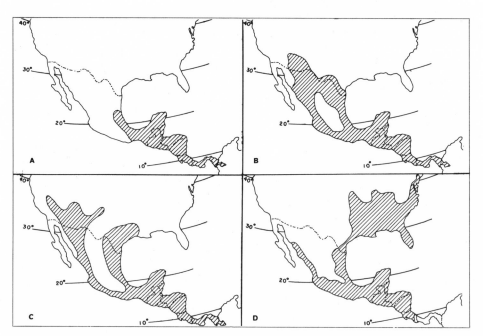

FIG. 3. Present Ranges of Some Predominantly Tropical Mammals of Northern Ancestry in North America

A, two species of Mazama; *B,* Nasua narica; *C,* Felis onca; *D,* Oryzomys palustris. *Redrawn from Hall and Kelson, 1959. Pleistocene records of* Felis onca *in the eastern part of the continent precisely match the recent distribution of* Oryzomys palustris *there (Hibbard et al., 1965, Fig. 8).*

In the Recent, at least, a tropical component of the North American native mammalian fauna definitely exists. There is some suggestion that similar conditions prevailed in the Tertiary. The late Eocene or earliest Oligocene sciuravid, *Floresomys,* is not known elsewhere. Of the six Central American Pliocene forms (Table 2) identified to species, either definitely or tentatively, four were regarded by their authors as distinct from those occurring to the north. The fragment identified as *Oxydactylus* sp. by Stirton is later in time than species of the genus occurring in the United States and may represent a distinct taxon. The commonest fossil in the small local fauna from Panama is the undetermined protoceratid, which Whitmore and Stewart were unable to refer to any northern form. [Since this went to press, Patton and Taylor (1971, p. 207n) have evidently identified this form as *Paratoceras,* a genus which ranges from Texas ". . . into Central America as far as Panama."] All taxa identified to genus, except *Floresomys,* are present in the north, but this is hardly surprising. Temperate and tropical North America today share 26 widely ranging genera of northern origin, nearly a quarter of the total (forms with a wide distribution are usually successful and hence numerous), and the number may well have been higher in the Tertiary—as it evidently was at times in the Pleistocene—when climates were less sharply zonal than they are today. The relations between tropical and temperate North America (used in the *geographic,* not the strictly *climatologic* sense) may then have resembled those between the Palearctic and Oriental regions in eastern China at the present time, with no sharp differentiation and considerable inter-digitation of taxa that were, in the main, characteristic of one or the other. A number of the distribution maps in Hall and Kelson (1959), four of which are shown in Fig. 3, reveal degrees of penetration of temperate North America by species that appear to be primarily tropical. Ameliora-tion of mean annual temperature with concomitant ecological changes would no doubt allow these and many other species, some of them now wholly tropical, to extend farther northward. Tertiary faunas within the United States contain hints of groups that may have been predominantly southern in distribution, e.g., the peculiar camels of the subfamily Florida-tragulinae that occur in the Miocene of Florida and of the Gulf Coastal Plain of Texas (Maglio, 1966; Patton, 1967).

To sum up, the North American tropical peninsula was evidently a fact of ancient geography, and there is convincing Recent and suggestive Tertiary evidence that its mammals are and were distinctive to some degree within the continental fauna as a whole.

THE MAMMALS OF TERTIARY SOUTH AMERICA

Discoveries of late Cretaceous mammals in Peru have recently been announced. One, *Perutherium* (Thaler, in Grambast et al., 1967), is represented by a mandibular fragment with two broken molars. As Thaler suggests, it seems to be a very small condylarth, more advanced than the latest Cretaceous *Protungulatum* (an arctocyonid) of North America. Sigé (1968) reports a dozen broken teeth of perhaps two species of very small marsupials, very similar to some North American late Cretaceous didel-phids. These finds do not conflict with the evidence previously provided by the early Tertiary mammals as to the original composition of the South American Tertiary fauna. The dating, at first based on charophytes which Grambast considered to be diagnostic, has been reinforced by egg-shell fragments considered to be dinosaurian. It is greatly to be hoped that further mammalian remains will be recovered at the locality.

The early Tertiary mammalian faunas, Riochican to Mustersan, con-sisted of marsupials, edentates of the suborder Xenarthra, and a variety of ungulates—and nothing else. These, the "ancient inhabitants," were already a diversified lot when we first encounter them, which suggests a late Cretaceous or early Paleocene arrival for their ancestors. Caviomorph rodents and platyrrhine primates make their first appearance in the Deseadan. Absence of rodents in South America for approximately an epoch after their appearance in the north profoundly affected faunal composition and diversity; certain marsupials and small notoungulates that had earlier moved into the rodent zone were long undisturbed in it.

The only other addition to the fauna prior to the interchange with North America was a group of extinct procyonids, the *Cyonasua* group, which is first met with in the middle Pliocene Huayquerian. Since no influx of other mammals accompanies any of these later additions it must be concluded that their ancestors were waif immigrants to the continent, Simpson's "old island hoppers" (1951, p. 385). The rodents and primates presumably arrived during the time represented by the long hiatus in the record between the Mustersan and Deseadan, and the extinct procyonids perhaps toward the end of the Miocene. Haffer (1970) has recently reviewed the late Cretaceous and Cenozoic geological history of northwestern Colombia. He finds evidence that ". . . toward the end of the Middle Eocene and again toward the end of the Middle Miocene . . ." there was ". . . a temporary discontinuous connection between northern Central America and the gently rising Andes of Colombia" (p. 622). The dating of these discontinuous connections, especially of the former, agree rather well with the appearances of the later waif immigrants. The discontinuous nature of the connections is underlined by the very small number of invasions associated with them.

The ancient inhabitants were, judged by the standard of contemporary continental faunas of the northern hemisphere, an unbalanced assemblage. Seven orders—Marsupialia, Edentata, Condylarthra, Notoungulata, Litopterna, Trigonostylopoidea, Xenungulata—are present in the Riochican; another, Astrapotheria, was surely in existence by Riochican time. The first four of these are known in the north, whereas the remainder, all ungulates, are exclusively South American. All families except Didelphidae are autochthonous. It has generally been assumed that so numerous a lot must have arrived via a land connection with another continent, and this view finds expression in most reviews of the South American fauna (e.g., Hoffstetter, 1954a; Thenius, 1964). But this conclusion does not necessarily follow from the evidence. The Panamanian bridge, established at the end of the Tertiary, resulted in an interchange that included members of nearly all the orders and over half of the families then living in North and South America. This was clearly not the case around the beginning of the Tertiary. Haffer (1970, p. 616) finds no geological evidence for a continuous connection in late Cretaceous and earliest Tertiary time. Darlington (1957) and Patterson (1957, 1958) have argued against a direct connection, suggesting that the ancestors of the ancient inhabitants were waif immigrants. As the former has very well expressed it, ". . . there is no certainty of just how many ancestral forms [of ancient inhabitants] there were or that they all came at exactly the same time, and there is some evidence that they were selected fractions of a more diverse fauna which existed in the main part of the world: the edentates and ungulates were apparently already edentates and ungulates (or protungulates) when they reached South America (this is indicated by certain related fossils, especially in North America), and some important Paleocene mammals apparently failed to reach South America, e.g., insectivores and early placental carnivores. The best explanation of all this seems to be that one or more marsupials, one or more edentates, and one or two or three or more ungulates reached South America about the beginning of the Tertiary, but not necessarily all at one time, and that they came across a water barrier which blocked other mammals" (p. 363-364). Although there may well have been more, the minimum number of successful landfalls required to account for marsupials, edentates, condylarths and notoungulates is four. The ungulate orders, other than the Notoungulata, could have arisen from immigrant condylarths within the continent. This was demonstrably true for the Litopterna and probably so for the others, which may be regarded as parts of an early radiation of large (for the time) herbivores. Comparable radiations took place on other continents; e.g., in Africa: Proboscidea, barytheres, deinotheres, moeritheres, Embrithopoda and Hyracoidea. The simple ordinal count in South America gives a rather exaggerated impression of the actual diversity. Three of the orders, Xenungulata, Trigonostylopoidea, and Astrapotheria, contained only one family that included only one or a few genera at any one time. Notoungulata, we suspect, arrived as such. Judging from their extraordinary diversity, manifest from the beginning of the record, they encountered abundant ecological opportunities in the continent. They may have arrived somewhat later than the rest. Failure to compete successfully with them may have been a factor in the marked decline of condylarths—*qua* condylarths as opposed to their litoptern descendents—in post-Casamayoran time.

The most telling evidence against direct land connection around the Cretaceous-Tertiary boundary is the absence of any representatives of the unguiculate therians, edentates alone excepted. Had any members of the early "insectivore" (s.l.) groups or any creodonts or carnivores reached South America it is most unlikely that the marsupials would have radiated within the carnivore adaptive zone. Absence of multituberculates, abundant in the north during the later Cretaceous and Paleocene, and of prosimians is also hard to explain on the land bridge hypothesis. They would surely have crossed it, had it been in existence; the rise of somewhat multituberculate-like and rodent-like marsupials might not have taken place in their presence.

The available data, while not conclusive, suggest North America as the continent of origin of the ancient inhabitants. There and only there are to be found in combination, and at more or less the right times, marsupials, edentates, condylarths and notoungulates. Didelphids are abundant and rather diversified in the late Cretaceous (Clemens, 1966) and persist into the Tertiary. Condylarthra (including the Arctocyonidae) occur in the Cretaceous (Sloan and Van Valen, 1965) and are common in the Paleocene. Notoungulates, belonging to a northern family, and edentates of the ancestral suborder Palaeanodonta are known in the late Paleocene; both groups are rare, the former exceedingly so, and their appearances in the northern record are essentially contemporaneous with their ap-

pearances in the southern. It is possible that they may have been predominantly tropical in North America. A North American origin is the
simplest, most consistent explanation of the known facts and we accept it
as a working hypothesis. North America seems the likely point of departure of the later waif immigrants—rodents, primates, and procyonids.

The hypothesis we adopt is not the only one possible, of course.
Eutherian and metatherian mammals may have been in existence throughout the latter half of the Cretaceous (Patterson, 1956; Slaughter, 1968),
and some of them could have reached South America quite early. It is thus
just conceivable that, for example, edentates and notoungulates arose
there and reached North America as waif immigrants from the south (cf.
Hoffstetter, 1970b,c). Until more is known of the Mesozoic history of
mammals in the southern continents, students of mammalian distribution
will labor at a disadvantage.

The faunal diversity encountered in the Riochican implies rapid
evolution during late Cretaceous and earlier Paleocene time. With adaptive zones and innumerable niches awaiting exploitation by mammals we
believe that this is precisely what did happen.

The Ancient Inhabitants

Marsupials (Figs. 4, 5)

On their arrival in South America, marsupials were presented with
opportunities second only to those encountered by their relatives that
reached Australia. They made the most of them, occupying the insectivore, sharing the carnivore and edging into the rodent adaptive zones.
The central stock of the order, the Didelphidae, could very well, as
Clemens (1966) suggests, have been derived from the North American
Cretaceous *Alphadon* (or relatives), with diversification coming after entry
into South America. The Riochican locality at Itaborai near Rio de
Janeiro has yielded a variety of true didelphines, no less than 13 genera
having been described from it (Paula Couto, 1952b, 1962). Among these
is a very curious form, *Derorhynchus*, which in the structure of its lower
jaw parallels the caenolestines to a certain extent. The abundance of
members of this subfamily at the Brazilian locality is in striking contrast
to the situation in Patagonia, where with the exception of the Casamayoran *Coona*, they are practically absent. Members of another subfamily, Microbiotheriinae, occur there in the Oligocene and Miocene.
Until rather recently it was supposed that microbiotheres had then died
out, but Reig (1955) has shown that the living *Dromiciops, Caluromys*
and *Glironia* are surviving members. Didelphines reappear in Argentina
in the Pliocene. Prior to the description of *Coona* and the discoveries at
Itaborai, this apparent temporal segregation led Patterson (1937) to the
erroneous suggestion that true didelphines were waif immigrants. The
Argentinian Pliocene didelphids are accompanied by an extinct subfamily, the Sparassocyninae, whose teeth suggest more exclusively pre-

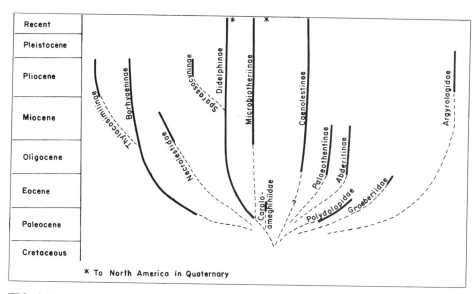

FIG. 4. SOUTH AMERICAN MARSUPIALS: TIME RANGES AND PHYLOGENY

daceous habits than is usual in the family (Reig, 1952). Completing the
roster of didelphid radiation known to date is the Casamayoran subfamily
Caroloameghiniinae, with one known genus. This apparently shortlived
lineage was adapted to an omnivorous or frugivorous diet, to judge from
molar structure (Simpson, 1948).

The carnivorous Borhyaenidae, in the course of their evolution, converged placental carnivores and paralleled their Australian relatives the
Dasyuridae. The latter set of resemblances was frequently cited in the
older literature as an indication of a relationship so close as to demand a
land connection between the two continents. The newer South American
evidence opposes this rather decisively. Primitive borhyaenids such as the
Casamayoran *Patene* approach didelphids closely enough to demonstrate
beyond reasonable doubt that the similarities were independently acquired
on the two continents (Simpson, 1941). Two subfamilies are known, one
of which, exemplified by the Pliocene *Thylacosmilus* (Riggs, 1934), converged saber-tooth cats to a remarkable degree in dental and some
cranial characters, although the feet were not at all felid-like. The more
orthodox subfamily, Borhyaeninae, would appear to have had a rather
complex phylogeny, but materials are insufficient for proper analysis of
it. A large, highly-specialized form, *Arminiheringia*, occurs together with
the small and primitive *Patene*—thus indicating that one lineage of large
forms evidently evolved from the beginning in step with such large early
ungulates as the Xenungulata. A generalized form, *Lycopsis*, occurs as
late as the Santacruzian, and so on. The size range, at least in the early
Tertiary, was in general comparable to that of the Carnivora. The giant
of the group, *Proborhyaena*, is Deseadan, and thereafter no really large

representatives are known. All borhyaenids whose limb bones have come down to us were rather short in the leg; there is no evidence that any of them were really cursorial.

An explanation of this fact, and also perhaps of the later Tertiary falling off in borhyaenid size, exists. The other occupants of the carnivore adaptive zone were members of a group of large birds, the phororhacoids, distant relatives of the living South American *Cariama*. Three families are known, two of them with two subfamilies (Patterson and Kraglievich, 1960); they were assorted into three size groups, medium, large and very large (in the mammalian context; for the avian, read "large," "very large," and "gigantic"); they are known to have ranged from Deseadan to Montehermosan. Although not yet recorded in the Pleistocene of South America, there is proof that they survived into that epoch: remains of one of them have been discovered recently in the earlier Pleistocene (C. E. Ray, pers. commun.) of Florida (Brodkorb, 1963). Two of the families, Phororhacidae and Psilopteridae, were swift and rather lightly built with long tarso-metatarsi; the third, Brontornithidae, included ponderous forms with massive beaks and tarsometatarsi of more Moa-like type. The former two were evidently the dominant cursorial carnivores of their time. The last, so far unknown subsequent to the Santacruzian, may have preyed to a large extent on glyptodonts, which then and earlier were relatively small and thin-shelled and still retained vestiges of the movable bands in the carapace inherited from their armadillo ancestry. By the Pliocene glyptodonts were larger and more heavily armored. (It is unusual to have to interrupt the flow of a mammalian narrative by a digression on birds, but Tertiary South America was an extraordinary continent.)

One borhyaenid character seems decidedly odd for a group of carnivores. The enamel on their canines was extremely thin and was rapidly worn away, the apices of the teeth becoming decidedly blunted as a result. In compensation the roots long remained open, permitting continued growth, and may possibly have so remained throughout life. This was certainly the case in the Thylacosmilinae, in which thin enamel was retained in open-rooted canines so long that they extended over the cranium practically to the occiput.

The sole known representative of a fossorial family that arose from the primitive didelphid stock is the Santacruzian *Necrolestes* (Patterson, 1958). A curious little creature with an upturned snout, it resembled the chrysochlorids and *Notorcytes* rather than the moles. The dentition is of the zalambdodont type. *Necrolestes* is only one of a number of fascinating creatures—*Groeberia,* the argyrolagids, and *Acamana* are others—that appear unheralded in, and as suddenly disappear from, the record, demonstrating as they pass how much remains to be learned.

Caenolestoid marsupials also underwent a radiation remarkable in its way even if less spectacular than the didelphoid one. The stem group is the primarily insectivorous subfamily Caenolestinae, a few members of which still survive. Two groups, the early Polydolopidae and the later

Abderitinae of the Caenolestidae (Simpson, 1928, 1939; Paula Couto, 1952a, 1962) were rather multituberculate-like. The resemblances, while not exact, extend to general skull shape, enlargement of anterior incisors and, in particular, of an enlarged pair of lower cheek teeth of cutting type, with ridges and serrations. Survival of the Abderitinae long after the arrival of rodents finds a parallel in North America in the survival of multituberculates into the late Eocene (Robinson, Black and Dawson, 1964) long after the rise of rodents there. The less specialized Palaeothentinae are intermediate between the multituberculate-like forms and the caenolestines. The Groeberiidae, known only from two species of *Groeberia* in the peculiar Divisadero Largo local fauna (Patterson, 1952; Simpson, 1970c), are possibly but by no means certainly caenolestoids. They are the most rodent-like marsupials so far known. Resemblances include an enlarged pair of upper and lower incisors of gnawing type with enamel limited to the anterior faces, conspicuous diastemata and four subequal cheek teeth. Major differences are the presence of a second, smaller pair of upper incisors and the position of the lower incisors, which instead of running back within the ramus as in rodents extend posteriorly along the median line in a prolongation of the symphysial region.

Origin of the caenolestoids has been much argued, some authors favoring relationship with the Australian phalangeroids. We believe, with others, that the ancestry of the caenolestoids lies within the early South American Didelphinae. The peculiar *Derorhynchus*, which, while clearly a didelphine, has some caenolestine features in the anterior portion of the mandible, indeed offers a hint as to the way in which some of the changes leading to the origin of the caenolestine stock might have come into being. The very real resemblances to phalangeroids we interpret as due to parallelism.

A fascinating addition to the already remarkable array of South American marsupials has recently been made. The Argyrolagidae, *Microtragulus* and *Argyrolagus*, had been known for nearly seventy years but only from fragments that revealed very little about them. Excellent new material found by Don Galileo J. Scaglia has enabled Simpson (1970a, b) to present a rather full account of these extraordinary creatures. They were small ricochetal forms with the features usual for that habitus, such as inflated epitympanic sinuses in the skull, reduced forelegs, elongate hindlegs and a very long tail. Striking characters include a reduced dentition—two incisors and five cheek teeth above and below on each side, all teeth rootless, a tubular bony snout anterior to the incisors, a large orbit with the eye in the posterior part and a masseter origin in the anterior, the temporal fossa reduced to the vanishing point, side digits of the hind foot lacking and metatarsals III and IV greatly elongated and so closely appressed as to form a pseudo-cannon bone. Argyrolagids display a decided convergence toward such ricochetal rodents as the kangaroo rat *Dipodomys* and certain jerboas. They appear suddenly in the Huay-

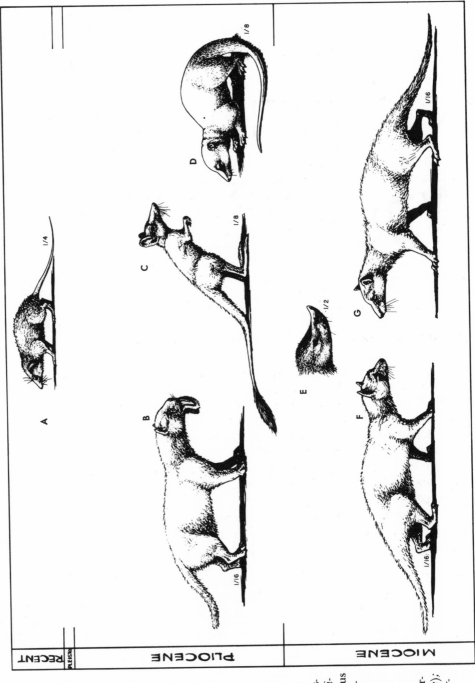

FIG. 5. RESTORATIONS
OF SOUTH AMERICAN
MARSUPIALS

Recent: A, Caenoles-
tes (Caenolestidae). *Pliocene: B,* Thylacosmilus
(Borhyaenidae); *C,* Ar-
gyrolagus (Argyrolagi-
dae); *D,* Lutreolina
(Didelphidae). *Mio-
cene: E,* Necrolestes
(Necrolestidae); *F,* Borhyaena (Borhyaenidae);
G, Prothylacynus (Bor-
hyaenidae).

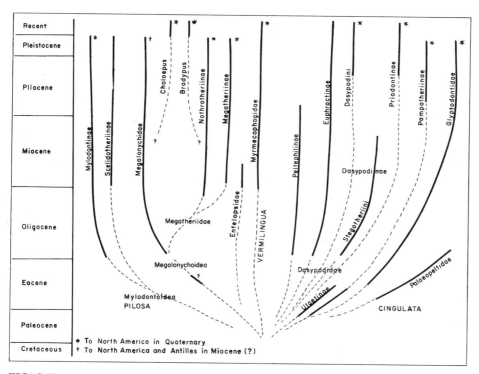

FIG. 6. XENARTHRANS: TIME RANGES AND PHYLOGENY

All tribes of armadillos are not shown. We recognize three in the Euphractinae: Euphractini, Eutatini, and Chlamyphorini; and two in the Priodontinae: Priodontini and Tolypeutini. Subfamilies of Glyptodontidae are not shown; they are: Propalaeohoplophorinae, Mustersan to Friasian; Sclerocalyptinae, Chasicoan to Lujanian; Doedicurinae, Huayquerian to Lujanian; Glyptodontinae, Montehermosan to Lujanian.

querian and have not so far been found in deposits later than the Uquian. So peculiar is the family that Simpson concludes that its ancestry probably arose within the Didelphidae, and that it represents a major division (superfamily in his usage) of the order.

Edentates (Xenarthra) (Figs. 6, 7)

No elements of the South American mammalian fauna are more characteristic than the members of the Xenarthra. Armadillos and glyptodonts, anteaters, ground sloths, and tree sloths together make up an assemblage unlike anything that evolved elsewhere in the world.

The North American Palaeanodonta have usually been placed in the Edentata, as a suborder, and regarded as survivors of the ancestral stock from which the Xenarthra arose. Emry (1970), largely on the basis of the newly discovered North American early Oligocene *Patriomanis*, which he refers to the Manidae, would suppress the suborder and refer the constituent families Metacheiromyidae and Epoicotheriidae to the Pholidota. As regards affinities with the pangolins he is, as he notes, in agreement

with Matthew (1918), although that author was equally as insistent on
xenarthran affinities as well. On the evidence presented by Emry, it
would seem reasonable to regard *Patriomanis* as a palaeanodont that was
convergent toward the pangolins in various features. As knowledge of
the palaeanodonts slowly increases, it is becoming apparent that the group
enjoyed a modest radiation during the first half of the North American
Tertiary.

The early record of the Xenarthra is unfortunately very defective.
Armadillo scutes occurring in the Riochican reveal that cingulate armor
was in existence by that time but tell us little else. Not until the Santacruzian does the armadillo record approach adequacy. The poorly known
palaeopeltids and the glyptodonts appear in the Mustersan; the record of
the latter, also, does not acquire substance until the Santacruzian. Ground
sloths are known from the Deseadan and anteaters from the Santacruzian.
Tree sloths are unknown as fossils.

Fortunately, a rather good specimen of *Utaetus*, a primitive armadillo,
is known from deposits of Casamayoran age (Simpson, 1948). While
definitely an armadillo, *Utaetus* does show a number of resemblances to
palaeanodonts, notably vestiges of enamel on the teeth. When adequate
specimens of contemporary members of the other groups are found, they
will in all probability be characterized by a similar combination of primitive and advanced characters. *Utaetus* and the Riochican scutes combine
to suggest a very rapid early radiation of small, originally unarmored
palaeanodonts at low hierarchic levels, followed by initial rapid evolution within those lineages that emerged from it. The ancestral palaeanodonts probably resembled the small North American epoicotheriids, and
may even have been members of that family.

The record of the armadillos, Dasypodidae, when it becomes clearly
decipherable in the Miocene, discloses some really remarkable extinct
forms and also a rather surprising number of gaps. Dasypodines, represented today by a genus that ranges from Patagonia to temperate North
America, are unknown prior to the Montehermosan and only one extinct
genus has so far turned up. The climatic tolerance now possessed by
Dasypus may be a relatively recent acquisition. *Tolypeutes* is unknown in
pre-Montehermosan time. The ancestry of *Priodontes*, the largest surviving armadillo, is a blank, and the curious little chlamyphorines are
likewise without representation. The extinct eutatines and their relatives,
the euphractines, have comparatively good records. Among the latter, the
very large *Macroeuphractus* of the Pliocene is outstanding, not only for its
size but for its closed dentition with incisiform and large caniniform
teeth. It may have been primarily a scavenger. The broad-skulled pelte-
philines also have a closed dentition, and an overlapping bite besides, but
their chief peculiarity, known in *Peltephilus*, is the possession of a pair
of scutes near the front of the head that are modified into sharp horns.
The very long snout and vestigial teeth of *Stegotherium*, as Scott (1937)
suggested, are indicative of a diet in which termites bulked large. The

real giants were the Pampatheriinae (Chlamytheriinae auct.), the later members of which approached the larger glyptodonts in size. A major hiatus in pampatherine history intervenes between Mustersan and Huayquerian time. Reference of the Eocene form to the group has been questioned but we are strongly inclined to credit it. Ameghino long ago suggested the pampatherines as ancestors of the glyptodonts, and he was probably right. In dental and basicranial structure they are the closest to the glyptodonts of any of the groups of armadillos. As such, their presence in Eocene (and earlier) deposits is to be expected. *Machlydotherium,* the genus in question, is represented by scutes and a tooth; both are pampatherine in structure.

Glyptodonts, Glyptodontidae, were the most heavily armored mammals that have ever existed. Starting as relatively small animals with comparatively weak armor, they achieved really large size and practical impregnability in the Pliocene and Pleistocene. Provided with a solid head shield, modifications of the cervical vertebrae serving to lower the head and shield to the anterior edges of the thick and solid carapace, and a heavily armored tail they were quite safe from predators—until the end of the Pleistocene. Members of the subfamily Doedicurinae had the end of the caudal tube studded with bosses or spikes, which greatly increased its effectiveness as a defensive weapon. Glyptodonts had complex teeth and could have subsisted to a considerable extent on grasses. They had no anterior teeth, but, as the African rhinoceros *Ceratotherium* demonstrates, it is quite possible to graze without them. Their apparent increase in numbers and diversity in post-Miocene time was perhaps associated with the rise of the pampas environment.

A third family of the Cingulata is the poorly known Palaeopeltidae. [We believe the higher taxa to have been oversplit in the infraorder Cingulata, and that the known groups can reasonably be arranged within three families (see Fig. 6).] An early Tertiary group, the Palaeopeltidae had simple, rather thin, featureless scutes and a short, deep, somewhat glyptodont-like facial region with subcircular teeth arranged in a continuous series. The best specimen consists of parts of a skull found together with a scute from the head shield and one from the carapace described by Kraglievich and Rivas (1951). These authors believed that the teeth, all but the last of which were broken off at the alveolar margin, agreed with the type of *Orophodon* Ameghino, based on a single tooth, and relegated *Palaeopeltis* to synonymy. Hoffstetter (1954b, 1956) showed that *Orophodon* was a ground sloth, but he believed, following earlier suggestions by Tournouër and Gaudry, that the scutes of *Palaeopeltis* were attributable to this genus and to the related *Octodontotherium;* the specimen described by Kraglievich and Rivas he placed in a new genus, *Pseudorophodon.* The solution of this tangle, which is crucial to an understanding of the Palaeopeltidae, lies, we believe, in the direct association of peculiar cingulate scutes with a peculiar cingulate skull shown by Kraglievich and Rivas' specimen. The finding of cranial fragments of *Orophodon* and *Octo-*

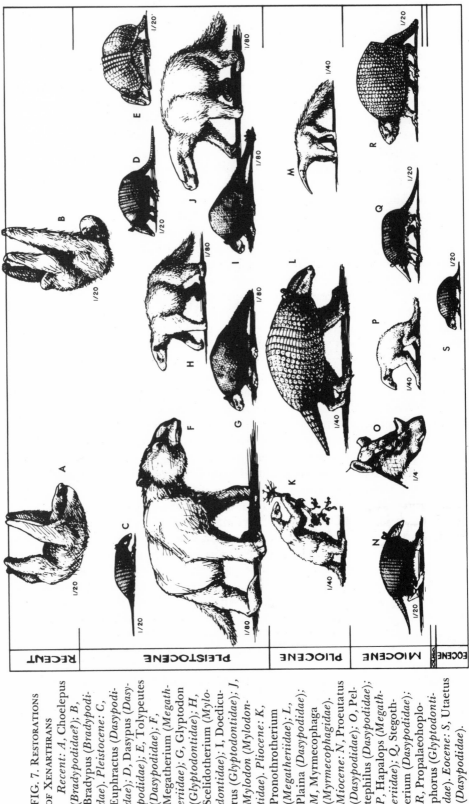

FIG. 7. RESTORATIONS
OF XENARTHRANS

Recent: A, Choelepus
(Bradypodidae?); B,
Bradypus (Bradypodi-
dae). Pleistocene: C,
Euphractus (Dasypodi-
dae); D, Dasypus (Dasy-
podidae); E, Tolypeutes
(Dasypodidae); F,
Megatherium (Megath-
eriidae); G, Glyptodon
(Glyptodontidae); H,
Scelidotherium (Mylo-
dontidae); I, Doedicu-
rus (Glyptodontidae); J,
Mylodon (Mylodon-
tidae). Pliocene: K,
Pronothrotherium
(Megatheriidae); L,
Plaina (Dasypodidae);
M, Myrmecophaga
(Myrmecophagidae).
Miocene: N, Proeutatus
(Dasypodidae); O, Pel-
tephilus (Dasypodidae);
P, Hapalops (Megath-
eriidae); Q, Stegoth-
erium (Dasypodidae);
R, Propalaeohoplo-
phorus (Glyptodonti-
dae). Eocene: S, Utaetus
(Dasypodidae).

dontotherium at the same locality as isolated scutes of *Palaeopeltis* is no indication that the scutes actually belong with the cranial fragments. With others, we believe *Octodontotherium* to be a mylodontid sloth, and refer *Orophodon* to the same family. *Palaeopeltis* stands as the name for the peculiar cingulate, with *Pseudorophodon* as a synonym.

Anteaters have a very poor record. The Santacruzian specimens indicate an animal intermediate in size between *Tamandua* and *Cyclopes*. A skull of *Myrmecophaga* from the Montehermosan of Catamarca, Argentina, has a rostrum that is relatively shorter than that of the living species but is otherwise nearly identical. The family has obviously had a long history but we are in the dark as to practically all of it. We agree with Hoffstetter (1954c) that the group merits infraordinal rank.

The very peculiar little *Entelops*, known only from a few Santacruzian specimens (Pascual, 1960) is another of the reminders of how much is yet to be learned. Possibly it represents a lineage that has survived from an early stage in pilosan differentiation.

Knowledge of the great sloth group, the infraorder Pilosa, begins in the Deseadan. [An astragalus has been claimed to come from the Musters formation, but may very well have been derived from overlying Deseado sediments.] By then the major dichotomy into mylodontoid and megalonychoid divisions had already been established, as, apparently, had the separation of the Mylodontidae into Scelidotheriinae and Mylodontinae. At least the Deseadan *Octodontotherium* appears to be, on cranial characters, a mylodontine. The two subfamilies differ notably in the muzzle, which is usually wide and flaring in mylodontines, narrow and more pointed in scelidotherines. The latter make their first certain appearance in the Santacruzian as relatively small forms and increase in size thereafter. *Octodontotherium* is as large as some Pliocene forms. Oddly, there is no record of mylodontines from the Deseadan to the Pliocene. Thereafter they are numerous and varied. As a group, mylodontoids differ from megalonychoids in having shorter forelegs, which suggests that they were more quadrupedal and less prone to stand erect.

Megalonychids, the stem group of their superfamily, are small when first encountered, and may have been partially arboreal. At some time in the mid-Tertiary one or more of them reached the Antilles as waif immigrants, initiating a minor radiation there. At about the same time the family evidently reached North America by the same means, judging from specimens found in the Pliocene of the United States that antedate establishment of the land connection between the continents. *Megalonyx* itself has never been found in South America and presumably evolved in the north from this waif ancestry. The post-Miocene history of the family in South America is somewhat obscure and the known material is in need of revision. Nothrotheres appear in the Coluehuapian and megatheres in the Santacruzian. The two groups appear to be closer to each other than either is to the ancestral megalonychids, especially in cranial structure. Both have good Pliocene and Pleistocene records. Nothrotheres did not attain great size whereas megatheres went on to become gigantic. It is curious and possibly significant that of the two tree sloths, *Choloepus* shows certain resemblances to the megalonychids whereas *Bradypus* is somewhat closer to the nothrotheres. Whether or not this is indicative of separate ancestry and subsequent parallelism is uncertain, but it does seem evident that tree sloth ancestry stemmed from the megalonychoid side of the ground sloth dichotomy.

Ungulates (Figs. 8-11)

The Condylarthra, important as ancestors, are themselves very poorly known. Only two genera have been recorded from post-Mustersan deposits: *Protheosodon* of the Deseadan of Patagonia, and *Megadolodus* (McKenna, 1956) of the Friasian of Colombia. Both are fairly large. To judge from hindleg and foot bones, *Protheosodon* may have resembled *Phenacodus* in general build (a restoration published by Loomis, 1914, Fig. 21, and constructed after *Theosodon*, a litoptern, is misleading). The South American condylarths are usually placed in a single family, Didolodontidae, but Paula Couto (1952c) has suggested that one genus, *Asmithwoodwardia*, is a member of the otherwise Holarctic Hypopsodontidae. This, if correct, would indicate that more than one condylarth immigration occurred. McKenna (1956), however, regards the resemblance as a probable case of parallelism and we tend to agree with him.

The Litopterna, grading out of the Condylarthra, underwent a minor radiation into three families, each somewhat diversified within itself. The least known of these is the Adianthidae, a group of small, evidently delicately-built creatures, within which three lineages can dimly be discerned (Simpson, Minoprio and Patterson, 1962). The Proterotheriidae, medium sized forms, were equid-like in build and foot structure, much less so in dentition; an enlarged sharp pair of incisors probably served as defensive weapons. The feet of the three-toed forms, such as the Santacruzian *Diadiaphorus*, were strikingly (if only superficially) similar to those of anchitherine horses, while the contemporary *Thoatherium* was monodactyl, going beyond equine horses in degree of reduction of the lateral digits. The Macraucheniidae, alone in the order, achieved large size, terminal forms equalling the larger true camels. They were the only South American ungulates known to have evolved a long, graceful neck, which accounts in large part for their rather camel-like appearance. The chief peculiarity displayed by them was a progressive reduction of the nasal bones accompanied by unmistakable evidence of the evolution of a short proboscis. Proterotherids and macrauchenids seem to have thrived in the evolving pampas areas, whereas adianthids, if any survived beyond the Miocene, have not as yet been found there.

The later and better known members of the order Astrapotheria were extraordinary looking animals with undershot jaws, large and sharp tusks, no upper incisors, a domed head and an inflated nasal region. From the

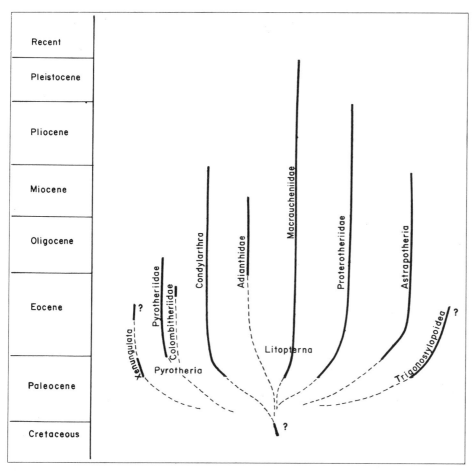

FIG. 8. SOUTH AMERICAN UNGULATES: TIME RANGES AND PHYLOGENY
   (*The Pyrotheria may prove to be notoungulates.*)

Deseadan on they come in two sizes, large and very large, the two apparently representing distinct lineages. The lower tusks were probably used
for rooting; along their front edges they frequently display grooves worn
into them by dirt-covered plants that had been held against them and the
lower incisors by the upper lip, and then pulled out by jerks of the head.
No astrapothere is known to have survived beyond Friasian time. There
is some degree of convergence between astrapotheres and amynodont
rhinoceroses in the skull and dentition.

The Trigonostylopoidea, a poorly known group, formerly included in
the Astrapotheria, was recently raised to ordinal rank by Simpson (1967).
Resemblances to astrapotheres, such as the presence of moderately enlarged upper and lower tusks followed by diastemata, appear to be more
than offset by differences in skull structure, especially in the basicranium.
Nothing is known of the postcranial skeleton.

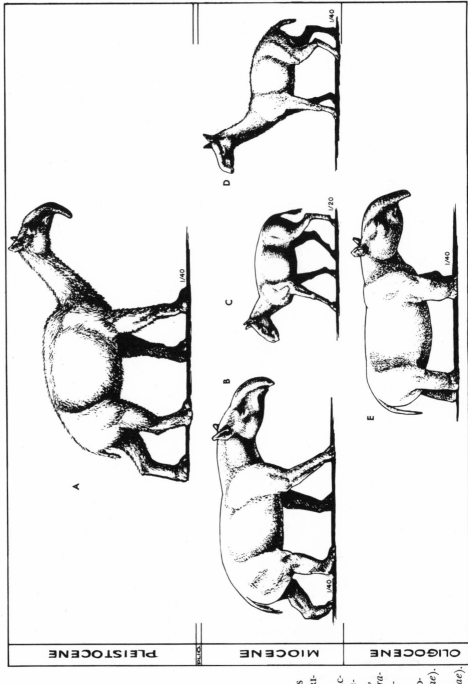

FIG. 9. RESTORATIONS OF SOME SOUTH AMERI-CAN UNGULATES

Pleistocene: A, Mac-rauchenia *(Macrauch-enidae). Miocene: B,* Astrapotherium *(Astra-potheriidae); C,* Tho-atherium *(Protero-theriidae); D,* Theoso-don *(Macraucheniidae). Oligocene: E,* Pyro-therium *(Pyrotheriidae).*

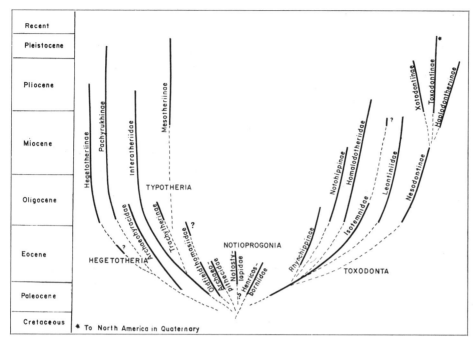

FIG. 10. NOTOUNGULATES: TIME RANGES AND PHYLOGENY
(*The pyrotheres may be referable to this order.*)

The Xenungulata is an order known essentially from one genus, the Riochican *Carodnia* (Paula Couto, 1952c). This was a large mammal with partially bilophodont cheek teeth, strong and sharp canines, rather chisel-like incisors, relatively slender limbs and pentadactyl feet. Members of the order no doubt played a role in the early faunas that was at least roughly comparable to those of pantodonts and uintatheres in the northern hemisphere.

The Pyrotheria, best known from the Deseadan *Pyrotherium*, were large mammals with long bodies, rather short and columnar legs, and large heads. The incisor teeth were specialized as short tusks, two pairs in the upper and one in the lower dentition; the cheek teeth were bilopho-dont. The skull suggests some inflation of the nasal area. Given this combination of characters, it is not surprising that some earlier students viewed the pyrotheres as related to the Proboscidea. Improved knowledge of pyrothere anatomy effectively disposed of the notion. The degree of convergence between the two orders is not very impressive. Nothing really convergent to a proboscidean has evolved anywhere. Early forms are poorly known; Hoffstetter (1970a) has described *Colombitherium*, which he places in a distinct family, from possible late Eocene beds in Colombia. The skull is known only in *Pyrotherium* and from but one specimen. Reexamination of this (Patterson and Maglio, in preparation) reveals enough in the way of notoungulate characters to suggest the possibility that pyrotheres may constitute another suborder of that remarkable group.

The ancestral stock of the enormously successful order Notoungulata underwent an early adaptational dichotomy into an ungulate series, the suborder Toxodonta (and possibly Pyrotheria also), and a rodent- and rabbit-like series, comprising the suborders Typotheria and Hegetotheria. One family, Notostylopidae, of the ancestral suborder Notioprogonia, also evolved in a rodent-like direction. Evolutionary trends among the rodent- and rabbit-like forms included enlargement of the anterior incisors, development of diastemata between these and the cheek teeth, acquisition by some of a sciurid-like zygomasseteric structure, retention of rabbit-like size generally (the approximately pig-sized mesotherids were the only fairly large forms), and attainment, in the pachyrukhine hegetotherids, of a hopping gait. The feet of the Santacruzian interatherids and hegetotherids are of a rather generalized, four-toed type, but those of *Miocochilius*, an interatherid from the La Venta fauna of Colombia, are highly specialized, the pes resembling that of tayassuid artiodactyls to a rather striking degree (Stirton, 1953b). Typotheres and hegetotheres were well adapted to their niches by Deseadan time and the groups then in existence do not appear to have been affected by the arrival of the rodents.

On the ungulate, or toxodont, side are a number of families descended from the generalized, highly variable, earlier Tertiary Isotemnidae, whose best known member is *Thomashuxleya* (Simpson, 1967). The Notohippidae show vague but far from precise resemblances to horses in the skull and the cropping incisor teeth. Homalodotheres converged chalicotheres, agriochoerids and the pantodont *Titanoides* in their possession of secondarily acquired claws in place of hoofs. These families and the lumbering leontiniids disappeared from the scene by or shortly after the close of the Miocene. It was otherwise with the toxondontids. Three subfamilies that arose from the ancestral Nesodontinae flourished during the Pliocene in the new environment afforded by the evolving pampas area (Pascual, 1965), and one of them, Toxodontinae, survived until the end of the Pleistocene. Alone among South American ungulates, the Toxodontidae include forms with small dermal horns resembling those of certain rhinoceroses. Members of the family also have a sharp, moderately projecting pair of lower incisors, again as in rhinoceroses with small horns. The incisors alone are effective weapons in these animals; used in conjunction with the horn they can be even more deadly. Glover (1955) quotes an observer, "T.S.," a civil servant in the India of the 1840's, who witnessed an encounter between an Indian rhinoceros and an elephant charged by it: ". . . the elephant immediately turned tail and bolted, but the rhinoceros was too quick for him, came up to the elephant in a few strides and with his tusks cut the fugitive so severely on the stern, nearly severing his tail, that he attempted to lie down under the pain. But the

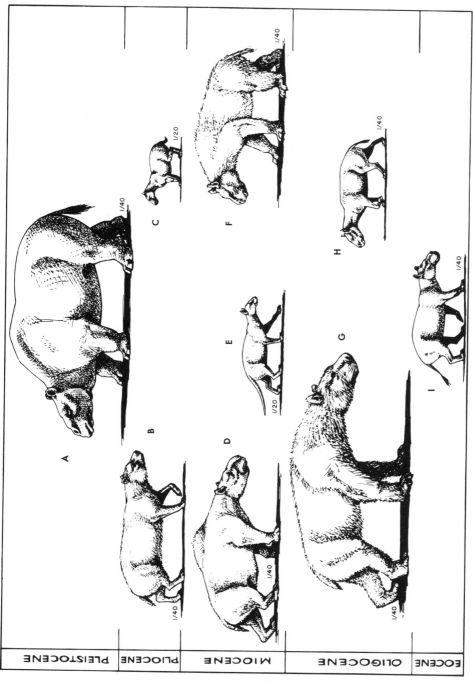

FIG. 11. RESTORATIONS OF NOTOUNGULATES

Pleistocene: A, Toxodon (Toxodontidae). Pliocene: B, Typotheriopsis (Mesotheriidae); C, Paedotherium (Hegetotheriidae). Miocene: D, Nesodon (Toxodontidae); E, Protypotherium (Interatheriidae); F, Homalodotherium (Homalodotheriidae). Oligocene: G, Scarrittia (Leontiniidae); H, Rhynchippus (Notohippidae). Eocene: Thomashuxleya (Isotemnidae). For Pyrotherium, possibly a member of this order, see Fig. 9, E.

PLEISTOCENE

PLIOCENE

MIOCENE

OLIGOCENE

EOCENE

rhinoceros was again too quick for him, and bringing his horn into play he introduced it under the elephant's flank; the horn tightened the skin and then with his frightful tusks he cut the poor animal so severely that his entrails came rolling about his legs as he fell . . ." p. 197. Those toxodontids similarly armed may have been relatively safe in the South America of bygone days.

The imposing roster of native South American ungulates may not be complete even now. The Divisadero Largo fauna includes fragmentary remains of *Acamana*, a large mammal that is probably an ungulate, but cannot on available evidence be referred to any known group (Simpson, Minoprio, and Patterson, 1962).

Bats

Bats have surely been present in South America since a very early time (Paleocene?) in the history of the order, and hence would qualify as ancient inhabitants, but as usual we know next to nothing of their history. The only positively determined Tertiary representative is *Notonycteris magdalenensis* Savage (1951), an extinct phyllostomatid closely related to *Vampyrum* and *Chrotopterus*, from the late Miocene of Colombia, Late Pleistocene finds, mostly from the Lagoa Santa caverns (Paula Couto, 1946), represent living forms.

Tropical South America, the Antilles, and Central America—the American Tropics—are remarkable for their possession of the richest microchiropteran fauna in the world. The area harbors over half (75) of the living genera (95) and over twice as many as occur in either Africa (24) or the Oriental Region (25) (data mainly from Simpson, 1945). The bats of the Antilles, which display degrees of endemicity at nearly all taxonomic levels (Table 4), suggest one possible factor that contributed to this richness. Bats can cross water barriers with a degree of ease unknown to terrestrial mammals, but the Antillean record conclusively demonstrates that they do not often do so. The several "strata" of endemicity shown by the West Indian forms suggests a long history of occasional successful colonizations by storm-transported bats at different times in the past. Throughout almost all of the Tertiary tropical America was sundered by a water-gap broad enough to serve as a barrier for Chiroptera. Storm transport with occasional establishment and subsequent separate evolution of southern forms in the north, and vice versa, would have contributed greatly to taxonomic diversity. This would also apply and with greater force, to birds (cf. Mayr, 1946, 1964). Tropical America has the richest bird fauna in the world.

The Later Waif Immigrants

Caviomorph rodents (Figs. 12, 13)

Despite incursions into the rodent adaptive zone by caenolestoids and small notoungulates—not, after all, incursions of a really major sort—the

TABLE 4

Endemicity in Antillean Chiroptera

Taxonomic Level	Endemic	Non-Endemic
Subfamily	1 endemic subfamily with 2 genera, 6 species (family present in North and South America)	
Genus	6 other endemic genera * with 19 species, 6 subspecies (subfamilies present in North and South America)	
Subgenus	2 endemic subgenera with 5 species (genus present in North and South America)	
Species	9 other endemic species with 4 subspecies (genera present in North and South America)	2 species also present in North and South America
	3 other endemic species with 7 subspecies (genera present in North America)	
Subspecies	8 other endemic subspecies (species present in North and South America)	1 subspecies also present in North and South America
	1 other endemic subspecies (species present in South America)	1 subspecies also present in South America

* Hall and Kelson (1959) and Hershkovitz (1958) are followed in recognizing Ariteus, Phyllops and Ardops as genera; Simpson (1954) regards them as subgenera of Stenoderma. Hershkovitz (1958) records the North American Centurio and the North and South American Micronycteris as occurring in the Antilles; neither is so listed by the other authors cited.

immigrant ancestors of what was to become the suborder Caviomorpha found a relatively clear field awaiting them. At the time of their first appearance in the Deseadan it is already possible, despite a pervasive underlying similarity, to recognize six of the living families and all four of the superfamilies (Wood and Patterson, 1959; Patterson and Wood, in preparation). This indicates an evolutionary pattern similar to that suggested by the ancient immigrant groups, namely, rapid early diversification followed by rapid initial evolution within niches. The ancestry of the group may well have lain in the primitive Holarctic family Paramyidae. The total absence of rodents in pre-Deseadan deposits, in which small mammals are not lacking, points to arrival of the ancestral caviomorphs at some time, probably early, in the interval between the mid-Eocene Mustersan and the early, although not earliest, Oligocene Deseadan. The view, sometimes put forward, that rodents were present in South America long prior to their first appearance in the record there strikes us as quite unrealistic. It has been suggested (Lavocat, 1969; Hoffstetter and Lavocat, 1970) that the caviomorphs are descended from the African phiomyids, the ancestral form or forms having reached South America by waif transport across a then much narrower South Atlantic Ocean. The evidence for this is tenuous (Wood and Patterson, 1970; Patterson and Wood, in preparation). The rodents from the Deseadan of Salla, Bolivia, which have been especially cited in this connection, belong to South American families—Echimyidae, Dasyproctidae and Dinomyidae—and do not show any compelling resemblances to the Phiomyidae.

The Deseadan octodontid *Platypittamys* is the most primitive caviomorph so far known. It is especially remarkable for the small size of the infraorbital foramen, which evidently did not transmit any part of the masseter muscle. Enlargement of the foramen and passage through it of the anterior portion of the deep masseter to the side of the face is characteristic of caviomorphs—and a point of resemblance to Old World "hystricomorphs." *Platypittamys* affords suggestive evidence that this specialization was acquired after the ancestral caviomorph stock had reached South America. It was persistently primitive in this feature since contemporary forms had very large infraorbital foramina. The early cavioids, particularly the Deseadan eocardiine *Chubutomys,* were remarkably advanced as regards acquisition of high-crowned cheek teeth.

Caviomorph diversification continued through the later Tertiary (Fig. 12). The climatic change that set in toward the end of the Miocene in the southern part of the continent appears to have affected the distribution of some forms and to have opened up possibilities to others, with rapid evolution evidently being involved in some cases. Octodontids, comparatively rare in the Oligocene and Miocene, increased markedly in the Pliocene. Pascual, Pisano and Ortega (1965) present evidence showing that the burrowing tuco-tucos, Ctenomyinae, may have descended from a Huayquerian species of the octodontine *Phtoramys*. The octodontid increase during the Pliocene in the Pampas region seems to have

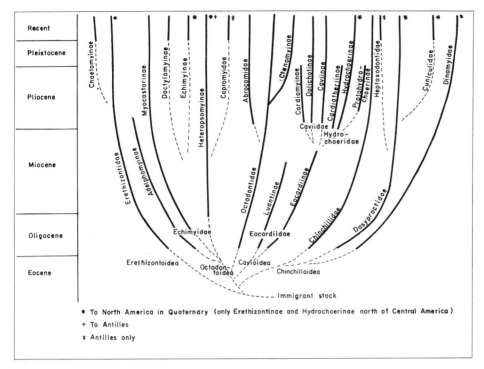

FIG. 12. CAVIOMORPH RODENTS: TIME RANGES AND PHYLOGENY

coincided with a retraction of Echimyidae in the area (Pascual, 1967); *Myocastor,* which we suspect (1968a) of being an echimyid, represents a lineage that did successfully adapt to the changed conditions. Dasyproctids and erethizontids, relatively abundant in the Santacruzean and earlier, are not at all or poorly represented in the Argentinian Pliocene, although the largest known erethizontid, *Neosteiromys,* occurred there. The cavoid group appears to have undergone a Pliocene radiation, the details of which are still being worked out. Chinchillids declined in diversity, only the ancestor of the living plains vizcacha occurring in Pliocene deposits. During the Pliocene some truly gigantic rodents existed. The largest dinomyid, *Telicomys,* was approximately as large as a small rhinoceros, and the somewhat cursorial hydrochoerid, *Protohydrochoerus,* attained the size of a tapir. The Caviomorpha still include more large forms than does any other major group of rodents, but these are a pale shadow of what has gone before.

Three groups of caviomorphs reached the Antilles as waif immigrants at some time or times in the mid-Tertiary. Two of these, the Capromyidae and the Heptaxodontidae, both so far unrecorded on the continent, have evolved there in isolation to family level. One caviomorph, *Erethizon,* has penetrated the boreal region of North America to the shores of the Arctic

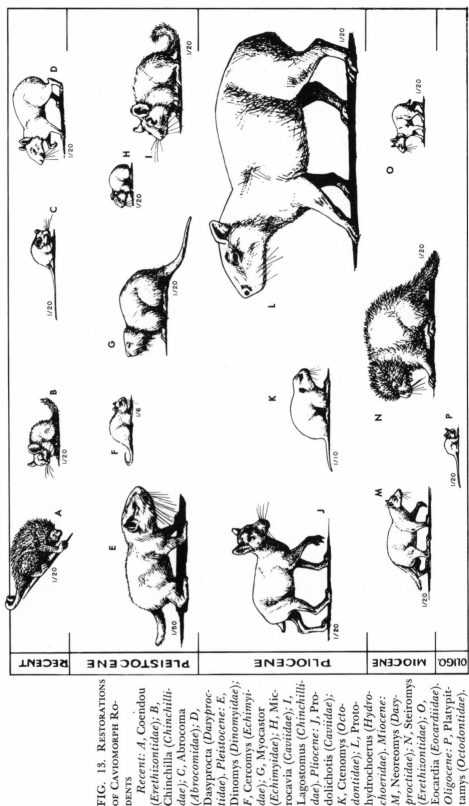

FIG. 13. RESTORATIONS
OF CAVIOMORPH RO-
DENTS

Recent: A, Coendou
(Erethizontidae); B,
Chinchilla *(Chinchilli-
dae); C,* Abrocoma
(Abrocomidae); D,
Dasyprocta *(Dasyproc-
tidae). Pleistocene: E,*
Dinomys *(Dinomyidae);
F,* Cercomys *(Echimyi-
dae); G,* Myocastor
(Echimyidae); H, Mic-
rocavia *(Caviidae); I,*
Lagostomus *(Chinchilli-
dae). Pliocene: J,* Pro-
dolichotis *(Caviidae);
K,* Ctenomys *(Octo-
dontidae); L,* Proto-
hydrochoerus *(Hydro-
choeridae). Miocene:
M,* Neoreomys *(Dasy-
proctidae); N,* Steiromys
(Erethizontidae); O,
Eocardia *(Eocardiidae).
Oligocene: P,* Platypit-
tamys *(Octodontidae).*

Ocean, an example of (geologically) rapid acquisition of cold temperature tolerance even more striking than that provided by *Dasypus*.

Platyrrhine Primates

The geologic range of South American primates, hitherto first recorded in the Colhuehuapian, has been extended by the welcome discovery of *Branisella* in the Deseadan of Bolivia (Hoffstetter, 1969). Two genera, *Homunculus* (Rusconi, 1935) and *Dolichocebus* (Kraglievich, 1951) are known from the Colhuehuapian. *Homunculus*, which survived through the Santacruzian, has generally been regarded as a cebid but Hershkovitz (1970) believes it to be "a highly evolved monkey of a primitive, non-cebid stock." *Dolichocebus* was regarded by Kraglievich, with reservation, as a callithricid; Hershkovitz believes it to be related to *Homunculus*. *Neosaimiri*, *Cebupithecia* (Stirton, 1951), and *Stirtonia* (Hershkovitz, 1970), all from the Colombian Fraisian, complete the roster of adequately known Tertiary forms. Stirton referred *Cebupithecia* to the Pithecinae; Hershkovitz regards both it and *Stirtonia* as representing subfamilies of their own. Various living forms have been recorded from the late Pleistocene Lagoa Santa caverns. One extinct genus, *Xenothrix* (Williams and Koopman, 1952), is known from Jamaica; Hershkovitz erects a family for it.

The impact of primates on the South American fauna is impossible to assess. The record gives no hint of any partially terrestrial offshoots such as have arisen among the Old World cercopithecids. In the arboreal sphere they may have displaced some unknown marsupials and edentates, and possibly they may have been one of the factors that in combination led to the remarkable adaptations of the tree sloths.

Gazin (1958) suggested that the ancestry of the platyrrhines might lie in the advanced prosimian Omomyidae (Hoffstetter remarks that *Branisella* seems to have been derived from this group). Since then the view that catarrhines also might have been derived from this family, via its Old World representatives, has been gaining ground among students of the order, although, as is the rule in work on this order, not without dissent.

It is interesting to reflect that two of the major radiations of primates that have come down to the present, the platyrrhine and the lemuroid, resulted from waif immigrations. Just conceivably, the catarrhine might fall into the same category. There is some rather suggestive evidence that Africa was isolated from Eurasia until some time in the later Oligocene (Patterson, 1965). As in South America, an indigenous group of rodents arrived in Africa as waif immigrants and omomyids might also have done so.

Procyonids of the *Cyonasua* Group

These, the latest of the waif invaders, evidently did not arrive early enough to have any major faunal impact. Only two genera are known,

TABLE 5

Hypsodonty (*) and hypselodonty (†) in South American ungulates

	Paleocene	Eocene	Oligocene	Miocene	Pliocene	Pleistocene
Litopterna						
Macraucheniidae					*	
Notoungulata						
Archaeohyracidae		*				
Hegetotheriidae			†			
Interatheriidae			†			
Mesotheriidae			†			
Notohippidae		*				
Toxodontidae						
Nesodontinae		*				
Toxodontinae					†	
Xotodontinae					†	
Haplodontheriinae					†	

Cyonasua, a rather generalized form, ranging from Huayquerian to Uquian, and *Chapalmalania,* Montehermosan. The latter is relatively gigantic, for a procyonid, and was originally described as a bear. New material enabled Kraglievich and Olizábal (1959) to make a correct familial assignment.

Some Features of the Tertiary Record

One or two striking features demand brief comment. One is the precocity shown by certain ungulates in the acquisition of high-crowned, or hypsodont, and rootless, or hypselodont, teeth (Table 5). Notohippids by mid-Eocene time were as advanced in this respect as equines were in the early Pliocene, about 30 million years later. By the Deseadan such teeth had been acquired by no fewer than six groups of ungulates, large and small, and this number stayed fairly constant through the Tertiary. Students of South America mammals are familiar with this situation. Some of them have commented on it, but the fact is not as widely known as it should be. Judged in the light of what was going on in the rest of the world it was extraordinary. Marked increase of tooth height in herbivores is generally believed to be an adaptation to nutritious but abrasive food, especially grasses. Impressed, we think overly impressed, by the excellent record of equid evolution in North America, some workers have dated the spread of grasslands from the Miocene, when horses began to acquire high-crowned teeth. The South American record suggests that grasses were present and in abundant quantity from very early in the Tertiary. Did South America differ in this respect from other continents? We doubt it, and prefer to suspect that ungulates elsewhere were slower to adapt to grass. Those artiodactyls capable of ruminating may have provided ex-

TABLE 6

The large native herbivores of South America

	Paleocene	Eocene	Oligocene	Miocene	Pliocene	Pleistocene
Ungulates						
Condylarthra						
Litopterna						
Macraucheniidae						
Trigonostylopoidea						
Astrapotheria						
Xenungulata						
Pyrotheria						
Notoungulata						
Mesotheriidae						
Isotemnidae						
Notohippidae						
Homalodotheriidae						
Leontiniidae						
Toxodontidae						
Inc. sed.						
Acamana						
Edentates						
Mylodontidae						
Megatheriidae						
Palaeopeltidae						
Glyptodontidae						
Dasypodidae						
Pampatheriinae						
Rodents						
Dinomyidae						
Hydrochoeridae						

ceptions. The existence of an evolutionary opportunity does not ensure that it will at once, or even soon, be seized. As a striking example of this, witness one South American group, the macrauchenids, whose record with regard to hypsodonty almost exactly parallels that of the horses.

Another remarkable feature is the variety of groups composing the "large herbivore" category (Table 6). In addition to seven ungulate orders, five families of edentates and even two of rodents have contributed to the total. For those accustomed to conditions in the northern continents, where "large herbivore," from the Oligocene on at least, means Artiodactyla and Perissodactyla supplemented by Proboscidea, this is somewhat unusual. The total number of families (12) is a little higher in the Deseadan than later because of the presence of a few archaic groups that made their last recorded appearance in that age. Thereafter, the number settled down around 10 until the end of the Tertiary. Seven continued well into or to the end of the Pleistocene. We stress this because there appears to be an impression that a notable reduction of large South American herbivores followed upon or shortly after establishment of the land connection with North America. By the time the bridge was established over half of the large herbivores were non-ungulates, and of these the large edentates survived but not the gigantic rodents, although the families to which they belonged did. Much of the large ungulate extinction took place during the later Tertiary and had, as far as the record goes, nothing to do with the faunal interchange.

THE LATE CENOZOIC FAUNAL INTERCHANGE WITH NORTH AMERICA

An interesting and unique faunal balance had been achieved toward the end of the Tertiary by the descendants of the ancient inhabitants and of the later waif immigrants. The South American fauna was greatly enriched and the old balance to some degree altered after the Bolivar geosyncline went out of existence and Panama was transformed from a jetty to a bridge in later Pliocene time. The long isolation of the continent was over, a permanent way was at last open for overland migration and a spectacular interchange of mammals began. The Neotropical mammalian fauna of Recent zoogeography is the product of this interchange and it is a very late event in earth history. No better example of a geologically sudden meeting of two radically different faunas exists in the geologic record. Documentation of it is fairly good, but a great deal remains to be learned. Our knowledge is very largely derived from localities north and south, respectively, of about latitude 25°; additional data for the Pliocene and earlier Pleistocene of the tropical areas are badly needed, particularly for North America.

Concerning all this, Hershkovitz has remarked: "Accounts of South American faunal histories have been based on the *assumption* that an Isthmian water gap nearly completely isolated North American mammals from South America . . . to the end of the Tertiary. The assumption was further complicated by the *notion* that establishment of a land connection between the continents near the end of the Pliocene initiated a wholesale interchange of faunas" (1969, p. 13, italics ours). The suggestion is conveyed that a dubious view is being foisted upon the scientific world merely by repetition. Statements such as "Simpson . . . has established as dogma . . ." (Hershkovitz, 1969, p. 14) and references to the "Simpson-Patterson time table" (Hershkovitz, 1966b, p. 744) purport to identify two of those concerned with the foisting and also to imply that there is something rather novel about the concept. However flattering such tributes may be to these authors they are quite undeserved; the idea was advanced before either of them was born.

How widespread such misapprehensions may be we do not know, but a brief review of the facts does seem desirable. The origin of the idea of a late land connection and extensive faunal interchange between the Americas can be rather precisely pinpointed. The original impetus came, perhaps, from malacology rather than paleontology. Von Ihering, working on freshwater mollusks, had noted major differences between the North and South American faunas, which led him to postulate a long separation and a recent connection of these continents. Thanks to the Ameghinos, the essential evidence for dating the connection, an outline of South American Tertiary history, was beginning to emerge and von Ihering felt able to conclude that the mammalian faunal interchange did not begin until the end of the Tertiary (von Ihering, 1890, p. 942). He then began a correspondence with Florentino Ameghino, in the course of which the latter stated, in a letter of June 24, 1891 (Torcelli, 1935, p. 141), "In short: only from the last part of the Miocene epoch [his dating of what is now the Montehermosan] do we see a mingling of faunas that places the communication between the two Americas beyond doubt." (A slightly modified version of this letter appeared as Ameghino, 1891.) By 1893, von Zittel, in his *Handbuch der Palaeontologie*, could say ". . . there was thus accomplished, toward the end of the Pliocene, one of the most remarkable migrations of faunas that geology has been able to record" (cf. our remarks, above!). By the early years of the 20th century the idea had become part of the common fund of paleontological information.

From the beginning, the concept was based on evidence and not on assumption. The extensive collections now available tell the same story as did the earlier and smaller ones; the working hypothesis of the early 1890's is now a well-tested theory. It is not to be overthrown by claims, which really are dogmatic assumptions, that Recent distributions provide a safer guide to history than does the factual evidence provided by an adequately documented fossil record. Hershkovitz (this volume, Chapter VII), rising blithely above such evidence, reasserts his earlier opinions. These can be taken seriously if and when fossils supporting them are found; in the meantime, we cannot do so.

The Extent of the Interchange

At the time the bridge came into existence 8 orders with 26 families were present in North America, and 7 orders with 26 families in South America (Table 7). Seven of the orders and 16 of the families of northern mammals participated to varying degrees in the interchange, as did 5 out of the 7 southern orders and 16 of their families. One of the northern orders, Insectivora, and 2 of the northern families, Soricidae and Heteromyidae, are confined to northwestern South America; neither is represented in the fossil record of the continent (another, Geomyidae, reaches eastern Panama but has not been recorded from adjacent Colombia).

[Two near misses in the fossil record deserve mention. Stirton and Gealey (1949) record remains of bison and mammoth in the late Pleistocene of El Salvador. Osborn (1929) described some tooth plate fragments of a mammoth said to have come from French Guiana. No other specimen having turned up anywhere in South America, the record has generally been discredited. The El Salvador find raises the faint possibility that a species of

TABLE 7

Interchange of mammalian families between South America and North America following establishment of the land connection

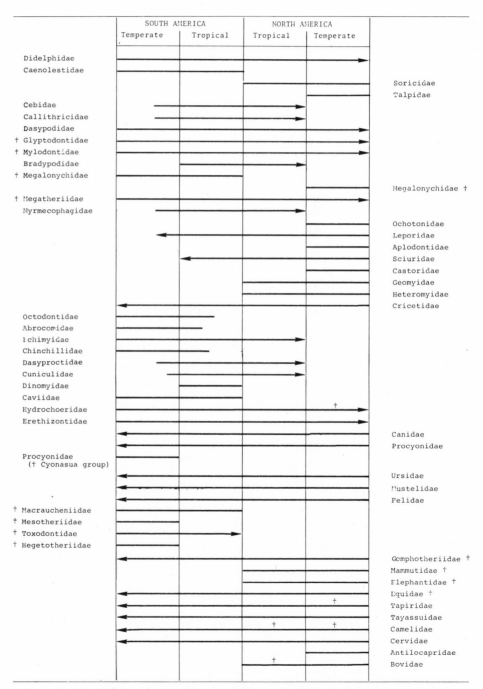

	SOUTH AMERICA		NORTH AMERICA	
	Temperate	Tropical	Tropical	Temperate

Didelphidae
Caenolestidae

Soricidae
Talpidae

Cebidae
Callithricidae
Dasypodidae
† Glyptodontidae
† Mylodontidae
Bradypodidae
† Megalonychidae

Megalonychidae †

† Megatheriidae
Myrmecophagidae

Ochotonidae
Leporidae
Aplodontidae
Sciuridae
Castoridae
Geomyidae
Heteromyidae
Cricetidae

Octodontidae
Abrocomidae
Echimyidae
Chinchillidae
Dasyproctidae
Cuniculidae
Dinomyidae
Caviidae
Hydrochoeridae
Erethizontidae

Canidae
Procyonidae

Procyonidae
(† Cyonasua group)

Ursidae
Mustelidae
Felidae

† Macraucheniidae
† Mesotheriidae
† Toxodontidae
† Hegetotheriidae

Gomphotheriidae †
Mammutidae †
Elephantidae †
Equidae †
Tapiridae
Tayassuidae
Camelidae
Cervidae
Antilocapridae
Bovidae

(†, *extinct—wholly, in the Americas, or in the region indicated*)

mammoth actually did extend its range for a brief period along the northern fringe of the continent.]

The remainder of the northern families penetrated South America deeply; genera of nearly all of them extend or extended beyond latitude 25° S. The southern immigrant families were less successful. Genera of only 7 of them now occur or are known to have occurred beyond latitude 25° N, the remainder are or were confined to tropical North America. Good reasons for this disparity exist. The Panama land bridge is deep in the tropics. Warm-adapted or warm-tolerant northern forms expanded southward into a very large tropical area, the southern forms into a much smaller one. North America during this time was subjected to periodic, large-scale continental glaciations with all their attendant effects; glaciation in South America was much less severe, being confined to the higher mountains and to southern Patagonia. The flanks of the Andean chain would have provided an excellent access route for southern North American forms not adapted to tropical forest habitats. In short, expansion of range was much easier for northern forms. Presumably the ranges of those South American immigrants (the majority) now confined to the North American tropics contracted and expanded as the continental ice sheets waxed and waned, but so far we have little evidence to document this. At the height of the glacial advances mean annual temperature may have been lowered by some 5° C in Central America. The world is now emerging from the latest of these advances and a number of present-day northern South American forms, of both northern and southern ancestry, may in the future expand northward into and beyond the Panamanian bridge (cf. Simpson, 1966).

With respect to the tempo of North American invasion (Table 8), the record shows a marked increase between the Montehermosan, in which only 5 northern genera—three cricetine rodents, a skunk and an extinct peccary have so far been recorded, and the Uquian in which 18 appear for the first time. This may reflect the real situation with some degree of accuracy, at least at the latitude of these faunas. Montehermosan faunas are rich and varied; they include over 80 genera of large, medium-sized and small mammals, and provide a good idea of South American faunal composition south of the tropical zone around the Pliocene-Pleistocene boundary. Uquian faunas, with some 50 genera, are not nearly as well known and it is rather likely that further collecting and discovery will increase the number of northern forms. Ten immigrant genera make their first appearance in the Ensenadan and 24 in the Lujanian. Eleven of the latter, however, are known only from the caves of Lagoa Santa, Brazil, and are today largely or wholly tropical. This suggests, as would be expected a priori, that many of the Recent tropical genera of northern ancestry may have been present in northern South America throughout much of Pleistocene time. In temperate North America the record shows a comparable if smaller increase in the number of southern forms: 2 in

TABLE 8

Time ranges of immigrant families in the Late Cenozoic of South America

	Montehermosan	Uquian	Ensenadan	Lujanian	Recent
Soricidae					1
Leporidae				1	1
Sciuridae				1	3
Heteromyidae					1
Cricetidae	4	5	5	6 10	40±
Canidae		2	2	5	6
Ursidae			1	1	1
Procyonidae (Pleistocene immigrants)			1	— — — 2	4
Mustelidae	1	3	4	4 6	7
Felidae		1	2	2	1
Gomphotheriidae		1	1	4	
Equidae		2	3	3	
Tapiridae		1	1	1	1
Tayassuidae	1	1	3	2	2
Camelidae		2	3	4	2
Cervidae		3	3	8	6

The numbers indicate genera recorded. A genus present in two or more Provincial Ages (see Table 1) is counted for each. A genus missing in an age but recorded in earlier and later ones is counted as present in that age. The late Lujanian records are for the Lagoa Santa caverns, Brazil.

the Blancan, 6 in the Irvingtonian, and 14 in the Rancholabrean (Hibbard, et al., 1965). These, however, were probably for the most part near their northern limits. The earlier Pleistocene deposits of southern North America, when and if made known, may well reveal a record more like that of South America with respect to numbers. As stressed above, emigration to South America was much easier than to temperate North America.

A large majority of the southern genera recorded in the Pleistocene of North America, 11 out of 15, are, or are known to have been, present in South America. Of the northern genera recorded in the southern continent a much smaller proportion, 24 out of 51, are, or are known to have been, present in North America. Hershkovitz (1966b) would interpret some at least of the genera so far unrecorded in the north as descendants of forms that reached South America in the Tertiary: "There is slight likelihood that the species and genera of cricetines, canids, procyonids, mustelids, deer, and others could have become peculiarly specialized for isolated niches in South America since the Pleistocene. The probability is even less that these species and genera invaded South America preadapted for distant and untried habitats and predestined to reach them after trials through hostile environments" (p. 746). It is possible that some of the northern genera, particularly of cricetines, may have evolved in the southern continent (as *Erethizon* may have done in the north; cf. White, 1968), but we agree with Hershkovitz to the extent of doubting that all, or even a large fraction, of those unknown in the north did so. Like him and others we regard tropical North America as a region of faunal differentiation throughout Tertiary time. Unlike him, we believe that it had no land connection to the south until the end of the Tertiary, and that it was there and not in unknown areas of South America that many of the Pleistocene immigrants or their ancestors lived. The Tertiary faunal record in both continents, we repeat, permits no other conclusion. Every one of the families mentioned by Hershkovitz in the passage just cited, with the exception of the immigrant procyonids, is represented in the early Pleistocene of Argentina. Had these families been present in the continent throughout the Pliocene it is inconceivable that no representatives of them would occur in Argentinian deposits of that age. Upon completion of the bridge the invaders that crossed it early would have had some 3 million years in which to become adapted to their various niches and habitats—and that was surely time enough. We now have supporting data. The tropical regions, to be sure, largely escaped the destructive effects of continental glaciations, but they did not come through the Pleistocene in undisturbed tranquility. Evidence is beginning to accumulate (it is summed up for South America by Vanzolini and Williams, 1970, pp. 92-108; see also Haffer, 1970, pp. 618-626; Vuilleumier, 1971) that the tropics underwent—no doubt repeatedly and, geologically speaking, very rapidly—wide-spread climatic fluctuations that resulted in expansions and contractions now of forest, now of non-forest. Under such conditions there is a likelihood that immigrants such as the cricetines, canids, and procyonids would have become specialized for niches within South America.

The number of South American genera of northern origin that have not hitherto been recorded in North America is likely to decrease in the future—and not solely as a result of new discoveries. All too much of the work done on the Pleistocene mammals of either continent has been carried out with little or no attention to forms occurring in the other. As examples of what may be expected when adequate intercontinental comparisons are made we cite Kraglievich's (1952) reference of *"Canis" texanus* to *Protocyon*, Kurtén's (1967) conclusion that *Arctotherium* and *Pararctotherium* constitute at most a subgenus of *Arctodus*, and Paula Couto's (1955) ranking of *Smilodon californicus* as a subspecies of *S. populator*. [*S. populator* is the species usually called *S. neogaeus;* Paula Couto has pointed out that *Hyaena neogaea* Lund 1839 is a *nomen nudum;* Churcher (1967) refers the Uquian *Smilodontidion* to *Smilodon;* if correct this is an earlier record for the genus than any in North America, but the possibility that *Smilodontidion* may actually be *Megantereon* merits consideration.]

Competition and Displacement Versus Enrichment

It seems to be the prevalent impression that following establishment of the Panamanian bridge the native South American fauna suffered a sharp decline due to inability to compete successfully with the invaders. The record bears this out only in part (Table 9). Direct competition there was, but mainly within one adaptive zone, the carnivore. The borhyaenid marsupials disappear at the end of Montehermosan time, displaced by placental carnivores. The more carnivorous didelphids, the Sparassocyninae (Reig, 1952), may also have been involved in this displacement. The bear-like procyonid *Chapalmalania* may have failed in competition with the immigrant *Arctodus*. (Hershkovitz, 1969, p. 65, states: "There is absolutely no evidence of mass extinctions or displacement of South American mammals as a result of supposed wholesale invasions by aggressive North American mammals during the Pliocene or early Pleistocene"; as regards the carnivore adaptive zone this is incorrect.)

Predation by the newly arriving carnivores may have contributed to some extinctions that occurred around the Pliocene-Pleistocene boundary. It is axiomatic that no predator can afford to exterminate its prey, but these predators were not in danger of doing that—they enjoyed an advantage: they were accompanying their usual prey and encountering new prey as they went. These they could have pursued to the point of great reduction or even extinction without seriously jeopardizing themselves. Furthermore, the new prey could have been at some disadvantage. Defensive and evasive behavior adapted to coping with the old set of predators, phororhacoid birds as well as marsupials, might have been less effective against the new. Proterotherids, hegetotherids, xotodontine and haplodontheriine toxodontids, and the gigantic rodents could have been affected by the new predation, and there may have been a connection between this and a decline in cavioid variety subsequent to the Montehermosan. It is at least permissible speculation.

Aside from the carnivorous forms, there was remarkably little carry-over of genera between Montehermosan and Uquian time (some 25%), which on the face of it might be interpreted as evidence of a considerable northern impact. Much of this turnover, however, may well be more apparent than real. About half of it was perhaps more or less "normal" for the time (both extinction and phyletic change were involved), to judge from what went on in other continents: e.g., in North America 38 per cent of the genera living during the Blancan have not been recorded in later deposits. For the rest, some is probably due to ignorance and accidents of sampling: Uquian and Ensenadan faunas are by no means as well known as Montehermosan, and smaller forms are poorly represented in them. Part may simply reflect artifacts of taxonomy: e.g., 8 genera of Montehermosan glyptodonts are followed by 10 different genera in later ages (glyptodonts lend themselves only too easily to the art of splitting). Whatever changes and readjustments may have gone on at lower

TABLE 9

Time ranges of native families in the Late Cenozoic of South America

	Montehermosan	Uquian	Ensenadan	Lujanian	Recent
Didelphidae	7	1	1	1　3	11
Borhyaenidae	5				
Caenolestidae	1				2
Argyrolagidae	2	1			
Cebidae				3	12
Callithricidae				1	1
Dasypodidae	10	7	6	10	8
Glyptodontidae	8	5	10	10	
Mylodontidae	4	5	4	4	
Megalonychidae	1			2	
Megatheriidae	2	2	1	4	
Bradypodidae					2
Myrmecophagidae	1			2	3
Erethizontidae				1	3
Octodontidae	8	3	1	1	6
Abrocomidae					1
Echimyidae	3	1	1	2　8	14
Caviidae	7	3	3	4	6
Hydrochoeridae	5	3	2	2	1
Dasyproctidae				2	3
Dinomyidae	1				1
Chinchillidae	1	2	1	1	3
Procyonidae (Cyonasua group)	2	1			
Proterotheriidae	3				
Macraucheniidae	2	2	2	1	
Mesotheriidae	1	1	1		
Hegetotheriidae	2	1			
Toxodontidae	4	1	1	2	

The numbers indicate genera recorded. A genus present in two or more Provincial Ages (see Table 1) is counted for each. A genus missing in an age but recorded in earlier and later ones is counted as present in that age. The late Lujanian records are for the Lagoa Santa caverns, Brazil.

taxonomic levels, a great majority of the families of native South American mammals present at the beginning of the interchange was represented throughout much or all of the Pleistocene, 79 per cent surviving until the end of the epoch. The major extinctions, mostly involving the larger forms and affecting both natives and immigrants, took place at that time (see further below, p. 298).

Following establishment of the bridge, then, there was considerably more intermixture and enrichment than there was competition and displacement. Two of the orders involved in the interchange, Edentata and Carnivora, exemplify these extremes. Every one of the five families of carnivores reached South America to the complete discomfiture of their southern vicars. Six out of the seven edentate families entered North America (there is at present no evidence that megalonychids participated in the Pleistocene interchange); members of four of these six families went on into the temperate zone, enriching the North American fauna without, apparently, causing any major disturbance in the previous balance. (The impact of the South American invasion on the late Pliocene and early Pleistocene mammals of tropical North America is of course wholly unknown. It is tempting to dream of lingering prosimians and palaeanodonts being displaced there by platyrrhines and xenarthrans.)

Each of these two orders, Edentata and Carnivora, illustrates one of two principal requirements for successful penetration into newly accessible regions. Continental faunas that have been evolving for millions of years are not wide open to invaders, but there will be gaps and chinks within them, portions of the environment not fully, perhaps not at all, exploited; some of their faunal elements may be less or more effective in the exploitation of niches, or even of a zone, than similarly adapted forms living elsewhere. When two such faunas become joined via a land connection those elements of each that are able to move into the gaps and chinks of the other, or are the better adapted to exploit zones or niches, will readily be able to invade. Patterson and Pascual (1963) have distinguished these as insinuators and competitors.

The other participants in the interchange, looked at in this light, appear to fall mainly into the insinuator category. Opossums, primates, echimyids, agoutis and pacas, capybaras, and porcupines have no discernible ecological vicars among northern forms; *Mixotoxodon* was not basically like any northern ungulate. Rabbits, among the northerners, resemble the pachyrukhine hegetotherids to a very considerable degree, but there is as yet no evidence that the two groups ever came into contact. On the record, *Sylvilagus* was a late comer that may have arrived after the extinction of the hegetotheres; one of its two South American species, *S. floridanus*, certainly appears to have been a very late arrival. *S. brasiliensis* seems not to invade the area of the rather hare-like *Dolichotis* (Hershkovitz, Chapter VII). Nothing like a squirrel had evolved in South America. Cricetines are the most successful of the northern invaders but their impact on the southern fauna is not easy to assess. Being small forms they do not appear to have affected the larger southern rodents in any major way. Among the smaller, the echimyids are presently in flourishing condition but octodontids may have suffered reduction in numbers and restriction of range. They were numerous during the Montehermosan (8 gen.) in what is now the Province of Buenos Aires, a region in which they are today only represented marginally by *Ctenomys*, whereas 8 genera of cricetines live there. Competition with the smaller caviids does not seem likely. The disappearance of caenolestines from the fossil record in post-Montehermosan time nearly coincides with the appearance of cricetines, and this may not be fortuitous (Pascual and Herrera, in prep.). On the whole, however, cricetines seem to have been predominantly insinuators. As such they enriched the South American fauna to a remarkable extent. As pointed out above (p. 284), the southern ungulate groups were much reduced in variety by the end of the Tertiary, only a few being in existence at the time of the connection. With the exception of the Proterotheriidae, these survived well into or throughout the Pleistocene. Proterotherids and deer might have competed to some extent, but this is highly conjectural. The vaguely camel-like macrauchenids and the invading camels would offhand seem the most likely competitors, yet the record does not bear the possibility out: macrauchenids and large species of *Palaeolama* coexisted. The invaders did not include anything closely resembling *Mesotherium* or the toxodontids (*Mixotoxodon* went north to Central America) and nothing in South America at the time resembled mastodonts, horses, tapirs or peccaries. Glyptodonts and ground sloths, the other large southern herbivores, were not affected by the interchange; nothing remotely like them arrived. The impression conveyed is that nearly all the northern ungulates expanded southward into ecological vacua. In fact this seems to have been the case for nearly all the noncarnivorous groups involved, both northern and southern. The degree to which these two great and long-separated faunas were open to penetration is remarkable, but not too surprising. In long-separated faunas most of the ecological analogues that evolve in each, among herbivores at least, will not be precisely similar or exploit the environment in precisely the same ways. Arrival of insinuators when isolation is ended will in general lead mainly to marginal competition and narrowing of niches.

Evolution of the northern invaders within South America is a subject that we cannot pursue here. Data essential to an understanding of it are largely lacking. As stated above, progress in this field will depend largely on studies of North American late Tertiary and early Pleistocene groups carried out with an eye to the ancestry of the southern emigrants, as well as on new discoveries in southern North America. Modern revisions of northern immigrant families are badly needed. This has been done for the mastodonts by Simpson and Paula Couto (1957) who find that there are three valid southern genera, *Stegomastodon*, *Cuvieronius* and *Haplomastodon* (a fourth, *Notiomastodon*, is of very dubious status), belonging to one subfamily, Anancinae, of the Gomphotheriidae. Generic differentiation was evidently accomplished before entry into South America, which was probably true of nearly all the invading families. The most likely exception is that most successful of all the immigrant groups, the cricetines.

The Cricetine Rodents

Within South America this subfamily is today represented by about 40 genera with some 180 species. These numbers may be reduced to some extent by future revisionary work, but the total will still remain extremely impressive. Practically all belong to one division of the subfamily that is characterized, although with exceptions, by possession of a complex penis (Hershkovitz, 1966a). This array is subdivided by him into a number of generic groups, at least 8, of which 5 are rather sparsely represented in tropical and 2 in temperate North America.

Hershkovitz (1966b) does not believe that all this differentiation went on in South America since the end of the Tertiary, and in this he is undoubtedly right. He does believe, however, that it took place in Tertiary South America from ancestors resembling the living Central American genera *Nyctomys* and *Otonyctomys* that reached the continent in the Miocene. North American representatives, *Oryzomys* and *Sigmodon*, are regarded as Pliocene waif immigrants from South America with other, and minor, expansions northward taking place after completion of the bridge (p. 732-739).

All this would be plausible if knowledge of the past were a blank. As matters stand we can only repeat once again that the fossil record is in contradiction. Had something like *Oryzomys* inhabited South America in the Miocene, cricetines would have appeared in deposits of that age and later, the caviomorphs would not have had things all their own way during the later Tertiary, and cricetine radiation on the continent would surely have gone beyond the generic group stage (cf. Koopman, 1964). Hershkovitz (1969, p. 22) believes that the effectiveness of the Bolivar gap as a barrier to cricetines is ". . . seriously compromised by the Patterson and Pascual premise that all other Tertiary mammals of South America and the West Indies are of waif origin." This is not so. The very small number of mammals that reached South America over the water gap during seventy million years is eloquent testimony to its effectiveness as a barrier. On the evidence, cricetines were not among those few mammals that succeeded in crossing it. In waif transport—the sweepstakes route —the odds against a successful landfall are heavy indeed. Such later Tertiary Central American cricetines as may have been carried out from land on natural rafts presumably perished at sea before reaching South America.

An hypothesis of cricetid distribution in the Americas that does agree with the fossil record is required, however, and one is offered here. Table 10 shows in condensed form the distribution of the living genera and

TABLE 10

Summary of American cricetid distribution

	North America	Central America	South America
Microtinae	9 (36)	1 (5)	—
Cricetinae (simple penis)	5 (43)	11 (81)	2 (2)
Cricetinae (complex penis)	2 (5)	5 (33)	36 (183)

Genera and species occurring in more than one area are counted in each

species. This illustrates the well-known fact that microtines are primarily northern (the species of *Microtus* in Central America are relicts that occur at high elevations) and that the simple penis cricetines are more northern in their distribution than the complex penis ones. Some form of temperature control seems to be involved here. Turning to consideration of the details (Tables 11, 12; data from Hall and Kelson, 1959; Cabrera, 1961; Hershkovitz, 1958, 1966a; Handley, 1966), this possibility receives further support. Each major cricetid group has at least one wide-ranging genus or species that exists over a broad climatic spectrum. These exceptions, and probable past ones which may have furthered cricetine diversification, do not obscure the general pattern, however. The simple penis cricetines appear in the main to be temperate to subtropical; a number of them now extend into the North American tropics, but it is noteworthy, to judge from the data compiled by Hall and Kelson, that a great many of these occur at higher elevations there. The complex penis forms are predominantly tropical, but with Andean elements, some of which extend to the extremity of the South American continent, where they have spread over Patagonia.

These distributions are at least broadly interpretable, it seems to us, in terms of the cooling of the northern hemisphere in the late Cenozoic. The microtines, to judge from the record, are a comparatively recent group, adapted mainly to boreal and cold temperate climates. With each glacial advance microtines would shift south impinging on simple penis cricetines and these in turn on complex penis cricetines. With each glacial retreat the reverse process would go on, with isolated populations left behind here and there. If temperatures continue to rise, a number of the present South American complex penis cricetines whose ranges extend north of the equator may well re-enter Central America.

Coming at the time it did, the land connection provided the complex penis cricetines with an escape hatch as well as a gateway to a great evolutionary opportunity. With a nearly clear field before them they began an evolutionary burst in South America that has resulted in the remarkable number of species in the present fauna. Adequate time and ecological opportunity for rapid evolution at the species level has been available. The question is: could the genera or a majority of them have been in

TABLE 11

Latitudinal ranges of American Cricetidae (complex penis)

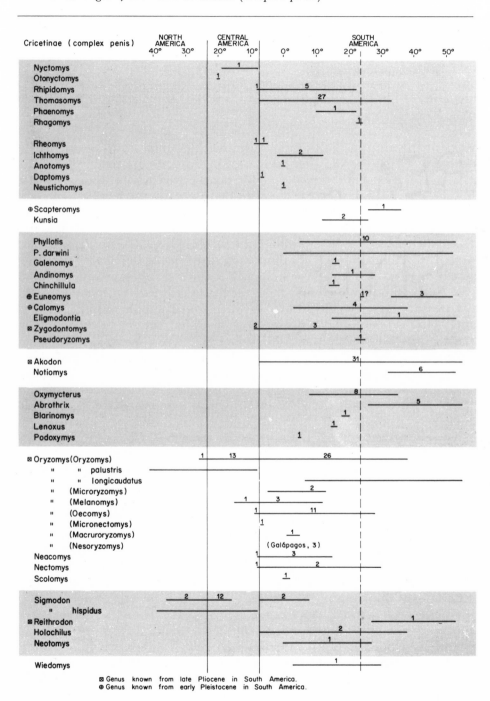

Cricetinae (complex penis)	NORTH AMERICA		CENTRAL AMERICA				SOUTH AMERICA			
	40°	30°	20°	10°	0°	10°	20°	30°	40°	50°
Nyctomys				1						
Otonyctomys			1							
Rhipidomys				1	5					
Thomasomys					27					
Phaenomys						1				
Rhagomys							1			
Rheomys			1	1						
Ichthomys					2					
Anotomys					1					
Daptomys				1						
Neustichomys					1					
⊕ Scapteromys								1		
Kunsia						2				
Phyllotis							10			
P. darwini										
Galenomys						1				
Andinomys							1			
Chinchillula						1				
⊕ Euneomys							1?	3		
⊕ Calomys						4				
Eligmodontia								1		
⊠ Zygodontomys			2		3					
Pseudoryzomys							1			
⊠ Akodon							31			
Notiomys								6		
Oxymycterus							8			
Abrothrix								5		
Blarinomys							1			
Lenoxus						1				
Podoxymys					1					
⊠ Oryzomys (Oryzomys)	1	13				26				
" " palustris										
" " longicaudatus						2				
" (Microryzomys)				1	3					
" (Melanomys)				1		11				
" (Oecomys)			1							
" (Micronectomys)										
" (Macruroryzomys)					1					
" (Nesoryzomys)			(Galápagos, 3)							
Neacomys			1	3						
Nectomys			1		2					
Scolomys				1						
Sigmodon		2	12		2					
" hispidus										
⊠ Reithrodon								1		
Holochilus						2				
Neotomys						1				
Wiedomys						1				

⊠ Genus known from late Pliocene in South America.
⊕ Genus known from early Pleistocene in South America.

TABLE 12

Latitudinal ranges of American Cricetidae (simple penis)

Cricetinae (simple penis)	80°	70°	60°	NORTH AMERICA 50°	40°	30°	CENTRAL AMERICA 20°	10°	SOUTH AMERICA 0°
Peromyscines									
Peromyscus (Peromyscus)				9			30		?
" " maniculatus									
" (Haplomylus)					11		1		
" (Podomys)						1			
" (Megadontomys)								4	?
" (Ochrotomys)					1				
Reithrodontomys				6			14		1
Baiomys						1	2		
Onychomys					2		2		
Scotinomys								4	
Neotomodon							1		
Neotomyines									
Neotoma				12			14		
Nelsonia							1		
Xenomys							1		
Ototylomys								3	
Tylomys								5	1
Microtinae									
Microtus (Microtus)				11			2		
" (Aulacomys)				1					
" (Chilotus)				1					
" (Stenocranius)			2						
" (Pitymys)					1		1		
" (Pedomys)					1	1			
" (Orthriomys)							1		
" (Herpetomys)							1		
Lagurus					1				
Phenacomys				4					
Neofiber						1			
Ondatra					2				
Synaptomys					2				
Clethrionomys				3					
Lemmus			2						
Dicrostonyx		3							

existence in North America at the end of the Tertiary? None of them has been found as fossils there with the exception of *Sigmodon* and *Oryzomys,* the only members of the group whose ranges are known to extend to the north temperate zone. In view of our virtually complete ignorance of the past microfauna of Central America this is not surprising. Records of *Zygodontomys, Akodon, Oryzomys* and *Reithrodon* in the Montehermosan and of *Scapteromys, Euneomys,* and *Calomys* in the Uquian (Hershkovitz, 1969, p. 22) suggest that these at least were by then differentiated in the north. Five of the generic groups recognized by Hershkovitz are represented by them. We suspect that a majority of the genera did arise in tropical North America. The region is a diverse one topographically and ecologically; 17 genera of cricetids live there today, represented, at any rate on paper, by 119 species. In pre-Pleistocene time when the tropical area was more extensive and the cricetine fauna predominantly a complex penis one the number of genera in the region could well have been considerably higher. Among them no doubt were some adapted to or tolerant of the higher elevations. While others were taking the forest road south these would have found the flanks of the Andean chain a ready highway and also an area for differentiation, in some cases to the generic level.

Hershkovitz (1969, p. 22) comments that our Table 11 (1968b) ". . . indicates that all South American cricetines had already pervaded South America by the time the intercontinental land bridge came into existence." It does nothing of the sort, of course; it merely shows the present latitudinal distribution of the complex penis cricetines and indicates the genera recorded in Montehermosan and Uquian deposits. These records suggest, correctly we think, that the spread of cricetines following establishment of the bridge was rapid. Noting the presence of these forms in late Pliocene deposits, Hershkovitz goes on to remark that: "In contrast, such cricetines are absent in known Middle American fossil deposits of any age." Since no identifiable rodent remains at all are known from the later Tertiary of Central America this piece of negative evidence has no significance whatever. Host-ectoparasite data have been interpreted by Wenzel and Tipton (1966) as pointing to an early arrival of cricetines in South America. The validity of the interpretation really depends on whether these rodents arrived before the bridge came into existence—and there is no direct evidence that they did.

Late Pleistocene Extinction

The dramatic extinctions, involving whole groups of large mammals of both northern and southern ancestry (Tables 5, 6) and practically confined to them, took place at the end of Pleistocene time. In various other parts of the world the same phenomenon occurs. Attention is once again being focused on this interesting fact, which has various implications (Deevey, 1967). A symposium volume on the subject has recently appeared, which should be consulted in this connection (Martin and Wright, 1967). The contributors to the volume are divided in their views, which fall into three main categories: man was the major factor in these extinctions; he was only one contributing factor; he was a very minor factor with climatic change playing the major role. South America serves as a test of these hypotheses. It was a part of the world in which the effects of Pleistocene glaciation were not as disruptive as in the northern hemisphere and to which man came very late.

The evidence would seem to indicate that climatic change can be ruled out as the primary cause, although various authors (e.g., Hoffstetter, 1954b) have so considered it. Guilday, for example, (1967, p. 133-134) suggests "near elimination of the Pampas as a major habitat" at the end of the Pleistocene, but we do not know of any good evidence for this, nor does he cite any. Even if such had happened, the scattered records show that large mammals of the same groups as those occurring in the Pampean region were widely spread over the northern and far larger part of South America. It is rather unlikely that the after-effects of the last glaciation would have differed in any major way from those followed upon earlier ones, and the large mammals survived these, whatever they may have been, with no marked diminution in variety. However, any late Pleistocene forms whose ranges had become restricted due to climatic fluctuations (p. 289) would have been vulnerable to a new and deadly predator.

We are driven, it seems, to consider man as a major, if not the major, factor. Whatever reluctance may be felt to attribute the extinction of horses to man (Martin, 1967) can hardly be carried over to such forms as glyptodonts and ground sloths. The latter, even though slow moving, were formidable animals, well armed with long claws. If their defensive behavior resembled that of anteaters, as it may have done, adults could easily have held their own against normal predators. Large and heavy adult glyptodonts had only to squat in order to render themselves safe from harm. Yet both would have been highly vulnerable to human hunters armed with projectiles, long-shafted spears and a capacity for team work. The extinction even of some of the larger predators may have been directly hastened by man. Extinction of large felines is not everywhere associated with the spread of advancing human cultures, but that of the rather slower, hence more vulnerable, sabertooth cats is. Conceivably, a prestige factor could have operated here. To adorn his neck with sabertooth canines may have been the ambition of many a young hunter (cf. Masai and lion, Turkana and leopard, etc.).

Radiocarbon dating in South America is still in its infancy. No such imposing body of data as that presented by Martin (1967) for North America is available. Information is beginning to come in, however. Human artifacts have been reported from Pikimachay Cave in highland Peru in association with megatherid and *Equus* remains from $19,620 \pm 3000$ to $14,170 \pm 180$ B. P. (MacNeish, Berger and Protsch, 1970; MacNeish, Nelken-Turner and Cook, 1970). Montané (1968) has recorded mastodont, *Hippidion*?, and *Antifer* in association with artifacts in central Chile at 11,380 B. P. These finds extend the earlier, undated record of horses and mylodontid sloths associated with artifacts in southern Chile (Bird and Bird, 1937) and Ubbelohde-Doering's report (1959) of artifacts, *Neochoerus* and *Pampatherium* (determinations by Dehm) in northern Peru. As more early archaeological sites are discovered and dates established, a picture broadly comparable to that for North America will surely emerge.

The late Pleistocene extinction left South America shorn of nearly all its really large mammals, but with a substantial fraction of old inhabitant and waif immigrant stock remaining. Marsupials are well represented by didelphids, and the few caenolestines serve as reminders of past diversity. Anteaters and tree sloths are still with us, and armadillos are in fairly flourishing condition. Caviomorph rodents are in good state and primates are doing rather well. Only the southern ungulates are entirely gone, and with them have passed at least half of the immigrants. Natives and invaders are now rather evenly balanced at the familial and generic levels—16 native families and approximately 80 genera against 14 immigrant families and approximately 80 genera, with cricetines contributing about half of the northern total.

SUMMARY

Of the three southern continents, South America was more isolated during the Tertiary than Africa, less isolated than Australia. Its record of Cenozoic mammalian life is better than that of either. This record suggests that around the beginning of the Cenozoic, South America received a few waif immigrants—marsupials, edentates, ungulates—that reached the continent across a water barrier. The source area was probably Central America, which formed a tropical North American peninsula until near the end of Tertiary time. A few later waif immigrants reached the continent across the water barrier—rodents and primates in the later part of the Eocene, and an extinct group of procyonids perhaps in the later Miocene. From the descendants of these few immigrants a balanced fauna evolved that was strikingly different in composition from those of other continents. The evolution of the various groups composing it is briefly presented and discussed. At the end of the Tertiary the isolation of the continent ended with the establishment of the Isthmus of Panama. Large scale faunal interchange between North and South America then began and is still going on. The Neotropical mammalian fauna dates from this time. Most of the northern participants in the interchange penetrated deeply into South America. The southern participants, advancing into a continent subjected to periodic continental glaciations, were less successful, the majority of them not penetrating beyond the tropical area. Competition and extinction during the faunal interchange went on mainly among the carnivores, the southern marsupials being replaced by the northern placentals. The spectacular extinctions, involving mainly large mammals of both northern and southern ancestry, came at the end of the Pleistocene; the arrival of man was probably a major factor.

ACKNOWLEDGMENTS

We wish to express our thanks to Miss Margaret Estey for the restorations, Mr. Laszlo Mészöly and Mr. Kazuna Tanaka for the drafting of the tables, Mrs. B. Gail Browne and Miss Julia Baldwin for their struggles with manuscript, and Professor Glenn L. Jepsen for the opportunity to examine material from the Deseadan of Bolivia.

LITERATURE CITED

(The more important earlier literature, to 1940, is given in Simpson, 1945.)

ALVAREZ, T. 1965. Catálago paleomastozoológico mexicano. *Inst. Nac. Antrop. Hist., Dept. Prehist., Pub.* 17: 1-70.

AMEGHINO, F. 1891. Determinación de algunos jalones para la restauración de las antiguas conexiones del continente sudamericano. *Rev. Argent. Hist. Nat.,* 1: 282-288.

BAIRD, D., M. WOODBURNE, and A. LAWRENCE. 1966. [Notice of *"Pyrotherium* and other mammals from Bolivia."] *Soc. Vert. Paleontol. News Bull.,* No. 77: 18.

BIRD, J. and M. BIRD. 1937. Human artifacts in association with horse and sloth bones in southern South America. *Science,* 86: 36-37.

BRODKORB, P. 1963. A giant flightless bird from the Pleistocene of Florida. *Auk,* 8: 111-115.

BRUNDIN, L. 1966. Transantarctic relationships and their significance, as evidenced by chironomid midges with a monograph of the subfamilies Podonominae and Aphroteniinae and the austral Heptagyiae. *Kungl. Svenska Vetensk. Handl.,* (4) 11: 1-472.

CABRERA, A. 1961. Catálago de los mamíferos de America del Sur. II. *Rev. Museo Argent. Cienc. Natur.,* 4: i-xxii, 309-732.

CHURCHER, C. S. 1967. *Smilodon neogaeus* en las barrancas costeras de Mar del Plata, Provincia de Buenos Aires. *Pub. Museo Munic. Cienc. Natur. Mar del Plata,* 1(8): 245-262.

CLEMENS, W. A. 1966. Fossil mammals of the type Lance formation, Wyoming. *Univ. Calif. Publ. Geol. Sci.,* 62: 1-122.

DARLINGTON, P. J., JR. 1957. *Zoogeography: The Geographical Distribution of Animals.* 675 p. John Wiley, New York.

DEEVEY, E. S. 1967. Introduction. In P. S. Martin and H. E. Wright (eds.), *Pleistocene Extinctions. The Search for a Cause,* p. 63-72. Yale Univ. Press, New Haven, Conn.

DURHAM, J. W., A. R. V. ARELLANO, and J. H. PECK. 1955. Evidence for no Cenozoic Isthmus of Tehuantepec seaway. *Bull. Geol. Soc. Am.,* 66: 977-992.

EMRY, R. J. 1970. A North American Oligocene pangolin and other additions to the Pholidota. *Bull. Am. Museum Natur. Hist.,* 142: 455-510.

EVERNDEN, J. F., D. E. SAVAGE, G. H. CURTIS, and G. T. JAMES. 1964. Potassium-argon dates and the Cenozoic mammalian chronology of North America. *Am. J. Sci.,* 262: 145-198.

FRIES, C. J., C. W. HIBBARD, and D. H. DUNKLE. 1955. Early Cenozoic vertebrates in the Red Conglomerate at Guanajuato, Mexico. *Smithson. Misc. Coll.,* 123: 1-25.

GAZIN, C. L. 1957. Exploration for the remains of giant ground sloths in Panama. *Smithson. Rept.* 1956: 341-354.

———. 1958. A review of the Middle and Upper Eocene primates of North America. *Smithson. Misc. Coll.,* 136(1): 1-112.

GLOVER, R. 1955. Weapons of the great Indian rhinoceros. *Oryx,* 3: 197.

GRAMBAST, L., M. MARTINEZ, M. MATTAUER, and L. THALER. 1967. *Perutherium altiplanense, nov. gen., nov. sp.,* premier mammifère Mesozoique de l'Amérique du Sud. *Comptes Rend. Acad. Sci (Paris),* 264: 707-710.

GUILDAY, J. E. 1967. Differential extinction during late Pleistocene and Recent times. In P. S. Martin and H. E. Wright (eds.), *Pleistocene Extinctions. The Search for a Cause,* p. 120-140. Yale Univ. Press, New Haven, Conn.

HAFFER, J. 1970. Geologic climatic history and zoogeographic significance of the Urabá region in northwestern Colombia. *Caldasia,* 10: 603-636.

HALL, E. R., and K. R. KELSON. 1959. *The Mammals of North America. Vol. 1, Marsupialia to Rodentia, Heteromyidae; Vol. 2, Rodentia, Castoridae to Artiodactyla.* The Ronald Press Co., New York.

HANDLEY, C. O. 1966. Checklist of the mammals of Panama. In R. L. Wenzel and V. J. Tipton (eds.) *Ectoparasites of Panama,* p. 753-795. Field Museum of Natural History, Chicago.

HARRINGTON, H. J. 1962. Paleogeographic development of South America. *Bull. Am. Assoc. Petrol. Geol.,* 46: 1773-1814.

HERRERO-DUCLOUX, A. 1963. The Andes of western Argentina. *Am. Assoc. Petrol. Geol. Mem.,* 2: 16-28.

HERSHKOVITZ, P. 1958. A geographic classification of neotropical mammals. *Fieldiana: Zool.,* 36: 579-620.

———. 1966a. South American swamp and fossorial rats of the scapteromyine group (Cricetinae, Muridae) with comments on the glans penis in murid taxonomy. *Z. Säugetierk.,* 31: 81-149.

———. 1966b. Mice, land bridges and Latin American faunal interchange. In R. L. Wenzel and V. J. Tipton (eds.), *Ectoparasites of Panama,* p. 725-751. Field Museum of Natural History, Chicago.

———. 1969. The Recent mammals of the Neotropical Region: a zoogeographic and ecological review. *Quart. Rev. Biol.,* 44: 1-70.

———. 1970. Notes on Tertiary platyrrhine monkeys and description of a new genus from the late Miocene of Colombia. *Folia Primatol.,* 12: 1-37.

HIBBARD, C. W., C. E. RAY, D. E. SAVAGE, D. W. TAYLOR, and J. E. GUILDAY. 1965. Quaternary mammals of North America. In H. E. Wright and D. G. Fray (eds.), *The Quaternary of the United States,* p. 509-525. Princeton Univ. Press, Princeton, N. J.

HOFFSTETTER, R. 1952. Les mammifères pleistocènes de la République de l'Equateur. *Mém. Soc. Géol. Fr., n.s.,* 31: 1-391.

———. 1954a. Les mammifères fossiles de l'Amérique du Sud et la biogéographie. *Rev. Gen. Sci.,* 61: 11-12.

———. 1954b. Les gravigrades cuirassés du Déséadan de Patagonie (note préliminaire). *Mammalia,* 18: 159-169.

———. 1954c. Phylogénie des édentés xénarthres. *Bull. Muséum Nat. Hist. Natur.* (2), 26: 433-438.

———. 1956. Contribution à l'étude des Orophodontoidea, gravigrades cuirassés de la Patagonie. *Ann. Paléontol.,* 42: 27-64.

———. 1968a. Un gisement de mammifères deseadiens (Oligocène inférieur) en Bolivie. *Comptes Rend. Acad. Sci. (Paris),* 267: 1095-1097.

———. 1968b. Ñuapua, un gisement de vertébrés Pleistocène dans le Chaco bolivien. *Bull. Muséum Nat. Hist. Natur.,* 40: 823-836.

———. 1969. Un primate de l'Oligocène inférieur Sud-Américain: *Branisella boliviana* gen. et sp. nov. *Comptes Rend. Acad. Sci. (Paris),* 269: 434-437.

———. 1970a. *Colombitherium tolimense,* pyrothérien nouveau de la formation Guandalay (Colombie). *Ann. Paléontol.,* 56: 149-169.

———. 1970b. Radiation initiale des mammifères placentaires et biogéographie. *Comptes Rend. Acad. Sci. (Paris),* 270: 3027-3030.

———. 1970c. L'histoire biogéographique des marsupiaux et la dichotomie marsupiaux—placentaires. *Comptes Rend. Acad. Sci. (Paris),* 271: 388-391.

HOFFSTETTER, R. and R. LAVOCAT. 1970. Découverte dans le Déséadien de Bolivie de genres pentalophodontes appuyant les affinités africaines des rongeurs caviomorphes. *Comptes Rend. Acad. Sci. (Paris),* 271: 172-175.

JACOBS, C., H. BÜRGL, and D. L. CONLEY. 1963. Backbone of Colombia. *Am. Assoc. Petrol. Geol. Mem.,* 2: 62-72.

KOOPMAN, K. F. 1964. Review of Hershkovitz, 1962, Evolution of Neotropical cricetine rodents with special reference to the phyllotine group. *Am. Mid. Natur.,* 71: 255-256.

KRAGLIEVICH, J. L. 1951. Contribuciónes al conocimiento de los Primates fósiles de la Patagonie. I. Diagnosis previa de un nuevo primate fósil del Oligoceno superior (Colhuehuapiano) de Gaiman, Chubut. *Com. Museo Argent. Cienc. Natur.,* 2: 55-82.

———. 1952. Un cánido del eocuartario de Mar del Plata y sus relaciones con otras formas brasileñas y norteamericanas. *Rev. Museo Munic. Cienc. Natur. Mar del Plata,* 1: 53-70.

KRAGLIEVICH, J. L., and A. G. DE OLIZÁBAL. 1959. Los prociónidos extinguidos del género *Chapalmalania* Amegh. *Rev. Museo Argent. Cienc. Natur.,* 6: 1-59.

KRAGLIEVICH, J. L. and S. RIVAS. 1951. *Orophodon* Amegh. representante de una nueva superfamilia Orophodontoidea del suborden Xenarthra (nota preliminar). *Com. Museo Argent. Cienc. Natur.*, 2: 9-28.

KURTÉN, B. 1967. Pleistocene bears of North America. 2. Genus *Arctodus,* short-faced bears. *Acta Zool. Fenn.,* No. 117: 1-60.

LAVOCAT, R. 1969. La systématique des rongeurs hystricomorphes et la dérive des continents. *Comptes Rend. Acad. Sci. (Paris),* 269: 1496-1497.

LEIDY, J. 1882. On remains of horses. *Proc. Acad. Natur. Sci. Phila.,* 1882: 290-291.

LLOYD, J. J. 1963. Tectonic history of the South Central-American orogen. *Am. Assoc. Petrol. Geol. Mem.* 2: 88-100.

LOOMIS, F. B. 1914. *The Deseado Formation of Patagonia.* 232 p. The Rumford Press, Concord, N. H.

MACNEISH, R. S., R. BERGER and R. PROTSCH. 1970. Megafauna and man from Ayacucho, Highland Peru. *Science,* 168: 975-977.

MACNEISH, R. S., A. NELKEN-TURNER and A. G. COOK. 1970. Second Annual Report of the Ayacucho Archaeological-Botanical Project, 1-46. Phillips Academy, Andover, Mass.

MAGLIO, V. J. 1966. A revision of the fossil selenodont artiodactyls from the middle Miocene Thomas Farm, Gilchrist County, Florida. *Brevoria, Museum Comp. Zool.,* No. 225: 1-27.

MARTIN, P. S. 1967. Pleistocene overkill. In P. S. Martin and H. E. Wright (eds.), *Pleistocene Extinctions. The Search for a Cause,* p. 75-120. Yale Univ. Press, New Haven, Conn.

MARTIN, P. S., and H. E. WRIGHT (eds.). 1967. *Pleistocene Extinctions. The Search for a Cause.* 453 p. Yale Univ. Press, New Haven, Conn.

MATTHEW, W. D. 1918. A revision of the Lower Eocene Wasatch and Wind River faunas. In W. D. Matthew and Walter Granger, *Part V. Insectivora (continued), Glires, Edentata. Bull. Amer. Museum Natur. Hist.,* 38: 565-657.

MAYR, E. 1946. History of the North American bird fauna. *Wilson Bull.,* 58: 3-41.

———. 1964. Inferences concerning the Tertiary American bird faunas. *Proc. Nat. Acad. Sci.,* 51: 280-288.

McGREW, P. O. 1944. An *Osteoborus* from Honduras. *Geol. Ser. Field Museum Natur. Hist.,* 8: 75-77.

McKENNA, M. 1956. Survival of primitive notoungulates and condylarths into the Miocene of Colombia. *Am. J. Sci.,* 254: 736-743.

MONTANÉ, J. 1968. Paleo-Indian remains from Laguna de Tagua Tagua, central Chile. *Science,* 161: 1137-1138.

MOOSER, O. 1959. Un équido fósil del genero *Neohipparion* de la Mesa Central de México. *An. Inst. Biol.,* 30: 375-388.

——. 1963. *Neohipparion monias* n. sp., équido fósil del Pliocene de la Mesa Central de México. *An. Inst. Biol.,* 34: 393-396.

NYGREN, W. E. 1950. Bolivar geosyncline of northwestern South America. *Bull. Am. Assoc. Petrol. Geol.,* 34: 1998-2006.

OLSON, E. C., and P. O. McGREW. 1941. Mammalian fauna from the Pliocene of Honduras. *Bull. Geol. Soc. Am.,* 52: 1219-1244.

OSBORN, H. F. 1929. New Eurasiatic and American proboscideans. *Am. Museum Novit.,* No. 393: 1-23.

PASCUAL, R. 1953. Sobre nuevos restos de sirenidos del Mesopotamiense. *Rev. Assoc. Geol. Argent.,* 3: 163-185.

——. 1960. Una nueva superfamilia "Entelopsoidea" descripción de la nueva especie *Entelops parodii. Acta Geol. Lilloana,* 3: 127-146.

——. 1961. Un nuevo Cardiomyinae (Rodentia, Caviidae) de la formación Arroyo Chasicó (Plioceno inferior) de la Provincia de Buenos Aires. *Ameghiniana,* 2: 61-71.

——. 1965. Los Toxodontidae (Toxodonta, Notoungulata) de la formación Arroyo Chasicó (Plioceno inferior) de la Provincia de Buenos Aires. Características geológicas. *Ameghiniana,* 4: 101-129.

——. 1967. Los roedores Octodontoidea (Caviomorpha) de la formación Arroyo Chasicó (Plioceno inferior) de la Provincia de Buenos Aires. *Rev. Museo La Plata (N.S.), Sec. Paleontol.,* 5: 259-282.

PASCUAL, R. and M. L. DIAZ DE GAMERO. 1969. Sobre la presencia del género *Eumegamys* (Rodentia, Caviomorpha) en la formación Urumaco del Estado Falcón (Venezuela). Su significación cronológica. *Bull. inform. Asoc. Venezolana Geol. Min. Pet.,* 12: 369-386.

PASCUAL, R., J. PISANO, and E. J. ORTEGA. 1965. Un nuevo Octodontidae (Rodentia, Caviomorpha) de la formación Epecuen (Plioceno medio) de Hidalgo (Provincia de La Pampa). Consideraciones sobre los Ctenomyinae Reig, 1958, y la morfología de sus molariformes. *Ameghiniana,* 4: 19-29.

PASCUAL, R., E. J. O. HINOJOSA, D. GONDAR, and E. TONNI. 1967. Las edades del Cenozoico mamalífero de la Argentina, con especial atención a aquellas del territorio bonaraerense. *An. Com. Invest. Cienc. Buenos Aires.* 1967: 165-193.

PATTERSON, B. 1937. Didelphines from the Pliocene of Argentina. *Proc. Geol. Soc. Am.,* 1936: 379.

——. 1952. Un nuevo y extraordinario marsupial deseadiano. *Rev. Museo Munic. Cienc. Natur. Mar del Plata,* 1: 39-44.

——. 1956. Early Cretaceous mammals and the evolution of mammalian molar teeth. *Fieldiana: Geol.,* 13: 1-105.

——. 1957. Mammalian phylogeny. In E. Mayr and J. Baer (eds.), *Premier Symposium sur la Spécificité Parasitaire des Parasites de Vertébrés,* p. 15-48. Paul Attinger, Neuchatel.

——. 1958. Affinities of the Patagonian fossil mammal *Necrolestes. Brevoria, Museum Comp. Zool.,* No. 94: 1-14.

——. 1965. The fossil elephant shrews (family Macroscelididae). *Bull. Museum Comp. Zool.,* 133: 297-335.

PATTERSON, B., and J. L. KRAGLIEVICH. 1960. Sistemática y nomenclatura de las aves fororracoideas del Plioceno argentino. *Pub. Museo Munic. Cienc. Natur. Mar del Plata,* 1: 1-49.

PATTERSON, B., and R. PASCUAL. 1963. The extinct land mammals of South America. *16. Internat. Zool. Congr.,* program vol.: 138-148.

——, and ——. 1968a. New echimyid rodents from the Oligocene of Patagonia, and a synopsis of the family. *Brevoria, Museum Comp. Zool.,* No. 301: 1-14.

——, and ——. 1968b. The fossil mammal fauna of South America, *Quart. Rev. Biol.,* 43: 409-451.

PATTON, T. H. 1967. Revision of the selenodont artiodactyls from Thomas Farm. *Quart. J. Fla. Acad. Sci.,* 29: 179-190.

PATTON, T. H., and B. E. TAYLOR. 1971. The Synthetoceratinae (Mammalia, Tylopoda, Protoceratidae). *Bull. Am. Museum Natur. Hist.,* 145: 119-218.

PAULA COUTO, C. DE. 1946. Atualização de nomenclatura genérica e específica usado por Herluf Winge, em "e museo lundii." *Est. Bras. Geol.,* 1(3): 59-80.

——. 1952a. Fossil mammals from the beginning of the Cenozoic in Brazil. Marsupialia: Polydolopidae and Borhyaenidae. *Am. Museum Novit.,* No. 1559: 1-27.

——. 1952b. Fossil mammals from the beginning of the Cenozoic in Brazil. Marsupialia: Didelphidae. *Am. Museum Novit.,* No. 1567: 1-26.

——. 1952c. Fossil mammals from the beginning of the Cenozoic in Brazil. Condylarthra, Litopterna, Xenungulata, Astrapotheria. *Bull. Am. Museum Natur. Hist.,* 99: 357-394.

——. 1955. O "tigre-dentes-de-sabre" do Brasil. *Inst. Bras. Bibl. Document.,* Bol. no. 1: 1-30.

——. 1962. Didelfídeos fósiles del Paleoceno de Brasil. *Rev. Museo Argent. Cienc. Natur.,* 8: 135-166.

REIG, O. A. 1952. Descripción previa de nuevos ungulados y marsupiales fósiles del Plioceno y del eocuartario argentinos. *Rev. Museo Munic. Cienc. Natur. Mar del Plata,* 1: 119-129.

——. 1955. Noticia preliminar sobre la presencia de microbiotherinos vivientes en la fauna sudamericana. *Invest. Zool. Chilenas,* 2: 121-130.

——. 1957. Nota previa sobre los marsupiales de la formación Chasicó. *Ameghiniana,* 1: 26-31.

REINHART, R. H. 1951. A new genus of sea cow from the Miocene of Colombia. *Univ. Calif. Publ. Bull. Dept. Geol. Sci.,* 28: 203-214.

RIGGS, E. S. 1934. A new marsupial saber-tooth from the Pliocene of Argentina and its relationship to other South American predaceous marsupials. *Trans. Am. Philos. Soc.,* n.s., 24: 1-32.

RIGGS, E. S., and B. PATTERSON. 1939. Stratigraphy of late Miocene and Pliocene deposits of the Province of Catamarca (Argentina) with notes on the faunae. *Physis,* 14: 143-162.

ROBINSON, P., C. C. BLACK, and M. D. DAWSON. 1964. Late Eocene multi-tuberculates and other mammals from Wyoming. *Science,* 145: 809-810.

RUSCONI, C. 1935. Las especies de Primates del Oligoceno de Patagonia (gen. *Homunculus*). "*Ameghinia,*" *Rev. Argent. Paleontol. Antropol.,* 1: 39-125.

SAVAGE, D. E. 1951. A Miocene phyllostomatid bat from Colombia, South America. *Univ. Calif. Publ. Bull. Dept. Geol. Sci.,* 28(12): 357-366.

SCHAUB, S. 1935. Säugetierfunde aus Venezuela und Trinidad. *Abh. Schweiz. Palaeont. Ges.,* 55: 1-21.

SCHUCHERT, C. 1935. *Historical Geology of the Antillean-Caribbean Region.* 811 p. John Wiley, New York.

SCOTT, W. B. 1937. *A History of Land Mammals in the Western Hemisphere.* 786 p. The Macmillan Co., New York.

SIGÉ, B. 1968. Dents de micromammifères et fragments de coquilles d'oeufs de dinosauriens dans la faune de vertébrés du Crétacé supérieur de Laguna Umayo (Andes péruviennes). *Comptes Rend. Acad. Sci. (Paris),* 267: 1495-1498.

SIMPSON, G. G. 1928. Affinities of the Polydolopidae. *Am. Museum Novit.,* No. 323: 1-13.

——. 1939. The development of marsupials in South America. *Physis,* 14: 373-398.

——. 1940. Review of the mammal-bearing Tertiary of South America. *Proc. Am. Philos. Soc.,* 83: 649-709.

——. 1941. The affinities of the Borhyaenidae. *Am. Museum Novit.,* No. 1118: 1-6.

——. 1945. The principles of classification and a classification of mammals. *Bull. Am. Museum Natur. Hist.,* 85: 1-350.

——. 1947. Holarctic mammalian faunas and continental relationships during the Cenozoic. *Bull. Geol. Soc. Am.,* 58: 613-688.

——. 1948. The beginning of the Age of Mammals in South America. *Bull. Am. Museum Natur. Hist.,* 85: 1-350.

——. 1951. History of the fauna of Latin America. In G. A. Baitsell (ed.), *Science in Progress* (7th Ser.), p. 369-408. Yale Univ. Press, New Haven, Conn.

——. 1956. Zoogeography of West Indian land mammals. *Am. Museum Novit.,* No. 1759: 1-28.

——. 1966. Mammalian evolution on the southern continents. *Neues Jahrb. Geol. Paläont. Abh.,* 125: 1-18.

——. 1967. The beginning of the Age of Mammals in South America, Part 2. *Bull. Am. Museum Natur. Hist.,* 137: 1-259.

——. 1970a. The Argyrolagidae, extinct South American marsupials. *Bull. Museum Comp. Zool.,* 139: 1-86.

——. 1970b. Additions to knowledge of the Argyrolagidae (Mammalia, Marsupialia) from the late Cenozoic of Argentina. *Breviora, Museum Comp. Zool.,* No. 361: 1-9.

——. 1970c. Addition to knowledge of *Groeberia* (Mammalia, Marsupialia) from the mid-Cenozoic of Argentina. *Breviora, Museum Comp. Zool.,* No. 362: 1-17.

SIMPSON, G. G., and C. DE PAULA COUTO. 1957. The mastodonts of Brazil. *Bull. Am. Museum Natur. Hist.,* 112: 127-189.

SIMPSON, G. G., J. L. MINOPRIO, and B. PATTERSON. 1962. The mammalian fauna of the Divisadero Largo formation, Mendoza, Argentina. *Bull. Museum Comp. Zool.,* 127: 237-293.

SLAUGHTER, B. H. 1968. Earliest known marsupials. *Science,* 162: 254-255.

SLOAN, R. E., and L. VAN VALEN. 1965. Cretaceous mammals from Montana. *Science,* 148: 220-227.

STIRTON, R. A. 1951. Ceboid monkeys from the Miocene of Colombia. *Univ. Calif. Publ. Bull. Dept. Geol. Sci.,* 28: 315-356.

——. 1953a. Vertebrate paleontology and continental stratigraphy in Colombia. *Bull. Geol. Soc. Am.,* 64: 603-622.

——. 1953b. A new genus of interatheres from the Miocene of Colombia. *Univ. Calif. Publ. Bull. Dept. Geol. Sci.,* 29: 265-348.

——. 1954. Late Miocene mammals from Oaxaca, Mexico. *Am. J. Sci.,* 252: 634-638.

STIRTON, R. A., and W. K. GEALEY. 1949. Reconnaissance geology and vertebrate paleontology of El Salvador, Central America. *Bull. Geol. Soc. Am.,* 60: 1731-1754.

THENIUS, E. 1964. Herkunft und entwicklung der südamerikanischen Säugetierfauna. *Z. Säugetierk.,* 29: 267-284.

TORCELLI, A. J. 1935. Obras completas y correspondencia científica de Florentino Ameghino. Volumen XXI. Correspondencia científica. Taller de impresiones oficiales, La Plata, p. 1-935.

UBBELOHDE-DOERING, H. 1959. Bericht über archäologische Feldarbeiten in Peru, II. *Ethnos,* 24: 1-32.

VAN COUVERING, J. A. 1972. Radiometric calibration of the European Neogene. In W. W. BISHOP and J. A. MILLER (eds.), *Calibration of Hominoid Evolution.* Wenner-Gren Foundation, New York. In press.

VAN FRANK, R. 1957. A fossil collection from northern Venezuela. 1. Toxodontidae (Mammalia, Notoungulata). *Am. Museum Novit.,* No. 1850: 1-38.

VANZOLINI, P. E. and E. E. WILLIAMS. 1970. South American anoles: the geographic differentiation and evolution of the *Anolis chrysolepis* species group (Sauria, Iguanidae). *Arq. Zool. S. Paulo,* 19: 1-124.

VON IHERING, H. 1890. Die geographische Verbreitung der Flussmuscheln. *Das Ausland, Jahrg.* 63: 941-944, 968-973.

VON ZITTEL, K. A. 1893. *Handbuch der Palaeontologie. I Abteilung. Palaeozoologie. IV Band. Vertebrata (Mammalia).* R. Oldenbourg, Munich.

VUILLEUMIER, B. T. 1971. Pleistocene changes in the fauna and flora of South America. *Science,* 173: 771-780.

WENZEL, R. L. and V. J. TIPTON. 1966. Some relationships between mammal hosts and their ectoparasites. In R. L. Wenzel and V. J. Tipton (eds.), *Ectoparasites of Panama,* p. 677-723. Field Museum of Natural History, Chicago.

WHITE, J. A. 1968. A new porcupine from the middle Pleistocene of the Anza-Borrego desert of California, with notes on mastication in *Coendou* and *Erethizon. Los Angeles Co. Museum Contrib. Sci.,* No. 136: 1-15.

WHITMORE, F. C., and R. H. STEWART. 1965. Miocene mammals and Central American seaways. *Science,* 148: 180-185.

WILLIAMS, E. E. and K. F. KOOPMAN. 1952. West Indian fossil monkeys. *Am. Museum Novit.,* No. 1546: 1-16.

WOOD, A. E., and B. PATTERSON. 1959. The rodents of the Deseadan Oligocene of Patagonia and the beginnings of South America rodent evolution. *Bull. Museum Comp. Zool.,* 120: 282-428.

—— and ——. 1970. Relationships among hystricognathous and hystricomorphous rodents. *Mammalia,* 34: 628-639.

WOODRING, W. P. 1954. Caribbean land and sea throughout the ages. *Bull. Geol. Soc. Am.,* 65: 719-732.

——. 1966. The Panama land bridge as a sea barrier. *Proc. Am. Phil. Soc.,* 110: 425-433.

VII

The Recent Mammals of the Neotropical Region: A Zoogeographic and Ecological Review

by Philip Hershkovitz

INTRODUCTION

The cartographer's line that divides the New World into continental South America and continental North America is unrelated to the biogeographical boundary between the two land masses. Until mid-Tertiary, the southern continent was geographically isolated from the northern by seas or straits covering what are now northwestern Colombia and parts of Middle America. Consolidation of the inter-American islands into a continuous land bridge established their identity as a zoogeographic province of South America. The present relationship of the Greater Antillean island chain to Middle and South America is roughly comparable to the one held by early Cenozoic Middle America to South America. To speak of Middle America or the West Indies as tropical parts of North America, as some zoologists do, is to confuse the geopolitical with the biogeographical.

The present account focuses on the recent mammals of South America, but in the context of the total tropical American zoogeographic area, or the Neotropical Region (defined below). Perhaps because Neotropical mammals are smaller, on the average, are more difficult to observe, hunt, or collect, and have been studied only meagerly, they are less known than the mammals of comparable areas elsewhere. Notwithstanding these facts, the animals are there, and they challenge the student to reconstruct the history of their origins, evolutions, and dispersals.

Resources used in attempting to solve the problems of when and where the modern mammalian fauna had its beginnings in Latin America, but especially in South America, are: the animals themselves, primary taxonomic revisions, phylogenetic and ecological studies, field observations, precise plottings of distributional patterns, and the geological data. Successive intercontinental faunal movements and the chronological sequence of faunal stratifications outlined below have been determined almost entirely on these foundations. The same grounds are used for tracing and indicating principal centers of colonization, radiation, and dispersal. The descriptions of widely separated and ecologically contrasting local biotic areas, each with its peculiar fauna, also provide insights into ecological and faunal successions through time. Space limitations permit only the most cursory survey of the animals themselves, and the briefest review of biological factors controlling their evolution and dispersal.

GEOGRAPHIC CLASSIFICATION OF MAMMALS

The following terms are used for the more important zoogeographic types of non-marine Recent mammals. Names, definitions and examples are from Hershkovitz (1958).

Cosmopolite: Any taxon whose range includes at least a tropical Region of either the Western or Eastern Hemisphere (i.e., Neotropical or Paleotropical), and a Holarctic (i.e., Nearctic or Palearctic) Subregion of the *other* Hemisphere.

Insectivora, Chiroptera, Carnivora, Lagomorpha and Rodentia are the most cosmopolitan orders of mammals. Some of their families, for example, Soricidae, Vespertilionidae, Canidae, Leporidae and Sciuridae, respectively, are likewise cosmopolites. In turn, certain genera of these families are also cosmopolites. The insectivore *Sorex,* broadly defined, is found in Paleotropica and Nearctica. Bats of the genus *Myotis* are common in all major zoogeographic regions. The canids *Canis* and *Vulpes* are widespread in the Nearctic and Palearctic Subregions and in the Paleotropical Region. *Sciurus* is the cosmopolite of the squirrel family. There are no cosmopolitan *species* of land mammals other than those whose dispersal was aided by man.

Regionalite: A taxon native to a zoogeographic Region to which it may be confined (*endemic*), or from which it may spread into another, usually contiguous Region (*excurrent*).

The edentate genus *Dasypus* is a neotropical regionalite, with one of its species, the nine-banded armadillo (*D. novemcinctus*), excurrent into the Nearctic Subregion. All other genera of the edentate order Xenarthra are endemic Neotropical regionalites, most of them endemic to the Patagonian Subregion.

Varicant: The name applied to any taxon occurring in contiguous Regions when it cannot be determined with certainty in which Region that taxon originated. A varicant is usually highly tolerant of fluctuating climatic conditions and is well distributed over a large part of each of the Regions it inhabits. The term "varicant" is from the Latin *varicare,* meaning "to straddle." It should not be confused with *vicarant* or *variant.*

The monotypic genus *Urocyon,* or gray fox, is a varicant. It ranges widely in the southern part of the Nearctic Subregion as it does in the northern part of the Neotropical Region. It may have originated in a zone of transition between the two areas or just within the border of either. The polytypic genus *Sylvilagus,* with species of rabbits widely distributed in both Regions, one endemic to the Neotropical Region, others to the Nearctic Subregion, is best classified as a varicant.

Endemic: Any taxon from species to phylum confined to a Region. An endemic is always a regionalite (*q.v.*). The term is not valid for an individual, a local population, a subspecies, or any other fraction of a true species.

Autochthon: A taxon that originated by evolution in a given geographic area. The term is here regarded as strictly synonymous with *native* or *indigene.*

Visitor: An individual or group of individuals of a given species, with temporary or non-breeding residence in a Region or any of its subdivisions. Many migratory Holarctic birds are *seasonal* visitors in the Neotropical or Paleotropical Region. They may be *incidental* or *accidental* visitors en route. As in the case of birds, migratory mammals (e.g., bats, cetaceans and others) may be regarded as natives of their breeding areas and as visitors in other areas inhabited by them.

Import: An individual or group of individuals of a given species introduced into a foreign area through human agency. Domesticated animals and pets, commensal *Rattus* and *Mus,* game and show animals, all enter the category of *import* in localities where they are not native. In a few places, notably islands, imports have become so well established since prehistoric times that their introduction by aboriginal man is unsuspected or practically impossible to prove. Imports, insofar as they can be recognized, are not taken into account in the definition of a natural faunal area.

EVOLUTIONARY CENTERS AND GLOBAL PATTERNS OF DISTRIBUTION

Introduction

Modern mammalian zoogeography is primarily concerned with the definition of faunal areas, centers of origin, past and present distributions, and the environmental factors controlling dispersal. Nearly all living species, most genera, and some orders or suborders of Neotropical mammalian regionalites, originated within the limits of their present geographic range. Some of the remainder may have originated in one part of what is now the Neotropical Region and spread into another in which they became endemic. Still others are survivors of former boreal American lineages, and a few high-ranking taxa could have originated on other continents. The abundant, even rich fossil *records* of mammals in some localities of North and South America provide surprisingly little, and in many crucial cases, no direct *evidence* of the place of origin of the hierarchies in question.

The provenance of the well-documented South American Cretaceous–early Tertiary mammalian fauna is unknown or disputed. The late Paleocene marsupials, edentates, and odd ungulates with which the record begins were already specialized. An upper Cretaceous condylarth from

Peru (Thaler in Grambast, 1967) is said to be more advanced than contemporaneous boreal American condylarths. Some marsupial, possibly
didelphid, mandibular fragments and teeth from the same locality and of
the same age, are said to agree best with similar elements from the late
Cretaceous of boreal America (Sigé, 1968). A later Tertiary fauna of
highly organized and greatly diversified simian primates, hystricomorphous and cricetine rodents, bats, and possibly others, arose from as yet
unidentified stock which could have lived in tropical America, boreal
America, or Africa. The uncertainties regarding their respective origins
seem to increase rather than decrease with each new discovery. Finally,
the living South American fauna is composed of descendents of as yet
unknown stirpes of the first two strata, and descendents of Middle American stocks. The latter attained South America and the West Indies by
overwater or land routes from late Miocene onward, radiated and spread
at different rates into a great diversity of niches. Whatever the pathways
of the founders, there can be no doubt that the survivors of all but the
latest arrivals evolved within the area they occupy now.

Some zoogeographers (e.g., Matthew, 1915; Simpson, 1950; and see
Patterson and Pascual, Chapter VI) accept as a working hypothesis that
the ancestral forms of the earliest known orders of South American land
mammals originated in a stable northern continent whether boreal America or Eurasia, and spread south. Present knowledge of paleogeography
and Mesozoic mammals strongly suggests, however, that most if not all
these ancient orders originated in one of the rifted or drifting continents
of the former Gondwanaland complex. The main tenets of each of the two
schools of thought regarding tropical American mammalian origins are
outlined below.

I. *Continental Stability—The Matthew Hypothesis: Origin of mammals
on stable northern continents separated by fixed ocean basins; intercontinental dispersal routes usually flowing southward*

The Hypothesis as propounded by W. D. Matthew (1915), consists of
four main propositions. (1) The northern portion of the earth has been
the primary center of evolution and dispersal of vertebrates. (2) Nearly
all mammals (and other vertebrates) of the southern continents are
descendents of migrants from the northern continents. (3) At any given
period, the most advanced and progressive forms would be those inhabiting the original centers of dispersal while the most primitive and unpro-
gressive forms would be those forced to the periphery of the range. (4)
Geographic distributions of extinct and extant animals can be explained
on the basis of stable continents and permanent oceans. Hypothetical
land bridges in tropical and southern regions connecting continents now
separated by deep seas are improbable and unnecessary to explain geographic distribution.

The Matthew Hypothesis also implies that until evidence to the contrary is forthcoming, the age and site of the oldest known representative

of a taxon must be taken as the time and place of origin of that taxon. This rule of thumb contradicts Proposition 3, although Matthew explains it otherwise.

II. *Continental Drift—The Wegenerian Theory: Origin of land animals on one of a northern or southern complex of more or less connected, or disconnected and drifting continents; intercontinental dispersal routes in any feasible direction.*

The Wegenerian Theory, as interpreted here, predicates that terrestrial forms of life, including all Mesozoic–early Tertiary mammals, originated in the primary land mass Pangaea, its rifted northern supercontinent Laurasia, or southern supercontinent Gondwanaland, or one of their rifted, drifted, or still drifting daughter continents.

The original theory of continental drift now stands on geological evidence alone. It appears to be well established and generally accepted by the vast majority of geologists [cf. Wegener, 1966 (1929, 1962); du Toit, 1937; Wilson, 1963; Hallam, 1967; Le Pichon, 1968; Hurley, 1968; Heirtzler, 1969; Bonatti, Ball, Schubert, 1970; Dietz and Holden, 1970a, b; Smith and Hallam, 1970; Horsfield and Dewey, 1971]. Recent discoveries and estimates insofar as they might relate to the history of South American mammals confirm the following tectonic movements and chronologies.

1. South American/African block split from Gondwanaland in Mesozoic–Permian and became widely separated at end of Triassic.
2a. South America began splitting from Africa in late Jurassic, but opening of the South Atlantic Ocean occurred mostly since early Cretaceous. According to Maxwell et al. (1970), separation between South America and Africa began during early Cretaceous, about 130 million years ago. Average annual rate of spread of Atlantic Ocean at about 30° south latitude, 2 cm. Spreading rate at end of the Eocene, 37 million years ago, 1.9 cm.; end of the Oligocene, 26 million years ago, 1.8 cm.; lower Miocene to end of the Aquitanian, 23 million years ago, 1.5 cm.; end of the Miocene, 6 million years ago, 2.0 cm.
2b. Drift between North America and Africa, according to Pitman, Talwani, and Heirtzler (1971), initiated about 180 million years ago; about 35 per cent of total drift between Africa and North America occurred in past 72 million years (since latest Cretaceous); approximately 70 per cent of total drift between Europe and North America occurred in same period.
3. South America completely isolated since Cretaceous until united with North America in late Tertiary.
4. Deep-sea cores from sub-Antarctic Pacific sector of southern oceans, according to Margolis and Kennett (1971), indicate cool southern oceans throughout much of Cenozoic with major cooling during early Eocene, late middle Eocene and Oligocene; warming trend from middle Miocene ending in late Miocene, followed by cooling, leading to Antarctica's Pleistocene glaciation. Glaciation on Antarctica prevailed throughout much of Cenozoic. [See Ramsay (1971) for summary and timetable of events which contributed to formation of the Atlantic Ocean.]

Discussion

The Matthew Hypothesis explicitly excludes the possibility of the origin of mammals of ordinal or subordinal grade in the Gondwanaland continents Antarctica, Australia, Africa south of the Sahara, India, and associated islands. It concedes the origin in situ of the ancient South American ungulates except the contemporaneous Condylarthra from which they are said to have evolved, and is vague or noncommittal about the origin of Proboscidea, Sirenia, and Chiroptera. The Hypothesis provides for explanations of past distributions of mammals on the basis of present geography. It allows for considerable interchange between a stable North America and Eurasia with successively divergent lines of dispersal flowing southward from northern centers of origin, creating the "Sherwin-Williams" effect. Close resemblances between higher mammalian categories on opposite shores of the South Atlantic Ocean are attributed to convergences and parallelisms.

Matthew's zoogeographic concepts have been grossly censured by Croizat (1958). Brundin (1966) found the same faults, failures, and contradictions but his somewhat less documented, albeit logical, organized, and tempered criticisms carry the conviction that Croizat's *jihad* fails to achieve. Darlington (1957:206, 327, 556, 566, 600) also reviewed Matthewian zoogeography and summarized some earlier critiques. His own zoogeographic views (cf. 1965: 210) require an immoderate back-dating of continental drift within an essentially Matthewian framework.

The Wegenerian Theory of continental drift, in contrast, implies the origin of mammals in any one of the ancient supercontinents or breakaway continents. Dispersal routes from evolutionary centers conform to whatever the rifting, drifting, or shifting positions of the continents were at the time. Close resemblances between higher mammalian categories of southern continents on opposite sides of the Atlantic are attributed to correspondingly close genetic relationships.

A direct relationship between drift and Mesozoic tetrapod distribution was initially rejected by most zoogeographers (cf. Mayr, 1952; Darlington, 1957, 1965). However, such recent discoveries as the lower Triassic remains of land-living amphibians and reptiles in Antarctica (Elliot et al., 1970), and congeneric cynodonts of the same time in Africa and Argentina (Bonaparte, 1967; Romer, 1968), upper Cretaceous dinosaurs in Madagascar and South America (Hoffstetter, 1961); the boa *Madtsoia* in upper Cretaceous of Madagascar and Paleocene–Eocene of Patagonia (Hoffstetter, 1961; Del Corro, 1968) have dispelled nearly all doubts, insofar as the nonmammalian vertebrates are concerned.

The role played by continental drift in mammalian distribution is still being debated. The Matthewian posture, consistently maintained by Simpson, was restated by him (1970: 48-49) in a recent review of extinct South American marsupials. "The evidence of the argyrolagoids [Marsupialia] agrees with and to that extent reinforces the view that South America had no land connection with either Australia or Africa during the late Mesozoic and Cenozoic. It thus adds a small additional item, of no great significance in itself, to the large body of evidence that Gondwanaland did not exist during these times and that continental drift did not then have any influence on land faunas and has little, if any, bearing on the present distribution of mammals. Whether Gondwanaland or continental drift or both occurred at earlier times and had some bearing on early Mesozoic and still older zoogeography is another matter not relevant here."

Argyrolagids actually contribute nothing in support of Simpson's sweeping statements regarding continental and faunal relationships. These marsupials are known from mid- or late Pliocene to early or mid-Pleistocene only (Simpson, 1970:1, 65). If it is assumed, as argued by Simpson (1970:48), that argyrolagids arose in South America during late Cretaceous or early Tertiary from didelphoid stock, then only the provenance of the latter is germane to the question of mammalian and continental relations during late Mesozoic or early Cenozoic.

Mammals originated during late Triassic when rifting of Gondwanaland began, and they were already widely dispersed, perhaps globally, by Early Cretaceous when drifting had become universal. If marsupials did not originate in South America, they may have entered that continent from boreal America or from Antarctica during the Cretaceous, possibly earlier. At either end they would have crossed a water gap, the southern much narrower than the northern (cf. Dietz and Holden, 1970a,b: Fig. 5). Access of marsupials to Australia would have been easier in late Mesozoic via Antarctica than any other hypothetical route. Africa may not have figured in marsupial dispersal but cannot be excluded from consideration. Simpson's reconstruction of mammalian dispersal routes during Cretaceous-Early Tertiary time rests on his belief that spreading seas between drifting Gondwanaland continents were barriers to faunal interchange, but that a land bridge connecting North and South America allowed interchange (cf. 1940a:685; 1940b: 157; 1950: 373, 385; 1965: 213; 1969: 895). The existence of this bridge has never been demonstrated.

If Simpson (1959) is correct in his disputed postulations that mammals are polyphyletic in origin, any part of the Laurasian and Gondwanaland supercontinents inhabited by therapsids, more specifically cynodonts, could have been a birthplace for one or more mammalian lineages. Ameghino's faith in South America as the cradle of mammalian origin would have found comfort in Romer's (1970) opinion that middle Triassic chiniquodontid cynodonts of South America lie close to and perhaps on the main evolutionary line leading to mammals. If mammals are monophyletic (cf. Hopson and Crompton, 1969), the supercontinent provided the unified geographic center for mammalian origin, and its sundered components offered the isolation for ordinal divergence.

The influence of Gondwanaland or continental drift on the past or present distribution of mammals cannot be dismissed categorically. Continental drift has played a large and important part in the evolution and dispersal of at least higher categories of mammals. How much bearing drift has had on the affinities of living South American mammals depends largely on the geographic origin of some and the interpretation of the relationship of others to similar-appearing mammals in Africa, or elsewhere. Simpson, in the works cited in this account, has analyzed a number of interpretations of resemblances and shown that most were incorrect or unacceptable. Others reviewed here appear to be worthy of serious consideration as alternatives to current hypotheses based mainly, if not solely, on the apriorisms of Matthewian zoogeography.

CONTINENTAL ORIGINS OF SOUTH AMERICAN MAMMALIAN ORDERS

Past and present species of South American mammals represent the 20 orders listed in Table 1. Of the total, 7 are believed to have originated in South America. An eighth, Primates, may have arisen in Africa, less likely, in one of the northern continents. One primate suborder, Platyrrhini, however, is surely a South American autochthon. A ninth order, Condylarthra, known since Cretaceous, may be boreal American or South American in origin. A few early Cretaceous teeth hint to the origin of Marsupialia in boreal America but the suborder Marsupicarnivora may be South American. The orders Chiroptera and Sirenia may have differentiated at an early date, the first on a rifted but as yet little drifted Gondwanaland continent, the second in a Gondwanaland, probably African, continental sea. Africa also appears to be the most probable birth place of the Proboscidea but entry of representatives of this order into South America was through North America during the Quaternary. Lagomorpha, Perissodactyla and Artiodactyla may have arisen in North America or Eurasia, as the case for each may prove to be. The cradle of the remaining orders, Insectivora, Rodentia, Carnivora and Cetacea is uncertain, however the fossil record may be interpreted. It seems certain, nevertheless, that all families of Carnivora entered South America from the north, as did some of the Rodentia, and one genus (*Cryptotis*) of Insectivora.

Separation of native Gondwanaland from native Laurasian mammals was assayed by Kurtén (1967, 1969) primarily on the basis of the oldest paleontological records. Kurtén did not discuss South American mammals in detail but our respective allocations coincide in the main. Histories of some of the more moot South American mammalian orders, or infraordinal groups, are discussed below.

Marsupialia (Marsupicarnivora)

The fossil record of marsupials points to a North American origin and most authors tend to accept this sign as conclusive. Kurtén (1967) indicates, however, that the Marsupicarnivora (I regard as a suborder) arose in Gondwanaland. If marsupials originated in North America they most likely entered Australia from South America. If they are southern or Gondwanaland in origin, boreal America was colonized by marsupials from South America. Contrary to arguments advanced by Simpson (1939), accumulated paleontological records indicate that marsupials were not present in Asia and the likelihood of their invasion of Australia by island-hopping or rafting from that continent is virtually excluded (cf. Cox, 1970). As for the supposed ecological discordance or incompatibility between marsupials and placentals, both kinds of animals can and do mix. They have been living side by side in tropical America since Paleocene if not Cretaceous. The recent rapid and pervasive spread of the opossum (*Didelphis virginianus*) in boreal America is being accomplished without evident prejudice to the native placental fauna. Conversely, the successful colonization of Australia by placental bats, murids and the dingo (cf. Gill, 1955) was effected without discernable detriment to native marsupials and monotremes.

For additional information and hypotheses on marsupial origin, dispersal routes or classification, see the preceding section (pp. 314, 316); also Keast, and Patterson and Pascual, Chapters II, V, and VI; Clemens (1968, 1970), Lillegraven (1969); Patterson (1967), Ride (1964), Simpson (1970).

Insectivora

Solenodon, living in Cuba and the Dominican Republic (Island of Haiti), and the recently extinct *Nesophontes* from Haiti, have no known western continental relatives, extant or extinct. McDowell (1958: 210), who reviewed the group, believes that *Solenodon* and *Nesophontes* "represent a line that separated from a pre-soricid stem not later than the upper Eocene, and there is no reason to believe that the divergence of the two genera did not take place in the West Indies." A close relationship between Antillean forms and African tenrecids was admitted but cranial characters, according to McDowell, indicate greater affinities with soricids. Accordingly, he referred both genera to the family Solenodontidae, superfamily Soricoidea, order Lipotyphla.

In his classification of the Insectivora and Deltatheridia, Van Valen (1967) treated *Nesophontes* as type of the new family Nesophontidae, in the superfamily Soricoidea, suborder Erinaceota, order Insectivora. *Solenodon* was made type of the Solenodontidae, in the superfamily Tenrecoidea, suborder Zalambdodonta, order Deltatheridia. Van Valen's arrangement of the Antillean insectivores in separate orders seems based partly on a question of molar cusp homologies, and partly on indecision. *Nesophontes* and *Solenodon* may have diverged widely enough dentally to justify their separation on the family level. Both, however, are zalambdodont insectivores apparently most nearly related to tenrecids (cf. Hershkovitz, 1971a). The African affinities, and the absence of near relatives in the Americas, suggest a Late Cretaceous to Early Tertiary Gondwanaland origin, followed, during the early stages of continental drift, by overwater colonization of the Antilles and possibly of an island of the Middle American complex (cf. Lloyd, 1963; Frieland and Dietz, 1971) but with survival only in the former.

TABLE 1

Possible centers of origin of Recent and extinct orders of South American mammals

	SA	Afr	Gond	bA	Laur	?
Marsupialia [1]						
Marsupicarnivora	+(?)			+(?)		+(?)
Paucituberculata	+			+(?)		
Insectivora						
Zalambdodonta		+(?)				+
Soricidae	+(?)	+(?)			+(?)	
Solenodontidae [2]	+(?)	+(?)				
† Nesophontidae[2]	+(?)	+(?)				
Chiroptera						
Microchiroptera [3]			++			
Primates						
Platyrrhini	+	+(?)				+(?)
Edentata (Xenarthra)	+					
Lagomorpha					+	
Rodentia						
Myomorpha						++
Sigmodontini	+	+				
Hystricomorpha						++
Cavioidea	+					
Carnivora						+
† Condylarthra	+(?)			+(?)		
† Litopterna	+					
† Trigonostylopoidea	+					
† Astrapotheria	+					
† Pyrotheria	+					
† Xenungulata	+					
† Notoungulata	+					
Proboscidea		+				
Perissodactyla					++	
Artiodactyla					++	

Sirenia [4]

Cetacea [4]

    Susuidae [5]

    Delphinidae

$+$

$+$

$+$

$+$

Key:

    SA = South America

    Afr = pre-Eocene Africa, except Proboscidea in Upper Eocene of N. Africa

    Gond = Gondwanaland, the pre-Tertiary southern supercontinent; as used here, a pre- or post-drift
        component continent

    bA = boreal America

    Laur = Either of the Laurasian continents, boreal America or Eurasia

    ? = Geographic origin not established, whatever the fossil evidence, if any.

    † = extinct

Footnotes

[1] *The above two subdivisions of Marsupialia are arranged by Ride (1964) as follows:*

    Marsupialia (Ride's superorder, my order)

    Marsupicarnivora Ride (Ride's order, my suborder)

        Didelphoidea

        Borhyaenoidea

        Dasyuroidea

    Paucituberculata (Ride's order, my suborder)

        Caenolestoidea (my superfamily to include Ride's families Caenolestidae and Polydolopidae)

    A revised classification based on serological data was offered by Kirsch (1968). It agrees essentially with Ride's insofar as American marsupials and related Australian marsupials are concerned except that bor-hyaenoids are ranked as a subdivision of didelphoids, which seems better. Kirsch also replaces Ride's Mar-supicarnivora with the name Polyprotodonta Owen, and includes his Peramelemorphia (bandicoots) as a suborder. Ride treats the bandicoots as a distinct order, the Peramelina Gray.

[2] *Possibly Middle American or West Indian, rather than South American, but included here be-cause of the possibility of African or trans-Atlantic origins.*

[3] *Includes 5 tropical American endemic families, all possibly South American in origin.*

[4] *Only fresh water forms are included in the continental fauna of South America. The orders may have originated, however, in one of the continental seas.*

[5] *Platanistidae of most authors.*

Chiroptera

Bats are essentially tropical land mammals and in the more favorable parts of their range may dominate other mammals in numbers and kinds. Temperate zones in all latitudes provide habitats for a comparatively few insectivorous species that migrate or hibernate when food is scarce or absent.

The oldest known bats, from the early Eocene of boreal America and the middle Eocene of Europe, were already highly specialized and peripheral in distribution. Differentiation of the order, therefore, must have occurred during Late Cretaceous or earliest Tertiary time, almost certainly in a tropical zone, most likely on a southern continent. Spread of bats into the remaining continents must have been rapid.

Of 14 extant families of the suborder Microchiroptera, the Vespertilionidae, Molossidae and Emballonuridae are the most primitive and global in distribution. The Megadermatidae and Rhinolophidae, known since Eocene, are confined to Eurasia, Africa, India, Australia and associated islands. Six progressive families, the Noctilionidae, Pteronuridae, Phyllostomidae, Natalidae, Furipteridae and Thyropteridae, are endemic to the New World tropics. One family, the Rhinopomatidae is essentially Asiatic with an extension into north Africa. Another family, the Nycteridae, is primarily African south of the Sahara, but with spread into the southeast Asian island chain. Of the remaining two families, the Myzopodidae are restricted to Madagascar, the Mystacinidae to New Zealand.

The Megachiroptera, with a single family known since middle Oligocene, is entirely Old World in distribution.

The distributional pattern of bats, as outlined above, suggests their origin on the southern supercontinent and spread to the northern. Endemicism begins with widespread drift and increases in direct proportion to the size of the isolated sister continents and the marine gaps between them. Endemicism is highest in South America, the most distantly isolated of the southern continents, and nonexistent in Africa, the least separated. Australia, with a large and varied bat fauna but no endemic families, is connected to tropical Asia by an island bridge with suitable habitats and easy passage for bats spreading into either continent from the other. Oceanic New Zealand, with two native species of mammals, both bats, one of the endemic family Mystacinidae, the other of the cosmopolitan Vespertilionidae, is isolated at the far extreme of the Australian region. In contrast, boreal America, at the opposite extreme of the global range, offers only peripheral habitats for some members of the cosmopolitan families Vespertilionidae and Molossidae, and the few Neotropical phyllostomatids and emballonurids that penetrated contiguous parts of Nearctica.

The global pattern of chiropteran distribution does not conform to tenets of the Matthew Hypothesis and Matthew himself (1915:227) evaded the question. Continental drift, on the other hand, offers the only explanation consistent with the realities of past and present distribution of bats.

For a synopsis of bat distribution and a tabulation of bat genera by zoogeographic regions, see Koopman (1970).

Primates

Prosimians and simians, the domesticated or cultured kinds omitted, are essentially tropical forest animals with some temperate climate or scrub-savanna tolerant forms occupying peripheral habitats. The earliest known primates, the prosimians, from the Paleocene of boreal America and Europe, are already highly specialized and none appears to be ancestral to any living primate. Eocene prosimians of boreal America, Europe, and Asia are quite monkey-like and some groups, particularly the vaguely defined Omomyidae, possess features which place them near but not on the line leading to higher monkeys. Late Oligocene to earliest Miocene saw the disappearance of ancient prosimians in the northern continents, the appearance of platyrrhines in tropical America, and catarrhines in Africa. Living lemuroids, lorisoids and tarsioids are descendents of tropical, probably Afro-South Asian prosimians. According to Szalay (1970), *Amphipithecus,* from the late Eocene of Burma, may be a lemuroid that disappeared without issue. Simons (1971), however, contends it may be the oldest known catarrhine.

It has been assumed on the basis of the chronology, abundance, and variety of the fossils, and the Matthew Hypothesis, that primates originated in the northern continents and spread into the southern. The tropical American invaders, according to the Hypothesis, gave rise to platyrrhines. Among those that spread into Africa and southeast Asia, some gave rise to modern lemuroids, galagoids, and the tarsier, and others evolved into catarrhines. The community of characters that distinguishes the independently evolved platyrrhines and catarrhines from all other primates is attributed, according to the Hypothesis, to initial convergence followed by parallel evolution.

The geographic and chronological sequences of the Hypothesis seem plausible. Notwithstanding this, the rich North American and Eurasian record of prosimians from late Paleocene onward demonstrates evolutionary trends toward increasing specialization away from, not toward, the simian facies, particularly with respect to dental systems and locomotor skeletons.

A second hypothesis postulates that prosimians arose in the rifted South American-African continents, possibly during the Cretaceous, and spread across both continents during early drift stages. Platyrrhines and catarrhines then evolved independently in isolated South America and Africa, respectively, perhaps during early Tertiary from closely related, possibly congeneric prosimian stocks. This hypothesis accounts for basic similarities without the need for initial convergence.

An extension or variation of the second hypothesis assumes that the ancestral platyrrhine and catarrhine stocks had already evolved to simian grade in rifted but not yet widely drifted South America-Africa. Fossils closing the anatomical gap between higher and lower primates have not been found but the gradient must have existed and can be demonstrated in living forms.

The first of the three hypotheses of primate origin and dispersal slights critical morphological facts. The other hypotheses, based on an idealized construction of evolutionary and geological sequences, may be inconsonant with the supposed chronology of either primate evolution or of continental drift, but not both. No satisfactory solution is possible before the real taxonomic and systematic problems at hand are solved. A sample of each follows.

Branisella boliviana Hoffstetter (1969), represented by a fragment of upper jaw from the lower Oligocene, is the oldest South American primate known. Its systematic position is uncertain. Should the animal prove to be prosimian, it cannot be assigned with certainty to any known family. If simian, its greatly reduced second upper premolar (pm$^{\underline{2}}$) deviates from the platyrrhine model but is intermediate between those of African Oligocene catarrhines in which pm$^{\underline{2}}$ is present and models in which it is absent.

A classification of higher primates (the Anthropoidea of many authors) based on the divergence of platyrrhines and catarrhines from a common simian, or even prosimian, stock implies a common ancestral center of origin. Only Africa, South America, or the two continents approximated provide the stage for this event. Paradoxically, advocates of this classification, such as Matthew (1915) and a multitude of others, point to Asia as the ancestral catarrhine center of origin and to South America as the independent center of platyrrhine origin.

Edentata (Xenarthra)

Edentates, order Edentata or Xenarthra, strictly speaking, evolved and radiated in South America since the Cretaceous or earliest Tertiary times before some of the species spread into North America and the West Indies during late Tertiary and most of the Quaternary. Until recently, the Palaeanodonta, known from the Eocene of boreal America, were regarded as ancestral to the older Xenarthra (cf. Patterson and Pascual, 1968: 422). A review of the accumulated evidence, however, led Emry (1970) to conclude that the "palaeanodonts are ancestral to manids (Pholidota) and probably not closely or at all related to the Xenarthra" (p. 488).

Rodentia

a. Sigmodontini (Cricetinae, Muridae)

Neotropical mice are the most primitive of living myomorphs and the most diversified of New World murids. Their Tertiary history is largely a blank. The oldest known fossils, from late Pliocene of the northern and southern extremes of the range, are practically indistinguishable from modern relatives. The Nearctic Peromyscini, known since Oligocene, are not ancestral to but could be derived from sigmodontines. They are characterized by a secondarily simplified glans penis and uncomplicated baculum, as contrasted with the complex glans and tridigitate baculum of other murids including the Sigmodontini. I have previously suggested (1969: 21) that complex penis cricetines may have originated in boreal America, spread into Eurasia and South America. They were then supposed to have disappeared from boreal America, presumably during Oligocene, when simple-penis-type Peromyscini suddenly replaced them. This reconstruction, seemingly the least implausible of several adaptable to the Matthew Hypothesis, is unconvincing. There is no evidence that South American sigmodontines existed in boreal America prior to their invasion of that continent in late Pliocene and there is no likelihood they gave rise to, or are descended from Eurasian cricetines. It is no more unlikely, possibly more likely, that sigmodontines were rafted from Africa to South America during early Tertiary (see following discussion). Similarities between sigmodontines and African (and Malagasy) cricetines heretofore attributed to parallelisms (cf. Hershkovitz, 1962: 107, 221) may require revision in the light of present suggestions. Peromyscines, with peculiarly simplified penis, are otherwise more or less generalized, and now regarded as isolated offshoots of Eurasian cricetines.

b. Hystricomorpha (*sensu lato*)

The history of Old and New World hystricomorphous rodents parallels that of platyrrhine and catarrhine primates, and possibly that of sigmodontine cricetine rodents, as well. The essentially South American hystricomorphs, currently classified in the suborder Caviomorpha, agree in fundamental characters with Old World forms assigned to the restricted suborder Hystricomorpha. Highly evolved representatives of each group appear suddenly in the early Oligocene, the one in southern South America, the other in northern Africa. The probability that caviomorphs or a likely ancestral form originated in boreal America and migrated into South America is not well founded. The probability that the group was established by African hystricomorphs rafted across the Atlantic has been proposed by a number of authors. Even Matthew (1915: 231) in the absence of other plausible explanations, admitted the proposition as a possibility. Simpson (1940a: 685) adopted it as such but later (1950: 386) rejected it. Most recently, Lavocat (1969), impressed by close resemblances between lower Oligocene phiomyids from Africa and contemporaneous hystricomorphous rodents from South America, suggested that westward trans-Atlantic rafting might have been accomplished between middle and late Eocene.

Wood and Patterson (1970) insist, however, that each world group arose independently from a northern ancestor and that recognized simi-

larities between them are parallelisms. They (1970: 633) also indicate that
the time-span involved in the prior origin and spread from either northern continent excludes the possibility of movements between southern
continents during the Eocene. In any case, the feasibility of rafting across
the broad and open sea is questioned. The estimated width of the Atlantic
at 30° S, they (Wood and Patterson, 1970: 639) point out, was already
3000 km during the Campanian (cf. Maxwell et al., 1970: 1057). Wood
and Patterson (1970: p. 634) also believe it "most unlikely" that "phiomyids should have a South American relationship when nothing else [of
the other 12 mammalian orders of the same late Eocene-early Oligocene
Fayum fauna] does." They also hold that the tetralophodont molar
pattern of the early Oligocene *Platypittamys* of South America is primitive, and that the *pentalophodont* pattern of early Oligocene Fayum
Phiomys is more advanced, or derived. The literature pertaining to the
origin, evolution, and dispersal of early hystricomorphous rodents is
cited by Wood and Patterson and need not be repeated here.

In rebuttal, Hoffstetter and Lavocat (1970) show that the pentalophodont molar enamel pattern is primitive and present in the oldest
known South American hystricomorphous rodents and that the molar
pattern and other characters of *Platypittamys* are more advanced. With
this I am in agreement (cf. Hershkovitz, 1948). It may also be argued that
successful rafting of the only rodent species of a sizeable fauna across a
large body of water, is neither surprising nor unprecedented. Contrary
to the opinion of Wood and Patterson (1970), it would be less likely,
rather than more so, for one or more non-rodents of the same fauna to
accomplish the same feat at the same time. Furthermore, the actual distance between the nearest points across the Atlantic could well have
been less than half the estimated width at 30° S (cf. Dietz and Holden,
1970a: Fig. 5). Assuming a prehystricomorphous ancestor, the time of
the supposed trans-Atlantic rafting can be predated without prejudice to
the claims of relationships between African and South American hystricomorphous rodents.

From the foregoing, it seems reasonable to entertain the hypothesis that
hystricomorphous or prehystricomorphous rodents arose in the rifted
South America-Africa mass, possibly during the Paleocene when separation of the continents at critical points was not too great. As presumed in
the case of early primates, one part of the still homogenous, albeit separated, stock gave rise to caviomorphs, the other to hystricomorphs. It is
virtually certain that the same grade of resemblances between past and
present African and South American hystricomorphous rodents would be
deemed phylogenetic in comparable boreal American and South American rodents.

THE NEOTROPICAL REGION

Neotropica as defined by its mammalian fauna, includes all of South
America; Middle America except the dry and temperate zone of northern

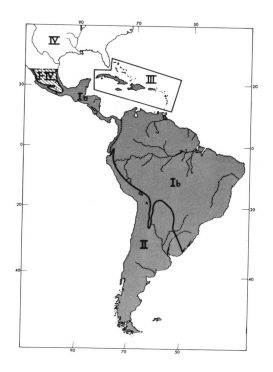

FIG. 1. Neotropical Region (Shaded) and Bordering Part of Holarctic Region

I, Brazilian Subregion (Ia = Middle American Province; Ib = South American portion); II, Patagonian Subregion; III, West Indian Subregion; IV, Holarctic Region: shown is part of Nearctic Subregion (boreal North America). I-IV (diagonals), Neotropical-Holarctic transition zone. (Modified from Hershkovitz, 1958.)

Mexico; continental islands off the Middle and South American coasts; and the oceanic Bahamas, West Indies, Galápagos and Falklands (Fig. 1). The mammals of the Region are terrestrial, volant or fresh-water forms. With exceptions noted below, whales, manatees, sea otters, seals, and sea lions are regarded as members of marine faunal areas which abut on continental zoogeographic regions and their insular districts. The shores where certain marine mammals breed and rear their young are transition zones between terrestrial (including streams and lakes) and marine faunal areas.

The genus is adopted here as common indicator for zoogeographic regions and subregions. The taxonomic and statistical data used in descriptions, comparisons, and analyses of North and South American mammals are taken from my geographic classification of Neotropical mammals (1958), unpublished notes, and taxonomic revisions listed in the bibliography; see also, Cabrera (1958, 1961a), Miller and Kellogg (1955), and Hall and Kelson (1959). For explanations of zoogeographic concepts see Hershkovitz (1958).

The Number and Kinds of Neotropical Mammals

The number and kinds of Neotropical orders, families, genera, and species of mammals are summarized in Table 2. The register of species and genera is presumed to be nearly complete for most orders. A predictably small percentage, perhaps less than 10 per cent, of the known total of

TABLE 2

Summary of the mammalian fauna of the Neotropical Region [1] *(Recent South America, Middle America, West Indies)*

Order and Family	Genera Total	Genera Endemic	Species Total	Species Endemic
Marsupialia				
* Didelphidae [2]				
Didelphinae	10	9	52	51
* Microbiotheriinae	1	1	1	1
* Caenolestidae	3	3	7	7
Insectivora [3]				
* Solenodontidae	1	1	2	2
Soricidae	1	—	8	8
Chiroptera				
Vespertilionidae	8	2	30	18
Molossidae	6	3	33	30
* Noctilionidae	1	1	2	2
Emballonuridae	9	9	17	17
* Thyropteridae	1	1	2	2
* Natalidae	1	—	1	—
* Furipteridae	2	2	2	2
Pteronotidae	2	1	7	6
Phyllostomidae				
Phyllostominae	11	10	34	34
* Glossophaginae	13	10	27	25
* Carolliinae	2	2	6	6
* Sturnirinae	1	1	9	9
* Stenoderminae	17	16	43	43
* Phyllonycterinae	3	3	6	3
* Desmodidae	3	3	3	3
Primates				
* Platyrrhini				
Callithricidae	4	4	15	15
Callimiconidae	1	1	1	1
Cebidae	11	11	26	26
Edentata (Xenarthra)				
* Myrmecophagidae	3	3	3	3
* Bradypodidae	2	2	3	3
* Dasypodidae [4]	9	8	20	16

* *Endemic with exceptions noted below.*

[1] *Majority of taxons have not been revised; figures given for genera and species are estimates of the number of valid groups.*

[2] *Except* Didelphis marsupialis, *excurrent in Nearctica.*

[3] *The extinct West Indian Nesophontidae with genus* Nesophontes, *comprising several nominal species, should perhaps be included with the Recent Neotropical fauna.*

[4] *Except* Dasypus novemcinctus (Dasypodidae), *excurrent in Nearctica.*

TABLE 2—*Continued*

Order and Family	Genera Total	Genera Endemic	Species Total	Species Endemic
Rodentia				
Sciuromorpha				
Sciuridae	5	3	18	16
Heteromyidae	2	1	8	6
Geomyidae	3	3	6	6
Myomorpha				
Muridae				
Cricetinae				
Sigmodontini	42	40	181	179
Peromyscini	8	4	41	34
Microtinae	1	—	1	1
* Caviomorpha [5]				
Erethizontidae	3	3	8	8
Caviidae	6	6	9	9
Hydrochaeridae	1	1	1	1
Dinomyidae	1	1	1	1
Dasyproctidae [6]	3	3	3	3
Chinchillidae	3	3	3	3
Myocastoridae	1	1	1	1
Capromyidae	6	6	15	15
Octodontidae	6	6	8	8
Ctenomyidae	1	1	25	25
Abrocomidae	1	1	2	2
Echimyidae	16	16	44	44
Heptaxodontidae	3	3	3	3
Lagomorpha				
Leporidae	1	—	2	1
Cetacea				
Susuidae	1	1	1	1
Delphinidae	1	1	1	1
Sirenia				
Trichechidae	1	—	1	1
Carnivora				
Canidae	7	6	13	12
Ursidae	1	1	1	1
Procyonidae	6	3	8	6
Mustelidae	9	4	15	11
Felidae	3	0	10	5
Perissodactyla				
Tapiridae	1	1	3	3
Artiodactyla				
Tayassuidae	1	—	2	1
Camelidae	2	2	4	4
Cervidae	6	5	11	10
Totals: 12 orders; 50 families				
(27 = endemic)	278	233	810	755

[5] *Not included*, Erethizon dorsatum (*Erethizontidae*), *a Nearctic endemic.*
[6] *Includes Agoutidae of recent authors.*

rodent species remains to be discovered in the field, among unidentified or misidentified museum specimens, or revived from the oblivion of synonymy. Some of the smaller marsupials may also have escaped detection but compared with rodents, the number must be far fewer.

The intensified study in recent years of the biology and distribution of bats is resulting in a significant increase in the number of recognized species and genera. The progress during the last three decades may be attributed in large part to the widespread use of fine mesh bird nets for bat collecting. The effect of this tool on the rapid advance in chiroptology is comparable to the impact of the snap-and-live traps on the advancements in rodent taxonomy and zoogeography during the first half of this century and the turn of the last.

There is little probability that more than a very few species (*sensu stricto*) larger than a cottontail rabbit remain unknown to science. This statement is made with the fact in mind that Baird's tapir (*Tapirus bairdi*), largest of Neotropical mammals, had not been identified as a member of the South American fauna until 1954, and that another ungulate, the dwarf Andean brocket, *Mazama chunyi*, was not described until 1959.

The vast majority of currently recognized Neotropical taxa, particularly of familial, generic, and specific grades, remain to be revised. A large number of the taxa will certainly be dropped as superfluous, while a smaller number will be erected as new. The net total may not differ significantly from that shown in Table 2.

Twelve of the 18 orders of living mammals are represented in the Neotropical Region. Not present are the relict orders Monotremata (spiny anteaters), Dermoptera (colugos or flying lemurs), Pholidota (pangolins or scaly anteaters), Hyracoidea (hyraxes or dassies), Tubulidentata (aardvark), and Proboscidea (elephants). The single living species of inland fresh-water manatee (Sirenia) and two fresh-water species of toothed whales (Cetacea) are included in the Neotropical fauna. Some species of Pinnipedia frequent coasts and continental islands of the Neotropical Region but are essentially marine in distribution. They are not counted as members of Neotropica. In comparison, the Holarctic Region has 13 orders of non-marine mammals, the Ethiopian 12, the Nearctic Subregion (of Holarctic) 8, and the Australian 4, excluding man and introduced species.

No single order of mammals is absolutely confined to the Neotropical Region. Nevertheless, endemism is extremely high. The autochthonous Xenarthra is virtually endemic with but a single species, the nine-banded armadillo (*Dasypus novemcinctus*), extending its range into Nearctica. Two subordinal groups, the Platyrrhini (Primates) and Caviomorpha (Rodentia) are also typically Neotropical although one species of the latter, the porcupine (*Erethizon dorsatum*), is wholly boreal. The Marsupialia is one of the oldest and most characteristic orders of Neotropical mammals, but it is even more representative of the Australian region. Of all Neotropical marsupials, only a species of opossum, genus *Didelphis,* ranges beyond into Nearctica. Of a total of 50 modern Neotropical mammalian families, 27 (or 54 per cent) are endemic. Of the total number of genera and species, approximately 83 per cent and 93 per cent respectively, are endemic (Table 2).

The Neotropical Region and the Nearctic Subregion, or boreal America (i.e., North America less Neotropical Middle America), are approximately equal in size. The Neotropical fauna, however, is more diversified, not only in terms of higher categories, but in species as well. It is also more densely populated in terms of number of individuals per species. Rodents predominate in both Regions but represent a higher proportion of the total fauna in temperate zones, irrespective of Region, than in tropical zones. Neotropical bats follow in number of species and individuals but in many parts of the tropical zones may be more diversified and abundant than rodents (Table 3).

The South American portion of what is now the Neotropical Region was colonized by the evolving mammalian fauna of Middle America and perhaps in small part by waifs from the Gondwanaland continents of Africa and possibly Antarctica. Middle America received its first mammals from boreal America, subsequent ones almost entirely from South America. The meager fauna of the West Indies consists of relicts of a mid-Tertiary fauna which lived on mainland coasts of the Caribbean and, perhaps, Mexican seas, and an odd assortment of mostly Quaternary Middle American waifs, strays, and imports.

In addition to works cited in the text, see Cabrera and Yepes (1940) for a popular account of the recent mammals of South America, Scott (1937), for the recent and extinct mammals, Darlington (1957) for general zoogeography, Simpson (1940a; 1950) for a history of Latin American mammals, Hershkovitz (1963a) for a preliminary report on present subject matter, and Hershkovitz (1966b) for an examination of opinions on intercontinental faunal interchange. The student will also be interested in a valuable collection of articles on South American geography, climate, flora, fauna, and ethnology written by respected authorities and compiled under the editorship of Steward (1950). Croizat (1958) has compiled an enormous amount of information on the history and distribution of Neotropical mammals. The student may find Croizat's violent reactions to orthodox zoogeography mind-reeling and he must decide for himself whether the rewards for patient sifting through disputatious ramblings are worth the effort.

Neotropical Subregions

Brazilian Subregion

The major topographic features of the Brazilian Subregion (Fig. 1), exclusive of its Middle American Province (see below), include the great arc of the Andes on the west and northwest, the Guianan highlands in the northeast, and the Brazilian highlands on the southeast (Fig. 10). Lying

TABLE 3

Comparison of each order of Neotropical mammals (first line of each couplet) with the Nearctic mammals (second line of couplet).

Diversity Rank *	Order	Families	Genera	Species	Percent of Species Total
1	Rodentia	17	112	378	46.6
1	*Rodentia*	*8*	*44*	*256*	*58*
2	Chiroptera	10	80	222	27.4
3	*Chiroptera*	*5*	*25*	*53*	*12*
3	Marsupialia	2	14	60	7.4
7	*Marsupialia*	*1*	*2*	*2*	*0.5*
4	Carnivora	5	26	47	5.8
4	*Carnivora*	*5*	*20*	*39*	*9*
5	Primates	3	16	42	5.2
—	*Primates*	*0*	*0*	*0*	*0*
6	Edentata (Xenarthra)	3	14	26	3.2
8	*Edentata (Xenarthra)*	*1*	*1*	*1*	*0.2*
7	Artiodactyla	3	9	17	2.1
6	*Artiodactyla*	*4*	*10*	*11*	*2*
8	Insectivora	2	2	10	1.2
2	*Insectivora*	*2*	*10*	*57*	*13*
9	Perissodactyla	1	1	3	0.4
—	*Perissodactyla*	*0*	*0*	*0*	*0*
10	Lagomorpha	1	1	2	0.2
5	*Lagomorpha*	*2*	*4*	*23*	*5*
11	Cetacea [1]	2	2	2	0.2
—	*Cetacea* [1]	*0*	*0*	*0*	*0*
12	Sirenia [1]	1	1	1	0.1
—	*Sirenia* [1]	*0*	*0*	*0*	*0*
Neotropical	12	50	278	810	100
Nearctic	*8*	*28*	*116*	*442*	*100*

* *The Neotropical orders are ranked according to their respective numbers of species, beginning with the most diversified order. The rank of the corresponding Nearctic order is shown by its number.*

[1] *Only strictly fresh-water, land-locked species are counted as members of continental faunas.*

between the highlands is the grand Rio Amazonas basin and the connecting Río Orinoco basin. Between the Andes and the Brazilian highlands lies the Paraná-Paraguay basin. The coastal plains are extensive in northern Brazil and the Guianas but are narrow at the foot of the Cordillera Oriental in northern Venezuela. However, the offshore Caribbean islands, including Trinidad, Tobago, Sparta, and Netherlands Antilles, are isolated extensions. The Lago Maracaibo basin of western Venezuela and the Río Magdalena basin in northern Colombia are broad, deep coastal valleys between the main chains of the northern Andes. The coastal plains of eastern Brazil are narrow but broaden in the extreme south and in

Uruguay, which is largely transitional between the Brazilian and Patagonian Subregions.

The vegetation (Fig. 2) of the Brazilian Subregion is highly diverse. It ranges from coastal mangrove swamps, deserts, lowland savannas, tree savannas, and scrub forests to coniferous deciduous and evergreen broadleaf forests. Uplands support vegetation characteristic of extremely dry to extremely humid tropical zones. Rain forests cover much of the Andes, the Guianan highlands and Brazilian coastal ranges. Scattered atop the Ecuadorian, Colombian, and Venezuelan Andes are alpine meadows and tundra, and many summits of Guianan highlands or "tepuis" are covered with scrub or grasses.

Of approximately 195 genera of mammals occurring in the South American portion of the Brazilian Subregion, fully one-third are endemic. Only 21 of the Neotropical genera, or nearly 11 per cent of the total, are excurrent in Nearctica. Nine genera which straddle Brazilia and Nearctica cannot be definitely classified as either Neotropical or Nearctic. They are termed varicants. Seven genera are extremely wide-ranging or cosmopolite; that is, they are represented in the Old World as well as the tropical region of the New World. Very few living species of proven or conceded Nearctic origin are also South American, perhaps only the river otter (*Lutra canadensis*), long-tailed weasel (*Mustela frenata*), puma (*Felis concolor*), and jaguar (*Felis onca.*)

The Brazilian Subregion comprises a number of Provinces, but only the Middle American Province has been defined in terms of its mammals (Hershkovitz, 1958, p. 596). The Province is discussed below (p. 338). Other parts of the Subregion are treated here simply as geographic tracts which may or may not coincide with zoogeographic Provinces or Districts. They are described under the separate headings: Brazilian Highlands and Bolivian Uplands, Amazon Valley, Orinoco Valley, Llanos, Guianan District, Paraná-Paraguay Valley District, Andes (part), and Páramos (part).

Patagonian Subregion

The Patagonian Subregion includes the páramos of Ecuador from the equator southward, the desert coast and puna zones of Peru, the alpine highlands of Bolivia, all Chile, the pastoral plains of Uruguay, and all Argentina except the subtropical forests of Misiones, Corrientes, and those of the eastern slopes of the Andes from Tucumán to Bolivia.

A broad transition zone between the Patagonian and Brazilian subregions extends from southeastern Brazil and Uruguay through Entre Rios and pastoral parts of the chaco of Argentina, Paraguay, and Bolivia; it interdigitates with the alpine and temperate forest zones of Bolivia, Peru, and southern Ecuador and overlaps the northern coast of Peru. In general, the mammals of the gallery forests along the banks of the northern Paraná and its tributaries are Brazilian; those of pastoral habitats between the streams are mainly Patagonian.

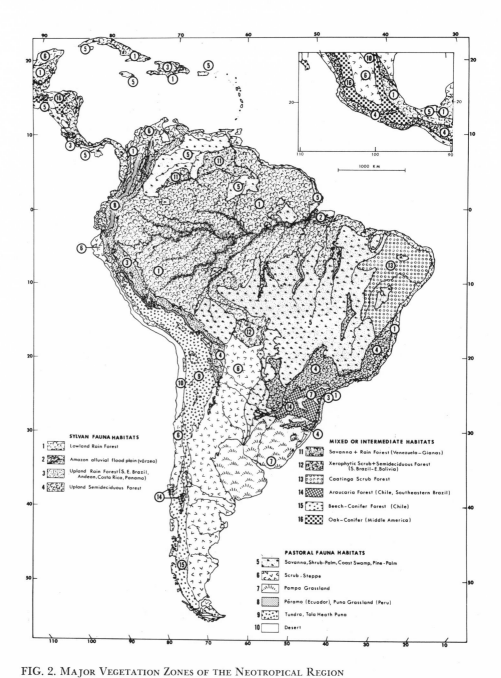

FIG. 2. MAJOR VEGETATION ZONES OF THE NEOTROPICAL REGION

Adapted from Sauer (1950), and from Leopold (1959) for Mexican portion. Except for thin coastal bands, many parts of pastoral zones, particularly Zones 5 in West Indies and most of Zone 6 in Colombia and Venezuela, are products of human disturbances.

The dominant topographic features of the Patagonian Subregion are the dry Pacific coastal plains and the Andean chain in the west, the Patagonian Plateau in the center and the vast low-lying Paraná basin and thin southern coastal strips on the east.

The vegetation of the Patagonian Subregion is predominantly pastoral. The pampas, or prairies, of northwestern Argentina and most of Uruguay are characterized by tall perennial grasses broken by wooded hills and thin lines of trees bordering the streams. Westward toward the Andes, the land becomes dry, its thin cover of scrub and grasses broken by bare salt pans in the north and center, and by desert in the south. Beyond the Andes, the narrow Pacific coast of Peru and northern Chile is desertic, but inland and to the north and south the waste gradually changes to scrublands. Continuing southward the xerophytic vegetation gives way to nearly continuous stands of beech-conifer forests. These extend from about 32° to 47° S in Chile and bordering parts of Argentina. The forest, in turn, is gradually replaced by tundra which covers the entire tip of the continent. The lower slopes of the Argentine side of the Andes are arid, with cactus and scrub growing to the headwaters of the main streams where the lower edge of the forest is met. The permanent snow line varies from 2500 meters above sea level in Neuquén to over 5000 meters between San Juán in Argentina and Coquimbo in Chile. The zone of tundra is narrowest in central Chile and expands northward into the tola heath puna of northern Chile, northwestern Argentina, western Bolivia, and southern Peru. Extension of the Patagonian vegetation with some of its fauna into the Andes of northern Peru and southern Ecuador to the equator results from deforestation, cultivation, and persistent burning with attendant dessication.

The vegetation of the Patagonian-Brazilian transition zone includes the scrublands of the Gran Chaco, bordering swamp-palm savannas of Argentina, Paraguay, Bolivia, and Brazil, and dense gallery forests along the Paraná and some tributaries. Man-made clearings advance the boundaries of the transition zone northward.

The mammalian fauna of the Patagonian Subregion is comparatively poor and largely insular. It consists of 76 genera, 56 per cent of which are confined to the area. None of the Patagonian species, with the possible exception of the jaguar and puma, originated outside the present limits of the Neotropical Region, but three genera of bats (*Myotis, Eptesicus, Tadarida*) and three genera of Carnivora (*Mustela, Lutra, Felis*) are cosmopolitan.

The most characteristic Patagonian mammals are the relict marsupials, edentates, and caviomorph rodents, which comprise 31 of the 76 genera, and the progressive cricetines with 21 genera. All non-volant Patagonian mammals are pastoral or versatile (see p. 369 ff.), and the 12 Patagonian genera of bats are insectivorous except for the blood-sucking *Desmodus*.

The faunas of some parts of the Patagonian Subregion will be examined under the separate headings: Paraná-Paraguay Valley District; Andes;

Páramos; Altiplano District. For a list of Patagonian mammals and comparisons with those of other Neotropical districts, see Hershkovitz (1958, pp. 599, 611).

West Indian Subregion

The West Indian Subregion consists of the chain of islands from the Bahamas and Cuba in the northwest to the Grenadas in the southeast. Little Swan Island may be included, if its capromyid rodent (*Geocapromys browni thorocatus*) is not an import. Trinidad, Tobago, Sparta and the Dutch West Indies are continental islands of the Brazilian Subregion.

The living mammalian fauna of the West Indies is comparatively small, apparently Middle and northern South American in origin, and preponderantly chiropteran in kind. Its 31 genera of bats, 8 of them endemic, make up 69 per cent of the total number of genera in the fauna. Two monotypic genera of Insectivora, *Solenodon* and *Atopogale* (regarded as congeneric by McDowell, 1958, p. 121) are the most peculiar and ancient of West Indian mammals. They have no near relatives on the mainland and would seem to be survivors of an early Tertiary Caribbean or Middle American fauna. The caviomorphs are the 3 living genera of Capromyidae (*Capromys, Geocapromys, Plagiodontia*), the aguti (*Dasyprocta,* Dasyproctidae), and an arboreal spiny rat (*Echimys,* Echimyidae). The capromyids and aguti were important game animals commonly domesticated and carried by man from island to island. Capromyids, like solenodonts, are relicts without near mainland relatives. The aguti, however, is possibly a recent mainland import. Spiny rats could have been rafted to Martinique from the continental islands of Trinidad or Margarita, or from the Venezuelan coast. Their habit of nesting in family groups in the hollows of tree trunks and branches lends them to this form of transportation and to successful colonization. The mouse opossum or marmosa (*Marmosa*) of the Grenadines is also a waif or import from Venezuela or its offshore islands. The history of the pygmy rice rat [*Oryzomys (Oligoryzomys) victus*] from St. Vincent, Lesser Antilles, may be nearly the same. The swamp rice rat (*Oryzomys palustris antillarum*) of Jamaica is a waif of Central American origin, but accidental importation by man cannot be ruled out. Finally, the opossum (*Didelphis marsupialis*), the armadillo (*Dasypus novemcinctus*), and the raccoon (*Procyon lotor*), all of the Lesser Antilles, are less likely to have been rafted than to have been introduced by man from the mainland. The first two were (and still are) commonly transported throughout the Neotropical Region for trade or food. The raccoon, though of the varicant genus *Procyon,* is very likely an import from Middle America or the Nearctic Subregion.

The total known West Indian mammalian fauna is an agglomeration of living and recently extinct elements. Among the living is an odd lot of the aforementioned marsupials, bats, rice rats, arboreal spiny rat, aguti, armadillo, and raccoon, all essentially forest dwellers. They are little if at all differentiated from their respective mainland relatives and could have been transported recently over water, through the air, or imported by man from the Caribbean or Mexican mainland. Also among the living, but more abundantly among the recently extinct, is a relict fauna of insectivores, bats, a primate, megalonychid ground sloths, caviomorph rodents and the giant arboreal cricetine rodent, *Megalomys* of South American affinities (Hershkovitz, 1970, p. 793). Except for absence of pre-Recent marsupials, forms of which may still turn up, this relict West Indian fauna is an exceptionally well-preserved and representative sampling of what the Late to Middle Tertiary Caribbean or Middle American *sylvan* fauna may have been. The striking similarities between the composition of this fauna and Upper Tertiary fauna of South America, and the close relationship between their respective taxons, suggest that the West Indian fauna is either derived from South America or, more likely, is a relict of a common Middle American fauna. A third possibility is that the Antillean fauna combines sylvan elements from both Middle and South America. To a large extent, the faunal relationship of the Greater Antilles to the tropical American mainland parallels that of Madagascar to the African mainland.

The nature of the dispersal routes from mainland to islands is still a subject for speculation. The arguments for and against land bridge or over-water dispersal are summarized by Simpson (1956), who favors the latter. Students considering the problem, however, have not always distinguished between modern (Strata IV, V), and relict (Strata II, III) West Indian species (see p. 347 and Fig. 5) or avoided anachronisms in relating the insular to the mainland faunas. Also, they may have overlooked the ecological factors controlling dispersal of individual species. The "imbalance" sometimes noted in the composition of the older West Indian mammalian fauna is misleading. Except for absence of marsupials, the relict West Indian fauna is representative of what the *sylvan* fauna of Middle and northern South America must have been during the Tertiary. Judged by this fauna, the West Indies then, as now, lacked suitable natural habitats for establishment of the grazing ungulates and their train of predators known to have occurred in Middle America and northern South America since the Miocene. If the West Indies is indeed, as it appears to be, a refugium of a mainland Tertiary sylvan fauna, it may be necessary to postulate the existence of a land bridge or a Caribbean Land at the time of the invasion (Barbour, 1916; Willis, 1932; Hummelinck, 1940; Anthony, 1942; Maldonado-Koerdell, 1964; Vinson and Brineman, 1963; Frieland and Dietz, 1971; also *in contra*, Patterson and Pascual, Chapter VI).

The predominant form of modern West Indian mammals is chiropteran. Present and future natural expansion of the West Indian fauna depends on continued fortuitous overwater and air-borne arrivals from the mainland, and from inter-island exchange. This straggling and uncertain method of increment is largely nullified by human interference and control of the environment. The overall result is that bats, the most successful colonizers in tropical regions, may increase in kind and numbers, even in urban and cultivated rural localities. At the same time the non-volant, non-imported, natural colonizers of the island are virtually doomed to extinction.

[Most of the above account is extracted, with modifications, from Hershkovitz (1958, pp. 600-605). For additional information on the zoogeography of West Indian mammals, faunal lists, and bibliographies, see Darlington (1938), Simpson (1956) and Koopman (1959.]

Middle America

a. The Zoogeographic Province

The faunal relationship between modern Middle American and northern South American mammals is so intimate that Middle America is now considered to be a zoogeographic province of the Brazilian Subregion of the Neotropical Region. The Province extends from Mexico at about 23° N on the Atlantic coast, 25° N on the Pacific coast, and 18° 22' N in the central highlands, southward into Central America and the coastal plains and low hills west of the Cordillera Occidental in Colombia and Ecuador.

Mexico and Central America are dominated by rugged highlands. Except for the broad limestone platform of Yucatán, plains and lowlands occur only as fringes along the coast and large rivers, and as intermontane basins. The vegetation zones of the tropical lowlands includes deserts, savannas, thorn forests, savanna-palm forests, rain forests, and mangrove swamps. Evergreen and deciduous forests cover the uplands and lower slopes of the mountains. They are replaced at higher altitudes, mostly north of Nicaragua, by oak-conifer forests. Scattered alpine meadows succeed the mountain forests above tree line. Eastern Panama and the Middle American portion of Colombia and Ecuador are coastal lowlands except for isolated chains of low hills and a single high range, the Serranía del Darién, with a few peaks barely rising above the tropical zone. Nearly all the land from eastern Panama southward is covered by tropical rain forests interspersed with swamps.

b. Geological History

Historically, Middle America consists of two parts. The northwestern portion, or nuclear Central America, extends from southern Mexico into southern Nicaragua. It may or may not have been isolated at times, possibly at the Isthmus of Tehuantepec, from the remainder of Mexico. The southeastern portion of the subregion varied in composition but generally consisted of most, sometimes all, of Panamá, Costa Rica, adjacent parts of Nicaragua, and a Western Archipelago. These lands, according to Lloyd (1963) were represented by a series of islands which varied in size and number from Jurassic to Pliocene when they united to form an uninterrupted link between South America and nuclear Central

America. The pre-Pliocene islands and the since-foundered Western Archipelago served as an island bridge between the continents. The zoogeographic implications of the two historically distinct portions of the Middle American Subregion have not been fully determined.

c. Faunal Relations

The great variety and numerical abundance of the mammals of the Middle American Province are characteristic of the Brazilian Subregion as a whole. The North American portion of the Province, though possessing less than one-twentieth of the area of Nearctica, contains 11 per cent more genera. Of its 138 genera, 109 (79%) are Neotropical regionalites. Twenty-two of the latter (16% of the total) range into Nearctica. In contrast, only 4 genera of strictly Holarctic mammals, and 9 cosmopolitan genera have penetrated the Middle American Province. This paucity of exotic elements plus an endemicism of 8 per cent (11 genera) underscore the nearly complete individuality of the North American fraction of the Middle American Province, as compared with the Nearctic Subregion of the Holarctic Region. All Holarctic and two cosmopolitan genera drop out in the South American portion of the Middle American Province and, in proportion to the total number of genera (195), they form an almost insignificant minority.

Some zoogeographers (cf. Schmidt, 1954, p. 328) treat Middle America as a part of the Nearctic Subregion transitional between Nearctica and Neotropica. Others include Middle America in the Neotropical Region but qualify it as historically the tropical part of Nearctica. The qualification is misleading. Middle America, exclusive of the central Mexican plateau which lies within Nearctica, supports substantial temperate and subtropical zone faunas composed almost entirely of autochthonous elements. These faunas may have been dominant before climatic change brought on their supplantation in the lowlands by a tropical zone fauna.

The Nearctic, as generally understood, refers to the Recent, not the historical, boreal American fauna. It is a Subregion of the circumpolar Holarctic Region. Its mammalian fauna is composed of living boreal American autochthons, and living postglacial elements from Eurasia and Middle America. Hibbard, Ray, Savage, Taylor, and Guilday (1965, p. 513) list 88 genera of living Nearctic mammals which were boreal American during the Wisconsin or earlier. Of this number, at least 9 genera of bats and rodents, one of opossum and one of armadillo are certainly tropical American elements which spread into boreal America during the Pleistocene. Not less than 17 genera of bats and rodents, a skunk (*Conepatus*), and a deer (*Odocoileus*) very probably do belong in this group. A few among the remaining 28 genera not listed by Hibbard et al., out of a total of about 116 now living in Nearctica, may yet prove to be preglacial autochthons. The living genera unknown as fossils in boreal America include 19 genera of bats, a marsupial (*Marmosa*), a peccary

(*Tayassu*), and 2 genera of carnivores (*Nasua, Herpailurus*), all of tropical origin, and 2 rodents (*Lagurus, Lemmus*) and 2 carnivores (*Alopex, Thalarctos*) of northern or Eurasian origin. Evidently, Nearctica, with 53 of its 116 genera of certain or probably tropical origin, has strong Middle American affinities. Paleontologists and some zoogeographers have stated the reverse, but relationships remain the same.

For detailed information on the geographic classification and distribution of living Middle American mammals see Hershkovitz (1958) and Baker (1963). Alvarez (1963) has discussed the northeastern limits of the Middle American Province for mammals, while Martin (1958) and Duellman (1965) have described the northern limits with particular reference to the herpetological fauna. Leopold (1959) has presented an excellent and handsomely illustrated account of the ecology and game animals of Mexico. A detailed and authoritative account of all aspects of Middle American natural history is contained in Wauchope and West (1964).

d. Ecological Relations

The historically and geographically distinct mammalian faunas of temperate, or boreal, America, and of Middle America are separated by a pronounced ecological barrier which lies athwart northern Mexico. The boundary between the faunas follows the contour dividing the subtropical deserts and temperate highland savannas on the north from the lowland tropical forests to the south. The dividing line is not static. Overlying it is a broad transition zone occupied by many species of both areas (Fig. 1). In the past, from Cretaceous to Recent, the border shifted from near the present boundary of the continental United States to its present position. Wherever the separation at any one time may have been, it seems to have been roughly the same for all classes of land-based vertebrates and, in the case of mammals, at least, of their ectoparasites as well (Wenzel and Tipton, 1966, pp. 714, 716).

The northern ecological barrier is, and has been since early Cenozoic, the broad and comparatively dry vegetation zone which, with a qualified exception of the narrow Gulf coast corridor, isolates the forest fauna of Middle America from that of boreal North America. The history of the phytogeographic regions, or geofloras, has been described by Axelrod (1958, pp. 434, 436) as follows:

> By Early Tertiary time the vegetation of North America comprised three geofloras, each of which represents a major vegetation type of wide geographic extent and relative uniformity that maintained its essential identity through time and space. Occupying the southern half of the continent was the broadleafed evergreen Neotropical-Tertiary Geoflora; at the north was the temperate, mixed deciduous Arcto-Tertiary Geoflora; and between them, centered in the southern Rocky Mountains and adjacent Mexico, the sclerophyllous and microphyllous Madro-Tertiary Geoflora was making its initial appearance. . . . The Madro-Tertiary Geoflora had already appeared on the drier borders of the North American tropics by the Middle Eocene, and probably occupied much of the southwestern United States and adjacent

Mexico by the close of the Oligocene. It extended its range northward and southward, as well as eastward and westward, in response to expanding dry climate in the succeeding Miocene epoch, and it attained an even wider distribution during the Pliocene as semi-arid climate continued to spread. The particular time it invaded a given region depended chiefly on climate, as determined by position with respect to latitude, mountains and the ocean. It was largely in the later Pliocene, as environmental diversity became more pronounced over western America, that the geoflora was segregated into a number of derivative communities of more restricted occurrences. Some Madro-Tertiary species survived down to the present in areas of their Tertiary distribution and became adapted to climates which differ from those of the Tertiary. But others that formerly ranged northward into California, Nevada, Utah, Colorado and Oklahoma now find their nearest relatives only in the mild-winter areas to southward, notably in the mountains from southern Arizona to western Texas, and in the structurally continuous ranges farther south which comprise the Sierra Madre of Mexico. It was from these mountains of southwestern North America, where many relicts of the Madro-Tertiary Geoflora now survive, that the term "Madro-" was derived. The name also seems appropriate because this region apparently was the general area of both its early evolution and subsequent radiation.

Three mammalian faunas correlated with the geofloras must have evolved in North America at the same time. The first was the northern, or boreal American, associated with the Arcto-Tertiary Geoflora. This was a "temperate" zone fauna. The second was the southern, or Middle American, linked with the Neotropical-Tertiary Geoflora. This was a tropical to temperate zone fauna. The "temperate" elements of the two faunas must not be confused. The intermediate Madro-Tertiary Geoflora supported a fauna which must have roughly paralleled or corresponded to the present transition Nearctic–Neotropical fauna. The composition of these faunas changed in time so that resemblance between the early Tertiary and the Recent boreal American mammalian faunas is minimal, probably verging on zero. In contrast, the Recent Middle American fauna retains descendents of many elements of older faunas.

The Middle American fauna associated with the Neotropical-Tertiary Geoflora almost certainly became established in late Mesozoic and early Tertiary. Presumably it arrived by a slow and sporadic filtering process from mainly boreal America and possibly in the case of a few elements, from South America. The composition of this old fauna can only be surmised from what is known of the Cretaceous and early Tertiary mammals of western United States and from the very different early Tertiary mammals of the southern half of South America. This Middle American fauna may have included representative and ancestral forms of the ancient marsupials, bats, edentates, primates, condylarths, rodents, and perhaps one or more of the ungulate orders Notoungulata, Litopterna, Astropotheria, Xenungulata, and Pyrotheria, which appear in Paleocene deposits of southern South America (but see p. 417).

Meanwhile, the fauna of boreal America was changing as a result of extinctions, evolution of surviving taxons and extensive exchange with adjacent parts of Eurasia. So great has been this exchange that boreal

America is now the Nearctic Subregion of the circumpolar Holarctic Region (cf. Hibbard et al., 1965; Burt, 1958, p. 152). Exchange with the evolving Middle American fauna also took place but was mainly limited during late Tertiary to xenarthrans, rodents, and bats from the south, and mostly browsing or grazing ungulates and their predators from the north (cf. Olson and McGrew, 1941; Stirton and Gealey, 1949; Stirton, 1953, 1954; Fries, Hibbard, and Dunkle, 1955; Whitmore and Stewart, 1965).

The historical biogeography of modern boreal American and Middle American mammals is largely concordant with that of the herpetofauna of the same regions, as outlined by J. M. Savage (1960, 1966). For other treatments of the subject see Tihen (1964) and Duellman (1965, 1966); Stuart (1966) gives the most recent account of the history of Central American environment; Martin and Harrell (1957) have discussed the relationships of the biota of Mexico and the United States; contributions edited by Wauchope and West (1964) on the geology, geography, climate, soil, hydrography, oceanography, fauna, flora, and biogeography of Middle America are invaluable.

FAUNAL ORIGINS AND DISPERSAL ROUTES

Intercontinental Faunal Movements

Accounts of South American faunal histories have been based on the assumption that an Isthmian water gap nearly completely isolated North American mammals from South America during the whole of the Mesozoic and the Cenozoic to the end of the Tertiary. The assumption was further complicated by the notion that establishment of a land connection between the continents near the end of the Pliocene initiated a wholesale interchange of faunas. As conceived by Simpson (1950, pp. 380-381; also 1965, p. 221; 1966, p. 9), ". . . the exchange was at first rather limited in scope and the full surge of intermigration did not occur until somewhat later, in unequivocably Pleistocene times. . . . Invasion occurred in both directions. By a moderate tabulation, fifteen families of North American mammals then spread [across the land bridge] into South America and seven families spread in the reverse direction. The main migrants to the south were rabbits, squirrels, field mice, dogs, bears, raccoons, weasels, cats, mastodons, horses, tapirs, peccaries, camels, and deer, including in most of these cases some variety of related forms."

This dramatic scene of the crossing of the Panamanian bridge is not consonant with the zoological, ecological, and geographic evidence, and with what is known of the ecological preferences, habits, and vagility of the animals concerned. For most mammals, the pre-Pleistocene shifting system of Isthmian sea channels (cf. Woodring, 1954, 1966; Lloyd, 1963; Whitmore and Stewart, 1965) may not have been more than minor obstacles and for some, such as otters and other aquatic and subaquatic animals, they may have been invitations. They were certainly no deterrent compared with the climatic barrier across northern Mexico, or with seas crossed by non-volant terrestrial mammals in reaching the Antilles, the Galápagos, the Philippines, Australia, New Guinea and other islands well off continental shelves. Evidently, animals with territories extending to the edge of the Isthmian waterways crossed opportunely. Rodents, armadillos, and anteaters are accomplished island hoppers, waifs, and swimmers. Rafts and shifting patterns of peninsulas and island chains provided additional means of access to opposing shores. Seemingly non-aquatic mammals, such as ground sloths and related edentates, were crossing the water gap, or gaps, from the middle Pliocene and possibly late Miocene, while monkeys crossed at various times since Oligocene or late Eocene. Bats, of course, may have been as evenly distributed in north-western South America and the Isthmian region during most of the Tertiary as they are today.

At the time of the Pliocene-Pleistocene transition when, according to Simpson, the full surge of intercontinental faunal exchange was about to begin, virtually all modern types of South and Middle American mammals had already become differentiated and most had reached nearly their past or present limits of dispersal (Hershkovitz, 1966b).

There is no likelihood that North American migrants could have spread throughout South America and radiated into the present multitude of highly specialized and peculiarly adapted species, genera, and supergeneric categories during the Pleistocene only. Hibbard et al. (1965, p. 520), in referring to the Pleistocene mammals of boreal America, concluded that "although mammalian evolution might have been accelerated during the Pleistocene in some groups, this time-span was so short that differentiation hardly ever went beyond the species-group level." Basing judgment on the differentiation of the ectoparasites of Neotropical cricetine rodents, Wenzel and Tipton (1966) suggested that dispersal of the cricetine mice into South America took place in the Miocene or earlier.

The final and still existing gap between the continents is the Bolívar geosyncline (Figs. 3 and 4). This, the Isthmian or Panamanian portal of some zoogeographers, extends, according to Nygren (1950, p. 1998), ". . . through coastal Ecuador and Colombia from southwestern Ecuador to the Golfo de Urabá. Six cross-basin highs separate the deeps within the trough. Marine sedimentation began in the south in the middle Eocene, gradually encroached northward, and continued intermittently on into the upper Miocene. Several unconformities of varying importance are present. Post-Miocene sedimentation is mostly nonmarine. During the early Tertiary the sediments were largely derived from the west, after the lower Miocene they were mostly from the east. Migration of terrestrial animals could have taken place through this area during the periods from upper Cretaceous to middle Eocene, middle Oligocene, lower Miocene, middle Miocene, and from upper Miocene to Recent."

Despite all evidence to the contrary, sheer dint of repetition [e.g., Simpson in at least six major articles; virtually all textbooks, short articles, and introductions by various authors, including Hershkovitz (1962: 18),

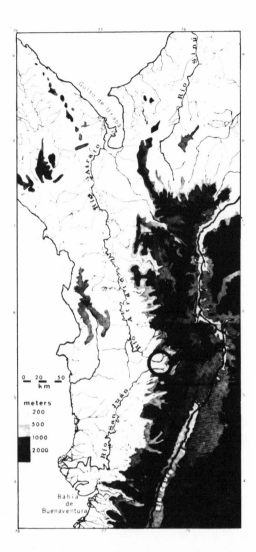

FIG. 3. Río Atrato-Río San Juán
Basins, Western Colombia

*The river channels follow the
axis of the Bolívar geosyncline.
Land bridge connecting Middle
and South America across the
former Isthmian seaway is the
narrow divide (circled) between
the rivers. The two river systems
with bordering swamps still inhibit
full interchange of mammalian
faunas between Middle and
South America.*

and most recently, Bianchi et al. (1971)] has established as dogma the
notion of a single grand intercontinental exchange of mammalian fauna
during the Pleistocene (cf. Keast, 1968, Abstract, p. 225; Chapter I).
Patterson and Pascual (1968) likewise adhere to the line the senior author
(Patterson) helped establish. My analysis of their concepts of intercontinental faunal movements and relationships concentrates on the special
treatment they give to South American cricetines (see below, p. 324, 354).

Primary Dispersal Routes

Movements of mammals into South America during the Quaternary were
mainly, if not entirely, via the Isthmian land bridge. From latest Cretaceous and during most of the Tertiary, access to the continent must have

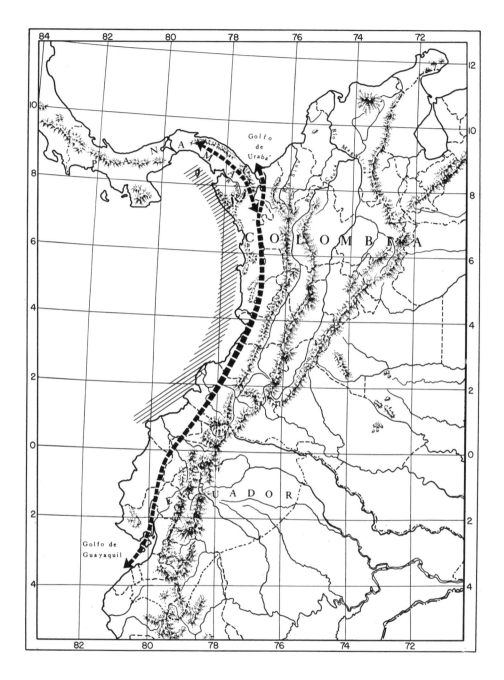

FIG. 4. Axis of Bolívar Geosyncline (Bars) and Western Tertiary Borderland (Diagonals), in Ecuador, Colombia, and Panama (Adapted from Nygren, 1950, Fig. 1)

The axis marks the extent of the Tertiary seaway which served as a faunal filter between Middle and South America. The trough has since been filled by sedimentation, mostly from the eastern border as the Andes rose while the western borderlands (diagonals) subsided. See Fig. 3 for present status.

been alternately by incomplete land routes and by fortuitous oversea routes involving rafting, waifing, wafting, and island hopping. Entry could have been gained either from Middle America or through the West Indian chain. The availability and greater proximity of habitats on the Caribbean coast of Colombia and Venezuela probably favored at times the Antillean route. This may indeed have been one approach used by migrants with living descendents occurring mainly or entirely east of the northern Andes. Terra firma gained, some animals spread southward, most likely along the eastern base of the rising Andes (cf. Harrington, 1962, p. 1802 ff.) as far as the Deseado massif in southern Patagonia. Others followed the same uplands southward to the Amazonas-Paraná divide in Bolivia, then turned east to reach the coastal highlands of Brazil. These postulated Tertiary highland routes persist today and, judged by modern faunas, some parts became primary evolutionary centers as well. Simpson (1965: 216) doubts that the "older mammals of the Brazilian uplands were derived from the Andes, as has been suggested, because those uplands were there and surely occupied by mammals of the older faunal stocks before the Andes existed." The older stocks to which Simpson refers are regarded by him as North American in origin, and his concept of the Andean uplands in this context, is as a Miocene–Quaternary phenomenon. It appears to me most unlikely, however, that the Brazilian highlands could have been inhabited by mammals of northern origin before the first colonizers or their descendents had crossed half the length of South America along an upland route available to them at the time of their entry from Middle America or, perhaps, the West Indies. The Andes, and here I follow the data compiled and illustrated by Harrington (1962, p. 1802), began to rise above sea level during late Cretaceous or earliest Paleocene. These dates, and there is evidence that the uplift may have occurred earlier in some part of the Andes, are early enough for bringing mammals to the Brazilian highlands along the suggested route. Recent discoveries of upper Cretaceous mammals in the Peruvian Andes (Thaler, 1967; Sigé, 1968) are confirmatory. Mammalian colonization of the Brazilian highlands in Cretaceous–early Tertiary by the oversea route from Africa was feasible, but Simpson has consistently denied the possibility of contributions from other Gondwanaland continents (see p. 317).

The uplands today begin at approximately the 200 meter contour line bordering the western Orinocoan, Amazonian, and Paranan basins. They rise westward into the Andes proper and eastward into the Brazilian highlands. The Guianan highlands east of the Rios Orinoco-Negro, however, appear to have been isolated from the mainstreams of terrestrial transcontinental traffic.

Large sections of the primary migration routes must have been obliterated and many of their local faunas destroyed or displaced as the result of diastrophic actions and climatic changes. Nevertheless, shifting faunal pockets persisted as foci of faunal contractions or expansions in the Amazonian uplands or Andean piedmont, the Amazonian-Paraná divide,

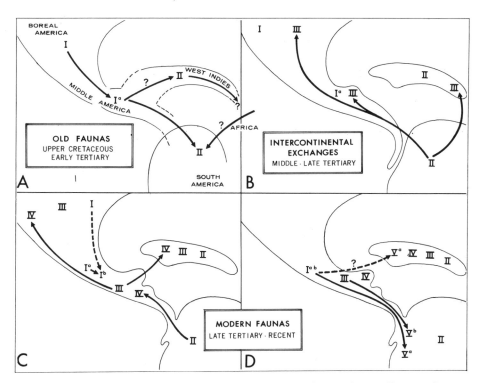

FIG. 5. MAIN INTERCONTINENTAL FAUNAL MOVEMENTS (ARROWS) AND FAUNAL STRATA (ROMAN NUMERALS)

Southward movements indicated in A go on in B. Northern movements indicated in C go on in D (see text below for explanation). Outlines of regions are stylized to indicate probable geographic relationships. Question marks in A indicate supposed West Indian land-bridge routes between Middle America and South America, and a possible trans-Atlantic route between drifting South America and Africa. Possible interchange between South America and Antarctica or Africa from Jurassic to late Cretaceous is not shown.

and the Brazilian highlands. This ancient route is paralleled by the present range of the primitive cricetine rodent genus *Thomasomys*, with its score or more of well-defined species.

Faunal Strata

Middle American, South American, and West Indian mammals can be sorted into five major faunal strata on the basis of origin, intercontinental relationships, degree of differentiation, and direction of migration of each taxon or phyletic line. The first three strata consist of extinct and living taxons, the last two of living animals only. Altogether, they form a mosaic reflecting dispersal routes in historical sequence (Fig. 5).

Stratum I^a—Ancestral Middle American fauna; derived from primitive boreal American and Eurasian stock, and possibly African and Antarctic stocks (Fig. 5A). There is not a single fossil record of this stratum, but see Stratum II, below.

Stratum I^b—Living Middle American fauna derived either from Stratum I^a, or late arrivals from boreal America, i.e., extrusive species. Examples: *Cryptotis* among insectivores; *Pipistrellus,* among bats; flying squirrel (*Glaucomys*), voles (Microtinae), white-footed mice (*Peromyscus*); coyote (*Canis*), striped skunk (*Mephitis*) (Fig. 5C).

Stratum II—Old South American (and West Indian) descendants of oversea or overland migrants from Stratum I^a in Middle America and, possibly, in Africa; evolved to generic, family, and ordinal grades. Examples: Cretaceous Condylarthra; living insectivore *Solenodon,* subordinally distinct from other North American Insectivora; extinct Jamaican monkey *Xenothrix,* family Xenothricidae. The Capromyidae, a family of caviomorph rodents now restricted to the West Indies may have evolved from Old Middle American (I^a) rather than South American (II) stock. Late Tertiary cricetine rodents, of African, Middle or South American origin, evolved to tribal grade in South America (Fig. 5A).

Stratum III—Early Middle American, boreal North American, and West Indian descendants of oversea migrants from Stratum II; evolution to species, genus, and subfamily grades. Examples: endemic West Indian subfamily of bats (Phyllonycterinae) and extinct genera of edentates; Middle American species or genera of bats, rodents, carnivores, ungulates, extinct edentates and others, the ranges of some extending into boreal North America (Fig. 5B).

Stratum IV—Modern Middle American and boreal American (and West Indian) populations of living species derived from Stratum II in northwestern South America and Stratum III in Middle America; differentiation to subspecies at most. Examples: some West Indian bats and marsupials; Middle American marsupials, bats, primates, edentates, rodents, lagomorphs, carnivores and others; boreal American opossum, armadillo, and sigmodont mice (Fig. 5C).

Stratum V^a—Modern South American and perhaps West Indian populations of living species derived from Strata I^{a, b} in Middle America; differentiation to subspecies at most. Examples: two South American species of cricetine rodents, one species each of insectivores, lagomorphs, tapirs, several of carnivores; also extinct horses and mastodons; possibly some West Indian bats (Fig. 5D).

Stratum V^b—Modern South American populations of living species derived from Stratum III in Middle America; differentiation to subspecies at most. Examples: Cottontop tamarin (*Saguinus oedipus oedipus*), perhaps black howler monkey, black white-fronted capuchin monkey, possibly black-eared opossum (*Didelphis marsupialis*), and other didelphids (Fig. 5D).

Strata I[a], II, and III became established in the Tertiary or before closure of the Bolívar portal. Strata I[b], IV and V[a, b] became established after completion of the intercontinental land bridge or during the Quaternary. West Indian mammals are derived from continental North and South America, but their faunal stratification is unique. Nevertheless, large-scale faunal movements between the continents may have been synchronous with particularly strong and successful invasions of the Antilles.

Intercontinental movements and faunal stratifications of living mammals are described below under their respective ordinal headings.

Marsupialia (Marsupicarnivora)

Marsupials are among the oldest and most primitive of living New World mammals and form at least three faunal strata. Elements of the original, presumably boreal, American didelphoid stock (Stratum I[a]), rafted into South America where some persisted as didelphoids but others differentiated into the shrew-like caenolestoids and the carnivore-like borhyaenoids. Together they formed Stratum II. Borhyaenoids disappeared but three genera of caenolestoids survive in temperate zones from Venezuela to Chile (Fig. 10). Among didelphoids, only the various kinds of opossums of the family Didelphidae are extant. Some of them reinvaded Middle America, perhaps in late Tertiary by the oversea route, to form Stratum III, but nothing firm supports the supposition. The alternative is that Middle American didelphids are components of Stratum IV, having spread comparatively recently (Pleistocene) from northwestern South America after the continents were connected. The common opossum, *Didelphis marsupialis* now ranges into the Lesser Antilles, and a Middle American offshoot (*D. virginianus, fide* Gardner, in prep.) into the Nearctic subregion as far as southern Canada. Some speculations on the origin and dispersal of marsupials are on p. 314, 316, 318.

Insectivora

A species of shrew, *Cryptotis thomasi,* with a multiplicity of specific names, lives in the upper subtropical and temperate zones of the Andes of Venezuela, Colombia and Ecuador. The species has been known from the temperate zone forests and fringing páramos at altitudes above 2000 meters. Heretofore unrecorded specimens were collected by me at Río Negrito, near Sonsón, 1750 meters altitude, and Ventanas, near Valdivia, 2000 meters, both localities in the forested subtropical zone of the Cordillera Central, Antioquia, Colombia. Very closely related and probably conspecific Middle American shrews are also highland dwellers. The distribution of all populations is disjunct. It appears that the original species invaded northwestern South America by the overland route (Stratum V[a]) when the climate was cooler. With rising temperature, shrews moved into higher altitudes and formed pinnacle populations (cf. Hershkovitz, 1962, p. 30).

The West Indian *Solenodon* (including *Atopogale*) and the recently extinct *Nesophontes* appear to be relics of a very early Tertiary insectivore stock with African tenrecid affinities (cf. p. 319). According to McDowell (1958, pp. 209-210), the West Indian insectivores probably diverged during early Tertiary from some boreal American soricoid stock and differentiated in the Greater Antilles. Wherever the place of origin, these insectivores belong to Stratum II.

Chiroptera

The native American bat fauna is ancient, and judged by the few known fossils, many if not most of the present genera were differentiated by or during the Middle Tertiary, the families in Early Tertiary. Five of the ten New World bat families are endemic (Table 1); the remainder are cosmopolitan. It would be difficult to establish which taxons originated where, but all must have been tropical or subtropical by present criteria. The greatest concentration in numbers and kinds of contemporary New World bats occurs in tropical northwestern South America and eastern Central America at the hub of intercontinental faunal exchange. Over 100 species are known from the area, more by far than the total number of species of any other New World order of mammals occupying the same or any other area of comparable size. The number and kinds of bats decrease with higher latitudes and higher altitudes. No more than seven species of bats have been recorded from all of Chile, and only three or four kinds of bats are known to range above tree line in any part of the Andes.

The great number and variety of bats on the Caribbean shores of Middle and South America favored colonization of the Greater and Lesser Antilles. The 30 living genera of bats on the various islands now constitute nearly three-fourths of the entire mammalian fauna of the West Indian Subregion. West Indian bats can be arranged in three groups. The first or oldest, derived from Stratum I^a or II, or from both, consists of the endemic phyllostomid subfamily, Phyllonycterinae, with the genera *Phyllonycteris* (=*Reithronycteris*) and *Erophylla*. The second group consists of five endemic phyllostomid genera. Four of them, *Brachyphylla, Ardops, Phyllops,* and *Ariteus,* are members of the widespread Neotropical subfamily Stenoderminae; the fifth, *Monophyllus,* belongs to the Glossophaginae, a subfamily of nectar-eating bats. This second group is also derived from continental Strata I^a or II, or from both, but at a later date than the first group. The third group, with more than a score of genera, represents all modern New World bat families except the Thyropteridae. Some species of group three are currently regarded as distinct from mainland forms, but most of them are indistinguishable.

Primates

Monkeys are widely distributed throughout the forested parts of the Brazilian Subregion. Of the three living New World families, the small squirrel-like marmosets, or Callithricidae, are most primitive and, judged by their distribution, probably South American in origin. Only one kind of marmoset, the bare-faced tamarin, *Saguinus oedipus geoffroyi,* ranges into Middle America but no farther than the Panamanian-Costa Rican border (Stratum III). Its parental South American stock (Stratum II) could not have been very different from living *Saguinus leucopus* of northern Colombia, and may have lived in the same general area east of the Bolívar Trough. The prototype of *S. oedipus geoffroyi* could have crossed the Bolívar Trough or Strait possibly before Late Pliocene. With closure of the intercontinental seaway, a breeding colony of *S. oedipus geoffroyi* became isolated in emergent habitats between the lower Ríos Atrato and Cauca and evolved into white-plumed *S. oedipus oedipus* (Stratum V[b]) (Fig. 6).

The family Cebidae comprises, apart from extinct forms, four genera of large-bodied prehensile-tailed monkeys and six genera of smaller non-prehensile tailed monkeys. All members of the small-bodied group are confined to South America, with the exception of some populations of night monkeys, or douroucoulis, *Aotus trivirgatus* (includes *bipunctatus*), and of squirrel monkeys, *Saimiri sciureus* (includes *orstedi*). Night monkeys west of the Río Atrato, in Colombia and Panama, are practically indistinguishable from night monkeys of the east bank of the same river (Hershkovitz, 1949, p. 399). Evidently, invasion of Middle America by *Aotus* is recent and may have been effected overland or by passive (e.g., by river cutoff) crossing of the Río Atrato.

Middle American squirrel monkeys, restricted to the narrow coastal zone of southeastern Costa Rica and southwestern Panama, are widely separated from their relatives of the same species east of the Andes. None occurs naturally in the eastern half of Panama, the Colombian Chocó, or elsewhere west of the Andes in South America with the exception of a hitherto unrecorded small population of squirrel monkeys I discovered in the upper Río Magdalena Valley, department of Huila, southern Colombia. This population is derived from and communicates with upper Amazonian *Saimiri sciureus* through low passes in the Cordillera Oriental. The same passes are used by *Aotus trivirgatus, Cebus apella, Lagothrix lagothricha,* and other mammals. The completely isolated range of Middle American *Saimiri sciureus* parallels that of the bush dog, *Speothos venaticus* (see p. 359). The peculiar distributional patterns suggest pre-Columbian introduction by man.

Three of the four living genera of the large-bodied prehensile-tailed cebids are represented in the Middle American Province by one or two species each. The Middle American black howler, *Alouatta villosa,* is the most primitive of three or four recognizable species of howlers. Its range extends from northern Mexico to southwestern Ecuador. *Alouatta seniculus* is most highly specialized and most widely distributed in the South American portion of the Brazilian Subregion. A few populations, however, gained access from the right bank of the Río Atrato to the left in Middle

352   PHILIP HERSHKOVITZ

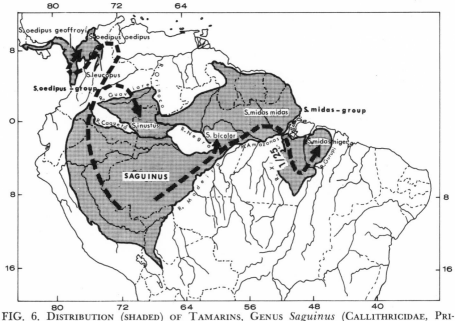

FIG. 6. DISTRIBUTION (SHADED) OF TAMARINS, GENUS *Saguinus* (CALLITHRICIDAE, PRI-
MATES)

*Probable dispersal routes (indicated by bars) from likely center of origin in the
southwestern Amazonian region. Western migrants following Andean base northward
differentiated into members of the S. oedipus group, eastern migrants crossing the
Amazonas evolved independently into the S. bicolor and S. midas groups. Note points
of Rio Amazonas crossing and recrossing at postulated river-bend cutoffs. (Map modified from Hershkovitz, 1966c.)*

American Colombia. Here they hold an enclave inviolate from neighboring bands of black howlers (*Alouatta villosa*) by virtue of their stentorian
vocalizations. *Cebus capucinus*, one of four living species of capuchins,
ranges from Honduras to northwestern Ecuador in the Middle American
Province. It also crossed the Atrato, presumably from left bank to right,
and spread east to the left bank of the Ríos Cauca and lower Magdalena in
Colombia. The common spider monkey, *Ateles paniscus*, ranges widely
throughout most forested parts of the Neotropical Region from southern
Mexico to southern Brazil. The relict *Brachyteles arachnoides*, confined to
southeastern Brazil, is on the verge of extermination. The two species of
woolly monkeys, genus *Lagothrix*, are confined to South America. One
of them inhabits the upper Amazonian, Orinocoan, and Magdalenan
river basins, the other is restricted to the Andes of northern Peru.

The foregoing suggests that the black capuchin, *Cebus capucinus*, and
the black howler, *Alouatta villosa*, may have evolved in Middle America
(Stratum III) possibly of old South American stock (Stratum II). There is
also an equal probability that the black howler, at least, is a direct descendant of old Middle American Stratum I stock. The status of Middle

American representatives of *Ateles paniscus* (includes *A. fusciceps* and *A. geoffroyi*) is problematical. The species here may belong to Faunal Stratum III, but spider monkeys of both sides of the Río Atrato almost certainly interbreed in nature. Invasions of South America by spider monkeys (*Ateles*) after completion of the Isthmian land bridge, constitute Stratum V[b]. Late invasions of Middle America by *Aotus* and colonization of the left shore of the lower Río Atrato by the red howler, *Alouatta seniculus,* contribute to Stratum IV.

Edentata (Xenarthra)

Edentates common to Middle America and northwestern South America are three anteaters of the family Myrmecophagidae *(Cyclopes didactyla, Tamandua tetradactyla, Myrmecophaga tridactyla)*, two sloths of the family Bradypodidae *(Bradypus tridactylus, Choloepus didactylus)*, and two armadillos of the family Dasypodidae *(Dasypus novemcinctus, Cabassous unicinctus)*. The taxa in question are unrevised, but it is evident that the species on both sides of the Isthmian Bridge are the same, and their distribution continuous. Thus, Middle American edentates ostensibly belong to Stratum IV, on the assumption that they are derived from South American Stratum II by the overland route. Except for the nine-banded armadillo *(Dasypus novemcinctus)*, modern xenarthrans did not spread beyond Middle America into boreal North America.

Rodentia

1. Sciuridae

Squirrels originated in the northern continents and differentiated widely, but only tree squirrels of the subfamily Sciurinae spread into Middle and South America. The invasions were probably multiple. The most distinctive of Neotropical Sciurinae is the pigmy squirrel, *Sciurillus guajanensis* Kerr, of the Guianan and Amazonian region. Its time-space separation from Middle America and absence of near relatives points to its great antiquity and an early arrival in South America, possibly together with ecologically related Middle Tertiary Primates. The extremely large *Sciurus spadiceus* and *S. igniventris* and the much smaller *S. aestuans* are also Amazonian and Guianan, but related forms occur in Middle America. Conceivably their ancestors, like the earlier prototype of *Sciurillus*, entered South America before the Andes arose as a barrier to the eastward spread of oversea migrants. Such squirrels belong to Stratum II. Two species, *Sciurus granatensis* and *Microsciurus flaviventris* (includes *alfari, boquetensis, isthmius*) range uninterruptedly in Middle America and northwestern South America, and from tropical lowlands to temperate zone forests. The first, having a typical Stratum V[a] distribution in northwestern South America, certainly spread overland from north to southeast. The second, with a wider range including the upper Amazonian region, may belong to the same Stratum as *S. granatensis;* or possibly originated in northwestern South America and then spread overland into Middle America.

2. Muridae (Cricetinae)

The two New World tribes of living cricetine rodents (Cricetinae, family Muridae) offer the best documented and least complicated examples of the five main faunal strata defined previously. The tribe Sigmodontini, characterized by an anatomically complicated glans penis with three digitate baculum, is essentially South American. The Peromyscini, characterized by a simplified glans penis with unbranched and usually elongate baculum is essentially North American. As shown elsewhere (Hooper and Musser, 1964, p. 52), the complex glans penis is the more primitive and the simple glans penis can be derived from it.

The Sigmodontini as such might well have originated in South America. There is absolutely no evidence for the occurrence of complex-penis-type cricetines in boreal America prior to the invasion by them in the Blancan, there is no indication these rodents arose in Middle America prior to their appearance in South America. Cricetines probably arose in the Old World, as likely in Africa as in Eurasia. If the ancestral sigmodontine stock did not enter South America through boreal America, it could have done so by rafting from Africa (see above, p. 324).

Adaptive radiation of the Sigmodontini in South America was pervasive. There are between 150 and 200 species (and possibly even more), representing about 40 genera (see Wenzel and Tipton, 1966, Errata: corrections for pp. 698, 716, 734). These mice occupy virtually every habitat capable of sustaining mammalian life. They are elements of Stratum II. Some early descendants of the original complex-penis-type colonizers invaded Middle America, ostensibly by crossing the seaway or Bolívar Trough. Others were rafted to the West Indies and the Galápagos Islands. Isolated from the parental stock, they differentiated into the species and genera of Stratum III. As I have shown elsewhere (1966b, 1970, 1971b), living cricetine genera of Stratum III are rice rats of the genera *Oryzomys, Nesoryzomys* and *Megalomys,* and cotton rats of the genus *Sigmodon.* The Middle and boreal North American species of *Oryzomys* are essentially palustrine or aquatic. The exterminated West Indian and Galápagos Island species of *Megalomys* were arboreal. The disappearing Galápagos Island *Nesoryzomys* is scansorial but primarily terrestrial. One extinct species of *Sigmodon* spread as far as Kansas during the Pliocene. The "fish-eating" mice of the icthyomine group range from northwestern South America into Mexico. The Middle American species currently assigned to *Rheomys* may have differentiated there and would belong in Stratum III.

Since closure of the Isthmian water gap during the Pliocene, thirteen more species of Sigmodontini spread overland from South America into

Middle America, where they form Faunal Stratum IV. The migrants are represented by 7 species of *Oryzomys,* and one each of *Nectomys, Neacomys, Rhipidomys, Sigmodon,* and *Zygodontomys.* Taxonomic differentiation between northwestern South American and Panamanian populations of each of the species is, at most, subspecific. Faunal flow in the opposite direction was insignificant. *Tylomys nudicaudatus* and *Aporodon mexicanus* are the only Peromyscini known to have crossed into northwestern South America, where they contribute to Faunal Stratum V.

The oldest known Sigmodontini are remains of specialized pastoral forms of *Zygodontomys, Akodon,* and *Reithrodon* (=*Proreithrodon* Ameghino), from the Montehermosan (late Pliocene) of Argentina, and *Scapteromys, Calomys* (=*Necromys* Ameghino) and *Euneomys* (=*Bothriomys* Ameghino) from the Uquian (early Pleistocene) of Argentina. These early and geographically peripheral grazing mice differ little from living species of the same genera inhabiting the same areas. The record of a Montehermosan *Oryzomys,* communicated by Prof. Oswaldo Reig to Patterson and Pascual (1968, p. 446) was based on a misidentification (Reig, pers. commun.). This clarifies the ecological problem presented by a sylvan cricetine in a pastoral habitat. The small mice of the subgenus *Oligoryzomys* did eventually invade grasslands but, evidently, not until the Pleistocene.

Patterson and Pascual (1968; Chapter VI) give the same historical data. They maintain, however, that the "fossil record is in contradiction" with the concept of an over-water colonization of South America by complex-penis-type cricetines prior to the late Pliocene. They argue that "had something like *Oryzomys* inhabited South America in the Miocene, cricetines would have appeared in deposits of that age and later" (1968, p. 444; Chapter VI, p. 294). Miocene fossils are indeed unknown, but South American records of cricetines from the late Pliocene onward are fully documented. In contrast, such cricetines are absent in known Middle American fossil deposits of any age.

Patterson and Pascual (op. cit.) offer a "hypothesis" of cricetine distribution in South America predicated on a land-bridge invasion, and geared to latitudinal temperature controls and probable invasion routes which recall late Pleistocene migrations of horses and mastodons. None of this is relevant to the prior origin of primitive tropical forest cricetines and to their subsequent radiation and dispersal, most of them into subtropical to temperate zone niches, rather than mainly tropical niches, as surmised by Patterson and Pascual, 1968, p. 444; Chapter VI; p. 294 ff.). These authors present evidence that extant South American genera of complex penis cricetines were already differentiated by late Pliocene in situ, and they show that the vast majority of the genera of complex-penis-type cricetines are restricted to continental South America. They fail to prove that these mice originated elsewhere and they fail to explain why these mice could not have originated where they are now. Instead, ecological factors favorable to a Middle American origin and differentiation of modern South American cricetine genera are recounted. This does not take into account my demonstration (1966b) that all known Middle and boreal American Sigmodontini can be derived from living South American types.

Furthermore, the unfounded assumption that the Isthmian channel was an effective barrier to cricetine expansion is seriously comprised by the Patterson and Pascual premise that all other Tertiary mammals of South America and the West Indies are of waif origin. Their own tabulation (1968, p. 446; Chapter VI, p. 297), which reveals more than may have been intended, indicates that all South American cricetines had already pervaded South America by the time the intercontinental land bridge came into existence, and that only two (not three) species of simple-penis-type cricetines penetrated northwestern South America thereafter. Finally, the inference of sigmodontine origins and distribution derived from host-ectoparasite relationships, unnoticed by Patterson and Pascual in their 1968 account, is cavalierly dismissed by them in the present one (p. 298). The host-ectoparasite relationships are summarized by Wenzel and Tipton (1966, p. 718) as follows:

> With very few exceptions, the ectoparasites of these complex-penis-type cricetine rodents belong to families and tribes or genera which are either restricted to or centered in South America, and whose closest relatives are in most cases Old World forms, especially of the Australian Region, but also of the Oriental and (to a much lesser extent) Ethiopian Regions. Only a very few parasites that are identifiable as Middle or North American, and these are obviously fairly recent intruders, occur on these hosts. Among these are the laelaptine mite *Eubrachylaelaps rotundus,* a few fleas of the genus *Pleochaetis,* another of the genus *Kohlsia,* and several rabbit fleas of the genera *Cediopsylla* and *Hoplopsyllus* (Subg. *Euhoplopsyllus*). The geographic and host distributions of lice like *Hoplopleura,* cited by Vanzolini and Guimarães (1955), must be reexamined.
>
> The complex-penis-type Cricetinae, like *Oryzomys* and *Sigmodon,* that occur north of Panama, can hardly be relicts of an old fauna that dispersed into South America, if their fleas (*Polygenis*) are an indication. *Polygenis* is an "expanding" South American genus which has, quite clearly, dispersed into Middle America along with complex-penis-type Cricetinae and caviomorph rodents from South America. Most of the Panamanian species probably dispersed very recently. In most cases they are not even subspecifically distinct from South American forms.
>
> Further, there seems to be little other reason to accept the Pliocene-Pleistocene transition as the principal time of dispersal of the ancestral complex-penis-type cricetine rodents (and possibly some other mammals too) into South America. Even if the fossil Cricetinae known from the Upper Pliocene of the Argentine (see following paper) reflect the first appearance of these rodents in southern South America, this may mark the end of a long "trail" of dispersal and evolution rather than the beginning (see Hershkovitz [1966b], pp. 727-732).

Chromosomes recently studied by Bianchi, Reig, Molina, and Dulout (1971), and the taxonomic and biogeographical data available to them, led these authors to conclude that the primitive, complex-penis-type cricetines (oryzomyines and thomasomyines) probably diversified in the highlands of northwestern South America. The derived, progressive akodont group of cricetines, they judge, must have radiated from the central Andean region in southeastern Peru, northern Chile, Bolivia, and northwestern Argentina. The time of these events is not given. The authors, who cite only Patterson and Pascual (1968) for general biogeographical data, presume that the ancestral South American cricetine originated in the southeastern or isthmian portion of Middle America but the question of its likely antecedents is left begging.

3. Heteromyidae

Spiny pocket mice (family Heteromyidae) are essentially North American. Only one genus, the Middle American *Heteromys* (Stratum I[b]), spread from Panama into western Colombia, western Ecuador, and northwestern Venezuela. Its distributional pattern is typical of Stratum V[a].

4. Geomyidae

North American pocket gophers (family Geomyidae) advanced southward to the eastern border of Panama, but not beyond. They represent faunal Stratum I[b], and potentially faunal Stratum V[a]. Despite the presence of a land bridge, tropical lowland rain forests (including flood plains of the Chocó) are barriers to fossorial mammals.

5. Caviomorpha (=Hystricomorpha)

Speculations regarding the origin of caviomorph rodents are outlined above (p. 325). The oldest known caviomorphs from the Oligocene of the southern half of western South America (Stratum II) were already highly diversified. The early history of their differentiation and radiation is lost, but the first stage may have been in northern South America. The boreal American porcupine *Erethizon* could be a relict of old Middle American invaders from South America. The prehensile-tailed porcupines (genus *Coendou*), to judge by present distribution, are more likely South American in origin. Interrelationships of the Middle American species of the genus have not been determined, but they would belong to faunal Stratum III or IV.

The capybara (*Hydrochaeris hydrochaeris*), aguti (*Dasyprocta leporina*), and paca (*Agouti paca*) are the only known living species of their kind, despite the multiplicity of their respective scientific names. All three are excellent swimmers, but the intimate relationship between the South and Middle American populations of these species indicates a comparatively recent overland or trans-Río Atrato migration into Middle America (Stratum IV).

Rat-like caviomorphs of the family Echimyidae are highly diversified but most of the species are unrevised, and little is known of their intergenic relationships. Of about a dozen valid genera, three are common to

Middle and South America, and two of them are monotypic. The arboreal *Diplomys caniceps* (includes *darlingi, labilis, rufodorsalis*) inhabits eastern Panama, western Colombia, and northwestern Ecuador. The spiny terrestrial *Hoplomys gymnurus* ranges from Nicaragua into western Colombia and northwestern Ecuador. Their respective distributional patterns indicate a Middle American origin (Stratum Iᵃ or Stratum III) with recent invasions of the South American portion of the Brazilian Subregion (Stratum Vᵃ or Vᵇ). The extinct West Indian echimyid rodents may be descendents of the same Middle American faunal stratum. *Proechimys*, with ten or more species, is represented in both Middle and South America by a species of the *P. guyannensis* complex and another of the *P. quadruplicatus* complex (Hershkovitz, 1948, pp. 130, 136). Their distributional pattern indicates a South American origin (Stratum II) and comparatively recent invasions of Middle America (Stratum IV) without important differentiation.

West Indian and Bahaman hutias of the family Capromyidae are relicts of an old caviomorph fauna which disappeared from the mainland. Their time of arrival in the West Indies is unknown, but access may have been by a Tertiary Caribbean land bridge or accidentally by sea. They form Stratum II if Middle America was their center of origin, or Stratum III if rafted from South America, whether directly or indirectly through Middle America. The history of the related and extinct West Indian Heptaxodontidae may be similar.

Lagomorpha

Rabbits (Leporidae, Lagomorpha) originated in boreal America. One species, the tapeti (*Sylvilagus brasiliensis*) or its prototype, entered South America, presumably by the oversea route, and spread throughout the Brazilian Subregion from Amazonian rain forest and lowland savannas to temperate zone forests and grasslands in the Andes (Stratum II). Completion of the Isthmian land bridge facilitated the return to Middle America (Stratum IV) of some populations of the tapeti. The Middle American cotton-tail, *Sylvilagus floridanus* (Stratum Iᵇ) is a recent colonizer of the woodlands and grasslands of northern Colombia and Venezuela, where it adds to Stratum Vᵃ. Tropical forests are barriers to its continued spread into suitable habitats in the interior of South America, including the Andean highland savannas (cf. Hershkovitz, 1950).

Carnivora

The South American dogs (Canidae) are *Speothos, Chrysocyon, Lycalopex* and *Atelocynus*, each with a single species, and *Dusicyon* (including *Cerdocyon*) with seven or eight coyote-like species. The genera are strongly marked, the first three being highly specialized for particular habitats. The relationships indicate an independent origin of each genus from old Middle American stock rather than divergence from a common South

American ancestor. Whatever the ancestry, the history of this mixed group of dogs was undoubtedly of long duration on both American continents.

A very different Neotropical species is the gray fox, *Urocyon cinereoargenteus*. It may have orginated in Middle America and spread during the Quaternary into Canada and northwestern South America. Its distributional pattern is that of a late or overland migrant from Middle America into South America (Faunal Stratum V^a). A second, more distantly related dog, the boreal North American coyote, *Canis latrans*, spread south into Middle America but only as far as Costa Rica.

Speothos venaticus is common throughout most of the South American portion of the Brazilian Subregion but is unknown west of the Andes except from a single locality in southeastern Panama. Whether this otherwise cis-Andean dog reached Panama by natural means or human agency remains to be verified. All other autochthonous South American dogs are widely separated either geographically or ecologically or by both means from the Middle American Province.

The family Ursidae is represented in South America by the spectacled bear, *Tremarctos ornatus*. It once ranged from the cold puna and páramo zones of the Andes to the tropical zone foothills and valleys in Venezuela, Colombia, Ecuador, Peru, and northwestern Bolivia. Persecution by man has largely exterminated the bear from all but the least accessible parts of the Andean temperate zone forests and bordering grasslands. Ursids are unknown from the Middle American Province, but a skull of *Tremarctos ornatus*, believed to have originated in the Serrania del Darién, Panama, may have been of an animal transported from northwestern Colombia (Hershkovitz, 1957, p. 122). During the Pleistocene, spectacled bears ranged from the southern United States into southern Bolivia, southeastern Brazil, and Buenos Aires Province, Argentina. Bears do not now and, as far as is known, never did occur naturally in Chile (Osgood, 1943, p. 237). Earliest North American records for the genus, according to Kurtén (1966, p. 7) are fragments from the Palm Springs formation, southern California, and bones of *Tremarctos floridanus* (*T. mexicanus* a synonym) from the younger Illinoisan of Florida. [Hibbard et al. (1965, p. 513) show *Tremarctos* appearing in the Yarmouth and "?" Kansan formations of Kansas without documentation.] Kurtén regards *T. floridanus* as divergent from the line leading to the South American *T. ornatus*. Delineation of the dispersal route of the latter, however, requires further clarification of the relationship between *Tremarctos* and the extinct South American *Arctotherium* and *Pararctotherium*, as recognized by Paula Couto (1960, p. 5).

Raccoons and their allies, family Procyonidae, are New World in origin and distribution. Asiatic pandas are not procyonids (Davis, 1965). The family may have originated in Middle America and radiated there in Early Pliocene (Stratum I) before elements invaded South America. A second radiation must have followed in South America (Stratum II). Today, two species of ring-tailed cats, *Bassariscus astutus* and *B. sumi-*

chrasti, are Nearctic and Middle American, respectively. One species of raccoon, *Procyon lotor,* is also Nearctic and Middle American. A second species, *P. cancrivorus,* is confined to the Brazilian Subregion and almost certainly originated in South America. The range of *P. cancrivorus* extends to Panama and bordering parts of Costa Rica (Stratum IV), where it overlaps that of the northern *Procyon lotor.* One species of coatimundi, *Nasua narica,* is entirely Middle American (western Colombia and western Ecuador included) in origin and distribution (see p. 362 below). A second species is Brazilian, the Middle American Province excluded. The third and last species, *Nasua* (or *Nasuella*) *olivacea,* is confined to temperate-zone Andean forests of Venezuela, Colombia, and Ecuador in a distributional pattern typical of relict Andean species of early faunas. The kinkajou, *Potos flavus,* of the forested parts of the Brazilian Subregion, ranges north into southern Mexico. This prehensile-tailed arboreal carnivore could have originated either in Middle or South America and then spread to the other continent by the overland or oversea route. The superficially similar and largely sympatric arboreal olingo, *Bassaricyon gabbi,* lives in upland tropical to temperate zone forests from Nicaragua into Venezuela, Colombia, Ecuador, Amazonian Peru, Bolivia and, possibly, British Guiana. Its distribution suggests high upper Amazonian origin with late overland colonization of Middle America.

The diversity of Neotropical weasels, skunks, and otters, family Mustelidae, points to a long and complex history. The four (or five) endemic genera, *Lyncodon, Galictis, Eira, Pteronura,* and *Grammogale* (=*Mustela?*), each with a single species, almost certainly evolved in South America and represent Stratum II. The giant otter, *Pteronura brasiliensis,* and the misnamed *Mustela (Grammogale) africana,* are restricted to the Brazilian Subregion east of the Andes. They are finely adapted to present habitats and are so different from their nearest living relatives that they appear to be relicts of an older fauna. *Galictis vittata* and *Eira barbara* are also peculiarly tropical American. Their spread from South America into Middle America was fairly recent and without marked differentiation. The huron *Galictis (Grisonella) cuja* is Patagonian (Stratum II). One genus of skunk, the monotypic *Conepatus,* is probably Middle American in origin, but its present range extends throughout South America and well into Nearctica. Middle American representatives of *Mephitis* and *Spilogale* (Stratum I[b]) may be late arivals from boreal North America. They range south to Nicaragua and Costa Rica respectively. *Mustela frenata* and *Lutra canadensis* (includes *annectens*) are possibly Middle American species which invaded boreal and South America (Stratum V[a]).

South American cats, family Felidae, are most likely products of two or three independent invasions each during a distinct climatological event. Prototypes of the small Patagonian colocolo (*Felis colocolo*), Geoffroy's cat (*F. geoffroyi*), the huiña (*F. guigna*), and the high Andean *F. jacobita,* may have invaded South America, possibly by the oversea route, during a cool period. There are no near relatives in Middle or boreal America.

FIG. 7. DISTRIBUTION OF
NEOTROPICAL TAPIRS, GENUS
Tapirus
    *Distributional pattern and
degrees of interspecific relations
indicate three independent and
widely spaced invasions of South
America.* T. bairdi *arrived last,
spread across the Río Atrato to
meet the secondary westward
spread of* T. terrestris *(arrows).
(Map adapted from Hershkovitz,
1954.)*

The second group, consisting of the jaguar, puma, ocelot, a margay (*Felis wiedi*) and the jaguarundi, are widely distributed in Middle America and South America. They probably invaded South America overland (or by crossing the Río Atrato) when tropical rain forests predominated. A second margay (*Felis tigrina*), confined to the Brazilian Subregion in South America, may be historically intermediate between the first and second groups.

Perissodactyla

Distributional patterns of the three living neotropical species of tapirs (Tapiridae) indicate three independent invasions of South America from Middle America (Fig. 7). The mountain tapir, *Tapirus pinchaque,* most primitive of living species, inhabits the temperate zone forests and bordering páramos of the Andes of Colombia and Ecuador. The Brazilian tapir, *Tapirus terrestris,* is widely dispersed throughout the Brazilian Subregion east of the Andes and in a small salient west of the Andes in northwestern Venezuela and northern Colombia. Baird's tapir, *Tapirus bairdi,* is essentially Middle American, with a range extending from Mexico into coastal Ecuador. In northwestern Colombia it advanced across the Río Atrato to the Río Sinú, where it meets on common ground with the Brazilian tapir (Hershkovitz, 1954). Prototypes of *Tapirus pinchaque* and *T. terrestris* almost certainly reached South America by the oversea route, but at widely separated periods when climates and continental topographies were significantly different. Which of the two species invaded South America first has not been determined. The third species, *Tapirus bairdi,* however, is clearly a late overland arrival in South America and corresponds to Faunal Stratum V[a]. Its crossing of the Atrato-San Juán "gap" must have been comparatively recent. The species has yet to reach the next important water gap, the Río Cauca-Magdalena, some 100 kilometers distant across lowlands. Interspecific competition is not a factor in limiting tapir dispersal.

Artiodactyla

Two species of peccaries, genus *Tayassu,* family Tayassuidae, range throughout the tropical zones of the Brazilian Subregion but the collared peccary, *Tayassu tajacu,* also occurs in bordering parts of Nearctica. The family originated in North America, but the genus *Tayassu* is probably a South American autochthon. Fossil peccaries are known from the upper Pliocene of Argentina. Their ancestors almost certainly invaded South America before closure of the Isthmian gap. According to Woodburne (1969, p. 125), "The lineage leading toward the collared peccary underwent most, if not all, of its evolution in South America." According to Simpson (1965, p. 226), *Tayassu* (and *Nasua*) are Nearctic autochthons "only recently incorporated into the Neotropical fauna, and they are simply spreading back within their native fauna in consequence of ecological reversions." Whatever Simpson means, it is a fact that *Tayassu* (and *Nasua*) have been recorded from the South American Pliocene and Pleistocene, respectively (cf. Simpson, 1945, p. 112; Paula Couto, 1952, p. 106; Woodburne, 1968, p. 32), but are unknown as fossils in Mexico (Alvarez, 1965, pp. 30, 54) and the United States (Hibbard et al., 1965, p. 513). Simpson's (1945, p. 146) listing of *Tayassu* from the North American Pleistocene appears to be based on the misidentified lower jaw of a domestic pig (*Sus scrofa*) reported by earlier authors (cf. Arata, 1964, p. 28). *Tayassu* (and *Nasua*) were correctly listed by me (1958, p. 608) among 22 genera of Neotropical regionalites excurrent into the Nearctic Subregion.

South American camelids, the llamas and vicuñas, are now confined to the Patagonian Subregion. Camelids arose in the Eocene of North America, but when and precisely where the first South American camels differentiated is unknown.

Deer (Cervidae) are represented by 11 species in the Neotropical Region, all autochthonous. Nine are restricted to South America. Pigmy deer, or pudus, genus *Pudu,* are well removed from all other deer and may be relicts of an old independent South American stock (Faunal Stratum II). One of the two species inhabits the temperate zone forests of Colombia and Ecuador, the other is confined to Chile. The ancestral pudu may have lived in equatorial lowlands during a cool epoch. With rising temperatures, some populations moved into higher altitudes and others moved southward into higher latitudes. Widely separated, each group evolved into the sharply defined modern species. The spike-antlered brockets, genus *Mazama,* are nearly related to the larger branch-antlered deer, but are more primitive; they probably stand near the ancestral line. Of four living species, three, including the pudu-like *Mazama chunyi* (cf. Hershkovitz, 1959), are restricted to South America.

The fourth, *Mazama americana*, is widely dispersed throughout the Brazilian Subregion including Middle America. Lack of any notable differentiation within the Middle American Province indicates a rapid spread from South America via the overland or trans-Río Atrato route (Stratum IV). The white-tailed deer, *Odocoileus virginianus*, is distributed from Canada southward to the north bank of the Amazon on the east and the Andes of northwestern Bolivia on the west. Its origin in Middle America is probable, and its spread into South America appears to be comparatively recent, possibly on two or more separate occasions (Stratum V[a]). The remaining branch-antlered deer (marsh deer, swamp deer, huemul, taruga), are eastern Brazilian and southern South American. They and related extinct forms became established during the Pleistocene. Whatever their history, the ancestral stock (Stratum II) had long preceded *Odocoileus* into South America, almost certainly by the oversea route.

EXTINCTIONS

Wholesale extinctions of South American mammals were said to have occurred during the late Pliocene-early Pleistocene as the result of large-scale invasions of aggressive North American mammals (Simpson, 1965, p. 222). The meager fossil record indicates, and present distributional patterns prove, that South American elements were spreading into Middle and boreal America and speciating at the same time Middle American elements were invading South America and speciating there. The interchange must have been sporadic and must have involved individuals or small groups of autochthonous species moving within the confines of an ecologically homogeneous, but sometimes geographically discontinuous, province. Displacements or extinctions of native species or populations of one continent as a direct result of invasion or competition by faunal elements of the other may well have been minimal and localized.

There is abundant evidence, on the other hand, that many large mammals, particularly herbivores, and their specialized predators, disappeared much later, during late Pleistocene and early Recent times, from all continents. The magnitude of extinctions in South America was probably of the same order as that of extinctions in North America during the same time. The records also indicate that extinctions among large boreal American genera which invaded South America during the Quaternary were no less than among resident South American genera allegedly exterminated by or because of them.

According to Martin (1966, p. 339), who supports his arguments with radiocarbon datings, early man may have been the principal cause of major extinctions during the late Pleistocene and into the Recent. Disappearance of game animals, particularly, followed the wave of human migration from Africa through Eurasia, North America, and into tropical America (see also Martin, 1958; Hester, 1960, p. 58; Hester, 1966, pp. 383-384; Müller-Beck, 1966, p. 191; Martin, 1967, p. 107).

TABLE 4

Major morphological types of Neotropical mammals

Representatives of certain Neotropical mammalian fauna, grouped by order and family. Primates are shown in Fig. 11 (p. 378), and cricetine rodents in Fig. 13 (p. 386). The English vernacular and the scientific names numbered below correspond to the numbers on Figs. 8A and 8B.

Order, Family and English Vernacular Name	Scientific Name	Head and Body Length (mm)	Tail Length (mm)	Weight	Ear Height (from notch) (mm)
MARSUPIALIA					
Didelphidae					
1. Common opossum	* Didelphis marsupialis	450	340	1.8 kg	—
2. Water opossum	* Chironectes minimus	315	375	0.8 kg	—
3. Murine opossum	* Marmosa murina	150	24	70 g	—
4. Squirrel-tailed opossum	Glironia venusta	185	210	—	—
5. Short-tailed opossum	* Monodelphis tricinctus	73	51	48 g	—
Caenolestidae					
6. Shrew-opossum	* Caenolestes fuliginosus	120	130	40 g	—
INSECTIVORA					
Solenodontidae					
7. Solenodon	Solenodon cubanus	300	225	—	—
Soricidae					
8. Shrew	* Cryptotis meridensis	95	27	12 g	—
CHIROPTERA					
Vespertilionidae					
9. Little black bat	* Myotis nigricans	44	40	—	12
10. Hoary bat	* Lasiurus cinereus	75	56	—	16
Molossidae					
11. Rat-tailed bat	Promops centralis	80	50	—	15
Noctilionidae					
12. Fish-eating bat	* Noctilio leporinus	100	25	—	26
Emballonuridae					
13. Sac-winged bat	* Peropteryx macrotis	47	13	—	13
Thyropteridae					
14. Disk-winged bat	* Thyroptera albiventris	41	28	—	12
Natalidae					
15. Funnel-eared bat	* Natalus stramineus	52	52	—	15
Phyllostomidae					
16. Giant spear-nosed bat	Vampyrum spectrum	150	—	—	40
17. Long-eared bat	* Lonchorhina aurita	65	50	—	27
18. Round-eared bat	* Tonatia sylvicola	75	20	30 g	38
19. Wrinkled-faced bat	Centurio senex	60	—	—	16
20. Nectar-eating bat	Choeronycteris mexicana	70	12	—	17
Desmodidae					
21. Vampire bat	* Desmodus rotundus	85	—	30 g	19
EDENTATA (XENARTHRA)					
Myrmecophagidae					
22. Giant anteater	* Myrmecophaga tridactyla	1050	650	20 kg	—
Bradypodidae					
23. Three-toed sloth	* Bradypus tridactylus	550	40	5 kg	—
Dasypodidae					
24. Nine-banded armadillo	* Dasypus novemcinctus	425	400	3 kg	—
25. Giant armadillo	Priodontes maximus	1000	500	60 kg	—
26. Three-banded armadillo	Tolypeutes tricinctus	400	60	—	—
27. Pichiciego	Chlamyphorus truncatus	125	35	—	—
RODENTIA					
Sciuridae					
28. Humboldt's squirrel	* Sciurus granatensis	230	200	400 g	—
Erethizontidae					
29. Prehensile-tailed porcupine	* Coendou prehensilis	460	465	—	—
Caviidae					
30. Wild cavy	* Cavia (porcellus) aperea	300	—	750 g	—
31. Mara	Dolichotis patagonum	740	45	15 kg	—

See Fig. 8A.

Measurements are taken in a straight line, usually rounded to the nearest 0.5 centimeter. All measurements are of fully adult males, caught in the wild. All bat heads are drawn to the same scale. Measurements of animals marked with an asterisk (*) were taken by the author; all measurements and specimens are now preserved in the Field Museum of Natural History.

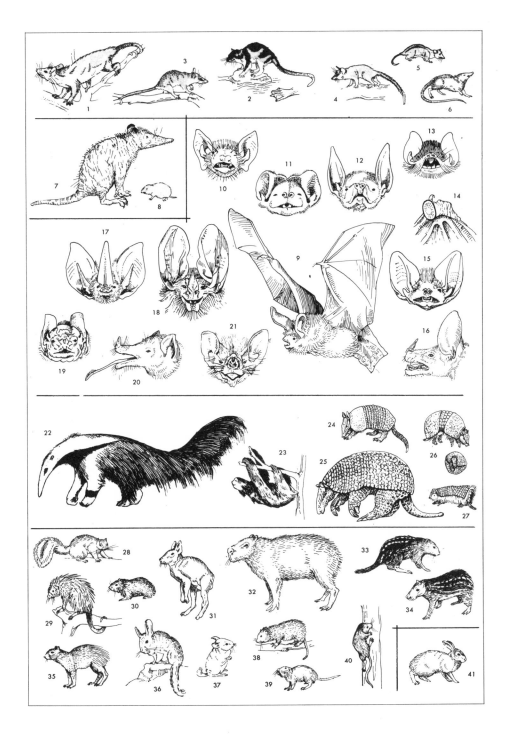

FIG. 8A. MAJOR MORPHOLOGICAL TYPES OF NEOTROPICAL MAMMALS
Numbers correspond to items in Table 4. See Table 4 (continued) for data corresponding to 32-41.

TABLE 4—*Continued*

Order, Family and English Vernacular Name	Scientific Name	Head and Body Length (mm)	Tail Length (mm)	Weight	Shoulder Height (mm)
RODENTIA (continued)					
Hydrochaeridae					
32. Capybara	* *Hydrochaeris hydrochaeris*	1200	63	48 kg	500
Dinomyidae					
33. Pacarana	*Dinomys branicki*	730	190	12 kg	—
Dasyproctidae					
34. Paca	* *Agouti paca*	665	15	10 kg	—
35. Agouti	* *Dasyprocta aguti*	600	20	5 kg	—
Chinchillidae					
36. Mountain viscacha	*Lagidium viscaccia*	400	335	1200 g	—
37. Chinchilla	*Chinchilla laniger*	260	125	750 g	—
Capromyidae					
38. Hutia	*Plagiodontia hylaea*	346	150	—	—
Ctenomyidae					
39. Tuco-tuco	*Ctenomys brasiliensis*	200	75	—	—
Echimyidae					
40. Arboreal spiny-rat	* *Echimys armatus*	220	230	230 g	—
LAGOMORPHA					
Leporidae					
41. Tapeti	* *Sylvilagus brasiliensis*	370	30	1.5 kg	—
CETACEA					
Susuidae					
42. Inia	[1] *Inia geoffrensis (immature)*	1626	—	37 kg	—
	[2] *Inia geoffrensis (mature)*	2743	—	—	—
Trichechidae					
43. River manatee	[3] *Trichechus inunguis*	2030	—	30 kg	—
CARNIVORA					
Canidae					
44. Savanna-dog	* *Dusicyon thous*	690	280	6 kg	—
45. Maned wolf	*Chrysocyon brachyurus*	925	445	23 kg	750
46. Bush dog	* *Speothos venaticus*	650	150	8 kg	—
Ursidae					
47. Spectacled bear	* *Tremarctos ornatus*	1390	40	125 kg	—
Procyonidae					
48. Cacomistle	*Bassariscus sumichrasti*	400	435	—	—
49. Crab-eating raccoon	* *Procyon cancrivorus*	600	280	5 kg	—
50. Kinkajou	* *Potos flavus*	450	510	3 kg	—
51. Coatimundi	* *Nasua nasua*	575	435	5 kg	—
Mustelidae					
52. Long-tailed weasel	* *Mustela frenata*	280	175	335 g	—
53. Tayra	* *Eira barbara*	650	440	5.5 kg	—
54. Patagonian huron	*Lyncodon patagonicus*	295	75	—	—
55. Hog-nosed skunk	* *Conepatus chinga*	415	195	4 kg	—
56. Flat-tailed otter	* *Pteronura brasiliensis*	860	510	16.5 kg	—
Felidae					
57. Ocelot	* *Felis pardalis*	725	320	9 kg	—
58. Pampa cat	*Felis colocolo*	640	280	6 kg	—
59. Jaguar	* *Felis onca*	1350	615	75 kg	—
60. Puma	* *Felis concolor*	950	700	40 kg	—
PERISSODACTYLA					
Tapiridae					
61. Brazilian tapir	* *Tapirus terrestris*	2000	100	250 kg	900
ARTIODACTYLA					
Tayassuidae					
62. Collared peccari	* *Tayassu tajacu*	1000	5	24 kg	—
Camelidae					
63. Guanaco	*Lama glama guanicoe*	1975	25	90 kg	1000
Cervidae					
64. White-tailed deer	* *Odocoileus virginianus*	1300	120	30 kg	750
65. Huemul	*Hippocamelus bisulcus*	1500	125	—	790
66. Pudu	*Pudu pudu*	820	40	11 kg	425

* *Measurements by author.*
[1] *Greatest circumference of body, 708 mm; measurements from Layne (1958).*
[2] *Measurements from Layne (1958).*
[3] *Greatest circumference of body, 1400 mm; measurements from Mohr (1957).*
  (*See Fig. 8A for 32-41; Fig. 8B for 42-65*).

FIG. 8B. Major Morphological Types of Neotropical Mammals (*continued*)
Numbers correspond to items in Table 4 (*continued*).

Axelrod (1967), judging from known Quaternary floras and faunas, decided that postglacial cold and aridity played important roles in the extinctions of large mammals previously adapted to equable climates. Postglacial decrease in humidity, however, aggravated by drastic seasonal fluctuations, might well have been the more important factor in the extermination of larger Middle and South American mammals. Axelrod notes that small boreal American mammals managed to survive the climatic crises because of behavioral and ecologic factors. The same factors and others, also apply to small South American species, as I noted elsewhere (1966a), and will discuss at greater length in following sections.

In addition to the factors already mentioned, Guilday (1967, p. 121) discusses habitat shrinkage and inability of the animal to adapt to new pressures or break through into a more favorable habitat. Slaughter (1967, p. 154) adds that failure to adjust mating behavior to a changing climate may have caused some species to disappear.

Simpson (1970:27) contributes a note, citing Gill (1955), that animals may disappear for causes unknowable. His example is the rat-sized Argentine marsupial superfamily Argyrolagoidea (2 genera, 4 to 6 species, Pliocene–Pleistocene), which "by all rules of analysis and theories of extinction . . . should have survived as did their close ecological analogues [jumping mice, pocket mice, kangaroo rats, jerboas, gerbils] in North America, Asia, Africa and Australia." Simpson observes that suitable argyrolagid habitats and communities are still preserved in South America but he is unaware that any other similarly adapted mammals ever occupied or survived in them. Simpson may not have considered the extant Patagonian gerbil-like *Eligmodontia* (Fig. 13c, and p. 387; also Hershkovitz, 1962, pp. 26, 178) which may well have been continuously contemporaneous and sympatric with the slightly more than twice as large argyrolagids.

Recent studies point to striking correlations between reversals of the earth's magnetic field and faunal extinctions during the Mesozoic and Cenozoic. As summarized by Hays (1971), extinctions of organisms may result from (1) increased cosmic radiation at the time of reversal, (2) the effect of climatic changes caused by reversals, and (3) the direct effect of reversals or low magnetic fields on the organisms. Crain (1971) believes that low or null radiation at the time of reversal rather than cosmic radiation, is the principal if not only cause for extinctions correlated with reversals. Still another consideration is the indirect effect of reversal on organisms with vital relationships, whether symbiotic, ecological, or through the food chain, with other organisms directly affected by reversal.

For a general account of recently extinct and vanishing mammals of the Western Hemisphere, see G. M. Allen (1942); for Pleistocene and Recent extinctions see Martin and Wright (1967). Literature cited by Axelrod (1967) includes an extensive bibliography on ecological factors involved in mammalian extinctions on continents other than South America.

Ecological Classification

Neotropical mammals (Table 4; Fig. 8A,B) may be classified as *sylvan, pastoral, fluviatile,* or *versatile,* according to their primary adaptations for locomotion, feeding, and the medium or media of food procurement. *Marine,* including transitional sea-shore mammals, are not regarded here as elements of the essentially terrestrial Neotropical fauna.

Sylvan mammals are primarily adapted for forest habitats. They may be terrestrial, arboreal, or aquatic, but not mainly subterranean. Many sylvan species survive destruction of natural forest habitats by accommodating themselves to similar or simulated habitats in jungle, scrubland, orchards, man-made buildings and, in the case of scansorial or arboreal species, to rock and cliff formations. True sylvan mammals are sylvan in origin, and comparatively generalized in structure. Except for a number of non-insectivorous bats, the molars of sylvan mammals retain a primitive tritubercular or quadritubercular design characterized by low crowns and raised cusps with interconnecting transverse ridges (cf. Fig. 9). Fore and hind feet are well developed, with all digits usually present; but the first digit of the forelimb, and rarely the first and fifth of the hind limb of many species, may be greatly reduced or absent. The tail is always present, except in certain bats, and is generally long.

Neotropical sylvan forms include all species of Marsupialia, although the common black-eared opossum (*Didelphis marsupialis*) is better classified as versatile (see below). All bats (Chiroptera) are historically sylvan, but many species, or populations, particularly cave dwellers, are adjusted to man-controlled environments. All monkeys and Neotropical Insectivora, Neotropical squirrels, cricetine mice of the thomasomyine and oryzomyine groups, and some genera of peromyscines are sylvan. Most Neotropical species of Carnivora may be historically sylvan, but many are now pastoral or versatile. Among canids, monotypic *Speothos* and perhaps the monotypic *Atelocynus* remain sylvan. Other sylvan carnivores are the procyonids, the bear *Tremarctos ornatus,* the mustelid tayra *(Eira barbara)* and the aquatic giant otter (*Pteronura brasiliensis*). Tapirs are omnivorous sylvan ungulates which commonly graze in bordering savannas.

Pastoral mammals are primarily adapted for living in deserts, rocklands, savannas (including pampas, prairies, meadows, tundra), scrublands, palm-savanna swamps, woodlands, thorn forests, and coniferous forests (see Fig. 2). They may also be at home on the grassy banks of forest streams, in forest clearings and succeeding second growths. Many are secondarily adapted for life in broad-leaf forests, particularly for grazing or browsing in evergreen forest canopies; others are frequently attracted to suitable fodder and fallen fruits periodically available on the forest fringe or floor. Pastoral mammals are usually terrestrial, but many are aquatic or sec-

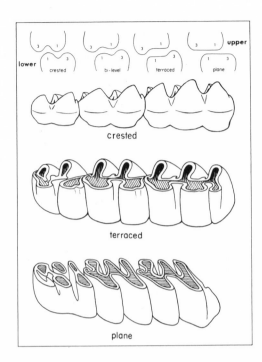

FIG. 9. EVOLUTIONARY STAGES OF
CRICETINE RODENT MOLARS
   *Evolution from generalized
sylvan (low-crowned crested or
brachyodont) for omnivorous food
habits, to specialized pastoral
(high-crowned plane or platy-
hypsodont) for grazing food habits.
Molars of other kinds of rodents,
and other mammals, most notably
ungulates, edentates, many bats,
also evolved through such stages.*

ondarily arboreal. All subterranean mammals of the Neotropical Region
are pastoral, but some species survive entrapment by succeeding forest.
   Pastoral mammals may be *progressive* offshoots of sylvan ancestry or
specialized descendents of progressive pastoral forms. Transition from
sylvan to pastoral life was made possible by transformation of crested,
low-crowned molars into flat high-crowned molars capable of grinding
and withstanding the attrition of tough fibrous vegetation, particularly
grasses and associated grit (Fig. 9). Changes in the remainder of the alimentary tract and modifications of limbs (Fig. 13), tail, and other parts
are also involved.
   Progressive pastoral species radiated into old or newly established
pastoral habitats along the forest edge. Initial changes in their dentition
and extremities were slight, and often subtle, but nevertheless crucial.
   The most numerous, ubiquitous, and representative progressive pastoral
mammals are members of the cricetine rodent genera *Calomys, Zygodontomys, Eligmodontia, Phyllotis, Akodon, Baiomys, Aporodon,* and possibly
others. Some of these mice spread from uplands to coastal plains and into
emerging river valleys, particularly along levees, as new habitats became
available. Others climbed into the highlands in the wake of retreating
glaciers to as high as 5000 meters above sea level, or to the highest altitudes
capable of sustaining mammalian life. Each lap or spurt in dispersal could
have been marked by explosive radiations with successive evolutionary
bursts on even higher planes of specializations.

Spike-antlered deer are outstanding examples of widespread progressive pastoral forms. The tiny pudus (*Pudu*) of the temperate Andean zones and the brockets (*Mazama*) are as much at home in forests as in bordering grasslands and thickets. They constitute a remote link between the ancestral sylvan stock and the larger branch-antlered deer of the wooded savannas of Middle and South America.

Living *specialized* pastoral cricetines include the species of the sigmodont, scapteromyine, oxymycterine, and ichthyomyine groups, and the akodonts *Notiomys, Thaptomys, Blarinomys, Hypsimys*, and many others. Neotropical species of spiny pocket mice (Heteromyidae), pocket gophers (Geomyidae), Caviomorpha (cavies, porcupines, tuco-tucos, agutis, spiny rats, chinchillas, etc.) and rabbits (Lagomorpha) have been pastoral as far back as their respective histories can be traced. Camelids, represented by the Patagonian llamas and vicuñas, should perhaps be classified as specialized pastoral forms. All Neotropical edentates or Xenarthra (armadillos, sloths, anteaters), are specialized pastoral descendents of pastoral ancestors known from the early Tertiary of South America.

Pastoral habitats, or savannas and deserts, are probably more extensive than any other vegetation type in South America (Goodland, 1966, p. 312). Nearly all of Argentina and Uruguay, one-half or more of Bolivia, Chile, and Venezuela, at least one-fifth of Brazil and Colombia, the entire coast, western uplands, and puna zone of Peru, the highlands of Ecuador, and large parts of the Guianas are savanna, scrub, prairie, meadow, tundra, or desert. Pastoral habitats were even more widespread during the Pleistocene. This may account for the predominance of pastoral mammals throughout most of South America and the secondary adaptations of many of them to newly established sylvan habitats.

Fluviatile mammals are strictly aquatic and are confined to streams and lakes. They do not ordinarily feed on land or move overland from one body of water to another. Fluviatile mammals of the Neotropical Region are the clawless manatee (*Trichechus inunguis*), and two freshwater cetaceans, the inia (*Inia geoffrensis*) and the Amazon river dolphin (*Sotalia fluviatilis*). All three species appear to be restricted to the Amazonian and Orinocoan basins of the Brazilian Subregion.

Versatile mammals are equally well adapted for living in sylvan and pastoral habitats and move freely from one to the other. The common opossum (*Didelphis marsupialis*), historically sylvan, and the nine-banded armadillo (*Dasypus novemcinctus*), historically pastoral, are rapidly spreading with nearly equal success into new pastoral and sylvan habitats. Many kinds of insectivorous, frugivorous, and omnivorous bats, and particularly the common blood-sucking vampire bat (*Desmodus rotundus*), readily adapt from their natural sylvan environment to pastoral ones where man-made structures, cultivated fruits, and concentrations of insects and domestic animals provide ideal cover and constant supplies of food. Predatory carnivores are difficult to categorize, but many species adjust their activities to whichever suitable sylvan or pastoral prey happens to be in greater supply or most vulnerable to capture. Versatile carnivores are particularly successful in cultivated country. Outstanding examples are the gray fox (*Urocyon cinereoargentatus*), bush dog (*Dusicyon thous*), raccoon (*Procyon cancrivorus*), weasel (*Mustela frenata*), otter (*Lutra canadensis*), all skunks, and many cats (e.g., jaguar, puma, ocelot, jaguarundi). A small number of cricetine rodents, notably some historically sylvan rice rats (*Oryzomys*) and progressive lauchas (*Calomys*), move freely from sylvan to pastoral habitats and in some parts of their range are commensal with man. Among ungulates, the peccaries (*Tayassu pecari*, *T. tajacu*) and brown brocket (*Mazama gouazoubira*) are as much at home in pastoral as in sylvan habitats.

Size

Small size characterizes nearly all living Neotropical mammals. Tapirs (the largest of Neotropical mammals) and guanacos (the tallest) are puny compared to extinct tropical American ungulates, and to living Holarctic and Ethiopian hoofed animals. Similar discrepancies exist between the living species of nearly all families of Neotropical mammals and those of the same families or ecological equivalents of other Regions or of pre-Recent South America. Even the boar-like capybara, largest of living rodents, is dwarfed by the rhinoceros-sized caviomorph *Eumegamys* of the South American Pliocene. Evidently, the large forms had disappeared, while the smaller, more primitive or generalized species survived. The smaller, in turn, would also tend to become larger, possibly to the point of extinction.

All mammals, it appears, tend to become larger in time. The larger individual that dominates the smaller possesses an advantage for self-preservation and propagation that translates into an evolutionary trend. Where selective pressures for small size should prevail, the trend toward larger size would be held in check, but not reversed. The small species remains small. It does not become smaller.

Geographic variation in body bulk or size of extremities reflects time in terms of the species' rate of dispersal in any direction. A high degree of correlation between larger size and higher latitudes or altitudes (Allen's rule) is explained by the fact that the vast majority of mammals originated in relatively warm habitats and many of them spread latitudinally or altitudinally into cooler or harsher peripheral habitats. Mammals spreading into warmer habitats, or moving cross-country within the same climatic zone, may also enlarge. Dispersal from highland or temperate climate habitats to lowland or tropical climate habitats is a common phenomenon in tropical latitudes. On the other hand, mammals of north temperate or arctic latitudes are specially adapted to withstand cold and they rarely, if ever, spread southward into warmer climates, winter migrations excepted. In any case, neither direction of dispersal nor climatic change is a factor in changing body size. Increase in bulk occurs in time with rate of change controlled by localized selective pressures.

Numbers of Species and Individuals

Variety, abundance, and year-round availability of food in the Neo-tropical Region supports many species and many individuals per species. For example, bats, which were primitively small insect-eaters, radiated in tropical rain forests into selective insect-eaters, specialized ripe fruit-, nectar-, flesh-, fish- or blood-eaters, and omnivores. There are no browsers, grazers, or seed eaters among the bats. Northern or temperate-zone bats remained, with few exceptions, insect-eaters, but acquired the ability to hibernate or migrate when their food supplies diminished or disappeared. As a consequence, temperate-zone bats are few in species and numbers. Tropical forest Chiroptera, in contrast, exceed any other mammalian taxon of temperate zone or latitude in number of species and individuals.

The Neotropical rodents are also highly diversified and often excessively abundant. In any one locality, under favorable circumstances, the individuals of one or two small rodent species may outnumber those of all other nonvolant mammalian species combined. Population highs generally follow protracted rainy seasons with unusual abundance of food; exceptionally dry or protracted dry seasons lead to drastic population declines. The periodic fruiting of particular plants, such as bamboo (e.g., *Merostachys*), promote population explosions or "ratadas" among some cricetine rodents. In tropical floodlands, ratadas may occur in forest canopies. For detailed accounts of rodent population fluctuations, see Hershkovitz (1962, p. 42) and Crespo (1966).

Year-round breeding by various populations of a Neotropical species tends to maintain the average number of individuals of the species uniformly high, and probably higher than in Nearctica. The numbers of individuals and sex ratios of a local population, however, fluctuate widely. Whatever the individual litter size of any species, the reproductive rate of Neotropical mammals must be as high as that of equivalent Nearctic forms.

Migrations

Mass migrations over great distances by living species of Neotropical mammals are unknown. Large herds of white-lipped peccaries wander seasonally in great circles attracted by dead or dying fish, mollusks, and other aquatic animals stranded in shallow pools left behind receding floods. Scores, perhaps hundreds, of miles are travelled over swamps and rivers in these erratic treks. Monkeys also seem to roam widely in search of the various fruits which ripen successively in different parts of the range throughout the year. The actual radius of the movements of a troop may be no more than a few miles, but individuals often shift from troop to troop. Many bats are migratory, but only species of the genus *Lasiurus*, with a continental range extending from Canada to Chile and Argentina, are suspected of migrating between northern and southern latitudes.

Hibernation

Hibernation or estivation, as regular seasonal phenomena have not been demonstrated in any Neotropical mammal. Nevertheless, cold-induced lethargy with lowered body temperature has been recorded for mouse-opossums (*Marmosa, Thylamys, Dromiciops*), a species of mastiff bat (*Molossus major*), sloths and other edentates (Wislocki and Enders, 1935), the common marmoset (*Callithrix jacchus*), and some species of Patagonian cricetine rodents (cf. Hershkovitz, 1962, p. 46; Morrison and McNab, 1967).

Adaptive Radiation

Marsupialia (Marsupicarnivora)

The Didelphidae and Caenolestidae are the surviving New World families of Marsupialia. Didelphids are typified by the common opossum (*Didelphis marsupialis*), oldest, largest and most versatile of living American marsupials (Fig. 16). Its similarity to the European red fox in size, shape of muzzle, large ears, musky odor, omnivorous diet, ubiquity, persistence, attraction to farmyards, and gastronomic predilection for roosting hens was already noted by Spanish colonists who dubbed the animal "zorra" or "raposa," both words meaning fox. The fox-like attributes, however, are mostly superficial. The common opossum with its unfox-like prehensile tail and adductible digits of fore and hind feet is also an expert climber and a diligent digger for crustaceans and other prey in river banks and shallow stream bottoms. The smaller *Lutreolina crassicaudata* is the marsupial equivalent of the placental weasel and is even called "comadreja" (=weasel) by Spanish-speaking natives. The pouched and pouchless four-eyed opossums *Philander* and *Metachirus*, respectively, are also weasel-like. The yapock (*Chironectes*) is the only truly aquatic didelphid. As swimmer, diver, slippery rock climber, and fish-eater, it compares favorably with placental otters. The woolly opossum (*Caluromys*) is the tropical American counterpart of the African lemuroids, particularly bush babies, family Galagidae. *Glironia* can be described as a marsupial tree shrew, paralleling the squirrel-like placental *Tupaia*. The many species of arboreal murine opossums (*Marmosa*) share habitats with similar-appearing Neotropical cricetine rodents of the genera *Rhipidomys, Oecomys*, and *Tylomys*. Functionally, ecologically, and even in gross form, however, murine opossums are more nearly like small lemurs—for example, the dwarf lemur (*Microcebus murinus*) of Madagascar. Short-tailed opossums of the genus *Monodelphis* are the smallest of the family, being vole-like in appearance and shrew-like in habits. The fat-tailed mouse-like *Dromiciops australis* of the bamboo thickets of the Andes of central Chile and neighboring Argentina is sole survivor of the didelphid subfamily Microbiotheriinae which flourished in South America during the Tertiary.

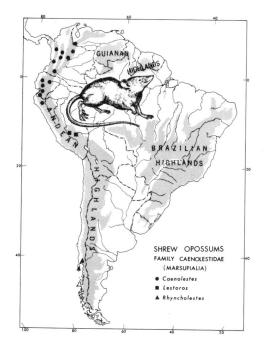

FIG. 10. Distribution of Shrew-
Opossums, Family Caenolestidae
*Relicts of an old South American
fauna, shrew opossums are confined
to high Andean altitudes and high
Chilean latitudes. Their distributional pattern parallels that of the
pigmy deer, genus* Pudu. *South
American highlands shaded.*

Living New World didelphids occupy many ecological niches but dominate none. They left untouched the vast majority of available and accessible mammalian habitats. Didelphids are essentially sylvan, but few of them
left the tropical forests for the less hospitable temperate-zone forests
and the more rigorous pastoral habitats. They did not radiate into
niches later occupied by ungulates, burrowers, jumpers, hoppers, terrestrial or arboreal springers, gliders, or flyers. They did not develop spines
or a scaly or horny armature. All didelphids are omnivorous, but none
evolved to replace the extinct Borhyaenidae, the marsupial equivalent
of a placental carnivore. A single living species, the common black-eared
opossum, *Didelphis marsupialis,* is as diversified in habits and habitats as
most didelphids combined. Stupid as *Didelphis marsupialis* may appear
to many human observers, it surpasses all other living didelphids, and
perhaps all other living mammals, in the combination of adaptability,
tenacity, viability, vagility, and phyletic longevity.

The Caenolestidae comprise several diprotodont, long-tailed, pouchless,
shrew-like species living in the Andean temperate-zone rain forest from
Venezuela to southern Chile. Caenolestids are generalized in form and
primitive in most respects. Their present distribution appears to be very
narrowly restricted ecologically (Fig. 10). Some species of the sympatric
cricetine rodents *Thomasomys* and *Abrothrix* are remarkably similar in
form and habits. Their superior numbers, at times reaching plague proportions, must exert powerful counter-pressures on caenolestid struggles
for survival. Essentially terrestrial, caenolestids are excellent and ready
climbers. Although omnivorous, they subsist largely on insects and worms.

Insectivora

The Neotropical Insectivora of Middle and South America comprise one or two species of small shrews of the genus *Cryptotis* (family Soricidae). The South American species *Cryptotis thomasi* is confined to upper subtropical and temperate-zone rain forests and bordering meadows in the Andes of Venezuela, Colombia, and Ecuador. It shares habitats in the upper limits of its range with marsupial shrews of the genus *Caenolestes* and mice of the genus *Thomasomys*. At lower levels, in upper subtropical forests, it crosses trails with the dominant white-throated rice rat, *Oryzomys albigularis*.

Chiroptera

Bats, next to rodents, are most varied, numerous, and pervasive. They comprise well over one-fourth of the total number of Neotropical species of mammals. Bats are primarily tropical, and their greatest radiation occurred in lowland rain forests, where the number of species and individuals of bats may equal and, in some cases, even exceed those of all other mammals combined. For example, Handley (1966) records 201 species (196 if revised) of native nonmarine mammals for Panama. Of these, 100 are bats and only 48 are rodents.

Year-round abundance of fruits, seeds, flowers, and animal prey, particularly insects, provides sustenance for bats of every dietary specialization. The kinds and numbers of bats diminish drastically toward higher latitudes in both the northern and the southern hemispheres where insects remain as the only constantly available food during the plant growing season. There is a comparable drop in variety and numbers of bats at higher altitudes in tropical latitudes, but representatives of all ecological types persist through the subtropical zone. A few species of insectivorous and rare frugivorous bats range into temperate-zone forests of the equatorial region, and only a limited number of insectivorous forms forage above tree line in páramos and punas.

Bats live in every Neotropical habitat from sea level to 5000 meters above sea level in the Andes, or to the highest altitudes capable of supporting warm-blooded animals. They live underground in caves, on the ground clinging to rocks and exposed roots, above ground in shrubs, in and on trees from trunks to the canopies of the tallest plants. Some bats roost during the day in the darkest recesses of caves and hollow trees, others where they are fully exposed to daylight but sheltered from the direct rays of the sun. Most kinds, however, rest diurnally in twilight zones of various intensities. Some bats are solitary except when mating, others roost in small colonies; still others cluster in groups of hundreds to tens of thousands of individuals. Each ecologically distinct compartment in a large hollow tree or in a cave can harbor a different bat species. Some caves shelter a dozen species or even more. Most species rest by clinging to rough surfaces with the claws of their feet, others support themselves with the claws of their fore and hind feet whether head-down, head-up, or horizontal. The disc-winged *Thyroptera* attach themselves to the smooth surfaces of rolled *Heliconia* leaves by means of suction pads at the base of each thumb and on each sole (Fig. 8A).

The more primitive forms, including all species of Emballonuridae, Vespertilionidae, Furipteridae, Natalidae, and Thyropteridae, are small and insectivorous. The Molossidae, also insectivorous, include large and small forms. The Phyllostomidae embrace the largest and most diversified of New World bats. Phyllostomids may be insectivorous, frugivorous, carnivorous, or omnivorous. The carnivorous false vampire, *Vampyrum spectrum,* with a wing spread of over 75 cm and a combined head and body length of nearly 15 cm, is the largest of New World bats. This hawk-like animal preys on other bats and other small mammals, birds, and insects. Fruit eaters (predominantly the subfamily Stenoderminae) prefer soft ripe fruit. I have never seen unripe or hard-coated fruit attacked by bats. Nectar-eaters (subfamily Glossophaginae) have long snouts and extensile tongues for inserting deeply into the corollas of flowers. Many flowering plants are dependent on these bats for cross pollination. Some insectivorous phyllostomids also eat fruit, but very little is known of specific feeding habits of most species of Phyllostomidae. Their diversity in shape, size, proportions, flight patterns, and roosts is greater than in any other family of bats. There is a corresponding diversity in their feeding and other habits.

The family Noctilionidae consists of one genus and two species, occurring throughout most of the Brazilian Subregion. The larger *Noctilio leporinus* is a fish-eater which hooks its prey by grappling with the large recurved claws of its feet while skimming over streams and ponds. It also eats insects, whereas the smaller species, *N. labialis,* seems to prefer them to fish.

Desmodidae is a family of three species of true vampire or blood-sucking bats, each the size of a mouse. *Desmodus rotundus* occurs almost everywhere in forest and pasture from Mexico to Chile and Argentina, from sea level to 3000 m or more above. It prefers mammalian blood and has a particular relish for that of humans and domestic cattle. *Diaemus youngi* is tropical and preys on birds, including poultry. *Diphylla ecaudata* is poorly known, but its habits are presumably like those of *Diaemus.* Vampires, with their peculiar dentition and thread-thin gullets, are so highly specialized for taking blood that they eat nothing else.

Primates

New World monkeys, suborder Platyrrhini, vary in size from the smallest of living primates to individuals about the size of a setter (Fig. 11). The size gradient reflects part of the evolution of primates in general, from the smallest and most primitive to the largest and most advanced. The size progression among living New World primates is surprisingly even

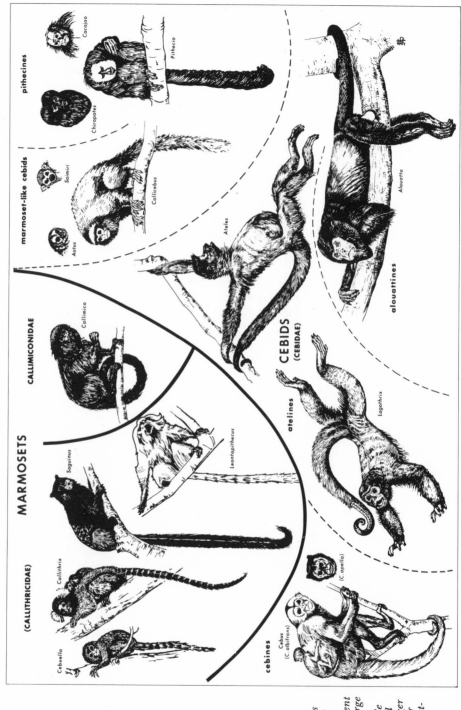

FIG. 11. NEW WORLD
PRIMATES

Representative species of platyrrhine monkeys arranged in systematic order. The rough gradient in size from small to large corresponds to the grouping. A sliding scale for size, however, is used for each group; the larger its members, the smaller the scale used for depicting each group. See Table 5 for measurements.

TABLE 5

Average sizes of representative New World Primates (Platyrrhini)[1]

English Vermacular Names	Scientific Names	Combined Head and Body Length [2]	Tail Length
	CALLITHRICIDAE		
Pigmy marmoset	*Cebuella pygmaea*	13 cm.	20 cm.
Common marmoset	*Callithrix jacchus*	20	31
Tamarins	*Saguinus*	23	35
Golden marmoset	*Leontopithecus rosalia*	24	34
	CALLIMICONIDAE		
Callimico	*Callimico goeldii*	23	31
	CEBIDAE		
Squirrel monkey	*Saimiri sciureus*	28	39
Night monkey	*Aotus trivirgatus*	30	36
Titis	*Callicebus*	32	42
Bearded Sakis	*Chiropotes*	41	41
Sakis	*Pithecia*	41	41
Uakaris	*Cacajao*	44	16
Capuchin monkeys	*Cebus*	40	43
Woolly monkey	*Lagothrix lagothricha*	43	61
Howler monkeys	*Alouatta*	50	65
Spider monkey	*Ateles paniscus*	48	75
Woolly spider monkey	*Brachyteles arachnoides*	58	72

(measurements in centimeters)

[1] *The measurements given are the averages of 10 or more adult males and females combined.*
[2] *Combined head and body length approximates sitting height; 1 inch = 2.54 centimeters.*

and is largely correlated with changes in forms of their locomotion and diet.

Marmosets, family Callithricidae, are the smallest of living primates and, except for the advanced architecture of their head with orbits set in front, are most primitive. They resemble tree squirrels in size, color pattern, and movements in general. Like squirrels, with which they coexist, marmosets can support the full weight of their bodies on the tips of the long sharp claws of their hands or feet. Unlike squirrels, however, the digits of marmosets are adductible; the great toe (though not the thumb) is opposable and is provided with a nail. These specializations, which permit grasping with both hands and feet are, collectively, among the most crucial characters for separating primitive primates from rodents and such Insectivora as tree shrews.

Marmosets are primarily insectivorous. Their small size, quick jerky movements, and sharp claws are adaptations for effective capture of insects, and their tritubercular molars are efficient tools for cracking the chitinous covering of arthropods. Marmosets also feed on other animals, including small birds and mammals, nestlings, lizards, and eggs, and they consume large quantities of fruit. The smallest and most primitive species is the pigmy marmoset (*Cebuella pygmaea*) of the upper Amazonian region. Its ecological niche is shared by mouse opossums (*Marmosa* spp.), arboreal mice (*Oecomys* spp., *Rhipidomys* spp.) and pigmy squirrels (*Sciurillus, Microsciurus*). Other marmosets are much larger than *Cebuella* but none surpasses in size the largest Neotropical squirrels. Marmosets of the genera *Callithrix* and *Saguinus*, the latter usually called tamarins, equal moderately large tree squirrels in size and occupy roughly similar ecological niches. The largest member of the family, the lion marmoset (*Leontopithecus rosalia*), is the most highly specialized. It possesses a large median ventral pharyngeal diverticulum, a character shared by few other primates. More notable, however, are the specializations of its long slender arm, narrow palm, and elongate middle fingers adapted for digging insects and grubs from under loose bark and from cracks or holes in tree trunks and branches. The lion marmoset has not gone nearly as far in this specialty as the lemuroid aye-aye of Madagascar, but its hand resembles closely that of the striped phalanger (*Dactylopsila*, Marsupialia) of New Guinea, which uses it in the same way.

The gradient of increasing size from largest marmoset to smallest of the marmoset-like cebids is almost imperceptible but nevertheless crucial (Fig. 11). It marks the passing of a threshold in arboreal support, locomotion, prehension, nutrition, and reproduction (Fig. 12).

The smaller marmoset-like cebids (*Aotus, Callicebus, Saimiri*), remain essentially quadrupedal but depart from marmosets in their greater reliance on hands for hoisting and climbing than on hind legs for springing. Pithecines (*Pithecia, Chiropotes, Cacajao*), the next larger group of cebids, have longer arms and are more proficient climbers. The arms of the larger and prehensile-tailed cebids (*Cebus, Lagothrix, Alouatta,*

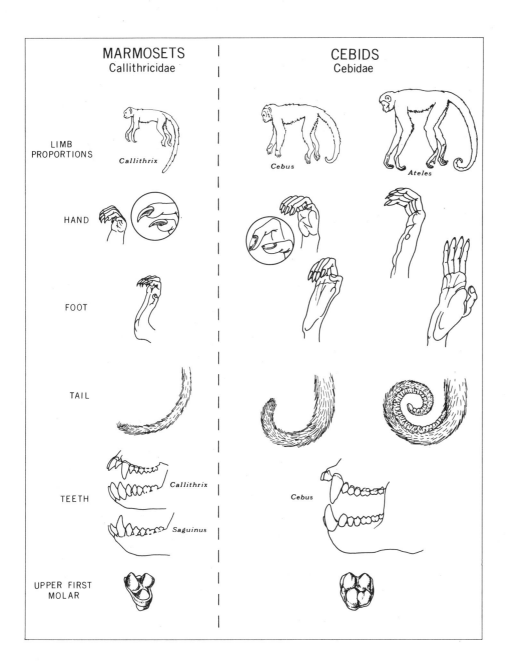

FIG. 12. EVOLUTIONARY CHANGES IN PLATYRRHINE BODY PROPORTIONS, HANDS, FEET, TAIL, AND TEETH CORRELATED WITH INCREASING BODY SIZE IN AN ARBOREAL HABITAT

Callithrix (*marmosets*) *are the size of the common gray squirrel,* Cebus (*capuchins*) *compare with terriers in size, and* Ateles (*spider monkeys*) *equal setters in size but not in bulk. As monkeys became larger, they needed more secure and powerful limbs for grasping and traveling in trees, and larger amounts of readily available and easily secured foods such as fruits and leaves. Because of the frequently flooded forest floor, New World monkeys evolved entirely above ground. Not drawn to scale.*

Ateles), may be nearly as long as the legs (e.g., *Cebus*) or longer than the legs (e.g., *Ateles*). Either front or hind limbs alone can support the body of the larger cebids in effective locomotion—the arms for brachiation, the legs for bipedal progression (Fig. 12).

For more effective support of the heavier body, the thumb followed the great toe to become opposable, thus endowing the hand with a locking grasp (Fig. 12). The claws themselves became obsolete in the process and were reduced to nails. As a result, the mainstay of arboreal support shifted from the grappling and clinging claws of marmosets to the grasping and clutching digits of cebids, and the whole hand became the equal of the whole foot in its adaptation for arboreal progression. In the final stage, represented by the brachiating spider monkey, the fore limb surpassed the hind limb in locomotory specialization. The palm and last four digits lengthened into an enormous grapnel-like organ for hooking onto the branches in locomotion. The now useless thumb was reduced or eliminated.

The tail also evolved with increasing body size from a mere balancing organ into serving as a clutching and prehensile limb, as well (Fig. 12). Specialization of the tail is least in *Cebus,* the smallest of prehensile-tailed cebids, and most in the largest cebids, the howlers and spider monkeys. The new caudal functions confer upon the larger cebids the balance, security, and agility of the smaller in arboreal support, prehension, and locomotion.

The quadritubercular molars (see Fig. 12) of the Cebidae, adapted for omnivorous but mainly vegetarian diets, are also correlated with larger body size and the need for bulkier and less mobile types of food. Smaller cebids such as the douroucouli (*Aotus trivirgatus*), titis (*Callicebus* spp.), and squirrel monkey (*Saimiri sciureus*) are still largely insectivorous, but more omnivorous, particularly frugivorous, than the trituberculate-toothed marmosets. At the other end, the larger prehensile-tailed cebids with terraced quadritubercular molars are even more frugivorous than insectivorous, the howler *(Alouatta* spp.) being entirely herbivorous and more browsing or leaf-eating than fruit-eating.

Reduction in litter size from two or three young per litter in marmosets to one per litter in cebids is also correlated with greater size. This is generally true of all mammals but is particularly significant in species which carry their offspring during the period of infancy.

Callimico is intermediate in size between the largest marmoset and smallest cebid. It has the non-opposable thumb and claws of marmosets but the more fluid movements of small non-prehensile tailed cebids. Its molars show transition from the tritubercular to the quadritubercular pattern. *Callimico* ranges widely in the upper Amazonian region from Colombia to Bolivia, but nothing is known of its habits in the wild. *Callimico* has been classified with marmosets by some authorities and with cebids by others. Those allocations seem to be dependent on similarities correlated with size rather than on phylogenetic considerations. Retention of the third molar and production of a single young per birth excludes an animal the size of *Callimico* from the marmoset family. The largest marmoset produces two young at a birth and the third molar was already lost in the smallest including, most probably, the ancestral species which could not have been larger than the pygmy marmoset. On the other hand, *Callimico* with its primitively structured extremities and tritubercular-quadritubercular molars might be regarded as a primitive cebid. A number of dental, cranial, and other characters still under study suggest, however, divergence from a pre-cebid stock and an evolution paralleling that of small platyrrhines generally.

Kinship between New and Old World monkeys is remote and resides in a common early Tertiary tarsioid stock. The remarkable parallelism in the evolution of platyrrhines and catarrhines derives from the conservation of primitive primate traits, primate evolutionary tendencies in general, and exposure to similar selective factors in tropical arboreal habitats.

There are no terrestrial platyrrhines and no prehensile-tailed catarrhines. The squirrel-like marmosets in the New World have no counterparts among Old World primates. The more arboreally adapted species of tree shrews (Insectivora sensu lato) approximate, however, the squirrel-like or marmoset habitus. The short-tailed or tailless Cercopithecidae, Pongidae, and Hominidae are hardly imitated by the two bob-tailed platyrrhine species of the genus *Cacajao*. These are simply more bipedal but no less arboreal than other American monkeys. Most lemuroids are nocturnal, but only the douroucouli (*Aotus trivirgatus*) among the platyrrhines has become somewhat lemur-like in its secondary adaptations for scotoptic vision and nocturnal habits. Finally, the brachiating gibbons and the leaping langurs and guerezas are large, powerful, Old World primates matched in locomotor agility only by the suggestively similar prehensile-tailed spider monkeys, *Ateles* and *Brachyteles*.

Edentata (Xenarthra)

Edentates, order Edentata originated in South or Middle America and, except for the nine-banded armadillo (*Dasypus novemcinctus*), are confined to the Neotropical Region. Living families are the sloths (Bradypodidae) with 3 species, the anteaters (Myrmecophagidae) with 3 species, and the armadillos (Dasypodidae) with perhaps 16 species.

Armadillos range in size from the tiny rat-sized fossorial pichi ciego (*Chlamyphorus truncatus*) to the boar-sized giant armadillo (*Priodontes maximus*). For all their range in size and variation in pattern of armored coats, armadillos are basically similar in form, terrestrial and fossorial modes of locomotion, and feeding habits. They are generally frugivorous and insectivorous, and opportunistic worm-, grub-, and carrion-eaters.

Anteaters show approximately the same range of size as armadillos. The giant anteater (*Myrmecophaga*) and lesser anteater (*Tamandua*) live and feed indiscriminately in pastoral and sylvan habitats. Both anteaters are diggers and climbers, the lesser anteater being aided in climbing by its scaly prehensile tail. A third species, the diminutive termite-eating silky anteater (*Cyclopes*), with remarkably prehensile tail, hooked claws, opposable foot pads, and swivel-jointed ankle bones, is strictly arboreal.

Sloths are highly specialized for arboreal life. They prefer tall timber and subsist mainly on leaves. Their grappling claws are basically of the same design as those of the grappling, ripping, and digging claws of ant-eaters and armadillos. A tail, long and powerful in most armadillos and all anteaters, is absent in sloths. Obsolescence of the tail in tree sloths began with the small, short-tailed ancestral ground sloths. These must have relied first on sitting tripodally, then standing bipedally, and finally, on greater size in order to feed on ever higher leaf-bearing branches. Long powerful arms and hooked claws helped bring to their mouths the more distant branches with heavier foliage. Seemingly, ground sloths were trapped in a vicious cycle of becoming larger to enable them to reach higher to get more browse to feed their ever enlarging bodies. On the other hand, another line of still small ground sloths benefited from its size and hooked claws by climbing into the very trees themselves, at first, perhaps, for escaping periodic floods, and then for browsing as well. When sloths came into contact with new environments and new and more powerful terrestrial predators, including man, the arboreal sloths survived but the ground sloths did not.

Rodentia

Rodents are the most widely distributed, varied, abundant, and successful of mammals. They live everywhere mammalian life is supported except in the sea and in the air. The Neotropical region is headquarters for mice of the subfamily Cricetinae (family Muridae) and home for all species of the suborder Caviomorpha save one, the boreal American porcupine, *Erethizon dorsatum.* Tree squirrels of the cosmopolitan family Sciuridae, and New World pocket mice (Heteromyidae) are also members of the Neotropical fauna. Introduced house mice (*Mus*) and rats (*Rattus*), and other exotics, are not considered here. The native rodent groups are briefly discussed under separate headings arranged in phylogenetic order.

1. Sciuridae

The Neotropical Sciurinae are typical tree squirrels. The essentially Nearctic flying squirrel, *Glaucomys volans,* however, penetrated Middle America as far as Honduras. The absence of ground squirrels in Middle America cannot be explained on ecological grounds alone. The time of arrival in Mexico may have been the crucial factor. Sciurines abound throughout the forested parts of the Brazilian Subregion, but neither tree squirrels nor ecological equivalents among other categories are present in the wooded areas of the West Indies and the extensive temperate zone forests of the Patagonian Subregion. The dominant Neotropical genus is *Sciurus* (sensu lato) with perhaps a dozen valid species of many sizes and colors. Pigmy squirrels of the monotypic genus *Microsciurus* are simply small mouse-sized tree squirrels. Even smaller is the relict *Sciurillus* of the Guianan and Amazonian regions. It is a miniature tree squirrel in habitus, but its cranial characters recall those of the equally small Oriental *Nanosciurus*. Two, three, or four species of tree squirrels may live side by side in some parts of the Neotropical Region, but rarely two of the same size. Notable exceptions are the two species of "giant" Amazonian squirrels, *Sciurus spadiceus* and *S. igniventris*. Both are as large as fox squirrels, similar in appearance inter se, and sympatric throughout most of their range. Neither these nor any other similarly related pairs of mammalian species support the notion of "character displacement."

2. Heteromyidae

Pocket mice occur in Middle America in the forms of *Liomys,* and the nearly related and similar appearing *Heteromys*. The latter also ranges into lowland Colombia, northwestern Ecuador, and northern Venezuela. Neotropical heteromyids live on forest floors and bordering fields. Their long thick tails and powerful hind legs equip them for leaping and bounding in flight, but *Liomys* and *Heteromys* are less specialized in these respects than related kangaroo rats, genus *Dipodomys,* of southwestern United States.

Burrowing pocket gophers, family Geomyidae, are mainly Nearctic, but three genera, *Orthogeomys, Heterogeomys*, and *Macrogeomys,* extend the range of geomyids to the eastern limits of Panama. Although common on the eastern slopes of the Serranía del Darién in Panama, *Macrogeomys* is not known to occur on the western or South American side. The burrowing caviomorph tucotucos, genus *Ctenomys,* of the Patagonian Subregion are strikingly similar in form, habits, and habitats.

3. Muridae (Cricetinae)

Mice, subfamily Cricetinae, are the dominant mammals of the Neotropical Region. They outnumber all others in diversity of species and numbers of individuals. More than 200 species represent two tribes, the essentially South American Sigmodontini and the almost wholly North American Peromyscini. Collectively, they comprise ten to twelve monophyletic aggregations or clusters of radiating species, and several aberrant species without close relatives. Each species (or sibling species group) of a cluster differs from other members of the same cluster by a complex of adaptive characters which fit it for a particular ecological niche. For example, rice rats of the oryzomyine cluster are essentially forest dwellers and are distributed from the eastern United States to the Straits of Magellan. The group includes some species adapted for terrestrial-cursorial or

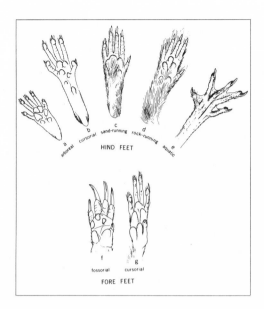

FIG. 13. ADAPTIVE RADIATION IN
CRICETINE RODENT FEET
    a, Oryzomys bicolor; b, O. albi-
gularis; c, Eligmodontia typus; d,
Galenomys garleppi; e, Nectomys
squamipes; f, Kunsia tomentosus;
g, Oryzomys albigularis; all plantar
surface of right foot except e (dorsal
surface to show webbing). (Adapted
from Hershkovitz, 1944, p. 24; 1960,
p. 524; 1962, p. 52; 1966a, p. 89.

for terrestrial-scansorial life, others for palustrine to aquatic life, and still others for the arboreal sphere (Fig. 13). The terrestrial-cursorial deep forest forms (e.g., *Oryzomys capito, O. albigularis*) are usually large-eared, long-tailed, narrow-footed, and digitigrade. The cursorial forest-edge types (subgenus *Melanomys*) are like the first but smaller-eared, shorter-tailed, and generally vole-like. Terrestrial scansorial oryzomyines are small, long-tailed, and broad-footed (e.g., *Oligoryzomys, Microryzomys*). The small, shorter-tailed spiny, *Acomys*-like *Neacomys* rarely climbs. Palustrine and aquatic rice rats (e.g., *Oryzomys palustris, Nectomys squamipes*) are usually small-eared, with water-shedding coats, long powerful tails, and oar-like hind feet with membranes stretched between the toes. The gray-brown upper parts and the silvery gray underparts of most aquatic oryzomyines are concealing. Arboreal oryzomyines [e.g., subgenus *Oecomys* (cf. Hershkovitz, 1958)] have long semi-prehensile tails covered, at least terminally, with long tactile hairs. Their feet are broad, with long and partially opposable outer digits, recurved claws, and enlarged plantar tubercles adapted for clutching slender branches and twigs. The short muzzle and enlarged eyes of these arboreal mice afford a wide field of frontal vision. The arboreal opposum-like *Megalomys* of the West Indies and Galápagos Islands is the largest oryzomyine and New World myomorph. It was exterminated by man during the last century. Oryzomyines may not have exploited every niche within their geographic range but they do occupy very many of them.

The thomasomyine cluster is closely related to, but less diverse than, the oryzomyines. Some of its species are the most primitive of living myomorphs. The forms of *Thomasomys* are mainly terrestrial-scansorial.

Others, especially those of the thomasomyine genus *Rhipidomys,* are specialized for arboreal life.

Radiation among the phyllotines, a group of pastoral cricetines, has been even wider than in oryzomyines. Most species of the Andean and Patagonian genus *Phyllotis* (cf. Hershkovitz, 1962) are short-tailed vole-like, terrestrial-cursorial inhabitants of grass and rock communities. One species, *Phyllotis griseoflavus,* is semi-arboreal. The large variegated Andean phyllotine, *Chinchillula sahamae,* is remarkably hamster-like. *Andinomys edax* is the Patagonian equivalent of Nearctic wood rats of the genus *Neotoma.* Superficially, *Pseudoryzomys wavrini* is practically indistinguishable from *Oryzomys palustris* in size, form, and external modifications for palustrine and aquatic life. The small desert-dwelling *Eligmodontia typus* is extraordinarily gerbil-like in size, color, elongated hind limbs, hairy plantar cushions, and habits. *Calomys laucha* is the common field and house mouse of the pampas and is almost indistinguishable in external characters and habits from the introduced house mouse, *Mus musculus.* Certain cranial, dental, and external characters of the high Andean phyllotine, *Galenomys garleppi,* recall those of the Arctic hare. These examples illustrate but do not exhaust the examples of ecological types of phyllotines.

Radiation within the pastoral sigmodont cluster of rodents parallels that of phyllotines. There are vole-like, hare-like, and aquatic forms.

The akodont cluster combines a number of short-tailed or vole-like species distributed throughout the grassy and gladed parts of the subtropical and temperate zones of South America. The long-clawed *Notiomys* diverges from the terrestrial-cursorial species of *Akodon* by its adaptations for fossorial life. The akodont *Blarinomys* is the most specialized mole-like cricetine on a continent where true moles are absent. Oxymycterines are long-clawed, shrew-like, semi-palustrine, insectivorous mice of akodont antecedents. In addition to insects, they favor earthworms, grubs, and small crustaceans.

Closely related to oxymycterines are the scapteromyines, a three-species cluster of the southern part of the Brazilian Subregion. Typical *Scapteromys* converges toward the shrew-like oxymycterine type but with modifications for life in both aquatic and arboreal environments. The second line of scapteromyines culminates in *Kunsia tomentosus,* at once the largest and most fossorial, or gopher-like, of living cricetines (cf. Hershkovitz, 1966a).

The ichythyomyine cluster comprises several species of otter-like or insectivore-like fish-eaters each particularly adapted for certain types of streams and climates. Their hind toes are fringed like those of their ecological equivalents among Insectivora, the European *Desmana* and *Galemys.*

The North American Peromyscini are represented in Middle America by the woodland vole *Scotinomys,* difficult to distinguish from such South American ecological equivalents as the akodont *Chalcomys.* The peromyscine *Baiomys* mimics nearly to perfection, in its superficial appearance and habits, the phyllotine *Calomys laucha* and its murine equivalent, *Mus musculus*. In both Middle America and northwestern South America, *Aporodon* agrees in superficial appearance, habits, and choice of habitats with small scansorial oryzomyine species of the genus *Microryzomys*. *Tylomys* and *Ototylomys* are large scaly-tailed arboreal peromyscines resembling murine opossums of the genus *Marmosa*.

Similarities in the adaptive characters of each of the diverse lineages of cricetine rodents are the results of convergence. Adaptive traits may conceal but do not obliterate any part of the unique combination of deep-seated skeletal, dental, external, and other fundamental characters common to the divergent members of a species cluster.

4. Caviomorpha (=Hystricomorpha)

Rodents of the suborder Caviomorpha radiated farther and in more directions than other comparable groups of living New World mammals. Whatever their origin, all present forms can be derived from pastoral terrestrial ancestors. They occupy all the more obvious kinds of non-volant pastoral and sylvan niches and perhaps some niches not yet classi-fied. Caviomorphs range in size from the small ground squirrel-like octo-donts to the giant of rodents, the boar-like capybara (*Hydrochaerus*). Cavies or wild guinea pigs (*Cavia*) resemble Holarctic pikas (Ochotonidae), but rock cavies (*Kerodon*) suggest rather the African rock dassies (Pro-caviidae). The coypu or nutria (*Myocastor*) is a valuable fur-bearer sur-passingly adapted for aquatic life. Colonies of them introduced into the United States and Eurasia have become firmly established, often to the detriment of similar native fur-bearers such as the muskrat and beaver. The fossorial tuco tuco (*Ctenomys*) is the Patagonian counterpart of the North American pocket gopher in size, form, function, social organization, local variation, and taxonomic confusion. The Patagonian "hares," *Doli-chotis* and *Pediolagus,* are caviomorph equivalents of North American jack-rabbits in general appearance and habits but their resemblance as well to kangaroos cannot be overlooked. Chinchillas and viscachas are the rock squirrels of the treeless Andes. Agutis (*Dasyprocta*) are three-toed forest ungulates corresponding to the African pygmy forest antelopes. The short-tailed, scurrying, bounding pigmy aguti or acuchy recalls Holarctic ground squirrels. The tailless spotted paca, characterized by a uniquely inflated cheek bone which functions as a resonating chamber, is the "chevrotain" of the Neotropical rain forest. The Andean pacarana (*Dinomys*) resembles the paca, but its somewhat shaggy coat, tail, and burrowing proclivities are quite marmot-like. A spotted coat similar to that of the paca and pacarana also distinguishes the young of peccary, tapir, and most deer. In addition to their digitigrade stance, all ungulate-like caviomorphs tend toward perissodactylism, with loss or obsolescence of one or both outer toes. The powerful hoof-like claws of these caviomorphs, however, are adapted for burrowing, but the forefeet still serve for hold-ing and manipulating foods.

The Echimyidae, or "spiny rats," are the most diversified of caviomorphs. The pelage of a majority of the 40-odd species may be only hispid or harsh, though in many it is soft or silky. The coat of the type species of the genus *Echimys*, however, is spiny, hence the vernacular group name. All living echimyids are confined to the Brazilian Subregion but some recently extinct ones were native to the Greater Antilles. Nearly all echimyids are forest-dwellers. Judged by their dentition and habits, all are primarily grazers and browsers. The most widespread are the terrestrial-cursorial rat-like species of the genus *Proechimys*. They are the basic source of protein for lowland predators of the Brazilian Subregion. The spiny pelage of *Proechimys* is too supple for protecting the body, but the tail, like that of lizards, can be neatly detached by a sharp tug. This may confer some advantage for survival, but fecundity appears to be the best defense of the many species of this genus. The truly spinous *Hoplomys* of the Middle American forest floor also possesses a disposable tail. In fact, any spiny-coated echimyid parts readily with part or all of its tail, or only the skin of the tail may be left in the predator's grasp. *Cercomys* is another terrestrial form, but it is soft-haired and specialized for leaping in open country. A number of other echimyids have become secondarily arboreal and, like their ground-dwelling pastoral ancestors, they graze and browse aloft in bamboos, palm fronds, and the canopies of hardwood trees. Some, like the spiny *Echimys*, shelter in tree hollows; others, like the large harsh-furred *Dactylomys*, *Kannabateomys*, and *Thrinacodus*, build large nests of bamboo leaves.

New World porcupines, family Erethizontidae, like echimyids, also appear to be secondarily arboreal. The small short-tailed Neotropical species *Echinoprocta rufescens* is confined to the Colombian Andes. The larger and more numerous prehensile-tailed forms range widely throughout the tropical forests of Neotropica but often take to the ground in tree-savanna country, or where there has been considerable deforestation. Indeed, the arboreal characters of porcupines appear to be superimposed on parts originally specialized for terrestrial or even fossorial habits. Thus, the palmar and plantar pads (though not the digits) of the plantigrade fore and hind feet are modified into the opposable grasping organs used in climbing. The long prehensile tail, judged by its structure and function, appears to have been secondarily acquired after the primitive tail disappeared. Reduction or loss of tail is common among caviomorphs. The supposed new porcupine tail curls in an unorthodox or reverse direction as compared with prehensile tails in other mammals and curvature of tails generally in fetal mammals. The prehensile tail of the Australasian murine rodents *Pogonomelomys* and *Melomys* also curves dorsally.

Lagomorpha

Two species of rabbits, family Leporidae, order Lagomorpha, are Neotropical. The tapeti *(Sylvilagus brasiliensis)* is endemic to the Brazilian Subregion. It lives in all terrestrial mammalian habitats from lowland desert or rain forest to grasslands bordering the upper limits of tree growth in the Andes. The cottontail *(Sylvilagus floridanus)* ranges from northwestern South America to southern Canada but is confined to woodland and savanna. The two rabbits are very similar, but the cotton-tail is, among other things, slightly larger and more aggressive. Where the two species meet the cotton-tail displaces the tapeti. Tropical forests, however, act as barriers to the spread of the cotton-tail, and preserve the tapeti from congeneric competition throughout most of its range (Hershkovitz, 1950, p. 328). On the other hand, the southward spread of the tapeti stops abruptly at the boundary of suitable pastoral habitats in the Patagonian Subregion occupied by the hare-like cavies *Dolichotis* and *Pediolagus,* and other leporine rodents of the suborder Caviomorpha. It appears that dispersal of the timid tapeti is controlled by other leporids or leporid-like competitors, while that of the bold cottontail depends on ecological factors only.

Carnivora

Thirteen species of native dogs (Canidae) live in the Neotropical Region, more than in any other comparable geographic area. The most characteristic New World dog is the coyote, *Canis latrans.* It is essentially Nearctic but penetrates as far south as Costa Rica in the Middle American Province of the Neotropical Region. The North and South American gray fox, *Urocyon cinereoargenteus,* is tentatively regarded as a Neotropical-Nearctic varicant but may prove to be a Middle American autochthon. The remaining 11 canine species are endemic to Neotropica, and all but *Speothos venaticus* are confined to continental South America. The stilt-legged maned wolf *(Chrysocyon brachyurus)* is adapted for hunting in the high grass campos of eastern and southern Brazil, and in the pampas and chaco of Argentina, Paraguay, Uruguay, and eastern Bolivia. The large, sleek-furred, extremely small-eared, blackish *Atelocynus microtis* appears to be specialized for life in tropical rain forests. The so-called deer dog (water dog, otter dog, or bush dog), *Speothos venaticus,* is the smallest of the Neotropical species, lives in tropical rain forests, hunts in packs, and swims with otter-like ease. The several species of the genera *Dusicyon* and *Lycalopex* are dog-like or coyote-like in general appearance and habits. Most Neotropical canids are avid fruit-eaters. Some, particularly *Dusicyon thous,* often knock down corn stalks to eat the ears.

Of 10 living species of bears, family Ursidae, 9 are Holarctic and 1 is Neotropical. The spectacled bear, *Tremarctos ornatus,* of the Andes of Venezuela, Colombia, Peru, and northern Bolivia, is the smallest and most arboreal member of the family.

The raccoons *(Procyon),* family Procyonidae, are bear-like; coatis *(Nasua),* the only diurnal members of the family, are closely related, but their form and behavior suggest Old World viverrids. The nocturnal and arboreal olingo *(Bassaricyon)* is fox-like in form and food habits. The kinkajou *(Potos),* most peculiar of procyonids, is one of the two truly prehensile-tailed species of living Carnivora. The other is the southeast Asian binturong (*Arctictis*, family Viverridae). The kinkajou is so lemuroid in aspect that early naturalists confused it with the African potto (*Perodicticus potto*). The kinkajou is, in fact, the nocturnal exploiter of the ecological niche worked during the day by prehensile-tailed cebids. The Central American ring-tailed cat, or cacomistle (*Bassariscus sumichrasti*), is cat-like in form, diet, and arboreal habits.

Neotropical Mustelidae comprise 12 wide-ranging species. Two kinds of weasels, both diurnal, occupy forests and savannas through tropical to temperate zones. Several kinds of otters, all diurnal, include *Lutra canadensis*, found in streams and lakes from Alaska to southern Brazil. The sea cat, *Lutra felina*, is a little marine otter of the west coast of southern South America. The giant flat-tailed Brazilian otter, *Pteronura brasiliensis*, largest of living Lutrinae, hunts in packs, driving fish ahead into the shallows of back-flowing channels. Skunks, wherever they occur, seem to obey their special routines. Only a single species of the hog-nosed type, genus *Conepatus*, is Neotropical. The skunk-like Patagonian huron (*Lyncodon*) and the widely dispersed grison (*Galictis*) look very much alike. The pattern of their grizzled caps and backs, contrasting with otherwise black bodies, recalls the African honey badger or ratel (*Mellivora capensis*). The tree-climbing, fruit-eating tayra (*Eira*) resembles the European marten and in some parts of its range is called "marta" by Spanish-speaking natives. Tayras often travel in pairs or small groups. Sometimes bands of ten or more individuals forage for fruit in tree tops.

Thirty-five living species of cats, family Felidae, are recognized, and 10 of them are native to the Neotropical Region. All feed on birds, rodents, reptiles, insects, or almost any animal they can kill. Each species, however, has its special prey. The jaguar (*Felis onca*), largest of New World cats and like the leopard in size, appearance, and ferocity, ranges from northern Argentina through the Brazilian Subregion and into contiguous parts of coastal Mexico and southwestern United States. The jaguar preys on cattle, tapirs, and crocodilians. Its favorite food, however, is peccary and its relationship to this species is comparable to that of wolves to moose, and of lynxes to rabbits. The puma (*Felis concolor*) ranges from British Colombia in Canada to the Straits of Magellan at the southern tip of South America, a range greater than that of any other terrestrial New World mammal. The favorite prey of this second largest of New World cats is deer. The lynx-sized jaguarundi (*F. yagouaroundi*) which, with the puma, are the only more or less uniformly colored New World cats, ranges from southwestern United States into northern Argentina. This least arboreal of Neotropical felids is partial to ground-nesting game birds and poultry. Among the smaller spotted cats, the ocelot (*F. pardalis*), and the domestic cat-sized Wied's margay (*F. wiedi*), both of the Brazilian Subregion and contiguous parts of coastal Mexico and southwestern United States, are forest canopy as well as ground hunters. Monkeys, birds, and arboreal lizards make up much of their fare. The tiger margay (*F. tigrina*) is confined to continental South America and is much less scansorial than Wied's margay. Four small tabby-cat-like species (*F. colocolo, F. guigna, F. geoffroyi*, and *F. jacobita*) are mainly northern Patagonian and transitional Brazilian. Ground-living birds and rodents, particularly caviomorphs, are mainstays of their diet.

Perissodactyla and Artiodactyla

Neotropical hoofed animals include the tapirs (family Tapiridae) of the order Perissodactyla or odd-toed ungulates, and the peccaries (Tayassuidae), vicuña and llamas (Camelidae), and deer (Cervidae), of the order Artiodactyla or even-toed ungulates. All conserve the basic terrestrial, cursorial, browsing, and grazing way of life, and all are prey; none prey.

A notable characteristic of Neotropical ungulates is small size. The living forms are dwarfed by the hoofed animals which preceded them in time and place, and they are smaller than corresponding living species of the same orders or families of similar habitats in other parts of the world.

Tapirs, the largest of Neotropical land mammals, are the smallest of the Perissodactyla, and the three Neotropical species are smaller than the Malay tapir, the only other living member of the family Tapiridae. All tapirs are omnivorous and remarkably similar in form and habits. Although essentially allopatric, each species is adaptable to the habitat of any of the others (Fig. 7).

The swine-like collared and white-lipped peccaries, *Tayassu tajacu* and *T. pecari*, are the smallest of living suoids save for the pigmy hog [*Sus (Porcula) salvania*] of the Indian Subregion. The two kinds of peccaries differ little in habitat and occupy similar if not practically identical niches in most of the Brazilian Subregion, where they are sympatric. Both are excellent swimmers and cross the largest of South American rivers routinely. The collared species travels in small herds, in pairs, or singly. It ranges throughout the tropical and lower subtropical zones of the Brazilian Subregion north into Mexico and the bordering parts of the United States. The white-lipped peccary normally travels in large herds, sometimes numbering hundreds of individuals. It is confined to the lowland tropics of the Brazilian Subregion.

New World Camelidae are the vicuña, the domesticated llama and alpaca, and the wild huanaco. The last, standing a little over one meter at the shoulders, is tallest of Neotropical mammals, but puny compared with Old World camels. The American camelids are hardy and thrive in pastures and climates where introduced domestic cattle cannot live.

Deer, family Cervidae, are the most diversified of New World ungulates. The two species of Andean hare-sized, spike-antlered pudus (*Pudu*) are smallest of living deer and, with the Asiatic chevrotains, the smallest of the Artiodactyla. The spike-antlered deer of the genus *Mazama* are intermediate in size between pudus and branch-antlered deer. Pudus and brockets are forest dwellers but the brown brocket (*Mazama gouazoubira*) also lives in open savanna country. Among branch-antlered deer, the pampa deer (*Ozotoceros bezoarticus*) is smallest. The white-tailed deer,

Odocoileus virginianus, is somewhat larger but averages much smaller in body and antler size than Nearctic races of the same species. The Andean taruga (*Hippocamelus antisensis*) similar in size, but the Patagonian huemul (*Hippocamelus bisculcus*) and the Brazilian marsh deer (*Blastocerus dichotomus*) are much larger. All branch-antlered deer feed in savannas and woodlands.

Periodicity of breeding among Neotropical deer is probably highly localized. Antler-shedding is irregular and, judged by my field observations and examination of hundreds of museum-preserved skulls, is an uncommon phenomenon in tropical latitudes. The pelage, however, probably molts with the change from the principal dry (summer) to wet (winter) seasons, but its character hardly changes. For example, white-tailed deer of the warm lowlands maintain a year-long short, thin, brownish "summer" pelage, and those of the cold Andean highlands wear a 12-month-long, thick, grayish "fall" or "winter" pelage.

Sirenia

Dugongs and manatees, order Sirenia, graze and browse in quiet waters along coasts and the mouths of large rivers. One species, the clawless manatee (*Trichechus inunguis*) of the Amazon and Orinoco Rivers, is a fresh-water faunal element of the Brazilian Subregion. The second living species in South American waters is the marine *Trichechus manatus.* It ranges from the Guianas to the West Indies and along the Caribbean, Gulf, and Atlantic coasts to North Carolina. Sirenians are the only herbivorous fluviatile or marine mammals.

Cetacea

The order Cetacea, essentially marine, is world-wide in distribution. Nearly half the known species visit the shores of the Neotropical Region, and many of them enter the mouths of the larger rivers. Of the few forms confined to freshwater, two are New World and endemic to the Brazilian Subregion. The inia (*Inia geoffrensis*), averaging about five and one-half feet in length, lives in the Amazon and Orinoco river systems, and the tucuxi (*Sotalia fluviatilis*), about four feet long, belongs to the Amazon River proper and the lower parts of its main tributaries.

Inia and tucuxi eat much the same food, but there is no social interaction between them. Both have long beaks, but that of the inia is proportionately longer, narrower, provided with sensory bristles, and used for bottom probing. For a detailed account of the South American river cetaceans, see Layne (1958) and Layne and Caldwell (1964).

SOME REGIONAL FAUNAL CENTERS

Brazilian Highlands and Bolivian Uplands

The Brazilian highlands, or Brazilian pre-Cambrian shields, extend from the state of Ceará south into Rio Grande do Sul, Brazil; from Ceará west, the highlands are defined by the 200 m contour through northern Piauí,

Maranhão, Mato Grosso, Rondônia, and continue into Bolivia to the Río Mamoré-Grande in the department of Beni and Santa Cruz, thence southeast across the Amazonas-Paraná divide, and, still following the 200 m contour, pass through eastern Paraguay and Misiones in Argentina to southwestern Rio Grande do Sul and some outlying hills in northern Uruguay.

The central mass of the Brazilian highlands is "campos," or grassland and tree-savannas. The northeastern portion was mainly "caatinga" or scrub forest but is now mostly treeless or cactus desert. Semideciduous forest covers much of the southeast in Espirito Santo and São Paulo, and rain forest exists along the coastal ranges. Large stands of araucarias and extensive prairies or pampas occur in Paraná, Santa Catarina, and Rio Grande do Sul. Most of the highlands range from 500 to 1000 m above sea level, but escarpments along the coast may rise over 2600 m. According to Bigarella and Andrade (1965), most of eastern Brazil to the Argentine Río de La Plata (3° S to 36° S) was semi-arid during the Pleistocene glaciations. They note, however, that "tropical humid conditions may have been restricted to smaller areas where topography was favorable for rainfall, and these areas were natural refuges for the flora and fauna" (p. 449).

The Brazilian highland fauna is mixed pastoral and sylvan and is more varied than that of any other part of the continent. Of 10 South American orders of land mammals, all but the Insectivora (limited to one northern Andean species) are represented in the Brazilian highlands. Of 43 South American land families, only 11 are absent. These are the mainly Andean or Patagonian Caenolestidae, Soricidae, Abrocomidae, Myocastoridae, Chinchillidae, Dinomyidae, Octodontidae, Heteromyidae, Ursidae and Camelidae, and the Amazonian Callimiconidae. These 11 families comprise less than 30 well-defined species.

The number of endemic genera and species in the Brazilian highlands is high despite the fact that the highlands constantly contribute samples of their fauna to surrounding districts. Endemics include the primates *Leontopithecus* (=*Leontideus*); members of the *Callithrix jacchus* complex; the large woolly spider monkey, *Brachyteles;* the cricetines *Phaenomys, Rhagomys, Thaptomys, Blarinomys* and *Juscelinomys;* the echimyids *Carterodon* and *Isothrix;* the erethizontid *Chaetomys;* and the caviid *Kerodon.* Genera which spread just beyond the confines of the highlands include the savanna and marsh deer (*Ozotoceros* and *Blastocerus,* respectively), three-banded armadillo (*Tolypeutes*), hairy armadillo (*Chaetophractus*), maned wolf (*Chrysocyon*), additional cricetines (*Kunsia, Wiedomys*), an echimyid (*Euryzygomatomys*), and numerous species of various orders and families.

A noteworthy part of the area under consideration is the western extreme, in the Bolivian uplands or Llanos de Mójos. Here, where the Rio Mamoré-Grande valley separates the Brazilian highlands from the Andean piedmont, waters of the Amazonas and Paraná connect at times in low marshes astride the divide. The Llanos de Mójos are dominated by swamp palm–savanna interspersed with forest islands. Beyond the northern boundary of the Llanos de Mójos lies an unbroken stretch of Amazonian forest. On the south is the scrub savanna of the Gran Chaco, and to the west rise the Andean rain forests.

It would seem that the recent fauna of this crossroads of the principal topographic and ecological features of South America is derived from all sides. The reverse is probably true. Terrestrial mammals of the Amazonas valley evolved from types such as occur in the Brazilian highlands and Andean piedmont of Bolivia. The largely pastoral fauna of the Paraná district (see below) can likewise be traced back to those of the surrounding highlands in Bolivia and Brazil. Most of the movement probably took place during the Pleistocene. Upon retreat of the glaciers and the advent of warmer temperatures, many highland or llano species moved southward into the higher latitudes of Patagonia, others climbed into higher altitudes in the Andes, and still others became adapted to the changing climate. Increasing aridity in the seasonally dry Brazilian-Bolivian uplands accelerated the evolution, particularly among cricetine rodents, of specializations for grinding and digesting dry tough grasses and shrubs found above ground and for burrowing beneath in search of tender roots, annelids, arthropods, and other invertebrates. Burrows and tunnels also served as refuges from predators and desiccating heat and winds. All the while, continued emergence and broadening of the flood plains through uplift and sedimentation of the Paraná River basin furnished new habitats for animals of the bordering highlands and gave impetus to the evolution of palustrine and aquatic forms.

The Amazon Valley

The Amazon valley is the densely forested flood plain of the Rio Amazonas basin. The Brazilian highlands form the southern boundary, the Guianan highlands the northern, and the Andes the western. The Amazon valley extends from the river's mouth on the Atlantic west to the base of the Peruvian Pongo de Manseriche, a straight line distance of over 3200 km with a rise of less than 150 m. The valley is widest between the upper Rio Madeira (Río Madre de Dios, Pando, Bolivia) and the upper Rio Negro (mouth of Río Casiquiare, Amazonas, Venezuela), a north-south distance of about 1500 km.

A comparatively narrow zone along the banks of the main stream and lower reaches of the tributaries is permanent swamp, or "igapó." Higher and roughly parallel to it is a seasonally flooded belt, the "várzea" (Fig. 14). Rising behind, between 100 and 200 m above sea level, is a wide and well-drained alluvial plain. The low uplands, beginning at altitudes varying from about 150 to 200 m above sea level, form the rim of the valley as well as the foot of the surrounding mountains and highlands.

The most dramatic phenomenon of the Amazon valley is its annual flooding. During high waters, much of the region takes on the aspect of a

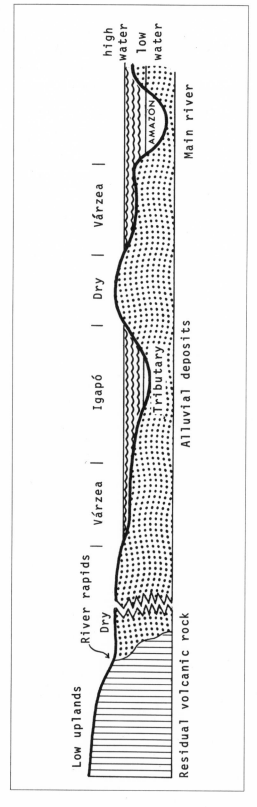

FIG. 14. Diagrammatic Cross-Section of Rio Amazonas Basin Showing Land Levels Relative to River Stages (After Stahelin and Everard, 1964)

Igapó is permanent swamp or floodland with few mammals, all aquatic; várzea is the forested higher, seasonally flooded plain with corresponding ebb and flow in numbers of its ground-dwelling mammals. The comparatively dry levees and alluvial uplands support a more stable association of ground-dwelling animals; higher uplands, at the base of the Andes, and Brazilian highlands are old established faunal centers. Igapós and várzeas increase the effect of the river as a barrier to spread of non-flying and non-aquatic mammals.

vast lake thickly studded with flooded, forested islands. The portion of the valley inundated does not ordinarily exceed 90 to 100 km in width at any one point across the main stream or large tributary. The total area under water, however, aggregates more than 250,000 km². The higher várzeas dry quickly, but flood waters stand for long periods in the low flat igapós. During the Pleistocene interglacials, flood waters rose higher, spread wider, and lasted longer. Minor streams may have been as large and may have exercised as effective control of mammalian distribution as primary tributaries do now.

The Amazon valley is one of the most important physiographic features of South America and was and remains the largest focus for mammalian colonization during the Quaternary. The valley is not, strictly speaking, a discrete zoogeographic province. It is, rather, the common drainage and sedimentary basin and territorial reservoir of three or four minor zoogeographic districts. With the Rio Negro it helps drain and demarcate the Guianan District to the northeast. With the Rio Madeira, it limits the central Brazilian highlands to the southeast. With both the Rio Negro and Rio Madeira and its western tributaries, it reaches into the upper Amazonian plains and the Andes. It has few terrestrial species of its own and no native terrestrial genera except possibly the uakaris (*Cacajao*), which may yet prove to be upland in origin. Even the fluviatile fauna is a small part of a vastly larger and widely disseminated fauna. The sirenian genus *Trichechus* ranges into the north Atlantic, *Sotalia* is a pantropical cetacean genus, and the endemic susuid cetacean *Inia* extends into the Orinoco basin and finds near relatives among southeast Atlantic (*Pontoporia*) and Asiatic members of the family.

Long before mammalian history began, in the Cambrian of 470 million years ago, the Amazonian basin, as reconstructed by Harrington (1962), was a narrow sea that extended from the Atlantic to the Pacific and isolated the northern Guianan part of South America from the southern. The sea had also invaded the Parnaiba and São Francisco basins. This state continued until late Pennsylvanian, 240 million years ago, when the sea abandoned the continental basins and the Amazonian valley may have become an inland brackish-water sea. Subsidence of the Andes in middle Cretaceous caused the sea to flood the Amazonian region in the areas of eastern Peru and Ecuador. The upper Amazon River, if such it was, then became, I suppose, an estuary of the Pacific, while the main basin may have remained a brackish swamp. The marine transgression held until upper Cretaceous or earliest Tertiary when, according to Harrington, an Andean uplift separated Amazonian from Pacific waters and the continent began to take on its modern form. The Amazonian basin from then on must have gradually succeeded from a brackish to fresh water swamp and lake stage perhaps little different from the present complex of anastomosing rivers, channels, lakes and swamps. As sedimentation provided ground for rooted terrestrial vegetation, habitats for land mammals became available. Unlike the páramos of the northern Andes and the iso-

lated forests of southern Chile, the Amazonian valley was surrounded by
highlands with pastoral and sylvan species preadapted to niches succeeding from brackish swamps to climax forest. The history of the Amazonian
flora is summarized by Camp (1952, p. 210, footnote) as follows:

> The flora of the tropical South American lowlands, especially that of the
> central Amazonian basin (and to a lesser extent the Orinoco basin), is highly
> heterogeneous, yet it is not a centrifugal flora; it is a centripetal flora,
> obviously having been derived (as the majority of lowland floras) from what
> might be called the "piedmont areas" of the surrounding uplands. Further-
> more, it is a recent flora, many groups being characterized by a series of
> often poorly delimited genera and species, apparently the result of yet active
> genic introgressions and unstabilized segregations. The flora of the central
> Amazonian basin appears to be no older than the late Pliocene, or perhaps
> even the Pleistocene, and for general complexity has its analogous counter-
> part in the Northern Hemisphere in the areas into which a similar but less
> rich heterogeneous assemblage migrated following the last glacial retreat.
> The reason for this is the relatively recent emergence of the central Amazonian
> basin following a series of inundations during the Tertiary.

The Amazonian basin was probably never completely submerged at
any one time during the Tertiary, but like the flora, the non-fluviatile
mammalian fauna of the Amazonian valley moved in from the peripheral
highlands. Terrestrial grazers, including semi-aquatic forms, spread downstream as grassy habitats became established on the rising levees. Succeeding grass-shrub habitats supplied cover and forage for non-aquatic grazers
and browsers. Forests which replaced or complemented the pastoral habitats provided niches for flying and arboreal species. The titi monkey is a
notable example of centripetal dispersal (Fig. 15). Predators followed
their accustomed prey, whatever the habitat. Terrestrial mammalian
habitats were established on higher ground first and advanced downstream, the sylvan succeeding the pastoral. The natural successional processes are continuous, reversible, and renovating, but the present overall
trend (except for human disturbance) is toward increasing sedimentation
and advancing forestation.

The characteristic and dominant mammals of the Amazonian valleys
are bats, primates, and the arboreal or scansorial forms of marsupials,
xenarthrans, rodents, and carnivores. The supremacy of the arboreal forms
may be attributed to the greater stability of the arboreal habitat with its
variety of cover, complex of travel routes, and year-round food supply.
The strictly terrestrial mammalian fauna is comparatively poor in variety
but the ubiquitous peccaries appear to be numerous; deer and tapir are
abundant, and numbers of certain rodents, especially those of spiny rats,
Proechimys, periodically attain plague proportions. Most terrestrial
mammals are secondarily adapted either for tree-climbing, swimming,
or both. Their specializations, however, are less for aquatic or arboreal
ways of life than for survival at flood times when no other way of life is
possible. Attrition, nevertheless, is high. Normal population densities of
ground based species are reestablished on flood plains during dry seasons

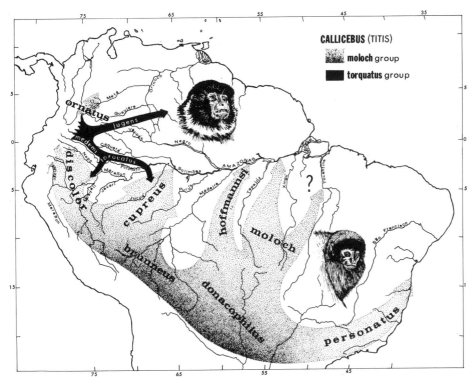

FIG. 15. DISPERSAL ROUTES OF TITIS, GENUS *Callicebus* (CEBIDAE—PRIMATES)

An example of centripetal dispersal from uplands to lowlands. Probable routes of
C. moloch *group are stippled, of* C. torquatus *group in solid black. Racial divergence*
of C. moloch *increases with downstream spread on opposite sides of barrier rivers.*
Origin of the C. torquatus *group from the* C. moloch *stock is indicated by the present*
hiatus between C. m. discolor *and* C. m. ornatus. *Chief differences between* C. moloch
and C. torquatus *are expressed in color pattern and average size. Subspecies are dis-*
tinguished by color variation within the pattern of each species. [Contrary to my
affirmation, (Hershkovitz, 1963b, p. 11), the range of C. torquatus lugens *and* C.
moloch ornatus *do overlap slightly in the Rio Guayabero-Sierra de la Macarena re-*
gion, as reported by Olivares (1962, p. 307) and F. Medem (pers. commun.).]

by incursions of new upland stock and explosive multiplication of lowland survivors.

Amazonian river otters are particularly adapted for aquatic life and
rarely leave their streams except for denning, mating, and breeding.
The otter-like marsupial *Chironectes minimus,* is similarly aquatic. It
has been recorded from broad and deep lower Amazonian streams but
its usual habitat in tropical or subtropical forests are swift-flowing rock-
strewn streams with stable banks suitable for denning.

The wholly aquatic or fluviatile forms are the inia (*Inia,* Susuidae),
river dolphin (*Sotalia fluviatilis,* Delphinidae), and the river manatee
(*Trichechus inunguis*). These freshwater forms presumably evolved
from brackish-water ancestors.

Mammalian evolution within the Amazonian valley has been of low taxonomic grade. Indeed, much of the speciation had already been accomplished in the uplands before the invaders converged on the bottom lands. In the case of wide-ranging cursorial animals such as peccaries, brockets, and tapirs, breeding could take place in the lowlands and flood plains between individuals derived from well-differentiated and geographically segregated highland populations.

The cursorial cricetine species complex typified by *Oryzomys capito*, affords remarkable examples of speciation, hybridization, and possible introgression throughout its range, but particularly in the Amazonian basin (cf. Hershkovitz, 1966a, p. 138). The same applies to members of the *Proechimys guyannensis* complex (Hershkovitz, 1948). On the other hand, bands of migratory populations of arboreal forms, particularly of smaller primate species, may become separated by the larger rivers. The farther downstream the migration the more effective the isolation and the greater the divergence between the advancing populations of opposite shores (see Fig. 15). The lower Rio Amazonas is the most formidable obstacle to dispersal of practically all arboreal and many terrestrial mammals. Large tributaries, such as the Japurá, Içá, and Negro on the North, the Ucayali, Juruá, Purús Madeira, Tapajóz, and Tocantins on the south, are also barriers, their effectiveness depending on their width and stream flow, the size of the animal, and historical factors. Crossings by rafts or by river cutoffs are probably frequent during floods, but the proportion of successful colonizations of opposite shores, especially by arboreal forms, is very small, to judge by present distributions of, for example, marmosets (cf. Hershkovitz, 1968). Bats, on the other hand, use streams as flyways. The few bat species at present known only from their type localities on the lower Amazon will no doubt prove to be wide-ranging; these are *Saccopteryx gymnura* Thomas, Santarém; *Depanycteris isabella* Thomas, Manacapurú; *Lichonycteris degener* Miller, Pará. *Eumops amazonicus* Handley, first known from Manaos, in 1955, was recently recorded from Panama (Handley, 1966, p. 773).

Absolutely nothing that is known of the fauna, ecology, and geology lends support to the assertion (Simpson, 1965, p. 217) that the "lowland rain forests with lateral and interior patches of savanna" of the Orinoco-Amazonas-Paraná basin are or ever were, a center of mammalian origin and dispersal. The few mammalian fossils known from the Amazon valley were picked up along the edges or banks of rivers in the upper Rio Purús and Juruá in the states of Amazonas and Acre, Brazil. With the exception of skull fragments of a manatee (*Trichechus*) and a tooth of a supposedly distinct inia-like cetacean, the fossils are of large land mammals (rodents, edentates, toxodonts, mastodonts) referred to genera or generic groups known from Andean or Pampean deposits. Paula Couto (1956, p. 110), who reviewed the Amazonian records, notes that they are "in part Tertiary (upper Miocene, Pliocene), and, in part, of Pleistocene aspect. Their stratigraphical origins are, however, in the most part, doubtful (most of them were collected on the edges of banks of the rivers after having been transported from their original sediments, and rolled down river)."

Orinoco Valley and Llanos

The Orinoco valley is an extension of the Amazon valley into eastern Colombia and western and northern Venezuela. It is bounded by the 100-200 m contour line of the Guianan highlands, the Andean foothills, and by the open sea on the northeast. The valley communicates with the Rio Negro of the Amazonian valley through the Casiquiare Canal. High waters in the upper Orinoco discharge through the canal into the Rio Negro, and vice versa. During floods, shallow boats or canoes can be navigated through the swamps and inundated forests from one watershed to the other.

The Llanos, which extend north and west of the Río Orinoco, are the principal topographic features of the Orinoco basin. They are flat grasslands dissected by the forest-lined tributaries of the Orinoco. Parts of the Llanos emerged from the sea during the Eocene upon uplift of the northern extremity of the Cordillera Oriental in northern Colombia. Continued uplift and deposition from erosion throughout the Tertiary gradually changed the shallow marine shelf to the annually flooded marshes and grasslands of the Quaternary (cf. Harrington, 1962).

The Llanos have no peculiar mammals. Sylvan species, most conspicuously the arboreal and volant ones, colonized the Llanos by spreading eastward through gallery forests from the base of the eastern Andes and the Serranía de la Macarena to the wooded shores of the Río Orinoco. Pastoral mammals, dominantly rodents, cotton-tail rabbits and deer, invaded from the Caribbean coast and occupied the extensive grasslands lying between the western tributaries of the Orinoco. The range of many sylvan species of the Llanos extends to the northwest bank of the Amazon valley and beyond. The same is true of virtually all bats, subaquatic species, the fluviatile inia (*Inia geoffrensis*), and probably also the Orinoco river dolphin (*Sotalia fluviatilis*) and the river manatee (*Trichechus inunguis*).

The fauna of the left bank of the Orinoco basin is primarily centripetal, and the main streams, like those of the Amazon valley, are barriers to many arboreal species or their races. On the other hand, the Orinoco delta proves to be the principal center of origin of the terrestrial mammals of Trinidad, and directly or indirectly, of Tobago. The Peninsula de Paría is another source of Trinidad mammals, particularly bats. Because of their insularity, Trinidad mammals differentiated more from the parental species of the Venezuelan coast than the latter did from their basic Andean ancestors.

Guianan District

The Guianan District in northeastern South America is defined by the interconnecting waters of the Río Orinoco, Casiquiare Canal, Rio Negro, and lower Amazonas. It encompasses Venezuela east and south of the Río

Orinoco, Brazil north and east of the Rio Amazonas–Rio Negro, and the three Guianan countries, Guyana, Suriname, and French Guiana. The dominant topographic features of the Guianas are the eroded tablelands or "tepuis" of the pre-Cambrian Guianan shield. These actually extend beyond the Guianan District into eastern Colombia in the form of broken mesetas, isolated hills, and ranges. Within the Guianas proper, the shield is subdivided by the south-flowing Amazonian Rio Branco in Brazil and the north-flowing Essequibo River in Guyana. Although structurally one of the oldest parts of South America, the Guianan District is superficially isolated from the rest of the continent by the interconnecting Amazonas-Orinoco river systems.

Tropical rain-forest covers most of the coast and main river valleys. Much of the interior lowlands and highlands is grassland. The altitudinal range of the Guianan District is sea level to 2772 m above (Mt. Roraima).

There is no indication that the Guianan District is, or ever was, a center of origin and dispersal of any line of Tertiary mammals, or of any superspecific taxon of Quaternary mammals. All known living species of Guianan mammals are derived from south of the Rio Amazonas or west of the Río Orinoco. Most of them are practically indistinguishable or are only subspecifically distinct from their extra-Guianan relatives. A small number have attained species grade, and one endemic cricetine rodent, *Podoxomys roraimae* Tate, is ostensibly generically distinct from all others. A few bat species (*Tonatia carrikeri, Bartionycteris daviesi, Lonchophylla thomasi, Phyllostomus latifolius, Myotis surinamensis, Eumops geijskesi,* and perhaps one or two more), known from only one or a few Guianan specimens, will certainly prove to be more widely distributed.

The lowland terrestrial species of the Guianas are virtually the same as those occurring in the surrounding faunal areas, but are fewer in number. The fauna of the interior savannas is particularly poor because of the limited or fortuitous means of access available to coastal savanna species. Some coastal pastoral cricetine mice, notably the wide-ranging, rapidly multiplying species of *Zygodontomys, Sigmodon* (includes *Sigmomys*), *Akodon,* and *Holochilus* (cf. Hershkovitz, 1955), invaded the grasslands by spreading along cleared or cultivated river banks. If confirmed, the absence of either of the Neotropical rabbits, the ubiquitous *Sylvilagus brasiliensis* or the strictly pastoral *S. floridanus,* would point to long isolation of the Guianan District from the mainstreams of mammalian dispersal. More impressive is the fact that the Guianas and the West Indies are the only major districts of the Neotropical Region with suitable habitats where skunks (*Conepatus*) are not known to occur.

Arboreal species, such as primates, whose horizontal spread is constrained by major waterways, appear to be most differentiated. The two species of Guianan marmosets or tamarins, *Saginus bicolor* and *S. midas,* are derived from more primitive tamarin stocks south of the Amazonas. The ancestors of both could have been shuttled from the southern to the Guianan shore of the Amazonas by a river bend cutoff (Fig. 6). Significantly, typical marmosets of the genus *Callithrix*, whose dispersal center is in the Brazilian highlands, did not reach the Guianas (cf. Hershkovitz, 1968). Among cebids, *Saimiri sciureus, Chiropotes satanas, Cebus apella, Ateles paniscus,* and *Alouatta seniculus* are generally distributed but are not more than slightly differentiated from relatives outside the Guianan district. They may have used the tamarin shuttle route for crossing the Amazonas. The night monkey, *Aotus trivirgatus,* one species of titi, *Callicebus torquatus* (Fig. 15), and possibly the capuchin, *Cebus albifrons,* seem to have entered the Guianas from west of the Orinoco. Neither species has spread eastward beyond the Essequibo-Branco Rivers. *Cebus nigrivittatus* may be autochthonous, although its range extends beyond the confines of the District to the northwest and southeast. *Pithecia pithecia* appears to be endemic, but a close comparison with *P. monacha* of the upper Amazonian region is needed.

The arboreal woolly opossum, *Caluromys philander,* may have originated in the Guianas, but it also occurs in Trinidad. The marsupial *Lutreolina crassicaudata turneri* Günther, from Guyana (British Guiana) is known from the type specimen only. The nearest known relatives of the same species occur south of a line drawn roughly from Rio de Janeiro, Brazil, west into Beni, Bolivia (specimen from San Joaquín, Beni, in the Field Museum). Presumably, geographically intermediate populations occur in the uplands of the Amazon and Orinoco basins.

The mammalian fauna of the Guianan highlands, or tepuis (1800-2600 m) is unimpressive. With two exceptions, it consists of wide-ranging species well represented in the tropical lowlands. The first exception is the white-eared opossum, *Didelphis albiventris,* collected by various American Museum of Natural History expeditions, at altitudes ranging from 100[?] to 2200 m above sea level.

> Specimens in the American Museum of Natural History from Brazil: Mt. Roraima (Arabupu, 4200 ft., 1; Towashing Stream, 5400 ft., 2; Glycon Ridge, 5900 ft., 1); Venezuela: (Mt. Duida, 3250-6600 ft., 8; Auyan Tepui, 1100-2200 m., 6; [?] Savanna Grande, 100 m., 1). These were misidentified as *Didelphis marsupialis* by Tate (1939, pp. 153, 160). The name *Didelphis azarae* Temminck, 1825, currently used for white-eared opossums, is based on several black-eared opossums, hence *Didelphis marsupialis* Linnaeus. The earliest valid name for the white-eared opossum appears to be *Didelphis albiventris* Lund, 1841.

Didelphis albiventris is widely distributed (Fig. 16) in the upper subtropical and temperate zones of the Andes, southern and southeastern Brazil, and bordering parts of the Patagonian Subregion.

The second oddity is the small cricetine, *Podoxomys roraimae.* This rodent, the only one of its genus, and known from 5 specimens, was taken near the summit of Mt. Roraima, approximately 2600 m above sea level, nearly at the highest point (2772 m) of the Guianan district. *Podoxomys roraimae* is a long-muzzled small-eared semi-fossorial species of the oxymycterine group. Species of the nearest related genus *Oxymycterus*

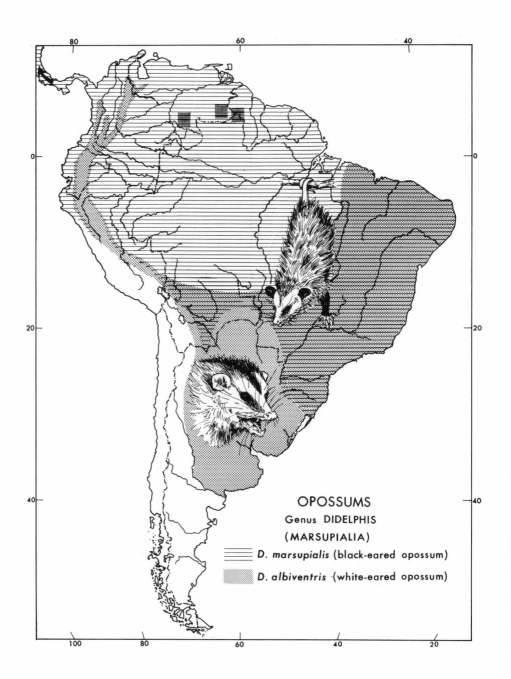

FIG. 16. NEW WORLD OPOSSUMS, GENUS *Didelphis* (MARSUPIALIA)

Temperate zone white-eared D. albiventris *can be derived from lowland black-eared* D. marsupialis *by complete depigmentation of external ear in young and adult.* D. albiventris, *formerly an inhabitant of lowland temperate zones, has spread into higher altitudes and higher latitudes as temperatures rose.* D. marsupialis *subsequently moved into the warm lowlands, possibly from Middle America. Note distribution of* D. albiventris *in high isolated Guianan tepuis.*

and the white-eared oppossum, *Didelphis albiventris,* are sympatric in many parts of their range in Andean Peru, upper Amazonian Bolivia, Paraguay, northern Argentina, Uruguay, and eastern Brazil from Rio Grande do Sul to Pernambuco. The climatic range of oxymycterines is tropical to temperate.

The Guianan *Didelphis albiventris* and *Podoxomys roraimae* are relicts of a temperate zone fauna which must have occupied the lowlands of the equatorial latitudes of South America. Many elements of this fauna moved southward or upward with retreating glaciers and rising temperatures; some became adapted to the changing environments and remained in situ; others disappeared. This temperate zone fauna in equatorial latitudes was and still is substantial and numbers hundreds of species. The paucity of the Guianan quota points to the faunistic poverty and long insularity of the Guianan District. Evidently, the history of Guianan mammals began during Pleistocene with a few strays. The modern balanced tropical lowland fauna could have accumulated since the Pleistocene, perhaps since latest Pleistocene.

The bird fauna of the isolated western Guianan table-top mountains shows similar distributional patterns, according to Mayr and Phelps (1967). The presence of 29 endemic species out of a total of 96 species in the region, designated Pantepui by the cited authorities, testifies to the greater power and effectiveness of avian colonization as compared with that of mammals.

Paraná-Paraguay Valley District

The Paraná-Paraguay valley is, next to the Amazon valley, the largest Neotropical river bottomland with a centripetal mammalian fauna. The valley begins in the marshlands drained by the northern tributaries of the Rio Paraguay in southwestern Mato Grosso, Brazil; southward it encompasses Paraguay, exclusive of its eastern and western highlands. It continues into the Argentine Chaco, the pampas west and southwest of the Río Paraná, and east into the Argentine mesopotamia, nearly all of Uruguay, and the bordering parts of Rio Grande do Sul, Brazil. The north to south extent of the valley is about 2300 km; the east to west extent, from Santiago del Estero, Argentina, to Rio Grande do Sul, Brazil, about 850 km; its altitudinal range is from sea level to 200 m above. The mammalian habitats are mainly pastoral, palustrine, and aquatic. Arboreal habitats occur as extensions of the upland forests on the northern and eastern periphery of the valley, and as gallery forests along the main streams.

The mammalian fauna of the Paraná-Paraguay valley is rich, varied, and derived from the surrounding highlands in the Brazilian and Patagonian Subregions. The species of the northern and eastern parts of the valley are dominantly Brazilian; those of the remaining parts are mixed or transitional, but with Patagonian elements preponderating in the extreme south and west. Many Brazilian taxons, from specific to ordinal rank (Primates), find their southern limits of distribution in the valley. Some Patagonian elements also reach their eastern or northern boundaries here. Valley endemism, if it occurs, is probably more apparent than real and is limited to a few rodents.

Marsupials are represented in the valley by the Brazilian *Didelphis* (2 species), *Marmosa* (2-4 species), *Monodelphis* (3 species), and the monotypic *Lutreolina, Metachirus, Philander,* and *Chironectes.* The last three genera terminate their ranges within the district. Five Brazilian primates, the cebids *Aotus trivirgatus, Callicebus moloch, Saimiri sciureus, Cebus apella,* and *Alouatta caraya,* find the southern limits of their range in the northern parts of the valley. Marmosets (Callithricidae) are absent. Like primates, eastern and southern Brazilian bat species, genera, and families begin to disappear in northern parts of the valley. Perhaps a score of species, mostly vespertilionids, molossids, the vampire (*Desmodus*), fish-eater (*Noctilio*), and a phyllostomid or two, occur in the southern part. The rich xenarthran fauna includes the greater and lesser anteaters, three-toed sloth *(Bradypus),* and 6 species of armadillos of the genera *Euphractus, Chaetophractus, Tolypeutes, Dasypus, Priodontes,* and *Cabassous.* No other faunal district has as many kinds of armadillos. The giant armadillo *Priodontes* and soft-tailed *Cabassous* reach the southern limits of their distribution in the valley.

The rodents of the District are highly diversified, but arboreal forms are few. The family Sciuridae, represented by *Sciurus aestuans,* terminates its distribution here, as do the following caviomorph families: the Erethizontidae, with the porcupine *Coendou;* the Echimyidae, with the arboreal *Kannabateomys* and terrestrial *Proechimys, Cercomys,* and *Euryzygomatomys;* the Hydrochaeridae, with the capybara (*Hydrochaeris*); the Dasyproctidae, with the aguti (*Dasyprocta*); and the Chinchillidae, represented by the viscacha (*Lagostomus*). The valley also harbors cavies (*Cavia*), Patagonian hares (*Pediolagus,* eastern limit), and coypu (*Myocastor*). The diversified cricetine fauna includes the terrestrial-cursorial *Oryzomys, Akodon, Calomys,* and *Zygodontomys;* the aquatic *Nectomys* and *Holochilus;* the fossorial *Kunsia;* and the saltatorial *Reithrodon.* All these cricetine mice range widely outside the valley, and all climb well when forced to escape the periodic inundations. Arboreal cricetines are the sylvan *Oryzomys concolor* and the pastoral *Phyllotis griseoflavus.* The latter frequently nests in trees but just as often shelters underground. *Scapteromys* is a swamp cricetine that is well-adapted for swimming, digging, and climbing. So far as is known, it is confined to the Paraná-Paraguay Valley District. The superficially similar palustrine *Pseudoryzomys* was at first known only from the Paraguay bottom-lands but has since been discovered in Beni, Bolivia [San Joaquín—specimen in the Field Museum of Natural History]. The range of the semi-aquatic *Akodon kempi* appears to be restricted to the Paraná delta and banks of the Río de La Plata, but this odd distribution may be a question of taxonomy rather than geography.

Carnivores are plentiful, with all Neotropical families present except bears. The Procyonidae, with the coati *(Nasua)* and raccoon *(Procyon)*, reach their southern limit here. Cats are most varied, with 8 species ranging in size from margay to jaguar (Cabrera, 1961b). Mustelids follow, with 6 species. Four or five kinds of dogs complete the order Carnivora. Although extensive and suitable habitats are available, fluviatile mammals (manatee, freshwater cetaceans) are absent. Ungulates, however, are numerous and include the Brazilian tapir and southernmost representatives of white-lipped peccaries, marsh deer, and pampa deer. The collared peccary and red and brown brockets, present in parts of the valley, also range beyond to the west and south.

Andes

The Andes extend the length of western South America, a distance of roughly 7000 km. The mountains attain their greatest height and width in the altiplano region of southern Peru, Bolivia, northern Argentina, and northern Chile. Their east-west breadth, in this area, is nearly 800 km, or more than twice the average. The passes lie above 4000 m and the average height of the crests is over 5000 m. The tallest peak, Mount Aconcagua, rises about 6700 m above sea level. The Caribbean portion of the Andes, in northern Colombia and Venezuela, averages much lower and forms three chains or cordilleras (Fig. 4). The two main inner valley streams unite in a common delta before emptying into the Caribbean. The rivers of the northern half of the outer slope of the western chain in Colombia also flow into the Caribbean, but the remaining western slopes of the Andes drain into the Pacific. The streams of the eastern and southern slopes in Venezuela and northern Colombia feed the Río Orinoco. The eastern Andes in southern Colombia, Ecuador, Peru, and northern Bolivia are drained by the Amazon. In southern Bolivia and Argentina, the Andes send their waters into the Atlantic via the Río Paraná and numerous shorter streams.

The tropical zone fauna of the northern Andes is identical to that of the surrounding uplands, or piedmont. The subtropical fauna derives directly from the tropical fauna, but it also includes a few relics of an older fauna. Three caviomorph rodents, the pacarana *(Dinomys branicki)*, mountain paca *(Agouti taczanowski)*, and the short-tailed porcupine *(Echinoprocta rufescens)*, are representative of the latter.

The temperate Andean forests contain many wide-ranging species derived from the lower zone fauna. In addition, they harbor distinctive elements of historically different faunas. The several species of the marsupial family Caenolestidae, confined to the temperate zone forests, are relics of the oldest South American mammalian fauna (Fig. 10). The Andean shrew, *Cryptotis thomasi*, the only species of South American Insectivora, is one of the latest arrivals in South America. It ranges from the upper subtropical altitudinal zone into the temperate. Evidently, the original lowland populations did not adapt to the climatic changes which forced their descendents into higher or cooler habitats. Middle American shrews of the same species group are also mountain dwellers. The simple-penis-type (or peromyscine) harvest mouse, *Aporodon mexicanus*, belongs to the same faunal stratum as the shrew and its ecological history is similar.

The pudu deer (*Pudu mephistopheles*), the Andean brocket (*Mazama rufina*), and the mountain tapir (*Tapirus pinchaque*), are characteristic species confined to the temperate rain forest, but the zoogeographic history of each may be distinct. The small olive coati, *Nasua (Nasuella) meridensis*, is another relict of an old temperate zone lowland fauna which climbed higher with rising temperatures. Forest-dwelling pastoral caviomorph rodents peculiar to the high northern Andes include the echimyid *Thrinacodus* and the small hairy porcupine, *Coendou vestitus*. Cricetine rodents usually range widely, but such native genera as *Chilomys*, *Anotomys*, and *Neusticomys* are confined to the temperate and upper subtropical forests of the northern Andes. *Thomasomys*, the most primitive of living cricetines, ranges through temperate zone forests from Venezuela into Bolivia, thence into the temperate zone upland forests of Misiones, Argentina, and Rio Grande do Sul, Brazil. A number of species of the sylvan *Oryzomys*, notably *O. albigularis*, and members of the generalized *Microryzomys* group, are indicators of temperate and upper tropical zone Andean forests from Venezuela to Bolivia.

A large part of the present tropical and subtropical faunas of the western slope of the northern Ecuadorian, Colombian, and Venezuelan Andes is derived from the Middle American Province, and the largest part of the faunas of the eastern slope is upper Amazonian. Some elements of each fauna in Colombia and Venezuela, however, crossed low passes or rounded the low northern terminals of the Andean chains and populated the inner valleys and outer slopes. Notwithstanding this, the original characteristics of tropical and subtropical faunas of eastern and western slopes are still marked. In contrast, the temperate forest fauna is fairly uniform from east to west. Páramos have no fauna proper but are exploited by a few fringe woodland or forest forms (see páramo, below).

The Andean slopes and connecting intermontane valleys of the tropical zones of eastern Peru are largely forested, their fauna derived from the Amazonian uplands or, more precisely, the eastern Andean piedmont. The subtropical and temperate-zone forest faunas of Peru and Bolivia are continuations of those of Ecuador, but with replacements of some species and additions of a few others. The general trend, however, is toward a small overall reduction in number of kinds from north to south. There is no close relationship or direct or indirect communication between the faunas of the eastern Andean base in Ecuador, Peru, and Bolivia, on the one hand, and those of the western Andean base and coast in Ecuador, Peru, and Chile, on the other.

The dry and largely treeless western Andean slopes of Peru and northern Chile rise from a narrow desertic coast. Its fauna is impoverished and of a mixed and problematic origin. A few species in the extreme north (squirrels, some mice, deer) are tag-ends of the Middle American or North Pacific coastal fauna. The remainder of the fauna appears to be essentially Patagonian. It may have originated in situ during the last glacial period, when the sea was lower and the coast wider.

Above tree line in Peru, Bolivia, northern Chile, and northern Argentina is the puna zone or "altiplano." Its mammals are discussed below under a separate heading.

The Andean fauna in Chile and Argentina becomes progressively poorer from north to south, particularly on the Pacific slope. The Chilean fauna differs from the Argentine less by what it has than by what it lacks. The extensive beech-conifer forests of southern Chile, bordered by sea on one side and by scrub steppes on the other side (the Fuegian of Osgood, 1943), has no proper fauna. Only three species of ubiquitous mice (*Oryzomys nigripes, Akodon longipilis, Akodon xanthorhinus*) and a wide-ranging canine (*Dusicyon culpaeus*) impinge upon the fringes of this forest.

The whole of the southern Andean region, for all its geographic variety and ecological diversity, supports a native fauna basically no different from and but little more varied than that of the relatively uniform life zone of the altiplano. Evidently, its recent mammalian habitats were established since the last glacial period. The centripetal fauna includes marsupials and edentates of the oldest strata, caviomorphs of the middle strata, and camelids of the latest strata. They may be derived from the Patagonian region east of the Andes which, according to Polanski (1965), was never glaciated during the Pleistocene. Endemics are the microbiotheriine marsupial *Dromiciops*, the caenolestid marsupial, *Rhyncholestes*, and the caviomorph rodents *Octodon*, *Spalacopus*, and *Aconaemys*. These could have originated in the uplands east of the Andes. The endemic cricetines *Irenomys* and *Notiomys*, and others, are probably old coastal elements which moved into the Andes as the glaciers retreated.

For accounts of Chilean mammals, see Osgood (1943) and Greer (1965).

Páramos

Isolated grasslands, or páramos, of various sizes are irregularly dispersed above tree line in the equatorial Andes of Venezuela, Colombia, and northern Ecuador. These páramos are cold and humid, and range from about 3800 m above sea level up to the limits of permanent snow or about 4700 m. Insofar as mammals are concerned, the páramos are new and largely unexploited habitats, formed in the wake of retreating glaciers. Temperatures frequently descend below freezing, usually during the night and commonly during the dry season. The characteristic plants are grasses (*Calamagrotis* and *Festuca*), low thick shrubs, small flowering plants and, typically, the velvety-leaved composite *Espeletia* or "frailejón" (cf. Cuatrecasas, 1958).

Páramos have no mammalian fauna of their own. Surrounding forests and deep valleys completely isolate the páramos from each other and from the lowland savannas with their pastoral faunas. The upper temperate zone forest is poor in mammals but harbors along its upper fringes a few elements which opportunely extend their range of activities into bordering parts of the páramos. The fringe fauna includes the browsing-grazing mountain tapir (*Tapirus pinchaque*), white-tailed deer (*Odocoileus virginianus*), red brockets (*Mazama americana* and *M. rufina*), pudu (*Pudu mephistopheles*), and tapetis (*Sylvilagus brasiliensis*). The puma (*Felis concolor*) follows the deer. A small vole-like species of the pastoral cricetine rodent genus *Akodon* appears to be common to most páramos. Other cricetines found along the forest fringes are tiny rice rats, genus *Oryzomys*, represented by species of the subgenera *Oligoryzomys* and *Microryzomys*. They are cursorial and scansorial and are equally at home in forest, scrubland, and fringing grassland. One or two small species of the sylvan scansorial genus *Thomasomys* complete the roster of true forest-páramo fringe rodents.

Mammals based on the forest fringe rarely wander across the páramos. Rather, they exploit the páramo gulleys, sheltered cliffs, and brush-lined streams near the forest edge; in the case of smaller species, particularly mice, they also exploit human habitations of mud and thatch. The animals may expand their range into the páramo grasses during population highs, but they disappear during the lows.

A few insectivorous bats of the vespertilionid genera *Myotis*, *Lasiurus*, and *Histiotus* are sometimes seen flitting across the páramos. Some of them may be migrants or waifs, others find regular or perhaps only periodic sustenance in the grasslands.

Deforestation of temperate zone forests and agriculture often result in a downward intrusion of páramo vegetation. Grass fires and stock-grazing may result in temporary upward extrusions of a few forest fringe conditions. Native mammals associated with those disturbed ecologies include some elements of fringe fauna, but the majority are hardy temperate-zone forest forms, and wide-ranging and rapidly spreading subtropical and tropical zone species. The more conspicuous of these are the white-eared opossum (*Didelphis albiventris*), shrew opossums (*Caenolestes* spp.), placental shrew (*Cryptotis thomasi*), vampire bat (*Desmodus rotundus*), harvest mouse (*Aporodon mexicanus*), margay (*Felis tigrina*), weasel (*Mustela frenat*a), hog-nosed skunk (*Conepatus chinga*), and others. The white-tailed deer may have gained access to páramos from lowlands by following the maze of pre-Columbian cultivated plots and deforested wastes. Alternatively, it may be regarded as a member of the same Pleistocene temperate zone fauna which includes shrews and harvest mice.

Destruction of temperate-zone forest buffers south of the páramos in Ecuador provided invasion corridors for some puna, or Patagonian, elements from Peru. The most notable intruder is *Phyllotis*, one of the characteristic cricetine genera of the Patagonian fauna. *Akodon mollis,* a common Patagonian cricetine, is also present in Ecuadorian páramos, and is probably the same species noted in Colombian páramos. The taruga deer (*Hippocamelus antisensis*) invaded Ecuadorian páramos from Peru. The wolf-like *Dusicyon culpaeus* is a Patagonian canid which extended its range as far north as the páramos of southern Colombia.

The taxonomy and distribution of the mammalian faunas of the northern Andes are fairly well documented. The ecological relationships summarized here, however, are based on personal observations of the native mammals of Colombia and Ecuador.

Altiplano District

The altiplano is the high Andean grassland or puna zone of Peru, western Bolivia, northern Chile, and northwestern Argentina. Like the páramos of the northern Andes, the altiplano as a biotic district was established in the wake of retreating glaciers. Unlike the páramos, however, the puna is replete with a pastoral–predator fauna derived from older habitats at lower elevations. Communication is still open between the altiplano and arid pastoral habitats of the Pacific coast to the west, the steppes of the Patagonian plateau to the south and southeast, and the upland scrublands of the Gran Chaco to the east.

The altiplano begins about 10° S, in the department of Pasco, Peru, and continues southward astride the crests of the Andes through western Bolivia to about 29° S, in Atacama, Chile, on the west, and San Juan, Argentina, on the east, a distance of over 2100 km. Its altitudinal range averages from 3700 to 4800 m above sea level. The extreme range is probably 3300 to 5000 m (or to the lower limits of permanent snow). Southward to the tip of the continent equivalent biotic zones descend to sea level. Temperature extremes in the altiplano range from about −18° C to +16° C. The average annual precipitation throughout the district is probably less than 300 mm, but more than 1100 mm has been recorded in some localities. The terrain is flat, rolling, or moderately to steeply inclined, and it is interrupted at irregular intervals by volcanic peaks and small lakes. The vegetation is poor and greatly reduced because of fires and overgrazing by domestic stock. The dominant plants are grasses (*Festuca, Poa, Bromus, Calamagrostis* and others) and tola, a name applied indiscriminately to woody plants or shrubs of the genera *Tetraglochin, Diplostephium, Baccharis, Adesmia, Senecio, Lepidophyllum*, etc. The yareta (*Azorella garita*) and cactus (*Opuntia*) are common in rocky situations.

The cold desertic altiplano is one of the most severe marginal mammalian habitats in the Neotropical Region. Sylvan species are completely lacking. There are no marsupials, insectivores, tapirs, or rabbits, and comparatively few species of bats, edentates, rodents, carnivores, and deer (Table 6). Notwithstanding, the altiplano supports a varied, well-adapted and peculiarly balanced fauna dominated by pastoral rodents. The few recognizable mammalian niches appear to be occupied, and an efficient predator–prey relationship operates between respective species. O. P. Pearson (1951, pp. 127-128), who spent many months in the altiplano studying its mammalian ecology, and whose concepts of it are closely followed here, gives this picture of the animal life:

> . . . At Caccachara, a location where altiplano conditions are perhaps somewhat accentuated, all the mammals have thick, warm fur, especially *Chinchillula, Lagidium, Phyllotis sublimis,* and the vicuña. Many are unusually adept at thriving on the meagre, armed, and pungent vegetation of the region. Viscachas eat almost every plant that grows there including leaves, bark, and blossoms of the prickly thorn-bush (*Senecio spinosus*), needle-sharp spears of *Oxychloe andina* and *Festuca orthophyllum,* and bark and blossoms of rank-smelling Senecios and Wernerias. Vicuñas thrive here where other large herbivores fail. I have seen a herd of 24 vicuñas feeding on a desert that would not conceal a mouse and which I would not have thought could feed a rabbit.

> Several of the altiplano mammals are protected against the cold by their diurnal habits. [The rodents] *Akodon amoenus* and *berlepschii, Phyllotis boliviensis, Punomys, Lagidium, Cavia,* and *Ctenomys* are diurnal and can retreat to their burrows at night when temperatures may drop as low as 0° F. The most difficult season for these diurnal animals is the summer (November to April) when at the higher altitudes it may hail, snow, or rain almost daily, usually in the afternoon. Consequently, diurnal animals must face melting snow and additional precipitation almost every day and they seem poorly equipped for life at this season. The fur of most [of] these animals wets easily; once wet the animal dies unless the sun is shining. From November 15 to December 11, 1946, it snowed or hailed every day at Caccachara. Wild viscachas lost weight during this time and it is not unlikely that if this weather had continued for another fortnight (as indeed it may have) many would have starved or died seeking food in the wet snow. Nocturnal mammals such as *Chinchillula, Phyllotis darwinii,* and *P. sublimis* must withstand extreme cold during the dry season, but they encounter better weather at night in the wet season than they would in the daytime. As far as is known none of the mammals avoids an unfavorable season by hibernating (for a possible exception see account of *Phyllotis sublimis*), and few store food (*Punomys* and possibly *Ctenomys*).

Forty-five species of mammals are recorded from the altiplano as here defined. These represent 28 genera, 13 families, and 5 orders (Table 6). Intensive and widespread collecting throughout the district comparable to Pearson's (1951; 1957) investigations in southern Peru and northwestern Bolivia may increase the known number of species considerably.

Altiplano bats are rare and have never been systematically collected with modern techniques. A species each of the genera *Histiotus* and *Eptesicus* is known from the district. Representatives of *Lasiurus* and *Myotis* may also occur. These bats are insect-eaters of the cosmopolitan family Vespertilionidae. The scarcity of bats in the high Andean steppes suggests that the animals may be migrants or wind-blown waifs, but the insect fauna is substantial enough to support a low population of permanent residents with solitary habits.

Hairy armadillos of the genus *Chaetophractus* have been recorded from the altiplano of northern Chile (Mann, 1945, p. 64), and from western Bolivia, as *C. nationi* (Thomas, 1894, p. 70), and *C. boliviensis* (Grandidier and Neveu-Lemaire, 1908, p. 5). The relationships of these to each other have not been made clear. The altiplano armadillos are insect-, worm-, and grub-eaters.

The altiplano ungulates include a species of branch-antlered deer, the taruga (*Hippocamelus antisensis*), and two camelids, the guanaco (*Lama guanicoe*) and the vicuña (*Vicugna vicugna*). The limits of the present geographic range of the vicuña coincide with those of the altiplano. In effect, this once wide-ranging species is now confined to the altiplano. Koford (1957), who monographed the life history of the vicuña, calculates an average density of one animal per 50 acres of range but up to one per 10 acres live in optimum sites. Vicuñas compete for food with guanacos, domestic alpacas, llamas, sheep, deer, and rodents.

The principal mammalian predators of altiplano ungulates are the puma (*Felis concolor*) and the wolf-like culpeo (*Dusicyon culpaeus*). Three small altiplano cats, *Felis guigna*, *F. colocolo*, and *F. jacobita*, subsist mainly on rodents and birds. Two mustelids, the weasel (*Mustela frenata*) and the grison (*Galictis cuja*), feed largely on rodents. A third mustelid, the hog-nosed skunk (*Conepatus chinga*), may take mice, but its usual provender consists of insects, worms, and grubs.

Rodents form the bulk of the altiplano fauna, about half the species being endemic. Field mice (Cricetinae) constitute 19 species, 10 being endemic; of the 9 genera, 4 are endemic. Six of the 13 caviomorph species, but none of the genera, are endemic.

The sharply defined monotypic cricetine genus *Punomys*, with no near relative, appears to be a relict of an old temperate-zone cricetine stock, now extinct. It forms the oldest faunal stratum of the altiplano. A second stratum, also of generic grade but of progressive pastoral stock, consists of two monotypic phyllotine genera, *Galenomys* and *Chinchillula*, and the monotypic sigmodont, *Neotomys*. Endemic species of wide-ranging genera make a more diversified third stratum. These are the phyllotines *Calomys sorellus*, *Phyllotis pictus*, *P. boliviensis*, and *P. sublimis;* the akodonts *Akodon berlepschi* and *A. jelskii;* the cavy *Microcavia niata;* and the tucotucos *Ctenomys opimus*, *C. peruanus*, *C. leucodon*, *C. frater*, and *C. lewesi*. Little weight is placed on the endemicity of tucotucos. Like their gopher equivalents in other parts of the world, nearly all local populations of the taxonomically unrevised tucotucos are described as "species." The vicuña (*Vicugna vicugna*) is technically a generic endemic, but the species itself probably originated elsewhere, perhaps in the lowlands during the Pleistocene (cf. Lopez Arangurén, 1930, p. 121).

Rodent colonization of the altiplano, as judged from present ecological conditions and faunal affinities, originated in lowland pastoral habitats and spread at irregular intervals into widely separated pockets at higher altitudes. Most cricetines evolved into the vole-like habitus. *Eligmodontia*, however, is gerbil-like, and *Galenomys* has leporine characteristics. The

TABLE 6

Altiplano mammals of Peru, Bolivia, Chile, and Argentina

Order	Family	Genus	Species	Nearest Lowland Relative
Chiroptera	Vespertilionidae	*Histiotus*	*macrotus*	*H. macrotus* to near sea level
		Eptesicus	*fuscus*	*E. fuscus* to sea level
Edentata (Xenarthra)	Dasypodidae	*Chaetophractus*	*nationi* (*boliviensis*)	*C. villosus* to sea level
Rodentia	Muridae	*Akodon*	*andinus*	—
			boliviensis (*puer*)	—
			olivaceus (*pacificus*)	*A. olivaceus* to sea level
			amoenus	*A. obscurus* to sea level
			berlepschi	*A. obscurus* to sea level
			jelskii	*A.* spp.
		Calomys	*sorellus*	*C. laucha* to sea level
			lepidus	*C.* spp.
		Eligmodontia	*typus*	*E. typus* to sea level
		Phyllotis	*darwini*	*P. darwini* to sea level
			osilae	*P. osilae* to 500 m
			pictus	*P.* spp.
			boliviensis	*P.* spp.
			sublimis	*P.* spp.
		Galenomys	*garleppi*	*Phyllotis* spp.
		Andinomys	*edax*	*A. edax* to 2000 m
		Chinchillula	*sahamae*	*Phyllotis* spp.
		Neotomys	*ebriosus*	*Reithrodon physodes* to sea level
		Punomys	*lemminus*	[?]
	Octodontidae	*Octodontomys*	*gliroides*	*O. gliroides* to under 1000 m
	Abrocomidae	*Abrocoma*	*cinerea*	*A. bennetti* to near sea level
	Caviidae	*Cavia*	*porcellus*	*C. porcellus* to near sea level
		Microcavia	*niata*	*M. australis* to sea level

TABLE 6—*Continued*

Altiplano mammals of Peru, Bolivia, Chile, and Argentina

Order	Family	Genus	Species	Nearest Lowland Relative
Rodentia	Caviidae	*Galea*	*spixi* (=*musteloides*)	*G. spixi* to near sea level
	Chinchillidae	*Chinchilla*	*lanigera* (includes *brevicaudata*)	*C. lanigera* to sea level
		Lagidium	*viscacia*	*L. viscacia* to near sea level (cf. Crespo, 1963)
	Ctenomyidae	*Ctenomys*	* *opimus* * *peruanus* * *leucodon* * *frater* * *lewesi*	Genus unrevised; related species to sea level
Carnivora	Canidae	*Dusicyon*	*culpaeus*	*D. culpaeus* to sea level
	Mustelidae	*Mustela*	*frenata*	*M. frenata* to sea level
		Galictis	*cuja*	*G. cuja* to sea level
		Conepatus	*chinga*	*C. chinga* to sea level
	Felidae	*Felis*	*guigna*	*F. guigna* to sea level
			colocolo	*F. colocolo* to sea level
			jacobita	*F. jacobita* above 1000 m. (cf. Cabrera, 1961b: 206)
			concolor	*F. concolor* to sea level
Artiodactyla	Cervidae	*Hippocamelus*	*antisensis*	*H. bisculcus* to sea level
	Camelidae	*Lama*	*guanicoe*	*L. guanicoe*
		* *Vicugna*	* *vicugna*	[*V. vicugna* sea level (Pleistocene)]
5	13	28	45	

Altiplano habitats range between 3300-5000 meters above sea level. Lowland representatives of the altiplano species, or nearest relatives, are listed to indicate the lower limits of altitudinal distribution. Endemic altiplano species are distinguished by an asterisk (*).

cavies can be compared to tiny ungulates in some cases, or to ground squirrels in others. The viscacha is quite hare-like, and the chinchilla displays qualities of the rabbit and the ground squirrel. Tuco-tucos correspond to the burrowing gophers of the Nearctic Subregion. There are no aquatic mammals in the altiplano and, needless to say, none is arboreal.

Wide-ranging species of rodents and other mammals which make up the final faunal stratum invaded the altiplano from all sides comparatively recently. Camelids, weasels, skunks, and others which first entered South America from the north may have colonized the Altiplano District from the north, west, or even the south, depending on the dispersal route available to each kind. The puma and other cats could have reached the altiplano from the humid forested eastern slopes as well as from the drier open country in other directions.

Some altiplano forms spread northward secondarily. The prototype of *Phyllotis darwini* is said to have advanced to the equator, differentiating into several highly localized species. The greater probability, however, is that the high Andean equatorial member of the *Phyllotis darwini* group is the more primitive form and that dispersal and differentiation was in a southward direction. *Akodon boliviensis* also has near relatives in the northern Andes but these, like *Akodon mollis* of northern Peru and Ecuador, may be peripheral. Described races of *Cavia porcellus* appear in isolated localities as far as the Bogotá region in Colombia, and in Venezuela and the Guianas. These cavies, however, have all the characteristics of feral populations of pre-Columbian domestic stock. Human intervention and the introduction of sheep promoted the northward spread of the culpeo (*Dusicyon culpaeus*) into southern Colombia, and of the colocolo, (*Felis colocolo*) in northern Ecuador.

Adaptations for lower atmospheric pressures at higher altitudes are not requisite for survival in the altiplano. Many altiplano species also live near or at sea level, wherever suitable food and cover are available. On the other hand, many sylvan species among marsupials, tapirs, rabbits, and rodents live at altitudes above 4000 m but for lack of proper food and cover could not survive at the same or lower altitudes in the altiplano. Where local conditions permit, however, forest fringe forms emerge into the periphery of punas and páramos. Table 6 lists the altiplano species (fringe forms excluded), with the lowland representatives of each; an asterisk (*) distinguishes endemic species. For life history accounts of some altiplano rodents, see Pearson (1948, for the viscacha; 1951; 1960, for the tucotuco).

SUMMARY

Biogeography

The Neotropical Region extends from tropical Mexico to the tip of South America and includes all continental islands and oceanic Bahamas, West Indies, Galápagos, and Falklands. The Subregions are the Brazilian,

Patagonian, and West Indian. The Region and its subdivisions are defined solely on the basis of living mammals.

Nearctic, as understood here, refers to the Recent not the historical boreal American fauna. The mammalian fauna of Nearctica is composed of living autochthonous, and living immigrant species from Eurasia and Middle America.

Modern Middle America is undoubtedly a zoogeographic province of the Brazilian Subregion. Cretaceous and Early Tertiary Middle America, then isolated from South America, was assumed to be the primary evolutionary and dispersal center for South American (and West Indian) mammals of boreal American extraction. This hypothetical fauna included marsupials, edentates, condylarths, protoungulates, primates, and rodents. Fossil evidence to support the assumption is absent. On the other hand, the geological and nonmammalian vertebrate fossil records lend credence to the view that Gondwanaland, or its rifted or drifted continents, particularly Antarctica and Africa, may be the source of some, if not all, the ancient South American mammalian fauna. Antarctica may have contributed the marsupials. Strong African affinities are evident in the West Indian insectivores, on the one hand and in the primates and hystricomorphous and myomorphous rodents of South America, on the other. Bats almost certainly originated in and spread with the drifting Gondwanaland continents. The known edentates and protoungulates are regarded as strictly South American in origin but their precursors more likely originated in a Gondwanaland than in a Laurasian continent. Origin of the condylarthra remains equivocal.

The Pliocene-Pleistocene date postulated for completion of the intercontinental land bridge has little or no biogeographic significance. A Miocene-Pliocene date for closure of the marine portals agrees more closely with the zoological evidence and geological hypotheses, but the question is academic. Virtually all lowland-inhabiting Middle American or South American mammals, past or present, crossed or could be passed over such minor water gaps as separated the continents during the Tertiary. Water gaps and land bridges per se had little or no long-range effects. Faunal exchange between and across the continents were and are primarily controlled by population pressures and ecological factors at the points of interchange.

There is no foundation for the widely cited notion that fifteen or sixteen North American and seven South American families of terrestrial mammals, with all the disparity of their ecological requirements, were confined within the narrow Panamanian Isthmus ready to "surge" across a newly completed intercontinental bridge, in unequivocally Pleistocene times (cf. Simpson, 1950, p. 381). Most of the mammals in question had already reached the limits of their distribution in North and South America by the end of the Tertiary.

At some time faunal movements took place from southwestern boreal America into northern Middle America, and from southern Middle

America into northwestern South America and the West Indies (mainly the Greater Antilles). A reverse movement from Middle America to boreal America followed after movements between Middle America and South America became a two-way exchange. At the same time, a few South American elements probably spread into the West Indies. Evidently, reverse movements from the West Indies to Middle America failed to occur. Spread from the West Indies to northern South America, however, was feasible and probably successful on a number of occasions.

The West Indian Subregion appears to be a refugium of a Middle American late Tertiary fauna. Some of its living species are waifs and imports from the Recent mainland fauna. The remaining species, living and extinct, are representative of the sylvan Miocene and Pliocene fauna of the Caribbean shores. Evidently, the West Indian Subregion lacked suitable habitats for grazing ruminants and associated carnivores.

In the absence of evidence to the contrary, it is assumed that in the past, just as now, successful colonizing movements were small-scale and sporadic and were usually into new and previously unexploited mammalian habitats.

Late Pleistocene extinctions of mammals in South America (as in North America, Eurasia, and Africa), were mainly of the larger, more specialized herbivores and their predators. Early man, as hunter and modifier of the environment, was certainly a persistent and effective exterminator. Postglacial decrease in humidity was probably the more important factor in eliminating species unable to adapt to changing conditions. There is absolutely no evidence of mass extinctions or displacement of South American mammals as a result of supposed wholesale invasions by aggressive North American mammals during the Pliocene or early Pleistocene.

Early and Middle Tertiary dispersal routes in South America followed the upland base of the rising Andes to the Amazonas-Paraná divide, thence south into Patagonia or east into the Brazilian uplands.

Andean and eastern Brazilian uplands became evolutionary centers. As habitats were made available, mammals spread from upland centers into mountains (or higher latitudes) and lowlands (or lower latitudes). With ebb and flow of Andean glaciers and bottom-land inundations through the ages, some phyletic lines found refugia, others retreated to uplands, still others disappeared.

The modern mammalian fauna of the Amazon valley is derived from the Brazilian and Andean uplands. Fauna of the Orinoco Valley Llanos moved in from the Andean uplands and Caribbean coast. The Guianan region is isolated from continental South America by the connecting Amazon and Orinoco rivers. Its living species are derived from south of the Río Amazonas or west of the Río Orinoco. The rich and varied mammalian fauna of the Paraná-Paraguay valley combines Patagonian and Brazilian upland elements. There is no evidence that the Orinoco-Amazon-Paraná basins are or were centers of mammalian evolution and dispersal.

The northern Andean páramos are postglacial temperate zone grasslands above tree line and without autochthonous fauna. Mammals of the
surrounding temperate zone forests are sylvan, but some species are
adapted to forest fringe habitats. Certain of these could evolve into a
pastoral páramo fauna.

The southern Andean puna zone or altiplano has an indigenous pastoral
fauna derived from the Pacific coast and Patagonian uplands through
connecting scrublands.

The postglacial beech-conifer forest of southern Chile and bordering
Argentina is completely isolated from northern forests and has no fauna
of its own. Glades, bamboo thickets, and other second growths are the only
niches occupied by some of the local pastoral mammals.

Ecology

Neotropical (and all other land mammals) are classified as *sylvan, pastoral,
fluviatile,* or *versatile.* Marine mammals are not elements of the essentially
terrestrial Neotropical fauna. *Sylvan* mammals are primarily adapted for
forest habitats; they are usually generalized in structure. *Pastoral* mammals are primarily adapted for living in open country, woodland, thornbush or coniferous forests, and may be secondarily adapted to evergreen
forests. Pastoral mammals may be *progressive* offshoots of sylvan ancestry
or *specialized* descendents of progressive forms. *Fluviatile* mammals are
strictly aquatic. They are the freshwater cetaceans and manatees. *Versatile* mammals are predators, omnivores, and scavengers. They are equally
well-adapted for sylvan and pastoral habitats and move freely from one
to the other.

Faunal Differentiation

Virtually all modern Neotropical genera were defined by the time of the
early Pleistocene, most of them since late Tertiary, Differentiation during
the Quaternary was of low taxonomic grade, mostly to species and subspecies. The influx of terrestrial mammals into new postglacial habitats
in temperate zones of the Andes and Patagonia and the humid tropical
Amazonian and Orinocoan basins was marked by limited local differentiation.

Living marsupials are remnants of a once-flourishing order. Extant
edentates hardly suggest the exuberance and diversification of the group
during the Tertiary. The Insectivora is represented by the single genus
Cryptotis in Middle America and northern South America. The Neotropical bat fauna is rich and highly specialized. The broad morphological gap between most related genera (or generic groups) and families of
bats is more likely the result of absolute extinction of intermediate forms
than acelerated evolution during the Quaternary. The chiropteran fossil
record is insignificant, but it is reasonable to assume that such peculiarly
tropical American families as the Phyllostomidae, Thyropteridae, Desmo-

didae, and Noctilionidae were no less diversified during the Tertiary than they are today.

New World families and genera of primates completed their radiation by the late Tertiary. Considerable speciation occurred during the Quaternary as the result of migrations from the southern parts of what is now the Brazilian Subregion into newly established and accessible arboreal habitats in the lower reaches of the Amazonian basin, the Orinocoan basin, the Guianas, and the inter-Andean and trans-Andean valley and coastal areas.

The Caviomorpha are ancient Middle American and South American rodents now widely dispersed throughout the Neotropical Region. Most living genera are strongly marked monotypes or relics of what was formerly a much richer suborder. Differentiation since the Tertiary does not seem to have gone beyond the species grade.

The mouse-like Cricetinae, a subfamily of the Muridae, are the dominant rodents of the Neotropical Region. By the end of the Tertiary, South American (i.e., complex-penis-type) cricetines of the tribe Sigmodontini, had virtually attained their present level of differentiation and limits of dispersal in North and South America. The much less diversified North American (i.e., simple-penis-type) cricetines of the tribe Peromyscini are widely distributed in North America, but representatives of only two Middle American species reached northwestern South America during the Quaternary. All Neotropical squirrels, family Sciuridae, are arboreal, most of them confined to tropical forests. With the probable exception of the South American *Sciurillus*, superspecific differentiation of Neotropical squirrels may have taken place during late Tertiary times in North America or Middle America. Speciation of most living South American forms probably occurred in situ since the Pliocene. The Heteromyidae and Geomyidae are Middle American, but only one or two species of the former invaded northwestern South America, their dispersal aided by man-made clearings and secondary growths.

The cotton-tail rabbit (*Sylvilagus floridanus*) followed the path of *Heteromys*, but not as far or as pervasively. Cotton-tails of some Caribbean islands may be imports. The tapeti, *Sylvilagus brasiliensis*, of an older faunal stratum, is almost certainly Middle American in origin but is now widely dispersed throughout the Brazilian Subregion.

Neotropical Carnivora are, for the most part, well differentiated from their boreal relatives. Many evolved to generic, and some to supergeneric grades.

Neotropical Perissodactyla are few. Horses were transient during the Pleistocene. Tapirs invaded the Brazilian Subregion on several occasions, perhaps since the Pliocene, each species finding its own habitat. A slight overlap in range of the two lowland species is secondary and recent.

Neotropical Artiodactyla are highly diversified, but their differentiation may have begun in boreal America. Tayassuids, camelids, and cervids entered Middle America and South America as such, attained their maximum diversification and dispersal in the late Pliocene and Pleistocene, and then declined.

ACKNOWLEDGMENTS

Financial support for technical assistance and preparation of this manuscript was received from the National Science Foundation Grant GB-2059 and the National Cancer Institute, Contract PH 43-65-1040.

The illustrations are by John Pfiffner and former Field Museum staff artist Marion Pahl. Assistance by Museum staff photographers Homer V. Holdren and John Bayalis, is gratefully acknowledged.

LITERATURE CITED

ALLEN, G. M. 1942. Extinct and vanishing mammals of the western hemisphere with the marine species of all oceans. 620 p. American Committee for International Wild Life Protection, Special Publ. No. 11, Lancaster, Pa.

ALVAREZ, T. 1963. The recent mammals of Tamaulipas, México. *Univ. Kansas Publ. Mus. Natur. Hist.*, 14(15): 363-437.

——. 1965. *Catálogo Paleomastozoológico Méxicano.* 70 p. Inst. Nac. Anthrop. Hist. México, Mexico City.

ANTHONY, H. E. 1942. Summary of the fossil land mammals of the West Indies. *Proc. 8 Am. Sci. Congr.*, 4: 359-363.

ARATA, A. 1964. A mistaken report of a peccary from the Pleistocene of Louisiana. *Tulane Stud. Geol.*, 2 (2): 28.

AXELROD, D. I. 1958. Evolution of the Madro-Tertiary geoflora. *Bot. Rev.*, 24 (7): 433-509.

——. 1967. Quaternary extinctions of large mammals. 42 p. Univ. California Publ. Sci. No. 72, Berkeley.

BAKER, R. H. 1963. Geographical distribution of terrestrial mammals in Middle America. *Am. Midl. Natur.*, 70 (1): 208-249.

BARBOUR, T. 1916. Some remarks upon Matthew's *Climate and Evolution. Ann. N. Y. Acad. Sci.*, 27: 1-15.

BIANCHI, N. O., O. A. REIG, O. J. MOLINA, and F. N. DULOUT. 1971. Cytogenetics of the South American akodont rodents (Cricetidae). I. A progress report of Argentinian and Venezuelan forms. *Evolution*, 25: 724-736.

BIGARELLA, J. J. and G. O. DE ANDRADE. 1965. Contribution to the study of the Brazilian Quaternary. International Studies of the Quaternary. Geol. Soc. America, Special Papers, No. 84, p. 431-451; New York.

BONAPARTE, J. F. 1967. New vertebrate evidence for a southern transatlantic connexion during the lower or middle Triassic. *Paleontology*, 10: 554-563.

BONATTI, E., M. BALL, and C. SCHUBERT. 1970. Evaporites and continental drift. *Naturwissenschaften,* 58 (3): 107-108.

BRUNDIN, L. 1966. Transantarctic relationships and their significance, as evidenced by chironomid midges with a monograph of the subfamilies Podonominae and Aphroteniinae and the austral Hepatagyiae. *Kungl. Svenska Vetensk. Handl.,* (4) 11: 1-472.

BURT, W. H. 1958. The history and affinities of the Recent land mammals of western North America. In C. Hubbs (ed.), *Zoogeography,* p. 131-154. Publ. 51, American Assoc. Adv. Sci., Washington, D.C.

CABRERA, A. 1958. Catálogo de los mamíferos de America del Sur. I. (Metatheria-Unguiculata-Carnivora). *Rev. Museo Argentino Cienc. Natur. "Bernardino Rivadavia," Zool.,* (1957), 4(1): 1-307.

———. 1961a. Catálogo de los mamíferos de America del Sur. II. (Sirenía-Perissodactyla-Artiodactyla-Lagomorpha-Rodentia-Cetacea). *Rev. Museo Argentino Cienc. Natur. "Bernardino Rivadavia," Zool.,* (1960), 4 (2): 309-732.

———. 1961b. Los félidos vivientes de la república argentina. *Rev. Museo Argentino Cienc. Natur. "Bernardino Rivadavia,"* Zool., 6 (5): 161-247.

CABRERA, A. and J. YEPES. 1940. *Mamíferos Sud-Americanos (Vida, Costumbres y Descripción).* 370 p. Historia Natural Ediar, Compañia Argentina de Editores, Buenos Aires.

CAMP, W. H. 1952. Phytophyletic pattern on lands bordering the south Atlantic basin. *Bull. Am. Museum Natur. Hist.,* 99, (3): 205-212.

CLEMENS, W. A., JR. 1968. Origin and early evolution of marsupials. *Evolution,* 22: 1-18.

———. 1970. Mesozoic mammalian evolution. *Ann. Rev. Ecol., Syst.* 1: 357-390.

COX, C. 1970. Migrating marsupials and drifting continents. *Nature,* 226: 767-770.

CRAIN, I. K. 1971. Possible direct causal relation between geomagnetic reversals and biological extinctions. *Bull. Geol. Soc. Am.* 82: 2603-2606.

CRESPO, J. A. 1963. Dispersión del chinchillón, *Lagidium viscacia* (Molina) en el noreste de Patagonia y descripción de una nueva subspecie (Mammalia: Rodentia). *Neotrópica,* 9 (29): 61-63.

———. 1966. Ecología de una communidad de roedores silvestris en el Partido de Rojas, Provincia de Buenos Aires. *Rev. Museo Argentino Cienc. Natur. "Bernardino Rivadavia,"* 1 (3): 79-134.

CROIZAT, L. 1958. *Panbiogeography, or an Introductory Synthesis of Zoogeography, Phytography, and Geology. Vol. 1, The New World.* 1018 p. (Privately published, Caracas.)

CUATRECASAS, J. 1958. Aspectos de la vegetación natural de Colombia. *Rev. Acad. Colombiana Cienc. Exact. Fis. Natur.*, 10 (40): 221-268.

DARLINGTON, P. J., JR. 1938. The origin of the fauna of the Greater Antilles, with discussions of dispersal of animals over water and through the air. *Quart. Rev. Biol.*, 13: 274-300.

——. 1957. *Zoogeography: The Geographical Distribution of Animals.* 675 p. John Wiley and Sons, Inc., N.Y.

——. 1965. *Biogeography of the Southern End of the World.* 236 p. Harvard University Press, Cambridge.

DAVIS, D. 1965. The giant panda. A morphological study of evolutionary mechanisms. *Fieldiana: Zool.*, 3: 1-339.

DEL CORRO, G. 1968. La presencia de *Madtsoia* Simpson (Boidae) en el Eoceno de Patagonia y en el Cretacio de Madagascar y algunos ejemplos de distribución disjunta. *Com. Mus. Argentino Cien. Nat. "Bernardino Rivadavia," Paleo.*, 1(3): 21-26.

DIETZ, R. S. and J. C. HOLDEN. 1970a. Reconstruction of Pangaea: breakup and dispersion of continents, Permian to present. *J. Geophys. Res.*, 75(26): 4939-4956.

——. 1970b. The breakup of Pangaea. *Sci. American*, 223 (4): 30-41.

DUELLMAN, W. E. 1965. A biogeographic account of the herpetofauna of Michoacán, México. *Univ. Kansas. Publ. Mus. Natur. Hist.*, 15 (4): 627-709.

——. 1966. The central American herpetofauna: an ecological perspective. *Copeia*, (4): 700-719.

DU TOIT, A. L. 1937. *Our Wandering Continents: An Hypothesis of Continental Drifting.* 366 p. Oliver & Boyd, London.

ELLIOT, D. H., E. H. COLBERT, W. J. BREED, J. A. JENSEN, and J. S. POWELL. 1970. Triassic tetrapods from Antarctica: evidence for continental drift. *Science*, 169: 1197-1201.

EMRY, R. J. 1970. A North American Oligocene pangolin and other additions to the Pholidota. *Bull. Am. Museum Natur. Hist.*, 142 (6): 455-510.

FRIELAND, G. L., and R. S. DIETZ. 1971. Plate tectonic evolution of Caribbean-Gulf of Mexico region. *Nature*, 232: 20-23.

FRIES, C., JR., C. HIBBARD, and D. H. DUNKLE. 1955. Early Cenozoic vertebrates in the red conglomerate at Guanajuato, Mexico. *Smithsonian Inst. Misc. Collections*, 123. (9): 1-25.

GILL, E. D. 1955. The problem of extinction, with special reference to Australian marsupials. *Evolution*, 9(1): 87-92.

GOODLAND, R. 1966. On the savanna vegetation of Calabozo, Venezuela and Rupununi, British Guiana. *Bol. Soc. Venezolana Cienc. Natur.*, 26 (110): 341-359.

GRAMBAST, L., M. MARTINEZ, M. MATTAUER, and L. THALER. 1967. *Perutherium altiplanense, nov. gen., nov. sp.*, première mammifère Mesozoique de l'Amerique du Sud. *Comptes Rend. Acad. Sci. (Paris)*, 264: 707-710.

GRANDIDIER, G. and M. NEVEU-LEMAIRE. 1908. Observations relatives à quelques tatous rares ou inconnus habitant la "puna" argentine et bolivienne. *Bull. Muséum Nat. Hist. Natur., Paris*, 14: 4-7.

GREER, J. K. 1965. Mammals of Malleco Province, Chile. *Publ. Museum Michigan State Univ., Biol. Ser.*, 3 (2): 51-151.

GUILDAY, J. E. 1967. Differential extinction during late Pleistocene and Recent times. In P. S. Martin and H. E. Wright, Jr. (eds.). *Pleistocene Extinctions; The Search for a Cause*, p. 121-140. Proc. 7. Intern. Assoc. Quaternary Research. Yale Univ. Press, New Haven.

HALL, E. R. and K. R. KELSON. 1959. *The Mammals of North America*. 2 vols. Ronald Press, New York.

HALLAM, A. 1967. The bearing of certain paleozoogeographic data on continental drift. *Paleogeogr. Paleoclimatol. Paleoecol.*, 3: 201-241.

HANDLEY, C. O., JR. 1966. Checklist of the mammals of Panamá. In R. L. Wenzel and V. J. Tipton (eds.), *Ectoparasites of Panamá*, p. 753-795. Field Museum Natur. Hist., Chicago.

HARRINGTON, H. J. 1962. Paleogeographic development of South America. *Bull. Am. Assoc. Petrol. Geol.*, 46 (10): 1773-1814.

HAYS, J. D. 1971. Faunal extinctions and reversals of the earth's magnetic field. *Bull. Geol. Soc. Am.*, 82: 2433-2447.

HEIRTZLER, J. R. 1969. Theory of sea-floor spreading. *Naturwissenschaften*, 56 (7): 341-347.

HERSHKOVITZ, P. 1944. A systematic review of the neotropical water rats of the genus *Nectomys* (Cricetinae). 88 p. Misc. Publ. Mus. Zool., Univ. Michigan, No. 58, Ann Arbor.

———. 1948. Mammals of northern Colombia. Preliminary report no. 2: spiny rats (Echimyidae), with supplemental notes on related forms. *Proc. U. S. Nat. Museum*, 97: 125-140.

———. 1949. Mammals of northern Colombia. Preliminary report no. 4: monkeys (Primates) with taxonomic revisions of some forms. *Proc. U. S. Nat. Museum*, 98: 323-427.

———. 1950. Mammals of northern Colombia. Preliminary report no. 6: rabbits (Leporidae), with notes on the classification and distribution of the South American forms. *Proc. U.S. Nat. Museum*, 100: 327-375.

———. 1954. Mammals of northern Colombia. Preliminary report no. 7: tapirs (genus *Tapirus*), with a systematic revision of American species. *Proc. U. S. Nat. Museum*, 103: 465-496.

——. 1955. South American marsh rats, genus *Holochilus*, with a summary of sigmodont rodents. *Fieldiana, Zool.*, 37: 639-673.

——. 1957. On the possible occurrence of the spectacled bear, *Tremarctos ornatus* (F. Cuvier), in Panamá. *Säugetierk. Mitt.*, 5 (3): 122-123.

——. 1958. A geographical classification of neotropical mammals. *Fieldiana: Zool.*, 36 (6): 581-620.

——. 1959. A new species of South American brocket, genus *Mazama* (Cervidae). *Proc. Biol. Soc. Washington*, 72: 45-54.

——. 1960. Mammals of northern Colombia. Preliminary report no. 8: arboreal rice rats, a systematic revision of the subgenus *Oecomys*, genus *Oryzomys*. *Proc. U.S. Nat. Museum*, 110: 513-568.

——. 1962. Evolution of neotropical cricetine rodents (Muridae) with special reference to the phyllotine group. *Fieldiana, Zool.*, 46: 1-524.

——. 1963a. The recent mammals of South America. *Proc. 16. Int. Congr. Zool.*, 4: 40-45.

——. 1963b. A systematic and zoogeographic account of the monkeys of the genus *Callicebus* (Cebidae) of the Amazonas and Orinoco River basins. *Mammalia*, 27 (1): 1-79.

——. 1966a. South American swamp and fossorial rats of the scapteromyine group (*Cricetinae, Muridae*) with comments on the glans penis in murid taxonomy. *Z. Säugetierk.*, 31 (2): 81-149.

——. 1966b. Mice, land bridges and Latin America faunal interchange. In: R. L. Wenzel and V. J. Tipton (eds.), *Parasites of Panamá*, p. 725-747. Field Museum Natur. Hist., Chicago.

——. 1966c. Taxonomic notes on tamarins; genus *Saguinus* (Callithricidae, Primates) with descriptions of four new forms. *Folia Primatol.*, 4: 381-395.

——. 1968. Metachromism or the principle of evolutionary change in mammalian tegumentary colors. *Evolution*, 22 (3): 556-575.

——. 1969. The evolution of mammals on southern continents. VI. The recent mammals of the Neotropical Region: A zoogeographic and ecological review. *Quart. Rev. Biol.*, 44 (1): 1-70.

——. 1970. Supplementary notes on Neotropical *Oryzomys dimidiatus* and *Oryzomys hammondi* (Cricetidae). *J. Mammal.*, 51(4): 789-794.

——. 1971a. Basic crown patterns and cusp homologies of mammalian teeth. In A. Dahlberg (ed.), *Dental Morphology and Evolution*, p. 95-149. Univ. of Chicago Press, Chicago.

——. 1971b. A new rice rat of the *Oryzomys palustris* group (Cricetinae, Muridae) from northwestern Colombia, with remarks on distribution. *J. Mammal.*, 52(4): 700-709.

HESTER, J. J. 1960. Late Pleistocene extinction and radiocarbon dating. *Am. Antiq.*, 26: 58-77.

——. 1966. Late Pleistocene environments and early man in South America. *Am. Natur.*, 100 (914): 377-388.

HIBBARD, C. W., C. E. RAY, D. E. SAVAGE, D. W. TAYLOR and J. E. GUILDAY. 1965. Quaternary mammals of North America. In H. E. Wright, Jr., and D. G. Frey (eds.), *The Quaternary of the United States,* Part 2, p. 509-525. Princeton Univ. Press, Princeton, N. J.

HOFFSTETTER, R. 1961. Nouveau restes d'un serpente boïdé (*Madtsoia madagascariensis* nov. sp.) dans le Cretacé Supérieure de Madagascar. *Bull. Muséum Nat. Hist. Natur.,* (2), 33, (2): 152-160.

———. 1969. Un primate de l'Oligocène inférieur Sud-Americain: *Branisella boliviana* gen. et sp. nov. *Comptes Rend. Acad. Sci. (Paris),* 269: 434-437.

HOFFSTETTER, R. and R. LAVOCAT. 1970. Découverte dans le Déséadien de Bolivie de genres pentalophodontes appuyant les affinités Africaines des rongeurs caviomorphs. *Comptes Rend. Acad. Sci (Paris),* 271: 172-175.

HOOPER, E. T. and G. G. MUSSER. 1964. The glans penis in neotropical cricetines (family Muridae) with comments on the classification of muroid rodents. 57 p. Misc. Publ. Museum Zool. Univ. Michigan, No. 123, Ann Arbor.

HOPSON, J. A. and A. W. CROMPTON. 1969. Origin of mammals. *Evolutionary Biol.,* 3: 15-72.

HORSFIELD, B. and J. DEWEY. 1971. How continents are made and moved. *Science Journal,* 7 (1): 43-48.

HUMMELINCK, P. W. 1940. *Studies on the Fauna of Curaçao, Aruba, Bonaire and the Venezuelan Islands. Vol. I.* 130 p. Martinus Nijhoff, The Hague.

HURLEY, P. M. 1968. The confirmation of continental drift. *Sci. American,* 218 (4): 52-62.

KEAST, A. 1968. Evolution of mammals on southern continents. I. The southern continents as backgrounds for mammalian evolution. *Quart. Rev. Biol.,* 43: 225-233.

KIRSCH, J. A. W. 1968. Prodromus of the comparative serology of Marsupialia. *Nature,* 217: 418-420.

KOFORD, C. B. 1957. The vicuña and the puna. *Ecol. Monogr.,* 27: 153-219.

KOOPMAN, K. F. 1959. The zoogeographical limits of the West Indies. *J. Mammal.,* 40 (2): 236-240.

———. 1970. Zoogeography of bats. In B. H. Slaughter and D. W. Walton (eds.), *About Bats,* p. 29-50. Southern Methodist University Press, Dallas.

KURTÉN, B. 1966. Pleistocene bears of North America. 1. Genus *Tremarctos,* spectacled bears. *Acta Zool. Fennica,* (115): 1-120.

———. 1967. Continental drift and the paleogeography of reptiles and mammals. *Comment. Biol. Soc. Sci. Fennica,* 31 (1): 1-8.

———. 1969. Continental drift and evolution. *Sci. American,* 220 (3): 54-64.

LAVOCAT, R. 1969. La systématique des rongeurs hystricomorphs et la dérive des continents. *Comptes Rend. Acad. Sci. (Paris),* 269: 1496-1497.

LAYNE, J. N. 1958. Observations on freshwater dolphins in the upper Amazon. *J. Mammal.,* 39 (1): 1-22.

LAYNE, J. N. and D. K. CALDWELL. 1964. Behavior of the Amazon dolphin, *Inia geoffrensis* (Blainville), in captivity. *Zoologica,* 49 (2): 81-108.

LEOPOLD, A. S. 1959. *Wildlife of Mexico. The Game Birds and Mammals.* 568 p. Univ. California Press, Berkeley.

LE PICHON, X. 1968. Sea-floor spreading and continental drift. *J. Geophys. Res.,* 73 (12): 3661-3697.

LILLEGRAVEN, J. 1969. Latest Cretaceous mammals of upper part of Edmonton Formation of Alberta, Canada, and review of marsupial-placental dichotomy in mammalian evolution. *Univ. Kansas Paleo. Contrib. Vert.,* 12 (50): 1-122.

LLOYD, J. J. 1963. Tectonic history of the south Central American orogen. In O. E. Childs and B. W. Beebe (eds.), *Backbone of the Americas,* p. 88-112. Mem. 2, Amer. Assoc. Petrol. Geol.

LOPEZ ARANGURÉN, D. J. 1930. Camélidos fósiles argentinos. *Anal. Soc. Cien. Arg.,* 109: 97-126.

MALDONADO-KOERDELL, M. 1964. Geohistory and paleogeography of Middle America. In R. Wauchope and R. C. West (eds.), *Handbook of Middle American Indians,* p. 3-32. Univ. Texas Press, Austin.

MANN, G. 1945. Mamíferos de Tarapacá. Observaciones realizadas durante una expedición al norte de Chile. *Biológica, Inst. Biol. Univ. Chile, Fasc.* 2: 23-98.

MARGOLIS, S. V. and J. P. KENNETT. 1971. Cenozoic paleoglacial history of Antarctica recorded in subantarctic deep-sea cores. *Am. J. Sci.,* 271: 1-36.

MARTIN, P. S. 1958. Pleistocene ecology and biogeography of North America. In C. Hubbs (ed.), *Zoogeography,* p. 375-420. Publ. 51, American Assoc. Adv. Sci., Washington, D. C.

———. 1966. Africa and Pleistocene overkill. *Nature,* 212 (5060): 339-342.

———. 1967. Prehistoric overkill. In P. S. Martin and H. E. Wright, Jr. (eds.), *Pleistocene Extinctions; The Search for a Cause,* p. 75-120. Proc. 7. Congr. Intern. Assoc. Quaternary Research. Yale Univ. Press, New Haven.

MARTIN, P. S. and B. E. HARRELL. 1957. The Pleistocene history of temperate biotas in Mexico and eastern United States. *Ecology,* 38: 468-480.

MARTIN, P. S. and H. E. WRIGHT, JR. 1967. *Pleistocene Extinctions; The*

Search for a Cause. Proc. 7. Congr. Intern. Assoc. Quaternary Research. Yale Univ. Press, New Haven.

MATTHEW, W. D. 1915. Climate and evolution. *Ann. N. Y. Acad. Sci.,* 24: 171-318.

MAXWELL, A. E., R. P. VON HERZEN, K. J. HSÜ, J. E. ANDREWS, T. SAITO, S. F. PERCIVAL, JR., E. D. MILOW, and R. E. BOYCE. 1970. Deep sea drilling in the South Atlantic. *Science,* 168: 1047-1059.

MAYR, E. (ed.). 1952. The problem of land connections across the South Atlantic, with special reference to the Mesozoic. *Bull. Am. Museum Natur. Hist.,* 99 (3): 79-258.

MAYR, E. and W. H. PHELPS, JR. 1967. The origin of the bird fauna of the south Venezuelan highlands. *Bull. Am. Museum Natur. Hist.,* 136 (5): 269-328.

McDOWELL, S. B., JR. 1958. The Greater Antillean insectivores. *Bull. Am. Museum Natur. Hist.,* 115 (3): 113-214.

MILLER, G. S., JR., and R. KELLOGG. 1955. List of North American Recent mammals. *Bull. U. S. Nat. Museum,* 205: 1-954.

MOHR, E. 1957. *Sirenen oder Seekühe.* Die neue Brehme-bucherei Bucherim, Heft 197, Wittenberg, Lutherstadt.

MORRISON, P. and B. K. McNAB. 1967. Temperature regulation in some Brazilian phyllostomid bats. *Comp. Biochem. Physiol.,* 21: 207-221.

MÜLLER-BECK, H. 1966. Paleo-hunters in America; origin and diffusion. *Science,* 152: 1191-1210.

NYGREN, W. E. 1950. Bolivar geosyncline of northwestern South America. *Bull. Am. Assoc. Petrol. Geol.,* 34 (10): 1998-2006.

OLIVARES, A. 1962. Aves de la región sur de La Macarena. *Rev. Acad. Colombiana Cienc. Exact. Fis. Natur.,* 11: 305-345.

OLSON, E. C. and P. O. McGREW. 1941. Mammalian fauna from the Pliocene of Honduras. *Bull. Geol. Soc. Am.,* 52: 1219-1244.

OSGOOD, W. H. 1943. The mammals of Chile. *Field Museum Natur. Hist., Zool. Ser.,* 30 (542): 1-268.

PATTERSON, B. 1967. Infraclass Metatheria. Superorder Marsupialia. In *The Fossil Record,* Part II (Mammalia), p. 763-787. Geol. Soc., London.

PATTERSON, B. and R. PASCUAL. 1968. Evolution of mammals on southern continents. V. The fossil mammal fauna of South America. *Quart. Rev. Biol.,* 43: 409-451.

PAULA COUTO, C. DE. 1952. As sucessivas faunas de mamíferos terrestres no continente Americano. 159 p. Publ. Avulsas Brasil. Museo Nac. No. 11, Rio de Janeiro.

——. 1956. Mamíferos fósseis de Cenozoico da Amazonia. 121 p. Bol. No. 3, Conseho Nac. Pesq., Rio de Janeiro.

——. 1960. Un urso extincto do Brasil. *Bol. Soc. Brasil. Geol.,* 9 (1): 5-27.

PEARSON, O. P. 1948. Life history of mountain viscachas in Peru. *J. Mammal.,* 29 (4): 345-374.

———. 1951. Mammals of the highlands of southern Peru. *Bull. Museum Comp. Zool.,* 106 (3): 117-174.

———. 1957. Additions to the mammalian fauna of Peru and notes on some other Peruvian mammals. *Breviora Museum Comp. Zool.,* 73: 1-7.

———. 1960. Biology of the subterranean rodents, *Ctenomys,* in Peru. *Mem. Museo Hist. Natur. "Javier Prado,"* 9: 1-55.

PITMAN, W. C., III., M. TALWANI, and J. R. HEIRTZLER. 1971. Age of the North Atlantic Ocean from magnetic anomalies. *Earth, Planet. Sci. Lett.,* 11 (3): 195-200.

POLANSKI, J. 1965. The maximum glaciation in the Argentine Cordillera. International Studies of the Quaternary. Geol. Soc. America Special Paper No. 84, 453-472; New York.

RAMSAY, A. T. S. 1971. A history of the formation of the Atlantic Ocean. *Advancement of Science,* 27 (133): 239-249.

RIDE, W. D. L. 1964. A review of Australian fossil marsupials. *J. Proc. Roy. Soc. West. Austral.,* 47 (4): 97-131.

ROMER, A. S. 1968. Fossils and Gondwanaland. *Proc. Am. Phil. Soc.,* 112 (5): 335-343.

———. 1970. The Chañares (Argentina) Triassic reptile fauna. VI. A chiniquodontid cynodont with an incipient squamosal-dentary jaw articulation. *Breviora,* No. 344: 1-18.

SAUER, C. O. 1950. Geography of South America. In J. H. Steward (ed.), *Handbook of South American Indians,* Part 6, p. 319-344. Bull. No. 143, Bur. Am. Ethnol., Smithsonian Inst., Washington, D. C.

SAVAGE, J. M. 1960. Evolution of a peninsular herpetofauna. *Syst. Zool.,* 9 (3/4): 184-212.

———. 1966. The origin and history of the Central American herpetofauna. *Copeia,* 1966 (4): 719-766.

SCHMIDT, K. P. 1954. Faunal realms, regions and provinces. *Quart. Rev. Biol.,* 29: 322-331.

SCOTT, W. B. 1937. *A History of Land Mammals in the Western Hemisphere.* Macmillan, New York. [Rev. ed.]

SIGÉ, BERNARD. 1968. Dents de micromammifères et fragments de coquilles d'oeufs de Dinosauriens dans la faune de Vertébrés du Crétacé supérieur de Laguna Umayo (Andes peruviennes). *Comptes Rend. Acad. Sci. (Paris),* 267: 1495-1498.

SIMONS, E. L. 1971. Relationship of *Amphipithecus* and *Oligopithecus.* *Nature,* 232: 489-491.

SIMPSON, G. G. 1939. The development of marsupials in South America. *Physis (Rev. Soc. Argentina Cien. Nat.),* 14: 373-398.

——. 1940a. Review of the mammal-bearing Tertiary of South America. *Proc. Am. Philos. Soc.,* 83 (5): 649-709.

——. 1940b. Mammals and land bridges. *J. Wash. Acad. Sci.,* 30: 137-163.

——. 1945. The principles of classification and a classification of mammals. *Bull. Am. Museum Natur. Hist.,* 85: 1-350.

——. 1950. History of the fauna of Latin America. *Am. Scientist,* 38 (3): 361-389.

——. 1956. Zoogeography of West Indian land mammals. *Am. Museum Novit.,* 1759: 1-28.

——. 1959. Mesozoic mammals and the polyphyletic origin of mammals. *Evolution,* 13: 405-414.

——. 1965. *The Geography of Evolution. Collected Essays.* 249 p. Chilton Books, Philadelphia.

——. 1966. Mammalian evolution on the southern continents. *Neues Jb. Geol. Paläontol.,* 125: 1-18.

——. 1969. South American mammals. In E. J. Fittkau, J. Illies, H. Klinge, G. H. Schwabe, and H. Sioli (eds.), *Biogeography and Ecology in South America,* p. 879-909. W. Junk, The Hague.

——. 1970. The Argyrolagidae, extinct South American marsupials. *Bull. Museum Comp. Zool.,* 139 (1): 1-86.

SLAUGHTER, B. H. 1967. Animal ranges as a clue to Late-Pleistocene extinction. In P. S. Martin and H. E. Wright, Jr. (eds.), *Pleistocene Extinctions; A Search for a Cause,* p. 155-167. Proc. 7. Congr. Intern. Assoc. Quaternary Research. Yale Univ. Press, New Haven.

SMITH, A. G. and A. HALLAM. 1970. The fit of the southern continents. *Nature,* 225: 139-144.

STAHELIN, R. and W. P. EVERARD. 1964. Forests and forest industries of Brazil. 50 p. Forest Resource Rep. No. 16, U. S. Dept. Agriculture, Washington, D. C.

STEWARD, J. (ed.). 1950. *Handbook of South American Indians. 6. Physical Anthropology, Linguistics, and Cultural Geography of South American Indians.* 715 p. Bull. No. 143, Bur. Am. Ethnol., Smithsonian Inst., Washington, D. C.

STIRTON, R. A. 1953. Vertebrate paleontology and continental stratigraphy in Colombia. *Bull. Geol. Soc. Am.,* 64: 603-622.

——. 1954. Late Miocene mammals from Oaxaca, México. *Am. J. Sci.,* 252: 634-638.

STIRTON, R. A. and W. K. GEALEY. 1949. Reconnaissance geology and vertebrate paleontology of El Salvador, Central America. *Bull. Geol. Soc. Am.,* 60: 1731-1754.

STUART, L. C. 1966. The environment of the Central American cold-blooded vertebrate funa. *Copeia,* 1966 (4): 684-699.

SZALAY, F. S. 1970. Late Eocene *Amphipithecus* and the origins of catarrhine primates. *Nature,* 227: 355-357.

TATE, G. H. H. 1939. The mammals of the Guiana region. *Bull. Am. Museum Natur. Hist.,* 76 (5): 151-229.

THOMAS, O. 1894. A new species of armadillo from Bolivia. *Ann. Mag. Natur. Hist.,* 13 (6): 70-72.

TIHEN, J. A. 1964. Tertiary changes in the herpetofauna of temperate North America. *Senckenbergiana Biol.,* 45 (3/5): 265-279.

VAN VALEN, L. 1967. New Paleocene insectivores and insectivore classification. *Bull. Am. Museum Natur. Hist.,* 135 (5): 217-284.

VINSON, G. L. and J. H. BRINEMAN. 1963. Nuclear Central America, hub of Antillean transverse belt. In O. E. Childs and B. W. Beebe (eds.), *Backbone of the Americas,* p. 101-112. Mem. Amer. Assoc. Petrol. Geol.

WAUCHOPE, R. and R. WEST. 1964. *Handbook of Middle American Indians. Vol. 1: Natural Environment and Early Cultures.* 570 p. Univ. Texas Press, Austin.

WEGENER, A. 1966. *The Origin of Continents and Oceans.* 246 p. Dover Pubs., New York. [New English translation of 1962 printing of 4th rev. ed. of *Die Entstehung der Kontinente und Ozeane,* published in 1929 by Friedrich Vieweg & Sohn].

WENZEL, R. L. and V. J. TIPTON. 1966. Some relationships between mammal hosts and their ectoparasites. In R. L. Wenzel and V. J. Tipton (eds.), *Ectoparasites of Panamá,* p. 677-723. Field Museum Natur. Hist., Chicago.

WHITMORE, F. C., JR. and R. H. STEWART. 1965. Miocene mammals and Central American seaways. *Science,* 148: 180-185.

WILLIS, B. 1932. Isthmian links. *Bull. Geol. Soc. Am.,* 43: 917-952.

WILSON, J. T. 1963. Continental drift. *Sci. Am.,* 208 (4): 86-100.

WISLOCKI, G. B. and R. K. ENDERS. 1935. Body temperature of sloths, anteaters, and armadillos. *J. Mammal.,* 16: 328-329.

WOOD, A. E. and B. PATTERSON. 1970. Relationships among hystricognathous and hystricomorphous rodents. *Mammalia,* 34 (4): 628-639.

WOODBURNE, M. O. 1968. The cranial myology and osteology of *Dicotyles tajacu,* the collared peccary and its bearing on classification. *Mem. S. California Acad. Sci.,* 7: 1-48.

——. 1969. A late Pleistocene occurrence of the collared peccary, *Dicotyles tajacu,* in Guatemala. *J. Mammal.,* 50 (1): 121-125.

WOODRING, W. P. 1954. Caribbean land and sea through the ages. *Bull. Geol. Soc. Am.,* 65: 719-732.

——. 1966. The Panama land bridge as a sea barrier. *Proc. Am. Philos. Soc.,* 110 (6): 425-433.

VIII Comparisons of Contemporary Mammal Faunas of Southern Continents

by Allen Keast

INTRODUCTION

The present contribution integrates certain facets of the chapters by Bigalke (Chapter IV), Keast (Chapter V), and Hershkovitz (VII), on the contemporary mammal faunas of Africa, Australia, and Neotropica, and uses this information (supplemented by additional data as necessary) to develop a series of broad concepts concerning evolutionary processes on those continents. Numerical comparisons are made of the relative richnesses of the three faunas, and of the proportions of the various taxonomic groups composing them. Faunal structure and composition are related to such environmental variables as the size of each continent, its latitudinal position, its physiographic diversity, its rainfall, and its dominant vegetation. Attention is focussed on the mammal groups that are endemic on each continent and those that have undergone major diversification and radiation on each continent. The major adaptive zones, or ways of life, and ecological niches are investigated to determine how they are subdivided within each fauna. Finally, some general matters such as the development of balance in faunas, and the concepts of what constitutes "saturation" and "unsaturation," are discussed.

The review is limited mainly to the Recent faunas since these can be more adequately compared. For details of the faunal histories of each continent, see Cooke (1968), Patterson and Pascual (1968), and Keast (1968b) and Chapters III, V, and VI of this book. The historical aspects of the evolution of the three continental faunas have also been briefly summarized by Simpson (1965, 1966). Some of the aspects of mammalian evolution in Africa, South America, and Australia, considered here, have been investigated for the avifaunas of these regions in two recent papers by the writer (Keast, 1972a,b).

NUMBERS OF FAMILIES, GENERA, AND SPECIES: AFRICA, SOUTH AMERICA
AND AUSTRALIA COMPARED

The contemporary mammal faunas of Africa, South America, and Australia are compared in Table 1. The data are taken from the chapters by Bigalke, Keast, and Hershkovitz. In all discussions and calculations Africa is taken as "the whole continent of Africa without the extreme northwest corner" (Bigalke), and without Madagascar. South America follows the classical limits of the Neotropical Region to include South America proper, Central America and the West Indies (Hershkovitz). Australia includes Australia proper, Tasmania, and New Guinea.

The continents could be delimited in any one of three ways: (1) strictly on the basis of continental limits; (2) as classic zoogeographic regions so that South America (=Neotropica) includes Central America north to the lowlands of Mexico, and the West Indies; and Africa (=Ethiopian Region) is Africa less the northwestern corner (which has partly a Palearctic fauna) but including Madagascar; and (3) the zoogeographic regions as defined less the West Indies on the one hand and Madagascar on the other, these two insular areas having an ancient history of isolation, and faunas so distinct that they constitute distinct subregions.

In the present series the guest authors were invited to delimit their areas of concern according to the evidence as they saw it. Hershkovitz has followed the second method and Bigalke the third. The complexities in delimiting the areas stem partly from relatively late changes in the continental limits and hence in the distribution of the faunas of these continents.

Only in the case of Australia do the historic and present-day continental boundaries and hence faunistic limits, correspond. "Australia," as used here, is the continent plus New Guinea and Tasmania. New Guinea, which has a rich fauna of its own, lies on the Australian continental shelf and has repeatedly been in contact with the mainland (probably four times during the Pleistocene, corresponding to the glacial lowerings in sea level). Moreover, as the fossil record has become better understood it has been found that various "endemic" New Guinea genera formerly occurred in southern Australia, and that at least one "southern Australian" genus (*Thylacinus*) occurred in New Guinea (references in Keast, Chapter V). Tasmania, of course, has a similar history of intermittent junction with Australia and has a purely Australian fauna.

Throughout the Tertiary, South America was isolated from North America by seas. Central America was a promontory of the latter; i.e., it represented the southern part of a "tropical North America." With the formation of the Panamanian Isthmus in the late Tertiary (apparently late Pliocene), Central America became, faunistically, part of South America, the latter gaining a second tropical fauna, so to speak. Accordingly, Simpson (1966) stresses that the Central American fauna has to be viewed in two ways: from the static (present day fauna) viewpoint and

TABLE 1

Comparisons of mammal faunas of the southern continents

	Africa [1]	*Neotropica*	*Australia*
No. of taxa at the ordinal and superfamily levels [2]	32	24	11
No. of families [3]	52	50	18
No. of genera	231	278	117 [5]
No. of superspecies	554	not available	218
No. of species	744	810	364
No. of families per 100,000 sq. mi.	0.45 *0.63* [4]	0.70	0.55
No. of genera per 100,000 sq. mi.	2.02 *3.0*	3.86	3.55
No. of superspecies per 100,000 sq. mi.	5.16 *7.2*	not available	6.66
No. of species per 100,000 sq. mi.	6.42 *9.2*	11.3	11.03
species/genera	3.24	2.91	3.11
species/superspecies	1.35	not available	1.67
genera/families	4.46	5.56	6.50
species/families	14.46	16.20	20.22

[1] AFRICA *does not include Madagascar;* NEOTROPICA *includes Central America and the West Indies;* AUSTRALIA *includes New Guinea.*

[2] *In this and the following tables the classification of Simpson (1945) is followed with minor modifications (i.e., Ride, 1964 is used with respect to marsupial classifications).*

[3] *Includes Sirenia and, in the case of Neotropica, two endemic freshwater cetaceans.*

[4] *Numbers in italics in the African column are calculations for the continent less the Sahara (i.e., zone with a rainfall of less than 5 inches per annum). This amounts to about 30% of the total continental area.*

[5] *Differs from Table 1 in Keast, Chapter V, in including the Sirenia.*

dynamic or historical aspects. South America is the only one of the three regions to have undergone an expansion in area.

Africa is now slightly smaller than it was during much of the Tertiary, Arabia having been detached. The "Ethiopian Region" may be defined as the whole of Africa less the Atlas region in the northwest; or it may be delimited alternatively by an imaginary line through the center of the Sahara (Darlington, 1957). Bigalke (Chapter IV) notes that, in the case of mammals, many Ethiopian elements reach the Mediterranean and that, while various Palearctic forms (bear, boar, deer, etc.) do occur in north-west Africa this segment cannot simply be regarded as part of the Pale-arctic region as in the case of birds, plants, and land snails. The relative distribution of the two elements in North Africa, he notes requires fuller study.

For the sake of consistency all calculations are based on the continental areas as defined by Bigalke, Hershkovitz, and Keast in this book. In order to make it clear that South America is used in the wider context the term "Neotropica" will be used for it. The areas of the two larger continents are taken as follows: *Africa*—the whole continent including the north-west corner (for the reasons stated above and because, at any event, the area is so small that its inclusion, or exclusion, makes no difference to the results), but not Madagascar; *Neotropica*—South America plus Central America north to include the lowlands of Mexico. The area of the West Indies is insignificant. If it is desired to develop a set of faunistic figures for continental South America (i.e., less Central America) this can readily be done by reference to the detailed distributional lists of mammals in Hershkovitz (1958). These show that Central America has 22 genera that do not occur further south.

The exclusion of the Madagascar fauna from Africa and the inclusion of the West Indian one with the Neotropical figures might seem anomalous. The West Indian fauna, however is most impoverished today and adds to the basic Neotropical fauna only one endemic family (2 genera) of Insectivora, one endemic subfamily and 8 endemic genera of bats, and 3 endemic genera of caviomorph rodents (Hershkovitz, 1958). Thus, inclusion of these forms would not significantly change the Neo-tropical figures. Madagascar, by contrast, has one endemic family of insecti-vores (10 genera), 3 endemic families of lemurs (10 genera), an endemic subfamily of cricetine rodents (7 to 8 genera), an endemic subfamily of viverrids (4 genera), and one endemic family and genus of bats (Bigalke, Chapter IV). About three-quarters of the 66 mammal species occurring on Madagascar are endemic. The addition of these to the African fauna (744 species) would give Africa a fauna of the same size as Neotropica (810 species).

Africa has 32 taxa at the ordinal and superfamily levels, South America 24, and Australia 11 (excluding Carnivora, the sole member of which, the dingo, was introduced by aboriginal man). See Table 1 for corresponding numbers of families, genera, superspecies and species.

In the numerical comparisons of families the classifications used in Bigalke, Hershkovitz, and Keast in their respective chapters on the con-temporary faunas are followed, except in the case of marsupials, where the Neotropical Paucituberculata and Didelphoidea, and the Australian Dasyuroidea are treated as superfamilies (Ride, 1964).

In a few cases the authors of the papers on the contemporary faunas differ from Cooke (Chapter III) and Patterson and Pascual (Chapter VI) who treat the fossil faunas in according family rather than subfamily status to a group (e.g., Protelidae instead of Protelinae), or the reverse. The differences in the two systems are relatively insignificant and can be ignored.

These latest figures indicate that, contrary to what has been believed (Keast, 1963; Simpson, 1966, p. 14) Neotropica has more, not fewer, mammal species than Africa. Australia of course, has materially fewer, about one-third the number of families and half the number of genera and species in Africa.

The question arises as to whether or not numerical calculations based on current taxonomics are reliable, i.e., have the taxonomics on the three continents reached a stage of sophistication and finality for the figures to be truly meaningful. Most of the African mammal groups and a number of the Neotropical and Australian-New Guinea ones, have been the subject of recent taxonomic revisions. In his African calculations Bigalke (Chapter IV) was able to draw upon a large series of recent, unpublished taxonomic works being carried out by an international committee under the sponsorship of the Smithsonian Institution, Washington, and the U.S.I.B.P. program. These include reviews of the rodents and bats, the most complicated groups taxonomically (see acknowledgements accompanying Bigalke's Chapter IV). Nevertheless, Bigalke writes (p. 144): "The taxonomy of many groups is far from settled so that the numbers of species, and especially of superspecies, must be regarded as provisional." In compiling his Neotropical figures Hershkovitz (Chapter VII) draws on published catalogues of primates and other groups. He writes (in his Table 2): "Majority of taxons have not been revised, figures given for genera and species are estimates of the number of valid groups." The Australian mammal taxonomy may be described as being in a "reasonable" state, although revisions of the rodents are badly needed. In his counts Keast (Chapter V) compensates somewhat for this by excluding forms of doubtful status, especially those that are the allopatric counterparts of others.

The "state" of mammalian taxonomics in each continent can be tested impartially by comparing the ratios of species to genera, genera to families, and species to families. If taxonomists in the different continents are applying uniform standards these should be roughly equivalent.

Table 1 shows the ratios, in the case of Africa, Neotropica, and Australia, to be as follows: species to genera, 3.24, 2.91 and 3.11; genera to families, 4.46, 5.56, 6.50; species to families, 14.46, 16.20, and 20.22. These correspond to a reasonable degree, particularly for Africa and Neotropica. This indicates that the comparative differences between the faunas of the three continents, particularly at the family and generic level, and the relationships between these and the surface areas of the continents, are real.

ENDEMISM IN THE THREE CONTINENTAL MAMMAL FAUNAS

The level of endemism in the mammal faunas of the three continents is summarized in Table 2. The figures for percentages of endemic families

	Africa	Neo-tropica	Aus-tralia
Total taxa at the ordinal and superfamily level	32	24	11
Total families	52	50	18
Total genera	231	278	117
Total species	744	810	364
% endemic taxa at the ordinal and superfamily levels	19	29	36
% endemic families	29	54	50
% endemic genera	72	84	89
% endemic species	90–95	94	95+
% families in endemic taxa at the ordinal and superfamily levels	21	42	50.
% genera in endemic families	17	37	54
% species in endemic families	11	34	41

TABLE 2

Endemism in the mammal faunas of Africa, Neotropica, and Australia

Continental limits are as defined in text.
Basic figures taken from the chapters of Bigalke, Hershkovitz, and Keast.
Groups that are obviously autochthonous to a continent but extend marginally beyond its limits (e.g., African Hyracoidea), and those in which a single species has recently extended beyond the continental limits (e.g., Neotropical Didelphidae) are here regarded as endemic.

and genera in Australia supersede those of Simpson (1961) quoted in Keast (Chapter VI), since Simpson's data refer to Australia only, not Australia plus New Guinea. Comparisons are developed in terms of taxa at the ordinal and superfamily levels rather than just families, in order best to bring out the degree of distinctness of each fauna.

Africa today has only one endemic order, the Tubulidentata which in the Pliocene extended to Europe and India: the Hyracoidea, however, should rightly be regarded as endemic. The percentage of endemism for all taxa at the ordinal and superfamily level is 19 (6 out of 32). Neotropica has 29% endemic taxa at the ordinal and superfamily levels. The more distinctive elements include the Paucituberculata (Caenolestoidea), Xenarthra, Platyrrhini, Caviomorpha (one species of which now reaches Hudson Bay), and Didelphoidea (also with one species in North America).

Australia has 4 endemic taxa at the ordinal and superfamily levels, the Monotremata, Dasyuroidea, Peramelina, and Phalangeroidea (to follow the classification of Ride, 1964) amounting to 36% of the total of 11.

At the family level Africa now has 15 endemic groups: Potamogalidae,

Chrysochloridae, Macroscelididae, Galagidae, Anomaluridae, Pedetidae, Thronomyidae, Petromuridae, Ctenodactylidae, Bathyergidae, Protelidae, Orycteropodidae, Procaviidae, Hippopotamidae, and Giraffidae (Bigalke, Chapter IV). These amount to 29% of the families. Two of these groups (Galagidae, Protelidae), however, are given subfamily status by some workers. There are 27 families of mammals endemic to Neotropica, if the Didelphidae, Dasypodidae, and Erethizontidae, one species of each of which reaches North America, be included. The endemics are: Didelphidae (centered today in South America but originating in North America in the Cretaceous and persisting there through much of the Tertiary; the present North American species is presumably a Pleistocene invader from Central America), Caenolestidae, Solenodontidae (West Indian and almost certainly of tropical North American—i.e., Central American—origin), Noctilionidae, Thyropteridae, Natalidae, Furipteridae, Desmodidae, Callithricidae, Callimiconidae (if this merits family rank), Cebidae, Myrmecophagidae, Bradypodidae, Dasypodidae (extending to continental North America), and 13 families of caviomorphs, one of which, as noted, now reaches the Arctic Ocean (Hershkovitz, Chapter VII). This is 54% of the total families, or 48% if didelphids, armadillos, and porcupines are excluded. Nine families are endemic to Australia: Tachyglossidae, Ornithorhynchidae, Dasyuridae, Thylacinidae, Peramelidae, Phalangeridae, Macropodidae, Vombatidae, Notoryctidae. This is equal to 50% of the total of 18.

At the generic level endemism is 72% for Africa, 84% for Neotropica, and 89% for Australia. At the species level it is probably 90-95% for Africa (author's estimate), 94% for South America (Hershkovitz, Chapter VII), and 95% or over for Australia (author's estimate).

Figures for percentage of a given category of taxa belonging to a particular endemic group (Table 2) reflect the above trends. Only 21% of African families belong to endemic taxa at the ordinal and superfamily levels whereas the figure is 42% for Neotropica and 50% for Australia. The percentages of genera belonging to endemic families are 17, 37, and 54, respectively, while the percentages of species belonging to endemic families is 11, 34, and 41.

These differences between the continents confirm what is known from the fossil record about their relative degrees of isolation during the Tertiary and Quaternary.

FAUNISTIC DIFFERENCES BETWEEN AFRICA, NEOTROPICA, AND AUSTRALIA

Table 3 lists the orders, suborders, and superfamilies of mammals occurring on each of the three continents; the numbers of families, genera, and species belonging to each; and expresses these data on genera and species as the percentage each taxonomic category represents of the continent's mammal fauna as a whole. Data on superspecies are not tabulated since these are available for Africa and Australia only. Hershkovitz (pers. com-

TABLE 3

Mammalian faunas of Africa, Neotropica, and Australia—a comparison of the groups occurring and their relative abundance (numbers in italics represent percentages)

	Africa			Neotropica			Australia		
	Families	Genera [1]	Species	Families	Genera	Species	Families	Genera	Species
MONOTREMATA									
Tachyglossidae and Ornithorhynchidae							2	3 2.6	4 1.1
MARSUPIALIA									
Marsupicarnivora [5]									
Dasyuroidea							3		
Dasyuridae								15 12.8	42 11.5
Thylacinidae								1 0.9	1 0.3
Notoryctidae								1 0.9	2 0.5
Didelphoidea				1	11 4.0	53 6.5			
Paucituberculata				1	3 1.1	7 0.9			
Peramelina							1	8 6.8	19 5.2
Phalangeroidea							3		
Phalangeridae								17 14.5	36 9.9
Macropodidae								16 13.7	42 11.5
Vombatidae								2 1.7	3 0.8
PLACENTALIA									
Insectivora									
Tenrecoidea	1								
Solenodontidae					1 0.4	2 0.2			
Potamogalidae		2 0.8	3 0.4						
Chrysochloroidea	1								
Chrysochloridae		3 1.2	16 2.1						

Taxon															
Erinaceoidea															
Erinaceidae	1	3	*1.2*	6	*0.8*										
Macroscelidoidea															
Macroscelididae	1	5	*2.4*	13	*1.7*										
Soricoidea															
Soricidae	1	7	*3.0*	56	*7.4*							1	*0.4*	8	*1.0*
Chiroptera															
Megachiroptera	1	13	*5.6*	26	*3.4*						1	5	*4.3*	25	*6.9*
Microchiroptera															
Emballonuroidea	2	3	*1.2*	9	*1.2*	2	10	*3.6*	19	*2.3*	1	2	*1.7*	2	*0.5*
Rhinolophoidea	4	8	*3.3*	44	*5.9*						2	2	*1.7*	15	*4.1*
Phyllostomatoidea	3					3	52	*18.7*	135	*16.7*					
Vespertilionoidea	2	18	*7.8*	95	*12.6*	5	18	*6.5*	68	*8.4*	2	12	*10.3*	47	*12.9*
Primates															
Prosimii															
Lorisidae+Galagidae	2	5	*2.0*	8	*1.1*										
Anthropoidea															
Platyrrhini	2					3	16	*5.8*	42	*5.2*					
Catarrhini															
Cercopithecidae		4	*1.7*	47	*6.3*										
Pongidae		2	*0.8*	3	*0.4*										
Edentata															
Xenarthra															
Myrmecophagoidea	1					1	3	*1.1*	3	*0.4*					
Bradypodoidea	1					1	2	*0.7*	3	*0.4*					
Dasypodoidea	1					1	9	*3.2*	20	*2.5*					
Pholidota	1	1	*0.4*	4	*0.5*										
Lagomorpha	1	2	*0.8*	10	*1.3*	1	1	*0.4*	2	*0.2*					
Rodentia															
Sciuroidea	1	7	*2.9*	31	*4.1*	1	5	*1.8*	18	*2.2*					
Geomyoidea	2					2	5	*1.8*	14	*1.7*					

TABLE 3—*Continued*

	Africa			Neotropica			Australia		
	Families	*Genera*[1]	*Species*	*Families*	*Genera*	*Species*	*Families*	*Genera*	*Species*
Anomaluroidea	2								
Anomaluridae		3 *1.2*	7 *0.9*						
Pedetidae		1 *0.4*	1 *0.1*						
Muroidea	3	43 *18.8*	151 *20.0*	1	51 *18.3*	223 *27.5*	1	31 *26.5*	124 *34.1*
Gliroidea (Muscardinidae)	1	1 *0.4*	7 *0.9*						
Dipodoidea	1	2 *0.8*	3 *0.4*						
African "Hystricomorph" rodents and others	6	16 *6.9*	27 *3.7*						
Neotropical Caviomorph rodents				13	51 *18.3*	123 *15.2*			
Cetacea				2					
Susuidae + Delphinidae					2 *0.7*	2 *0.2*	(1)²	(1) *0.9*	(1) *0.3*
Carnivora	2			4					
Canoidea									
Canidae		5 *2.0*	11 *1.4*		7 *2.5*	13 *1.6*			
Ursidae					1 *0.4*	1 *0.1*			
Procyonidae					6 *2.2*	8 *1.0*			
Mustelidae		7 *2.9*	7 *0.9*		9 *3.2*	15 *1.9*			
Feloidea	4			1					
Viverridae		18 *7.6*	37 *4.9*						
Hyaenidae		2 *0.8*	3 *0.4*						
Protelidae		1 *0.4*	1 *0.1*						
Felidae		2 or 3³ *1.2*	10 *1.3*		3 *1.1*	10 *1.2*			
Tubulidentata	1	1 *0.4*	1 *0.1*						
Proboscidea	1	1 *0.4*	1 *0.1*						
Hyracoidea	1	3 *1.2*	11 *1.4*						
Sirenia	2	2 *0.8*	2 *0.2*	1	1 *0.4*	1 *0.1*	1	1 *0.9*	1 *0.3*

Taxon									
Perissodactyla									
Equoidea									
Equidae	1	1 0.4	5 0.7						
Tapiroidea									
Tapiridae	1								
Rhinocerotoidea									
Rhinoceratidae	1	2 0.8	3 0.4			2 0.2			
Artiodactyla									
Suiformes									
Suoidea									
Suidae	1	3 1.2	3 0.4						
Tayassuidae	1	1 0.4							
Anthracotherioidea	1	1 0.4							
Hippopotamidae	1	2 0.8				2 0.2			
Tylopoda									
Camelidae	1				2 0.7	4 0.5			
Ruminantia									
Traguloidea									
Tragulidae	1	1 0.4				1 0.1			
Cervoidea									
Cervidae	1				6 2.2	11 1.4			
Giraffoidea									
Giraffidae	1	2 0.8				2 0.2			
Bovoidea	1	28 11.4	78 10.4						
Total	52	231	744	50	278	810	18	117[4]	364

[1] Numbers of genera in the various families are taken from the chapter by Bigalke. In the few cases where these are not detailed (cf. in the Gerbillinae) the Preliminary Identification Manual of African Mammals (J. Meester, 1968), currently being circulated by the Smithsonian Institution, has been consulted.

[2] Canidae from Australia are shown in brackets as species was introduced by original man.

[3] Number of genera of African Felidae is 3 if Panthera is recognized as genus to which the lion belongs; if the lion is assigned to genus Felis, number of genera of African Felidae is 2.

[4] Differs from Table 1 in Keast (Chapter VI) in including Sirenia.

[5] In using the term "Marsupicarnivora" to group the Australian Dasyuroidea and the South American Didelphoidea and Paucituberculata, the classification of Ride (1964) has been followed. Later serological work, however, indicates that the Paucituberculata represent a different lineage from the Dasyuroidea and Didelphoidea (Hayman, Kirsch, Martin, and Waller, 1971).

mun.) stresses that it would be misleading to attempt to develop such figures for Neotropica at the present time.

In terms of numbers of genera and species it is obvious that the dominant mammals of Africa are insectivores, bats, catarrhine monkeys, murine and cricetine rodents, viverrids, and bovids. In Neotropica, the dominant mammals are didelphoids, bats, platyrrhine monkeys, edentates, cricetine rodents, and caviomorph rodents. In Australia, the dominant mammals are dasyuroid marsupials, perameloids, phalangers, kangaroos, bats, and murine rodents and their derivatives. When these data are presented in terms of the percentages of the total fauna, murine rodents, bovids, bats and insectivores emerge as the dominant mammals of Africa. Insectivores, however, are a very insignificant part of the Neotropical fauna and are totally absent from Australia. Bovidae and Viverridae, absent from Neotropica and Australia, account for very significant percentages of the African fauna. In the case of Neotropica, microchiropteran bats constitute the largest percentage of the fauna; megachiropteran bats, present in Africa and Australia, are absent from Neotropica. Cricetine and caviomorph rodents are the next most important components of the Neotropical fauna. Didelphoids and edentates, significant in Neotropica, are absent in Africa and Australia, as are deer. The Australian fauna, of course, is dominated by dasyuroid, perameloid, and phalangeroid marsupials; marsupials are completely lacking in Africa, while Neotropica has representatives of two groups of marsupials—the didelphoids (as indicated above) and the caenolestoids.

Groups occurring on only one of the three southern continents, but today shared with one or more northern ones are: *Neotropica and the Holarctic*—Ursidae, Procyonidae, Camelidae, Cervidae, Phyllostomidae, Heteromyidae, and Geomyidae (North American families reaching Ecuador and Panama, respectively), with the essentially Neotropical Didelphidae, Erethizontidae, Tayassuidae, and Dasypodidae being represented in North America by single species; *Neotropica and Asia*—Tapiridae; and *Africa and Eurasia*—Proboscidea, Viverridae, Hyaenidae, Equidae, Tragulidae, and Bovidae (the last extending to North America). Present-day distributions are, of course, somewhat at variance with the fossil ones (e.g., the Camelidae arose in North America but are now absent there; the Giraffidae and Hippopotomidae formerly occurred in Africa and Eurasia, but do not now occur in the latter, and so on). For discussion of past distributions see the chapters of Cooke, Patterson and Pascual, and Keast in this book.

Mammal groups shared by the southern continents are: *Africa and Neotropica*—Soricidae (marginal in the latter), Primates (separate groups), Leporidae, Sciuridae, Mustelidae, and Canidae; *Africa and Australia*—Megachiroptera; *Africa, Neotropica, and Australia*—Microchiroptera and muroids (the latter are exclusively cricetines in the case of South America and murines in Australia, while Africa has a mixed fauna); *Neotropica and Australia*—marsupials.

Many factors may combine to influence the numerical richness of faunas and the kinds of forms that occur. Of importance in the case of the three southern continents are: (a) surface area; (b) proximity to other continents, i.e., opportunity for recruitment by colonization from outside; (c) area within the tropics; (d) diversity of living areas (in terms of physiography, climate, and vegetation); (e) past and present opportunities for developing new species within the continent; and (f) late Pleistocene extinctions.

Continental Area

The areas of the three continents as defined are: Africa without Madagascar, 11,458,000 square miles; Neotropica, 7,161,000 square miles; and Australia, 3,255,000 square miles.

When the numbers of families are considered relative to these areas (Table 1) Africa is found to have 0.45, Neotropica 0.70, and Australia 0.55 families per 100,000 square miles. See Table 1 for corresponding figures for genera, superspecies, and species.

By dealing with faunas *en bloc* in this way we are, for the moment, ignoring the obvious fact that the richness of Neotropica is due to its very large fauna of rodents and bats (Table 3). The question may well be asked whether, in terms of its area, Africa is not carrying less than its potential capacity of mammals. There are three reasons for postulating that it is: (a) the Sahara Desert covers about 30% of the continent's total surface—an area roughly equivalent to the whole of Australia; (b) this desert has an average rainfall of less than 5 inches and supports a negligible mammal fauna; (c) the extension of the Sahara to its present limits is a relatively recent phenomenon and is part of a wider series of climatic changes that, in addition, almost eliminated the Congo rain forests between 75,000 and 52,000 years ago (Moreau, 1966).

Accordingly, it is relevant to develop a set of figures for the "relative faunistic richness" of Africa exclusive of the Sahara Desert. This area would correspond to the "Ethiopian Region" of old workers. When this is done the number of families per 100,000 sq. miles rises to 0.63, similar to the figure for Neotropica. The figure for number of superspecies rises to 7.2%—slightly greater than that for Australia; those for genera and species to 3.0 and 9.2, respectively—half-way between the figures for Africa as a whole and those for Neotropica and Australia. In other words, if "Africa" is restricted to that part of the continent south of the Sahara the numbers of families occurring on each continent becomes almost directly proportional to surface area, as does the number of superspecies (data for Africa and Australia only). The number of genera and species in Ethiopian Africa is only about 80% of that which might be expected on the basis of the South American and Australian figures.

If the desert area is excluded from Africa, it might be argued that the figures for Australia, which is today almost one-third desert, should be similarly corrected. Since the desert of Australia has the smallest mammal fauna of any of the major vegetation formations on the continent (Keast, Chapter V), this would make Australia relatively richer. Exclusion of the desert segment is not justified, however, since most of the so-called Australian desert is vegetated, and mostly has an average annual rainfall of 8 to 10 inches (compared to less than 4 inches over much of the Sahara—see Table 4) and parts of it have a relatively good mammal fauna (see lists of species in Finlayson, 1961).

The relationship between area and numbers of species has received little attention from biologists working on continental faunas. In later years a number of workers have considered it relative to the much simpler insular situation. Here it has been found that if ecological conditions are uniform, the number of plant and animal species increases in approximately a logarithmic manner with increasing area (Preston, 1962; Wilson, 1961; MacArthur and Wilson, 1963). More recently, Mayr (1965) has examined a range of island bird faunas (e.g., those of solitary, well-isolated islands; single islands near mainlands or large archipelagos; and islands in the Gulf of Guinea). He has indicated that in birds, which he suggests could be unique in this regard, there is a high level of extinction and species turnover due to such factors as competition from new colonists, climatic changes, and biotic changes. It would be worth attempting an elaboration of the "fauna-area" models developed for island faunas for the more complicated continental situations.

Proximity to Other Continents: Faunistic Recruitment from Outside

The spatial relationships of the southern continents to each other, and to northern continents, have already been discussed (Keast, 1968a; Chapter I). Their different degrees of isolation not only underlie differences in the basic stocks that populated each continent at the end of the Cretaceous or beginning of the Tertiary, but also the frequency with which new groups were able to colonize them subsequently. Thus, in the case of Africa, the original stocks were supplemented by a range of new forms from Eurasia in the late Oligocene and again at the end of the Miocene, at which times there were apparently temporary land, or island, connections with the north (Cooke, Chapter III). Isolation was apparently complete thereafter until the late Pliocene. South America was spatially isolated until the late Tertiary. Primates and "Old South American" rodents arrived, presumably by rafting, in the middle Tertiary, as did procyonids in the Miocene. With the formation of the Panamanian land bridge, however, there was a great influx of new forms. This is generally regarded as having occurred in the Late Pliocene and Pleistocene, but Hershkovitz (Chapter VII) suggests that the exchange began earlier.

The timing and duration of this interchange is the subject of basic disagreement between Simpson (1950) and Patterson and Pascual (1968) on the one hand, and Hershkovitz (1966a, 1969) on the other (see also chapters in this book); hence they must be reviewed in some detail.

Simpson and Patterson and Pascual give a late Pliocene date for the completion of the Panamanian land bridge, on the basis of the fact that (1) Late Miocene and Early Pliocene fossil assemblages of Colombia and Venezuela contain only South American mammals (lists in Savage, 1951; Stirton, 1953; McKenna, 1956); (2) Miocene and early Pliocene assemblages from Central America (then a promontory of North America) contain only North American forms (lists in Whitmore and Stewart, 1965; Olson and McGrew, 1941; Frick, 1929); and (3) Late Pliocene and Pleistocene deposits as far south as Argentina show a sudden infusion of North American elements. The mammals that first appear in the South American fossil record at this time are "rabbits, squirrels, field mice, dogs, bears, raccoons, weasels, cats, mastodons, horses, tapirs, peccaries, camels, and deer, including in most of these cases some variety of related forms" (Simpson, 1950, p. 380). As a result of the exchange South America received no fewer than 7 orders and 16 families of North American mammals (Simpson, 1950; Patterson and Pascual, Chapter VI). About half the present Neotropical genera have developed from Late Pliocene or Quaternary North American invaders (about 35% are of mid-Tertiary North American ancestry, and 15% are derived from early Tertiary South American stocks, according to Simpson, 1966).

Simpson (1966) sees most of the South American–North American interchange as occurring during the Pleistocene: ". . . the exchange was at first rather limited in scope and the full surge of intermigration did not occur until somewhat later, in unequivocally Pleistocene times" (p. 380). Patterson and Pascual (1968 and Chapter VI) agree with Simpson's general conclusions.

Hershkovitz (1966a, 1969 and Chapter VII), while not denying the broad facts of late Tertiary enrichment, takes vigorous issue with the others that most of the colonization was Pleistocene. He bases his views on the high level of distinctness and diversification attained by the invaders since their arrival in South America and the well-known capacity of various groups of mammals to cross water gaps. He argues (with some justification) that if (1) primates and precaviomorphs colonized South America across extensive water gaps in the Oligocene, as Simpson states in his various papers; (2) procyonids reached South America and ground sloths North America in the Miocene; (3) the West Indies acquired a diverse fauna by rafting (Simpson, 1956); (4) various African mammals colonized Madagascar; and (5) rodents reached the Galapagos across a thousand miles of ocean, and have repeatedly colonized Australia, then surely the late-Tertiary enrichment of South America began ahead of the completion of the land bridge. A progressive enrichment must have begun much earlier and been accelerated as the water gap narrowed. He suggests, moreover, that the land bridge was completed earlier than Simpson suggests, probably at about the Miocene-Pliocene junction.

In his earlier (1966a) paper, Hershkovitz has suggested a possible time scale for the arrival of the various groups in South America: *mid-Tertiary* —ancestors of the distinctive squirrel, *Sciurillus; Miocene*—cricetine rodents; *Middle or Late Pliocene*—first canids, mustelids, and cervids; *Late Pliocene*—tapirs, bears, cats; *Pleistocene*—horses, mastodons, and camels; *since the Early Pleistocene*—soricids (*Cryptotis*), rabbits and the spiny mouse, *Heteromys*. He stresses that colonization and differentiation of the cricetines was progressive; thus the Sigmodontini attained virtually their present level of differentiation and limits of dispersal in both continents by the end of the Tertiary, while the Peromyscini only reached northwestern South America during the Quaternary (Hershkovitz, 1969; Chapter VII).

Reconciliation of the opposing views is dependent both on better stratigraphic data as to the precise dating on the closure of the Central American land bridge and fuller consideration of the relative capacities of the different groups of mammals to cross water gaps.

The former is still not available and there is some difference of opinion among geologists as to when the land bridge was completed. All the more recent writers show it as Pliocene—see Harrington (1962), Woodring (1964), and others listed in Patterson and Pascual (1968 and Chapter VI). An earlier worker, Nygren (1950), however, postulated that mammals could have intermittently crossed the Bolivar geosyncline during the Tertiary. It is interesting to note that a study of Central American marine mollusks has shown that the Caribbean contained many Pacific elements until the late Pliocene, and none thereafter, apparently confirming marine continuity across the area until that time (Woodring, 1964).

The mammals (apart from bats) that have demonstrated an ability to colonize across tracts of sea in different parts of the world are the following: insectivores (Madagascar, Indonesia, West Indies); primates (Madagascar, West Indies, Jamaica); hippopotamus (Madagascar); pigs (note monotypic *Babyrousa babyrussa* on Celebes and adjacent islands, and the wide dispersion of *Sus verrucosus* through the islands to the east of Wallaces' Line); elephants (see *Stegodon* on the Celebes and Timor); rodents (universally, but only members of specific groups), a few marsupials but especially *Phalanger* (islands to north of Australia), and squirrels (East Indies). Timor has a deer that could have been introduced by man. The above list is certainly sufficiently large to support Hershkovitz's contention that a variety of groups possibly colonized South America ahead of the completion of the land bridge. Their absence from the fossil record does not disprove this, of course. At the same time, as testified to by the 15-mile-wide Macassar Strait between Borneo and the Celebes, a narrow water gap can be a tremendous barrier to mammalian colonization. See Simpson (1952) for a discussion of the probabilities of mammalian dispersal across water gaps in geologic time.

If, in fact, the majority of the colonists from North America did not reach South America until the late Pliocene and Pleistocene their distinctness has to be explained. Patterson and Pascual suggest that many had already differentiated in Central America (tropical North America at that time). They feel that their appearance, as such, in late Pliocene assemblages in Argentina, along with the first large herbivores, supports this. Hershkovitz (Chapter VII), while agreeing that various groups (e.g., many canid genera) are probably of Central American origin, interprets the cricetine rodent evidence in the opposite way—that is, as confirming a long period of evolution in South America ahead of the formation of the land bridge. Either way, there was undoubtedly rapid evolution and diversification in many mammal groups in South America during the Pleistocene.

To sum up, it reasonably can be assumed that: (1) as suggested by the paleontological record, the completion of the Middle American land bridge was a Pliocene phenomenon; (2) some of the smaller mammals perhaps reached South America before this, and have thus had a longer period to evolve there than the paleontological record indicates. Cricetine rodents, otters, and squirrels are likely examples. They could not have diversified significantly before the Pliocene, however; otherwise they would surely have shown up in fossil assemblages such as those of the La Venta, which are fairly rich in caviomorph rodents. Irrespective of the time of arrival of the first colonizers, any early colonization must have been dwarfed by the vast interchange that followed formation of the land bridge; (3) few, if any, of the larger-bodied North American mammals reached South America before the land bridge—these animals fossilize well and would surely have shown up in the early Pliocene fossil record had they been present; (4) many of the more distinctive South American endemic genera of mammals originated in "tropical North America"; (5) most of the remarkably diverse South American cricetines as well as certain other groups, developed their morphological, habitat, and ecological specializations, and their patterns of allopatry, within South America. Some of these features point to moderately long occupancy as well as rapid diversification.

Australia was completely isolated throughout the Tertiary and Quaternary. The only land mammals to reach the continent, accordingly, have been bats and muroids. The latter entered, by rafting, at the end of the Miocene or during the Pliocene, later waves arriving during the Pleistocene.

The groups of animals that reached these continents at the different times became integrated into the fauna in due course. While each continent developed its own endemic orders, superfamilies, and families, the total diversity of each continent, at the higher category level, to a degree reflects its opportunities for obtaining additional orders and families from outside.

While there has been a considerable settling down within the Neotropical mammal fauna since the Pleistocene, with many groups becoming extinct, the continent possibly still benefits, numerically speaking, from its late Tertiary–Pleistocene enrichment from North America. This may partly explain why it is richer than Africa (less the Sahara) per unit area in terms of numbers of families (0.70 per 100,000 square miles compared to 0.63), and genera (3.86 compared to 3.0)—see Table 1.

The mammal faunas of each of the three continents were greatly enriched, numerically speaking, by the arrival of muroids towards the end of the Tertiary. (Africa had already received cricetids in the Miocene.) The muroids, with their potential for dividing up the environment into a large number of small niches, have undergone a striking radiation and diversification on each continent (see discussion below). It would be interesting to speculate on how the numbers of species of mammals on each continent compared *prior to* the arrival of the muroids, but that lies beyond the scope of the present study.

Area within the Tropics

Neotropica has the most extensive latitudinal range, from 24° N to 55° S, a distance of about 5450 miles. Africa ranges from 33° N to 34° S, or about 4620 miles. Australia (plus New Guinea) ranges from the equator to 44° S (3035 miles) and Australia alone from 10° S to 44° S, 2346 miles (Table 4). 78% of Africa, 70% of Neotropica, and 40% of Australia-New Guinea (33% of Australia without New Guinea), lie within the tropics.

These differences in latitudinal range influence faunistic diversity in various ways. Since Neotropica extends farthest south, any generalized cooling or "climatic deterioration" would affect a greater proportion of this continent than either of the others. This effect is increased by the presence of the high Andes, with their permanent snows and resultant cold winds. Africa, by contrast, straddling the equator, obviously occupies a highly favorable latitudinal position. Its fauna was obviously largely insulated against the cold periods of the Pleistocene, which were, of course, not nearly as severe as those in the northern continents (discussions in Moreau, 1966; Simpson, 1966; Axelrod, 1967). Of particular interest here are Axelrod's deductions concerning the benefits of the consistently equable climates of Africa. The transequatorial position of Africa also means that even though the tropical and subtropical belts may have been compressed from time to time during the Pleistocene they would never have been squeezed almost off the edge of the continent (as could conceivably have applied in the Texas-Alabama section of North America). Moreover, in the course of the north-south climatic sweeps of the Pleistocene a corridor (see "drought corridor" in Bigalke, Chapter IV) must have brought the northern and southern savannah into contact, permitting reconstitution of their faunas. There was no parallel in the case of Neotropica.

Tropical regions are widely recognized as having richer faunas than those of temperate regions. The link is not, of course, by any means absolute, since montane massifs, when present, would create areas where conditions were temperate, not tropical. Likewise, diversity varies with

TABLE 4

Some physiographic and vegetational characteristics of the southern continents

	Africa	*Neotropica*	*Australia*
Area (sq mi)	11,458,000	7,161,000	3,254,650 (Australia alone: 2,950,000)
Latitudinal range	33°N–34°S	24°N–55°S	0°–44°S (Australia: 10°S–44°S)
% of area within tropics (approx.)	78	70	40 (Australia alone: 33)
% above 5000 ft elevation (approx.)	3.5	7	2 (almost all in New Guinea)
Rainfall: % continental area with avg. annual rainfall of >60 inches	9	39	7
40–60 inches	19	29	9
20–40 inches	21	14	28
10–20 inches	9	4	27
5–10 inches	9	9	29
<5 inches	31	2	1
% rain forest (approx.)	9	32	4.5 (almost all in New Guinea)
% woodland and open forest (approx.)	31	22	20
% savannah, grassland, low-scrub steppe, and moorland (approx.)	19	38	23
% desertic vegetation (approx.)	30	3	30

AFRICA *dos not include Madagascar;* NEOTROPICA *includes Central America and West Indies;* AUSTRALIA *includes New Guinea.*

vegetation type. A tropical rain forest is richer than tropical savannah woodland in numbers of species of plants, insects, birds, bats, and arboricolous mammals. Deserts, tropical or otherwise, have poor faunas. Accordingly, percentage of area within the tropics is, in itself, of only limited significance. As can be seen from the maps in Keast (Chapter I) tropical rain forest covers only a relatively small area of the African tropics but much of the South American. Savannahs, with their magnificent faunas of large herbivores, dominate the African tropics.

Another feature of the transequatorial position of Africa is that there is some duplication of vegetation belts in comparable latitudes to the north and south of the equator. This means that there is partial duplication of mammal faunas with development of a series of "vicarious species pairs." Africa is unique in having no fewer than three desert, or semi-desert, grassland mammal faunas: the Somali Arid fauna in the northeast (reviewed in Keast, 1965), the Saharan fauna in the north and northwest, and the Kalahari fauna in the southwest. For the position of these three arid areas see Fig. 1 in Keast (1968a, and Chapter I). Their distinctive faunal elements are listed in the chapter by Bigalke. The first two have a number of distinctive endemic bovids, apart from other forms. The Somali and Kalahari faunas, aside from the fact that each possesses unique species, have a series of disjuncts (listed in Bigalke, Chapter IV) at the species and race levels.

Continental South America differs from Africa in that the tropical habitat (rain forest, woodland), and high rainfall zones, extend to its northern limits. There is, therefore, neither a broad temperate nor a desert belt in the north of the continent to "duplicate" those in the south. Latitudinal effects in Australia are largely restricted to a clearcut zonation of the rainfall and vegetation belts.

Physiography and Faunistic Diversity

The three continents differ strikingly in their physiography. South America alone has a great south-north mountain range, the Andean Cordillera. This extends the length of the continent, a distance of about 4300 miles and in the south (Altiplano region) has a width of almost 500 miles. The highest peaks reach nearly 23,000 ft, and there are extensive areas above 10,000 ft. By contrast, both Africa and Australia are relatively flat, being eroded peneplains, although the former is largely uplifted flat-land, the latter mostly low-lying flat-land.

Some concept of the relative physiographic diversity of each of the southern continents can be obtained by calculating the percentage of each over 5000 ft in height (Table 4). This comes to about 3.5% in the case of Africa, perhaps 7% in continental South America, and under 2% in Australia–New Guinea (almost all of which is New Guinea). As H. B. S. Cooke (pers. commun.) has pointed out to me, however, if the 3500 ft contour line is taken as the basis for comparison, a different picture emerges. A higher proportion of Africa than South America is now seen to be "elevated." This is also brought out in the discussions of Moreau (1966, p. 13 and 14).

While South America certainly has the greatest physiographic diversity in terms of altitude, Africa is unique in having a great many isolated mountain massifs and isolated volcanic peaks, which rise to heights of 9,000 to 18,000 ft. Included here are the Abyssinian plateaus, the Ruwenzoris, and Mounts Elgon, Kenya, Kilimanjaro, and Meru, in eastern Africa, the great line of highlands that form the eastern edge of the Congo basin, the Cameroon and Banso-Bamenda highlands in west Africa, the Ahaggar and Tibesti in the central Sahara, and the Grand Atlas highlands in northwestern Africa (Moreau, 1966).

The great expanse of the Altiplano of South America has permitted the development of a high grassland fauna in South America not duplicated either in Africa or Australia. This segment, which is about the size of California and has a height of 11,000 to 14,000 ft, has a fauna of 45 species, 28 genera, 13 families, and 5 orders of mammals (Hershkovitz, Chapter VII). Rodents form the bulk of the fauna, about half the species are endemic, and three "faunal strata" can be recognized.

The Andes also affect the distribution of mammals in various other important ways. They are the only mountains on the southern continents to support a comprehensive series of altitudinal life zones similar to those in the Himalayas and Rockies. Altitudinal zonation in mammals is reviewed in detail by Hershkovitz (Chapter VII), and has been discussed for birds by Chapman (1917, 1926). The Andes form a distributional barrier between east and west. Thus, "a large part of the present tropical and subtropical faunas of the western slope of the northern Ecuadorian, Colombian, and Venezuelan Andes is derived from the Middle American Province, and the largest part of the faunas of the eastern slope is upper Amazonian" (Hershkovitz, Chapter VII, p. 408). The isolated massifs of Africa, covered for the most part with highland rain forest, have a distinctive montane avifauna (Moreau, 1966). This does not extend to mammals, however, only the Abyssinian Highlands being an important center of endemism—for a detailed review of the montane mammal faunas of Africa, see chapter by Bigalke. The massifs add little to the faunistic diversity of the African continent.

Australia has no significant mountains and the Great Divide, extending from north to south adjacent to and parallel to the east coast, reaches only 7000 ft in height and has negligible areas above 5000 ft. New Guinea has a central backbone of high mountains, with several peaks reaching 15,000 ft; the present elevation stems from the Pleistocene. There is some altitudinal zonation of bird species and a minor degree of zonation in mammals (e.g., in phalangers of the genus *Pseudocheirus*). Altitudinal zonation on the Australian mainland is limited to a very few birds and reptile species (mostly Tasmanian forms that extend northward along the tops of the mountains). The Great Divide does, however, make a marked contribution to the ecological diversity of the Australian biotic scene by its influence on rainfall patterns. Almost all the eucalypt forests and rain forests lie between the Great Divide and the sea. The Great Divide, moreover, has functioned as a refuge area that has permitted the persistence of forms against encroaching aridity—note, for example, the more extensive western distribution of forest mammals in the late Pleistocene (faunal list for Lake Menindee in Tedford, 1967).

Vegetation and Faunistic Diversity

Table 4 brings out that striking differences in average annual rainfall characterize Africa and Neotropica. Thus, in the case of the latter 39% of the land area receives more than 60 inches per annum, and an additional 29% between 40 and 60 inches, compared to 9% and 19% respectively,

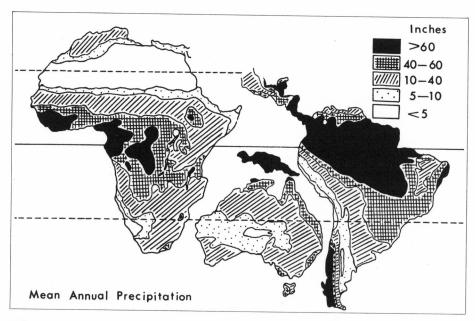

FIG. 1. MAPS OF AVERAGE ANNUAL RAINFALL FOR AFRICA, SOUTH AMERICA, AND
AUSTRALIA

*South America is by far the best-watered of the continents and has the largest segment
of tropical rain forest (see map in Chapter 1). By contrast, about 30% of Africa is extremely arid (annual rainfall of less than 4 inches). The Australian so-called "desert"
is not nearly as arid as much of the Sahara and mostly has an annual rainfall of 8–10
inches. Arid terrain is very restricted in South America. The maps bring out why
mammals adapted to rain forest are prominent in the South American fauna and why
savannah and woodland elements are dominant in Africa. The major rainfall (and
hence vegetation belts) follow a clear-cut zonal pattern in Australia and west Africa.
There are three distinct isolated arid areas or deserts in Africa, each with a number of
endemic faunal elements. This "duplication" includes antelopes. In Australia the
southwest, northwest, and southeast "corners" of the continent (and to some extent the
northeast), have a slightly higher rainfall than the intermediate areas and function as
refuges. (Adapted from Times Atlas, 1958).*

for Africa. The figures for Australia are 7% and 9%. In Africa, by contrast,
31% receives less than 5 inches of rainfall per annum, compared to 2%
of Neotropica, and 1% of Australia. Percentage figures for area receiving
between 5 and 10 inches per annum are 9% for Africa and Neotropica
and 29% for Australia. (Figures are calculated from the rainfall maps in
the *Times Atlas*, 1958). Average annual figures, of course, are only one
aspect of rainfall. Effectiveness in terms of plant growth varies with latitude, seasonal distribution of the rain, and other factors. Average figures
are sufficient, however, for the broad picture. Fig. 1 compares the distribution of the rainfall belts on the three continents. A marked zonal pattern
is characteristic of Africa and Australia and this, in turn, is reflected in
zonation of the major vegetation types (Fig. 1 in Chapter I). In Africa

the distribution of many mammal species, in turn, closely follows these zones (Fig. 2, p. 479).

In Table 4 an attempt is made to show the approximate percentages of the three continents covered by four broad vegetation categories: tropical rain forest, woodland-open forest, savannah-scrub and savannah-grassland, and desertic vegetation.

Comparative data on the contemporary vegetation of the three continents is basic to an understanding of the kinds of mammals that occur on each. While the continents have many similarities (e.g., in the occurrence of tropical rain forest and desertic vegetation), each has formations not duplicated on the others (e.g., palm forest in South America, eucalypt forest in Australia). An attempt must be made, therefore, to group a diversity of vegetation formations into fewer and broader categories to permit quantitative comparisons. This must be done, moreover, with due acknowledgment of the way that mammals "see" or use vegetation.

On the basis of African and Australian experience it would be appropriate to consider "tropical rain forest," "woodland," "savannah steppe and grassland," and "arid vegetation" as the basic categories. The faunas of these are largely distinct and the terms have generally accepted meanings. Closer inspection, however, shows most world vegetation maps (especially in the South American segment) to be based partly on structural and partly on floristic criteria. Kuchler (1954) has stressed the shortcomings of this and Cochrane (1963) has stressed the need for developing a world map based purely on structural features. Other problems, of course, are that many areas are covered not by a single vegetation formation but by a mosaic of formations, as Dansereau (1958) has stressed; and the existence, in places, of extensive transitional zones. Again, in some of the lesser known areas, vegetation limits are inserted not by actual mapping but by projection on the basis of climatic belts.

Original sources used in developing the figures in Table 4 are as follows: *Africa*—UNESCO Vegetation Map (Keay, 1959) and the map in Clark (1967); *Australia*—the map of Cochrane (1963), and that of Wood (1950); *Neotropica*—the map of Hershkovitz (Chapter VII) which is based mainly on Sauer (1950) and Leopold (1959). In trying to arrive at a simplified grouping of the South American vegetation formations a number of other South American vegetation maps have been consulted, including those in Smith and Johnston (1945), Hueck (1966), and Walter (1964), and I have had the benefit of discussions with B. Maguire of the New York Botanical Gardens, and P. Dansereau of the University of Montreal. This has been necessary because of the complex nature of the South American vegetation categories and patterns.

The groupings used in obtaining the percentages in Table 4 are as follows: (1) *Tropical rain forest*—forest of tall broad-leafed trees with a continuous canopy (this category has the same meaning on the three continents). (2) *Woodland, open forest, and scrub forest*—a continuous (or nearly continuous) covering of large or medium-sized trees, a discontinuous canopy, and a substratum of grass or shrubs (i.e., two distinct structural layers are present). Included here are the *Brachystegia-Isoberlinia* and Mopani woodlands of Africa, the tropical and temperate savannah woodlands of Australia, the dryer sclerophyll (eucalypt) forests of Australia, and the South American caatinga, semideciduous forests, high cerados, oak-conifer forests, *Araucaria* forests, palm forests, and thorn forests. (3) *Savannah, grassland,* and *scrub steppe*—the Sahel and Sudanese savannahs of Africa, the temperate savannah grasslands and high veldt of Africa, the Australian savannah grassland, and the llanos, pampas, Altiplano, open planato, low cerados, and scrub savannah and steppe of South America are grouped here. The criterion is the dominance of a low plant layer, most of it less than about a meter high (i.e., there is only one major feeding zone, in the vertical sense). Scattered trees are, of course, a feature of some savannah. (4) *Desertic vegetation*—the sparse xeric vegetation of arid areas. Dansereau (1958) defines desertic vegetation as woody and/or succulent plants very widely scattered, with ephemerals abundant after rain. In the map in Keast (Chapter I) the category has been extended to include the Australian porcupine grass (*Triodia*) areas.

These groupings, especially the second and third, include a range of dissimilar elements. Structurally there is a good general resemblance between the African Guinea Savannah (*Brachystegia-Isoberlinia* zone) and the South American caatinga (P. Dansereau, pers. commun.) and between the former and the Australian tropical savannah woodland (writer's observations). Other South American formations like the palm forests are quite distinct floristically and structurally and, doubtless, in their capacity to support a diverse fauna of mammals. In the third category the grouping of the South American grasslands of the llanos, pampas, and altiplano along with the rather different scrub savannah or steppes and low cerados is somewhat artificial (B. Maguire, pers. commun.). The Patagonian arid belt may alternatively be regarded as desert or semidesert (as by Smith and Johnston, 1945, and as shown in Fig. 1 of Chapter I) or as dry grassland (as by the writer in the calculations in Table 4). The rainfall of most of this region is only about 8 inches per annum, but it is as effective as perhaps 12 inches nearer the tropics, since it lies at relatively high latitudes.

Smaller highly distinctive vegetation formations like the *Nothofagus* forests of South America and Australia, and the wet sclerophyll forests of Australia, are not included in Table 4.

The figures confirm the prominence of tropical rain forests in South and Central America, about 32% of the land area being covered by them, compared to 9% of Africa, and perhaps 4.5% of Australia–New Guinea (mostly in the latter). (For visual comparisons see the rain forest map of the world in Richards, 1952, and Fig. 1 in Chapter I). By contrast, woodland and open forest cover about 22% of Neotropica, 20% of Australia, and 31% of Africa. Savannah, grassland, and low shrub steppe cover about 19% of Africa, 23% of Australia, and 38% of Neotropica. Included in the last figure, however, are the extensive cold, windswept, and floristically relatively homogeneous high grasslands and moors of the Altiplano. This contrasts with the tropical and subtropical savannahs of Africa in being very poor habitat for large herbivores. What grasslands do occur in the warmer parts of Neotropica differ from those of Africa in two ways: Either they are recent, as shown by the fact that they have not, as yet, built up any endemic species (see discussion of the Parámos in Hershkovitz, Chapter VII); or they are mostly subject to seasonal flooding.

Of the South American rain forests, those of the Amazon, of course, dominate. This is "the most extensive continuous rain-forest in the world. . . . in its greatest east-west extent this forest approaches 2200 miles, and in a north-south direction . . . it exceeds 1200 miles" (Smith and Johnston, 1945, p. 14).

Desertic vegetation covers about 30% of Africa, 3% of Neotropica and, if *Triodia* areas be included, about 30% of Australia. The latter figure is deceiving, however, since virtually all the Australian "desert" has between 5 and 10 inches of rainfall per year (8 inches is a fair average), whereas the Sahara averages less than 5 inches per annum. These differences are strikingly brought out in the map of arid and semi-arid regions in Walter (1964).

These profound differences in vegetation obviously explain some of the more striking differences in the mammal faunas of Africa and Neotropica (Table 3). Bats are richly developed in tropical rain forests and Neotropica has 222 species of bats compared to 174 in Africa. When writing of South American bats, Hershkovitz (Chapter VII, p. 376) states: "Bats are primarily tropical, and their greatest radiation occurred in lowland forests, where the number of species and individuals of bats may equal and, in some cases, even exceed those of all other mammals combined." Primates are also largely inhabitants of tropical rain forest. Here, however, the Neotropical fauna (16 genera, 42 species) is little different numerically from the African one (11 genera, 58 species). A proportion of the 378 species of Neotropical rodents are rain-forest dwellers and included here, besides squirrels are most of the 40-odd species of Echimyidae and various muroids, especially the primitive thomasomyines and oryzomyines (Hershkovitz, 1966b; Chapter VII; pers. commun.). From among Africa's 227 rodent species, however, only the squirrels, anomalurids, and to some extent the muscardinids, are rain-forest dwellers. The muroids have not, by contrast, radiated in this biome to any extent (Bigalke, Chapter IV).

The great differences in numbers of artiodactyls between Neotropica and Africa (e.g., 6 genera and 11 species of deer, plus two camelids, in the former, and 28 genera and 78 species of bovids in the latter—Table 3), can also be explained on the basis of habitat differences. African bovids are mostly inhabitants of woodland, savannah, and grassland, and there are several distinctive desert species. These habitats cover 80% of Africa (perhaps 9,300,000 square miles), compared to less than 60% of Neotropica (possibly about 4,300,000 square miles). As a group, the cervids have not shown the capacity to radiate under open country conditions as have the bovids, although they occur in grassland in Asia, and P. Hershkovitz (pers. commun.) informs me that some South American deer are grassland inhabitants. The reason for the poor contemporary South American large herbivore fauna cannot clearly be seen. Many of the Pleistocene invaders (e.g., equids), like the endemics that survived through to that period, are extinct. Bovids have never reached the continent.

Opportunities for Developing New Species within Continental Limits

Basic to a continent building up a rich and diversified fauna are opportunities for evolving new species by the isolation of populations and progressive differentiation so that, eventually, they can no longer interbreed with the parental stocks. When a large segment of a particular vegetation formation, and along with it the accompanying fauna, becomes isolated, many species may differentiate simultaneously. If the isolation continues for a very long time whole faunas may come to be partly duplicated.

The most important case of partial duplication of faunas in the southern continents are those of Australia and New Guinea. Of the total 364 species occurring in the whole region 188 are confined to Australia and 128 to New Guinea (Keast, 1968b). While a considerable proportion of the elements are differently adapted (e.g., inhabit the Australian eucalypt forests, woodlands, and grasslands, or New Guinea rain forests and mountainous areas, respectively) and would still remain distinct even if the land masses were joined, others inhabit equivalent vegetation formations in the two areas (e.g., rain forest and, in a few instances, woodland) and hence partly duplicate each other. This duplication of a portion of the mammal faunas of Australia and New Guinea makes this region faunistically rather richer than it would otherwise be.

The rain forests on each of the three continents are somewhat broken up into isolated blocks, with a degree of faunistic duplication and contemporary speciation. In the case of Africa, Bigalke (Chapter IV) quotes the work of Booth (1954) and Misonne (1963) indicating there were three isolated centers of differentiation of rain forest mammals in Pleistocene times, these corresponding approximately to Liberia, the high forests of the Cameroons (which are still separated by the Dahomey savannah gap), and the Ituri-Maniema section of the Upper Congo. These areas differ both in their faunas and in overall richness. Included in the groups that have differentiated in them are monkeys and duikers (Cephalophinae). The isolated eastern rain forest blocks of Africa have no endemic mammals; by contrast, various distinctive endemic bird species have evolved here. The Abyssinian Highlands, however, are a fairly important center of regional mammal endemism. (For attempted reconstructions of former vegetation patterns in Africa see Cooke, 1964, and Clark, 1967.) In Neotropica, the Central American and Brazilian rain forests are isolated and are faunistically markedly different. The tropical and subtropical rain forest faunas of the western slopes of the Andes in Ecuador, Colombia, and Venezuela, are derived from the Central American rain forests and are distinct from those of the eastern slopes which are Amazonian in origin (Hershkovitz, 1969). The isolated, or near-isolated, coastal rain forests of southeastern Brazil show various marked floristic differences from those of the Amazon (B. Maguire, pers. commun.). Differences in the mammal faunas would appear to be largely limited to the race level although no proper analysis has yet been made (P. Hershkovitz, pers. commun.).

The southern temperate (*Nothofagus*) rain forests of Chile and Argentina (see distribution map in Osgood, 1943) are effectively isolated from the equatorial rain forests to the north by the high Andes and "rain shadow" desert. The *Nothofagus* forests have various endemic birds and frogs (Vuilleumier, 1967) but they lack a proper mammal fauna (discussions in Hershkovitz, 1969, p. 58). Vuilleumier (1967) estimates that these forests have been isolated since at least the Pliocene, and probably the Miocene. In Australia the New Guinea and north Queensland rain forests are, as noted, isolated by Torres Strait. There is a moderate level of faunistic duplication, and some contemporary speciation (e.g., in the genus *Pseudocheirus*—see Keast, Chapter V) occurring between them.

The vegetation maps suggest a fair measure of continuity of the woodlands within Africa and Australia. Australian woodland (and eucalypt forest) birds show some tendencies to be isolated in peripheral "refuge areas" in the east, southwest, northwest, and northeast, of the continent (Keast, 1961). There are also some examples among the mammals of this sort of isolation, particularly with respect to the eucalypt forests in the south (Keast, 1963; Chapter V). The desert grasslands of Africa occur as three extensive tracts in the southwest, northeast, and north and northwest of the continent. The grasslands of Australia are largely continuous. In the woodlands and grasslands of both continents there is much species replacement, plus additions to the fauna, from south to north. This suggests separate centers of origin in the south and north. Bigalke (Chapter IV) suggests that this isolation came about by an eastward extension of the forest zone towards the coast, and that it may have occurred repeatedly, with each of the major Quaternary climatic fluctuations. The grasslands of South America form a series of isolated tracts: the extensive Altiplano in the south has a distinctive fauna, which is derived from the pampas and other areas to the east, but the extensive Paramos of the northern Andes and llanos of the Orinoco basin are comparatively recently established grasslands and lack endemic mammals (Hershkovitz, Chapter VII). In Africa, as noted, a measure of species duplication, as well as isolation and speciation, is occurring in the isolated Somali Arid, Saharan, and Kalahari Arid Zones. In addition to these, Africa provides a considerable number of cases of disjunct distributions (with or without differentiation) among mammals. Bigalke (1968 and Chapter IV) discusses some of these, and Clark (1967) provides a number of range maps.

Of great importance in explaining present-day species diversity are data on vegetation distribution in the past, and hence opportunities for speciation. This whole subject has received considerable attention from Moreau (1966), while Cooke (1964) and Butzer (in Clark, 1967) have produced series of hypothetical temperature, rainfall and vegetation maps for different stages of the Pleistocene. These show that the position and distribution of the major vegetation areas have changed considerably through to modern times. One of the most interesting maps is that of Balinsky (reproduced in the Chapter by Bigalke) of the "drought corridor" along which faunas moved between the Somali Arid and Kalahari Arid Zones, and that intermittently in the past disrupted the *Brachystegia* and its accompanying fauna (Moreau, 1966).

Extinction and Faunal Diversity

"Extinction is perhaps the most elusive of all evolutionary phenomena" (Mayr, 1965, p. 1587); this certainly applies in the case of the mammal faunas of the southern continents. Like the northern ones, they suffered a significant reduction in the number of large forms, mostly herbivores. Most of this apparently occurred in the period between 20,000 and 10,000 years before present (B. P.) in the case of Neotropica and Australia, but was rather earlier in Africa. Accounts of this are to be found in Martin (1966) for Africa, in the chapter by Patterson and Pascual for South America, and in Tedford (1967), Merrilees (1968), and Keast (Chapter V) for Australia. Extinction was moderate in Africa and Australia but drastic in South America. There is now an extensive (and controversy-laden) literature on the reasons for these faunistic reductions: climatic change (Axelrod, 1967), the hunting activities of primitive man (Martin, 1967), or habitat change as a result of man's activities (Merrilees, 1968), are favored theories. Part of the problem is, of course, to explain the persistence of the magnificent African large mammal fauna. Axelrod (1967) sees this largely as an expression of a continuing equable climate, stemming from the continent's transequatorial position. Martin (1967), however, feels that the important difference between Africa and South America is that the fauna of the former evolved with man and has had a long period to adjust to him, whereas in South America man was a late invader and the "inexperienced" fauna was no match for the efficient hunter. Guilday (1967) suggests that "habitat shrinkage" has been important in the elimination of South American forms; Patterson and Pascual (Chapter VI), however, have reservations about this, pointing out that this has not been demonstrated for the latter half of the Pleistocene. It might be noted, in passing, that during the glacial periods, when the sea level fell by up to 300 ft, the southern parts of the pampas would have been considerably increased in area to the east, to judge from the position of the 100 m line on bathymetric charts. There must have been progressive changes (e.g., overall shrinkage) in the total area of prime large herbivore habitat (especially tropical savannah) in South America between the Oligocene and Pliocene, to judge from the early and progressive elimination of many of the distinctive quadrupedal and cursorial endemic ungulates. Thus, reference to the phylogenetic trees in the chapter by Patterson and Pascual show that it is necessary to go back to the Miocene in South America to get an assemblage of endemic large herbivorous mammals equivalent to that of Africa today. Significantly, at this time Patagonia was subtropical (Patterson and Pascual, Chapter VI). By the late Pliocene only a few groups of autochthonous large herbivores survived. By the Pleistocene *Toxodon* and *Macrauchenia* were apparently reduced to a couple of species each. The ground sloths and glyptodonts, however, reached their peak in size then, along with a considerable level of diversity.

Just how the habitat requirements of the ground sloths and glyptodonts compared with that of the earlier cursorial quadrupeds is a matter for speculation. Many of the former were, of course, browsers. Nevertheless, it is tempting to postulate, as Guilday (1967) does, that by the Pleistocene, when man arrived, the optimum large herbivore habitat had already shrunk to a series of pockets (especially in the tropics and subtropics). Patterson and Pascual (Chapter VI) make an interesting point in stressing how vulnerable the lumbering and slow-moving ground sloths and glyptodonts would have been to human predation. The unique armor-plating of the glyptodonts, which had apparently evolved as a defense against the large carnivorous phororacoid birds was now little help against a new predator that could roll them over and thrust a spear into the vulnerable underside. They draw attention to cases of extinct herbivore remains being found in association with human artifacts.

Tedford (1967) regards climatic change as the major late factor reducing and modifying the Australian Pleistocene large herbivore fauna and, in the case of this continent at least, the present writer agrees with him.

There is abundant evidence for a drastic climatic deterioration in the Late Pleistocene–Early Recent. Included are various cases of shrinkages in the ranges of various small-bodied mammals, species that should have been little affected by man and his activities—e.g., the rat *Mastacomys*, and the mouse-sized phalanger *Burramys;* the larger *Sarcophilus* and *Phascolarctos* may perhaps also be included here. Geological evidence includes the huge dry lakes and dead river systems of the interior. Support also comes from relict plant distributions—e.g., disjunct distributions in northern South Australia (Crocker and Wood, 1948), relict stands of palms and cycads in the Macdonnell Ranges in central Australia (Keast, 1959), and the confinement of forest and woodland faunas to peripheral refuges (Chapter V).

Simpson (1966), it might be noted, does not regard the late Pleistocene-Recent extinction in Africa as significantly greater than what might be expected from a normal turnover rate. The "exceptional" extinctions of

Neotropica he attributes to a natural correction of a positive faunal im-balance produced by the incursion of North American forms, and those of Australia to a "climatic and faunistic change that was not merely accelerated but revolutionary" (Simpson 1966, p. 15).

In a recent analysis of population turnover in the late Cenozoic land mammals of North America, Webb (1969) argues that "extinction-origina-tion" is part of the normal evolutionary process, that some die-offs can readily be linked to climatic changes, and that the late Pleistocene extinc-tions of North America were part of a trend that began long before the earliest men appeared on the continent.

Recently, two papers by geologists (Hays, 1971; Crain, 1971) have ap-peared that correlate periods of massive faunal extinction with periods of sudden change in the Earth's magnetic field. Hershkovitz briefly sum-marizes this evidence in Chapter VII (p. 368). The idea does not, as yet, enjoy support among biologists.

Summary

It will be seen from the above that numerical and other differences in the mammal faunas of Africa, Neotropica, and Australia, stem from a variety of factors: continental area, proximity to an adjacent continent, latitudinal position, percentage of land area within the tropics, physio-graphic diversity, dominant vegetation type, potential (past and present) for developing new species, and different degrees of extinction in the immediate past.

The numerically large mammal fauna of Neotropica stems from its large numbers of rodents and bats. The strikingly diverse fauna of Africa is the result of exceptional survival from the Pleistocene. It also has a unique fauna of large herbivores. Australia has a reasonably rich and diverse fauna for its size, but there are various deficiencies. For example, there is no large cat-like carnivore or large scavenger. The large terrestrial and carnivorous phalangeroid *Thylacoleo*, however, apparently filled these roles in the Pleistocene.

RADIATION AND DIVERSIFICATION

The degree of morphological and ecological differentiation achieved by the various mammal groups on each of the continents, the ecological roles filled by each, and the major ecological counterparts on the different continents will now be reviewed below.

Monotremata

(Australia)

The Australian monotremes occupy two distinct ecological zones. The specialized aquatic platypus (*Ornithorhynchidae*) is a bottom feeder, tak-ing worms, crayfish, and small mussels by means of its leathery ducklike bill. The food niche somewhat duplicates that of certain ducks. No aquatic marsupial has evolved in Australia like the Neotropical *Chironectes*. Australia, of course, also lacks water-shrews, otter-shrews and such aquatic mustelids as the mink and otter. The only other Australian aquatic mammal is the large water-rat (*Hydromys*, Hydromyinae). This is a somewhat diversified carnivore that eats fish, crayfish, mussels and young water birds (Fleay, 1949a).

The echidnas (Tachyglossidae) are almost exclusively ant- and termite-feeders, obtaining these with the aid of strong claws and powerful digging limbs. They occupy all latitudes and a wide range of habitats from rocky desert to rain forest and mountains. This is possible in part because of the protective covering of quills, the ability to roll into a ball, and the ability to dig rapidly. One marsupial (*Myrmecobius*, Myrmecobiinae) is also an ant- and termite-eater; it is confined, however, to dry parts of southern Australia where there are fallen logs for shelter.

The ecological counterparts of the echidnas and *Myrmecobius* in Africa are the aardvarks (Tubulidentata) and pangolins (Pholidota), and in Neotropica the Myrmecophagidae (Xenarthra).

Dasyuroidea

(Australia)

The smaller members of this Australian group of 17 genera and 45 species occupy the niches of shrews and weasels, and the larger ones those of terrestrial and arboreal African genets (Viverridae) and larger mongooses, and Holarctic mustelids like *Martes* (Keast, Chapter V). The thylacine (Thylacinidae) is ecologically and structurally a wolf. *Sarcophilus*, the size of a small terrier dog, is a somewhat specialized scavenger with a skull form and heavy peglike premolars convergent with those of *Gulo* (Mustelidae), and *Crocuta* (Hyaenidae). The long-snouted *Myrmecobius* is an ant- and termite-feeder.

The marsupial mole (*Notoryctes*), like the African Chrysochloridae and Holarctic Talpidae, is structurally highly specialized for its subterranean insectivorous way of life. It has a restricted desert range; possibly the peramelids, which obtain some of their prey by digging, in part overlap it ecologically.

Caenolestoidea and Didelphoidea

(Neotropica)

The caenolestoid (paucituberculate) marsupials (3 genera, 7 species—Hershkovitz, Chapter VII) are generalized shrew-like marsupials restricted to the temperate rain forests. They are terrestrial and subsist largely on insects and worms.

The didelphoids, with 11 genera and 53 species (Hershkovitz, Chapter VII), are a diverse group of predominantly rain forest dwellers. Some

(*Lutreolina, Philander, Metachirus*) are superficially weasel-like. The fish-eating aquatic *Chironectes* is the ecological counterpart of an otter, while *Glironia* can be described as the counterpart of a tree-shrew (Hershkovitz, Chapter VII). *Caluromys* is superficially convergent with African galagos, the murine opossums (*Marmosa*) with dwarf lemurs, while *Monodelphis* is vole-like (Hershkovitz, Chapter VII). Too little is known of the diets of most genera to allocate them to ecological categories. Most, however, are definitely omnivorous.

The caenolestoids and the didelphoids represent the survivors of the earliest South American marsupial stocks, both being known as fossils from the Paleocene (Patterson and Pascual, Chapter VI).

Perameloidea

(Australia)

This endemic Australo-Papuan group (8 genera, 19 species) ranges in body size from a rat to a rabbit. The nocturnal perameloids have long snouts and moderately strong, digging forelimbs. They are generally considered omnivorous. Detailed food studies on the Tasmanian species (Heinsohn, 1966), however, show them to live on insects, earthworms, and gastropods, and only seasonally to take other items (berries in this case). The bandicoots are the nearest Australian ecological counterparts of South American armadillos. They have obviously had a long and continuous history on the Australian continent.

Phalangeroidea

(Australia)

The diverse, forest-dwelling phalangers (17 genera, 36 species) range in size from a small mouse to a large cat (Keast, Chapter V). The group is mainly herbivorous and omnivorous. Some genera, however, are almost entirely insectivorous—e.g., the mouse-sized pigmy possums *Cercartetus* and *Eudromicia* (Hickman and Hickman, 1960) and the larger striped possums, *Dactylopsila* and *Dactylonax* (Fleay in Troughton, 1948), which, like the Malagasy lemur *Daubentonia*, have greatly elongated fourth fingers for extracting insects from crevices. Nectar ranks high in the diet of a few Australian phalangers, e.g., the tiny, long-snouted honey phalanger (*Tarsipes*). The largest-bodied group, the tropical cuscuses (*Phalanger*) live on fruits and berries, leaves, large insects, birds, and eggs (Fleay, 1949b). The koala is a highly specialized herbivore, its diet being limited to the leaves of perhaps ten species of *Eucalyptus*. Accordingly, different Australian phalangers occupy the food niches of herbivorous and omnivorous monkeys, herbivorous tree sloths and squirrels, and insectivorous marmosets, pottos, and tree shrews.

The phalangers obviously have had a long and continuous history on the Australian continent and their progressive evolution has been carried out in the absence of competitors. Unfortunately, since the fossil record of Australian mammals does not definitely extend back beyond the beginning of the Miocene (Ride, 1968; Keast, Chapter V), little or nothing is known of intermediate stages.

The terrestrial saltatory kangaroos and wallabies (16 genera, 42 species) range in size from small potoroos about the size of a hare and which inhabit thickets, to 5 to 6 ft-tall plains-dwelling kangaroos. Except for one or two small, primitive forms, the group is exclusively herbivorous. The macropodids, accordingly, are the Australian ecological counterparts of the artiodactyls, perissodactyls and, to some extent, the lagomorphs. The different genera are specialized for life in thickets, forest, woodland, grassland, or on rocky outcrops. One genus, *Dendrolagus,* has secondarily become arboreal. Some living macropodids are largely grazers and some are part browsers, part grazers. It is worth noting that the short-headed sthenurines, which are regarded as a predominantly browsing line, are extinct.

The macropodids were present, as such, at the beginning of the Miocene. Thereafter they underwent progressive differentiation. The greatest dergee of diversification, which included the production of giant short-headed browsers, was achieved in the Pleistocene. They are highly successful today and remain the dominant terrestrial herbivores of the Australian continent.

The wombats (Vombatidae), with 2 genera and 3 species, are moderately large-bodied, quadrupedal, terrestrial herbivores. They shelter by day in burrows and have large, continuously-growing incisors of the rodent type that permit them to eat roots and coarse herbage. Wombats were already well differentiated when they first appeared in the fossil record (mid-Miocene).

Insectivora

(Africa, Neotropica)

The African Insectivora belong to 5 families, 20 genera (8.6% of the total genera), and 94 species (12.6% of total species): otter shrews (Potamogalidae), 2 genera and 3 species; golden moles (Chrysochloridae), 3 and 16; hedgehogs (Erinaceidae), 3 and 6; elephant shrews (Macroscelididae), 5 and 13; and true shrews (Soricidae), 7 and 56 (Bigalke, Chapter IV). The potomogales inhabit forest and feed on aquatic invertebrates. The subterranean golden moles consume earthworms and other invertebrates. The hedgehogs feed mainly on invertebrates but are somewhat omnivorous. The partly saltatorial, kangaroo-like elephant shrews are insectivorous but apparently may also take some plant material (Patterson, 1965). The small soricid shrews are insect eaters and predators.

In the fossil record macroscelids are recognizable from the early Oligocene (Patterson, 1965), and chrysochlorids, potamogalids, soricids, and erinaceids from the early Miocene (Cooke, Chapter III).

Insectivora are somewhat marginal in Neotropica where the only species are recent invaders from North America. The West Indies, however, have distinctive endemic genera. Insectivora are absent from Australia where the small terrestrial "mouse-sized" dasyurids fill their ecological role. The terrestrial shrew niche in Neotropica is filled in part by caenolestids and oxymycterine rodents (Hershkovitz, Chapter VII) and, probably marginally, by opportunistic mammals like the armadillos. Ichthyomyine cricetines utilize the water-shrew niche.

The absence of a mole in the contemporary fauna of South America is surprising in view of the success of the contemporary African chrysochlorids. A "marsupial mole," *Necrolestes,* occurred in the Miocene and apparently died out even though it had no competitors (Patterson, 1958). It represented an interesting case of parallelism with the contemporary Australian marsupial mole (*Notoryctes*). Today, a cricetine rodent, *Blarinomys,* partly fills the mole niche (Hershkovitz, Chapter VII).

Chiroptera

(Africa, Neotropica, Australia)

Africa has 13 genera of Megachiroptera (5.6% of the total mammal genera) and 26 species (3.4% of total); and 8 families, 29 genera (12.3% of total) and 148 species (19.7% of total) of Microchiroptera. Neotropica lacks Megachiroptera, but there is a very diverse fauna of Microchiroptera belonging to 10 families, 80 genera (28.8% of total genera), and 222 species (27.4% of total). Australia has 5 genera (4.3% of the total genera) and 25 species of Megachiroptera (6.9% of total), and 5 families, 16 genera (13.7% of total), and 64 species (17.5% of total) of Microchiroptera.

On each continent the majority of the bats are insectivorous, but there is also a range of fruit, nectar, and pollen eaters, and one or two that are carnivorous on other bats (not yet proven in the case of Africa). The fruit-eating Megachiroptera may have a wingspan of up to 4 ft. In Neotropica the Microchiroptera have moved into the frugivorous niches but they have not evolved the large size of the Megachiroptera. (The largest Neotropical bat, the carnivorous *Vampyrum spectrum,* has a wingspan of about 30 in). One group, the bizarre mouse-sized vampires (Desmodidae), have become blood-suckers. It has been suggested (K. Koopman, pers. commun.) that this group is derived from fruit-eaters that lapped juice. There are also fish-catching bats like *Noctilio leporinus* (Noctilionidae) which use the large recurved claws on their feet for this activity.

Despite similar histories of Tertiary isolation Australia and Neotropica differ with respect to their bat faunas. The Australian bat fauna is characterized by a low level of endemicity (no families and 29% of genera endemic; New Zealand, however, does have one endemic family). The Neotropical bat fauna shows marked endemicity (56% of endemic families and 87% endemic genera, Simpson, 1966). Simpson accounts for the situation in Australia (which he suggests may have involved 20 to 30 colonizations down the island chain from Asia) by the fact that the exchanges were entirely within the same climatic zone. Any south-north movement between or through the Americas would, by contrast, involve the crossing of decidedly different climatic and ecological zones. A more important reason, however, would seem to be that the vast tropical belts of Central America and South America have long been a major center of endemism and radiation for tropical bats. The area of the tropical rain forest belt of Australia and New Guinea is, by contrast, insignificant. It is very possible, of course, that some of the genera shared by Australia and southeast Asia originated in the former.

Bats obviously have had a long history on each of the southern continents. The fossil record is, however, so limited that the evolution of many of the contemporary groups cannot be traced. At the same time, there is no reason to believe necessarily that the chiroptera may have had a Gondwanan origin, as suggested by Hershkovitz (Chapter VII). The Australian bats do not have any South American affinities; rather they represent an attenuation of the oriental fauna.

Primates

(Africa, Neotropica)

Africa has 11 genera and 58 species of Primates (amounting to 4.5% of total genera and 7.8% of total species). Neotropica has 16 genera and 42 species (5.8% of total genera and 5.2% of total species).

Africa has 5 genera and 8 species of nocturnal Prosimii: the slothlike lorisids (Lorisidae) are mainly carnivorous in diet, while the agile galagos (Galagidae), ranging between a mouse and a rabbit in size, are omnivorous. The cercopithecid monkeys (4 genera and about 47 species), are diurnal and feed on leaves, fruit, flowers, and to a limited extent on eggs and other animal foods (Bigalke, Chapter IV). The 5 species of non-forest monkeys include terrestrial and omnivorous baboons. The large chimpanzee and gorilla are omnivorous and herbivorous, respectively.

The Neotropical primates belong to 3 families, one of which is monotypic. The marmosets (Callithricidae), with 4 genera and 15 species, the smallest of living primates, resemble tree squirrels, tree shrews, and the smallest Malagasy lemurs in size and form; they are primarily insectivorous but also eat small birds, mammals, lizards, eggs, and large quantities of fruit (Hershkovitz, Chapter VII). The lion marmoset, *Leontopithecus rosalia,* has a "long slender arm, narrow palm, and elongate middle fingers for digging insects and grubs from under loose bark and from cracks or holes" (Hershkovitz, Chapter VII, p. 380), an adaptation somewhat reminiscent of the elongated "digging fingers" of *Dactylopsila* and *Daubentonia.* The Cebidae (11 genera, 26 species) range from small predominantly insectivorous species to large omnivorous or herbivorous ones.

The New World platyrrhine and Old World catarrhine monkeys have evolved to roughly the same evolutionary level. There are, however, no terrestrial platyrrhines and no prehensile-tailed catarrhines, and South America has developed no counterparts of the pongids. With only one exception, the platyrrhines, like the Old World monkeys, are diurnal. The more primitive primates like the pottos, galagos, tarsiers, and various lemurs, by contrast, are nocturnal.

Primates occur in the early Oligocene both in Africa and South America, presumably, in the latter case, arriving as waif immigrants from North America. Some authorities suggest direct colonization from Africa (Chapters II and VII); others, however, disagree (Chapters II and VI).

Pholidota and Tubulidentata

(Africa)

These two groups constitute the African "anteaters." The pangolins (Pholidota) are African and Asian, and have 4 species in Africa, 2 of which are arboreal and 2 terrestrial. They have elongated muzzles, long retractable tongues, and strong digging claws. The surviving monotypic aardvark (Tubulidentata) is a large, burrowing animal.

There are no pholidotids in the African fossil record and they may have arived during the Pliocene. The aardvarks are almost certainly an endemic group, with a long history on the continent prior to the first fossil record in the early Miocene (Cooke, Chapter III). At least four lineages are present in the late Tertiary, one of which is Madagascan (B. Patterson, pers. commun.).

Edentata (Xenarthra)

(Neotropica)

The contemporary Neotropical edentates fall into three distinctive families that represent the terminal members of long evolutionary lines (see Patterson and Pascual, Chapter VI). The anteaters (Myrmecophagidae), with 3 genera and 3 species, are known from the Miocene. The leaf-eating tree sloths (Bradypodidae), 2 genera and 3 species, are known only from the Recent, but belong to a group that extends back to the early Oligocene. The armadillos (Dasypodidae), with 9 genera and 20 species in the existing fauna, are known from the Paleocene. The living armadillos, which range up to small pig size, are generalized and opportunistic feeders, taking insects, worms, berries, and carrion.

Lagomorpha

(Africa, Neotropica)

Africa has 2 genera and 10 species of lagomorphs (accounting for 0.8% and 1.3% of the total genera and species, respectively). Neotropica has only 2 species of rabbits, the endemic *Sylvilagus brasiliensis* and the boreal North American *S. floridanus*, restricted to the far north (Hershkovitz,

Chapter VII). Hershkovitz makes the interesting observation that the latter species replaces the former wherever they meet and that, in Patagonia, *S. brasiliensis* stops abruptly at the boundary of suitable habitats occupied by the hare-like cavies *Dolichotis* and *Pediolagus,* and other leporine-like caviomorphs. Ochotonid lagomorphs appear in the African fossil record in the early Miocene but became extinct on the continent by the end of that period. Leporids appear in the early Pliocene record presumably as invaders from the Holarctic (Cooke, Chapter III), where they are known as far back as the late Eocene (Wood, 1957). The contemporary African lagomorph fauna is made up of rock hares (*Pronolagus*), three species of which occupy hilly terrain; the "Bunyoro rabbit" (*Poelagus*) in forest country; the Bushman hare (*Bunolagus*) in arid South Africa; and true hares (*Lepus*), 5 species, occupying open habitats (Bigalke, Chapter IV).

The success of the European rabbit (*Oryctolagus cuniculus*) in Australia, following its establishment in 1859, provides an example of the adaptive superiority of an animal that had evolved in the highly competitive background of a large continent, over comparably adapted members of an isolated insular fauna. Along with sheep, it drastically changed habitats by eliminating the cover on which the native Australia mammals depended. In this changed habitat, but also in natural areas, the rabbit used its phenomenal reproductive capacity (commonly more than 4 litters a year with 6 to 8 young per litter, compared to 2 young per year in the case of the smaller macropodids) to build up a population estimated at hundreds of millions by 1950. One of the significant aspects of the fertility of the rabbit is its ability to recover rapidly from droughts. The native marsupials (small macropodids and bandicoots like *Macrotis* and *Choeropus*) could not persist in the degraded habitat. A survey by Marlow (1958) has shown that 51% of the marsupials of New South Wales have become extinct since 1910, almost all of them inhabitants of the woodland-grassland belt where the rabbit is most common.

Some measure of biological control of the rabbit has been achieved by introduction of the virus disease, myxomatosis, which is epizootic in *Sylvilagus brasiliensis* (Ratcliffe, 1959).

Rodentia

(Africa, Neotropica, Australia)

Africa has 14 families of rodents, 73 genera (31.4% of the total genera), and 227 species (30.4% of total). Neotropica has 17 families, 112 genera (40.2% of total genera), and 378 species (46.6%). Australia has one family, 31 genera (26.5% of total), and 124 species (34.1%). The richness of the larger continents stems from there being more than one faunal stratum on each, an older one of distinctive endemics, and one or more of recent immigrants (Neotropica has two clear faunal strata; Africa since the Miocene appears to have received several immigrant groups at various times).

The South American "old endemics," the Caviomorpha, were already recognizable in the early Oligocene (Deseadan fauna) as 5 families and 4 superfamilies (Wood and Patterson, 1959).

Most authors have accepted a North American origin for the ancestral caviomorphs. Recent data on sea-floor spreading, suggesting that South America and Africa were connected until the Cretaceous, has produced some support for the alternative theory, that they had an African origin (discussions in Chapters II, VI, VII, and above). Patterson and Pascual (Chapter VI) suggest that, on anatomical evidence, the African and Neotropical "hystricomorph" rodents are probably not very closely related.

In Africa the "old endemics" are known as far back as the beginning of the Oligocene (Phiomyidae). The surviving families Thryonomyidae and Petromuridae are surely of phiomyid ancestry. The endemic Pedetidae and Anomaluridae are probably of African origin. The Ctenodactylidae are immigrants from Asia that appear in Africa towards the end of Miocene time, and the Bathyergidae, now endemic to Africa and known from early Miocene time, may possibly be of Asiatic origin as well. The Cricetinae and Sciuridae are recorded in the late Miocene and Pliocene of Africa. There are no Tertiary records of murids and hystricids (Lavocat, 1967). *Hystrix* is known from the Late Miocene or Early Pliocene of north Africa.

There are various collections of small mammals, mostly rodents and insectivores, from the African Miocene that have yet to be classified (H. B. S. Cooke, pers. commun.). Likewise Pleistocene rodents from South America require much additional work (B. Patterson, pers. commun.).

In both continents the "old groups" persist in a wide range of morphological types and utilize a diversity of ecological niches. The old African groups belong to five families and the South American caviomorphs to 13 families (11 in Patterson and Pascual, Chapter VI). Significantly, however, most of these families are now reduced to relics with just a few (often highly successful) terminal forms. The African Pedetidae and Petromuridae are monotypic; the Rhizomyidae and Thryonomyidae are represented each by one genus and two species (Bigalke, Chapter IV). Within the caviomorphs the Hydrochoeridae, Dinomyidae, Abrocomidae, Myocastoridae and Ctenomyidae (the last two are regarded as subfamilies of the Echimyidae and Octodontidae, respectively, by Patterson and Pascual, Chapter VI), are represented by single species, and the Erethizontidae, Dasyproctidae, Chinchillidae, and the Antillean Heptaxodontidae, each by three monotypic genera.

African murines (sensu strictu) are first known in the African fossil record in the Pleistocene but possibly arrived from Eurasia as early as the beginning of the Pliocene (Cooke, Chapter III). They were preceded by cricetines which are known as late Miocene fossils. Unfortunately, the considerable gaps in the African fossil record, particularly in the Pliocene, do not permit us to say to what extent there was a usurpation of cricetine roles by murines after the arrival of the latter.

The precise time of arrival of the second stratum of rodents in South America is a matter of disagreement. Patterson and Pascual, drawing on fossil data, place it as late Pliocene, the time of completion of the land bridge (see Chapter VI). Thus, cricetines are absent from Miocene and earlier Pliocene deposits containing rich faunas of rodents. The first cricetines appear in late Pliocene deposits in Argentina simultaneously with the first large North American mammals. Hershkovitz (Chapter VII), on the other hand, argues strongly that, because of the degree of differentiation achieved by cricetines in South America, entry must have been earlier: he suggests adventitious colonization by the first groups no later than the Miocene. The well-known capacity of some rodents to cross water gaps, and the fact that procyonids apparently reached South America in the Miocene could be interpreted as supporting Hershkovitz's convictions. Patterson and Pascual (Chapter VI) suggest that the major groups and most of the genera had already differentiated in tropical North America prior to the formation of the land bridge, in what is now Central America, and that from there they colonized South America. They note that the first (late Pliocene) deposits in the South American pampas contain a fair proportion of the distinctive genera, supporting the idea that they had already differentiated before arriving on the continent. The date of the initial cricetine colonization of South America must remain an open question at present.

Simpson (1961) has given a Miocene date for the first wave of "island-hopping" murine colonizers of Australia. The first fossils are, however, in the New Guinea Pliocene (Plane, 1967), and a late Pliocene fossil assemblage in southern Victoria has so far revealed no fossil rodents (Lundelius and Turnbull, 1967). It is not until the Pleistocene that rodents are abundant. In view of this and their relatively minor differentiation in Australia (one or two endemic subfamilies and various endemic genera) a Pliocene colonization date is more reasonable. At the same time, the existence of these endemic genera would tend to confirm that much of the generic evolution in South American rodents may be Pliocene and post-Pliocene.

The "old rodent" fauna of Africa includes the squirrel-like *Petromus* (Petromuridae), the large *Thryonomys* (Thryonomyidae), the rabbit-sized saltatorial *Pedetes* (Pedetidae), and the Anomaluridae, with their resemblances to flying squirrels. The members of the "second stratum" include the highly specialized subterranean mole rats (Bathyergidae) that feed on roots and tubers (Pienaar, 1964), and the ctenodactylids that resemble hyraxes both in form and ecology (Bigalke, Chapter IV). The South American caviomorphs are exceedingly diverse morphologically and ecologically, ranging from the size of ground squirrels to the 30-inch-long boar-like capybara (*Hydrochoerus*) whose "food niche" is suggestive of that of an African hippopotamus (K. Koopman, pers. commun.). Different groups of caviomorphs suggest North American pikas, African hyracoids, pocket gophers, and jack rabbits; the long-legged aguti (*Dasy-*

procta) suggests an African pigmy antelope (Hershkovitz, Chapter VII). The forest-dwelling echymyids (spiny rats) have radiated into about 44 species and the 8 species of porcupines include specialized rain forest types.

Since their establishment, the muroids of Africa, Neotropica, and Australia have radiated in spectacular fashion. Today Africa has 43 genera of muroids (18.8% of the total genera) and 151 species (20.0%). Neotropica has 51 genera (18.3%) and 223 species (27.5%). These represent three groups: "old South American" cricetines, 42 genera; Recent (?Pleistocene land-bridge) peromyscines, 8 genera (only 2 of which get into northern South America); and microtines, one genus (P. Hershkovitz, pers. commun.). Australia, whose faunas have been built up both by colonization and radiation within the continent, has 31 genera (26.5%) and 124 species 34.1%). African murines range in size from small mice to the giant rat (*Cricetomys*), with a head and body length of 16 inches. Most of the generalized "rats and mice" live in woodland, savannah, and desert; they have not, in contrast with Neotropical counterparts, radiated in rain forest to any extent (Bigalke, Chapter IV). The Neotropical cricetines, which comprise 10 to 12 radiating aggregations or clusters of species are discussed by Hershkovitz (Chapter VII). Different groups are convergent in body form and ecology with Nearctic wood rats (*Neotoma*), gerbils, voles, gophers, and small hares, while oxymycterines are shrew-like, feeding largely on earthworms, grubs, and small crustaceans. In the absence of moles, one genus (*Blarinomys*) has become mole-like. The ichthyomyine group comprises species of otter-like or insectivore-like fisheaters adapted for stream life.

In the Australian rodents only two endemic subfamilies have evolved. The carnivorous Hydromyinae, some of which are adapted for aquatic life, include a few shrew-like forms (e.g., *Microhydromys*), and have diversified mostly in New Guinea; the "Pseudomyinae" (see Simpson, 1961) are Australian. The other rodents are typical Murinae. Some Australian desert species, like their counterparts in North America, Africa and South America, have become independent of exogenous water (MacMillan and Lee, 1967; Koford ,1968).

The Sciuridae have radiated into 7 genera (2.9% of the total fauna), and 31 species (4.1%) in Africa since their arrival in the early Pliocene. In South America, where they have certainly been since the Pleistocene, and possibly from the Miocene (Hershkovitz, Chapter VII), 5 genera (1.8% of the fauna), with 18 species (2.2% of the fauna) are recognized by Hershkovitz (Chapter VII). The two faunas are comparable in that tree squirrels represent a dominant arboreal group of forest herbivores. Africa has terrestrial squirrels.

To sum up, rodents are the only mammalian group (apart from bats) that have radiated on all of the three southern continents and hence offer an oportunity for a three-way comparison. Africa and Neotropica have older strata showing that colonization occurred early in the Tertiary and by the Oligocene the rodents had undergone radiation; all three continents have Pliocene-Pleistocene strata or, in the case of South America, possibly Miocene-Pliocene strata (Hershkovitz, Chapter VII). The older groups on the larger continents are represented in the contemporary faunas by a diversity of families: most are relicts and are now represented by one or two, or a relatively few, species—although these, like the African *Pedetes,* may be numerous and successful. (The Neotropical echimyids, with about 40 species, are an exception.) The "old rodents" of Africa and Neotropica occupy a wide range of niches; the newer muroids tend to occupy the "typical rodent" adaptive zone, although they overlap the other groups to some extent. In Africa and Neotropica some older lines are convergent with hyracoids and lagomorphs. Africa has the fossorial mole rats. The Neotropical caviomorphs have succeeded in entering the "ungulate" adaptive zone. (There was a wider range of very large caviomorphs in the Pliocene than today.) The late evolution of large-bodied rodents in South America apparently occurred coincidentally with a progressive reduction in the number of native ungulate groups during the Miocene. Their ecology was presumably somewhat intermediate between that of muroids and that of ungulates. The "old rodents" of Africa and Neotropica have also produced some comparable body forms (Simpson, 1962).

"Typical rats and mice" (Cricetinae and Murinae) have undergone a late radiation on each of the continents. The group now accounts for 18.8% of genera of mammals in Africa, 18.3% in Neotropica, and 26.5% in Australia. In terms of proportion, muroid species represent 20.0%, 27.5% and 34.1%, respectively, of each continent's total fauna. The continents differ in that Africa has a combined fauna of cricetines, which arrived in the Miocene (49 species of gerbils, 2 species of cricetines, sensu strictu), and 82 species of murines—all of which are not recorded in the fossil record before the Pleistocene but could have arrived in the Pliocene (Cooke, Chapter III). Neotropica, on the other hand, has only cricetines, while Australia has only murines and their derivatives.

Carnivora

(Africa, Neotropica, Australia)

The Canidae have 5 genera (amounting to 2.0% of the total genera) and 11 species (1.4%) in Africa, and 7 genera (2.5%) and 13 species (1.6%) in South America. Australia has one species, *Canis familiaris dingo,* introduced by aboriginal man.

The African canids fall into three groups: omnivorous foxes (*Vulpes, Fennecus, Otocyon*) that eat invertebrates, small vertebrates, berries, etc.; somewhat larger jackals that live on small and medium-sized vertebrates, invertebrates, carrion, and minor quantities of vegetable matter (Shortridge, 1934; Stevenson-Hamilton, 1957; Grafton, 1965; Bigalke, Chapter IV); and the hunting dog (*Lycaon*), a large-bodied pack hunter that preys almost exclusively on gazelles. The morphologically diverse Neotropical canids include the shortest-legged and the longest-legged members of the family. The rain-forest-dwelling *Speothos* has a forelimb-spine ratio of 51-54% (Hildebrand, 1952), and "hunts in packs and swims with otter-like ease" (Hershkovitz, Chapter VII, p. 390). The stilt-legged, 4-ft-long savannah-dwelling maned wolf, *Chrysocyon,* has a forelimb-spine ratio of 89-96% (Hildebrand, 1952). *Speothos* is omnivorous; *Chrysocyon,* the largest canid, subsists on rabbits, rodents, frogs, birds, and some fruit (Walker and Paradiso, 1968). Other Neotropical canids are coyote-like in appearance, food, and habits (*Dusicyon, Lycalopex*), while the long-legged Andean fox (*Cerdocyon*) is jackal-like, and the pampas gray fox, *Pseudo-lopex,* is chiefly a rodent feeder (Hershkovitz, pers. commun.). Neotropica differs from Africa in having specialized rain-forest species (*Speothos, Atelocynus*), and in lacking a large predatory form corresponding to the African *Lycaon,* the Holarctic wolf, and the Australian marsupial *Thyla-cinus.* The large borhyenids that served this predatory role died out in the Pliocene ahead of the arrival of the North American Pleistocene dire wolf (*Aenocyon*), that enjoyed a brief period in Peru and elsewhere (Patterson and Pascual, Chapter VI).

Canids have been in Africa since at least early Miocene (Cooke, Chapter III) and presumably in South America since the formation of the Middle American land bridge. Most of the Neotropical canid genera are quite similar to North American ones, if Miocene genera be included (B. Patterson, pers. commun.). The latest canids to reach South America are the gray fox (*Urocyon*), which Hershkovitz (Chapter VII) suggests may actually be a Middle American autochthon that spread simultaneously south and north, and the coyote, *Canis latrans,* which now occurs as far south as Costa Rica.

The strictly carnivorous Felidae are equally developed in Africa (2 genera—3 if *Panthera* be admitted, 10 species) and Neotropica (3 genera, 10 species). In both continents there is a full range of size forms, with species ranging from that of a domestic cat to the largest of the contemporary carnivores (lion and leopard in Africa; jaguar and puma in South America). The smaller cats prey largely on small rodents and birds, the large ones on ungulates. Most species have their own special prey. African felids are predominantly savannah forms. The long-legged cheetah (*Acinonyx*) which has forsaken the usual "crouch and lie in wait" method of hunting for running down the prey, is unique. Neotropica has no counterparts of the lion, *Felis leo.* Felids are known from the early Miocene in Africa (Cooke, Chapter III). They presumably entered South America with the formation of the Panamanian land bridge in the late Pliocene.

The Mustelidae have 7 genera and 7 species in Africa, and 9 genera and 15 species in Neotropica. They are first known in the African fossil record in the middle of the Pliocene but aparently entered the continent from Eurasia at the beginning of that period (Cooke, Chapter III). Contemporary genera include *Mellivora* (honey badger), otters (*Lutra,*

Aonyx), and the long-bodied weasel-like *Poecilogale* and *Poecilictis*, and the skunk-like *Ictonyx*. The first recorded mustelid in the South American fossil record is a skunk from the Montehermosan of the late Pliocene (Patterson and Pascual, Chapter VI). The contemporary fauna includes otters, weasels, skunks, and the martin-like *Eira*.

The African Viverridae (18 genera, 37 species) apparently entered Africa from Eurasia at the end of the Oligocene (Cooke, Chapter III). Fifteen of the 18 contemporary genera are confined to the continent (Bigalke, Chapter IV). There are several different lines of specialization with the genets and their relatives (Viverrinae) accounting for 4 genera and 12 to 14 species, and the mongooses (Herpestinae) accounting for about 13 genera and 22 species. The Paradoxurinae is represented by the nocturnal tree civet, which consumes rodents and vegetable matter for the most part.

Bigalke (Chapter IV) reviews the ecology and radiation of the Viverrinae and Herpestinae in detail. Genets are mainly nocturnal and are essentially or completely carnivorous, being predatory on rodents and roosting birds; they also consume eggs and, possibly, berries and other vegetable material. They are common in forested areas, woodlands, and savannah. The rare Congo forest dwelling *Osbornictis*, however, is aquatic and largely a fish-eater. The large terrestrial civet (*Viverra*) consumes a variety of invertebrates, small vertebrates, eggs, fruits, berries, etc. The mongooses are morphologically generalized, largely terrestrial, and diurnal inhabitants of the arid and savannah zones. Differences in feeding habits are partly a function of size, the largest species (*Herpestes ichneumon* and *Ichneumia albicauda*) living partly on hares and guinea fowl, whereas the smaller ones take insects and, to a limited extent, reptiles, birds, small rodents, and eggs.

The interrelationships between the Viverridae (an African-Oriental group) and Mustelidae, their structural and ecological counterparts in the northern continents, is interesting. Both groups are obviously highly efficient, aggressive, and opportunistic, and have succeeded in the "competitive backgrounds" of large continental areas. Viverrids reached Africa at the end of the Oligocene, presumably from Eurasia (Cooke, Chapter III), the mustelids (also from Eurasia) not until the early Pliocene. The former (including genets, mongooses, etc.) are the dominant "medium-sized" terrestrial and arboreal carnivores and omnivores of Africa, and in this general area they have diversified greatly. The late-arriving mustelids have apparently been unable to make any real headway in this adaptive zone against the viverrids (this is also largely true of the Oriental region). There are no martin-like or fisher-like mustelids in Africa, and the two genera of weasels are specialized forms. (Hyenas, of course, are the counterparts of the scavenging wolverine, *Gulo*.) Most of the African mustelids occupy niches from which the viverrids are largely absent, e.g., those of the honey badger and aquatic otters. It is possible that mustelids have proven the more successful in the aquatic role. The only truly aquatic viverrid, the Congo forest-dwelling and fish-eating *Osbornictis,* is very rare, and there is one mongoose (*Atilax*) which is semi-aquatic. (The potamogales or water-shrews constitute a small-bodied but old African group; they feed largely on invertebrates and presumably would also be competitors of any of the more generalized viverrids tending to assume a more aquatic role.)

It is also significant that the mustelids, despite being in Africa since the early Pliocene, have not radiated at the species level; there are 7 genera and 7 species (excluding Palearctic forms confined to the far north of the continent).

The Procyonidae of Neotropica represent a series of distinctive elements. Some apparently arrived in this southern continent as waif colonizers in the Miocene. Of the fossil genera (*Cyonasua* group) *Cyonasua* was rather generalized and *Chapalmalania* had the dimensions of a bear (Patterson and Pascual, Chapter VI). The contemporary fauna includes typical raccoons (*Procyon*), terrestrial carnivores, gregarious and omnivorous coatis (*Nasua*), which also get most of their food (fruit, insects, mollusks) from the ground, and the olingo (*Bassarycion*) which Hershkovitz (Chapter VII) likens ecologically to a nocturnal fox. The kinkajou (*Potos*) is nocturnal and morphologically lemuroid: it exploits the ecological niche worked during the day by the prehensile-tailed cebids. The nocturnal cacomistle (*Bassariscus*) is "nocturnal and cat-like in form, diet, and arboreal habits" (Hershkovitz, Chapter VII).

The Neotropical region has a single ursid, the Andean-dwelling *Tremarctos* which is the smallest and most arboreal member of the family. It is a surviving relict of a North American genus that presumably entered the continent after completion of the land bridge.

Neotropica lacks any counterpart of the African Hyaenidae, large-bodied scavengers and hunters with exceptionally massive jaws and teeth for crushing bone. The Protelidae of Africa, represented by the monotypic *Proteles,* are largely termite feeders. Like the hyenas, to which it is related, it is mainly a savannah form.

To sum up, Africa with 35 genera and 69 species, has a slightly more diverse fauna of Carnivora than Neotropica (26 genera and 47 species). The continents differ in the particular families that occur in each and, where families are shared, in the extent to which they have radiated and in the diversity of morphological types produced. This means that the many carnivore niches and feeding zones are differently divided up on the two continents. In addition, it is apparent that Africa, with its vast areas of savannah and its diversity of prey species, has several carnivore niches not available in contemporary South America. The latter, for example, has no large running carnivores comparable to the African hunting dog, *Lycaon,* the cheetah, *Acinonyx,* or large-bodied scavengers. It is interesting to note that the Australian dasyuroids, that fill the carnivore (and, in part, the insectivore) niche on that continent, have produced a series of size and structural counterparts of weasels, genet or martin, the wolf, and a somewhat different but equivalent animal to the wolverine and hyena. This indicates that the carnivore adaptive zones or ways of life are roughly equivalent on the three continents.

Hyracoidea and Proboscidea

(Africa)

These two groups are old African elements, being well-represented in the Fayum Oligocene. Both had early radiations. Three genera and 11 species make up the contemporary hyracoids. Two of the genera are social rock dwellers and the other a non-social tree-dweller; all are herbivorous, but occasionally insects are eaten (Sale, 1965). The proboscidians are represented by the very successful *Loxodonta,* an adaptable and highly diversified browser and grazer.

The continued success of these groups in Africa in the face of successive invaders and more newly evolved forms is interesting. The hyracoids were most diversified in the Oligocene, the 6 genera and 24 species including "giant" forms (Cooke, Chapter III). Subsequently, in the rock-dwelling habitat that is occupied by most contemporary species they have obviously withstood the impact of successive groups of rodent competitors (e.g., Petromuridae, Ctenodactylidae), early lagomorphs (the picas, a group which is now extinct in Africa although still extant in the Holarctic region), and later lagomorphs—the rock hares (*Pronolagus*). All these groups have food and cover requirements similar to the rock-dwelling hyraxes and it says a lot for the versatility of this group that it has been able to maintain high population levels despite these competitors. The proboscideans remained a diversified group in Africa throughout the latter half of the Tertiary and the Pleistocene.

South American Ungulates

There are three species of tapir (mostly allopatric), two peccaries, four camelids (only two of which are wild), and eleven species of deer constituting the ungulate fauna of Neotropica. The deer are partly separated on the basis of habitat: there are predominantly forest, woodland, and grassland species. These large herbivores are the survivors of a much richer Pleistocene fauna that included, in addition, a number of extinct groups of northern ancestry and some surviving old South American faunas.

African Artiodactyla and Perissodactyla

The contemporary African ungulates are comprised of 5 equid species (largely allopatric in range), 2 rhinoceroses, 3 suids (all that remain of a rich Pleistocene fauna), 2 hippos, one tragulid, 2 giraffes, and 78 bovid species. The rhinocerotids, suids, tragulids, and bovids probably colonized the continent from Eurasia or Asia at the end of the Oligocene, the equids and giraffids at the end of the Miocene (Cooke, Chapter III).

Camels are known at the beginning of the Pleistocene. Today Africa alone maintains a rich and diversified large herbivore fauna similar to that present in North America and South America during the Pleistocene. Bigalke (Chapter IV) provides a detailed account of the distribution and general ecology of contemporary bovids.

Considerable evolutionary and ecological interest lies in unravelling the specializations of the large African herbivores and the mechanisms that permit the continent to support so many species. For this reason, and to further highlight the differences between the African and Neotropical large herbivore faunas the writer develops this subject (a review of which will be published at a later date) further than Bigalke has done. In brief, the mechanisms are as follows:

(1) *Habitat specialization.* Different vegetation formations commonly have distinct groups of species. Thus, in Nigeria (Fig. 2; see also data from Rosevear, 1953), the Sahel Savannah, Sudanese Savannah, Guinea Savannah, tropical rain (along with montane) forests, and rivers and marshes, are populated by distinct groups of large herbivore species.

(2) *The occupation of different sub-zones within a vegetation formation.* In the woodlands of Zambia the oribi (*Ourebia ourebi*) inhabits dambos (grassy drainage channels), Sharpe's grysbok (*Raphicerus sharpei*) inhabits thick grassy and scrubby sections, and the klipspringer (*Oreotragus oreotragus*) inhabits rocky outcrops (Ansell, 1960).

(3) *Duplication of faunas in equivalent vegetation formations or life zones in the south and north of the continent.* There are distinct Saharan, Somali Arid, and Kalahari-Karoo groups of species, for example.

(4) *Specialization for feeding at different levels.* The giraffe (*Giraffa camelopardalis*) is the highest feeder (up to 18 ft), the gerenuk (*Litocranius walleri*) is a relatively high feeder (4 to 8 ft), the kudu (*Tragelaphus strepsiceros*) feeds at intermediate levels (3 to 6 ft), and so on. There is a large number of grazing species. The warthog (*Phacochoerus aethiopicus*) obtains a proportion of its food (tubers and roots) below ground.

(5) *Specialization for grazing as opposed to browsing.* Most species, however, combine the two in varying proportions.

(6) *Development of food preferences.* Some degree of preference in choice of plants or growth stage may be exercised (see Talbot and Talbot, 1962). Commonly, however, there is a considerable degree of overlap in the range of food plants eaten (Lamprey, 1963; Van Zyl, 1965).

(7) *Seasonal patterns of environmental utilization.* The excellent survey of the Rukwa Valley fauna by Vesey-Fitzgerald (1950) brings out that elephant and buffalo feed, at different seasons, in the woodland, flood plain, drainage channels, etc., changing their diet as they do so. Other species (e.g., topi) follow different routines, while others (e.g., giraffe) feed in the same area all year.

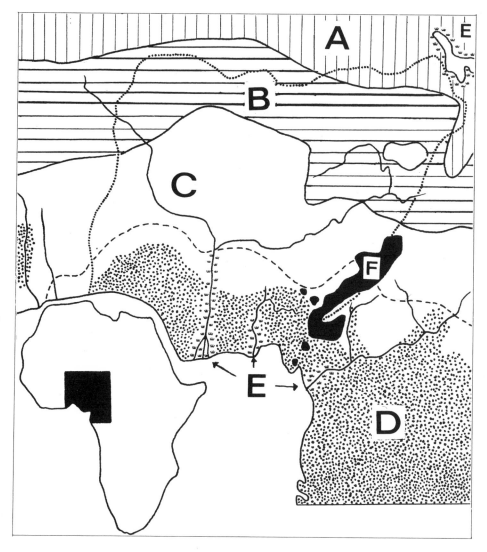

FIG. 2. Types of Vegetation and Distribution of Artiodactyls in West Africa

Rainfall and vegetation belts lie in broad east-west bands. While some large herbivores range through several of these zones, others closely follow the limits of one or another of them: The Sahel Savannah (A) is populated by the dama gazelle (Gazella dama), dorcas gazelle (G. dorcas), and white oryx (Oryx dammah); the Sudanese Savannah (B) by the Senegal hartebeeste (Damaliscus korrigum), red-fronted gazelle (Gazella rufifrons), and kob (Adenota kob); the Guinea Savannah (C) by the western hartebeeste (Alcelaphus buselaphus), red-flanked duiker (Cephalophus rufilatus), and giant eland (Taurotragus derbianus); the tropical rain forest (D) and montane forest (F) by about 7 species of duikers (Cephalophus callipygus, C. dorsalis, C. jentinki, C. leucogaster, C. niger, C. silvicultor, C. zebra), the water chevrotain (Hyemoschus aquaticus), and red river hog (Potamochoerus larvatus); and the rivers and marshes (E) by the hippopotamus (Hippopotamus amphibius), and sitatunga (Limnotragus spekii).

Specialization to habitat is one of the mechanisms enabling Africa to support such a diverse fauna of large herbivores. (Based on distributional data in Rosevear, 1953.)

(8) *Extensive seasonal migrations.* These may entail journeys of hundreds of miles so that different parts of the species range are utilized at different times of the year. This is seen in Saharan antelopes like the addax (Gillet, 1967), in Kalahari species (e.g., Eloff, 1959), and in East African grassland wildebeeste (Talbot and Talbot, 1963).

In effect, the patterns of environmental utilization in the African ungulates are complex and sophisticated, and nothing similar is seen in contemporary ungulate faunas elsewhere, except possibly in the Oriental region. Individually, none of the adaptations is unique—e.g., similar habitat specializations are seen in Australian macropodids (see Calaby, 1966). The present integrated pattern of balanced relationships, however, obviously reflects a long evolutionary history under relatively equable environmental conditions. I suspect that in Recent Africa we are seeing what was the rule during the Tertiary in other continents.

THE DEVELOPMENT OF BALANCE IN FAUNAS

The present synthesis provides opportunity for the discussion of two fundamental questions: (1) how do the proportions of species occupying the various basic mammalian adaptive zones ("ecological categories") on the three continents compare; and (2) are these in a state of "balance" with each other on each of the continents?

As used by paleontologists, "balance" is a term that is applied to continental faunas (it has been used especially with respect to the northern continents) to contrast them to the nature of island faunas (unbalanced). Continents have the full range of insectivores, carnivores, and herbivores; islands, however, despite a measure a radiation, have characteristically only achieved an unbalanced sample of these. Both Australia and South America and, presumably, Africa were unbalanced in the insular sense at the beginning of the Tertiary; subsequently, from dissimilar and randomly selected stocks, they built up highly diversified faunas. In the case of South America the evolving fauna of marsupial insectivores and carnivores, archaic ungulates, and ancestral edentates was later supplemented by rodents, primates, and one or two other stocks. Australia achieved a balance with marsupials alone—at least until the arrival of rodents in the Pliocene. Africa had a more complex history. Initially it must have achieved a state of "balance" with creodonts, primates, primitive insectivores, and an assortment of archaic ungulate stocks. With each major inroad of new forms from outside, the balance would have been upset and a new state, with a new combination of mammal types would have been achieved.

Apart from colonizations from outside, major periods of extinction and the evolution of more efficient ecological types within the continent would have had widespread effects and initiated widespread adjustments.

As noted, despite the very different faunas of the three continents and their different histories, ecological equivalents or counterparts (in the food sense) are readily recognizable; e.g., the Australian arboricolous phalangers occupy the same range of "food niches" as do the Neotropical and African monkeys. Commonly, these counterparts can also be recognized (at least in part) on morphological criteria—note the tendency towards long snouts and digging forelimbs in small to medium-sized terrestrial omnivores (armadillos, Australian bandicoots), the repeated development of a fossorial type of body form, diagnostic nature of dentition, etc.

The present comparison, which admittedly is capable of refinement and elaboration, has been developed both on the basis of structure and on published data concerning food habits and general ecology of the groups. Fourteen ecological catagories or divisions have been set up (Table 5). These form the basis of natural groupings, e.g., "terrestrail omnivores," "anteaters," "large terrestrail herbivores," which tend to have a range of morphological attributes in common.

The basic food data on which the table is based come from Bigalke (Chapter IV), Keast (Chapter V), Hershkovitz (Chapter VII), and a variety of reference works and journals including Shortridge (1934), Ansell (1960), and the *East African Wild Life Journal,* for Africa; Pearson (1951) and Walker and Paradiso (1968), for Neotropica; and Jones (1923, 1924, 1925), and Troughton (1948), for Australia. Results of the analysis by ecological categories are as follows:

Small terrestrial insect eaters and predators. This category makes up 7.4% of the genera and 10.0% of the species in Africa; 2.1% of the genera and 2.2% of the species in Neotropica, and 8.6% of the genera and 9.3% of the species in Australia. The groups filling this role are: Africa—soricids, erinaceids, and macroscelidids; Australia—the smaller dasyures (Phascogalinae of older classifications); Neotropica—caenolestids, a few of the smaller didelphids, and cricetines of the genus *Oxymycterus* (Hershkovitz, Chapter VII).

The high figures for Africa result partly from the very rich fauna of soricids (7 genera and 56 species), and it is obvious that this family is very diversified. There is a fair level of allopatry. Nevertheless, the figures are not unduly out of line with those for Australia, where a diversity of small dasyurid marsupials occupy this adaptive zone. The real incongruity surrounds Neotropica. Soricids barely penetrate South America, and although there is a range of small-bodied insectivorous marsupials, these are much fewer than in Australia. It is probable, accordingly, that a variety of omnivorous rodents (plus, of course, the larger-bodied armadillos) penetrate this adaptive zone. The study of the food ecology of South American rodents is still in its infancy.

Fossorial mole-like insectivores. In Africa 1.3% of genera and 2.1% of species come into this category: less than 1% do so in the case of Australia where only the monotypic marsupial *Notoryctes* occupies the adaptive zone. Neotropica lacks mole-like insect-eaters although a marsupial "mole," *Necrolestes,* occurred in the Miocene. In their absence a few

TABLE 5

Genera and species occupying major adaptive zones: Africa, Neotropica, and Australia compared

	Africa		Neotropica		Australia	
	Genus (Total No. 231)	*Species (Total No. 744)*	*Genus (Total No. 278)*	*Species (Total No. 810)*	*Genus (Total No. 117)*	*Species (Total No. 364)*
Small insect-eaters and predators (shrews, etc.)	17 7.4	78 10.0	6 2.1 + oxymycterine rodents	18 2.2	10 8.6	34 9.3
Fossorial moles	3 1.3	16 2.1	nil	nil	1 0.8	1 0.3
Rodents occupying the mole niche	nil	nil	one species of *Blarinomys*		nil	nil
Specialized ant and termite feeders	3 1.3	6 0.8	3 1.1	3 0.4	3 2.6	4 1.1
Small to medium-sized terrestrial omnivores	13 5.4	28 3.7	17 6.1	31 3.8	9 7.6	20 5.5
Typical muroid rodents	46 20.0	159 21.1	51 18.3	223 27.5	31 26.5	124 34.1

Misc. rodents, non-muroid	5 *2.1*	21 *2.8*	36 *12.9*	102 *12.6*	nil	nil
Rabbit-sized herbivores	12 *5.0*	30 *4.0*	12 *4.3*	17 *2.1*	4 *3.4*	7 *1.9*
Medium to large terrestrial herbivores	40 *16.7*	95 *12.5*	13 *4.7*	23 *2.8*	12 *10.3*	32 *8.8*
Fossorial herbivores (under-ground feeding)	4 *1.7*	15 *2.0*	*Ctenomys partly occupies this adaptive zone*		nil	nil
Arboreal herbivores, omni-vores and insect eaters	19 *7.8*	93 *12.3*	32 *11.5*	106 *13.1*	18 *15.4*	40 *11.0*
Carnivores, weasel to fox-sized	17 *7.1*	36 *4.8*	17 *6.1*	32 *4.0*	4 *3.4*	7 *1.9*
Carnivores and scavengers, large	4[2] *1.7*	7 *0.9*	1 *0.3*	2 *0.04*	1[1] *0.8*	1[1] *0.03*
Bats, fruit and blossom feeding	13 *5.6*	26 *3.4*	30 *10.8*	80 *9.9*	5 *4.3*	25 *6.9*
Bats, insectivorous	29 *12.3*	148 *19.6*	50 *18.0*	143 *17.7*	16 *13.7*	64 *17.6*

Numbers in italics are percentages.

[1] *Does not include the dingo, introduced by aboriginal man.*

[2] *If lions be regarded as generically distinct this figure would be 5.*

cricetine rodents show adaptations towards the mole niche, *Blarinomys* being the most specialized of these (Hershkovitz, Chapter VII).

Specialized ant and termite feeders. In Africa 1.3% of genera and 0.8% of species fit into this category. For Neotropica the corresponding figures are 1.1% and 0.4%, and in Australia they are 2.6% and 1.1%. The adaptive zone is occupied by the pangolins, aardvark, and *Proteles* in Africa, the Myrmecophagidae in Neotropica, and echidnas and *Myrmecobius* in Australia.

Small to medium-sized terrestrial omnivores. In Africa these account for 5.4% of genera and 3.7% of species, in Neotropica for 6.1% and 3.8%, respectively, and in Australia 7.6% and 5.5%. The figures are broadly comparable. The groups filling the role are as follows: *Africa*—many mongooses (except the larger, predatory species and a few highly specialized ones); *Neotropica*—procyonids (mainly herbivorous), armadillos (mainly insectivorous), and terrestrial mustelids like *Conepatus* (skunk) and *Lyncodon*; *Australia*—the bandicoots (Peramelidae) and the potoroine macropodid *Hypsiprymnodon*. Some rodents, of course, impinge on this ecological category but, for simplicity, these are treated separately.

The "terrestrial omnivore" category overlaps the "terrestrial carnivores, weasel to fox-sized," so that allocating some of the Herpestinae becomes somewhat arbitrary: likewise some of the small canids, placed here under the latter, have strong omnivorous tendencies.

"Typical" rats and mice (muroids). The muroid faunas of the three continents are as follows: *Africa*—20% of genera and 21.1% of species; *Neotropica*—18.3% and 27.5%; *Australia*—26.5% and 34.1%. The level of agreement is good. Neotropica, however, has a large fauna of caviomorphs (especially 16 genera and 44 species of Echimyidae), which total about 12.9% of genera and 12.6% of species (Table 5). These occupy a wide range of ecological niches (including those of gophers and ground squirrels). Virtually all are larger than the muroids. The rat-sized echimyids are largely forest dwellers and while undoubtedly overlapping the muroid adaptive zone probably do not compete with them to a marked extent.

Rabbit-sized herbivores. In Africa this category accounts for 5.0% of genera and 4.0% of species; Neotropica, 4.3% and 2.1%, and Australia 3.4% and 1.9%. The figures are comparable. The groups filling the role are: *Africa*—hyracoids, leporids, and ctenodactylid, petromyid, and pedetid rodents; *Neotropica*—the Chinchillidae and Caviidae, and two leporids; *Australia*—the potoroine macropodids, less the omnivorous *Hypsiprymnodon*.

Medium-sized to large terrestrial herbivores. Figures here are: Africa, 16.7% of genera and 12.6% of species; Neotropica, 4.7% and 2.8%; Australia, 10.3% and 8.8%. The figures emphasize the striking richness of the large herbivore fauna of Africa and the impoverishment of the

Neotropical one. The Australian macropodids, the dominant "large herbivores" of that continent, are much smaller in body size than their ecological counterparts in Africa. The groups occupying this adaptive zone are: *Africa*—all the Artiodactyla (large and small) and Perissodactyla, plus a proboscidian; *Neotropica*—tapirs, peccaries, deer, camels, and a few large caviomorphs, i.e., the capybara (Hydrochoeridae), and *Agouti* and *Dinomys* (Dasyproctidae)—forms that are as large as the smaller African antelopes (dikdiks, tragulids); *Australia*—Macropodinae (other than the tree-kangaroos, *Dendrolagus*), and wombats (Vombatidae).

Fossorial herbivores that feed underground. This category, represented by African mole rats (Bathyergidae, Rhizomyidae) is apparently restricted, in ultimate form, to Africa. About 1.7% of genera and 2.0% of species belong to it. The South American tuco-tucos (Ctenomyidae) apparently only do some of their feeding underground. Thus, Walker and Paradiso (1968) give their diet as roots and tubers and mention that individuals are seldom seen more than a foot from the mouths of their burrows; Pearson (1951), by contrast, refers to them stripping large areas of grass and hence being major competitors of the vicuñas. One or two of the Neotropical cricetine rodents are seasonally fossorial, notably *Kunsia tomentosus* (Hershkovitz, Chapter VII), but there does not seem to be any data as to whether or not they feed underground. There are no subterranean herbivorous mammals in Australia. In some places large cockatoos (Psittaciformes) dig for the more superficial roots and tubers.

Arboreal (climbing) herbivores and omnivores. In Africa 7.8% of genera and 12.3% of species fit into this category; in Neotropica the figures are about 11.5% and 13.1%; and in Australia they are 15.4% and 11.0%, respectively. These percentages are broadly comparable. The high figure for genera in Australia is due to the fact that many are monotypic or have only two or three species. The groups filling these adaptive zones are: *Africa*—monkeys, galagos and pottos, squirrels and anomalurids, and the tree dassie; *Neotropica*—monkeys (including the insectivorous marmosets), squirrels, arboreal porcupines, the mustelid *Eira*, tree sloths, and perhaps two-thirds of the didelphoids; *Australia*—Phalangerinae and Phascolarctinae, and tree kangaroos (*Dendrolagus*).

Terrestrial carnivores, weasel to fox-sized. These make up about 7.1% of African mammals at the generic, and 4.8% at the species level; for Neotropica the figures are 6.1% and 4.0%, respectively; for Australian they are 3.4% and 1.9%. The figures for the two larger continents are comparable but Australia is clearly deficient. Birds of prey dominate this adaptive zone in Australia. The reasons would appear to be two-fold. Rodents, which are prominent in the diet of these mammals, are recent arrivals in Australia (probably in the Pliocene and did not assume a dominant position until the Pleistocene). Secondly, most mammalian predators are forest species: there are no savannah and desert equivalents of the mobile foxes among the Australian marsupials.

The forms occupying this adaptive zone are: *Africa*—genets, a few mongooses (especially the larger ones), mustelids, foxes, small jackals, and the smallest felids; *Neotropica*—mustelids, the smaller canids and felids, and weasel-like didelphoids such as *Lutreolina, Philander,* and *Metachirus* (see Hershkovitz, Chapter VII); *Australia*—dasyuroids such as *Dasyurus* and *Dasyurops, Phascogale tapoatafa,* and *Sarcophilus.*

Carnivores and scavengers, large. This category makes up about 1.7% of the African genera and 0.9% of species; the Neotropical figures are 0.3% and 0.4%, respectively; and the Australian ones are 0.8%, and 0.03%. If the dingo (*Canis*), introduced by aboriginal man, be included the Australian figures would be doubled. Until the Early Recent this continent supported a large carnivorous phalangerid, *Thylacoleo,* that possibly occupied a niche that was part-felid, part-hyenid.

The groups occupying the large carnivore adaptive zone are: *Africa*—large felids, the canid *Lycaon,* and hyenids; *Neotropica*—large felids only (the ursid *Tremarctos* and the canid *Chrysocyon* are omnivores and the mammal prey of the latter is of small size—Walker and Paradiso, 1968); *Australia*—*Thylacinus* (marsupial wolf). The higher percentage and greater diversity of large carnivores in Africa are linked, of course, to the continent's large and rich herbivore fauna. The relationship between numbers of predator and prey species is presumably more geometric than arithmetic. Where herbivore density is inadequate to support a large mammalian scavenger, as in Neotropica and Australia, the mobile birds of prey fill the role.

Bats, fruit and blossom feeding. The fruit and blossom feeding Megachiroptera account for about 5.6% of genera and 3.4% of species in Africa, and 4.3% and 6.9%, respectively, in Australia. The adaptive zone is filled by Microchiroptera in Neotropica, these mainly belonging to the subfamilies Stenoderminae and Glossophaginae (Hershkovitz, Chapter VII). There are 30 genera and 80 species in these groups, amounting to 10% of the total genera and species. Most Neotropical fruit and blossom feeding bats also consume insects (P. Hershkovitz, pers. commun.).

Bats, insectivorous. Microchiroptera make up about 12.3% of genera and 19.6% of the African mammal species, and 13.7% and 17.6%, respectively, of the Australian ones. The figures for Neotropica, less Stenoderminae and Glossophaginae, are 18% for genera and 17.7% for species. The African and Australian figures are comparable. When the part-nectarivorous and part-frugivorous groups are included Neotropica· has a distinctly larger small-bat fauna.

This rather arbitrary breakdown of the mammal faunas of Africa, South America, and Australia, in terms of adaptive zones occupied, permits a number of conclusions to be drawn:

(1) All the adaptive zones are occupied on each continent (as would be expected) but, in the case of some, the number or overall proportion of

groups and genera occupying them varies greatly. In most cases this can be directly linked to the characteristics of the particular continent. Thus the predominance of savannah in Africa (and its presumed long continuous history) accounts for the dominance of savannah lines like the macroscelids, chrysochlorids, bovids, and the carnivores associated with the latter. By contrast, the deficiencies of Neotropica and Australia in fossorial, mole-like insect-eaters, is somewhat puzzling. Thus, the Australian marsupial mole, *Notoryctes,* is confined to areas of desert sand, and perhaps a quarter of the Australian continental area. Neotropica, as noted, had a marsupial "mole" in the Miocene. Mole niches in these two continents would seem to remain largely unoccupied, although in Neotropica in later times rodent species have invaded them.

(2) Current ecological knowledge is too scanty to adequately allocate many of the smaller mammals to specific adaptive zones or ecological categories. This can be done with fair precision, however, for the larger forms.

(3) It is obvious that particular adaptive zones and ways of life may be quite differently utilized on the different continents. Australia, for example, has no tree-top browsing ungulate, hence this adaptive zone is utilized by small-bodied climbing forms. Again, the adaptive zones may be differently divided up between families. Some of the larger caviomorph rodents in Neotropica are the ecological equivalents of some of the smaller bovids in Africa. African rodents, by contrast, are all relatively small-bodied. Extinct caviomorphs reached even larger size; e.g., the Pliocene *Telicomys* was the size of a small rhinoceros and *Protohydrochoerus* the size of a tapir (see Chapter by Patterson and Pascual), notwithstanding the existence, at the time, of a diverse fauna of endemic Neotropical ungulates.

With such variables as the above operating, the question then presents itself as to whether comparable figures for percentage of fauna occupying the above 15 "adaptive zones" in Africa, Neotropica, and Australia, can be expected, and whether or not we can learn anything about the meaning of "balance" from this approach. Interestingly, the correlations are fairly good.

In five of the above 15 categories—"ant and termite feeders," "small to medium-sized terrestrial omnivores," "typical rats and mice (muroids)," "rabbit-sized herbivores," and "arboreal (climbing) herbivores, omnivores, and insect-eaters"—the percentages of genera and species are roughly similar on each of the three continents. In the case of another four, two of the continents are in broad agreement (see "small insect-eaters and predators"—Africa and Australia; "carnivores, weasel to fox-sized"—Africa and Neotropica; "bats, fruit and blossom feeding"—Africa and Australia; and "bats, insectivorous"—Africa and Australia). Of the remaining categories three are of little significance ("fossorial moles," "rodents occupying the mole niche," and "fossorial herbivores") and were included only to bring out the occurrence of certain special morphological types on one or another of the continents.

Faunal features peculiar to one continent, as noted, are the great richness of Africa in terms of large herbivores, and to a lesser extent large carnivores; the exceptional prominence of rodents and bats in Neotropica; and the impoverishment of Australia in terms of mammalian carnivores. Most of these features, however, can be accounted for, either by basic differences in the three continents as living areas (e.g., in vegetation), or on historic grounds.

To sum up, the three continents have very different faunas. The vast bulk of the mammals have, in the course of their evolution, specialized in the direction of one or another of these zones. Despite the continents differing as living areas there is a tendency for the occupants of several of the basic adaptive zones to make up comparable proportions of each of the faunas.

Probably a couple of semi-independent variables are involved in attaining this state. One is a direct area effect. Thus, the number of available muroid, small terrestrial omnivore, and insectivorous bat niches (or ecological opportunities) is probably partly a function of continental area. These small-bodied forms can be thought of as dividing up the ecosystem spatially into a large number of small packages. They also have the capacity to radiate quickly to fill up all these available niches. There is little or no evolutionary lag in the case of these rapidly-reproducing and opportunistic small-bodied mammals. The ultimate number of species that will evolve depends, of course, among other things, on the relative extent to which optimal habitats are developed on the particular continent. This accounts for the larger number of small bats in Neotropica. In contrast with the above are the large-bodied mammals, which reflect not only current ecological opportunities but, because of their slower evolutionary rates, also reflect historic factors (e.g., past ecological "bottlenecks") as well.

This discussion brings out fairly clearly that the term "balance," as applied to faunas by vertebrate paleontologists and zoogeographers, is relative. Continental faunas are "balanced" because they are large, diversified, and because all of the more obvious "adaptive zones" are occupied. This state will be achieved because continental areas are sufficiently large to permit active speciation and radiation. Islands are usually too small for this and, because of their isolation, receive only a limited number of colonizers from outside. The fauna of New Zealand could be described as "unbalanced" in that mammals are absent (except for two species of bats) and their adaptive zones are occupied by birds. But the fact that animals, irrespective of the group, have moved in to occupy the vacant niches means that a state of balance has been achieved. All faunas, continental and insular are, of course, in a state of dynamic evolution and change as new forms are constantly appearing to challenge, or supplement, preexisting ones. The concept of "balance" in faunas, while real enough in the broad sense, is hardly a static phenomenon.

Simpson (1962) has introduced the terms "saturated," "unsaturated," and "supersaturated" to describe faunas. When a fauna, such as the contemporary West Indies mammal fauna, lacks certain basic ecological components or is apparently "out of balance," it is unsaturated. As an example of a supersaturated fauna Simpson gives the Pleistocene large mammal fauna of South America, following its supplementation by North American forms. (At this time 16 additional mammal families were added to the fauna.) The continent then had 36 families, compared to 23 in the Mid-Miocene, 25 in the Mid-Pliocene, and 30 today. The concept of saturation in faunas is closely interrelated with that of balance and hence must be examined briefly here. Two questions must be asked: (1) Is the concept of saturation a real or viable one? (2) What does it mean, ecologically speaking?

One of the best examples of an "unsaturated" fauna today is the large herbivore fauna of Neotropica. Simpson does not use it as an example but it meets the basic requirements. First, there are only 20 species of artiodactyls and perissodactyls (tapirs, tayassuids, camels and deer), compared to 95 in Africa (horses, rhinoceroses, suids, hippos, tragulids, giraffes, and bovids). However, South America has only 58% of the land area of Africa; hence, strictly on the basis of area, 55 species might be expected. Woodland, grassland and arid grassland, the main large herbivore habitats, cover about 80% of Africa and 60 to 65% of Neotropica. This means that a fauna of 30 to 35 species is more in line with expectations. (Actually, what work has been done on the relationship of numbers of species to area suggests that the relationship is more geometric than arithmetic).

On this reasoning Neotropica should have over 30 species of large herbivores. Since there are but 20 species now, the large herbivore fauna of South America then is definitely "unsaturated." Second, the fauna today is markedly deficient compared to what it has been in the past. Throughout the Tertiary the continent enjoyed a diverse fauna of endemic ungulates and large non-ungulate herbivores. In the early Pleistocene there was a fauna as rich in *major categories* of animals as that of Africa today. Lists in Boule and Thevenin (1920), largely drawn together from Ameghino's works, show that the pampas alone supported a large herbivore fauna as follows: proboscideans (1 gen., 2 sp.), equids (3 and 6), tayassuids (1 and 1), cervids (1 and 4), camels (3 and 3), macrauchenids (1 and 2), toxodons (1 and 1), typotheres (1 and 1), glyptodonts (3 and 6), and ground sloths (6 and 9). This comes to 8 orders, 22 genera, and 34 species. If the northern invaders be discounted this still leaves 5 orders, 13 genera, and 19 species of autochthons. These figures also prove that the large herbivore fauna of South America is now "unsaturated."

The largest continuous area of grassland in South America today is the pampas, and this is where the large herbivores should be concentrated. There are, however, only 4 species in the pampas and the altiplano combined, the deer *Ozatoceros bezoarticus* and *Hippocamelus antisiensis*, and the camelids *Lama guanicoe* and *Vicugna vicugna.* Do the pampas therefore contain a large number of unoccupied "niches?" The answer seems to be that the "large herbivore" niches have been partly invaded by a diverse fauna of rodents. Hershkovitz (Chapter VII) has reviewed the highly diversified pampean rodent fauna, which includes a wide range of cricetines as well as caviomorphs. Various writers have suggested that rodents compensate for the shortage of large herbivores (e.g. Dorst, 1967, p. 168). Others have referred to competition for herbage between rodents and ungulates in the grasslands of South America—note, for example, the remarks of Pearson (1951, p. 157) about the interaction of tucotucos (*Ctenomys*), alpacas, llamas, and sheep, on the plains of the Altiplano. Included in the large rodents that may, in part, utilize the large herbivore niches are the Patagonian hare, *Dolichotis patagonum,* that attains the length of 30 inches, the nutria (*Myocastor coypus*) and the viscacha (*Lagostomus*), 20 inches in length, and *Pediolagus,* the size of a jack rabbit. Added to this are the burrowing tucotucos (*Ctenomys*), which have massive heads and bodies 8 inches in length.

No biomass figures are available for the pampas rodents and ungulates to compare with those for the African grasslands. (Hershkovitz quotes Koford's figure for vicuña as one animal per 50 acres but up to one per 10 acres in optimum areas.)

Several other interesting features of the pampas fauna may be noted. There were still larger-bodied rodents in the Pliocene, e.g., giant dinomyids, but by the Pleistocene, when the fauna became a blend of South American and North American elements, these had become extinct. In the Pliocene, moreover, the pampas supported 8 genera of octodontid rodents, the same number of genera as of cricetines today (Patterson and Pascual, Chapter VI). Secondly, the caviomorph rodents of the Pleistocene, at the time when the pampas supported a diverse ungulate fauna, were of the same basic types as today. Lastly, the pampas now support a high biomass of cattle and horses (which was probably still higher when Darwin visited the area), showing that these grasslands are, in effect, prime ungulate habitat.

If, as it appears, rodents fill the ecological role of ungulates on the pampas today, they presumably exploit the habitat in quite a different way. Prior to the arrival of European stock they had presumably built up a biomass approximating that which the habitat could support. This would mean that the pampas were not "unsaturated" in terms of carrying capacity or amount of energy turnover but only (possibly) in the range of major morphological types that they had the potential to support.

These considerations raise various interesting problems. Have the pampas changed in such a way since the Pleistocene (or Pliocene) that they now favor caviomorph rodents rather than ungulates? Alternatively, since there is now evidence that man lived in association with some of the extinct large herbivores (see Patterson and Pascual, Chapter VI), is their absence today a purely artificial phenomenon, a secondary result of the advent of man? The fact that the pampean large mammal fauna changed markedly from the Miocene and Pliocene to the Pleistocene, with large ungulates being largely eliminated in favor of giant ground sloths and glyptodonts supports the former argument. On the other hand, subsequent to the formation of the Panamanian land bridge a variety of northern forms, proboscideans and horses among them, successfully became established in the area. As noted, Simpson (1962), in using the term "supersaturated" to describe the South American large mammal fauna established after this entry, infers that the carrying capacity of the continent was exceeded, at least on the long-term basis. In view of the fact that these northerners persisted for probably a million years or so, however, this concept seems hard to justify.

This throws us back to a consideration of a range of fundamental problems. To what extent does the presently impoverished large herbivore fauna of South America reflect deficiencies in the carrying capacity of the continent, as compared to historic factors, the advent of man included? How does the pattern of utilization of a habitat by ungulates and rodents compare? To what extent are ungulates and rodents or, for that matter, ungulates and herbivorous insects, in competition? (Note the spectacular increase in plant growth in Natal which followed the elimination of termites by insecticides—see Coaton, 1958). Are the three general body-size categories to be found in terrestrial herbivorous mammals, as represented by rodent, lagomorph, and ungulate, of any basic metabolic or ecological significance, or is it just a matter of chance that the faunas of the most continents, "exposed" to faunistic interchange, sort out in this way.

These considerations are all relevant to an understanding of the differences in the carrying capacity of the South American pampas, in terms of large herbivores, as between the Pliocene, Pleistocene, and present, and compared to the African savannah today.

SUMMARY

(1) The mammal faunas of Africa, Neotropica, and Australia differ fundamentally in their compositions. While some groups (muroids, bats) occur on each continent, many of the more important adaptive zones (definition in Simpson, 1944), or ecological roles (e.g., small terrestrial omnivores, arboreal herbivores and omnivores, anteaters) are filled by quite different groups on the three continents. Associated with this are basic differences in the dominant groups, i.e., those that have the largest numbers of genera and species.

(2) Different factors have been important in achieving a position of dominance on each continent. In Australia, total isolation permitted the survival of a predominantly marsupial fauna, and today this group occupies all the major adaptive zones, except for those of rodents and bats. In Neotropica, by contrast, where primates have been since the Oligocene,

this group long ago took over the arboreal omnivore adaptive zone occupied by the Phalangeridae in Australia. The fossil records of the southern continents provide many examples of older groups being subsequently replaced by later, better adapted forms or, at least, forms better adapted to changing conditions. Examples are the replacement of hyaenodontids by modern carnivores in Africa during the Miocene (these groups were clearly direct ecological counterparts), and the progressive replacement of quadrupedal diprotodontid herbivores by bipedal, saltatorial macropodids in Australia in the late Tertiary and Pleistocene. At the same time there are many demonstrations of old groups, while not maintaining a dominant position, at least continuing to be successful despite the repeated invasion of new forms from outside or the development of new types within the continent. The African hyracoids, elephant shrews (Macroscelididae) and, of course, primates are examples. Another situation is represented by the Viverridae and Mustelidae in Africa. These are, broadly speaking, ecologically equivalent groups. Both evolved in large land masses in the middle Tertiary and are vigorous, opportunistic, and well adapted. Viverrids reached Africa at the end of the Oligocene and radiated widely. Mustelids did not arrive, apparently, until the early Pliocene. In the ensuing period the latter have only been able to gain a minor foothold in the terrestrial "medium-sized carnivore and omnivore" adaptive zone. This is an interesting demonstration of an older group of inhabitants maintaining its position, in part, by having occupied almost the full range of niches in an adaptive zone so that the latecomer is disadvantaged.

(3) Interaction or competition with later forms is by no means the only reason for groups losing their dominant position (and in many cases eventually becoming extinct). There is a marked difference between the Oligocene and early Pliocene faunas of South America. In the course of this change the South American fossil record is sprinkled with cases of whole groups formerly dominant becoming greatly reduced in importance or extinct, in the apparent absence of direct competitors.

(4) Differences in the dominant groups in the three continents means that the major ways of life are utilized differently by comparable groups on each. Thus, while the Neotropical armadillos and Australian marsupial bandicoots, both of which have long snouts and strong digging forelimbs are, as groups, the nearest counterparts to each other, no single species could be selected from the one and said to be the direct ecological equivalent of a particular species of the other. This is partly because armadillos have a range of structural, physiological, ecological, and behavioral attributes different from bandicoots, and partly because, during the course of their radiation the species have divided up the "terrestrial omnivore" zone in a somewhat different way from the bandicoots. Notwithstanding this when one compares the arboreal African cercopithecid monkeys, Neotropical cebid monkeys, and Australian phalangers, it is

found that within each group are species that are predominantly frugivorous, predominantly leaf-eating, or insectivorous, and others that combine these foods in similar ways.

(5) Groups common to two or more of the continents have commonly radiated in different ways on each. Only in Africa have the primates given rise to a series of distinctive terrestrial forms (baboons, large pongids), and only in Neotropica has a small-bodied insectivorous line of monkeys (the marmosets) emerged. While many of the felids and canids on these two continents are equivalent, only in Africa does a large hunting dog (*Lycaon*), and long-legged hunting cat (*Acinonyx*) occur.

(6) The three faunas are "structurally" similar. Despite the prolonged isolation of Australia, mammals there occupy the same range of adaptive zones as on the other continents. All the continents have the same recognizable combinations of basic "ecological categories" of mammals, e.g., "large carnivores," "small terrestrial insect-eaters," "specialized anteaters," and so on.

(7) Each continent has a number of unique mammals, both morphologically, and ecologically. Only Africa has a treetop-browsing ungulate (giraffe); only Neotropica has vampire and fish-catching bats, and only Australia has a mammal that is, ecologically, as much a duck as it is anything else (platypus).

(8) By grouping the genera and species of the three continents into 15 basic adaptive zones or ecological ("food niche") groups, and expressing each of these as a percentage of the whole, an attempt is made to determine if, in the evolution of a fauna, these tend to assume a certain relation to each other. These ecological categories, which were designated on morphological criteria as well as food data, included "small insect eaters and predators," "fossorial mole-like insect-eaters," "specialized ant and termite feeders," "small to medium-size terrestrial omnivores," "typical" rats and mice, "insectivorous bats," "medium-sized to large terrestrial herbivores," and so on. Five of the 15 categories proved to make up roughly equivalent percentages of the genera and species in the 3 continental faunas, while in another 5 of the categories 2 of the 3 continental faunas were in agreement.

It is suggested that two factors may be involved in the evolution of this partial "balance," a direct area effect (i.e., the number of insectivorous bat and muroid "niches" may be proportional to continental area), and an intergroup effect (i.e., there is a link between the number of predator and prey species, as well as the number of individuals; this link is very likely geometric rather than directly arithmetic, however).

(9) The degree of endemism in the mammal faunas of the three continents accords with what is known about the relative isolation of each in the historic past. With respect to taxa at the ordinal and superfamily

level endemism is 19% for Africa, 29% for Neotropica, and 36% for Australia: at the family level 29%, 54%, and 50%. The percentage of families belonging to endemic taxa at the ordinal and superfamily level is 21% for Africa, 42% for Neotropica, and 50% for Australia.

(10) The numbers of families in each continent per 100,000 square miles of area is 0.45 (0.63 without the Sahara) for Africa, 0.70 for Neotropica, and 0.55 for Australia; at the generic level the figures are 2.02 (3.0), 3.86, and 3.55. Species figures are 6.42 for Africa (9.2 for Africa less the Sahara), 11.3 for Neotropica and 11.03 for Australia. There would thus appear to be a good level of consistency. Neotropica owes its richness to an exceptionally large fauna of rodents and bats; it is, however, markedly deficient in certain other groups, e.g., large herbivores. Africa has the most diverse fauna, a high level of survival of large forms from the Pleistocene, and is strikingly rich in large herbivores.

(11) The factors influencing the richness of a continental fauna are many. These include area of the continent, its capacity to support a diverse fauna which is, in turn, influenced by percentage of area covered by the different vegetation formations (especially tropical rain forest), latitudinal position, area that lies within the tropics, degree of vegetational and physiographic diversity, proximity of other major land masses (from which new forms may colonize the continent), degree of "duplication" of faunas within the continent (Africa, because of its trans-Equatorial position not only has separate temperate faunas to the north and south but has three isolated areas of desert with partially distinct faunas), the opportunities for developing new species within the continent, and amount of extinction in the immediate past.

(12) Striking differences in the rainfall, and hence development of the different vegetation types, are reflected in the *kinds* of mammal faunas that occur on each continent, and in their specializations and adaptations. Thus about 68% of Neotropica has a rainfall greater than 40 inches per annum, compared to about 28% of Africa and 16% of Australia; 31% of Africa has a rainfall of less than 5 inches per annum, compared to about 2% of Neotropica and 1% of Australia. In accordance with this an estimated 32% of Neotropica is covered with tropical rain forest, compared to perhaps 9% of Africa, and 4.5% of Australia (including New Guinea). About 50% of Africa and Australia are covered by savannah, steppe, grassland, and desertic vegetation, compared to perhaps 41% of Neotropica.

Rain forest mammals are unusually prominent in the Neotropical fauna. Inhabiting this formation are a good proportion of the didelphoids, most of the bats, the monkeys, tree sloths, most echimyids, squirrels, perhaps 10% to 20% of the muroids, many of the mustelids, most of the procyonids, canids, and felids, two of the tapirs, the peccaries, and several of the deer. An arbitrary count, without the bats, shows about 90 genera (33% of the total genera) and 300 species (40%) to be rain forest inhabitants. If bats are included the figures would approach 50% at the generic and 60% at the species level.

Most of the dominant groups of African mammals are savannah forms —e.g., the chrysochlorids, the hedgehogs, the elephant shrews (11 of 13 species), the leporids, a good proportion of the muroids, the bathyergid mole rats, all the canids, most mongooses, the hyenas, most of the felids, most hyracoids, the equids, rhinos, and about 80% of the bovids. In addition, several groups that are not particularly open-country forms have produced specialized savannah derivatives; the cheetah among the felids is an example. Savannah groups in Africa account for about 105 of the 231 genera (nearly 45%), and about 290 of the 744 species (about 40%).

The isolated Australian mammal fauna is a fairly good balance of savannah and forest elements, notwithstanding that grassland and "desert" cover about 53% of the land area. The diversity of the forest fauna stems from the rich development of rain forest elements in New Guinea, their partial duplication in the smaller rain forest areas of Australia proper, and in the rich and varied eucalypt forest fauna of the latter.

(13) To sum up, a great many of the faunistic features of the three continents can be explained in terms of measureable present-day phenomena such as continental area, proportion of each continent with high and low annual rainfall rates, percentage of each continent covered by rain forest, as compared to savannah, etc. Such a clear-cut link between fauna and environment supports the argument that environmental change is the greatest single cause of faunal turnover (extinction and replacement) on continents. The phenomenon certainly requires more study (though note the paper of Webb, 1969, concerning the late Cenozoic turnover in North America). Turnover rate has recently received some attention in the case of island faunas (e.g., Mayr, 1965).

ACKNOWLEDGMENTS

I should like to express my sincere thanks to Professor John A. Moore, Program Organizer for the XVI International Congress of Zoology, for his invitation to organize this Symposium, and to the Editors of *The Quarterly Review of Biology* for being so kind to publish it in expanded and updated form.

Successful completion of the present synthesis and summary would not have been possible without the kindness of various colleagues who read and criticized the manuscript. Included here are Professors Bryan Patterson and Ernst Mayr of Harvard University; Professor H. B. S. Cooke of Dalhousie University, Dr. Philip Hershkovitz of the Field Museum of Natural History, Chicago, and Dr. Karl Koopman of the American Museum of Natural History, New York. Dr. Bassett Maguire of the New York Botanical Gardens and Dr. Pierre Dansereau of the University of Montreal gave up their time to discuss certain botanical aspects. I am indebted to all of these workers, and to Professor Patterson in particular.

Needless to say, in the case of controversial issues, the weighing of the evidence and the ensuing shortcomings, are my own.

The work was carried out while the author was in receipt of a research grant from the National Research Council of Canada.

LITERATURE CITED

ANSELL, W. F. H. 1960. *Mammals of Northern Rhodesia.* 155 p. Government Printer, Lusaka.

AXELROD, D. I. 1967. Quaternary extinctions of large mammals. *Univ. Calif. Publ. Geol. Sci.,* 74: 1-42.

BIGALKE, R. C. 1968. The contemporary mammal fauna of Africa. *Quart. Rev. Biol.,* 43: 265-300.

BOOTH, A. H. 1954. The Dahomey Gap and the mammalian fauna of the West African forests. *Rev. Zool. Bot. Afr.,* 1, 3-4: 305-314.

BOULE, M., and A. THEVENIN. 1920. *Mammifères fossiles de Tarija.* 225 p. Mission Scient. G. de Créqui-Montfort et E. Sénechal de la Grange. Imprimerie Nationale, Paris.

CALABY, J. H. 1966. Mammals of the Upper Richmond and Clarence Rivers, New South Wales. Division of Wildlife Res. Tech. Paper No. 10, C.S.I.R.O., 1-55.

CHAPMAN, F. M. 1917. Distribution of bird life in Colombia. *Bull. Am. Museum Natur. Hist.,* 36: 1-729.

———. 1926. The distribution of bird life in Ecuador. Part I. *Bull. Am. Museum Natur. Hist.,* 55: 133-144.

CLARK, J. D. 1967. *Atlas of African Prehistory.* 62 p. Univ. Chicago Press, Chicago.

COATON, W. G. H. 1958. The hodotermitid harvester termites of South Africa. Science Bull. No. 375, 112 p. Department of Agriculture, Union of South Africa.

COCHRANE, G. R. 1963. A physiognomic vegetation map of Australia. *J. Ecol.,* 51: 639-655.

COOKE, H. B. S. 1964. The Pleistocene environment in southern Africa. In D. H. S. Davis (ed.), *Ecological Studies in Southern Africa,* p. 1-23. W. Junk, The Hague.

———. 1968. The fossil mammal fauna of Africa. *Quart. Rev. Biol.,* 43: 234-264.

CRAIN, I. K. 1971. Possible direct causal relation between geomagnetic reversals and biological extinctions. *Bull. Geol. Soc. Am.,* 82: 2603-2606.

CROCKER, R. L. and J. G. WOOD. 1947. Some historic influences on the development of the South Australian vegetation communities. *Trans. Roy. Soc. S. Austral.,* 71: 91-136.

DANSEREAU, P. 1958. A universal system for recording vegetation. Contrib. Inst. Bot. Univ. Montreal, No. 72.

DARLINGTON, P. J. 1957. *Zoogeography: The Geographical Distribution of Animals.* John Wiley and Sons, N. Y.

DORST, J. 1967. *South America and Central America. A Natural History.* 298 p. Random House, New York.

ELOFF, F. C. 1959. Observations on the migration and habits of the antelopes of the Kalahari Gemsbok Park—Parts 1 and 2. *Koedoe,* 2: 1-51.

FINLAYSON, H. H. 1961. On central Australian mammals. Part IV, The distribution and status of central Australian species. *Rec. S. Austral. Museum,* 14: 141-191.

FLEAY, D. 1949a. The shy Australian water rat. *Animal Kingdom,* 52: 54-58.

——. 1949b. That curious marsupial, the cuscus. *Animal Kingdom,* 52: 22-25.

FRICK, C. 1929. New remains of trilophodont-tetrabelodont mastodons. *Bull. Am. Museum Natur. Hist.,* 59: 527-533.

GILLET, H. 1967. The Scimitar Oryx and the Addax in the Tchad Republic. Parts I and II. *African Wild Life,* 20: 103-115; 21: 191-196.

GRAFTON, R. N. 1965. Food of the black-backed jackal: a preliminary report. *Zool. Afr.,* 1: 41-54.

GUILDAY, J. E. 1967. Differential extinction during late-Pleistocene and Recent times. In P. S. Martin and H. E. Wright (eds.), *Pleistocene Extinctions: The Search for a Cause,* p. 121-140. Yale Univ. Press, New Haven.

HARRINGTON, H. J. 1962. Paleogeographic development of South America. *Bull. Am. Assoc. Petrol. Geol.,* 46: 1773-1814.

HAYMAN, D. L., J. A. W. KIRSCH, P. G. MARTIN, and P. F. WALLER. 1971. Chromosomal and serological studies of the Caenolestidae and their implications for marsupial evolution. *Nature,* 231: 194-195.

HAYS, J. D. 1971. Faunal extinctions and reversals of the earth's magnetic field. *Bull. Geol. Soc. Am.,* 82: 2433-2447.

HEINSOHN, G. E. 1966. Ecology and reproduction of the Tasmanian bandicoots (*Perameles gunni* and *Isoodon obesulus*). *Univ. Calif. Publ. Zool.,* 80: 1-96.

HERSHKOVITZ, P. 1958. A geographic classification of Neotropical mammals. *Fieldiana: Zool.,* 36: 581-620.

——. 1962. Evolution of neotropical cricetine rodents (Muridae) with special reference to the phyllotine group. *Fieldiana Zool.,* 46: 1-524.

——. 1966a. Mice, land bridges and Latin American faunal interchange. In R. Wenzel and V. J. Tipton (eds.), *Ectoparasites of Panama,* p. 725-747. Field Museum of Natural History, Chicago.

——. 1966b. South American swamp and fossorial rats of the scapteromyine group (Cricetinae, Muridae) with comments on the glans penis in murid taxonomy. *Sonderdruck aus Z. f. Säugetierk.,* 31: 81-149.

——. 1969. The recent mammals of the neotropical region: a zoogeographic and ecological review. *Quart. Rev. Biol.,* 44: 1-70.

HICKMAN, V. V. and J. L. HICKMAN. 1960. Notes on the habits of the Tasmanian dormouse phalangers *Cercartetus nanus* (Desmarest) and *Eudromicia lepida* (Thomas). *Proc. Zool. Soc. Lond.*, 135: 365-374.

HILDEBRAND, M. 1952. An analysis of body proportions in the Canidae. *Am. J. Anat.*, 90: 217-256.

HUECK, K. 1966. *Die Wälder Südamerikas. Ökologie, Zusammensetzung und wirtschaftliche Bedeutung.* Gustav Fischer, Stuttgart.

JONES, F. WOOD. 1923, 1924, 1925. *The Mammals of South Australia. Parts I, II, III.* Government Printer, Adelaide.

KEAST, A. 1959. Relict animals and plants of the Macdonnell Ranges. *Austral. Museum Mag.*, 13: 81-86.

——. 1961. Bird speciation on the Australian continent. *Bull. Museum Comp. Zool., Harvard Coll.*, 123: 305-495.

——. 1963. The mammal fauna of Australia. *Proc. 16. Intern., Congr. Zool.*, 4: 56-62, 149.

——. 1965. Interrelationships of two zebra species in an overlap zone. *J. Mammalogy*, 46: 53-66.

——. 1968a. The southern continents as backgrounds for mammalian evolution. *Quart. Rev. Biol.*, 43: 225-233.

——. 1968b. Australian mammals: zoogeography and evolution. *Quart. Rev. Biol.*, 43: 373-408.

——. 1972a. Faunal elements and evolutionary patterns; some comparisons between the continental avifaunas of Africa, South America, and Australia. *Proc. 15 Intern. Ornith. Congress.* The Hague. In press.

——. 1972b. Ecological opportunities and dominant families, as illustrated by the Neotropical Tyrannidae (Aves). In T. Dobzhansky, M. K. Hecht, and W. C. Steere (eds.), *Evolutionary Biology*, Vol. 5. Appleton-Century-Crofts, New York. In press.

KEAY, R. J. W. 1959. *UNESCO Vegetation Map for Africa.* Oxford University Press, London.

KOFORD, C. B. 1968. Peruvian desert mice: water independence, competition, and breeding cycle near the Equator. *Science*, 160: 552-553.

KUCHLER, A. W. 1954. Plant geography. In P. E. James and C. E. Jones (eds.), *American Geography, Inventory and Prospect*, p. 428-441. Syracuse Univ. Press, Syracuse, N.Y.

LAMPREY, H. F. 1963. Ecological separation of the large mammal species in the Tarangire Game Reserve, Tanganyika. *E. Afr. Wildlife J.*, 1: 63-92.

LAVOCAT, R. 1967. Les microfaunes du Neogène d'Afrique orientale et leurs rapports avec celles de la region Palearctique. In W. W. Bishop and J. Desmond Clarke (eds.), *Background to Evolution in Africa*, p. 57-72. Univ. Chicago Press, Chicago.

LEOPOLD, A. 1959. *Wildlife of Mexico. The Game Birds and Mammals.* 568 pp. Univ. California Press, Berkeley.

LUNDELIUS, E. L., and W. D. TURNBULL. 1967. Pliocene mammals from Victoria, Australia, *39. Congr. Austral. N.Z. Assoc. Adv. Sci.:* K. 9 [Abstract].

MACARTHUR, R. H., and E. O. WILSON. 1963. An equilibrium theory of insular zoogeography. *Evolution,* 17: 373-387.

MACMILLEN, R. E., and A. K. LEE. 1967. Australian desert mice: independence of exogenous water. *Science,* 158: 383-385.

MARLOW, B. J. 1958. A survey of the marsupials of New South Wales. *J. C.S.I.R.O. Wildlife Res.,* 3: 71-114.

MARTIN, P. S. 1966. Africa and Pleistocene overkill. *Nature,* 212: 339-342.

———. 1967. Prehistoric overkill. In P. S. Martin and H. E. Wright (eds.), *Pleistocene Extinctions: The Search for a Cause,* p. 75-120. Yale Univ. Press, New Haven.

MAYR, E. 1965. Avifauna; turnover on islands. *Science,* 150: 1587-1588.

MCKENNA, M. 1956. Survival of primitive notoungulates and condylarths into the Miocene of Colombia. *Am. J. Sci.,* 254: 736-743.

MEESTER, J. 1968. *Preliminary Identification Manual for African Mammals.* Smithsonian Institution, Washington.

MERRILEES, D. 1968. Man the destroyer: late Quaternary changes in the Australian marsupial fauna. *J. Roy. Soc. W. Austral.,* 51: 1-24.

MISONNE, X. 1963. Les rongeurs du Ruwenzori et des régions voisines. Exploration du Parc National Albert (Deuxième Série), Fasc. 14. Institut des Parcs Nationaux du Congo et du Rwanda, Bruxelles.

MOREAU, R. E. 1966. *The Bird Faunas of Africa and Its Islands.* 424 p. Academic Press, London.

NYGREN, W. E. 1950. Bolivar geosyncline of northwestern South America. *Bull. Am. Assoc. Petrol. Geol.,* 34: 1998-2006.

OLSON, E. C., and P. O. McGREW. 1941. Mammalian fauna from the Pliocene of Honduras. *Bull. Geol. Soc. Am.,* 52: 1219-1243.

OSGOOD, W. H. 1943. The mammals of Chile. *Field Museum Natur. Hist. Publ. Zool. Ser.* No. 30: 1-268.

PATTERSON, B. 1958. Affinities of the Patagonian fossil mammal *Necrolestes. Breviora Museum Comp. Zool. Harvard Coll.,* 94: 1-14.

———. 1965. The fossil elephant shrews (Family Macroscelididae). *Bull. Museum Comp. Zool. Harvard Coll.,* 133: 297-335.

PATTERSON, B., and R. PASCUAL. 1968. The fossil mammal fauna of South America. *Quart. Rev. Biol.,* 43: 409-451.

PEARSON, O. P. 1951. Mammals in the highlands of southern Peru. *Bull. Museum Comp. Zool. Harvard Coll.,* 106: 117-174.

PIENAAR, U. DE V. 1964. The small mammals of the Kruger National Park—a systematic list and zoogeography. *Koedoe,* 7: 1-29.

PLANE, M. D. 1967. Stratigraphy and vertebrate fauna of the Otibanda formation, New Guinea. *Bull. Bur. Min. Res. Canberra,* 86: 1-64.

PRESTON, F. W. 1962. The canonical distribution of commonness and rarity: Parts I, II. *Ecology,* 43: 185-215, 410-432.

RATCLIFFE, F. N. 1959. The rabbit in Australia. In A. Keast, R. L. Crocker, and C. S. Christian (eds.), *Biogeography and Ecology in Australia,* p. 545-564. Junk, The Hague.

RICHARDS, P. W. 1952. *The Tropical Rain Forest.* University Press, Cambridge.

RIDE, W. D. L. 1964. A review of the Australian fossil marsupials. *J. Roy. Soc. W. Austral.,* 47: 97-131.

——. 1968. The past, present, and future of Australian mammals. *Austral. J. Sci.,* 31: 1-11.

ROSEVEAR, D. R. 1953. *Check List and Atlas of Nigerian Mammals.* Government Printer, Lagos.

SALE, J. B. 1965. The feeding behaviour of rock hyraxes (genera *Procavia* and *Heterohyrax*) in Kenya. *E. Afr. Wildlife J.,* 3: 1-18.

SAUER, C. O. 1950. Geography of South America. In J. H. Steward (ed.), *Handbook of South American Indians,* Part 6, p. 319-344. Bull. No. 143, Bur. Am. Ethnol., Smithsonian Inst., Wash.

SAVAGE, D. E. 1951. Report on fossil vertebrates from the upper Magdalena Valley, Colombia. *Science,* 144: 186-187.

SHORTRIDGE, G. C. 1934. *The Mammals of South West Africa—A Biological Account of the Forms Occurring in that Region.* 2 vols. 779 p. William Heinemann, London.

SIMPSON, G. G. 1944. *Tempo and Mode in Evolution.* 237 pp. Columbia Univ. Press, New York.

——. 1945. The principles of classification and a classification of mammals. *Bull. Am. Museum Natur. Hist.,* 85: 1-350.

——. 1950. History of the fauna of Latin America. *Am. Sci.,* 361-389.

——. 1952. Probabilities of dispersal in geologic time. In E. Mayr (ed.), *The Problem of Land Connections Across the South Atlantic with Special Reference to the Mesozoic,* p. 163-176. Bull. Am. Museum Natur. Hist., No. 99; N.Y.

——. 1956. Zoogeography of West Indian land mammals. *Am. Museum Novit.,* 1759: 1-28.

——. 1961. Historical zoogeography of Australian mammals. *Evolution,* 15: 431-446.

——. 1962. *Evolution and Geography: An Essay on Historical Biogeography with Special Reference to Mammals.* 64 p. Univ. of Oregon Press, Eugene.

——. 1965. *The Geography of Evolution.* 249 p. Chilton Books, New York, [Republication of Simpson, 1966, below.]

——. 1966. Mammalian evolution on the southern continents. *N. Jb. Geol. Palaeont. Abh.,* 125: 1-18.

SMITH, A. C., and I. M. JOHNSTON. 1945. A phytogeographic sketch of

Latin America. In F. Verdoorn (ed.), *Plants and Plant Science in Latin America*, p. 11-18. Chronica Botanica Co.

STEVENSON-HAMILTON, J. 1957. *Wild Life in South Africa.* 400 p. Cassell, London.

STIRTON, R. A. 1953. Vertebrate paleontology and continental stratigraphy in Colombia. *Bull. Geol. Soc. Am.,* 52: 1219-1243.

TALBOT, L. M., and M. H. TALBOT. 1962. Food preferences of some east African wild ungulates. *E. Afr. Agric. For. J.,* 27: 131-138.

——, and ——. 1963. The wildebeest in Western Masailand. *Wildlife Monogr.,* 12: 1-88.

TEDFORD, R. H. 1967. The fossil Macropodidae from Lake Menindee, New South Wales. *Univ. Calif. Pub. Geol. Sci.,* 64: 1-156.

TIMES PUBLISHING CO. 1958. *Times Atlas.* Bartholomew Edition, London.

TROUGHTON, E. 1948. *Furred Animals of Australia.* 376 p. Angus and Robertson, Sydney.

VAN ZYL, J. H. M. 1965. The vegetation of the S. A. Lombard Nature Reserve and its utilization by certain antelope. *Zoologica africana,* 1: 55-72.

VESEY-FITZGERALD, D. F. 1960. Grazing succession among East African game animals. *J. Mammalogy,* 41: 161-172.

VUILLEUMIER, F. 1967. Phyletic evolution in modern birds of the Patagonian forests. *Nature,* 215: 247-248.

WALKER, E. P., and J. L. PARADISO. 1968. *Mammals of the World.* Vols. I and II. 1500 p. Johns Hopkins Press, Baltimore.

WALTER, H. 1964. *Die Vegetation der Erde in öko-physiologischer Betrachtung.* Band I. Gustav Fischer, Jena.

WEBB, S. D. 1969. Extinction-origination equilibria in Late Cenozoic land mammals of North America. *Evolution,* 22: 688-702.

WHITMORE, F. C., JR., and R. H. STEWART. 1965. Miocene mammals and Central American seaways. *Science,* 148: 328-329.

WILSON, E. O. 1961. The nature of the taxon cycle in the Melanesian ant fauna. *Am. Natur.,* 95: 169-193.

WOOD, A. E. 1957. What, if anything, is a rabbit? *Evolution,* 11: 417-425.

WOOD, A. E., and B. PATTERSON. 1959. The rodents of the Deseadan Oligocene of Patagonia and the beginnings of South American rodent evolution. *Bull. Museum Comp. Zool. Harvard Coll.,* 120: 281-428.

WOOD, J. G. 1950. Vegetation map of Australia. In G. W. Leeper (ed.) *The Australian Environment,* p. 77-96. C.S.I.R.O., Melbourne, and Univ. Melbourne Press. [Second edition.]

WOODRING, W. P. 1964. Caribbean land and sea through the ages. *Bull. Geol. Soc. Am.,* 65: 719-732.

Author Index

Index to Scientific
and Vernacular Names

Numbers in italics correspond to pages on which animal is illustrated; numbers in boldface type correspond to those portions of the text where the more extensive or significant discussions appear. Semicolons are used to mark the breaks between chapters for most series of entries; when the series is exceptionally long, however, the entries are grouped and spaced by chapter.

Subject Index

For complete entries corresponding to taxa, see Index to Scientific and Vernacular Names